Lecture Notes in Computer Science · 3287

Commenced Publication in 1973
Founding and Former Series Editors:
Gerhard Goos, Juris Hartmanis, and Jan van Leeuwen

Editorial Board

David Hutchison
Lancaster University, UK

Takeo Kanade
Carnegie Mellon University, Pittsburgh, PA, USA

Josef Kittler
University of Surrey, Guildford, UK

Jon M. Kleinberg
Cornell University, Ithaca, NY, USA

Friedemann Mattern
ETH Zurich, Switzerland

John C. Mitchell
Stanford University, CA, USA

Moni Naor
Weizmann Institute of Science, Rehovot, Israel

Oscar Nierstrasz
University of Bern, Switzerland

C. Pandu Rangan
Indian Institute of Technology, Madras, India

Bernhard Steffen
University of Dortmund, Germany

Madhu Sudan
Massachusetts Institute of Technology, MA, USA

Demetri Terzopoulos
New York University, NY, USA

Doug Tygar
University of California, Berkeley, CA, USA

Moshe Y. Vardi
Rice University, Houston, TX, USA

Gerhard Weikum
Max-Planck Institute of Computer Science, Saarbruecken, Germany

Alberto Sanfeliu
José Francisco Martínez Trinidad
Jesús Ariel Carrasco Ochoa (Eds.)

Progress in Pattern Recognition, Image Analysis and Applications

9th Iberoamerican Congress
on Pattern Recognition, CIARP 2004
Puebla, Mexico, October 26-29, 2004
Proceedings

 Springer

Volume Editors

Alberto Sanfeliu
Universitat Politècnica de Catalunya
Institut de Robòtica i Informàtica Industrial (IRI)
Dept. d'Enginyeria de Sistemas, Automàtica e Informàtica Industrial (ESAII)
Parc Tecnològic de Barcelona, Edifici U
St. Llorens i Artigas 4-6, 08028 Barcelona, Spain
E-mail: sanfeliu@iri.upc.es

José Francisco Martínez Trinidad
Jesús Ariel Carrasco Ochoa
National Institute of Astrophysics, Optics and Electronics (INAOE)
Computer Science Department
Luis Enrique Erro No. 1, 72840 Sta. Maria Tonantzintla, Puebla, Mexico
E-mail: {fmartine, ariel}@inaoep.mx

Library of Congress Control Number: 2004113938

CR Subject Classification (1998): I.5, I.4, I.2.10, I.2.7

ISSN 0302-9743
ISBN 3-540-23527-2 Springer Berlin Heidelberg New York

Springer is a part of Springer Science+Business Media

springeronline.com

© Springer-Verlag Berlin Heidelberg 2004
Printed in Germany

Typesetting: Camera-ready by author, data conversion by Olgun Computergrafik
Printed on acid-free paper   SPIN: 11335887   06/3142   5 4 3 2 1 0

Preface

First of all, we want to congratulate two new research communities from Mexico and Brazil that have recently joined the Iberoamerican community and the International Association for Pattern Recognition. We believe that the series of congresses that started as the "Taller Iberoamericano de Reconocimiento de Patrones (TIARP)", and later became the "Iberoamerican Congress on Pattern Recognition (CIARP)", has contributed to these group consolidation efforts. We hope that in the near future all the Iberoamerican countries will have their own groups and associations to promote our areas of interest; and that these congresses will serve as the forum for scientific research exchange, sharing of expertise and new knowledge, and establishing contacts that improve cooperation between research groups in pattern recognition and related areas.

CIARP 2004 (9th Iberoamerican Congress on Pattern Recognition) was the ninth in a series of pioneering congresses on pattern recognition in the Iberoamerican community. As in the previous year, CIARP 2004 also included worldwide participation. It took place in Puebla, Mexico. The aim of the congress was to promote and disseminate ongoing research and mathematical methods for pattern recognition, image analysis, and applications in such diverse areas as computer vision, robotics, industry, health, entertainment, space exploration, telecommunications, data mining, document analysis, and natural language processing and recognition, to name a few.

CIARP 2004 was organized by the Computer Science Department of the National Institute of Astrophysics, Optics and Electronics (INAOE), the Center for Computing Research of the National Polytechnic Institute (CIC-IPN) and the University of Las Americas, Puebla (UDLAP), and was sponsored by the Institute of Cybernetics, Mathematics and Physics of Cuba (ICIMAF), the Center of Applications of Advanced Technology of Cuba (CENATAV), the University of La Salle, Mexico (ULSA), the Autonomous University of Puebla (BUAP), the International Association for Pattern Recognition (IAPR), the Cuban Association for Pattern Recognition (ACRP), the Portuguese Association for Pattern Recognition (APRP), the Spanish Association for Pattern Recognition and Image Analysis (AERFAI), the Special Interest Group on Pattern Recognition of the Brazilian Computer Society (SIGPR-SBC), and the Mexican Association for Computer Vision, Neurocomputing and Robotics (MACVNR).

We received contributions from 18 countries. In total 158 papers were submitted, out of which 87 were accepted for publication in these proceedings and for presentation at the conference. The review process was carried out by the Scientific Committee, each paper being assessed by at least two reviewers who, in conjunction with other reviewers prepared an excellent selection dealing with ongoing research. We are especially indebted to them for their efforts and the quality of the reviews.

Three professors were invited to give keynote addresses on topics in pattern recognition: Dr. Josef Kittler, Professor at the School of Electronics and Physical Sciences, University of Surrey, UK, Dr. Alberto Del Bimbo, University of Florence, Italy, and Dr. Eduardo Bayro Corrochano, Computer Science Department, Center of Research and Advanced Studies, Guadalajara, Mexico.

We would like to thank the members of the organizing committee for their enormous efforts that allowed for an excellent conference and proceedings.

October 2004

Alberto Sanfeliu
José Francisco Martínez-Trinidad
Jesús Ariel Carrasco-Ochoa

Organization

CIARP 2004 was organized by the Computer Science Department of the National Institute of Astrophysics Optics and Electronics (INAOE), the Center for Computing Research of the National Polytechnic Institute (CIC-IPN) and the University of Las Americas, Puebla (UDLAP).

General Conference Co-chairs

José Francisco Martínez-Trinidad	Computer Science Department, National Institute of Astrophysics, Optics and Electronics (INAOE), Mexico
Jesús Ariel Carrasco-Ochoa	Computer Science Department, National Institute of Astrophysics, Optics and Electronics (INAOE), Mexico
Alberto Sanfeliu	Institute of Robotics and Informatics (IRI), Department of Automatic Control (ESAII), Universitat Politècnica de Catalunya, Spain
Juan Luis Díaz de León Santiago	Center for Computing Research (CIC), National Polytechnic Institute (IPN), Mexico
Ma. del Pilar Gómez Gil	University of Las Americas, Puebla (UDLAP), Mexico

Iberoamerican Committee

José Ruiz-Shulcloper	Cuban Association for Pattern Recognition (ACRP)
Nicolás Pérez de la Blanca	Spanish Association for Pattern Recognition and Image Analysis (AERFAI)
Aurélio Campilho	Portuguese Association for Pattern Recognition (APRP)
Eduardo Bayro-Corrochano	Mexican Association for Computer Vision, Neurocomputing and Robotics (MACVNR)
Díbio Leandro Borges	Special Interest Group on PR of the Brazilian Computer Society (SIGPR-SBC)
Gregory Randall	University of the Republic, Uruguay
Gonzalo Rojas	Pontifical Catholic University of Chile
Bertille Adelaïde-Louviers	Université des Antilles et de la Guyane, Guadeloupe, France

Local Committee

Aurelio López López	INAOE, Mexico
Carlos Alberto Reyes García	INAOE, Mexico
Jesús Antonio González Bernal	INAOE, Mexico
Guillermo de Ita Luna	INAOE, Mexico
Leopoldo Altamirano Robles	INAOE, Mexico
Luis Villaseñor Pineda	INAOE, Mexico
Manuel Montes y Gómez	INAOE, Mexico
Olac Fuentes Chávez	INAOE, Mexico
Rodrigo Montufar Chaveznava	INAOE, Mexico

Local Arrangements Committee

Carmen Meza Tlalpan	INAOE, Mexico
Gorgonio Cerón Benítez	INAOE, Mexico
Gabriela López Lucio	INAOE, Mexico

Scientific Committee

Alarcón, V.	UDLAP, Mexico
Alquézar Mancho, R.	Universitat Politècnica de Catalunya, Spain
Altamirano, L.	INAOE, Mexico
Araújo, H.	Universidade de Coimbra, Portugal
Bayro-Corrochano, E.	Centro de Investigación y Estudios Avanzados-Gdl, Mexico
Bloch, I.	École Nationale Supérieure des Télécomm., France
Borges, D.L.	Pontifícia Universidade Católica do Paraná, Brazil
Caldas Pinto, J.R.	Instituto Superior Técnico, Portugal
Campilho, A.	Universidade do Porto, Portugal
Cano-Ortiz, S.D.	Universidad de Oriente, Cuba
d'Ávila-Mascarenhas, N.D.	Universidade Federal de São Carlos, Brazil
Del Bimbo, A.	Università di Firenze, Italy
Desachy, J.	Université des Antilles et de la Guyane, Guadeloupe, France
Díaz de León Santiago, J.L.	CIC-IPN, Mexico
Escalante Ramírez, B.	Universidad Nacional Autónoma de México, Mexico
Facon, J.	Pontifícia Universidade Católica do Paraná, Brazil
Fuentes, O.	INAOE, Mexico

Gibert, K.	Universitat Politècnica de Catalunya, Spain
Goldfarb, L.	University of New Brunswick, Canada
Gómez Gil, M.P.	UDLAP, Mexico
Gómez-Ramírez, E.	Universidad La Salle, Mexico
Gordillo, J.L.	Instituto Tecnológico y de Estudios Superiores de Monterrey, Mexico
Grau, A.	Universitat Politècnica de Catalunya, Spain
Guzmán Arenas, A.	CIC-IPN, Mexico
Kirschning, I.	UDLAP, Mexico
Kasturi, R.	University of South Florida, USA
Kittler, J.	University of Surrey, UK
Koschan, A.	University of Tennessee, USA
Lazo-Cortés, M.	Instituto de Cibernética, Matemática y Física, Cuba
Levashkine, S.	CIC-IPN, Mexico
Lira-Chávez, J.	Universidad Nacional Autónoma de México, Mexico
López López, A.	INAOE, Mexico
Lorenzo-Ginori, J.V.	Universidad Central de Las Villas, Cuba
Marques, J.S.	Instituto Superior Técnico, Portugal
Medioni, G.	University of Southern California, USA
Moctezuma, M.	Universidad Nacional Autónoma de México, Mexico
Novovicova, J.	Institute of Information Theory and Automation, Czech Republic
Padilha, A.J.M.N.	Universidade do Porto, Portugal
Pérez de la Blanca, N.	Universidad de Granada, Spain
Pina, P.	Instituto Superior Técnico, Portugal
Pla, F.	Universidad Jaume I, Spain
Randall, G.	Universidad de la República, Uruguay
Reyes, C.A.	INAOE, Mexico
Riazanov, V.	Computing Center of Russian Academy of Sciences, Russia
Ritter, G.	University of Florida, USA
Rodríguez, R.	ICIMAF, Cuba
Rojas Costa, G.M.	PUC, Chile
Ruiz-Shulcloper, J.	Instituto de Cibernética, Matemática y Física, Cuba
Sanfeliu, A.	Universitat Politècnica de Catalunya, Spain
Sanniti di Raja, G.	Instituto di Cibernetica, CNR, Italy
Serra, J.	École des Mines de Paris, France
Shirai, Y.	Osaka University, Japan

Sossa Azuela, J.H.	CIC-IPN, Mexico
Starostenko, O.	UDLAP, Mexico
Taboada Crispi, A.	Universidad Central de Las Villas, Cuba
Valev, V.	Saint Louis University, USA
Vidal, E.	Universidad Politécnica de Valencia, Spain
Villanueva, J.J.	Universidad Autónoma de Barcelona, Spain

Additional Referees

Aguado Behar, Alberto
Arias Estrada, Miguel O.
Biscay Lirio, Rolando
Fernández, Luis Miguel
García-Reyes, Edel B.
Gelbukh, Alexander
Gil-Rodríguez, José Luis
Medina Urrea, Alfonso

Montes y Gómez, Manuel
Montufar Chaveznava, Rodrigo
Pons Porrata, Aurora
Sánchez Díaz, Guillermo
Sierra Martínez, Gerardo
Silva-Mata, Francisco J.
Urcid Serrano, Gonzalo
Villaseñor Pineda Luis

Sponsoring Institutions

Institute of Cybernetics, Mathematics and Physics of Cuba (ICIMAF)
Center of Applications of Advanced Technology of Cuba (CENATAV)
University of La Salle, Mexico (ULSA)
Autonomous University of Puebla, Mexico (BUAP)
International Association for Pattern Recognition (IAPR)
Cuban Association for Pattern Recognition (ACRP)
Portuguese Association for Pattern Recognition (APRP)
Spanish Association for Pattern Recognition and Image Analysis (AERFAI)
Special Interest Group on PR of the Brazilian Computer Society (SIGPR-SBC)
Mexican Association for Computer Vision,
    Neurocomputing and Robotics (MACVNR)

Table of Contents

Use of Context in Automatic Annotation of Sports Videos

Ilias Kolonias, William Christmas, and Josef Kittler

Center for Vision, Speech and Signal Processing,
University of Surrey,
Guildford GU2 7XH, UK
{i.kolonias,w.christmas,j.kittler}@surrey.ac.uk
http://www.ee.surrey.ac.uk/CVSSP/

Abstract. The interpretation by a human of a scene in video material is heavily influenced by the context of the scene. As a result, researchers have recently made more use of context in the automation of scene understanding. In the case of a sports video, useful additional context is provided by formal sets of rules of the sport, which can be directly applied to the understanding task. Most work to date has used the context at a single level. However we claim that, by using a multilevel contextual model, erroneous decisions made at a lower can be avoided by the influence of the higher levels. In this work, we explore the use of a multilevel contextual model in understanding tennis videos. We use Hidden Markov models as a framework to incorporate the results of the scene analysis into the contextual model. Preliminary results have shown that the proposed system can successfully recover from errors at the lower levels.

1 Introduction

Constructing cognitive vision systems which can extract knowledge from visual data so as to derive understanding of the scene content and its dynamics, as well as to facilitate reasoning about the scene, has recently moved to the top of the research agenda of the computer vision research community. One of the many potential applications of such systems is to provide automatic annotation of videos so that the user can retrieve the desired visual content using iconic or linguistic queries in a user-friendly way. This would help to facilitate access to the huge quantities of video information currently stored in archives (and growing daily) and make its retrieval more efficient.

However, it is generally accepted that automatic analysis and interpretation of video is a challenging problem in computer vision for a number of reasons. First of all, there is no direct access to 3D information, as video material is invariably captured using a monocular camera. Second, as the camera is not under our control, we are not able to invoke the active vision paradigm which might help us to interpret a scene by directing the camera to observe each scene object from different views. Third, very little is typically known about the camera system that captured the data.

A. Sanfeliu et al. (Eds.): CIARP 2004, LNCS 3287, pp. 1–12, 2004.

On the positive side, a video captures contextual information which can be made to play a crucial role in the cognitive process. The merit of contextual information in sensory data perception has been demonstrated in application domains such as optical character recognition (OCR) and speech processing. For instance, in the former case, sequences of interpreted characters must constitute valid words. Thus, neighbours (preceding and ensuing characters) convey crucial contextual information for the correct recognition of each character. Similarly, at the next level, language grammar provides context aiding the correct interpretation of words by restricting the admissible sequences of word types and form. At the language understanding level, the circumstances relevant to the subject of discourse furnish contextual clues enabling a text processing system to gain understanding of the content.

In contrast, the use of context in visual data processing is less prevalent. Historically, the focus has been on dealing with the 3D nature of objects under varying illumination which makes object recognition in computer vision a much harder problem than OCR or speech perception. Moreover, in classical computer vision scenarios, such as a robot assembly cell or an office, both spatial and temporal context are relatively limited. For instance, key, books, cups can be placed almost anywhere and the scenes are largely static. Consequently, there are hardly any scene evolution rules that would restrict scene events in a productive way to assist interpretation. The lack of motivation for contextual processing has limited the development of tools that could be used to model and exploit contextual information in a routine manner.

However, in a number of application domains addressed more recently the contextual information is much richer and can play an important role in scene interpretation. A typical example is sports videos where the scene evolution is governed by strict rules. In this paper we explore the role of context in scene interpretation, with a focus on tennis videos. We demonstrate that in this event-driven sport, the detection of visual events and highlights, as well as the symbolic interpretation of the state of play, can be aided by contextual decision making. We construct a multilevel contextual model of tennis game evolution based on the hidden Markov model approach. We then use this model to annotate a tennis video. We show that the model has the capacity to derive the correct interpretation of the scene dynamics, even in the presence of low-level visual event detection errors.

The paper is organised as follows. In Section 2 we review related work. The contextual model adopted is developed in Section 3. The resulting interpretation scheme is described in Section 4. The method is evaluated experimentally in Section 5. Conclusions are drawn in Section 6.

2   Related Work

In order to provide a high-level analysis of video material, there has to be some means of bridging the gap between the contextual information generated by the visual processing modules and the set of assumptions that humans make when viewing the same material. In general, these assumptions are often fuzzy and ill-defined, which makes the bridging task difficult. However, as we have mentioned, in the case of sports material, we are helped by the existence of a set of well-defined rules that govern the progress of a sporting event; these rules can potentially provide strong additional context. For these reasons, Hidden Markov Models (HMMs) and other variants of Dynamic Bayesian Networks (DBNs) are often employed to bridge the semantic gap in sports video analysis. There have been several successful attempts of such use of HMMs in relation to the analysis and annotation of sporting events. Here we discuss some of this work, in particular relating to tennis [1, 2], snooker [3], Formula 1 racing [4] and baseball [5]. The hand gesture recognition system of [6] is also relevant.

- In [4] the authors are developing a complete cognitive audio/visual system for the analysis of videos of Formula 1 race events. They extract semantic information from both the audio and the visual content of the sequence, and annotate the material by detecting events perceived as highly important. For example they include visual events such as overtaking, and cars running off the road. In addition, as the sequences used came from off-air video, they also extracted and used textual information about the race, including the drivers' classification and times. Since off-air material was used, the audio part of the sequences was dominated by the race commentary; from that, features such as voice intensity and pause rates were used. Having extracted all of this information, the authors attempted to infer events of semantic importance through the use of Dynamic Bayesian Networks, inferring content semantics either by using audio and video information separately or combining this information in the temporal domain. Both approaches yielded promising results when tested on simple queries (for example finding shots in the Formula 1 race where a car runs out of the race track).
- In [1] Petkovic et al. use HMMs in order to classify different types of strokes in tennis games, using the body positions of the players. The hit types detected include fore-hands, back-hands, serves, etc. To do this, the authors initially segmented the players out of the background; then they used Fourier descriptors to describe the players' body positioning; finally they trained a set of HMMs to recognise each type of hit. The results of this work show that this method can be quite successful in performing the recognition task it was designed for.
- Kijak et al. [2] also use an HMM to classify a tennis game into these scenes: first missed serve, rally, replay, and commercial break. In this work they used the HMM to fuse both visual cues, including dominant colours, spatial coherency and camera motion activity, and audio cues, including speech, applause, ball hits, noise and music. A second level of HMM is also used in this method, to reflect the syntax of a tennis game.
- Video footage of snooker is used in the work of [3]. The white ball is detected and tracked, and its motion analysed to identify the strategy of the player. The table is partitioned into five strategic areas, which are used by a set of four HMMs to classify the play into five categories: shot-to-nothing,

in which a shot pots a single coloured ball, but with no further strategic benefit; building a break by keeping the white ball in the centre of the table; conservative play (similar to the shot-to-nothing, but with no coloured ball potted); escaping from a snooker; and a miss, in which no collision is detected. The maximum likelihood measures from each HMM are compared to generate the classification.

- The work of Chang et al. [5] describes a method to extract highlights from baseball games. They use a fusion of static and dynamic information to classify the highlights into home run, good hit, good catch and within-diamond play. The static information is represented as statistical modules in the form of histograms, that can be classified into seven different types of play. The dynamic information is in the form of a set of HMMs, one for each highlight type. Each HMM models the transitions between the types of play that are representative of the corresponding highlight.
- In [6], the authors use HMMs to analyse hand gestures. Their framework decomposes each complex event into its constituent elementary actions. Thus in one of the examples the authors have used, a gesture is broken down into simple hand trajectories, which can be tracked more successfully via HMMs. Then, they apply Stochastic Context-Free Grammars to infer the full gesture. Such a paradigm can be compared to a tennis match;if we consider all elementary events leading up to the award of a point in a tennis match to be the equivalent of the elementary gestures in this work, and the tennis rules related to score keeping as an equivalent of the grammar-based tracking of the full gesture the authors have implemented, we can easily see the underlying similarities between the authors' work and reasoning on tennis video sequences.

Although these examples are a small subset of the applications that these inference tools have been tested upon, in each case the HMM (or DBN) provides a useful mechanism for classifying a sequence of detected events with labels that have some semantic content. However we note that in general the HMMs are working at a single semantic level. Thus if mistakes occur, higher level information cannot be brought to bear to influence the decision making. (The exception is [2]), although it is not clear to what extent the higher-level HMM is being used to drive decision making in the lower level one.) In any sports activity, there exists a set of rules that, in the case of professional events, can more or less be relied upon. In particular, in the case of a professional tennis tournament there exists a rich and complex set of formal rules that can be structured in a hierarchical fashion. In the work of [4] these rules are not exploited at all, and in our own previous work, only rules at the lowest level, relating to the award of points, are used.

3   Contextual Model

As we have seen, a large body of work has been done in the area of creating decision-making schemes; one of the most important pieces of work has been the introduction of Hidden Markov Models (HMMs) [7, 8]. A formal definition of a Hidden Markov Model would be that it is a doubly stochastic process where we can *only* observe the outcomes of *one* of the processes; the underlying stochastic process *cannot* be directly observed, but can only be *inferred* through the existing observations, as if it was a function of the latter. A typical example of an HMM could be to consider ourselves in a room and be told about the results of a die being rolled in another room; since we don't know *how* the die is rolled, we have to consider this procedure as a stochastic process – as is the outcome of the die roll itself. Since we only know the outcome of the latter process, the system (the roll and the result processes) is properly described by a Hidden Markov Model. The notation most commonly used in the literature for the parameters in HMMs is the following:

- N, the number of distinct states in the model. In the context of a tennis match, it could be a set of possible playing states within a point (like expecting a hit, point to one player etc.)
- M, the number of distinct observation symbols for each state, i.e. the alphabet size. In this context, this could include the set of possible events within a tennis match.
- τ, the length of the observation sequence – in the scope of this analysis, it would be the length of a play rally.
- i^t will be the hidden state of the HMM at time t. Hence, $1 \leq i_t \leq N$.
- $P(i^t = k)$ denotes the probability of the state having the label k at time t.
- O_t will be the observation symbol at time t – equivalent to '*what was observed at time t?*'

When using HMMs to perform inference on a given problem, their most useful feature is their ability to calculate the *most likely* state sequence from an observation sequence. This is done by applying the *Viterbi algorithm*[9, 10], an inductive algorithm based on dynamic programming.

The Markov property for the sequence of hidden states $i_1, \cdots, i_\tau$ and the related observation sequence $O_1, \cdots, O_\tau$ for any $\tau \geq 2$ can be stated as

$$P(i^\tau | i^1, \cdots, i^{\tau-1}) = P(i^\tau | i^{\tau-1})$$

Assuming stationarity for i^τ, we can write, for $\tau \geq 2$ and $1 < k_1, k_2 \leq N$,

$$P(i^\tau = k_1 | i^{\tau-1} = k_2) \equiv P(k_1 | k_2)$$

Now, the previous state of the process is characterised by the (known) probability measure $P(i^{\tau-1} | O_1, \cdots, O_{\tau-1})$. Thus the *a priori* probability at time τ, which is $P(i^\tau | O_1, \cdots, O_{\tau-1})$, will be given by

$$P(i^\tau = k_1 | O_1, \cdots, O_{\tau-1}) = \sum_{k_2=1}^{N} P(k_1 | k_2) \cdot P(i^{\tau-1} = k_2 | O_1, \cdots, O_{\tau-1})$$

If we also assume that that $O_1, \cdots, O_\tau$ are conditionally independent, ie. that

$$P(O_\tau | i^\tau, O_1, \cdots, O_{\tau-1}) = P(O_\tau | i^\tau)$$

the *a posteriori* probability at time τ will be given by

$$P(i^\tau|O_1,\cdots,O_\tau) = \frac{P(i^\tau|O_1,\cdots,O_{\tau-1}) \cdot P(O_\tau|i^\tau)}{\sum_{k=1}^{N} P(O_\tau|i^\tau = k) \cdot P(i^\tau = k|O_1,\cdots,O_{\tau-1})}$$

This probability will be the optimal decision criterion at time τ and, at the same time, the *a priori* probability for time $\tau + 1$.

The Viterbi algorithm is appropriate for discovering the sequence of states that will yield a *minimum* path cost for the sequence. However, this is the case where we *only* want to extract the current state by *only* looking at the current observation symbol. This approach is bound to yield a large number of errors if faced with erroneous input data; therefore, we will need to compensate for that fact in some way if we are to use HMMs in a real-world system. There are two main methods of achieving this:

- Using multiple hypotheses for the evolution of a given sequence – in this case, we allow more than one event sequence to develop and be updated simultaneously, and we *eliminate* those where a transition from its previous state to its current one is *not allowed*.
- Directly taking under consideration the fact that the system will be using more than one observation to perform inference for a given event while developing the appropriate mathematical formulation of this problem. That means that we need to assume that the Markov processes that describe the problem can use the subsequent event in order to decide whether the current one is valid or not. This mode of decision is known in the literature as the *look-ahead ahead decision mode for a Markov chain* and is analysed in detail in [11]. In our context, *both the observation* (ie. the game event) *and the state* (ie. state of play) sequences would fall into this category.

The baseline technique can be generalised so as to also include *future* observation patterns, like $O_{\tau+1}$, in a similar way it can be generalised for higher-order Markov sources. Let us assume that, in time τ, a decision has to be made on classifying an input pattern O_τ. The decision can then *be postponed* until *the next pattern*, $O_{\tau+1}$, is also observed. Therefore, the probability required now is $P(i^\tau|O_1,\cdots,O_\tau,O_{\tau+1})$. For that to be calculated, $P(i^\tau|O_1,\cdots,O_\tau)$ is also required; this is calculated as we have previously seen. Therefore

$$P(i^\tau|O_1,\cdots,O_\tau,O_{\tau+1}) = \frac{P(i^\tau|O_1,\cdots,O_\tau) \cdot P(O_{\tau+1}|i^\tau)}{\sum_{k=1}^{N} P(O_{\tau+1}|i^\tau = k) \cdot P(i^\tau = k|O_1,\cdots,O_\tau)}$$

and, since $O_1,\cdots,O_{\tau+1}$ are independent,

$$P(i^\tau|O_1,\cdots,O_\tau,O_{\tau+1}) = \frac{P(i^\tau|O_1,\cdots,O_\tau) \cdot P(O_{\tau+1}|i^\tau)}{\sum_{k_1=1}^{N} \sum_{k_2=1}^{N} P(O_{\tau+1}|i^{\tau+1} = k_1) \cdot P(k_1|k_2) \cdot P(i^\tau = k_2|O_1,\cdots,O_\tau)}$$

4   Proposed Scheme

In our context (the analysis of tennis video sequences), the rules of the game of tennis provide us with a very good guideline as to what events we will have to be capable of tracking efficiently, so as to follow the evolution of a tennis match properly. Such events would include:

– The tennis ball being hit by the players
– The ball bouncing on the court
– The players' positions and shapes (that is, body poses)
– Sounds related to the tennis match (either from the commentary or the court)

These events can be used as a basis on which to perform reasoning for events of higher importance, like awarding the current point from the events witnessed during play. Based on them, the full graphical model for the evolution and award of a point in a tennis match is illustrated in the graph of Figure 1.

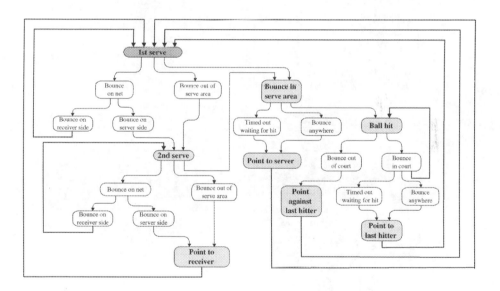

Fig. 1. Graphical model for awarding a point in a tennis match

As we can readily see from this diagram, it is a graphical model where a number of loops exist; the state transitions drawn with **bold** lines indicate where these loops close. Moreover, this graphical model *only* tackles the problem of awarding a single point in the match; there is some more detail to be added to it if we wish to include the awarding of games, sets or the full match. How these stages are going to be implemented will be discussed in more detail later in this section. Finally, this figure also shows us that, in order to address the problem of 'understanding' the game of tennis more effectively, we will have to convert this complex evolution graph into a set of simpler structures.

Thus, we propose to replace the original scene evolution model with a set of smaller models, each one trying to properly illustrate a certain scenario of the match evolution. The most important thing we need to ensure during this procedure is that, when we combine all of the models in this set, we *must* have a model equivalent to the original one (so that it reflects the rules of tennis). The set of sub-graphs proposed to replace the original one is illustrated in Figure 2.

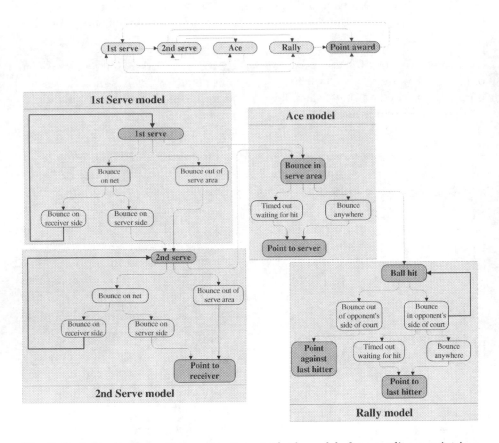

Fig. 2. Switching model and its respective set of sub-models for awarding a point in a tennis match, as separated out from the original graphical model

As we can see from the set of models above, we have opted for a more 'perceptual' way of selecting the set of event chains that will formulate the new model set for our purposes. This design strategy is going to be particularly helpful in the (quite frequent, as it is expected) cases where the system receives a query to extract sequences which contain some specific event; since the scene description will consist of a series of events occurring in the match, such queries can be dealt with relatively easily. Moreover, choosing to break the initial graph down to a number of sub-graphs and train each one of them separately will be beneficial in many more different ways. Some of the resulting benefits are:

- Using probabilistic reasoning tools (like HMMs) will allow for correction of wrongly detected elementary events within the game – so we can have a point correctly awarded even if we haven't tracked *all* events accurately from the start.
- Since the models are simpler, we will *not* have to acquire a huge training data set; a relatively small amount of data per model will suffice for our analysis. This will also make the training procedure a *much less* computationally expensive process as well – due to both the reduced volume of the training data and the simplicity of the models as well.
- In some cases, we can *considerably speed up* the training process due to prior knowledge for this type of content. For example, the amount of statistics available for events occurring in a tennis match helps us get a very good initial estimate for the HMM parameters *without* the need of a training process; we only need to pick up some existing measurements for this purpose.
- It will be *easier* to determine which areas (ie. sub-models) of the reasoning engine need to be improved to boost the overall performance of the system and which low-level feature extraction modules are more suspect to produce misleading results – so that we can either improve them or replace them with a different approach.

Since the detection of such elementary events will be done using machine vision algorithms and techniques, we are bound to encounter event detection errors in the process. Hence, another crucial issue is to examine the robustness of the proposed scheme to false events in its input. To address this, it has been decided that the system will be implemented through the use of *Hidden Markov Models with a look-ahead decision mechanism*, therefore allowing us to take into account events that occur *after* the one currently examined. This will help the system establish whether the current event can actually occur or it needs to be corrected and re-examined, as the rules of tennis will allow us to detect and correct contradictory hypotheses. The length of the look-ahead window has been limited to 1 event forward, thus allowing us to correct isolated errors – if we encounter 2 or more consecutive errors, the output will generally *not* be correct. However, there are two reasons for this choice:

- If the length of the look-ahead window is too large, small rallies (like aces) with errors in them may be wrongly interpreted. That can happen as, at the end of the chain, the Viterbi algorithm will *not* have enough evidence to correct errors. For cases like this, we will need to implement an error-correcting scheme on top of the proposed method, that will rely on different context – as will be discussed later on.
- Out of the events required for correct evolution tracking in this context, the type of events that is *clearly* most susceptible to errors is the ball bounces – the difficulty of tracking a ball in a tennis sequence stemming from the fact

that it is a very small, fast-moving object. However, since *only one bounce* can occur between two successive player hits if the point is still to be played, detecting a player hit (*not* a serve) automatically removes the chance of a point being awarded, even if the bounce point is wrongly detected (or not detected *at all*).

This graph will be implemented through using a *'switch'* variable to select which of the constituent sub-models will be used to model the scene at a given moment. Therefore, the proposed system's structure is similar to a Switching HMM. As soon as we have determined which way the points are going to be awarded, we can move on to the award of games and sets in the match. This can either be done through the use of probabilistic reasoning tools (such as HMMs), or with simpler, rule-based tools – such as grammars. The latter is possible due to the fact that at this level of abstraction in modelling tennis game sequences, it is the rules of the game of tennis that stipulate the evolution of the scene rather than low-level events in it. However, since the uncertainty stemming from the successful (or unsuccessful) detection of the elementary events mentioned above *cannot always* be considered to have been effectively addressed in the lower-level stages of the reasoning process (ie. up to the level of point awarding), we will *have to* opt for using probabilistic tools to perform higher levels of reasoning for these video sequences. However, the fact that these models will *directly* correspond to the rules of tennis and that most of the spurious low-level data have already been corrected will allow for far greater confidence in the output of the higher-level system.

5   Results and Discussion

The scheme described above has been tested on one hour's play from the Men's Final of the 2003 Australian Tennis Open. The sequence contained a total of 100 points played – equivalent to approximately one and a half sets of the match. Out of these 100 exchanges, a total of 36 were played on a second serve. The data that was used as input in this experiment were *ground-truth, hand-annotated event chains* from the broadcast match video in the first case, and the same data with *one* error per point sequence randomly inserted into it in the second. Therefore, we have examined *both* the ability of the proposed scheme to model the evolution of the match accurately *and* the robustness of it at the same time. To do that, we had to introduce four sets of models – one for every combination of which player serves and which side of the court he/she serves from (left or right). Moreover, in the second case, we limited the system to *only* check the next event for error correction. In those 100 exchanges, we have intentionally left in a few *unfinished* points, so as to examine whether the selection of the hidden states for these models can lead to an accurate representation of the scene at *any* given time – *not only* at the end of the scene. They were 4 in total – 2 leading to a second serve and 2 were cut short while still on play. An overall view of the results is given in Tables 1 and 2 below.

Table 1. Total results for Ground-Truth Data

	Ground Truth	Correctly Awarded	Wrongly Awarded	Not awarded (still on play)
Near Player Points	59	59	0	0
Far Player Points	37	37	0	0
Unfinished Points	4	4	0	n/a
TOTAL	100	100	0	0

Table 2. Total results for Data with Errors Inserted

	Ground Truth	Correctly Awarded	Wrongly Awarded	Not awarded (still on play)
Near Player Points	59	57	0	2
Far Player Points	37	35	1	1
Unfinished Points	4	3	1	n/a
TOTAL	100	95	2	3

As we can see in Table 1, *all* of the points were successfully tracked by the proposed system when ground-truth data were used, whereas in the case of errors in the data set (shown in Table 2), we did have some errors in recognition. This happened because of the fact that, in those points, the *very last* event on the chain was wrong – and since there was no 'future' to the event sequence after that event, the system had no way of inferring that this was wrong. However, this is a predictable problem, because this event is the deciding one for the point and the uncertainty in it *cannot* be removed; therefore, the uncertainty will propagate to the decision *for this level* as well. This observation shows that the application of a similar error-correcting scheme on top of the proposed system (in which point award is to be processed) will further enhance the robustness of the system.

6   Conclusions

As we can readily see from the results shown above, the proposed system has tackled the problem of tracking the evolution of a tennis match very effectively. Whereas in the case where no error input has been provided, such accuracy serves only to illustrate that the use of such an approach is not inherently wrong; it is the performance of the proposed scheme when errors were added in the observation sequences that makes it seem a very promisimg solution for a fully automated evolution tracking system for tennis vidoos.

However, there are still some issues to be addressed in this area. First of all, the aim of developing such an automatic evolution tracking scheme is for use as an automatic video annotation system, in conjunction with a set of fully automatic low-level feature extraction tools that will be able to detect the basic events required for input to the proposed system. As in any fully automatic computer vision system, the low-level feature extraction tools are bound to produce recognition errors which will propagate to the proposed decision-making scheme. Therefore, and although some testing has already been carried out for the proposed scheme, it is essential that the proposed scheme is also tested with the actual low-level feature extraction tools integrated into it, so that we can have a clearer view of what errors occur in the lower levels and provide accurate statistics about the performance and robustness of the higher levels of the inference engine as a whole.

Moreover, the proposed system is only the first step in a hierarchical model that will fully describe the evolution of a tennis match – it will only cover the award of a single point in the match. The creation of a full system will require the design of a similar error-correcting scheme to award games, sets and finally the match – and which will all rely on the efficiency of this method.

Acknowledgements

This work has been supported by the EU IST-2001-34401 Project VAMPIRE.

References

1. Petkovic, M., Jonker, W., Zivkovic, Z.: Recognizing strokes in tennis videos using Hidden Markov Models. In: Proceedings of Intl. Conf. on Visualization, Imaging and Image Processing, Marbella, Spain. (2001)
2. Kijak, E., Gravier, G., Gros, P., Oisel, L., Bimbot, F.: HMM based structuring of tennis videos using visual and audio cues. In: Proceedings of the IEEE International Conference on Multimedia and Expo (ICME'03). (2003)
3. Rea, N., Dahyot, R., Kokaram, A.: Modeling high-level structure in sports with motion-driven HMMs. In: Proceedings of the IEEE International Conference on Acoustics, Speech, and Signal Processing (ICASSP 2004), Montreal, Quebec, Canada (2004)
4. Petkovic, M., Mihajlovic, V., Jonker, W., Djordjevic-Kajan, S.: Multi-modal extraction of highlights from TV Formula 1 programs. In: Proceedings of the IEEE International Conference on Multimedia and Expo. Volume 1. (2002) 817–820
5. Chang, P., Han, M., Gong, Y.: Extract highlights from baseball game video with hidden Markov models. In: Proceedings of the International Conference on Image Processing (ICIP'02), Rochester, New York (2002)
6. Ivanov, Y., Bobick, A.: Recognition of Visual Activities and Interactions by Stochastic Parsing. IEEE Transactions on Pattern Analysis and Machine Intelligence 22 (2000) 852–872
7. Rabiner, L.R., Juang, B.H.: An introduction to Hidden Markov Models. IEEE Signal Processing Magazine 61 (1986) 4–16
8. Dugad, R., Desai, U.B.: A tutorial on Hidden Markov Models. Technical Report SPANN-96-1, Signal Processing and Artificial Neural Networks Laboratory Department of Electrical Engineering Indian Institute of Technology – Bombay Powai, Bombay 400 076, India (1996)
9. Viterbi, A.: Error bounds for convolutional codes and an asymptotically optimum decoding algorithm. IEEE Transactions on Information Theory 13 (1967) 260–269
10. Forney, G.D.: The Viterbi algorithm. Proceedings of the IEEE 61 (1973) 263–278
11. Devijver, P.A., Kittler, J.: Pattern Recognition – A Statistical Approach. Prentice Hall International, London, UK (1982)

Content Based Retrieval of 3D Data

Alberto Del Bimbo and Pietro Pala

Dipartimento Sistemi e Informatica
Università di Firenze
via S.Marta 3, 50139 Firenze, Italy
{delbimbo,pala}@dsi.unifi.it

Abstract. Along with images and videos, 3D models have recently gained increasing attention for a number of reasons: advancements in 3D hardware and software technologies, their ever decreasing prices and increasing availability, affordable 3D authoring tools, and the establishment of open standards for 3D data interchange.

The ever increasing availability of 3D models demands for tools supporting their effective and efficient management. Among these tools, those enabling content-based retrieval play a key role.

In this paper we report on our experience in developing models to support retrieval by content of 3D objects. Particularly, we present three different models for representing and comparing the content of 3D objects. A comparative analysis is carried out to evidence the actual potential of the proposed solutions.

1 Introduction

Digital multimedia information is nowadays spreading through all sectors of society and collections of multimedia documents are being created at an increasing pace in several domains. However, in order to exploit the valuable assets contained in these ever growing collections, some tool should be available to support users in the process of finding information out of these data. In recent years, as a result of the efforts spent in the attempt of finding solutions to this problem, many systems have been developed that enable effective retrieval from digital libraries, covering text, audio, images, and videos.

Beside image and video databases, archives of 3D models have recently gained increasing attention for a number of reasons: advancements in 3D hardware and software technologies, their ever increasing availability at affordable costs, and the establishment of open standards for 3D data interchange (e.g. VRML, X3D).

Acquisition of the 3D model of an object, capturing both object geometry and its visual features (surface color and texture), can be achieved through many different techniques, including CAD, 3D laser scanners, structured light systems and photogrammetry. The selection of the most appropriate technique depends on application specific quality requirements. Furthermore, these techniques result in a large variety of models, differing in terms of their representation (e.g. point clouds, voxels, analytical functions), of their resolution and size, of the presence, nature, and amount of noise and artifacts.

A. Sanfeliu et al. (Eds.): CIARP 2004, LNCS 3287, pp. 13–24, 2004.

Thanks to the availability of technologies for their acquisition, 3D models are being employed in a wide range of application domains, including medicine, computer aided design and engineering, and cultural heritage. In this framework the development of techniques to enable retrieval by content of 3D models assumes an ever increasing relevance.

This is particularly the case in the fields of cultural heritage and historical relics, where there is an increasing interest in solutions enabling preservation of relevant artworks (e.g. vases, sculptures, and handicrafts) as well as cataloguing and retrieval by content. In these fields, retrieval by content can be employed to detect commonalities between 3D objects (e.g. the "signature" of the artist) or to monitor the temporal evolution of a defect (e.g. the amount of bending for wooden tables).

Methods addressing retrieval of 3D models can be distinguished based on different aspects, such as the type of representation used for geometry, the use of information about models' aspect (i.e. colour and/or texture), the need for manual annotation.

Description and retrieval of 3D objects based on description and retrieval of 2D views has been addressed in [1] and [2]. However, the effectiveness of these solutions is limited to description and retrieval of simple objects. In fact, as complex objects are considered, occlusions prevent to capture distinguishing 3D features using 2D views.

Description of 3D surface data for the purpose of recognition or retrieval has been addressed for some time. A few authors have investigated analytical 3D models, but this is not always a viable solution, as there are many limitations in providing parameterizations of arbitrary models. In [3] retrieval of 3D objects based on similarity of surface segments is addressed. Surface segments model potential docking sites of molecular structures. The proposed approach develops on the approximation error of the surface. However, assumptions on the form of the function to be approximated limit applicability of the approach to special contexts.

Much attention has been recently devoted to free-form (i.e. polygonal) meshes. While this representation of 3D models poses major hurdles to development and implementation of algorithms, it is indeed the most appealing field of application. The system developed within the Nefertiti project supports retrieval of 3D models based on both geometry and appearance (i.e. colour and texture) [4]. Also Kolonias et al. have used dimensions of the bounding box (i.e. its aspect ratios) and a binary voxel-based representation of geometry [5]. They further relied on a third feature, namely a set of paths, outlining the shape (*model routes*). In [6] a method is proposed to select feature points which relies on the evaluation of Gaussian and median curvature maxima, as well as of torsion maxima on the surface. In [7], Elad et al. use moments (up to the 4-7th order) of surface points as basic features to support retrieval of 3D models. Differently from the case of 2D images, evaluation of moments is not affected by (self-)occlusions.

In this paper we report on the use of three models for representing the content of a 3D object for the purpose of supporting retrieval by object similarity.

The three models are based on projection of surface curvature information and spin images. Projection of surface curvature information is obtained by warping object surface until it becomes a function on the sphere. Then, information about curvature is projected onto a 2D curvature map that retains information about curvature distribution on the original object surface. Content of the 2D curvature map is described using two different techniques: histograms of map tiles and weighted walkthroughs of map regions.

The third model for content representation is based on spin images. These capture geometric properties of 3D objects regardless of surface curvature. Since object description based on spin images entails a huge amount of information, feature extraction and clustering techniques are used to meet the specific storage and efficiency requirements of content-based retrieval.

The paper is organized as follows: Sec.2 describes some pre-processing steps that are necessary to apply both curvature maps and spin images techniques; Sec.3 expounds on computation of curvature maps from 3D object meshes; Sec.4 describes how to use curvature maps for description of 3D objects content; Sec.5 introduces extraction of spin images from 3D objects; Sec.6 describes how to use spin images for description of 3D objects content; finally in Sec.7 a comparative analysis among the proposed techniques is presented.

2   Preprocessing

High resolution 3D models obtained through scanning of real world objects are often affected by high frequency noise, due to either the scanning device or the subsequent registration process. Hence, smoothing is required to cope with such models for the purpose of extracting their salient features.

Selection of a smoothing filter is a critical step, as application of some filters entails changes in the shape of the models. For instance, mean or Laplacian smoothing cause shrinking of the model (a known problem, which has been pointed out – for example – in [6]). In Laplacian smoothing, every vertex x is moved from its original location by an offset $\Delta(x)$; the offset is determined as a function of the neighbouring vertices of x, and a parameter λ controls the strength of the filter. To avoid shrinking, we adopted the filter first proposed by Taubin [8]. This filter, also known as $\lambda|\mu$ filter, operates iteratively, and interleaves a Laplacian smoothing weighed by λ with a second smoothing weighed with a negative factor μ ($\lambda > 0$, $\mu < -\lambda < 0$). This second step is introduced to preserve the model's original shape.

An additional pre-processing step is employed to reduce the complexity of the model (in terms of the number of vertices). To this end, an algorithm performing an iterative contraction of vertex pairs (i.e. edges) is used: first, all edges are ranked according to a cost metric; then, the minimum cost vertex pair is contracted; finally, the costs are updated [9]. The algorithm is iterated until a predefined stop criterion is met: In our experiments, the stop criterion was set in terms of the number of polygons of the final model.

2.1   Curvature Estimation

Estimation of surface curvature at a generic vertex v_i of the mesh is accomplished by considering variations of surface normal over the *platelet* V^{v_i} of vertex v_i. This guarantees less sensitivity to noise and acquisition errors.

In particular, surface curvature in correspondence with the i-th vertex v_i of the mesh $\mathcal{M}$ is estimated by considering versor $v_i^{\perp}$, that is, the normal to $\mathcal{M}$ at point v_i. Then , the *platelet* V^{v_i} of vertex v_i is considered. This is defined as the set of all mesh vertices around v_i. Given a generic vertex of the platelet $v_j \in V^{v_i}$ let $v_j^{\perp}$ be the normal to $\mathcal{M}$ at point v_j. Mesh curvature γ_{v_i} at vertex v_i is estimated as:

$$\gamma_{v_i} = \frac{1}{2} \frac{\sum_{v_j \in V^{v_i}} |v_i^{\perp} - v_j^{\perp}|}{|V^{v_i}|} \tag{1}$$

It can be shown that with this definition, the value of γ_{v_i} is always in $[0, 1]$.

3   Curvature Maps

Given a 3D object, construction of its curvature map relies on warping object surface until it becomes a function on a sphere and then projecting curvature information onto a 2D image. Mesh deformation is obtained by iteratively applying a smoothing operator to the mesh. In general, application of a smoothing operator is accomplished by updating the position of each vertex of the mesh according to the following formula:

$$\mathcal{M}(v_i) \otimes \omega = \frac{\mu}{\sum_{v_j \in V^{v_i}} w_j} \sum_{v_j \in V^{v_i}} w_j * v_i - v_i \tag{2}$$

being weights $\omega = \{w_j\}$ characteristic of each operator and μ a parameter used to control the amount of motion of each vertex and to guarantee stability and continuity of the smoothing process.

Under the assumption of low μ values, the iterative application of the smoothing operator to every vertex of the mesh is equivalent to an elastic deformation process. During the deformation process each vertex of the mesh should be moved in order to satisfy two sometimes opposite requirements: mesh regularization and curvature minimization. As demonstrated in previous work [10], application of *Laplacian Smoothing*, *Taubin Smoothing*, or *Bilaplacian Flow* operators increases mesh regularization but may result in unnatural deformations of the original mesh. Differently, application of *Mean Curvature Flow* operator doesn't guarantee mesh regularization.

To achieve both regularization and smoothing of the original mesh, the proposed solution develops on the application of two distinct operators at each step of the iterative deformation process. In particular, Laplacian and Gaussian smoothing operators are used in combination to achieve both mesh smoothing and regularization. Application of the two operators is iterated until the average value of vertex motion falls below a predefined threshold τ.

3.1 Mapping

Projection of a curved surface is a well known problem in cartography [11]. There are many different projections used to map (a part of) the globe onto a plane, but their description is far beyond the scope of this paper. In our approach, we have selected the Archimedes projection (also known as the Lambert equal-area projection). Similarly to the Mercator projection, the Archimedes projection is a cylindrical projection. In particular, it is the projection along a line perpendicular to the axis connecting the poles and parallel to the equatorial plane. Thus, a point on the sphere with latitude Θ and longitude Φ, is mapped into the point on the cylinder with the same longitudinal angle Θ and height $sin(\Phi)$ above (or below) the equatorial plane.

A major advantage of the Archimedes projection is that it is an area preserving projection: all regions on the surface of the sphere are mapped into regions on the map having the same area. This guarantees that, regardless of the position on the sphere, the relevance of any region is the same both on the sphere and on the map.

4 From Curvature Maps to Content Descriptors

Ideally, once a 3D model is represented through a 2D curvature map, any approach supporting image retrieval by visual similarity could be used to evaluate the similarity between two 3D models. In fact, this can be achieved by computing the similarity of the corresponding maps.

In the proposed approach, information about curvature maps is captured at two distinct levels: tiles obtained by a uniform tessellation of the map, and homogeneous regions obtained by segmenting the map. In the former case, we use histograms to capture global properties of map tiles, whereas in the latter case we rely on weighted walkthroughs to describe spatial arrangement and local properties of regions on the map. Details on the two techniques are provided hereafter.

4.1 Histogram-Based Description of Map Tiles

A generic histogram H with n bins is an element of the histogram space $\mathcal{H}^n \subset \mathbb{R}^n$. Given an image and a quantization of a feature space, histogram bins count the number of occurrences of points of that quantized feature value in the image.

Histograms also support a multi-resolution description of image features. Given a partitioning of an image into n fine-grained tiles, histograms provide a representation for the content of each of these tiles.

In order to compute the similarity between two histograms, a norm must be defined in the histogram space. In our experiments the *Kolmogorov-Smirnov* distance was adopted. Thus, the distance between two histograms H and H' is computed as follows:

$$\mathcal{D}_{KS}(H, H') = \max_i(\check{h}_i, \check{h}'_i) \tag{3}$$

being $\check{h}_i$ and $\check{h}'_i$ i-th element of the cumulated histogram of H and H', respectively (i.e. $\check{h}_i = \sum_{k=1}^{i} h_k$).

Computing the distance between two maps requires to find the best tiles correspondence function. This is defined as the permutation $p : \{1, \ldots, n\} \rightarrow \{1, \ldots, n\}$ that minimizes the sum of distances between corresponding tiles.

The solution p is approximated through a *greedy search* approach that requires to scan all tiles in the first map in a predefined order and associate to each tile the most similar tile not yet associated in the second map. This pairwise NN association yields a suboptimal solution.

4.2   Weighted Walkthroughs Description of Map Tiles

Description of map content through histograms is not able to capture neither the spatial arrangement nor the local properties of individual regions of the map. In some cases this can be a limitation, since information about individual regions and their spatial arrangement in the map is strictly related to information about shape and structure of the original 3D mesh. To overcome these limitations, the coarse description of map content is complemented with a local approach capturing local properties of individual regions in the map as well as their spatial arrangement.

Local description of map content is based on weighted walkthroughs technique [12]. In particular, description of map content is accomplished by segmenting the map into regions characterized by uniform curvature values. For each region, information about region area and average curvature is retained. Furthermore, for each pair of regions, their relative position is captured through a 3×3 array corresponding to the weighted walkthroughs for the two regions.

The use of weighted walkthroughs enables description of map content in the form of an attributed relational graph. Graph vertices correspond to regions of the map and are labelled with the region's area and average curvature. Graph edges retain information about the relative position of regions they link and are labelled with the corresponding 3×3 weighted walkthroughs.

The descriptor of content of a generic map can be represented as $\langle R, f, w \rangle$, being R the set of regions in the map, f the set of visual features capturing the appearance of each region (in our case region area and average curvature), and w the set of weighted walkthroughs capturing the relative position of each region pair.

Computation of the similarity between two descriptors of map local content is equivalent to an error correcting subgraph isomorphism problem [13], which is an NP-complete problem with exponential time solution algorithms [14].

In the proposed approach, identification of the optimal node association function is accomplished through the technique presented in [15]. This is based on a look-ahead strategy that extends classical state-space search approaches.

5   Spin Images

Spin images were introduced by Johnson and Hebert to support recognition of single objects in complex scenes [16]. Basically, spin images encode the density of mesh vertices projected onto an object-centred space: the three-dimensional mesh vertices are first mapped onto a two-dimensional space defined w.r.t. to the object itself; the resulting coordinates are then used to build a two-dimensional histogram.

More precisely, let $O = \langle p, n \rangle$ an *oriented point* on the surface of the object, where p is a point on the surface of the object and n the normal of the tangent plane in p. For a generic oriented point O, a *spin map* can be defined, which maps any point x in the three-dimensional space onto a two-dimensional space according to the following formula (see also Fig. 1 for notation):

$$S_O(x) \to [\alpha, \beta] = [\sqrt{\|x - p\|^2 - (n \cdot (x - p))^2}, n \cdot (x - p)]$$

In other words, the oriented point defines a family of cylindrical coordinate systems, with the origin in p, and with the axis along n. The spin map projection of x retains the radial distance (α) and the elevation (β), while it discards the polar angle.

To produce a *spin image* of an object, a spin map is applied to points comprising the surface of the object. Hence, given a mesh representation of the object, the spin image can be obtained by applying the map to the vertices comprising the mesh. A simple binary image can be obtained by discretizing the projected coordinates and by setting the corresponding point on the image. However, more refined grey-level spin images encoding a measure of the density of vertices that insist upon the same image point are usually employed. To construct such an image, the projected coordinates α and β of each mesh vertex are used to update the two-dimensional histogram $I(i, j)$ (i.e. the spin image) according to a bi-linear interpolation scheme that spreads the contribution of each vertex over the nearest points on the grid induced by the quantization of the image space.

Most outstanding characteristics of spin images are invariance to rigid transformations (as a consequence of the adoption of an object-centred coordinate system), limited sensitivity to variations of position of mesh vertices (which might result from the adoption of different sampling schemes), flexibility (since no hypotheses are made on the surface representation), and ease of computation.

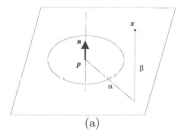
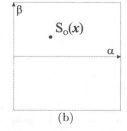

(a)   (b)

Fig. 1. Given an oriented point $\langle p, n \rangle$ on the object surface, a generic point x is mapped on point $[\alpha, \beta]$ on the spin map, being $[\alpha, \beta]$ the radial distance and the elevation of x w.r.t. to $\langle p, n \rangle$. a) the object centred 3D coordinates system, and b) the spin map coordinate system.

6 From Spin Images to Content Descriptors

Spin images provide a powerful means to describe three-dimensional objects. However, the fact that many spin images are typically produced for a single object, and the fact that each image implies considerable storage requirements, prevent us to use them directly as descriptors for retrieval purposes. Therefore, we decided to rely on more compact descriptions extracted from spin images, synthesizing the content of each spin image. Our descriptor for spin images was inspired by region descriptions such as grid-based techniques or the shape matrix [17]. Instead of sampling the shape at the intersection between radial and circular lines, we decided to measure the relative density encompassed by each of the regions defined by those lines, so as to provide a more precise description of the spin image. We have defined three independent sets of regions for the spin image: sectors of circular crowns for both the half-plane with $\beta > 0$ and the half plane with $\beta < 0$, and circular sectors. Each of these sets defines a descriptor ($C^p = \langle cp_1, \ldots, cp_{np} \rangle$, $C^n = \langle cn_1, \ldots, cn_{nn} \rangle$, and $S = \langle s_1, \ldots, s_{ns} \rangle$, respectively), whose components represent the amount of surface points (or vertices) whose projections fall within the corresponding crown/sector.

Based on results of some preliminary experiments we chose $np = nn = ns = 6$ as these represent a satisfactory trade-off between compactness and selectivity of the representation. Hence, a 18-dimensional descriptor $D = \langle C^p, C^n, S \rangle$ is evaluated for each spin image.

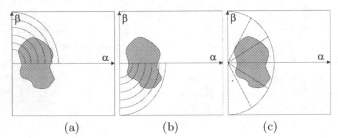

    (a)   (b)   (c)

Fig. 2. Compound object descriptors comprise descriptors for a) np crowns in the half-plane $\beta > 0$, b) nn crowns in the half-plane $\beta < 0$, c) ns sectors. In our experiments $np = nn = ns = 6$.

In order to avoid use of one spin image descriptor for each mesh vertex, spin image descriptors are subject to clustering. For this purpose we relied on fuzzy clustering [18], which is an extension to c-means procedure that avoids partitioning feature vectors into *hard* or *crisp* clusters. Through clustering, we represent the original set of spin image descriptors $\{SI_1, \ldots, SI_m\}$ ($SI_i \in \mathbb{R}^{18}$) – each descriptor being associated with one mesh vertex – with a compact set represented by the clusters' centers.

Computation of the similarity between two 3D objects is accomplished by comparing their descriptors, each descriptor being in the form of a set of cluster centers $\mathcal{D} = \{D_i, i = 1 \ldots\}$.

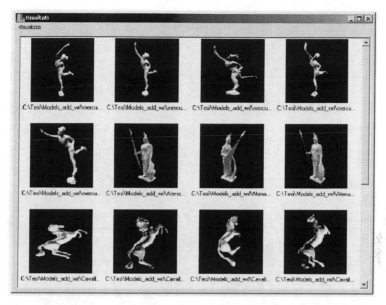

Fig. 3. Retrieval of Mercur statues using spin images. All models of the Mercur statues are retrieved first, followed by models of other statues which display similar shapes.

Computing the distance Δ between two descriptors $\mathcal{D}$ and $\hat{\mathcal{D}}$ requires to find the best cluster-center correspondence function. This is defined as the permutation $p : \{1, \ldots, l\} \to \{1, \ldots, k\}$ that minimizes the sum of distances between corresponding cluster centers.

7   Comparative Analysis

Approximately 300 models were collected to build the test database. These comprise four classes of models: taken from the web, manually authored (with a 3D CAD software), high quality 3D scans from the De Espona 3D Models Encyclopedia[1], and variations of the previous three classes (obtained through geometric deformation or application of noise, which caused points surface to be moved from their original locations).

Fig.3 shows a retrieval example using spin images. The query is the model of a statue portraying Mercur. The result set displays all models of the Mercur statue in the first five positions. In general, all retrieved models feature similar shapes, characterized by a main body and protrusions that resemble Mercur's elongated arm and leg. Fig.4 shows a retrieval example where the model of a Satyr's bust is used as a query. The result set displays all models of the Satyr's bust in the first five positions. Other models reproducing busts are also retrieved.

Among the different techniques reviewed in Section 1, we selected the curvature histograms [19] and moments of surface points [7] for a comparative as-

---

[1] http://www.deespona.com

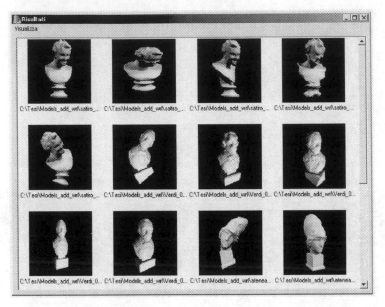

Fig. 4. A retrieval example, using the model of a Satyr's bust as the query. Other models of the Satyr's bust are retrieved first, followed by models of other busts.

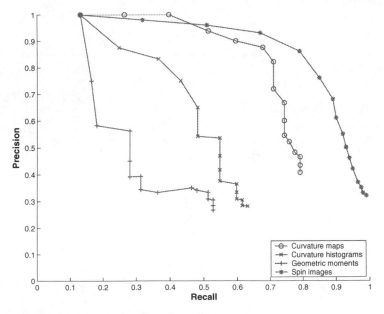

Fig. 5. Comparison of precision/recall figures for the four methods: curvature histograms, moments, weighted walkthroughs of curvature maps and spin images.

sessment. Performance comparison is assessed through four sample queries that were submitted to each of the four retrieval engines. Average precision vs. recall curves are shown in Fig. 5.

The comparative evaluation shows that retrieval based on spin images performs better than all the other three approaches. In particular, performance of approaches based on curvature histograms and 3D moments is particularly critical. This may be accounted to the fact that these two methods only provide a global description of the object, and this is often unappropriate for discrimination of different models.

References

1. S. Mahmoudi, M. Daoudi, "3D models retrieval by using characteristic views", in *Proc. of 16th Int'l Conf. on Pattern Recognition*, Vol.2, pp.457-460, 11-15 Aug, 2002.
2. R. Ohbuchi, M. Nakazawa, T. Takei, "Retrieving 3D Shapes based on Their Appearance", in *Proc. of MIR'03*, Berkeley, CA, USA, Nov. 2003, pp.39-46.
3. H.P. Kriegel, T. Seidl, "Approximation-Based Similarity Search for 3D Surface Segments", *GeoInformatica Journal*, 2(2):113-147, Kluwer Academic Publisher, 1998.
4. E. Paquet, M. Rioux, "Nefertiti: a query by content system for three-dimensional model and image database management", *Image Vision and Computing*, 17(2):157-166, 1999.
5. I. Kolonias, D. Tzovaras, S. Malassiotis, M. G. Strintzis, "Content-Based Similarity Search of VRML Models Using Shape Descriptors", in *Proc. of International Workshop on Content-Based Multimedia Indexing*, Brescia (I), September 19-21, 2001.
6. F. Mokhtarian, N. Khalili, P. Yeun, "Multi-scale free-form 3D object recognition using 3D models", *Image and Vision Computing*, 19(5):271-281, 2001.
7. M. Elad, A. Tal, S. Ar, "Content Based Retrieval of VRML Objects - An Iterative and Interactive Approach", *EG Multimedia*, September 2001, 97-108.
8. G. Taubin, "A Signal Processing Approach to Fair Surface Design", *Computer Graphics (Annual Conference Series)*, 29:351–358, 1995.
9. M. Garland, "Multiresolution Modeling: Survey & Future Opportunities", in *Proc. of Eurographics'99*, September 1999.
10. A.G. Belyaev, I.A. Bogaevski, Y. Ohtake, "Polyhedral Surface Smoothing with Simultaneous Mesh Regularization", in *Proc. of Geometric Modeling and Processing 2000. Theory and Applications*, Hong Kong, China, April 10-12, 2000, pp.229-237.
11. J.P. Snyder, L.M. Bugayevski, *Map projections – a reference manual*, Taylor & Francis, 1995.
12. A. Del Bimbo, E. Vicario, "Using weighted spatial relationships in retrieval by visual contents", in *Proc of the IEEE Workshop on Content-Based Access of Image and Video Libraries (CBAIVL'98*, Santa Barbara, CA, pp.35-39, June 1998.
13. M.A. Eshera, K.-S. Fu, "A Graph Measure for Image Analysis", *IEEE Trans. on Systems, Man and Cybernetics*, 14(3):398-407, May/June 1984.
14. M.R. Garey, D. Johnson, "Computer and Intractability: A Guide to the Theory of NP-Completeness", Freeman, San Francisco, 1979.
15. S. Berretti, A. Del Bimbo, E. Vicario, "Efficient Matching and Indexing of Graph Models in Content-Based Retrieval", *IEEE Trans. on Pattern Analysis and Machine Intelligence*, 23(10):1089-1105, October 2001.

16. A. E. Johnson, M. Hebert, "Using Spin-Images for efficient multiple model recognition in cluttered 3-D scenes", *IEEE Transactions on Pattern Analysis and Machine Intelligence*, 21(5):433-449, 1999.
17. A. Goshtasby, "Description and descrimination of planar shapes using shape matrices", *IEEE Transactions on PAMI*, 7:738-743, 1985.
18. J.C.Bezdek, J.Keller, R.Krishnapuram, N.R.Pal, *Fuzzy Models and Algorithms for Pattern Recognition and Image Processing*, Kluwer Academic Publisher, Boston, 1999.
19. J.-Ph. Vandeborre, V. Couillet, M. Daoudi, "A Practical Approach for 3D Model Indexing by combining Local and Global Invariants", in *Proc. of the 1st Int'l Symp. on 3D Data Processing, Visualization, and Transmission (3DPVT'02)*, 2002.

Clifford Geometric Algebra: A Promising Framework for Computer Vision, Robotics and Learning

Eduardo Bayro-Corrochano

Computer Science Department, GEOVIS Laboratory
Centro de Investigación y de Estudios Avanzados
CINVESTAV, Guadalajara, Jalisco 44550, Mexico
edb@gdl.cinvestav.mx
http://www.gdl.cinvestav.mx/~edb

Abstract. In this paper the authors use the framework of geometric algebra for applications in computer vision, robotics and learning . This mathematical system keeps our intuitions and insight of the geometry of the problem at hand and it helps us to reduce considerably the computational burden of the problems. The authors show that framework of geometric algebra can be in general of great advantage for applications using stereo vision, range data, laser, omnidirectional and odometry based systems. For learning the paper presents the Clifford Support Vector Machines as a generalization of the real- and complex-valued Support Vector Machines.

1 What Is Clifford Geometric Algebra?

Let $\mathcal{G}_n$ denote the geometric algebra of n-dimensions – this is a graded linear space. As well as vector addition and scalar multiplication we have a non-commutative product which is associative and distributive over addition – this is the *geometric* or *Clifford product*. A further distinguishing feature of the algebra is that any vector squares to give a scalar. The geometric product of two vectors a and b is written ab and can be expressed as a sum of its symmetric and anti-symmetric parts $ab = a \cdot b + a \wedge b$. The outer or wedge product of two vectors is a new quantity which we call a *bivector*. We think of a bivector as a oriented area in the plane containing a and b, formed by sweeping a along b. The outer product is immediately generalizable to higher dimensions – for example, $(a \wedge b) \wedge c$, a *trivector*, is interpreted as the oriented volume formed by sweeping the area $a \wedge b$ along vector c. The outer product of k vectors is a k-vector or k-blade, and such a quantity is said to have *grade* k. A *multivector* (linear combination of objects of different type) is *homogeneous* if it contains terms of only a single grade.

In an n-dimensional space we can introduce an orthonormal basis of vectors $\{\sigma_i\}$, $i = 1, ..., n$, such that $\sigma_i \cdot \sigma_j = \delta_{ij}$. This leads to a basis for the entire algebra:

$$1, \quad \{\sigma_i\}, \quad \{\sigma_i \wedge \sigma_j\}, \quad \{\sigma_i \wedge \sigma_j \wedge \sigma_k\}, \quad ..., \quad \sigma_1 \wedge \sigma_2 \wedge ... \wedge \sigma_n. \quad (1)$$

A. Sanfeliu et al. (Eds.): CIARP 2004, LNCS 3287, pp. 25–36, 2004.

Note that the basis vectors are not represented by bold symbols. Any multivector can be expressed in terms of this basis. In this paper we will specify a geometric algebra $\mathcal{G}_n$ of the n dimensional space by $\mathcal{G}_{p,q,r}$, where p, q and r stand for the number of basis vector which squares to 1, -1 and 0 respectively and fulfill n=p+q+r. Its even subalgebra will be denoted by $\mathcal{G}^{+}_{p,q,r}$. For example $\mathcal{G}^{+}_{0,2,0}$ has the basis

$$\{1, \quad \sigma_1, \quad \sigma_2, \quad \sigma_1 \wedge \sigma_2\}, \tag{2}$$

where σ_1^2=-1,σ_2^2=-1. This means $p=0$, $q=2$ and $r=0$. Thus the dimension of this geometric algebra is $n=p+q+r=2$.

In the n-D space there are multivectors of grade 0 (scalars), grade 1 (vectors), grade 2 (bivectors), grade 3 (trivectors), etc... up to grade n. Any two such multivectors can be multiplied using the geometric product. Consider two multivectors $\boldsymbol{A}_r$ and $\boldsymbol{B}_s$ of grades r and s respectively. The geometric product of $\boldsymbol{A}_r$ and $\boldsymbol{B}_s$ can be written as

$$\boldsymbol{A}_r \boldsymbol{B}_s = \langle \mathbf{AB} \rangle_{r+s} + \langle \mathbf{AB} \rangle_{r+s-2} + \ldots + \langle \mathbf{AB} \rangle_{|r-s|} \tag{3}$$

where $\langle \boldsymbol{M} \rangle_t$ is used to denote the t-grade part of multivector $\boldsymbol{M}$, e.g. consider the geometric product of two vectors $\boldsymbol{ab} = \langle \boldsymbol{ab} \rangle_0 + \langle \boldsymbol{ab} \rangle_2 = \boldsymbol{a} \cdot \boldsymbol{b} + \boldsymbol{a} \wedge \boldsymbol{b}$.

For an detailed introduction to geometric algebra the reader should resort to [1–3].

2   Body-Eye Calibration

The so-called hand-eye calibration problem involves the computation of the transformation between a coordinate system attached to a robotic hand and the camera on top of it. Since we want calibrate a binocular head with a mobile robot, from know on we will call this task as the body-eye calibration problem.

The robot-to-sensor relation can be seen as a series of joints $J_1, J_2, ..., J_n$ (where a rotation about joint J_i affects all joints $J_{i+1}, ..., J_n$) and a measurement system U which is rigidly attached to the last joint J_n. The problem can be stated as the computation of the transformations $\boldsymbol{M}_1, \boldsymbol{M}_2, ..., \boldsymbol{M}_{n-1}$ between the robot frame and the last joint and the transformation $\boldsymbol{M}_n$ between the last joint and the measurement device U, using only data gathered with U. The procedure consists of two stages. The first stage computes the *screw axes* of the joints, and the second stage uses these axes to compute the final transformation between the coordinate systems.

2.1   Screw Axes Computation

To compute the axes of rotation, we use a motion estimator, for details see [2]. Each joint J_i is moved in turn while leaving the rest at their home position (see Figure 1.a) . From the resulting motor $\boldsymbol{M}_i$, the axis of rotation $\boldsymbol{S}_i$ can be extracted, , for details see [2]. For our particular robot, the sequence of motions is presented in Figure 1.b.

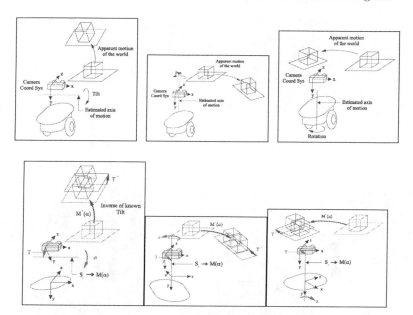

Fig. 1. (a) (*upper row*) Estimation of the screw axes. (b) (*lower row*) Correction of the rotation and relocation of the screw axes.

2.2   Calibration

Our algorithm will produce a set of lines S_i in the camera's coordinate system. Once these axes are known, the transformation taking one point x_k measured in the camera's framework to the robot's coordinate system is easy to derive, provided that we know the angles α_i applied to each joint J_i. Basically, the algorithm undoes the implicit transformations applied on the camera's framework by first rotating about joint J_k and then translating the joint (and the framework, along with the rest of the joints) to the origin (see Figure 1.b).

The functions used in our algorithm are defined as follows:

$$\texttt{nearest}(x) = \frac{(\bar{e} \cdot x) \cdot x}{\bar{e} \cdot [(\bar{e} \cdot x) \cdot x]}, \tag{4}$$

$$\texttt{makeTranslator}(t) = 1 + \frac{t}{2}\bar{e}, \tag{5}$$

$$\texttt{lineToMotor}(L^a, \alpha) = \cos(\frac{\alpha}{2}) + \sin(\frac{\alpha}{2})[\bar{e} \wedge (e_{123}m) - (e_{123}n)], \tag{6}$$

where $L^a = m + e \wedge n$, and $n = 1$. The function $\texttt{nearest}(x)$ returns the point on x which is nearest to the origin, $\texttt{makeTranslator}(t)$ returns a translator displacing by an amount t, and $\texttt{lineToMotor}(L^a, \alpha)$, simply returns a motor that rotates α radians about the axis L^a.

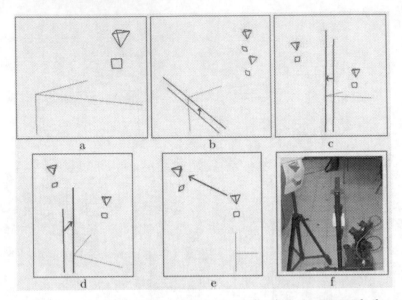

Fig. 2. (a) Reconstruction without calibration. (b–d) Relocation of the screws. (e) Comparison of the final reconstruction with the real view.

3   Inverse Kinematics and Object Manipulation

In this section we show how to perform certain object manipulation tasks in the context of conformal geometric algebra. First, we solve the inverse kinematics for a Pan-Tilt unit so that the binocular head will be able to follow the end-effector and to position the gripper of the arm in a certain position in space. Then, we we show how to grasp an object in space.

3.1   Inverse Kinematics for a Pan-Tilt Unit

In this task we apply a language of spheres for solving the inverse kinematics, this can be seen as an extension of an early approach [1], when a language of points, lines and planes were used instead.

In the inverse kinematics for a pan-tilt unit problem we aim to determine the angles θ_{tilt} and θ_{pan} of stereo-head, so that the cameras fix at the point p_t. We will now show how we find the values of θ_{pan} and θ_{tilt} using the conformal approach. The problem will be divided in three steps to be solved.

Step 1: Determine the point p_2.
When the θ_{tilt} rotes and the bases rotate (θ_{pan}) around the l_y (see Fig.3.a), the point p_2 describes a sphere s_1. This sphere has center at the point p_1 and radius d_2.

$$S_1 = p_1 - \frac{d_2^2}{2} e_\infty \qquad (7)$$

Fig. 3. a) Point p_2 given by intersection of the plane π_1 and the spheres s_1 and s_2. (b) Algorithm simulation showing the sphere containing the cube. (c) Image of the object we wish to grasp with the robotic arm. (d) The robot "Geometer" grasping a wooden cube.

Also the point p_t can be locked from every point around it. that is the point p_2 is in the sphere:

$$S_2 = p_t - \frac{d_3^2}{2}e_\infty \tag{8}$$

Where d_3 is the distance between point p_t and the cameras, and we can calculate d_3 using a Pythagorean theorem $d_3^2 = D^2 - d_2^2$, where D is the direct distance between p_t and p_1. We have restricted the position of the point p_2, but there is another restriction: the vector going from the p_2 to the point p_t must be live at the plane π_1 generated by the l_y axis ($l_y^* = p_0 \wedge p_1 \wedge e_\infty$) and the point p_t, as we can see in Fig. 3.a So that p_2 can be determined by intersecting the plane π_1 with the spheres s_1 and s_2 as follows

$$\pi_1^* = l_y^* \wedge p_t, \qquad P_{p2} = s_1 \wedge \pi_1 \wedge s_2. \tag{9}$$

Step 2: Determine the lines and planes.
Once p_2 have been determined, the line l_2 and the plane π_2 can be defined. This line and plane will be useful to calculate the angles θ_{tilt} and θ_{pan}.

$$l_2^* = p_1 \wedge p_2 \wedge e_\infty, \qquad \pi_2^* = l_y^* \wedge e_3. \tag{10}$$

Step 3: Find the angles θ_{tilt} and θ_{pan}.
Once we have all the geometric entities, the computation of the angles is a trivial step.

$$\cos(\theta_{pan}) = \frac{\pi_1^* \cdot \pi_2^*}{|\pi_1^*| |\pi_2^*|}, \qquad\qquad \cos(\theta_{tilt}) = \frac{l_1^* \cdot l_y^*}{|l_1^*| |l_y^*|}. \tag{11}$$

3.2   Grasping an Object

Other interesting experiments involve tasks of grasping objects. First, we consider only approximately cubic objects (i.e., objects with nearly the same width, length, and height). We begin with four non-coplanar points belonging to the corners of the object and use them to build a sphere. With this sphere, we can make either a horizontal or transversal section, so as to grasp the object from above, below, or in a horizontal fashion. Figure 3.b shows the sphere obtained using our simulator; the corners of the cube are shown in Figure 3.c; and Figure 3.d shows the robot arm moving its gripper toward the object after computing its inverse kinematics.

4   Learning: Clifford Valued Support Vector Machines

In this section we will present the Clifford valued Support Vector Machine (CSVM). A CSVM will be a multivector generalization of the real and complex valued Support Vector Machines [4].

4.1   Linear Clifford Support Vector Machines for Classification

For the case of the Clifford SVM for classification we represent the data set in a certain Clifford Algebra G_n where $n = p + q + r$, where any multivector base squares to 0, 1 or -1 depending if they belong to p, r, or s multivector bases respectively. Each data ith-vector has multivector entries $\boldsymbol{x}_i = [\boldsymbol{x}_{i1}, \boldsymbol{x}_{i2}, ..., \boldsymbol{x}_{iD}]^T$, where $\boldsymbol{x}_{ij} \in G_n$ and D is its dimension. Thus the ith-vector dimension is D$\times 2^n$. Each data ith-vector $\boldsymbol{x}_i \in \mathcal{G}_n^D$ of the N data vectors will be associated with their labels as follows: $(\boldsymbol{x}_{i1}, \boldsymbol{y}_{i1}),(\boldsymbol{x}_{i2}, \boldsymbol{y}_{i2}),...,(\boldsymbol{x}_{ij}, \boldsymbol{y}_{ij}),...,(\boldsymbol{x}_{iD}, \boldsymbol{y}_{iD})$, where each $\boldsymbol{y}_{ij} = y_{ij_s} + y_{ij_{\sigma_1}} + y_{ij_{\sigma_2}} + ... + y_{ij_I} \in \{\pm 1 \pm \sigma_1 \pm \sigma_2 ... \pm I\}$, where the first subindex s stands for scalar part. The 2^n classification problem is to separate these multivector-valued samples into 2^n groups by selecting a right function from the set of functions $\{f(\boldsymbol{x}) = \boldsymbol{w}^{*T}\boldsymbol{x} + b, \ \boldsymbol{x}, \boldsymbol{w} \in \mathcal{G}_n^D, \ \boldsymbol{b} \in \mathcal{G}_n^D$. The optimal weight vector will be

$$\boldsymbol{w} = [\boldsymbol{w}_1, \boldsymbol{w}_2, ..., \boldsymbol{w}_D]^T \in \mathcal{G}_n^D. \tag{12}$$

Let us see in detail the last equation

$$f(\boldsymbol{x}) = \boldsymbol{w}^{*T}\boldsymbol{x} + \boldsymbol{b} = [\boldsymbol{w}_1^*, \boldsymbol{w}_2^*, ..., \boldsymbol{w}_D^*][(\boldsymbol{x}_1, \boldsymbol{x}_2, ..., \boldsymbol{x}_D]^T + \boldsymbol{b}$$

$$= \sum_{i=1}^{D} \boldsymbol{w}_i^* \boldsymbol{x}_i + \boldsymbol{b}, \tag{13}$$

where $\boldsymbol{w}_i^* \boldsymbol{x}_i$ corresponds to the Clifford product of two multivectors and $\boldsymbol{w}_i^*$ is the conjugated of the multivector $\boldsymbol{w}$.

We introduce now a structural risk functional similar to the real valued one of the SVM and use loss function similar to the *function insensitive* ξ of Vapnik.

$$min \quad \frac{1}{2}\boldsymbol{w}^{*T}\boldsymbol{w} + C \cdot \sum_{j=1}^{l} \xi_i^2 \tag{14}$$

$$subject\,to \quad Coef_s(y_{ij})Coef_s(f(\boldsymbol{x}_{ij})) \geq 1 - Coef_s(\xi_{ij})$$
$$Coef_{\sigma_1}(y_{ij})Coef_{\sigma_1}(f(\boldsymbol{x}_{ij})) \geq 1 - Coef_{\sigma_1}(\xi_{ij})$$
$$\ldots$$
$$Coef_I(y_{ij})Coef_I(f(\boldsymbol{x}_{ij})) \geq 1 - Coef_I(\xi_{ij})$$
$$Coef_s(\xi_{ij}) \geq 0, \; Coef_{\sigma_1}(\xi_{ij}) \geq 0, \; ..., \; Coef_I(\xi_{ij}) \geq 0, \; j = 1, ..., l,$$

where the subindex $i = 1, ..., D$.

The dual expression of this problem can be derived straightforwardly. Firstly let us consider the expression of the orientation of optimal hyperplane.

Since the $\boldsymbol{w}_i = [\boldsymbol{w}_{i1}, \boldsymbol{w}_{i2}, ..., \boldsymbol{w}_{iD}]^T$, each of the $\boldsymbol{w}_{ij}$ is given by the multivector

$$\boldsymbol{w}_{ij} = w_{is} + w_{i\sigma_1}\sigma_1 + ... + w_{i\sigma_n}\sigma_n + w_{i\sigma_1\sigma_2}\sigma_1\sigma_2 + ... + w_{iI}I. \tag{15}$$

Each component of these weights are computed as follows:

$$w_{is} = \sum_{j=1}^{l}\Big((\alpha_{is})_j(y_{is})_j\Big)(x_{is})_j, \; w_{i\sigma_1} = \sum_{j=1}^{l}\Big((\alpha_{i\sigma_1})_j(y_{i\sigma_1})_j\Big)(x_{i\sigma_1})_j \;...,$$

$$w_{iI} = \sum_{j=1}^{l}\Big((\alpha_{iI})_j(y_{iI})_j\Big)(x_{iI})_j. \tag{16}$$

According the Wolfe dual programing [4] the dual form reads

$$min \quad \frac{1}{2}(\boldsymbol{w}^{*T}\boldsymbol{w}) - \sum_{j=1}^{l}\Big(\sum_{i=1}^{D}\Big((\alpha_{is})_j + ... + (\alpha_{i\sigma_1\sigma_2})_j + ... + (\alpha_{iI})_j\Big)\Big) \tag{17}$$

subject to $\boldsymbol{a}^T \cdot \boldsymbol{1} = 0$, where the entries of the vector

$$a = [\boldsymbol{a}_s, \boldsymbol{a}_{\sigma_1}, \boldsymbol{a}_{\sigma_2}, ..., \boldsymbol{a}_{\sigma_1\sigma_2}, \boldsymbol{a}_I] \tag{18}$$

are given by

$$a_s^T = \Big[[(\alpha_{1s1})(y_{1s1}), (\alpha_{2s1})(y_{2s1}), ..., (\alpha_{Ds1})(y_{Ds1})], ...,$$
$$[(\alpha_{1sl})(y_{1sl}), (\alpha_{2sl})(y_{2sl}), ..., (\alpha_{Dsl})(y_{Dsl})]\Big],$$
$$a_{\sigma_1}^T = \Big[[(\alpha_{1\sigma_11})(y_{1\sigma_11}), (\alpha_{2\sigma_11})(y_{2\sigma_11}), ..., (\alpha_{D\sigma_11})(y_{D\sigma_11})], ...,$$

$$[(\alpha_{1\sigma_1 l})(y_{1\sigma_1 l}), (\alpha_{2\sigma_1 l})(y_{2\sigma_1 l}), ..., (\alpha_{D\sigma_1 l})(y_{D\sigma_1 l})]\Big]$$

$$\boldsymbol{a}_I^T = \Big[[(\alpha_{1I_1})(y_{1I_1}), (\alpha_{2I_1})(y_{2I_1}), ..., (\alpha_{DI_1})(y_{DI_1})], ...,$$

$$[(\alpha_{1I_l})(y_{1I_l}), (\alpha_{2I_l})(y_{2I_l}), ..., (\alpha_{DI_l})(y_{DI_l})]\Big], \tag{19}$$

note that each data *ith*-vector, $i = 1, ... N$, has D multivector entries and after the training we take into account not N but l *ith*-vectors which is the number of the found support vectors each one belonging to $\mathcal{G}_n^D$. Thus $\boldsymbol{a}^T$ has the dimension: $(D \times l) \times 2^n$, the latter multiplicand corresponds to the length of a multivector of $\mathcal{G}_n$.

In $\boldsymbol{a}^T \cdot \mathbf{1} = 0$, $\mathbf{1}$ denotes a vector of all ones, and all the Lagrange multipliers should fulfill $0 \leq (\alpha_{is})_j \leq C$, $0 \leq (\alpha_{i\sigma_1})_j \leq C$, ..., $0 \leq (\alpha_{i\sigma_1\sigma_2})_j \leq C$, ..., $0 \leq (i\alpha_I)_j \leq C$ for $i = 1, ..., D$ and $j = 1, ..., l$.

We require a compact an easy representation of the resultant *GRAM matrix* of the multi-components, this will help for the programing of the algorithm. For that let us first consider the Clifford product of $(\boldsymbol{w}^{*T}\boldsymbol{w})$, this can be expressed as follows

$$\boldsymbol{w}^*\boldsymbol{w} = \langle \boldsymbol{w}^*\boldsymbol{w}\rangle_s + \langle \boldsymbol{w}^*\boldsymbol{w}\rangle_{\sigma_1} + \langle \boldsymbol{w}^*\boldsymbol{w}\rangle_{\sigma_2} + \ldots + \langle \boldsymbol{w}^*\boldsymbol{w}\rangle_I. \tag{20}$$

Since $\boldsymbol{w}$ has the components presented in equation (16), the equation (20) can be rewritten as follows

$$\boldsymbol{w}^*\boldsymbol{w} = \boldsymbol{a}_s^{*T}\langle \boldsymbol{x}^*\boldsymbol{x}\rangle_s \boldsymbol{a}_s + ... + \boldsymbol{a}_s^{*T}\langle \boldsymbol{x}^*\boldsymbol{x}\rangle_{\sigma_1\sigma_2}\boldsymbol{a}_{\sigma_1\sigma_2} + ... + \boldsymbol{a}_s^{*T}\langle \boldsymbol{x}^*\boldsymbol{x}\rangle_I \boldsymbol{a}_I +$$

$$\boldsymbol{a}_{\sigma_1}^{*T}\langle \boldsymbol{x}^*\boldsymbol{x}\rangle_s \boldsymbol{a}_s + ... + \boldsymbol{a}_{\sigma_1}^{*T}\langle \boldsymbol{x}^*\boldsymbol{x}\rangle_{\sigma_1\sigma_2}\boldsymbol{a}_{\sigma_1\sigma_2} + ... + \boldsymbol{a}_{\sigma_1}^{*T}\langle \boldsymbol{x}^*\boldsymbol{x}\rangle_I \boldsymbol{a}_I +$$

$$\tag{21}$$

$$\boldsymbol{a}_I^{*T}\langle \boldsymbol{x}^*\boldsymbol{x}\rangle_s \boldsymbol{a}_s + \boldsymbol{a}_I^T\langle \boldsymbol{x}^*\boldsymbol{x}\rangle_{\sigma_1}\boldsymbol{a}_{\sigma_1} + ... + \boldsymbol{a}_I^{*T}\langle \boldsymbol{x}^*\boldsymbol{x}\rangle_{\sigma_1\sigma_2}\boldsymbol{a}_{\sigma_1\sigma_2} + ... + \boldsymbol{a}_I^{*T}\langle \boldsymbol{x}^*\boldsymbol{x}\rangle_I \boldsymbol{a}_I.$$

Renaming the matrices of the t-grade parts of $\langle \boldsymbol{x}^*\boldsymbol{x}\rangle_t$, we rewrite previous equation as:

$$\boldsymbol{w}^*\boldsymbol{w} = \boldsymbol{a}_s^{*T}\boldsymbol{H}_s\boldsymbol{a}_s + \boldsymbol{a}_s^{*T}\boldsymbol{H}_{\sigma_1}\boldsymbol{a}_{\sigma_1} + ... + \boldsymbol{a}_s^{*T}\boldsymbol{H}_{\sigma_1\sigma_2}\boldsymbol{a}_{\sigma_1\sigma_2} + ... + \boldsymbol{a}_s^{*T}\boldsymbol{H}_I\boldsymbol{a}_I +$$

$$\boldsymbol{a}_{\sigma_1}^{*T}\boldsymbol{H}_s\boldsymbol{a}_s + \boldsymbol{a}_{\sigma_1}^{*T}\boldsymbol{H}_{\sigma_1}\boldsymbol{a}_{\sigma_1} + ... + \boldsymbol{a}_{\sigma_1}^{*T}\boldsymbol{H}_{\sigma_1\sigma_2}\boldsymbol{a}_{\sigma_1\sigma_2} + ... + \boldsymbol{a}_{\sigma_1}^{*T}\boldsymbol{H}_I\boldsymbol{a}_I +$$

$$\boldsymbol{a}_I^{*T}\boldsymbol{H}_s\boldsymbol{a}_s + \boldsymbol{a}_I^{*T}\boldsymbol{H}_{\sigma_1}\boldsymbol{a}_{\sigma_1} + ... + \boldsymbol{a}_I^{*T}\boldsymbol{H}_{\sigma_1\sigma_2}\boldsymbol{a}_{\sigma_1\sigma_2} + ... + \boldsymbol{a}_I^{*T}\boldsymbol{H}_I\boldsymbol{a}_I. \tag{22}$$

These results help us finally to rewrite equation (17) as a compact equation as follows

$$min \quad \frac{1}{2}\boldsymbol{w}^{*T}\boldsymbol{w} + C \cdot \sum_{j=1}^{l} \xi_i^2 = \frac{1}{2}\boldsymbol{a}^{*T}\boldsymbol{H}\boldsymbol{a} + C \cdot \sum_{j=1}^{l} \xi_i^2 \tag{23}$$

$$subject\,to \quad Coef_s(y_{ij})Coef_s(f(\boldsymbol{x}_{ij})) \geq 1 - Coef_s(\xi_{ij}), \tag{24}$$

where $\boldsymbol{a}$ is given by equation (18).

H is a positive semidefinite matrix which is the expected *Gramm* matrix. This matrix in terms of the matrices of the t-grade parts of $\langle x^*x\rangle_t$ is written as follows:

$$
H = \begin{bmatrix}
H_s H_{\sigma_1} H_{\sigma_2} \cdots \cdots \cdots \cdots H_{\sigma_1\sigma_2} \cdots H_I \\
H_{\sigma_1}^T H_s \cdots H_{\sigma_4} \cdots H_{\sigma_1\sigma_2} \cdots H_I H_s \\
H_{\sigma_2}^T H_{\sigma_1}^T H_s \cdots H_{\sigma_1\sigma_2} \cdots H_I H_s H_{\sigma_1} \\
. \\
. \\
. \\
H_I^T \cdots H_{\sigma_1\sigma_2}^T \cdots\cdots\cdots\cdots H_{\sigma_2}^T H_{\sigma_1}^T H_s
\end{bmatrix}, \tag{25}
$$

note that the diagonal entries equal to H_s and since H is a symmetric matrix the lower matrices are transposed.

The optimal weight vector w is as given by equation 12.

The threshold $b \in \mathcal{G}_n^D$ can be computed by using KKT conditions with the Clifford support vectors as follows

$$
\begin{aligned}
b = &\begin{bmatrix} b_1 b_2 b_3 \ldots b_D \end{bmatrix} \\
&- \big[(b_{1s} + b_{1\sigma_1}\sigma_1 + \ldots + b_{1\sigma_1\sigma_2}\sigma_1\sigma_2 + \ldots + b_{1I}I) \\
&\quad (b_{2s} + b_{2\sigma_1}\sigma_1 + \ldots + b_{2\sigma_1\sigma_2}\sigma_1\sigma_2 + \ldots + b_{2I}I)\ldots \\
&\quad (b_{Ds} + b_{D\sigma_1}\sigma_1 + \ldots + b_{D\sigma_1\sigma_2}\sigma_1\sigma_2 + \ldots + b_{DI}I) \\
= &\sum_{j=1}^{l} (y_j - w^{*T}x_j)/l.
\end{aligned} \tag{26}
$$

The decision function can be seen as sectors reserved for each involved class, i.e. in the case of complex numbers $(\mathcal{G}_{1,0,0})$ or quaternions $(\mathcal{G}_{0,2,0})$ we can see that the circle or the sphere are divide by means spherical vectors. Thus the decision function can be envisaged as

$$
\begin{aligned}
y = csign_m\big[f(x)\big] &= csign_m\big[w^{*T}x + b\big] \\
&= csign_m\Big[\sum_{j=1}^{l}(\alpha_j \circ y_j)(x_j^{*T}x) + b\Big],
\end{aligned} \tag{27}
$$

where m stands for the state valency, e.g. bivalent, tetravalent and the operation "$\circ$" is defined as

$$
\begin{aligned}
(\alpha_j \circ y_j) =&< \alpha_j >_0 < y_j >_0 + < \alpha_j >_1 < y_j >_1 \sigma_1 + \\
&\ldots + < \alpha_j >_{2^n} < y_j >_{2^n} I,
\end{aligned} \tag{28}
$$

simply one consider as coefficients of the multivector basis the multiplications between the coefficients of blades of same degree. For clarity we introduce this operation "$\circ$" which takes place implicitly in previous equation (16).

Note that the cases of 2-state and 4-state (Complex numbers) can be solved by the multi-class real valued SVM, however in case of higher representations like the 16-state using quaternions, it would be awkward to resort to the multi-class real valued SVMs.

The major advantage of this approach is that one requires only one CSVM which even can admit multiple multivector inputs. A naive and time consuming approach will be to use a a set of real valued SVM.

4.2   Nonlinear Clifford Valued Support Vector Machines for Classification

For the nonlinear Clifford valued classification problems we require a Clifford valued kernel k($\boldsymbol{x}$,$\boldsymbol{y}$). In order to fulfill the Mercer theorem we resort to a component-wise Clifford-valued mapping

$$\boldsymbol{x} \in G_n \xrightarrow{\phi} \varPhi(\boldsymbol{x}) = \varPhi_s(x) + \varPhi_{\sigma_1}\sigma_1 + \tag{29}$$
$$... + \varPhi_{\sigma_1}\sigma_2(x)\sigma_2 + ... + I\varPhi_I(x) \in G_n.$$

In general we build a Clifford kernel $k(x_m, x_j)$ by taking the Clifford product between the conjugated of $\boldsymbol{x}_m$ and $\boldsymbol{x}_j$ as follows

$$k(x_m, x_j) = \varPhi(\boldsymbol{x})^* \varPhi(\boldsymbol{x}), \tag{30}$$

note that the kind of conjugation operation ()* of a multivector depends of the signature of the involved geometric algebra $\mathcal{G}_{p,q,r}$.

Quaternion-valued Gaussian window Gabor kernel function (we use here $\boldsymbol{i} = \sigma_2\sigma_3$, $\boldsymbol{j} = -\sigma_3\sigma_1$, $\boldsymbol{k} = \sigma_1\sigma_2$):

The Gaussian window Gabor kernel function reads

$$k(\boldsymbol{x}_m, \boldsymbol{x}_n) = g(\boldsymbol{x}_m, \boldsymbol{x}_n)exp^{-i\mathbf{w}_0^T(\boldsymbol{x}_m - \boldsymbol{x}_n)} \tag{31}$$

where the normalized Gaussian window function is given by

$$g(\boldsymbol{x}_m, \boldsymbol{x}_n) = \frac{1}{\sqrt{2\pi}\rho}exp^{\frac{||\boldsymbol{x}_m - \boldsymbol{x}_n||^2}{2\pi^2}} \tag{32}$$

and the variables $\boldsymbol{w}_0$ and $\boldsymbol{x}_m - \boldsymbol{x}_n$ stand for the frequency and space domains respectively.

As opposite as the Hartley transform or the 2D complex Fourier this kernel function separates nicely the even and odd components of the involved signal, i.e.

$$k(\boldsymbol{x}_m, \boldsymbol{x}_n) = k(\boldsymbol{x}_m, \boldsymbol{x}_n)_s + k(\boldsymbol{x}_m, \boldsymbol{x}_n)_{\sigma_2\sigma_3} + k(\boldsymbol{x}_m, \boldsymbol{x}_n)_{\sigma_3\sigma_1} + k(\boldsymbol{x}_m, \boldsymbol{x}_n)_{\sigma_1\sigma_2}$$
$$= g(\boldsymbol{x}_m, \boldsymbol{x}_n)cos(\mathbf{w}_0^T\boldsymbol{x}_m)cos(\mathbf{w}_0^T\boldsymbol{x}_m) + g(\boldsymbol{x}_m, \boldsymbol{x}_n)cos(\mathbf{w}_0^T\boldsymbol{x}_m)sin(\mathbf{w}_0^T\boldsymbol{x}_m)\boldsymbol{i}$$
$$+g(\boldsymbol{x}_m, \boldsymbol{x}_n)sin(\mathbf{w}_0^T\boldsymbol{x}_m)cos(\mathbf{w}_0^T\boldsymbol{x}_m)\boldsymbol{j} + g(\boldsymbol{x}_m, \boldsymbol{x}_n)sin(\mathbf{w}_0^T\boldsymbol{x}_m)sin(\mathbf{w}_0^T\boldsymbol{x}_m)\boldsymbol{k}.$$

Since $g(\boldsymbol{x}_m, \boldsymbol{x}_n)$ fulfills the Mercer's condition it is straightforward to prove that $k(\boldsymbol{x}_m, \boldsymbol{x}_n)_u$ in the above equations satisfy these conditions as well.

After we defined these kernels we can proceed in the formulation of the SVM conditions. We substitute the mapped data $\varPhi(\boldsymbol{x}) = \sum_{u=1}^{2^n} < \varPhi(\boldsymbol{x}) >_u$ into the linear function $f(\boldsymbol{x}) = \boldsymbol{w}^{*T}\boldsymbol{x} + \boldsymbol{b} = \boldsymbol{w}^{*T}\Phi(\boldsymbol{x}) + \boldsymbol{b}$. The problem can be stated similarly as equations (15-17). In fact we can replace the kernel function in equations 24 to accomplish the Wolfe dual programming and thereby to obtain the kernel function group for nonlinear classification

$$\boldsymbol{H}_s = [k_s(\boldsymbol{x}_m, \boldsymbol{x}_j)]_{m,j=1,...,l} \tag{33}$$
$$\boldsymbol{H}_{\sigma_1} = [k_{\sigma_1}(\boldsymbol{x}_m, \boldsymbol{x}_j)]_{m,j=1,..,l}$$
$$...$$
$$\boldsymbol{H}_{\sigma_n} = [k_{\sigma_n}(\boldsymbol{x}_m, \boldsymbol{x}_j)]_{m,j=1,..,l} \cdot$$
$$H_I = [k_I(\boldsymbol{x}_m, \boldsymbol{x}_j)]_{m,j=1,..,l} \cdot$$

In the same way we use the kernel functions to replace the the dot product of the input data in the equation (27). In general the output function of the nonlinear Clifford SVM reads

$$\boldsymbol{y} = csign_m\Big[f(\boldsymbol{x})\Big] = csign_m\Big[\boldsymbol{w}^{*T}\Phi(\boldsymbol{x}) + \boldsymbol{b}\Big]$$
$$= csign_m\Big[\sum_{j=1}^{l}(\alpha_j \circ \boldsymbol{y}_j)(k(\boldsymbol{x}_j, \boldsymbol{x}) + \boldsymbol{b}\Big]. \tag{34}$$

where m stands for the state valency.

Next we present the well known 2-D spiral problem to the 3-D space. This experiment should test whether the CSVM would be able to separate three 1-D manifolds embedded in $\mathbb{R}^3$. In Figure 4 on can see that the problem is nonlinear

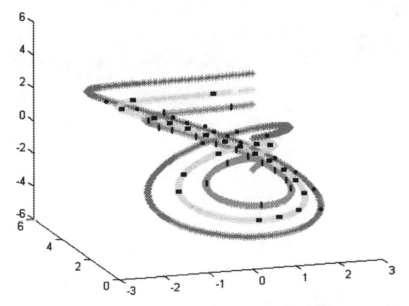

Fig. 4. 3D spiral with three classes. The marks represent the support vectors found by the CSVM.

separable. The CSVM used the kernel given by the equation 33. The CSVM found 16 support vector for $f_1(t)$, 21 support vector for $f_2(t)$ (in the middle) and 16 support vector for $f_3(t)$. Note that the CSVM indeed manage to separate the three classes. If we think in a real valued SVM (naive approach), one will require to do the job three SVMs.

5   Conclusions

In this article we have chosen the coordinate-free system of Clifford or geometric algebra for the analysis and design of algorithms useful for perception, action and learning.

Future intelligent machines will necessarily require of a powerful geometric language for reasoning at high level. The author believes that Clifford geometric algebra is a promissory mathematical system for representing and processing complex geometric data in real time.

Acknowledgment

I am very thankful to my PhD students: Leo Reyes Lozano, Julio Zamora Esquivel and Nancy Arana Daniel who provided me with experimental results useful for illustrating the application of geometric algebra in robotic vision and learning. Eduardo Bayro Corrochano, was supported by the project 49 of CONACYT-Fondo Sectorial de Investigación en Salud y Seguridad Social.

References

1. Bayro-Corrochano E. 2001. *Geometric Computing for Perception Action Systems*, Springer Verlag, Boston.
2. Bayro-Corrochano E. Conformal geometric algebra for robot perception. To appear in the *Hanbook on Computational Geometry for Patter Recognition, Computer Vision, Neuralcomputing and Robotics*, Eduardo Bayro-Corrochano (ed.), Chap. 11, Springer Verlag, Heidelberg, 2004.
3. H. Li, D. Hestenes and A. Rockwood. Generalized homogeneous coordinates for computational geometry. In Geometric Computing with Clifford Algebra, G. Sommer (Ed.), Springer-Verlag, pp. 27-59, 2001.
4. V. Vapnik. Statistical Learning Theory. Wiley, New York, 1998.

Adaptive Color Model for Figure-Ground Segmentation in Dynamic Environments*

Francesc Moreno-Noguer and Alberto Sanfeliu

Institut de Robòtica i Informàtica Industrial, UPC-CSIC
Llorens Artigas 4-6, 08028, Barcelona, Spain
{fmoreno,asanfeliu}@iri.upc.es

Abstract. In this paper we propose a new technique to perform figure-ground segmentation in image sequences of scenarios with varying illumination conditions. Most of the algorithms in the literature that adapt color, assume smooth color changes over time. On the contrary, our technique formulates multiple hypotheses about the next state of the color distribution (modelled with a Mixture of Gaussians -MoG-), and validates them taking into account shape information of the object. The fusion of shape and color is done in a stage denominated 'sample concentration', that we introduce as a final step to the classical CONDENSATION algorithm. The multiple hypotheses generation, allows for more robust adaptions procedures, and the assumption of gradual change of the lighting conditions over time is no longer necessary.

1   Introduction

Color is a visual cue that is commonly used in computer vision applications, such as object detection and tracking tasks. In environments with controlled lighting conditions and uncluttered background, color can be considered a robust and invariant cue, but when dealing with real scenes with changing illumination and confusing backgrounds, the apparent color of the objects varies considerably over time. Thus, an important challenge for any tracking system to work in real unconstrained environments, is the ability to accommodate these changes. In the literature, the techniques that cope with change in color appearance can be divided in two groups. On the one side, there is a group of approaches that search for color constancy (e.g. [2]). But in practice, these methods work mostly on artificial and highly constrained environments. On the other hand, there are the techniques that generate a stochastic model of the color distribution, and adapt this model over time, usually based on weighting functions of previous color distributions [6][7][8]. The drawback in all of these approaches is that they assume that color varies slowly and that it can be predicted by a dynamic model based in only one hypothesis. However, this assumption is not enough to cope with general scenes, where the dynamics of the color distribution might follow an unknown and unpredictable path.

---

* This work was supported by CICYT projects DPI2001-2223 and DPI2000-1352-C02-01, and by a fellowship from the Spanish Ministry of Science and Technology.

A. Sanfeliu et al. (Eds.): CIARP 2004, LNCS 3287, pp. 37–44, 2004.

Fig. 1. Example frames of a sequence with time-varying color illuminant and its corresponding color distributions (in normalized rg color space).

In order to cope with these drastic changes, we propose a framework that uses multiple hypotheses about the future state of the color distribution. In a previous work [5], we have suggested a similar multihypotheses framework to track objects in which color could be approximated by an unimodal distribution, represented by a histogram. The main contribution of the present paper consists of applying the fusion of shape and color information in a final stage of the CONDENSATION algorithm (that we call 'sample concentration') in order to deal with multicolored objects. To achieve this, the color of the object (and background) has been approximated by a MoG, which number is automatically initialized by an unsupervised algorithm. At each iteration, an offline learned dynamic model will generate the hypotheses about probable future states of the Gaussian mixture, that will be weighted depending on 'the quality' of the a posteriori probability map of the object computed with each of them.

A detailed description of the method is explained in the following sections. In Section 2 the object color model and initialization is given. The process of adjusting the color parameters over time to a dynamic model is explained in Section 3. And next, in Section 4, the complete tracking algorithm and model adaption is described in detail. Results and conclusions are presented in Sections 5 and 6, respectively.

2   Color Model

In order to represent the color distribution of a monochrome object, color histograms have been demonstrated to be an effective technique (e.g. [5]). However, when the object to be modeled contains regions with different color, the number of pixels representing each color can be relatively low and a histogram representation may not suffice. In this case, a better approach is to use Gaussian Mixture models. The conditional probability for a pixel $\mathbf{x}$ belonging to a multi-colored object $\mathcal{O}$ is expressed as a sum of M_o Gaussian components:

$$p\left(\mathbf{x}|\mathcal{O}\right) = \sum_{j=1}^{M_o} p\left(\mathbf{x}|j\right) P\left(j\right) \tag{1}$$

Similarly, the background color will be represented by a mixture of M_b Gaussians.

2.1   Model Order Selection

Similar to the problem of selecting the number of bins in histogram models, using MoG conceals the challenge of choosing the number of Gaussian components that

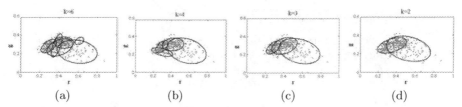

(a)   (b)   (c)   (d)

Fig. 2. Fitting a *MoG* to color data in *rg* colorspace. (a) Initialization with $K = 6$ components. (b),(c),(d) are three intermediate steps. The best estimate is the one corresponding to $K = 4$ components.

better adjust the data. In [7], the model order is selected by iteratively applying the EM algorithm and splitting those components having lower a posteriori probability $p(\mathcal{O}|\mathbf{x})$. We have observed that this method generates too many components, some of them unnecessary, increasing the computational cost of the segmentation stage.

We suggest the use of the method proposed in [3], based on a *Minimum Message Length* (MML) criteria that is implemented by a modified EM algorithm. This algorithm performs much more stable and generates an initial set with a lower number of gaussian components than in [7]. In Fig. 2, we show several steps of the fitting process. The algorithm begins with a large number of components (introduced by the user), and iteratively performs an annihilation of those components that are not supported by the data.

2.2 Figure-Ground Segmentation

In order to segment the object of interest from the background we model both color distributions by *MoGs* and compute the a posteriori probability that a pixel $\mathbf{x}$ belongs to the object using the Bayes rule:

$$p(\mathcal{O}|\mathbf{x}) = \frac{p(\mathbf{x}|\mathcal{O})\,P(\mathcal{O})}{p(\mathbf{x}|\mathcal{O})\,P(\mathcal{O}) + p(\mathbf{x}|\mathcal{B})\,P(\mathcal{B})} \tag{2}$$

where $\mathcal{B}$ refers to the background, and $P(\mathcal{O})$, $P(\mathcal{B})$ represent the prior probability of object and background, respectively. These values are approximated to the expected area of the object in the search region (Fig. 3).

(a)   (b)   (c)   (d)   (e)

Fig. 3. *MoGs* of $\mathcal{O}$ (the can) and $\mathcal{B}$, and probability density maps. (a) Original image. (b) Crosses and dashed lines correspond to $\mathcal{B}$ pixels and $\mathcal{B}$ Gaussian components, respectively, and points and continuous lines are $\mathcal{O}$ pixels and Gaussians. (c) $p(\mathbf{x}|\mathcal{O})$ (d) $p(\mathbf{x}|\mathcal{B})$ (e) $p(\mathcal{O}|\mathbf{x})$. Brighter points correspond to more likely pixels.

2.3   Model Paramaterization

Once we have learnt the initial configuration of the MoG for $\mathcal{O}$ and $\mathcal{B}$, we parameterize them with the following state vector:

$$\mathcal{X}_\varepsilon = [\mathbf{p}_\varepsilon, \mu_\varepsilon, \lambda_\varepsilon, \theta_\varepsilon] \qquad (3)$$

where $\varepsilon = \{\mathcal{O}, \mathcal{B}\}$, and $\mathbf{p}_\varepsilon = [p_\varepsilon^{(1)}, \cdots, p_\varepsilon^{(M_\varepsilon)}]$ contains the prior probabilities of each component, $\mu_\varepsilon = [\mu_\varepsilon^{(1)}, \cdots, \mu_\varepsilon^{(M_\varepsilon)}]$ are the centroids of each gaussian, the eigenvalues of the principal directions are represented by $\lambda_\varepsilon = [\lambda_\varepsilon^{(1)}, \cdots, \lambda_\varepsilon^{(M_\varepsilon)}]$ and $\theta_\varepsilon = [\theta_\varepsilon^{(1)}, \cdots, \theta_\varepsilon^{(M_\varepsilon)}]$ are the angles between the principal axis of each component with the horizontal. Observe the interest of having a low number of gaussian components in order to reduce the dimensionality of this state vector. The algorithm described in section 2.1 works properly in the sense that allows us to select the lowest number of gaussian components that best represent the data.

3   Learning the Dynamical Model

One of the stages of the tracking algorithm, consists of propagating the state vector from Eq. 3, in order to generate multiple hypotheses about the future configuration of the MoG. In order to formulate these hypotheses we formalize a dynamic motion model in terms of an auto-regressive Markov process. We model color dynamics as a 2nd order process, represented by the expression:

$$\mathcal{X}_{\varepsilon,t} = A_0 \mathcal{X}_{\varepsilon,t-2} + A_1 \mathcal{X}_{\varepsilon,t-1} + D_0 + B_0 \mathbf{w}_t \qquad (4)$$

where the matrices A_0, A_1 represent the deterministic component of the model, D_0 is a fixed offset, and $B_0 \mathbf{w}_t$ is the stochastic component, with $\mathbf{w}_t$ a vector of standard normal random variables with unit standard deviation and $B_0 B_0^T$ is the process noise covariance. The parameters A_0, A_1, B_0 and D_0 are learned a priori using the MLE algorithm described in [1]. In order to generate the training data we use a hand-segmented sequence, where the initial MoG configuration is fitted using the unsupervised algorithm described in Section 2.1 and to fit the subsequent components we use the EM algorithm. In Fig. 4 we show the evolution of the training parameters for the $\mathcal{O}$ and $\mathcal{B}$ color distributions.

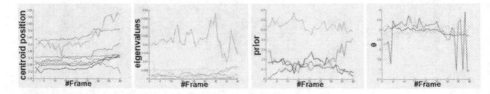

Fig. 4. Evolution of the Foreground parameters for the color distribution of a hand-segmented training sequence. There are shown the results for the 4 components of the MoG.

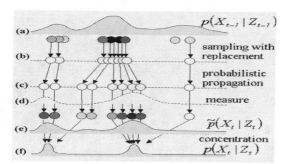

Fig. 5. One iteration of the implemented tracking algorithm for the one-dimensional case. The weight of each sample is represented by its gray level. The classical implementation of the CONDENSATION algorithm uses the steps (a)-(e). In our algorithm, we have added the 'concentration' step, where the samples are redirected to the local maxima.

4 The Tracking Algorithm

The basic steps of the tracking algorithm follow the typical procedure of the particle filters, but we introduce a modification similar to the idea presented in the algorithm ICONDENSATION [4], and in order to 'direct' the search for the next iteration we concentrate the future hypotheses on those areas of the state-space containing more information about the posterior probability $p(\mathbf{x}|\mathcal{O})$ (Fig. 5). Moreover, in this final stage we fuse object color and shape information. Next, we will briefly describe each one of the steps of the tracking algorithm:

1. **Probability Density Function of Color Distribution.** At time t, there are available from the previous iteration a set of N samples $\mathcal{S}_{t-1}^{(n)}$ ($n = 1, \ldots, N$) with the same structure than $\mathcal{X}$ (eq. 3), parameterizing N color distributions (Fig. 5a). Each sample has an associated weight $\pi_{t-1}^{(n)}$. The whole set represents an approximation of the a posteriori density function $p(\mathcal{X}_{t-1}|\mathcal{Z}_{t-1})$ where $\mathcal{Z}_{t-1} = \{z_0, \ldots, z_{t-1}\}$ is the history of the measurements. The goal of the algorithm consists of constructing a new sample set $\{\mathcal{S}_t^{(n)}, \pi_t^{(n)}\}$ for time t.

2. **Sampling from** $p(\mathcal{X}_{t-1}|\mathcal{Z}_{t-1})$**.** The next step in the estimation of $p(\mathcal{X}_t|\mathcal{Z}_t)$ consists of sampling with replacement N times the set $\{\mathcal{S}_{t-1}^{(n)}\}$, where each element has probability $\pi_{t-1}^{(n)}$ of being chosen (step (b) from Fig. 5). This, will give us a set $\{\mathcal{S'}_{t-1}^{(n)}\}$ of MoGs parameterizations. Those samples having higher weights may be chosen several times, so the new set can have identical copies of elements. On the other hand, those distributions having lower weights may not be chosen.

3. **Probabilistic Propagation of the Samples.** Each sample $\mathcal{S'}_t^{(n)}$ is propagated according to the dynamic model learnt during the training stage (eq. 4):

$$\tilde{\mathcal{S}}_t^{(n)} = A_0 \mathcal{S'}_{t-2}^{(n)} + A_1 \mathcal{S'}_{t-1}^{(n)} + D_0 + B_0 \mathbf{w}_t \tag{5}$$

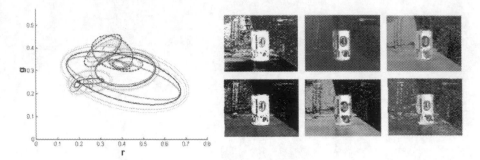

Fig. 6. Left: Ten samples of MoG from the set $\{\mathcal{S}_{t-1}^{(n)}\}$. The gray level is proportional to the weight of the samples. Right: Posteriori probability maps $p\,(\mathcal{O}|\mathbf{x})$, computed with different $MoGs$.

4. **Measure and Weight.** In this step, each element $\tilde{\mathcal{S}}_t^{(n)}$ has to be weighted according to some measured features. From the propagated samples $\tilde{\mathcal{S}}_t^{(n)}$ we construct the corresponding MoG, that are used to compute the probability maps $p\,(\mathcal{O}|\mathbf{x})$, for each sample (Fig. 6). The goal is to assign higher weights to the samples $\tilde{\mathcal{S}}_t^{(n)}$ generating 'better' segmentations of the tracked object. This is done assigning to each sample $\tilde{\mathcal{S}}_t^{(n)}$ the following weight:

$$\pi_t^{(n)} = \frac{\sum_{\mathbf{x}\in W} p\,(\mathcal{O}|\mathbf{x})}{N_w} - \frac{\sum_{\mathbf{x}\notin W} p\,(\mathcal{O}|\mathbf{x})}{\overline{N_w}} \qquad (6)$$

where W is the interest region around the previous object position (where we predict that will be the object), and N_w, $\overline{N_w}$ are the number of image pixels in and out respectively, of this interest region.

5. **Sample Concentration.** In the last stage of the algorithm (Fig. 5f) we concentrate the samples around the local maxima, so that in the following iteration the hypotheses are formulated around these more likely regions of the state space. In our case, this is absolutely necessary because our state vector $\mathcal{X}$ has high dimensionality (proportional to the number of gaussian components), and if we let the samples move freely, uniquely governed by the dynamic model, the number of hypotheses needed to find the samples representing a correct color configuration, is extremely high. The 'concentration' is performed with the following steps:

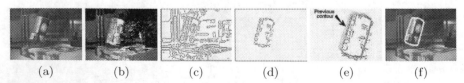

(a)   (b)   (c)   (d)   (e)   (f)

Fig. 7. Steps to extract the exact position of the object fusing color segmentation and accurate adjustment by deformable contours (commented in the text).

Fig. 8. Fitted contour and $p\left(\mathcal{O}|\mathbf{x}\right)$ map on a sequence with gradual change of illuminant and object position.

(a) The maximum from the set of weights $\{\pi_{t-1}^{(n)}\}$, $n = 1, \ldots, N$ is taken, and using morphologic operations over its probability map image (Fig. 7b), a coarse approximation of the object shape is obtained.

(b) With this rough shape, we eliminate noisy edges from the original image (Fig. 7c,d).

(c) The contour of the object in the previous iteration, is used as initialization of a snake, that is adjusted to the previous edge image (Fig. 7e). The fusion of color segmentation and shape information increases the robustness of the system, because even when the color hypotheses give a highly rough estimation, they can be corrected using the contour information.

(d) Once the object has been accurately detected (Fig. 7f), its color distribution is extracted. A MoG is fitted to this distribution (using the EM algorithm), giving a state vector $\mathcal{S}_t^*$. Samples $\widetilde{\mathcal{S}}_t^{(n)}$ are 'concentrated' on this new distribution as follows:

$$S_t^{(n)} = (1 - a)\widetilde{S}_t^{(n)} + a\mathcal{S}_t^* \tag{7}$$

where the parameter a governs the level of concentration. In our experiments we have set $a = 0.8$.

5   Results

In this section, three different experimental results are presented in order to illustrate the robustness and different capabilities of our system. In the first experiment (Fig. 8) we show how the method is able to face a gradual change of illumination and object position. The second experiment (Fig. 9) corresponds to a sequence with an abrupt change of both position and illumination. Fig. 9a and Fig. 9b correspond to the two consecutive frames presented to the algorithm. The a posteriori map of the best hypothesis (Fig. 9c) is used to discriminate false edges and fit a deformable contour (Fig. 9d,e). In this experiment we have constrained the fitting process to affine deformations. Finally, in the third experiment (Fig. 10) we show the performance of our system in a natural and cluttered scene, where we track the movement of an hippopotamus in the water. Observe that although the high level of noise and clutter from the scene the algorithm is able to perform a good tracking.

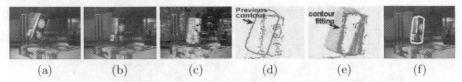

| (a) | (b) | (c) | (d) | (e) | (f) |

Fig. 9. Results of an abrupt change of illuminant and object position (commented in text).

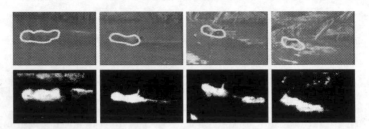

Fig. 10. Fitted contour and $p(\mathcal{O}|\mathbf{x})$ map of a natural sequence.

6   Conclusions

In this paper we have presented a new approach to the multi-colored object tracking under varying illumination environments that dynamically accommodates the color and shape of the object of interest. The main contribution of this work is the fusion of the shape and color information in the probabilistic framework offered by the particle filter formulation. We also introduce the concept of 'concentration' in the last stage of the CONDENSATION algorithm, what makes the system able to cope with a state vector of high dimensionality.

References

1. A.Blake, M.Isard, "Active contours", *Springer*, 1998.
2. G.D.Finlayson, B.V.Funt, K.Barnard, "Color Constancy under Varying Illumination", *Proc. ICCV*, pp.720-725, 1995.
3. M.A.T.Figueiredo, A.K.Jain, "Unsupervised Learning of Finite Mixture Models", *Trans.PAMI*, Vol.24, num.3, pp.381-396, 2002.
4. M.Isard, A.Blake "Icondensaton: Unifying Low-Level and High-Level Tracking in a Stochastic Framework", *Proc. ECCV*, Vol.1, pp.893-908, 1998.
5. F.Moreno-Noguer, J.Andrade-Cetto, A.Sanfeliu "Fusion of Color and Shape for Object Tracking under Varying Illumination", *Proc.IBPRIA, LNCS 2652, Springer*, pp.580-588, 2003.
6. L.Sigal, S.Sclaroff, V.Athitsos, "Estimation and Prediction of Evolving Color Distributions for Skin Segmentation under Varying Illumination", *Proc.CVPR*, Vol.2, pp.152-159, 2000.
7. Y.Raja, S.McKenna, S.Gong, "Colour Model Selection and Adaption in Dynamic Scenes", *Proc.ECCV*, Vol.1, pp.460-475, 1998.
8. J.Yang, W.Lu, A.Waibel, "Skin-color modeling and adaption", *Proc.ACCV*, Vol.2, pp.687-694, 1998.

Real-Time Infrared Object Tracking
Based on Mean Shift

Cheng Jian and Yang Jie

Institute of Image Processing & Pattern Recognition, Shanghai Jiaotong University,
Shanghai 200030, China
{ch_jian,jieyang}@sjtu.edu.cn

Abstract. The mean shift algorithm is an efficient method for tracking object in the color image sequence. However, in the infrared object-tracking scenario, there is a singular feature space, i.e. the grey space, for representing the infrared object. Due to the lack of the information for the object representation, the object tracking based on the mean shift algorithm may be lost in the infrared sequence. To overcome this disadvantage, we propose a new scheme that is to construct a cascade grey space. The experimental results performed on two different infrared image sequences show our new scheme is efficient and robust for the infrared object tracking.

1 Introduction

Object tracking is a hot topic in computer vision, image sequence analysis, video processing and compression, and perceptual user Interface. The essence of the object tracking is to determine the position of the object in the images. The mean shift algorithm is a nonparametric statistical method for seeking the nearest mode of a point sample distribution, which originally advocated by Fukunaga [1], and extended and brought to the attention of the image processing community by Yizong Cheng [2]. Recently, this algorithm has been adopted as an efficient technique for a wide variety of application, such as image segmentation, and appearance-based object tracking by G. R. Bradski [3], D. Comaniciu and Peter Meer [4, 5, 6].

Real-Time infrared object tracking is an important and challenging research task in many military applications. Infrared object tracking primarily addresses to localize and track the infrared thermal object in the infrared image sequences [7, 8]. Unfortunately, there are some disadvantages for the infrared image, such as extremely low signal to noise ratio (SNR), severe background clutter, non-repeatability of the target signature, and high ego-motion of the sensor. Commonly, many infrared object tracking algorithms are imposed different constraints, such as no drastic change of the object feature [7], and no sensor ego-motion [8]. In this paper, we follow the 'mean shift' tracking approach, which was proposed by D. Comaniciu et al. [5, 6]. Due to the nature of the infrared image, we choose the grey space as the feature space. In contrast to the color space, the lack of the information to represent the object will lead to the failure to track the infrared object. In order to overcome the disadvantage, we propose a new scheme that is to construct a cascade grey space. Then, the infrared object can be represented in the cascade grey space. The experimental results performed on two different infrared image sequences show our new scheme is efficient

A. Sanfeliu et al. (Eds.): CIARP 2004, LNCS 3287, pp. 45–52, 2004.
© Springer-Verlag Berlin Heidelberg 2004

and robust for the infrared small object tracking, and infrared object tracking in the severe clutter background.

2 Nonparametric Density Estimation and Mean Shift

There are several nonparametric methods available for probability density estimation [9, p.81]. Kernel estimation is one of the most popular techniques. Let $\{x_i\}_{i=1...n}$ be an arbitrary set of n points in the d-dimensional space R^d, the multivariate kernel density estimator with kernel K(x) and windows radius (i.e. bandwidth) h, in the point x is defined as [9, p.110]

$$\hat{p}(x) = \frac{1}{nh^d} \sum_{i=1}^{n} K(\frac{x - x_i}{h}) \tag{1}$$

There are several commonly used kernels, such as Epanechnikov kernel, and Normal kernel, etc. The Epanechnikov kernel is an optimum kernel that yields minimum mean integrated square error (MISE)

$$K_E(x) = \begin{cases} \frac{1}{2} c_d^{-1}(d + 2)(1 - \|x\|^2) & if \ \|x\| < 1 \\ 0 & otherwise \end{cases} \tag{2}$$

where c_d is the volume of the unit d-dimensional sphere, e.g., $c_1=2$, $c_2=\pi$, $c_3=4\pi/3$.

Let us introduce the profile [2] of a kernel K as a function k: $[0, \infty) \to R$ such that $K(x) = k(\|x\|^2)$. For example, according to (2) the Epanechnikov kernel is

$$k_E(x) = \begin{cases} \frac{1}{2} c_d^{-1}(d + 2)(1 - x) & if \ x < 1 \\ 0 & otherwise \end{cases} \tag{3}$$

Employing the profile notation we can write the density estimate (1) as

$$\hat{p}_K(x) = \frac{1}{nh^d} \sum_{i=1}^{n} k(\left\| \frac{x - x_i}{h} \right\|^2) \tag{4}$$

Let us denote

$$g(x) = -k'(x) \tag{5}$$

assuming that the derivative of k exists for all $x \in [0, \infty)$, except for a finite set of points. A kernel G can be defined as

$$G(x) = Cg(\|x\|^2) \tag{6}$$

where C is normalization constant.

Then, the estimate of the density gradient can be defined as the gradient of kernel density estimate (4)

$$\hat{\nabla}p_K(x) \equiv \nabla\hat{p}_K(x) = \frac{2}{nh^{d+2}}\sum_{i=1}^{n}(x-x_i)k'(\left\|\frac{x-x_i}{h}\right\|^2) = \frac{2}{nh^{d+2}}\sum_{i=1}^{n}(x_i-x)g(\left\|\frac{x-x_i}{h}\right\|^2)$$

$$= \frac{2}{nh^{d+2}}\left[\sum_{i=1}^{n}g(\left\|\frac{x-x_i}{h}\right\|^2)\right]\left[\frac{\sum_{i=1}^{n}x_i g(\left\|\frac{x-x_i}{h}\right\|^2)}{\sum_{i=1}^{n}g(\left\|\frac{x-x_i}{h}\right\|^2)} - x\right] \tag{7}$$

where $\sum_{i=1}^{n}g(\left\|\frac{x-x_i}{h}\right\|^2)$ can be assumed to be nonzero. Then, the last bracket in (7)

contains the sample mean shift vector

$$M_{h,G}(x) \equiv \frac{\sum_{i=1}^{n}x_i g(\left\|\frac{x-x_i}{h}\right\|^2)}{\sum_{i=1}^{n}g(\left\|\frac{x-x_i}{h}\right\|^2)} - x \tag{8}$$

Obviously, the value of $\hat{p}_K(x)$ will reach maximum when $M_{h,G}(x)$ equals zero. Moreover, the mean shift procedure is defined recursively by computing the mean shift vector $M_{h,G}(x)$, and a proof of the convergence can be found in [2].

3   Infrared Object Tracking

In our infrared object-tracking scenario, we follow the 'mean shift' tracking approach, which was proposed by D. Comaniciu et al. [5, 6]. In the mean shift object-tracking algorithm, there are three basic steps. Firstly, in order to characterize the object, a specific feature space must be chosen. In [3] the HSV color space was chosen, and in [5, 6] the RGB color space was chosen. In infrared object tracking, we choose the grey space as the feature space. After choosing the feature space, the object model q and the object candidate p are be represented by its probability density function (pdf) in the feature space. Secondly, for measuring the similarity between the object model and the object candidate, the similarity function must be defined. Alike [5, 6], the Bhattacharyya coefficient is chosen. Thirdly, it is to determine the location corresponding to the object in the current frame. In mean shift tracking algorithm, this step uses the gradient information, which is provided by the mean shift vector.

In our infrared object-tracking algorithm, there is a new idea: We choose the grey space as the feature space. In contrast to the color space, the lack of the information to represent the object will lead to the failure to track the object. In order to overcome the disadvantage, we propose a new scheme that is to construct a cascade grey space. The core of this scheme is that the infrared image is convoluted in the x-direction and y-direction to generate two grey sub-spaces by a specific one-dimensional filter. The cascade grey space is made of these two grey sub-spaces.

3.1 Infrared Object Representation

To represent the infrared object, we choose the grey space as the feature space in the infrared grey image sequence. Moreover, to satisfy the low-computational cost imposed by real-time processing, we employ the m-bin histogram to estimate the discrete density in the chosen feature space.

(1) Cascade Grey Space Construction

There are three sub-spaces, i.e. Red, Green, and Blue in the RGB color space, or Hue, Saturation, and Value in the HSV color space. However, there is a singular grey space in the grey infrared image. Due to this nature of the infrared grey image, we have to choose the grey space as the feature space. In contrast to the color space, there is a disadvantage of the information lack for the object representation in the grey space. With this disadvantage, the infrared object tracking will be lost in singular grey space. In order to overcome this shortcoming, we propose a new scheme in which we try to construct a cascade grey space. How to construct the cascade grey space through the singular grey space?

Our scheme to construct the cascade grey space mainly relies on the filtering method. Firstly, two specific one-dimensional filters must be defined. Here, we define two one-dimensional filters, i.e. filterX and filterY. Especially, filterX equals to the transpose of the filterY (i.e. filterX = filterY^T). One sub-space will be obtained by performing filtering with filterX in the x-direction of the infrared grey image. Similarly, performing filtering with filterY in the y-direction will make another subspace. After these two filtering operation, we obtain two infrared grey sub-spaces, which generate a cascade grey space. Then, the representation of the infrared object is credible in the cascade grey space. Moreover, the infrared object tracking is robust in our new scheme. We found that the performance of the tracker will be determined to a great extent by the choice of the filter in the infrared object-tracking scenario. Because there are low signal to noise ratio (SNR) and severe background clutter in the infrared image, the chosen filter to construct the cascade grey space should make the infrared small object prominent and weaken the background clutter, such as the Gabor filter, and the high-pass Butterworth filter.

(2) Object Model and Candidate Representation

Let $\{x_i\}_{i=1\ldots n}$ be the pixel locations of the object model, centered at x_0. Before calculating the histogram, we employ an isotropic kernel with a convex and monotonic decreasing kernel profile k(x) to assign a smaller weight to the locations farther from the center. Here, we choose the Epanechnikov kernel to represent the infrared object. Furthermore, the function b: $R^2 \rightarrow \{1 \cdots m\}$ is the index of the histogram bin at the location x_i in the quantized feature space, h is the radius of the kernel profile and δ is the Kronecker delta function. The probability of the quantized grey vector u in the object model is given by

$$\hat{q}_u(x_0) = C_m \sum_{i=1}^{n} k\left(\left\|\frac{x_0 - x_i}{h}\right\|^2\right)\delta[b(x_i) - u] \tag{9}$$

where C_m is the normalization constant, and $C_m = \dfrac{1}{\sum\limits_{i=1}^{n} k(\left\|\dfrac{x_0 - x_i}{h}\right\|^2)}$.

Similarly, the object candidate, centered at y in the current frame, is defined by

$$\hat{p}_u(y) = C_c \sum_{i=1}^{n} k\left(\left\|\frac{y - x_i}{h}\right\|^2\right) \delta[b(x_i) - u] \tag{10}$$

where C_c is the normalization constant, and $C_c = \dfrac{1}{\sum\limits_{i=1}^{n} k(\left\|\dfrac{y - x_i}{h}\right\|^2)}$. Note that C_c

does not depend on y, since x_i and y are organized in a regular image lattice. Therefore, C_c is a constant with a given kernel and window radius h.

3.2 Similarity Measurement Based on Bhattacharyya Coefficient

The mean shift object-tracking algorithm is an appearance based tracking method and it employs the mean shift iterations to find the object candidate that is the most similar to a given model in terms of intensity distribution. In [5, 6] the similarity between the distributions of the object model and candidates is expressed by a metric based on the Bhattacharyya coefficient. At location y, the sample estimate of the Bhattacharyya coefficient for object model density q_u and object candidate density $p_u(y)$ is given by

$$\hat{\rho}(y) \equiv \rho[\hat{p}(y), \hat{q}] = \sum_{i=1}^{m} \sqrt{\hat{p}_u(y)\hat{q}_u} \tag{11}$$

Then, the distance between two distributions can be defined as

$$d(y) = \sqrt{1 - \rho[\hat{p}(y), \hat{q}]} \tag{12}$$

In the infrared object tracking, to measure the similarity between the object model and candidate, we likewise define the metric based on the Bhattacharyya coefficient.

3.3 Object Localization

In the mean shift object-tracking algorithm, the object localization procedure starts from the position y_0 of the object in the previous frame and searches in the neighborhood. According to section 3.2, the most probable location y of the object in the current frame is obtained by minimizing the distance (12). Minimizing the distance is equivalent to maximizing the Bhattacharyya coefficient (11). In this procedure, the probabilities $\{\hat{p}_u(\hat{y}_0)\}_{u=1...m}$ of the object candidate at location y_0 in current frame must be computed at first. Then, using Taylor expansion around the value $\hat{p}_u(\hat{y}_0)$, the first-order approximation of the Bhattacharyya Coefficient is obtained

$$\rho[\hat{p}(y),\hat{q}] \approx \frac{1}{2}\sum_{u=1}^{m}\sqrt{\hat{p}_u(\hat{y}_0)\hat{q}_u} + \frac{1}{2}\sum_{u=1}^{m}\hat{p}_u(y)\sqrt{\frac{\hat{q}_u}{\hat{p}_u(\hat{y}_0)}} \qquad (13)$$

Then, introducing (10) in (13), we obtain

$$\rho[\hat{p}(y),\hat{q}] \approx \frac{1}{2}\sum_{u=1}^{m}\sqrt{\hat{p}_u(\hat{y}_0)\hat{q}_u} + \frac{C_c}{2}\sum_{i=1}^{n}w_i k\left(\left\|\frac{y-x_i}{h}\right\|^2\right) \qquad (14)$$

where $\quad w_i = \sum_{u=1}^{m}\delta[b(x_i)-u]\sqrt{\frac{\hat{q}_u}{\hat{p}_u(\hat{y}_0)}} \qquad (15)$

Therefore, to minimize the distance (12), the second term in (14) has to be maximized, the first term being independent of y. The second term in (14) represents the density estimate computed with kernel profile k(x) at y in the current frame, with the data being weighted by (15). According to (8), the maximization can be efficiently achieved based on the iterative procedure of the mean shift vector

$$\hat{y}_1 = \frac{\displaystyle\sum_{i=1}^{n}x_i w_i g\left(\left\|\frac{\hat{y}_0 - x_i}{h}\right\|^2\right)}{\displaystyle\sum_{i=1}^{n}w_i g\left(\left\|\frac{\hat{y}_0 - x_i}{h}\right\|^2\right)} \qquad (16)$$

where y_1 is the new location of the object in the current frame.

4 Experiments

Here, we exhibit the experimental results of the different infrared image sequences in our new scheme. Because one limitation of the mean shift tracking method is that at least some part of the object in the next frame should reside inside the kernel, we suppose that the object motion is continuous. There are two infrared image sequences: the first experiment deals with the infrared small object sequence, and the second experiment is to apply our new scheme to tracking the infrared object in the severe clutter background. These experiment are implemented on the MATLAB 6.1 platform with the Pentium IV 2.4GHz. The object model is chosen by hand in the first frame in our experiments. In the grey cascade space, the object model and the object candidate are represented by the histogram with 32×32 bins.

The infrared small object sequence has 120 frames of the 130×100 pixels in this experiment, and the radius h of the object model is $(h_x, h_y) = (14, 10)$. In order to make the infrared small object prominent, we choose one-dimensional Gabor filter to filter the infrared image in direction-x and direction-y for constructing the cascade grey space. In this experiment, the new scheme is capable of tracking at 10 fps (frames per second). The tracking result is shown every 30 frames in the Fig. 1.

The infrared object sequence with the severe clutter background has 300 frames of the 400×300 pixels, and the radius h of the object model is $(h_x, h_y) = (42, 25)$. Due to

Fig. 1. The infrared small object tracking results, from left to right, is the 1st, 30th, 60th, 90th, 120th frame.

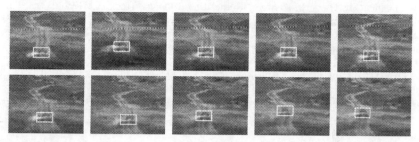

Fig. 2. The tracking result in the severe clutter background, the first row from left to right is the 1st, 30th, 60th, 90th, 120th frame, and the second row from left to right is the 150th, 180th, 210th, 240th, 270th frame.

the severe clutter background, we must try to weaken the clutter background to make the object tracking robust. In order to weaken the clutter background, we choose the one-dimensional high-pass Butterworth filter to filter the infrared image in direction-x and direction-y for constructing the cascade grey space. In this experiment, the new scheme is capable of tracking at 6 fps. The tracking result is shown every 30 frames in the Fig. 2.

The two experimental Results show that our opposed scheme is successful and indicate that our scheme is insensitive to the low SNR and the clutter background. Due to the mean shift gradient-descent seeking the object region in the feature space, the mean shift iterative processes rapidly converge in our two experiments. Therefore, our new scheme for the infrared object tracking can satisfy real-time processing.

5   Conclusion

We propose a new scheme in the infrared object tracking based on the mean shift algorithm. In our scheme, we construct a cascade grey space as the feature space for representing the infrared object. For the different infrared image sequence, we choose different filters to generate different cascade grey spaces. In order to demonstrate the performance of our scheme, we choose two kinds of infrared image sequence. The experimental results show our new scheme is efficient and robust for the infrared small object tracking and the severe clutter background.

References

1. K. Fukanaga, L. D. Hostetler: The Estimation of the Gradient of a Density Function, with Application in Pattern Recognition. IEEE Trans. Information Theory, 1975, Vol. 21: 32-40
2. Yizong Cheng: Mean Shift, Mode Seeking, and Clustering. IEEE Trans. Pattern Analysis and Machine Intelligence, 1995, Vol.17, No.8: 790-799

3. G. R. Bradski: Real Time Face and Object Tracking as a Component of a Perceptual User Interface. Proc. IEEE Workshop on Applications of Computer Vision, Princeton, (1998) 214-219
4. D. Comaniciu, P. Meer: Mean Shift: A Robust Approach towards Feature Space Analysis. IEEE Trans. Pattern Analysis and Machine Intelligence, 2002, 24(5): 603-619
5. D. Comaniciu, V. Ramesh, P. Meer: Real-Time Tracking of Non-Rigid Objects Using Mean Shift. Proc. IEEE Conference on Computer Vision and Pattern Recognition, 2000, 142-149
6. D. Comaniciu, V. Ramesh, P. Meer: Kernel-Based Object Tracking. IEEE Trans. Pattern Analysis and Machine Intelligence, 2003, Vol. 25, No.5: 564-577
7. H.Shekarforoush, R. Chellappa: A Multi-Fractal Formalism for Stabilization, Object Detection and Tracking in FLIR Sequence. IEEE International Conference on Image Processing, 2000, Vol. 3
8. D. Daviesy, P. Palmery, M. Mirmehdiz: Detection and Tracking of Very Small Low Contrast Objects. Ninth British Machine Vision Conference, 1998
9. Andrew R. Webb: Statistical Pattern Recognition, Second Edition. Weily, 2002

Optimal Positioning of Sensors in 2D

Andrea Bottino and Aldo Laurentini

Dipartimento di Automatica e Informatica, Politecnico di Torino
Corso Duca degli Abruzzi, 24 – 10129 Torino, Italy
{andrea.bottino,aldo.laurentini}@polito.it

Abstract. Locating the minimum number of sensors able to see at the same time the entire surface of an object is an important practical problem. Most work presented in this area is restricted to 2D objects. In this paper we present a sensor location algorithms with the following properties. In principle, the algorithm could be extended to 3D objects. The solution given by the algorithm converges toward the optimal solution when increasing the resolution of the object. Limitations due to real sensors can be easily taken into account.

1 Introduction

Sensor planning is an important research area in computer vision. It consists of automatically computing sensor positions or trajectories given a task to perform, the sensor features and a model of the environment [1]. Sensor panning problems require considering a number of constraints, first of all the visibility constraint. Although in general the problem addressed is 3D, in some cases it can be restricted to 2D [2,7,11]. This is for instance the case of buildings, which can be modeled as objects obtained by extrusion. Placing sensors able to see entirely a 2D environment is similar, but not equal, to the popular Art Gallery Problem [4, 5], referring to the surveillance, or "covering" of polygonal areas with or without polygonal holes. The difference is that we are interested in observing only the *boundary* of the object. In addition, the task of our sensors could be to observe the exterior boundary of a set of general polygons (this problem is known as the fortress problem for a single polygon). Then, our 2D visibility problem can be called the internal or external edge covering problem. At present, no finite exact algorithm exists able to locate a minimum unrestricted set of guards (sensors) in a given polygon. In addition, no approximate algorithm with guaranteed approximation has been found. A detailed analysis of the edge covering problem compared with the classic Art Gallery problem is reported in [3]. Among other results, it is shown that in general a minimal set of guards for the Art Gallery problem is not minimal for the interior edge covering, and that also the edge covering problem is NP-hard. However, edge covering admits a restriction which makes practical sense and allows to construct a finite algorithm which supplies a minimum set of viewpoints able to cover internal or external polygonal boundaries. The restriction is that each edge must be observed entirely by at least one guard. It allows finding one or more sets of regions where a minimal set of viewpoints can be independently located. Observe that this idea is related with the practical requirement of observing a feature in its entirety [14]. In addition the solution provided by the algorithm asymp-

A. Sanfeliu et al. (Eds.): CIARP 2004, LNCS 3287, pp. 53–58, 2004.

totically converges to the optimal solution of the unrestricted problem if the edges are subdivided into shorter segments. Finally, the algorithm can easily take into account several other constraints.

2 The Positioning Algorithm

Here we briefly present the essentials of the 2D sensor-positioning algorithm. The steps of the algorithm are as follows.

1. Divide the space into a partition Π of maximal regions such that the same set of edges is completely visible from all points of a region.
2. Find the dominant zones (a zone Z of Π is dominant if no other zone Z* exists which covers the edges of Z plus some other).
3. Select the minimum number of dominant zones able to cover all the faces.

The idea of partition Π has also been proposed, in restricted cases, in [11] and [12]. Step 1), and 2) of the algorithm, as shown in the paper, can be performed in polynomial time. Step 3) is an instance of the well known set covering problem, which in the worst case is exponential. However, covering the edges using the dominant zone only usually substantially reduces the computation complexity. In addition, in many cases several dominant zones are also *essentials*, that is cover some edges not covered by any other dominant zone, and must be selected. Finally, polynomial selection algorithms exist with guaranteed performance (see [13]).

In the following paragraph we will detail the steps of the algorithm. The environment is assumed to consist of simple polygons. Partition Π is built by means of a particular set of lines, called the *active visibility lines*. Each resulting region will be associated with the list of the edges that are completely visible from that zone. This set can be built traversing the partition graph from an initial region whose set of visible edges is known. Observe that interior inspection is similar, with a polygon enclosing the workspace and defining the outer border.

2.1 Visibility Lines

A *visibility line* (VL) relative to an edge divides the space into areas where the edge is completely visible and areas where it is partially or totally hidden. The VLs relative to an edge start at one of its vertices and lye in the half plane opposite to the inner side of the object, as respect to the edge. The angle between this line and the edge is in the range [0,π]. Also, each of this lines has a positive side, which is the side closer to the originating edge. Examples can be seen in Fig. 1, where the arrows mark the positive side of the VLs.

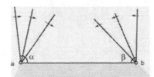

Fig. 1. VLs corresponding to the boundaries (a and b) of an edge

Each VL can have an *active* and an *inactive* part. Only the active VLs will be the effective boundary of the region of complete visibility of the edge they are related to. Active VLs can be found in two cases:

1. when the angle with its originating edge is π and the line does not enter the object in the proximity of the originating vertex (Fig. 2(a))
2. when the line is passing through another vertex of the object and, in the neighbourhood of this vertex, the inner side of the object lies on the negative side of the line (Fig. 2(b)). The inactive part of the VL is the segment connecting the originating and the intersecting vertices, while the active part is the remaining part of the VL

In both cases, any active VL stops if it intersects the object somewhere else (see for instance Fig. 2(a)).

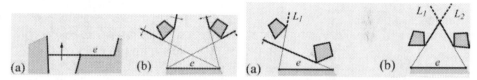

Fig. 2. (a) active VL making an angle of π with edge *e*. (b) VLs related to edge *e*; the active part of each line is bold. The arrows mark the positive side of the active VLs

Fig. 3. Extra conditions to identifiy active VLs. (a) active VL intersecting an inactive VL. (b) two active VLs intersecting. The dashed lines represent inactive VLs

Two other conditions must be checked to identify an active VL:

1. if an active VL relative to an extreme of an edge intersect the inactive part of a VL relative to the other extreme of the same edge, then the second active VL is indeed inactive (e.g. L_1 in Fig. 3(a) is inactive)
2. if the active parts of two VL relative to the two extremes of the same edge intersect somewhere, then they both stop at the intersection point (e.g. L_1 and L_2 segments in Fig. 3(b) are not active)

We can associate to each active VL an operator $\wedge$, where $\wedge j$ means that the line is the boundary between a region where edge j is hidden and a region where the edge j is visible. The operator has also a direction, which points at the area where the edge is visible. In Fig. 4, we can see an example, where the operator $\wedge$ is applied to the VLs related to edges 5 and 8.

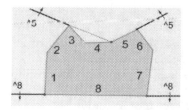

Fig. 4. Some active VLs (thick lines) and associated operators $\wedge$

2.2 The Partitioning Algorithm

Given the definition of active VL and operator $\wedge$, we can outline our partitioning algorithm:

```
1. found all the active VLs and the associate operator ^
2. intersect all the active VLs and subdivide the plane in regions
3. select one region and compute the set of visibile edges V(e1,…,en)
   for that zone
4. visit all the regions and compute their set of visible edges with
   the following rules:
   a. when crossing a boundary between R1 and R2 in the direction of
      the operator ^, the operand (j) is added to the set of visible
      edges of R2
   b. when crossing a boundary between R1 and R2 in the opposite di-
      rection of the operator ^, the operand (j) is removed from the
      set of visible edges of R2
```

An example of how the algorithm works is shown in Fig. 5, where the starting region has been marked with a different color. Note that several active VLs can be overlapping (or, in other words, we can have single VLs with multiple operators $\wedge$ associated). The dominant zones are highlighted by boxing their list of visible edges. The dominant zone in the upper left corner of the figure is also essential, and therefore it must be selected in the solution. It immediately comes that also the zone in the lower right corner must be selected to cover edges 6 and 7. The algorithm has been implemented, and some examples are shown in Fig. 6. For each example, the partition Π is shown, and the dominant regions that have been selected to cover all the edges are highlighted. In table 1 the number of objects, edges, regions of the partition and sensors placed for each case are summarized.

To find the active VLs, $O(n^2)$ pair of vertices must be considered. Checking if a line intersects the polygon at one the vertices can be done in constant time. For each edge, checking the extra conditions and finding the active segment requires intersecting each line with any other and sorting the intersections. Overall $O(n^2)$ VLs can be obtained in $O(n^3\log n)$ time. A classic algorithm can create the partition Π in $O(n^4)$ time. The partition can also be constructed by a plane sweep algorithm in $O(p \log p)$ time, where p is the number of vertices of the partition (regions and edges also are $O(p)$) [8]. The total time for computing partition Π is $O(n^3\log n + p \log p)$. Computing the visible edges of the starting region takes $O(n^2)$ time [9]. The time required for traversing the partition is $O(p)$ [10]. The overall time bound of step 1 is $O(n^3\log n + p \log p + p)$. To find d dominant zones, we must compare the sets of visible edges of each region. This process can be shortened if we observe that a necessary condition for a region to be dominant is that all the positive crossing directions of the edges of the region lead to the interior of the region (except for the edges of the objects). Given c candidate found with this rule, d dominant regions can be found in $O(nc^2)$ time [3]. Steps 1 and 2 of the algorithm requires $O(n^3\log n + p \log p + p + nc^2)$ time. Step 3 requires, in the worst case, exponential time. However, an interesting alternative could be using a greedy heuristic, which selects the region covering the largest number of uncovered edges each time, requiring polynomial time.

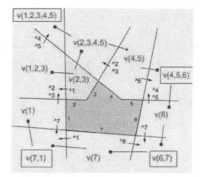

Fig. 5. Example of region labeling. The starting region is marked with a different color. The dominant zone are the one whose visible edges list is surrounded by a box

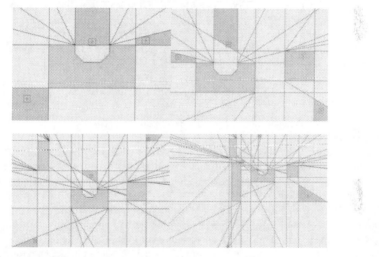

Fig. 6. Various examples showing several objects, the corresponding VLs and space partition, the dominant zones selected (drawn with a different background); for each zone, the cross represent a possible placement of a sensor

3 Conclusions

In this paper a method for positioning a minimum number of sensors into a polygonal environment has been presented for some sample cases. The approach has been implemented and results have been presented. Future work will be focused on extending the algorithm to 3D, maintaining the general idea of the 2D approach, that is: computing a partition Π of the viewing space of maximal regions Z_i, finding the dominant zones and selecting the minimum number of dominant zones able to cover all the faces. The idea is to find a suitable definition for active visibility surfaces, equivalent to the active VLs for the 2D case, in order to subdivide the space into regions where the same set of surfaces is completely visible.

Table 1. Total number of objects, edges, Active VLs, regions and sensors needed to cover all the edges of the objects of the examples of Fig. 6

Objects	Edges	Active VLs	Regions	Sensors
1	10	17	23	3
2	14	33	68	3
3	18	61	168	3
4	22	80	275	4

References

1. Scott W.R, Roth G. (2003) View Planning for Automated Three-Dimensional Object Reconstruction and Inspection. ACM Computing Surveys, Vol. 35(1), pp. 64–96
2. Kazakakis G. D., Argyros A.A. (2002) Fast positioning of limited visibility guards for inspection of 2D workspaces. Proc. Conf. On Intelligent Robots and Systems, pp.2843-2848
3. Laurentini A. (1999) Guarding the walls of an art gallery. The Visual Computer, vol.15, pp.265-278
4. O'Rourke J.(1987) Art gallery theorems and algorithms. Oxford University Press, New York
5. Shermer T.(1992) Recent results in art galleries. IEEE Proc. Vol. 80, pp.1384-1399
6. Nemhauser G., Wolsey L. (1988) Integer and Combinatorial Optimization. John Wiley& Sons
7. Danner T., Kavraki L.E. (2000) Randomized planning for short inspection paths. Proceedings. ICRA '00, vol. 2, pp. 971 – 976
8. Gigus Z, Canny J, Seidel R (1991) Efficiently computing and representing aspect graphs of polyhedral objects. IEEE Trans Patt Anal Machine Intell 13:542–551
9. Preparata F, Shamos M (1985) Computational geometry: an introduction. Springer, Berlin, Heidelberg, New York
10. Baase S (1988) Computer algorithms. Addison-Wesley, New York
11. Talluri R., Aggarwal J.K.(1996) Mobile robot self-location using model-image feature correspondence. IEEE Trans. On Robotics and Automation, 12(1), pp.63-77
12. Simsarian K.T., Olson T. J., Nandhakumar N. (1996) View-invariant regions and mobile robot self-localization, IEEE Trans. Robot. and Automat., vol. 12(5), pp. 810-816
13. Nemhauser, Wolsey L. (1988), Integer and Combinatorial Optimization. John Wiley pag.466
14. K. Tarabanis, R.Y.Tsai, and Anil Kaul, (1996) Computing occlusion-free viewpoints. IEEE Trans. Pattern Analysis and Machine Intelligence, 18(3).pp.279-292

Computer Vision Algorithms Versus Traditional Methods in Food Technology: The Desired Correlation

Andrés Caro Lindo[1], Pablo García Rodríguez[1], María Mar Ávila[1],
Teresa Antequera[2], and R. Palacios[3]

[1] University of Extremadura, Computer Science Dept.
Escuela Politécnica, Av. Universidad s/n, 10071 Cáceres, Spain
{andresc,pablogr,mmavila}@unex.es
[2] University of Extremadura, Food Technology,
Facultad Veterinaria, Av. Universidad s/n, 10071 Cáceres, Spain
tantero@unex.es
[3] "Infanta Cristina" University Hospital, Radiology Service, Badajoz, Spain

Abstract. Active Contours represent a common Pattern Recognition technique. Classical active contours are based on different methodologies (variational calculus, dynamic programming and greedy algorithm). This paper reviews the most frequently used active contours in a practical application, comparing weights, manually obtained by food technology experts, to volumes, automatically achieved by computer vision results. An experiment has been designed to recognize muscles from Magnetic Resonance (MR) images of Iberian ham at different maturation stages in order to calculate their volume change, using different active contour approaches. The sets of results are compared with the physical data. The main conclusions of the paper are the excellent correlation established between the data obtained with these three non-destructive techniques and the results achieved using the traditional destructive methodologies, as well as the real viability of the active contours to recognize muscles in MR images.

1 Introduction

Active Contours (or snakes) is a low level processing technique widely used to extract boundaries in many pattern recognition applications [4, 8]. In their formulation, active contours are parameterized curves, defined by an energy function. By minimizing this energy function, the contour converges, and the solution is achieved. An Active Contour is represented by a vector, $v(s)$, which contains all of the n points of the snake. The functional energy of this snake is given by:

$$E = \int \left[E_{int}(v(s)) + E_{image}(v(s)) \right] ds \qquad (1)$$

where E_{int} and E_{image} are the internal and external energy of the contour, respectively.

Energy-minimizing Active Contour models were proposed by Kass *et al.* [11]. They developed a controlled continuity spline which can be operated upon by internal

A. Sanfeliu et al. (Eds.): CIARP 2004, LNCS 3287, pp. 59–66, 2004.

contour forces, images forces, and external forces which are supplied by an interactive user, or potentially by a higher level process. An algorithmic solution involves derivation of this objective function and optimization of the derived equation for finding an appropriate solution. However, in general, variational approaches do not guarantee global optimality of the solution [1].

On the other hand, Amini *et al.* [1] also proposed a dynamic programming algorithm for minimizing the functional energy. However, the proposed algorithm is slow, having a great complexity. Williams and Shah [15] developed a greedy algorithm which has performance comparable to the dynamic programming and variational calculus approaches.

Active Contours could be used as a pattern recognition technique. A practical application of them could be employed to recognize muscles of Iberian ham images [5, 6]. Particularly, Iberian ham images have been processed in this research. The evolution of the ripening of this meat product has been studied, acquiring images in different stages during the maturation process. The ripening of the Iberian ham is a lengthy procedure (normally 18-24 months). Physical-chemical and sensorial methods are required to evaluate the different parameters in relation with quality, being generally tedious, destructive and expensive [2]. Traditionally, the maturation time is fixed when the weight loss of the ham is approximately 30% [7]. So, other methodologies have long been awaited by the Iberian ham industries.

The use of image processing to analyze Iberian products is quite recent. Processing images from Iberian ham slices taken by a CCD camera is a first approach. However, although Computer Vision is essentially a non-destroying technique, ham pieces must be destroyed to obtain images using these techniques.

On the other hand, MRI (*Magnetic Resonance Imaging*) offers great capabilities to non-invasively look inside the bodies. It is widely used in medical diagnosis and surgery. It provides multiple planes (digital images) of the body or piece. Its application to the Food Technology is still recent and it is confined for researching purposes.

In this work, three algorithm paradigms in active contours have been developed, *variational calculus*, *greedy algorithm* and *dynamic programming*, in order to recognize the two main muscles structures in the Iberian ham (*biceps femoris* and *semimembranosus* muscles). The experiment has been designed having Magnetic Resonance (MR) images from four different stages during the maturation of the ham (*raw, post-salting, semi-dry and dry-cured*). The first goal of this work is to recognize muscles processing MR images, in order to determine the volume of ham, and to study their changes during the ripening process. This objective is an attempt to provide a computer vision alternative to the traditional methods of determining the optimal ripening time. Anyway, the main contribution of the work is the satisfactory relationship (statistical correlation) between the volume and weight of these two muscles. The volume has been obtained by Computer Vision techniques (Active Contours), and the weight has been achieved by manual methods (extracting physically the muscles and weighing them in scales). The fine correlation coefficients obtained in this work verify that Computer Vision methods could be used properly as an alternative to the traditional and destructive customs.

2 Materials

The presented research is based on MRI sequences of Iberian ham images. A technique to recognize the main muscle form (*biceps femoris* and *semimembranosus*) is employed. Six Iberian hams have been scanned, in four stages during their ripening time. The images have been acquired using an MRI scan facilitated by the "Infanta Cristina" Hospital in Badajoz (Spain). The MRI volume data set is obtained from sequences of T1 images with a FOV (*field-of view*) of 120x85 mm and a slice thickness of 2 mm, i.e. a voxel resolution of 0.23x0.20x2 mm. As a result, a great image database is obtained. The total number of images used in this work is 600 for the *biceps femoris*, and 504 for the *semimembranosus* muscle. So, the total amount of images is 1104.

3 Methods

Three different algorithm paradigms in active contours (*variational calculus, greedy algorithm* and *dynamic programming*) have been proven in order to obtain results using several methodologies (section 3.1). Afterwards, the practical application of these three methodologies over MR Iberian ham images from different maturation stages will be shown in 3.2.

3.1 Classical Active Contour Approaches

An Active Contour is represented by a vector, v, of points [4]. The complete energy functional in all the developed methods is given by:

$$E = \sum \{\alpha E_{cont} + \beta E_{curv} + \gamma E_{image}\} \qquad (2)$$

The internal energy of the contour consists of continuity energy (E_{cont}) plus curvature energy (E_{curv}). E_{image} represents the proper energy of the image [12, 16]. All the energy terms are normalized to produce similar effects to the solution. α, β and γ are values chosen to control the influence of the three energy terms [13, 14].

Although most of the active contour algorithm and practical approaches consider a fixed number of n points for the snake, the three different active contour approaches developed in this work maintain a variable number, n, of points of the snake. This is the best way to ensure the finest muscle recognition. To achieve that, two distances have been consider, d_{max} and d_{min}. When two consecutive points of the snake exceed the maximum distance between points d_{max}, a new point appears between the two original points. In such a way, when two consecutive points go beyond the minimal distance d_{min}, one of them disappears. As a result, the total number of points of the snake varies, adjusting perfectly the final snake to the pattern.

The variational calculus approach is based on the finite difference method proposed by Kass et al. [11]. The equation (1) is solved iteratively by matrix inversion, using the *lower and upper triangular decomposition*, a well-known technique in linear algebra. A detailed description of the principle behind this numerical method is described in [10, 16]. The initial group of results has been achieved using this method.

On the other hand, the developed dynami programming approach is based on the method proposed by Amini [1]. Although it is natural to view energy minimization as a static problem, to compute the local minima of a functional such as equation (1) a dynamical system can be constructed, governed by the function and allowing the system to evolve to equilibrium. Following these ideas, a dynamic programming active contour has been designed and used to reach a set of results.

Finally, the implemented greedy algorithm approach is based on the Williams and Shah's proposals [15]. This technique achieves the final solution by steps, trying to take always an optimal decision for each stage. The algorithm considers a square neighborhood for each point of the snake. The energy function is computed for the current location of v_i and each of its neighbors. The location having the smallest value is chosen as the new position of v_i. Using this methodology, the last active contour approach has been developed obtaining the last set of results.

3.2 Practical Application: Active Contours on Iberian Ham MRI

An experiment was designed using the three considered methods above to study the ripening process of the hams. Four stages were selected: *raw*, *post-salting*, *semi-dry* and *dry-cured*, acquiring MR images of the hams in each of the stages. These images have been processed using non-destructive computer vision techniques, as the three Active Contour approaches presented in 3.1. The initial analysis began with 15 hams in the raw stage. Moreover, three of these hams were destroyed being extracted the muscles by an expert in each stage, to make the chemical analysis on *biceps femoris* and *semimembranosus* muscles. These two muscles were weighed too, for each of the three analysed hams. The chemical analysis implies the destruction of the considered ham, so, there only were 12 hams in the post-salting stage, 9 in the semi-dry stage, and finally 6 hams in the dry-cured stage. Therefore, there only are MR images for the six considered Iberian hams in all the four stages.

As a previous step, a pre-processing stage is introduced, in order to obtain the values used as image energy. In addition, the initial snakes for all the images have been previously calculated too.

Once the complete database of images and the initial values of the snakes for these images are obtained, the application of Active Contours to compute the area of the muscle is needed. Every of the three active contours methods exposed above (variational calculus, greedy algorithm and dynamic programming) have been developed, obtaining three different sets of results.

Each of the obtained final snakes determines the surface of the muscle over the image. The final step computes surfaces and volumes for the extracted muscles. Calculating the surface of the final snake obtained for each image is possible to determine the volume for the muscle.

Eventually, in average, the error made has been estimated at less than 10%, considering the manual expert delineation of the muscles compared with the final area of the snake-segmented muscle.

Figure 1 contains MR images with the final snake for both *biceps femoris* (a) and *semimembranosus* (b) muscles.

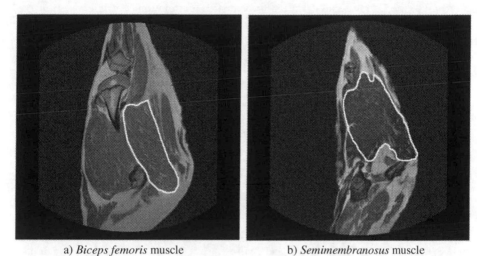

a) *Biceps femoris* muscle   b) *Semimembranosus* muscle

Fig. 1. Illustration of Iberian ham MR images, which include the detection of the muscles

4 Results and Discussion

The practical application of the three active contour approaches computes the volume of the Iberian ham *biceps femoris* and *semimembranosus* muscles during their ripening stages. These three sets of results have been obtained by means of Computer Vision techniques. Considering the results reached by the three different Active Contour techniques, it is particularly interesting to emphasize that they are certainly similar, independently of what method is used. They have been compared with the physical data, which have been obtained manually weighing the two muscles for all the three hams.

Table 1. Correlation coefficient (Correlation) and Pearson's correlation coefficient (Pearson) for the *Biceps Femoris* and *Semimembranosus* muscles

Method	*Biceps Femoris* muscle		*Semimembranosus* muscle	
	Correlation	Pearson	Correlation	Pearson
Variational	0.963	0.928	0.823	0.678
Dynamic	0.971	0.932	0.825	0.681
Greedy	0.965	0.944	0.821	0.674

So, different ways to obtain the data have been considered: manual and destructive techniques to weigh the hams, and automatic and non-destructive methods to compute volumes. The relationship between volumes and weights is shown in Table 1. This table shows the correlation coefficient [3] and the Pearson's correlation coefficient [3] achieved by the three methods. Both correlation coefficients, which mathematically vary from -1 to 1, are greater than 0.67 in all being the obtained results. That implies a good / excellent correlation between the data sets under consideration, according to the Colton's classification for statistical correlation coefficients [9].

Table 2 and 3 show the correlation coefficient in all the four maturation stages (raw, post-salting, semi-dry and dry-cured) for the *Biceps Femoris* and *Semimembranosus* muscles, respectively. Again, the obtained results could be considered as remarkable.

Table 2. Correlation coefficient (Corr.) and Pearson's correlation coefficient (Pearson) for the *Biceps Femoris* muscle

Method	Raw		Post-salting		Semi-dry		Dry-cured	
	Corr.	Pearson	Corr.	Pearson	Corr.	Pearson	Corr.	Pearson
Variational	0.841	0.708	0.900	0.811	0.870	0.758	0.915	0.838
Greedy	0.851	0.724	0.905	0.819	0.873	0.762	0.906	0.822
Dynamic	0.865	0.748	0.927	0.860	0.857	0.735	0.902	0.814

Table 3. Correlation coefficient (Corr.) and Pearson's correlation coefficient (Pearson) for the *Semimembranosus* muscle

Method	Raw		Post-salting		Semi-dry		Dry-cured	
	Corr.	Pearson	Corr.	Pearson	Corr.	Pearson	Corr.	Pearson
Variational	0.682	0.465	0.848	0.720	0.798	0.638	0.889	0.791
Greedy	0.681	0.464	0.859	0.739	0.806	0.650	0.886	0.785
Dynamic	0.683	0.466	0.915	0.837	0.817	0.668	0.896	0.803

Figure 2 shows the statistical correlation coefficients obtained between the three different Active Contour methods (variational calculus, greedy algorithm and dynamic programming) and the physical data, for the *biceps femoris* muscle. Both physical and computer vision results are certainly comparable. Moreover, a tendency line has been added in Figure 2, in order to show the predisposition of the data.

Similarly, figure 3 shows the same results corresponded to semimembranosus muscle. The physical extraction of this last muscle by Food Technology experts is a complex procedure. For this reason, these results are not as good as the data obtained for the biceps femoris muscle. However, there is a high correlation too.

The results in figures 2 and 3 show the good correlation between the Computer Vision results and the physical data, from the initial phase (raw) to the last stage (dry-cured), 21 months after the initial stage. Therefore, a significant relationship has been established and corroborated in this work: weight (manually obtained) and volume (automatically obtained) of the Iberian ham are correlated.

5   Conclusions

The real viability of the three classical active contour approaches for muscle recognition in MRI has been proved in this paper. An excellent correlation between the data

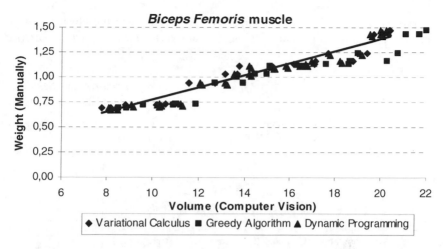

Fig. 2. Correlation coefficient for the *biceps femoris* muscle, in all the ripening stages

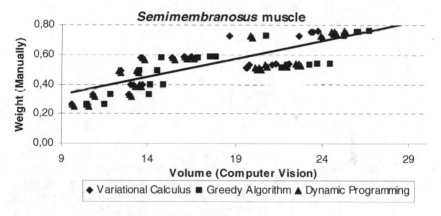

Fig. 3. Correlation coefficient for the *semimembranosus* muscle, in all the ripening stages

obtained with these three non-destructive techniques and the results achieved using the traditional methodologies have been reached. These significant correlations demonstrate the robustness of the employed methodology. Additionally, the practical feasibility of applying Computer Vision techniques to automate the ripening process of the Iberian ham constitutes a key finding in this research. Such computer vision techniques will introduce new and alternative methods for future work, which have long been awaited for the meat industries.

Acknowledgments

The authors wish to acknowledge and thank the support of the "Dehesa de Extremadura" brand name and the "Hermanos Alonso Roa" company from Villar del Rey

(Badajoz) to our study. In addition, this research has been funded by the Junta de Extremadura (Regional Government Board) under the IPR98A03P- and 2PR01C025-labeled projects.

References

1. Amini, A.A., Weymouth, T.E. and Jain, R.: Using Dynamic Programming for Solving Variational Problems in Vision, IEEE Transactions on Pattern Analysis and Machine Intelligence, Vol. 12, (1990), 855-867
2. Antequera, T., López-Bote, C.J., Córdoba, J.J., García, C., Asensio, M.A., Ventanas, J. and Díaz, Y.: Lipid oxidative changes in the processing of Iberian pig hams, Food Chem., 54, (1992), 105
3. Berry, D.A. and Lindgren, B.W.: Statistics. Theory and method, Duxbury, (1996)
4. Blake, A. and Isard, M.: Active Contours. Springer, London – UK, (1998)
5. Caro, A., Rodríguez, P.G., Cernadas, E., Durán, M.L., Antequera, T.: Potencial Fields,as an External Force and Algorithmic Improvements in Deformable Models, Electronic Letters on Computer Vision and Image Analisys, Vol. 2(1), (2003), 23-34
6. Caro, A., Rodríguez, P.G., Ávila, M., Rodríguez, F., Rodríguez, F.J.: Active Contours Using Watershed Segmentation, IEEE 9th Int. Workshop on Systems, Signal and Image Processing, Manchester - UK, (2002), 340-345
7. Cava, R. and Ventanas, J., Dinámica y control del proceso de secado del jamón ibérico en condic. naturales y cámaras climatizadas, T. jamón ibérico, Mundi Prensa, 260-274, (2001)
8. Cohen, L.D.: On Active Contour Models and Balloons, Computer Vision, Graphics and Image Processing: Image Understanding , Vol. 53(2), (1991), 211-218
9. Colton, T.: Statistical in Medicine. Little Brown and Co., Boston – USA, (1974)
10. Courant, R. and Hilbert, D., Methods of Mathematical Physics, Interscience, Vol. 1, New York, (1953)
11. Kass, M., Witkin, A. and Terzopoulos, D.: Snakes: Active Contour models, Proceedings of First International Conference on Computer Vision, London, (1987), 259-269
12. Kichenassamy, S., Kumar, A., Olver, P., Tannenbaum, A. and Yezzi, A.: Gradient Flows and Geometric Active Contour Models, Int. Conf. on Computer Vision, (1995), 810-815
13. Larsen, O.V., Radeva, P. and Martí, E.: Guidelines for Choosing Optimal Parameters of Elasticity for Snakes, Int. Conf. Computer Analysis and Image Processing, (1995), 106-113
14. Ranganath, S.: Analysis of the effects of Snake Parameters on Contour Extraction, Proc. Int. Conference on Automation, Robotics, and Computer Vision, (1992), 451-455
15. Williams, D.J. and Shah, M.: A Fast Algorithm for Active Contours and Curvature Estimation, C. Vision, Graphics and Im. Proc.: Im. Understanding, Vol. 55, (1992), 14-26
16. Xu, C. and Prince, J. L.: Gradient Vector Flow: A New External Force for Snakes, IEEE Proc. on Computer Vision and Pattern Recognition, (1997), 66-71

Radiance Function Estimation for Object Classification

Antonio Robles-Kelly and Edwin R. Hancock

Department of Computer Science,
University of York,York YO1 5DD, UK
{arobkell,erh}@cs.york.ac.uk

Abstract. This paper describes a simple method for estimating the surface radiance function from single images of smooth surfaces made of materials whose reflectance function is isotropic and monotonic. The method makes use of an implicit mapping of the Gauss map between the surface and a unit sphere. By assuming the material brightness is monotonic with respect to the angle between the illuminant direction and the surface normal, we show how the radiance function can be represented by a polar function on the unit sphere. Under conditions in which the light source direction and the viewer direction are identical, we show how the recovery of the radiance function may be posed as that of estimating a tabular representation of this polar function. A simple differential geometry analysis shows how the tabular representation of the radiance function can be obtained using the cumulative distribution of image gradients. We illustrate the utility of the tabular representation of the radiance function for purposes of material classification.

1 Introduction

The modeling of surface reflectance is a topic that is of pivotal importance, and has hence attracted considerable effort in both, computer vision and computer graphics communities. Broadly speaking, the methods used to model or approximate the bidirectional reflectance distribution function (BRDF) can be divided into those that are physics-based, semi-empirical or empirical in nature. Although the literature from physics is vast, it is perhaps the work of Beckmann on smooth and rough surface reflectance that is the best known in the vision and graphics communities [1]. Despite being based upon physically meaningful surface parameters, the Beckmann theory is intractable for analysis problems since it relies on the evaluation of the Kirchhoff wave scattering Integral. Further, it breaks down when either the surface roughness or the scattering angle are large. However, recently, Vernold and Harvey [2] have overcome this latter problem by developing a model which accounts for self shadowing on rough surfaces. By contrast, in the graphics community it is the development of computationally efficient tools for the purposes of realistic surface rendering that is of primary interest, and hence it is empirical models that have been the focus of activity [3, 4]. One of the most popular models is that developed by Phong [4]. However,

A. Sanfeliu et al. (Eds.): CIARP 2004, LNCS 3287, pp. 67–75, 2004.

neither the models developed in physics nor the computational models developed in graphics are well suited for surface analysis tasks in computer vision. It is for this reason that Wolff [5] and Nayar and Oren [6] have developed phenomenological, or semi-empirical, models that account for departures from Lambertian reflectance. Despite these efforts, the physical and phenomenological modeling of the BRDF remains an elusive task. An alternative is to empirically estimate or to learn the BRDF under controlled lighting and viewing conditions of rough and specular objects [7–11]. There have also been attempts to model the reflectance properties of human skin from real-wold imagery [12, 13]. Hertzmann and Seitz [14] have shown how the BRDF can be recovered making use of a reference object and multiple views of the scene.

The main problem with existing approaches is that the BRDF has four degrees of freedom that correspond to the zenith and azimuth angles for the light source and the viewer relative to the surface normal direction. As a result, the tabulation of empirical BRDF's can be slow and labour intensive. Furthermore, extensive lighting control and prior knowledge of the surface geometry is often required for the BRDF estimation process.

In this paper, we focus our attention in estimating the radiance function from single images without the use of expensive cameras and complex calibration procedures. Hence, we are interested in a computationally cheap alternative to the complicated setups employed by measurement-intensive approaches. Of course, acquiring a BRDF for purposes of photorealistic rendering from a single image is hard due to technical issues. Here, we aim at recovering a qualitatively good estimate that can be used for purposes of object classification or material library indexing.

We present an essentially non-parametric method for estimating the reflectance function from image data that avoids using basis functions or a predetermined parameterisation of the BRDF to characterise the specular spike and limb. Our method makes implicit use of the Gauss map, i.e. the projections of the surface normals onto a unit sphere. We map implicitly the brightness values for a single image onto locations on the unit sphere which have identical surface normal directions. Under conditions in which the light source and the viewer directions are identical, we show how the reflectance function can be represented by a polar function on the unit sphere. We pose the problem of recovering the reflectance function as that of estimating a tabular representation of this polar function. To overcome the problem that we do not have the field of surface normals at hand, under conditions of isotropic reflectance, we show how to estimate the zenith angles on the unit sphere using image brightness gradients. A simple analysis shows how the tabular representation of the reflectance function can be obtained using the cumulative distribution of image gradients.

2   Preliminaries

In this section, we provide the background for our method. Our overall aim is to make an estimate of the reflectance distribution function from a single image of a piecewise smooth surface. We limit our study to those surfaces whose reflectance function is isotropic and monotonic. Surfaces of this kind are those of shiny and moderately rough objects, terse objects and mate materials. Examples of these are porcelain, smooth terracotta, plastics, etc.

We simplify the problem of estimating the radiance function by using the differential properties of the Gauss map of the surface under study onto a unit sphere. For an orientable surface $S \in \Re^3$, the Gauss map $G : S \mapsto \hat{S}$ maps points on the surface S onto locations on the unit sphere $\hat{S}$ which have identical surface normal directions. Our aim is to use correspondences between surface normal directions to map brightness values from the image onto the unit sphere. The polar distribution of brightness values on the unit sphere $\hat{S}$ is the radiance function for the surface. To avoid ambiguities, we assume that points on the surface with identical surface normal directions have identical brightness values.

Of course, when only a single image is at hand, the mapping of the brightness values from the image onto the unit-sphere is not straightforward. In fact, the task of estimating surface normal directions from measured brightness values is an underconstrained one, which has preoccupied researchers in the field of shape-from-shading for several decades. Even for surfaces which exhibit simple Lambertian reflectance, the problem is not tractable in closed-form. Furthermore, for non-Lambertian reflectance the situation is more complex. In the case of non-Lambertian reflectance, provided that the reflectance properties of the surface are isotropic and homogeneous, the problem is simplified considerably if the viewer and light source directions are identical. The isotropy assumption will ensure that circles of latitude on the unit sphere will still have constant brightness. The problem of recovering the distribution of the brightness with respect to the latitude becomes that of estimating the zenith angle from the distribution of brightness values.

Hence, we limit our discussion to the case where the image plane Π is chosen so that the viewer direction vector $\boldsymbol{V}$ and the light-source direction vector $\boldsymbol{L}$ are coincident, i.e. $\boldsymbol{L} = \boldsymbol{V}$. Suppose that the point p on the unit sphere has zenith angle θ and azimuth angle α. Under the Gauss map, the brightness value associated with this point is denoted by the polar radiance function $f_O(\theta, \alpha) = I$, where I is the measured brightness at the point s in the image of the surface S. Thus, when the viewer and light source directions are identical, then provided that the reflectance process is isotropic, the distribution of radiance across the unit sphere can be represented by a function $g(\theta)$ of the zenith angle alone. As a result, the observed brightness values mapped onto the unit sphere by the Gauss map G can be generated by revolving the function $g(\theta) = f_O(\theta, 0)$ in α about the axis defined by the viewer and light source directions. The problem of describing the brightness distribution over the Gauss sphere hence reduces itself to that of approximating the function $g(\theta)$ and computing its trace of revolution.

To develop our analysis, and to show how to map brightness values onto the unit sphere, it will prove useful to consider the image of the unit sphere under orthographic projection onto the plane $\hat{\Pi}$ that is perpendicular to the viewer direction. The Cartesian image can be represented using the polar coordinates of the unit sphere and is given by $I_{\hat{\Pi}}(\sin(\theta)\cos(\alpha), \sin(\theta)\sin(\alpha)) = f_O(\theta, \alpha)$. In fact, when the light source and viewer directions are identical, then the image is circularly symmetric and we can write $I_{\hat{\Pi}}(\sin(\theta)\cos(\alpha), \sin(\theta)\sin(\alpha)) = g(\theta)$.

3   Radiance Function Estimation

When the viewer and light source directions are identical, then the task of estimating the radiance function reduces to that of estimating the distribution of brightness values with respect to the zenith angle on the unit sphere, i. e. to estimate $g(\theta)$. We show how this can be performed by using the differential structure of the observed brightness on the image plane Π. Hence, we commence by rewriting $g(\theta)$ as the integral of the partial derivative of the observed brightness with respect to the angular variable θ. To do this, we assume the radiance function $f_O(\theta, \alpha)$ to be monotonically decreasing for $\theta \in [0, \frac{\pi}{2}]$ and write

$$g(\theta) = \frac{1}{2\pi} \int_0^{2\pi} \left(f_O(0, \alpha) + \int_0^\theta \frac{\partial f_O(\theta, \alpha)}{\partial \theta} d\theta \right) d\alpha \tag{1}$$

In other words, the generating function $g(.)$ on the unit sphere can be expressed in terms of the cumulative distribution of the derivatives of the radiance function or, alternatively, the derivatives of the image brightness.

We now turn our attention to the image of the unit sphere on the plane $\hat{\Pi}$. Suppose that $F(r, \theta)$ is a parametric polar function that represents the distribution of radiance values over the image of the unit sphere. The radial coordinate of the function is the Euclidean distance between the point p and the center-point of the unit sphere $\hat{S}$ on the viewer plane $\hat{\Pi}$, i.e. $r = \sin(\theta) = \sqrt{(\sin(\theta)\cos(\alpha))^2 + (\sin(\theta)\sin(\alpha))^2}$. Hence

$$F(r, \theta) = \begin{bmatrix} r \\ g(\theta) \end{bmatrix} = \begin{bmatrix} \sin(\theta) \\ \frac{1}{2\pi} \int_0^{2\pi} \left(f_O(0, \alpha) + \int_0^\theta \frac{\partial f_O(\theta, \alpha)}{\partial \theta} d\theta \right) d\alpha \end{bmatrix} \tag{2}$$

As noted earlier, since the surface normals are not at hand, the correspondences between locations on the surface and the unit sphere are not available. Hence, the quantity θ is unkown. In other words, the function $F(r, \theta)$ only allows the surface S to be mapped onto the unit sphere $\hat{S}$ in an implicit manner.

To overcome this lack of correspondance information, we commence by showing the relation between the image brightness gradient and the function $g(\theta)$. Let the magnitude of the brightness gradient be given by

$$| \nabla I | = \sqrt{\left(\frac{\partial I}{\partial x} \right)^2 + \left(\frac{\partial I}{\partial y} \right)^2}$$

Since the image is circularly symmetric, the image gradient can be rotated about the z-axis without any loss of generality. We align the image gradient with the azimuth direction using the rotation matrix R_z, which rotates the vector ∇I by an angle α in a clockwise direction about the z-axis. The image brightness derivatives may be related to those of the function $g(\theta)$ using the inverse Jacobian J^{-1} via the following matrix equation

$$
R_z \begin{bmatrix} \frac{\partial I}{\partial x} \\ \frac{\partial I}{\partial y} \end{bmatrix} = J^{-1} \begin{bmatrix} \frac{\partial g(\theta)}{\partial \theta} \\ \frac{\partial g(\theta)}{\partial \alpha} \end{bmatrix} \tag{3}
$$

Using the rotation on the image plane and the coordinate transformation between the image plane and the unit sphere, we find that

$$
|\nabla I| = \frac{1}{\cos(\theta)} \frac{\partial g(\theta)}{\partial \theta} = \frac{\partial g(\theta)}{\partial \sin(\theta)} \tag{4}
$$

In this way, we can relate the image gradient to the derivative of the function $g(\theta)$ with respect to the zenith angle θ. In terms of finite differences, the relationship between the magnitude of the image gradient and the changes $\Delta g(\theta)$ in $g(\theta)$ and $\Delta \sin(\theta)$ in θ is the gradient of the function $F(r, \theta)$, i.e. $|\nabla I| = \frac{\Delta g(\theta)}{\Delta \sin(\theta)}$. The image gradient ∇I can be computed using the formula

$$
\nabla I = \frac{1}{\delta} \begin{bmatrix} I(j+1, k) - I(j-1, k) \\ I(j, k+1) - I(j, k-1) \end{bmatrix} \tag{5}
$$

where δ is the spacing of sites on the pixel lattice. Furthermore, on the unit sphere $\hat{S}$, it is always possible to choose points to be sampled so that the difference in brightness is a constant τ. As a result, we can write

$$
\Delta \sin(\theta) = \frac{\tau}{|\nabla I|} \tag{6}
$$

To recover θ from the expression above we perform numerical integration. To do this, we sort the image gradients according to the associated image brightness values. Accordingly, let ∇I_l be the image gradient associated with the brightness value l. The numerical estimate of $\sin(\theta)$ is then given by

$$
\sin(\theta) = \int_{l-0}^{l=m} \frac{\tau}{|\nabla I_l|} dI_l + \kappa \approx \sum_{l=0}^{m} \frac{\tau}{|\nabla I_l|} + \kappa \tag{7}
$$

where κ is the integration constant and m is the maximum brightness value for the surface under study. Hence, we can use the cumulative distribution of inverse gradients to index the zenith angle on the unit sphere. This indexation property means that we can approximate the function $F(r, \theta)$, or equivalently $g(\theta)$, by tabulation.

To pursue this idea, in principle, we only require a single image gradient corresponding to each of the distinct brightness levels in the image. In practice, we make use of the cumulative distribution of image gradients in order to minimise the approximation error by averaging. Let $Q_l = \{s \mid I = l\}$ be the set of pixels with brightness value l. For the brightness value $l = g(\theta)$, the average gradient is given by

$$
h(l) = \frac{\sum_{s \in Q_l} |\nabla I|}{|Q_l|} \tag{8}
$$

The distribution of average gradients is then stored as a vector h. Zero entries of the vector, which correspond to brightness values that are not sampled in the image, can cause divide-by-zero errors when the radiance function is computed. To overcome this problem, we smooth the components of the vector by performing piecewise linear interpolation of the adjacent non-zero elements. The resulting vector is denoted by $\hat{h}$. With the average image gradient at hand, we define the tabular approximation $\hat{F}$ to $F(r, \theta)$ as the set of Cartesian pairs

$$\hat{F} = \{((\tau \sum_{i=0}^{l} \hat{h}(l)^{-1} + \kappa), l); l = 0, 1, 2, \ldots, n_{max}\} \tag{9}$$

All that remains is to compute the constants τ and κ. We do this by making use of the maximum and minimum values of $\sin(\theta)$ for $\theta \in [0, \frac{\pi}{2}]$. Since the maximum and minimum values of $\sin(\theta)$ are unity and zero when $\theta = \frac{\pi}{2}$ and $\theta = 0$, we can set κ to unity and evaluate the numerical integral for $l = m$, which yields

$$\tau = -\left(\sum_{i=0}^{m} \hat{h}(i)^{-1}\right)^{-1} \tag{10}$$

4   Experiments

In this section, we illustrate the utility of the method for purposes of classification of shiny and rough materials. To this end, we have computed a set of pairwise distances for eight terracotta and porcelain objects captured using a simple setup which comprises only a Olympus

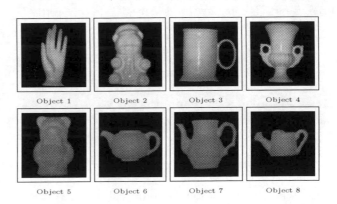

Fig. 1. Images used in our experiments.

E10 digital camera and a collimated 200W white tungsten light source. With the images at hand, we compute a similarity measure between pair of objects making use of the the reflectance map on the sphere computed from the reflectance function delivered by our method. This similarity measure is then used for purposes of separating images of shiny objects from those that correspond to rough objects.

The process described above is as follows. We compute a distance matrix D whose entry $d(a, b)$ is given by the error between the reflectance-map spheres corresponding to the objects indexed a and b. Hence, for a pair of reflectance-map spheres with a set of sample points Ω projected onto the pixel lattice, the pairwise distance is given by $d(a, b) = \frac{1}{|\Omega|} \sum_{q \in \Omega} | I_a(u) - I_b(u) |$, where $I_a(u)$ and $I_b(u)$ are the measured brightness values at the point q on the pixel lattice whose coordinates are $u = (i, j)$. With the matrix of pairwise distances at hand, we compute an affinity matrix W. Ideally, the smaller the distance, the stronger the weight, and hence the mutual affinity to a cluster. The affinity weights are required to be in the interval $[0, 1]$. Hence, for the pair of reflectance spheres indexed a and b the affinity weight is taken to be $W(a, b) = \exp\left(-k \frac{d(a,b)}{\max(D)}\right)$ where k is a constant.

For visualisation purposes, we have performed multidimensional scaling (MDS) [15] on the pairwise distance matrices. We have done this in order to embed the reflectance-map spheres in an eigenspace. Broadly speaking, the method can be viewed as embedding the objects in a pattern space using a measure of their pairwise similarity to one another. It is interesting to note that when the distance measure used is the L2 norm, then MDS is equivalent to principal components analysis.

In the top row of Figure 2, we show, from left-to-right, the distance matrix, the affinity matrix and the MDS plot for the eight porcelain and terracotta objects. The indexing of the objects corresponds to that shown in shown in Figure 1. Based on the visualisation provided by MDS, it is clear that the reflectance function delivered by our method may be suitable for the purposes of separating shiny and rough objects. It is important to stress that, since the distance has been computed using the reflectance map on the sphere, computed from the input images, and not the images themselves, we are effectively capturing the differences in the reflective properties of the objects and not only the differences in color.

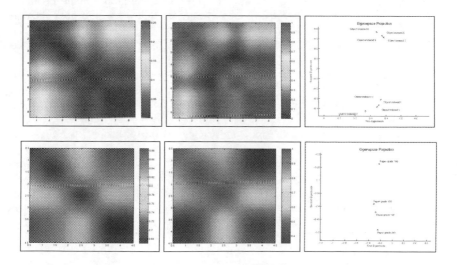

Fig. 2. Left-hand column: Distance matrices; Middle column: affinity matrices; Right-hand column: MDS plots.

To take our analysis further, we have performed experiments on four sandpaper rolls whose grades are 100, 150, 180 and 240. In the bottom row of Figure 2, we show the distance matrix, the affinity matrix and the MDS plot for the four sandpaper rolls. From the MDS plot its clear that the eigenspace embeddings describe a scattering that is in close accordance with a straight line. Further, the distribution of the distances describes a trace whose arrangement suggests an ordering from course to fine in the eigenspace, and hence, a way of classifying by grade the sandpaper rolls.

5   Conclusions

In this paper, we have presented a novel approach for approximating the radiance functions and hence the BRDF of objects whose reflectance is isotropic and monotonic from a single image. Although the new method is applicable only when the light source and viewer directions are approximately equal, it can be used as a computationally cheap alternative to other methods which use measurement-intensive approaches. Thus, the reflectance function estimated using the method may be used for tasks which require a computationally cheap estimate of the reflectance properties of the object, such as material classification.

References

1. P. Beckmann and A. Spizzochino. *The Scattering of Electromagnetic Waves from Rough Surfaces*. Pergamon, New York, 1963.
2. C. L. Vernold and J. E. Harvey. A modified beckmann-kirchoff scattering theory for non-paraxial angles. In *Scattering and Surface Roughness*, number 3426 in Proc. of the SPIE, pages 51–56, 1998.
3. R. L. Cook and K. E. Torrance. A reflectance model for computer graphics. *ACM Trans. on Graphics*, 1(1):7–24, 1982.
4. B. T. Phong. Illumination for computer generated pictures. *Communications of the ACM*, 18(6):311–317, 1975.
5. L. B. Wolff. On the relative brightness of specular and diffuse reflection. In *Int. Conf. on Comp. Vision and Patt. Recognition*, pages 369–376, 1994.
6. S. K. Nayar and M. Oren. Visual appearance of matte surfaces. *SCIENCE*, 267:1153–1156, 1995.
7. S. Westin, J. Arvo, and K. Torrance. Predicting reflectance functions from complex surfaces. In *SIGGRAPH 92 Conference Proceedings*, pages 255–264, 1992.
8. X. He, P. Heynen, R. Phillips, K. Torrance, D. Salesin, and D. Greenberg. A fast and accurate light reflection model. In *Siggraph 92 Conference Proceedings*, volume 26, pages 253–254, 1992.
9. G. J. Ward. Measuring and modeling anisotropic reflection. *Computer Graphics*, 26(2):265–272, 1992.
10. E. P.F. Lafortune, Sing-Choong Foo, K. E. Torrance, and D. P. Greenberg. Nonlinear approximation of reflectance functions. In *SIGGRAPH 97 Conference Proceedings*, pages 117–126, 1997.

11. K. J. Dana and S. K. Nayar. Correlation model for 3d texture. In *Int. Conf. on Comp. Vision*, pages 1061–1066, 1999.
12. S. R. Marschner, S. H. Westin, E. P. F. Lafortune, K. E. Torrance, and D. P. Greenberg. Image-based brdf measurement including human skin. In *10th Eurographics Rendering Workshop*, 1999.
13. P. Debevec, T. Hawkins, C. Tchou, H.-P. Duiker, W. Sarokin, and M. Sagar. Acquiring the reflectance field of a human face. In *SIGGRAPH 2000*, pages 145–156, 2000.
14. A. Hertzmann and S. M. Seitz. Shape and materials by example: A photometric stereo approach. In *Int. Conf. on Comp. Vision and Patt. Recognition*, pages 533–540, 2003.
15. I. Borg and P. Groenen. *Modern Multidimensional Scaling, Theory and Applications*. Springer Series in Statistics. Springer, 1997.

Detecting and Ranking Saliency
for Scene Description

William D. Ferreira and Díbio L. Borges

Pontifical Catholic University of Paraná (PUCPR)
Laboratory for Vision and Image Science
Rua Imaculada Conceicao, 1155, CEP 80215-901 Curitiba, Pr Brazil
{wdferreira,dibio}@ppgia.pucpr.br

Abstract. There is a long tradition in Computational Vision research regarding Vision as an information processing task which builds up from low level image features to high level reasoning functions. As far as low level image detectors are concerned there is a plethora of techniques found in the literature, although many of them especially designed for particular applications. For natural scenes, where objects and backgrounds change frequently, finding regions of interest which were triggered by a concentration of non-accidental properties can provide a more informative and stable intermediate mechanism for scene description than just low level features. In this paper we propose such a mechanism to detect and rank salient regions in natural and cluttered images. First, a bank of Gabor filters is applied to the image in a variety of directions. The most prominent directions found are then selected as primitive features. Starting from the selected directions with largest magnitudes a resultant is computed by including directional features in the image neighborhood. The process stops when inclusion of other points in the region makes the resultant direction change significantly from the initial one. This resultant is the axis of symmetry of that salient region. A rank is built showing in order the salient regions found in a scene. We report results on natural images showing a promising line of research for scene description and visual attention.

1 Introduction

Deciding upon what it is really important in a scene and how to extract and reason about that information can be regarded as a summary of all Computational Vision research. The idea behind saliency works is that it would be possible to find regions of interest (ROI) which are more important than others, and possibly to work towards understanding a scene without much trouble with segmentation or getting stuck with low level features uncertainty.

More recently many works have appeared in the literature proposing saliency detectors and visual attention mechanisms. In [4] Kadir and Brady show a saliency detector that starts by finding corners in the image and then analyzes the optimal scale by maximizing entropy surrounding that corner area. Many applications for the detector are given in their paper. Other interest points could

A. Sanfeliu et al. (Eds.): CIARP 2004, LNCS 3287, pp. 76–83, 2004.
© Springer-Verlag Berlin Heidelberg 2004

be used in the first step of a similar saliency detector, however one has to consider their intrinsic properties especially if the final task would be retrieval or visual attention. In [9] one can find an evaluation of many known interest point detectors. Reisfeld et. al. have proposed in [8] a symmetry transform which works as a saliency detector by looking for centers of symmetrical patterns in an image. Another approach to saliency has been to use more than one low level feature such as color, texture, or an edge map, and propose a way to weight and integrate those measures in order to reach a decision about the ROI. [2] and [6] are examples of that type of approach. Ranking ROI can be considered a way to compress an image, and special purpose compress algorithms based on visual saliency have been proposed. An example of such work is [10] which finds ROI in the wavelet space and use the saliency to order and divide blocks to be decomposed and reconstructed regarding their importance, or saliency rank.

Directional features are important cues in visual perception. In [1] a Self-Organizing Map (SOM) is proposed as a classification tool to detect salient structures in infrared images. The features considered as inputs to the SOM are directional and they are extracted using Gabor filters. The saliency detector proposed by us here considers directional features extracted by Gabor filtering as first primitives, and then build a novel algorithm to detect and rank a salient region by finding the more significant directions and their resultants, and finally using them as an axis of symmetry for scaling the region to be selected.

The remainder of this paper is organized as follows. Next section gives details of the proposed saliency detector dividing it into four main steps. Section 3 shows results on natural images of the detector and compares to another saliency detector proposed in [4]. Section 4 summarizes the main conclusions.

2 A Saliency Detector for Directional Visual Attention

Saliency frequently serves the purpose of compressing data by prioritizing non-redundancy. In order to understand a scene with unexpected and cluttered data as it is common in a natural image, the Human Visual System (HVS) seems to fixate around, or prioritize local information on an image. We offer here no general solution to the scene description problem, since it is known to be a kind of a local-global cycle depending on the visual task being realized [5, 11]. Our proposal is to have a saliency detector constructed around a property, believed to be present in many mammals visual system [3], that is to respond strongly to oriented patterns. By detecting and ranking salient regions in a scene, further tasks such as recognition and retrieval, or others in Active Vision which rely on visual attention may be achieved more efficiently.

We propose a saliency detector that finds and ranks regions upon which there is a strong directional feature. For this we begin by applying a bank of Gabor filters in the image, then we select the directions with highest probability. A region growing process considers then the peaks of the magnitude as seeds and compute a resultant direction until it finds an end point, or a consistently different direction. This resultant will be the axis of symmetry of the salient region found, and both its magnitude and final diameter grown will act as saliency importance, making it possible to rank the regions for visual attention or recognition tasks.

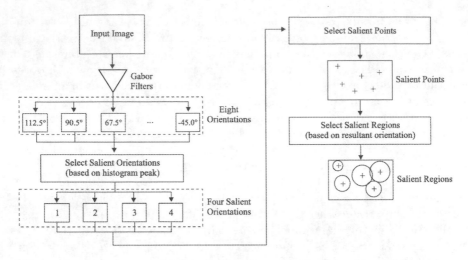

Fig. 1. General architecture of the proposed model.

Figure 1 shows a functional diagram for the proposed saliency detector. We give more details of it in the next sections dividing it into four steps: 1) Image filtering; 2) Preferred orientations; 3) Salient points; and 4) Salient regions.

2.1   Image Filtering

Directionality is one of the most important features to human visual perception [3], and some studies suggest that primitives of image representation in human vision have a wavelet form as Gabor filters or wavelets.

Gabor filters are a group of wavelets which can produce magnitude outputs favoring specific resolutions and orientations. A set of filtered images can be obtained by convolving an image with Gabor filters, and each of the images will represent the information at certain scale and orientation. The first step of our approach is to run Gabor filters using 1 scale, and 8 equally distant orientations (from 112.5° to -45.0°). A two dimensional Gabor function $g(x, y)$ and its Fourier transform $G(u, v)$ can be written as

$$g(x,y) = \left(\frac{1}{2\pi\sigma_x\sigma_y}\right) exp\left[-\frac{1}{2}\left(\frac{x^2}{\sigma_x^2} + \frac{y^2}{\sigma_y^2}\right) + 2\pi jWx\right] \qquad (1)$$

$$G(u,v) = exp\left\{-\frac{1}{2}\left[\frac{(u-W)^2}{\sigma_u^2} + \frac{v^2}{\sigma_v^2}\right]\right\}, \qquad (2)$$

where $\sigma_u = 1/2\pi\sigma_x$ and $\sigma_v = 1/2\pi\sigma_y$, and W is the frequency of the filter. A mother Gabor wavelet can be obtained by dilations and rotations of $g(x, y)$ through the function

$$g_{mn}(x,y) = a^{-m}G(x',y'), \; a > 1, m, n = integer$$
$$x' = a^{-m}(x\cos\theta + y\sin\theta), \; and \; y' = a^{-m}(-x\sin\theta + y\cos\theta), \qquad (3)$$

where $\sigma = n\pi/K$ and K is the total number of orientations. In our approach, for each input image $I(i,j)$ with dimension m x n, a set of filtered images ($O = \{O_1, O_2, O_3, ..., O_8\}$) is obtained by convolving I with Gabor filters in 8 orientations (equally spaced form 112.5° to -45.0°), 1 scale and filters dimension 60. The set of filtered images O is passed to the next step for selecting the orientations.

2.2   Preferred Orientations

Starting from the group of eight filtered images (O), obtained in previous step, a full histogram with the eight filtered images is computed. The four (4) highest peaks of this histogram are selected as the preferred orientations. Beginning by the filtered images from the previous step $O_1, O_2, O_3, ..., O_8$, the histogram (H) is an array defined by the Equation 4.

$$H(k) = \sum_{i=1}^{m} \sum_{j=1}^{n} O(i, j), k = 1, 2, 3, ..., 8 \tag{4}$$

The four (4) highest values in H are the chosen histogram peaks, with corresponding orientations.

2.3   Selecting Salient Points

There are $m*n$ points in each chosen orientation given by the previous step. These points are joined in a new image named P. In the case where points will have responses in more than one orientation, the orientation with the largest magnitude value will be the one selected. In this way the image P has dimension mxn, i.e. the same dimension of the input image I.

2.4   Selecting Salient Regions

The regions in our model are based on the resultant orientation. For selecting the salient regions the points obtained in the previous step are classified on order of importance, i.e. depending on the magnitude of its directional feature, and around each point a seed salient region is selected with ray r equals one, i.e. the selected region corresponds to a square matrix with dimension $m'xn'$ which is then called candidate region (ρ). For the experiments shown here the initial salient region ($r = 1$) has $m' = 6$ and $n' = 6$. Each point $\rho(i,j)$ in candidate region has its corresponding orientation called $\theta(i,j)$.

The resultant orientation RO is computed in candidate region using Equation 5. If the RO has a value which diverts more than 22.5° of the central point orientation, the growing process stops. However, if the mentioned condition is not fulfilled, the candidate region ray is increased of one unit ($r = r + 1$), and the process is repeated.

$$RO = \arctan\left(\frac{\sum_{i=1}^{m'}\sum_{j=1}^{n'} \rho(i,j) \times \sin(\theta(i,j))}{\sum_{i=1}^{m'}\sum_{j=1}^{n'} \rho(i,j) \times \cos(\theta(i,j))}\right) \tag{5}$$

In the experiments shown here candidate regions grow until size 64x64, however an automatic stop criterion for this could be further explored looking at redundancy, either for recognition or retrieval tasks. Figure 2 shows a complete example, highlighting the outputs of the four steps of the method.

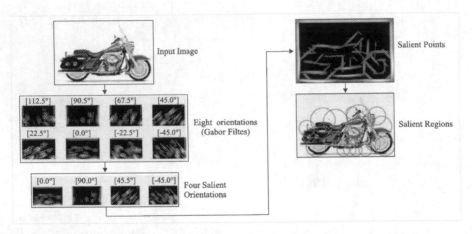

Fig. 2. An example of the steps of the proposed saliency detector.

3   Results on Natural Images

Natural images are usually cluttered because of sunlight and textured objects appearing at different distances. We tested the proposed saliency detector in a variety of natural images and show here some typical results. For these experiments the maximum size of the region would have diameter of 64 pixels. For the scale of the images shown this diameter finds meaningful regions, although this variable can be set differently depending on the image size, scale, and task it is aimed at describing.

Other saliency detectors have been proposed in the literature, and as we commented before each prioritizes either an specific feature to be searched for, or an integration model. Visually comparing results would serve more to enhance what each considers more salient and stable. In [4] Kadir and Brady propose an entropy based saliency detector, which starts at finding corners in an image and then enlarge its window until entropy is maximized. In Figures 3, 4, and 5 it is shown results with both saliency detectors for comparison. Numbers appearing on the regions borders indicate their importance rank in our detector.

Kadir and Brady Feature Detector   Our Detector

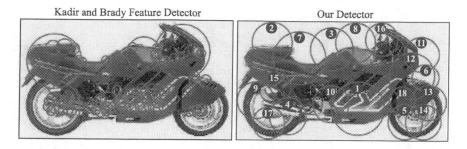

Fig. 3. Results of both saliency detectors (Kadir and ours) on images with object and clear background.

The Figure 3 shows an image with clear background, and it is observed that Kadir and Brady feature detector selects important regions to characterize the image. However, important regions were detected by the proposed model also, and the number of regions selected by it is less than Kadir and Brady feature detector. The reduced number of regions is an important characteristic to diminish redundancy.

Kadir and Brady Feature Detector   Our Detector

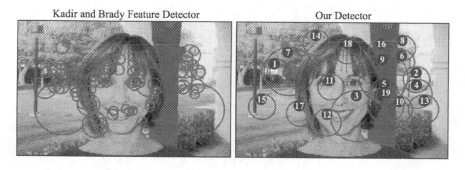

Fig. 4. Results of both saliency detectors (Kadir and ours) on images with object and cluttered background.

It is possible to verify in Figure 4 that in an image with textured background the feature detector proposed by Kadir and Brady selects large regions on the background, and it leaves out important regions in the face area, like mouth, nose and hair. Those regions are regarded as salient in the detector here proposed as shown in Figure 4. In the car sequence images of Figure 5 stability of the regions selected can be observed in our detector by looking at regions 1 and 4. Their relative importance and size remain closely similar (from one frame to the other), while the other detector changes its consideration on the object car.

As it can verified by the examples shown the proposed saliency detector finds very interesting and informative regions in natural and cluttered scenes. For the purpose of demonstration we have also included results of another known

Kadir and Brady Feature Detector   Our Detector

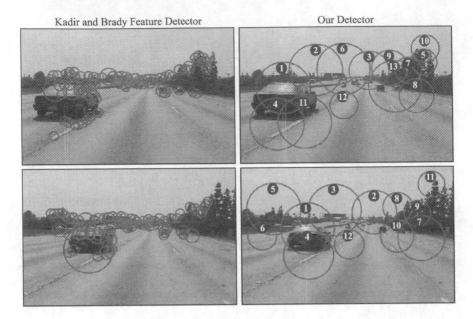

Fig. 5. Results of both saliency detectors (Kadir and ours) on a sequence of images with objects in different positions and cluttered background.

saliency detector [4] from the literature. Our proposed saliency detector prioritizes direction and symmetry notions, and serves the purpose of a reliable tool for scene description, especially if meant to visual attention tasks in Active Vision, recognition, and retrieval. Next section summarizes our main conclusions and point to future work.

4   Conclusions and Future Work

In this paper we have presented a region saliency detector based on the idea that regions of interest in a natural scene can be found around oriented patterns. A complete approach using Gabor filtering initially to locate the main responses to orientations, and then a selection and growing process using a resultant direction as an axis of symmetry of the region of interest is built and tested. Further, a recognition or retrieval process can make efficient use of such a scheme, since no segmentation is necessary for finding and ordering those regions as it was shown here.

Visual attention mechanisms and saliency provide a new paradigm for scene description in Computational Vision research, and there is an increase of interesting solutions appearing in the literature more recently. Unveiling the integration of attention models and saliency in the Human Visual System (HVS) is yet an out of reach target, and saliency detectors such as the one here proposed are meant to be just one of the useful mechanisms to be further explored. Future work is planned exploring the output regions of the detector for recognition and retrieval.

Acknowledgements

This research is in part supported by a grant from PUCPR (PRPPG Research Fund), and a grant from CNPq - MCT - Brazil to DLB.

References

1. M. Carreira, M. Mirmehdi, B. Thomas, and J. Haddon. Grouping of Directional Features using an Extended Hough Transform. In *Proc. of Int. Conf. on Pattern Recognition (ICPR)*, pages 990-993, 2000.
2. A. Dimai. Invariant Scene Description based on Salient Regions for Preattentive Similarity Assessment. In *Proc. of Int. Conf. on Image Analysis and Processing (ICIAP)*, pages 957-962, 1999.
3. D. Hubel. *Eye, Brain, and Vision*. W. H. Freeman and Company, USA, 1995.
4. T. Kadir and M. Brady. Saliency, Scale and Image Description. *Int. Journal of Computer Vision*, vol.45, n.2, pages 83-105, 2001.
5. S. Kosslyn. *Image and Brain*. MIT Press, USA, 1994.
6. J. Luo and A. Singhal. On Measuring Low-Level Saliency in Photographic Images. In *Proc. of the IEEE Conf. on Computer Vision and Pattern Recognition (CVPR)*, pages 1084-1089, 2000.
7. D. Marr. *Vision: A Computational Investigation into the Human Representation and Processing of Visual Information*. W. H. Freeman and Company, USA, 1982.
8. D. Reisfeld, H. Wolfson, and Y. Yeshrun. Context Free Attentional Operators: the Generalized Symmetry Transform. *Int. Journal of Computer Vision*, vol. 14, pages 114-130, 1995.
9. C. Schmid, R. Mohr, and C. Bauckhage. Evaluation of Interest Point Detectors. *Int. Journal of Computer Vision*, vol. 37, No. 2, pages 151-172, 2000.
10. T. Slowe and I. Marsic. Saliency-based Visual Representation for Compression. In *Proc. of the IEEE Conf. on Computer Vision and Pattern Recognition (CVPR)*, pages 554-557, 1997.
11. S. Ullman. *High-level Vision*. MIT Press, USA, 1996.

Decision Fusion for Object Detection and Tracking Using Mobile Cameras

Luis David López Gutiérrez and Leopoldo Altamirano Robles

National Institute of Astrophysics Optics and Electronics, Luis Enrique Erro No 1,
Santa Maria Tonantzintla, Puebla, 72840 México
luis_david@ccc.inaoep.mx, robles@inaoep.mx

Abstract. In this paper an approach to the automatic target detection and tracking using multisensor image sequences with the presence of camera motion is presented. The approach consists of three parts. The first part uses a motion segmentation method for targets detection in the visible images sequence. The second part uses a background model for detecting objects presented in the infrared sequence, which is preprocessed to eliminate the camera motion. The third part combines the individual results of the detection systems; it extends the Joint Probabilistic Data Association (JPDA) algorithm to handle an arbitrary number of sensors. Our approach is tested using image sequences with high clutter on dynamic environments. Experimental results show that the system detects 99% of the targets in the scene, and the fusion module removes 90% of the false detections.

1 Introduction

The task of detecting and tracking regions of interest automatically is a fundamental problem of computer vision; these systems have a great importance in military and surveillance applications. A lot of work has already been carried out on the detection of multiple targets. However, detection and tracking of small, low contrast targets in a highly cluttered environment still remains a very difficult task.

The most critical factor of any system for automatic detection is its ability to find an acceptable compromise between the probability of detection and the number of false target detection. These types of errors can generate false alarms and false rejections. In a single sensor detection system, unfortunately, reducing one type of error comes at the price of increase the other type. One way to solve this problem is to use more than one sensor and to combine the data obtained by these different expert systems. In this paper we propose an approach to solve the automatic detection problem of objects using decision fusion, our principal contribution is improve the target detection and tracking results without specialization of the algorithms for a particular task; the approach was tested on a set of image sequences obtained from mobile cameras.

The paper is organized as follows. Section 2 introduces the models which are considered, and briefly they are described. Section 3 shows an overview of the approach. Sections 4 and 5 describe the algorithms used to detect objects of interest in visible and infrared image sequences respectively. Section 6 describes the method for combining the results obtained by the two algorithms. Several results that validate our approach are reported in section 7, and finally section 8 contains concluding remarks.

A. Sanfeliu et al. (Eds.): CIARP 2004, LNCS 3287, pp. 84–91, 2004.

2 Background

Parametric motion model: The parametric motion model $\bar{w}_\theta$ represent the projection of the 3D motion field of the static background [1], where $\bar{w}_\theta$ denotes the modeled velocity vector field and θ the set of model parameters. The parametric motion model is defined at pixel p = (x,y) as:

$$\bar{w}_\theta(p) = \begin{pmatrix} a_1 + a_2 x + a_3 y \\ a_4 + a_5 x + a_6 y \end{pmatrix} = \begin{bmatrix} u(p) \\ v(p) \end{bmatrix} \tag{1}$$

Where $\theta = (a_i)$, i = 1..6, is the parameter vector to be estimated.

Motion estimation: To estimate a motion model θ_k we use a gradient-based multi-resolution robust estimation method described in [2]. To ensure the goal of robustness, we minimize an M-estimator criterion with a hard-redescending function [3]. The constraint is given by the usual assumption of brightness constancy of a projected surface element over its 2D trajectory [4]. The estimated parameter vector is defined as:

$$\hat{\theta} = \underset{\theta}{\text{argmin}}\ E(\theta) = \underset{\theta}{\text{argmin}} \sum_{p \in R(t)} \rho(DFD_\theta(p)) \tag{2}$$

Where $DFD_\theta(p)=I_{t+1}(p + \bar{w}_\theta(p))-I_t(p)$, and p(x) is a function which is bounded for high values of *x*. The minimization takes advantage of a multiresolution framework and an incremental scheme based on the Gauss-Newton method. More precisely, at each incremental step k (at a given resolution level, or from a resolution level to a finer one), we have: $\theta = \hat{\theta}_k + \Delta\theta_k$. Then, a linearization of $DFD_\theta(p)$ around $\hat{\theta}_k$ is performed, leading to a residual quantity $r_{\Delta\theta k}(p)$ linear with respect to $\Delta\theta_k$:

$$r_{\Delta\theta(p)} = \nabla I_t(p + \bar{w}_{\hat{\theta}k}(p)) \cdot \bar{w}_{\Delta\theta k}(p) + I_{t+1}(p + \bar{w}_{\hat{\theta}k}(p)) - I_t(p) \tag{3}$$

Where $\nabla I_t(p)$ denotes the spatial gradient of the intensity function at location p and at time t. Finally, we substitute for the minimization of $E(\theta_k)$ in (2) the minimization of an approximate expression E_a, which is given by $E_a(\Delta\theta_k)$ $= \sum \rho(r_{\Delta\theta k}(p))$. This error function is minimized using an Iterative-Reweighted-Least-Squares procedure, with 0 as an initial value for $\Delta\theta_k$ [1]. This estimation algorithm allows us to get a robust and accurate estimation of the dominant motion model between two images.

Mixture Gaussian background model: Mixture Models are a type of density model which comprise a number of component functions, usually Gaussian. These component functions are combined to provide a multimodal density [5]. The key idea of background model is to maintain an evolving statistical model of the background, and to provide a mechanism to adapt to changes in the scene. There are two types of background model:

Unimodal model: each pixel is modeled with a single statistical probability distribution (Gaussian distribution) $\eta(X, \mu t, \Sigma t,)$, where μt and Σt are the mean value and covariance matrix of the distribution at frame t respectively. Pixels where observed colors are close enough to the background distribution are classified as background points, while those too far away as foreground points.

Multimodal model: a mixture of multiple independent distributions is necessary to model each pixel. Each distribution is assigned a weight representing its priority. A pixel is classified as a background point only if the color observed matches with one of the background distributions. A new distribution of the observation should be imported into the background model if none of the distributions matches it.

Joint Probabilistic Data Association: The Joint Probabilistic Data Association (JPDA) algorithm considers the problem of tracking T targets in clutter [6]. $x^t(k)$ ($1 \leq t \leq$ T) denotes the state vectors of each target t at the time of the kth measurement. The target dynamics are determined by known matrices F^t and G^t and random noise vectors $w^t(k)$ as follows:

$$X^t(k+1) = F^t(k)x^t(k) + G^t(k)w^t(k) \tag{5}$$

where $t = 1, \ldots ,T$. The noise vector $w^t(k)$ is stochastically independent Gaussian random variables with zero mean and known covariance matrices. Let m_k denotes the number of validated returns at time k. The measurements are determined by

$$z_l(k) = H(k)x^t(k) + v^t(k) \tag{6}$$

where $t = 1, \ldots ,T$, and $l = 1, \ldots ,m_k$. The H(k) matrix is know, each $v^t(k)$ is a zero-mean Gaussian noise vector uncorrelated with all other noise vectors, and the covariance matrices of the noise vectors $v^t(k)$ are know.

The goal of JPDA is to associate the targets with the measurements, and to update those estimates. The actual association of targets being unknown, the conditional estimate is determined by taking a weighted average over all possible associations. An association for the kth observation is a mapping $a:\{1, \ldots , T\} \rightarrow \{0, \ldots , m_k\}$ that associates the target t with the detection a(t), or 0 if no return is associated with the tth target.

Let $\theta_a(k)$ denotes the event that "a" is the correct association for the kth observation. And $\hat{x}_l^t(k \mid k)$ denotes the estimate of $x^t(k)$ given by the Kalman filter on the basis of the previous estimate and the association of the tth target with the lth return. The conditional estimate $\hat{x}^t(k \mid k)$ for $x^t(k)$ given Z^k is

$$\hat{x}^t(k \mid k) = \sum_{l=0}^{m_k} \beta_l^t(k)\hat{x}_l^t(k \mid k) \tag{7}$$

where $\beta_l^t(k) = \sum_{a:a(t)=l} P(\Theta_a(k) \mid Z^k)$ is the conditional probability of the event $\theta_l^t(k)$ given Z^k. The set of probabilities $\beta_l^t(k)$ can be computed efficiently as the permanents of a set of sub-matrices.

Multi-sensor data fusion: The multi-sensor data fusion is defined as the process of integrating information from multiple sources to produce the most specific and comprehensive unified data about an entity, activity or even [7].

Fusion processes are often categorized as low, intermediate or high level fusion depending on the processing stage at which fusion takes place [7].

Low level fusion, also called data fusion, combines several sources of raw data to produce new raw data that is expected to be more informative and synthetic than the original inputs. *Intermediate level fusion*, also called feature level fusion, combines various features. Those features may come from several raw data sources or from the same raw data. *High level fusion*, also called decision fusion combines decisions coming from several experts. Methods of decision fusion include voting methods, statistical methods, fuzzy logic based methods, and machine learning methods.

3   Overview of the Approach

Figure 1 shows an overview of the method. The proposed algorithm consists of three independent parts. The first part finds the camera motion, and detects the mobile targets in the visible image sequence. The second part detects the mobile target in the infrared image sequence. Each part of the algorithm behaves as an expert, indicating possible presence of mobile targets in the scene; Decision fusion is used to combine the outcomes from these experts.

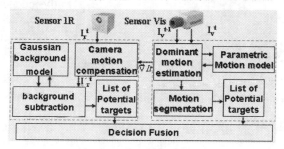

Fig. 1. Overview of the approach.

4   Targets Detection in Visible Images

Mobile objects in the visible image sequences are detected performing a thresholding on the motion estimation error, where the mobile objects are the regions whose true motion vector does not conform to the modeled flow vector.

In [8] is shown through the analysis of the results of different kinds of optical flow estimation algorithms, that $\| \vec{\tilde{I}}(p) \|^2$ is indeed a proper measure of the reliability of the estimation of the normal flow u_n, thus, the motion error is calculated using the following weighted average, which is proposed in [9]

$$Mes_{\hat{\Theta}_t}(p) = \frac{\Sigma_{q \in F(p)} \left(\| \vec{\tilde{I}}(q) \|^2 \times | FD_t(q) | \right)}{Max(\Sigma_{q \in F(p)} \| \vec{\tilde{I}}(q) \|^2, n \times G_m^2)} \tag{8}$$

Where $F(p)$ is a small neighborhood around p which contains n points, and G_m is a constant which accounts for noise in the uniform areas. An interesting property of this local measure is the following. Let us suppose that the pixel p and its neighborhood undergoes the same displacement of magnitude δ and direction $\vec{u}$. In [1] there were derived two bounds $l(p)$ and $L(p)$ such that, whatever the direction $\vec{u}$ might be, the following inequality holds:

$$0 \le l(\mathrm{p}) \le Mes_{\hat{\Theta}_t}(\mathrm{p}) \le L(\mathrm{p}) \tag{9}$$

The bounds used in the experiments are given by:

$$\begin{cases} l(p) = \eta \delta \sqrt{\lambda'_{min}(1-\lambda'_{min})} \\ L(p) = \delta \sqrt{1-\lambda'_{min}} \end{cases} \text{ with } \eta = \frac{\Sigma_{q \in F(p)} \| \vec{\nabla} \tilde{I}(q) \|^2}{Max(\Sigma_{q \in F(p)} \| \vec{\nabla} \tilde{I}(q) \|^2, n \times G_m^2)} \text{ and } \lambda'_{min} = \frac{\lambda_{min}}{\lambda_{max}+\lambda_{min}}$$

Where λ_{min} and λ_{max} are respectively the smallest and highest eigenvalues of the following matrix (with $\tilde{I}(q)$ = Image at time q and $\nabla \tilde{I}(q) = (\tilde{I}_x(q), \tilde{I}_y(q))$:

$$M = \begin{pmatrix} \Sigma_{q \in F(p)} \tilde{I}_x(q)^2 & \Sigma_{q \in F(p)} \tilde{I}_x(q) \tilde{I}_y(q) \\ \Sigma_{q \in F(p)} \tilde{I}_x(q) \tilde{I}_y(q) & \Sigma_{q \in F(p)} \tilde{I}_y(q)^2 \end{pmatrix} \tag{10}$$

Figure 2 shows the results of the target detection method in the visible sequence in presence of one target.

(a) Visible image sequence.   b) Detected target.

Fig. 2. Motion segmentation results in the Ship sequence.

5   Targets Detection in Infrared Images

Mobile objects in the infrared image sequences are detected determining the background in the image, and subtracting it to the original image, which has been preprocessed to eliminate the camera motion, this preprocessing step use information of the dominant motion calculated in the last module.

(a) Infrared image sequence.   (b). Detected target.

Fig. 3. Background model results in the boat sequence.

The background is obtained using a statistical model to classify pixels (see section 2). Each pixel is modeled as a mixture of 3 Gaussian models [10]. This process has three main stages:

1. Gaussian model initialization.
2. Background detection.
3. Update of the background estimation.

Figure 3 shows the results of the target detection method in the infrared sequence in presence of one target.

6 Decision Fusion

The first and second parts of the approach behave as experts indicating the possible position of mobile targets in the scene. The final decision is reached by fusing the results of these experts.

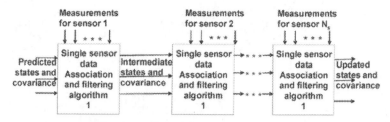

Fig. 4. Multi-sensor Fusion Architecture.

Figure 4 shows the sequential Multi-Sensor Data Fusion architecture [11] used to combine the individual target detecting results. The initial state of the tracking algorithms is obtained using a weighted "k out of N" voting rule. The combination of the measurements is done; making Ns (Number of sensors in the system) repetitions of the JPDA algorithm (see section 2).

The fusion algorithm works on the basis of the following equations.

Let m_{ki}, i = 1, 2, . . . ,Ns, the number of validated reports from each sensor i at time k. The measurements are determined by

$$z_i^l(k) = H_i(k)x^t(k) + v_i^l(k) \tag{11}$$

where t=1, ... ,T, i =1, ... ,Ns, and l =1, ..., m_{ki}. The measurement $z_i^l(k)$ is interpreted as the lth measurement from the ith sensor at time k. Generalizing from the single-sensor case, the $H_i(k)$ matrices are known, and $v_i^l(k)$ are stochastically independent zero-mean Gaussian noise vectors with known covariance matrices. The observation at time k is now

$$Z(k) = (z_1^1(k),...,z_{mk1}^1(k), z_1^2(k),...z_{mk1}^2(k),..., z_1^{Ns}(k),...,z_{mk1}^{Ns}(k)) \tag{11}$$

The conditional estimate of the fusion algorithm is given by:

$$\hat{x}^t(k\,|\,k) = \sum_L \beta_L^t(k)\hat{x}_L^t = \sum_t \prod_{i=1}^{Ns} \beta_L^t(k)\hat{x}_L^t \tag{13}$$

Where the sums are over all possible sets of associations L with target t.

7 Results

In this section, we will show the experimental results of our approach. The algorithm was tested with a database of two multi-spectral image sequences. The weather conditions were: winds of 30 to 70 km/hour, and variable lighting. The boat sequence was used to characterize the results of the motion segmentation algorithm.

Table 1 shows the principal features and results of the two first blocks. In the table, Pd is the probability of detection and NFt is the average number of false targets per image. The figures 5(a) and 6(a) show an image of the Boat and People sequence respectively. By applying the algorithms described in section 4 and 5 the objects are detected in each frame, figures 5(b) and (c) show the target detection results using the Boat sequence, figure 6(b) and (c) show the target detection results using the People sequence.

Table 1. Results of different experts.

Sequence	Size	Frames	Targets	Sensor	Pd (%)	NFt
Boat	640 x 480	150	1	Visible	96	2.0
				Infrared	100	1.5
People	640 x 480	150	2	Visible	99	1.5
				Infrared	98	0.6
Ship	640 x 480	50	2	Visible	95	5.2

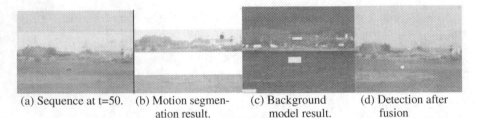

(a) Sequence at t=50.   (b) Motion segmen-   (c) Background   (d) Detection after
                          ation result.   model result.   fusion

Fig. 5. Target detection results in the boat sequence.

In table 2, results after the decision fusion are shown. In both sequences, the fusion improves results. The data association step in the fusion module reduces the number of false targets creating gating regions and considering just the measurements that fall in that region. The fusion module improves the target state estimation by processing sequentially the sensors detection, in this module if an target was not detected in a sensor, the information about it stays and the following sensor is processing, this way to combine the information improves the probability of detection, because the target must be loosed in all sensors to lose it in the fusion decision result. Figure 5(D) and 6(D) shows these results graphically.

Table 2. Results after fusion.

Sequence	Processing average time	Pd (%)	NFt
Boat	4.3 seg.	100	0.5
People	4.1 seg.	99	0.1

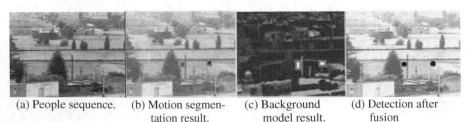

(a) People sequence.   (b) Motion segmen-   (c) Background   (d) Detection after
                         tation result.   model result.   fusion

Fig. 6. Target detection results in the people sequence.

8 Conclusions

In this paper an approach to improve target detection process using decision fusion is proposed. The approach was tested using multi-spectral image sequences from moving cameras. Experimental results show that targets detection algorithms detects in average 97% of the targets in the worse case, and in the better one detects 99.5%. The fusion module detects in the worst case 99% of the targets and 100% in the better one, while the 90% of the false targets are removed. This results show the advantages of this approach for automatic detection and tracking. It has been shown that this approach performs better that either tracker in isolation. Most importantly the tracking performance is improved without specialization of the tracking algorithms for a specific task; it remains to develop an algorithm to handle target occlusion and to reduce the processing time.

References

1. J. Odobez, P. Bouthemy. Direct incremental model-based image motion segmentation analysis for video analysis Signal Processing. Vol 66, pp 143-155, 1998
2. J. Odobez, P. Bouthemy. Robust multiresolution estimation of parametric motion models. JVCIR, 6(4) pp 348-365, 1995.
3. P.J. Hubert. Robust statistics. Wiley, 1981.
4. Horn, Shunck. Determining optical flow. Artificial Intelligence, vol 17 pp 185-203, 1981
5. C. Stauffer, Adaptive background mixture models for real-time tracking. In Proceedings of the IEEE Conference on Computer Vision and Pattern Recognition, pp 246-252, 1999.
6. Bar-Shalom, T. Fortmann. Tracking and data association, Academic Press, San Diego, 1988.
7. E. Waltz and J. Llinas, Handbook of multisensor data fusion, CRC Press, 2001.
8. J. Barron, D Fleet, S. Bauchemin. Performance of optical flow techniques. International Journal of Computer Vision. 12(1) pp 43-77, 1994.
9. M. Irani, B. Rousso, S. Peleg. Computing occluding and transparent motion. Intern. J. Comput. Vis. 12(1) pp 5-16, 1994.
10. C. Stauffer, W. E. L. Grimson, Learning patterns of activity using real time tracking. IEEE trans. PAMI, val 22, no. 8, pp 747-757, Aug, 2000.
11. L. Pao, S. O'Neil. Multisensor Fusion algorithms for tracking. Proc. of American Control Conference. pp. 859–863, 1993.

Selection of an Automated Morphological Gradient Threshold for Image Segmentation*

Francisco Antonio Pujol López[1], Juan Manuel García Chamizo[1],
Mar Pujol López[2], Ramón Riza Aldeguer[2], and M.J. Pujol[3]

[1] Depto. Tecnología Informática y Computación
Universidad de Alicante, Ap. Correos 99, 03080 Alicante, España
{fpujol,juanma}@dtic.ua.es
[2] Depto. Ciencia de la Computación e Inteligencia Artificial
Universidad de Alicante, Ap. Correos 99, 03080 Alicante, España
{mar,rizo}@dccia.ua.es
[3] Depto. Matemática Aplicada
Universidad de Alicante, Ap. Correos 99, 03080 Alicante, España
mjose@ua.es

Abstract. Segmentation is an essential part of practically any automated image recognition system, since it is necessary for further processing such as feature extraction or object recognition. There exist a variety of techniques for threshold selection, as it is a fast, simple and robust method. Threshold value will have considerable effects on the boundary position and overall size of the extracted objects. In this work, we propose an automated thresholding selection, which takes into account the local properties of a pixel. To do this, the algorithm calculates the morphological gradient and Laplacian and, afterwards, chooses a suitable threshold after estimating the lowest distance between the ideal segmentation and the morphological gradient thresholding segmentation.

1 Introduction

The recognition of objects in images is a non-trivial task. Machine learning research involves training a classifier with data obtained from known images, and then predicting the label of test samples from unseen images. The task of decomposing an image into distinctly different but homogeneous parts is called image segmentation, and the process of extracting information from these regions that define their unique properties is called feature extraction.

Image segmentation has been the subject of intensive research and a wide variety of segmentation techniques have been reported in the literature (see [1]). It is a crucial issue since it is the first step of the image understanding process, and all others steps, such as feature extraction and recognition, depend heavily on its results.

* This work has been supported by the Spanish (CICYT), project TIC2001-0245-C02-02 and by the Generalitat Valenciana, projects GV04B685,GV04B634.

A. Sanfeliu et al. (Eds.): CIARP 2004, LNCS 3287, pp. 92–99, 2004.

In general, the segmentation algorithms are based on two important criteria: the homogeneity of the region and the discontinuity between adjacent disjoint regions. Although many image segmentation approaches deal with these problems ([2], [3]), it is difficult to satisfy all the properties for the optimal set of segmented regions. The resulting segmented images generally depend on the predetermined threshold values. So the algorithm often fails due to it either merges regions that must be divided or separates connected regions.

Consequently, in this work, we propose a fast, robust method for image segmentation that takes into account some local properties of every pixel to calculate a well-suited threshold; thus, our segmentation scheme gives good results even when the tests are performed with noisy real-world images. The paper is organized as follows: Firstly, we define a method to obtain the morphological gradient threshold (MGT) image segmentation in Section 2. As a result, each of the steps necessary to develop this algorithm are explained in Section 3. Then, Section 4 establishes a measure related to the appropriateness of our technique. Afterwards, in Section 5 the experimentation is widely illustrated to verify the accomplishment of our research objectives. Finally, we conclude with some important remarks in Section 6.

2   MGT Algorithm for Image Segmentation

Designing an image segmentation scheme needs the consideration of two features of visual recognition: cost and uncertainty. Visual recognition is generally costly because the image data is large. Visual information contains uncertainty from many sources such as discretization. In general, the more observation a vision system performs, the more information is obtained, but the more cost is required. Thus, a trade-off must be considered between the cost of visual recognition and the effect of information to be obtained by recognition. In relation to this, some of the most popular approaches which provide low computation times and good information are the threshold techniques and the edge-based methods [4].

Threshold techniques, which make decisions based on local pixel information, are effective when the intensity levels of the objects are exactly outside the range of the levels in the background. These thresholding algorithms are simple and give very good results, but deciding the threshold values is not easy. Specially, this is a really serious problem for an automated vision system, as the system should decide the threshold values taking its own decision.

On the other hand, edge-based methods (e.g., gradient operators) focus on contour detection. They involve finding the edges of objects in the image and using this edge information to achieve the complete boundaries for the main objects in the image. Edge detection has many problems, especially when working with noisy images, since it could even fragment the true edges.

To overcome these problems, we propose a method that combines both thresholding and gradient operators: the so-called Morphological Gradient Threshold (MGT) segmentation, as described in Table 1. It consists of 7 main steps, where the gradient and the Laplacian are calculated in terms of Mathematical

Morphology operations and the optimal threshold value is selected by measuring the lowest distance between the ideal segmentation and a collection of MGT segmented images.

Table 1. MGT segmentation algorithm.

Step 1. Image smoothing.
Step 2. Global dilation and erosion.
Step 3. For every pixel, create a list of symbols by means of the Morphological
        gradient and the Morphological Laplacian.
Step 4. Creation of a pixel-symbol map.
Step 5. Binarization of the pixel-symbol map.
Step 6. Computation of a suitable measure to obtain the optimal threshold.
Step 7. Obtention of the MGT segmented image.

Next, a more detailed description of this process is found.

3   Construction of a Pixel-Symbol Map

3.1   Image Smoothing and Derivative-Based Operations

In every digital image there is a certain amount of white noise. To avoid the noise effects, which only consume computation time and affect the real image features, an initial filtering process has to be applied. There are many algorithms to accomplish this task; in our approach a Gaussian filter has been chosen, since it preserves many of the image features while its computational cost can be assumed in a real-time environment. For more information see [5].

Once the noise is eliminated, the point is how to create the pixel-symbol map. To do this, let us consider first the computation of some derivative-based operations, i.e., the gradient and the Laplacian.

As mentioned before, edge detection is a main problem in image analysis. There are many approaches to obtain edges by means of the gradient of an image (e.g., Prewitt or Sobel operators). Among all of these methods we find the morphological gradient, which uses the Mathematical Morphology operators.

Mathematical Morphology (MM) is a geometric approach in image processing and, originally, it was developed as a tool for shape analysis. The two elementary operations in MM are erosion and dilation [6]; from this two primitives, more complex operations are constructed, such as opening, closing and top-hat. Therefore, one can define the morphological gradient of an image X by a structuring element (SE) B, $\rho_B(X)$, as:

$$\rho_B(X) = \frac{1}{2}(\delta_B(X) - \varepsilon_B(X)) \, . \tag{1}$$

where $\delta_B(X)$ and $\varepsilon_B(X)$ are, respectively, the dilation and the erosion of an image X by a SE B.

It is well-known that MM has not been usually utilized when working with real-time images, as it has a very high running time. In [6] it is described an algorithm which overcome this problem by taking into account all the pixels in an image at the same time.

Let us consider that an image is dilated, using a line-segment SE that consists of two points separated by n pixels. Then, we define a projection matrix, M_p, built from the original image moved $n + 1$ points to the right/left, depending on the location of the SE center. Considering a binary image, one should do the logical operation OR between the original image and the moved one in order to obtain the required dilation. This method can be extended to dilations with any 2-D SE and, more generally, to the erosion, where the logical operation AND is used instead of the OR one. In gray-scale images, OR/AND operations should be replaced by the supremum/infimum ones. The computational cost of this approach is even 50% better than the classical MM method [6].

The following step is to calculate the second derivative, the Laplacian. Again, we have chosen a morphological implementation for the Laplacian, as we can use with costless time the previously pre-calculated erosion and dilation. Thus, the morphological Laplacian of an image X by a SE B, $\Lambda_B(X)$, is defined as:

$$\Lambda_B(X) = \frac{1}{2}(\delta_B(X) + \varepsilon_B(X)) - X . \tag{2}$$

The results for a gray-scale image after these initial steps are shown in Fig. 1, where the SE B is a 3×3 square.

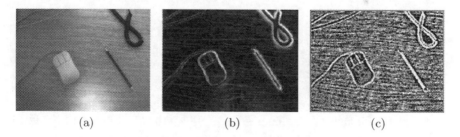

(a)   (b)   (c)

Fig. 1. A real image: (a) Original image. (b) $\rho_B(X)$. (c) $\Lambda_B(X)$.

3.2 The Pixel-Symbol Map

The next task is building a map that characterizes properly the pixels for a good segmentation. Thus, the pixel symbol map $m(x, y)$ is obtained as follows.

$$m(x,y) = \begin{cases} 128 & \text{if} & \rho_B(x,y) < MGT, \\ 255 & \text{if} & \rho_B(x,y) \geq MGT \text{ and } \Lambda_B(x,y) \geq 0, \\ 0 & \text{if} & \rho_B(x,y) \geq MGT \text{ and } \Lambda_B(x,y) < 0 \end{cases} \tag{3}$$

where MGT is the morphological gradient threshold and (x, y) is a pixel in X. The resulting image has three different gray-levels, according to if a pixel belongs to an object, to the background or to the borders.

The choice of the threshold value is one of the most difficult tasks, since the final result is high dependent on many factors, such as lighting conditions, objects texture or shading. Fig. 2 shows the results of the construction of the pixel-symbol map for the image in Fig. 1, with several different MGT values.

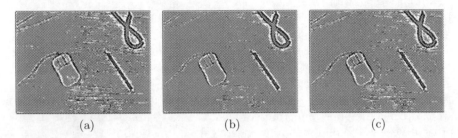

(a)   (b)   (c)

Fig. 2. The pixel-symbol map $m(x,y)$ with different MGT values: (a) Gradient mean. (b) $MGT = 0.9 * \max(\rho_B(x,y))$. (c) $MGT = 0.8 * \max(\rho_B(x,y))$.

Though many practical systems utilize an experimentally obtained threshold, in this work we consider the use of an automated thresholding system. This method takes into account a binary image metrics to compare the segmentation results and, afterwards, to establish the quality level of the obtained segmentation, as it is described in the following section.

4   A Measure of the Quality of the Segmentation

A main problem in computer vision is to be able to compare the results using a proper metrics. This will quantify the differences between two images and, if binary images are used, the method would be both easily implementable and low computationally complex. In our system we are interested in measuring the distance between image G (the map after gradient thresholding) and image A (the ideal segmentation). Thus, it will establish the optimal MGT value.

Hence, the map must be binarized first. To do this, we must recall that $m(x,y)$ has only 3 gray-levels (Eq. (3)): 0, 128 and 255. For simplicity, let us consider that the threshold is the same as in the construction of $m(x,y)$, i.e., the gradient threshold MGT. The results of this process are shown in Fig. 3.

Next, a reliable measure to compare the obtained image segmentation with an ideal segmentation must be selected.

As proved in [7], a good error measurement for binary images is $\Delta^p(A,G)$, defined as the pth order mean difference between the thresholded distance transforms of two images: A (the ideal segmentation) and G (the binary pixel-symbol map). Let us define first some previous terms:

– Let X denote the pixel raster.
– A binary image $A \subseteq X$ is a set $A = \{x \in X : A(x) = 1\}$.

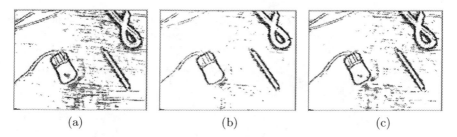

(a)   (b)   (c)

Fig. 3. Binarization with different MGT values: (a) Gradient mean. (b) $MGT = 0.9 * \max(\rho_B(x,y))$. (c) $MGT = 0.8 * \max(\rho_B(x,y))$.

If $\varrho(x,y)$ is the distance between two pixels x and y, the shortest distance between a pixel $x \in X$ and $A \subseteq X$ is defined as:

$$d(x, A) = \inf\{\varrho(x, a) : a \in A\}.$$ (4)

Then, for $1 \leq \varrho \leq \infty$ we define:

$$\Delta^p(A, G) = \left[\frac{1}{N} \sum_{x \in X} |w(d(x, A)) - w(d(x, G))|^p\right]^{1/p}.$$ (5)

where N is the total number of pixels in X and $w(t) = \min(t, c)$, for $c > 0$.

Intuitively, $\Delta^p(A, G)$ measures the suitability of an estimated image to be used instead of the real one.

Now, we can evaluate the goodness of our segmentation scheme.

5   Experiments

Let us show now the results of some experiments completed for our model. The tests have been performed with a set of real images, whose pixel-symbol maps have been calculated for different MGT values. Then, after applying the binarization process, the distance $\Delta^p(A, G)$ has been computed.

Table 2 shows the results for the image in Fig. 1, where $p = 2, c = 5$.

Table 2. Results obtained after the segmentation process.

MGT value	Distance $\Delta^p(A, G)$
Gradient mean	0.6038
$MGT = 0.95 * \max(\rho_B(x,y))$	0.2722
$MGT = 0.9 * \max(\rho_B(x,y))$	0.1988
$MGT = 0.85 * \max(\rho_B(x,y))$	0.3412
$MGT = 0.8 * \max(\rho_B(x,y))$	0.3704

As shown, the lowest distance is obtained when $MGT = 0.9 * \max(\rho_B(x,y))$. Fig. 4 compares the ideal segmentation and the MGT segmentation with the lowest $\Delta^p(A, G)$. Intuitively, if we compare the previous results in Fig. 3, the selected MGT value is quite similar to the ideal segmentation.

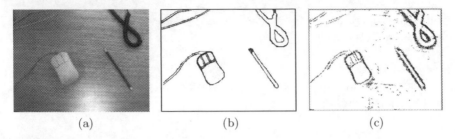

(a)   (b)   (c)

Fig. 4. (a) Original image. (b) Ideal segmentation. (c) MGT segmentation.

Let us consider now a more complex real image in order to confirm the accuracy of our technique to give an automated extraction of the threshold value with the best behavior. Fig. 5 and Table 3 show the results.

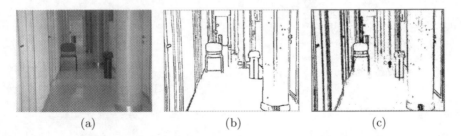

(a)   (b)   (c)

Fig. 5. (a) Original image. (b) Ideal segmentation. (c) MGT segmentation.

Table 3. Results obtained after the segmentation process.

MGT value	Distance $\Delta^p(A, G)$
Gradient mean	0.5526
$MGT = 0.95 * \max(\rho_B(x, y))$	0.3115
$MGT = 0.9 * \max(\rho_B(x, y))$	0.2245
$MGT = 0.85 * \max(\rho_B(x, y))$	0.2731
$MGT = 0.8 * \max(\rho_B(x, y))$	0.3219

The minimum distance is obtained again when $MGT = 0.9 * \max(\rho_B(x, y))$ and, as a consequence, we can conclude that the parameters used for this segmentation are near optimal, as they have a behavior very close to ideal segmentation.

Nevertheless, the threshold could be adaptively updated so as to assume the real conditions in which every image has been taken by the vision system.

6   Conclusions

In this paper, we have described a novel approach to image segmentation based on the selection of a suitable morphological gradient threshold. To do this, global morphological operators have been used to compute the gradient and the Laplacian and, after a proper binarization, the distance between the ideal segmentation and the MGT segmentation has been computed. As a consequence, the gradient threshold with the lowest distance has been selected as the optimal threshold value. Experimental results show that our model is fast and robust and could be applied for real-time imaging.

As a future work, we propose to extend the results of our research to object classification and recognition. It would be so desirable to consider new simulation experiments with different environments, such as image sequences obtained from a camera placed in a robot platform, where real-time constraints have a great influence in the final recognition results.

References

1. Pal, N.R., Pal, S.K.: A review on image segmentation techniques. Pattern Recognition, **9** (1993) 1277–1294
2. Arques, P., Compañ, P., Molina, R., Pujol, M., Rizo, R.: A cybernetic approach to the multiscale minimization of energy function: Grey level image segmentation. Kybernetes, **31** (2002) 596–608
3. Arques, P., Compañ, P., Molina, R., Pujol, M., Rizo, R.: Minimization of an energy function with robust features for image segmentation. Kybernetes, **32** (2003) 1481–1491
4. Ouadfel, S., Batouche, M.: MRF-based image segmentation using ant colony system. Electronic Letters on Computer Vision and Image Analysis **2** (2003) 12–24
5. Basu, M., Su, M.: Image smoothing with exponential functions. International Journal of Pattern Recognition and Artificial Intelligence, **15** (2001) 735–752
6. Pujol, F., García, J. M., Fuster, A., Pujol, M., Rizo, R.: Use of mathematical morphology in real-time path planning. Kybernetes, **31** (2002) 115–123
7. Pujol, F., Pujol, M., Llorens, F., Rizo, R., García, J. M. : Selection of a suitable measurement to obtain a quality segmented image. In Proc. of the 5th Iberoamerican Symposium on Pattern Recognition, Lisbon, Portugal, (2000) 643–654

Localization of Caption Texts in Natural Scenes Using a Wavelet Transformation*

Javier Jiménez and Enric Martí

Centre de Visió per Computador – Dept. Informàtica, UAB
Edifici O – Campus UAB, 08193 Bellaterra (Barcelona) – Spain
{Javier.Jimenez,Enric.Marti}@cvc.uab.es

Abstract. Automatic extraction of text from multimedia contents is an important problem that needs to be solved in order to obtain more effective retrieval engines. Recently, Crandall, Antani and Kasturi have shown that a direct analysis of certain DCT coefficients can be used to locate potential regions of caption text in MPEG-1 videos. In this paper, we extend their proposal to wavelet-coded images, and show that localization of text superimposed in natural scenes can also be effectively and efficiently performed by a wavelet transformation of the image followed by an analysis of the distribution of second order statistics on high frequency wavelet bands.

Keywords: Natural-scene statistics, text localization, text segmentation, wavelets, texture analysis, image analysis, computer vision.

1 Introduction

Digital video and still images have become popular, with an increase of media that content-based image retrieval systems are being required to access. Automatic extraction of text from multimedia images is an important problem that needs to be solved in order to obtain more effective high-level retrieval engines.

Previous proposals for text segmentation mostly assumed graphic documents or were developed to work with very structured images and simple distributions of colors (a survey of classical techniques that still are up-to-date can be found in [1]). New functional categorizations [2] recognize photographic images as a second major group, characterized by more colors, less structure and smooth transitions between elements.

To face the problem of extracting text that has been superimposed over natural images, methodologies from texture-segmentation contexts view the text as a texture and apply classical texture segmentation techniques, making very few assumptions about the image. Though textural analysis can be done directly over the input image [3, 4], most of these techniques apply some kind of transformation to the data in order to provide a more efficient representation, for example

---

* This work has been supported by the Spanish *Ministerio de Ciencia y Tecnología* under grants TIC2003-09291 and TIC2000-0399-C02-01.

A. Sanfeliu et al. (Eds.): CIARP 2004, LNCS 3287, pp. 100–107, 2004.

using Fourier [5], co-occurrent matrices [6], Gabor filters [7], or wavelets [8]. Recently, Crandall, Antani and Kasturi [9] have shown that a direct analysis of certain DCT coefficients can be used to locate potential regions of caption text in MPEG-1 video frames.

In this paper, we extend the proposal by Crandall, Antani and Kasturi [9] to wavelet-coded images, and show that localization of caption text superimposed in natural scenes can also be efficiently performed by a wavelet transformation of the image followed by an analysis of the distribution of second order statistics on high frequency wavelet bands. Examples of caption text addressed in this work can be seen in Fig. 1.

(a) Hateren composition [10] (b) Brodatz composition [11]

(c) Movie credits   (d)Web banner

Fig. 1. Examples of caption texts over natural backgrounds

The rest of this paper is organized as follows. In Sect. 2, the previous approach of Crandall, Antani and Kasturi [9] for text localization, which is the base of our proposal, is summarized. In Sect. 3, the new method for text localization is described. Experimental results are reported and discussed in Sect. 4. Conclusions are set out in Sect. 5.

2   A Previous Approach for Text Localization in DCT-Coded Images

The DCT became popular because of its energy packing capabilities while approaching a statistically optimal transform (the KLT) in decorrelating a signal governed by a Markov process; and because efficient algorithms for fast computation of the DCT are known, based on one-dimensional filtering transformations [12].

Recently, Crandall, Antani and Kasturi [9] have proposed a method to detect and locate caption text of arbitrary size and orientation in 8x8 DCT-coded images, like JPEG for still images and MPEG-1 for video. Specifically, the DCT F_b of an 8x8 image block f_b is given by

$$F_b[u,v] = \sum_{m=0}^{M-1} \sum_{n=0}^{N-1} f_b[m,n]\widetilde{\psi}_{u,v}[m,n]\,, \qquad (1)$$

with

$$\widetilde{\psi}_{u,v}[m,n] = \cos(\frac{(2m+1)u\pi}{2M})\cos(\frac{(2n+1)v\pi}{2N})\,. \qquad (2)$$

The m and n variables stand for the discrete spatial coordinate positions within each input image block f_b; u and v variables are the coordinate positions within the corresponding transformed block F_b; and $M = N = 8$ stand for the horizontal and vertical dimensions of each block.

In [9], the coefficients $F_b[u,v]$ of transformed blocks are directly analyzed in order to locate potential elements of text. A postprocessing is also suggested in order to integrate the detected regions of text and reject false positives while, in parallel, an analysis at different resolutions allows to detect letters of different sizes.

3   A New Method for Text Segmentation Using Wavelets

The method proposed by Crandall, Antani and Kasturi [9] is based on Eq. 1, which is equivalent to an inner product in each sub-block image space $\Omega = \{0,\ldots,7\} \times \{0,\ldots,7\}$ with a base given by an orthornormal system of cosinus functions (Eq. 2).

Analogously, a wavelet transformation (described in Sect. 3.2) can be viewed as an inner product with a biorthonormal system of wavelet and scale functions [13]. The fundamental difference between both approaches is the selection of a specific representation. This common formulation allows us to extend the text localization method proposed in [9] from DCT-coded images to wavelet-coded images.

The next subsections describe step by step our proposed method, which consists in a color space transformation to obtain a gray-level image, followed by a wavelet transformation, and finally a statistical analysis of high frequency wavelet bands to locate potential regions of text.

3.1   Color Space Transformation

This step only needs to be done in the case of color images, and consists in a transformation from RGB to YCbCr, which decorrelates the dependencies between color components into luminance and chrominance bands. Since the chrominance components are less sensitive to the human visual system (HVS) than the luminance component, we will work with the luminance band alone.

3.2   Wavelet Transformation

In this step, a wavelet transformation is used to decorrelate spatial dependencies and obtain a more sparse representation of the gray image.

Olshausen et al. [14, 15] found that localization, orientation and band-pass properties of certain wavelets agree with processes of the human visual system (HVS) and at the same time provide sparse representations for natural images. The Daubechies family of wavelets is indicated as suitable for this kind of image and, in order to choose a specific one, Wang [16] recommends *db8* and *db4*, which give better results than *Haar* [13, 17]. Other approaches make use of these wavelets for text segmentation and recognition tasks, but differ from our proposal in the target context or in the overall methodology: Menoti et al. [8] use Haar wavelets to locate text in postal envelopes; Bhattacharya et al. [18] use Daubechies *db4* wavelets to recognize handprinted numerals; Li and Doermann [19] suggest the use of *db4* wavelets, combined with a neural network, to classify text regions in digital video.

Based on these previous studies, in our experiments (reported in the next section) we choose transforming the input image by Mallat's algorithm with a *db4* wavelet filter [13, 17]. Let $\psi(x)$ be an orthonormal wavelet and let $\varphi(x)$ be its associated scaling function, such that there exists two square-summable functions, g and h, with

$$\psi(x/2) = 2 \sum_{k} g[k]\varphi(x - k) \tag{3}$$

$$\varphi(x/2) = 2 \sum_{k} h[k]\varphi(x - k) \tag{4}$$

Then Mallat's algorithm defines four sub-bands F^{LL}, F^{HL}, F^{LH} and F^{LL}, to form the global transform F:

$$F^{LL}[m, n] = \sum_{j} h[j] \sum_{i} h[i] f[2m - i, 2n - j]$$

$$F^{HL}[m, n] = \sum_{j} h[j] \sum_{i} g[i] f[2m - i, 2n - j]$$

$$F^{LH}[m, n] = \sum_{j} g[j] \sum_{i} h[i] f[2m - i, 2n - j] \tag{5}$$

$$F^{HH}[m, n] = \sum_{j} g[j] \sum_{i} g[i] f[2m - i, 2n - j]$$

Notice that Mallat's algorithm decimates the signal, but in order to improve the localization one can obviate the decimation or previously double the size of the gray image.

3.3   Feature Extraction and Classification

Our approach extends naturally to wavelet-coded images the text texture energy (TTE) descriptors from DCT coefficients proposed by Crandall, Antani and

Kasturi [9]. To this end, a map of local standard deviations on the LH and HL bands[1] is calculated, having the same dimensions as any of the four wavelet sub-bands. Fig. 2 shows typical histogram distributions of these feature maps.

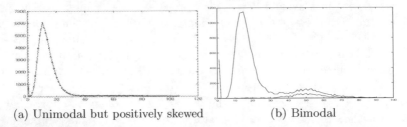

(a) Unimodal but positively skewed   (b) Bimodal

Fig. 2. Feature distributions of Figs. 1a and 1b. Two curves are represented, the major one is the overall histogram (background and text classes) while the other refers only to the text

We have found through different tests with natural images that the global distribution commonly appears as the composition of one or two bell-shaped non-gaussian distributions. In the unimodal case the text becomes blurred into the overall distribution (as in Fig. 2a). In the bimodal case each heap corresponds with one class (see Fig. 2b). In either case, the right part of the global distribution mostly corresponds with the text, and a first separation between classes in this space with a threshold umbralization is similar to using the TTE with DCT coefficients [9]. The two classes overlap only with certain non-natural distributions, making the separation more difficult or impractical (as in Fig. 6). Fig. 3 shows binarization results with Fig. 1 samples.

4   Experimental Results

To assess the overall performance of the method proposed in Sect. 3, we have built a test set using the first 50 natural images of the publicly available van Hateren's collection [10], where we have superimposed a constant caption text as in Fig. 1a. A detected pixel is counted as *correctly detected* if it is marked in the ground truth, or as *false positive alarm* if it is not. Non-detected pixels which have been marked in the ground truth are counted as *missed*. To perform the evaluation, the number of correctly detected, false positive alarms, and missed pixels are counted. The results are expressed as recall and false positive (FP) error rates: The recall is defined as the number of correctly detected pixels divided by the number of correctly detected and missed pixels, while the FP rate is defined as the number of false alarms divided by the number of pixels in the image. In this way, good performance corresponds to high recall with low FP

---

[1] Empirically we found that the inclusion of the HH band in this map does not improve the results.

Fig. 3. Localizations without further postprocessing (see Fig. 1)

rate. Note that a recall index alone is insufficient to measure actual performance, since a recall of 100% could be trivially obtained by classifying every pixel as text.

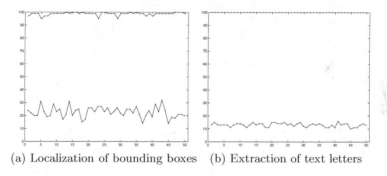

(a) Localization of bounding boxes   (b) Extraction of text letters

Fig. 4. Performance evaluation using the van Hateren's collection

Two performance evaluations are commonly done using the precision and recall indices introduced above: localization of bounding boxes and extraction of text letters. For localization, Fig. 4a shows an average recall rate of 98.78% (upper curve) at the cost of 22.68% of false positives (lower curve). For text extraction, Fig. 4b shows a maximum recall (100%) at the cost of a 13.06% of false positives.

Fig. 5 exhibits similar results with a second test set of 50 images, formed using Brodatz textures [11] with caption text that has been superimposed as in Fig. 1b. An evaluation by bounding boxes (Fig. 5a) show a recall rate of 81.74% (upper curve) with an FP rate of 8.48% (lower curve). Let us highlight the fact that there appear four *outsiders* – that is, four images that sit far apart from the rest – as the one in Fig. 6.

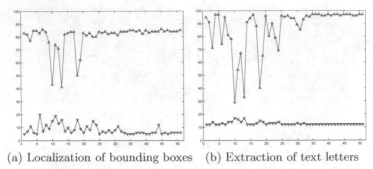

(a) Localization of bounding boxes   (b) Extraction of text letters

Fig. 5. Performance evaluation with a second, more difficult, test set of Brodatz textures. One of the compositions appears in Fig. 6

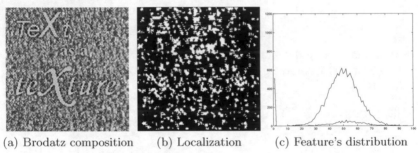

(a) Brodatz composition   (b) Localization   (c) Feature's distribution

Fig. 6. Unusual test result. Fig. 6a is a particular Brodatz composition where the superimposed text is difficult to be perceived visually. The localization given in Fig. 6b is one of the worst results obtained. Fig. 6c shows how the background's distribution overlaps the text's distribution

5   Conclusions

In this paper we have shown that localization of caption text can be done using wavelet transformations in an analogous way to the method proposed by Crandall, Antani and Kasturi [9] to analyze DCT-coded images. The proposed method has a linear complexity (with respect to the size of the input image) and experimental results show its viability for fast localization of text that has been superimposed over natural scene backgrounds. This method could be particularly well suited to deal with images that have been coded using modern systems based on wavelets, like JPEG2000 and MPEG-4.

References

1. O'Gorman, L., Kasturi, R., eds.: Document Image Analysis. IEEE Computer Society Press (1997) Published as Technical Briefing.
2. Hu, J., Bagga, A.: Categorizing images in web documents. IEEE Trans. on Multimedia (2004) 22–30

3. Allier, B., Duong, J., Gagneux, A., Mallet, P., Emptoz, H.: Texture feature characterization for logical pre-labeling. In: Proc. of Int. Conference on Document Analysis and Recognition. (2003) 567–571

4. Zhong, Y., Karu, K., Jain, A.K.: Locating text in complex color images. In: Proc. of Int. Conference on Document Analysis and Recognition. (1995) 146–149

5. Patel, D.: Page segmentation for document image analysis using a neural network. Optical Engineering **35** (1996) 1854–1861

6. Payne, J.S., Stonham, T.J., Patel, D.: Document segmentation using texture analysis. In: Proc. of Int. Conference on Pattern Recognition. (1994) 380–382

7. Jain, A.K., Bhattacharjee, S.K.: Address block location on envelopes using Gabor filters. Pattern Recognition **25** (1992) 1459–1477

8. Menoti, D., Borges, D.L., Facon, J., Britto, A.S.: Segmentation of postal envelopes for address block location: an approach based on feature selection in wavelet space. In: Proc. of Int. Conf. on Document Analysis and Recognition. (2003) 699–703

9. Crandall, D., Antani, S., Kasturi, R.: Extraction of special effects caption text events from digital video. Int. Journal on Document Analysis and Recognition **5** (2003) 138–157

10. van Hateren, J.H., Ruderman, D.L.: Independent component analysis of natural image sequences yields spatio-temporal filters similar to simple cells in primary visual cortex. Proc. of the Royal Society of London, Series B **265** (1998) 2315–2320

11. Brodatz, P.: Textures: A photographic Album for Artists and Designers. Dover Publications, N.Y. (1966)

12. Rao, K.R., Yip, P.: Discrete Cosine Transform. Algorithms, Advantages, Applications. Academic Press (1990)

13. Mallat, S.: A Wavelet Tour of Signal Processing. Academic Press (1998)

14. Olshausen, B.A., Field, D.J.: Sparse coding with an overcomplete basis set: a strategy employed by V1. Vision Research **37** (1997) 3311–3325

15. Olshausen, B.A., Field, D.J.: Natural image statistics and efficient coding. Network Computation in Neural Systems **7** (1996) 333–339

16. Wang, J.Z.: Integrated Region-based Image Retrieval. Kluwer Academic Publishers, The Netherlands (2001)

17. Mallat, S.: A theory for multiresolution signal decomposition: the wavelet representation. IEEE Trans. on Pattern Analysis and Machine Intelligence **11** (1989) 674–693

18. Bhattacharya, U., Chaudhuri, B.B.: A majority voting scheme for multiresolution recognition of handprinted numerals. In: Proc. of Int. Conference on Document Analysis and Recognition (ICDAR). (2003) 16–20

19. Li, H., Doermann, D.S.: Automatic identification of text in digital video key frames. In: Proc. of Int. Conference on Pattern Recognition. (1998) 129–132

A Depth Measurement System with the Active Vision of the Striped Lighting and Rotating Mirror

Hyongsuk Kim[1], Chun-Shin Lin[2], Chang-Bae Yoon[1],
Hye-Jeong Lee[1], and Hongrak Son[1]

[1] Division of Electronics and Information Engineering,
Chonbuk National Univ., Republic of Korea
hskim@moak.chonbuk.ac.kr
[2] Department of Electrical and Computer Engineering
University of Missouri-Columbia,
Columbia, MO 65211 USA
LinC@missouri.edu

Abstract. A depth measurement system that consists of a single camera, a laser light source and a rotating mirror is investigated. The camera and the light source are fixed, facing the rotating mirror. The laser light is reflected by the mirror and projected to the scene objects whose locations are to be determined. The camera detects the laser light location on object surfaces through the same mirror. The scan over the area to be measured is done by mirror rotation. Advantages are 1) the image of the light stripe remains sharp while that of the background becomes blurred because of the mirror rotation and 2) the only rotating part of this system is the mirror but the mirror angle is not involved in depth computation. This minimizes the imprecision caused by a possible inaccurate angle measurement. The detail arrangement and experimental results are reported.

1 Introduction

Active lighting [1-6] techniques have been used extensively in vision applications for depth measurement and 3-D surface reconstruction. Although measuring the distance and orientation of a planar surface using nonstructured lighting [1] is possible, many studies in this area focused on structured lighting. Multiple striped lights [2,3] and rectangular grid of lines [4] are examples of light patterns. The spatial resolution is usually low using multiple or grid of lines. There are also potential ambiguities in matching stripe segments resulting from object surfaces at different depth [7]. An alternative is to use a single light stripe and have it swept over the scene [5][6] by rotating the light projector. One possible drawback of this method is that the image of projected light could be blurred due to its movement. This deteriorates the measurement precision. Another issue arises from the accuracy of the light projection angle. These systems make use of the principle of triangulation to compute depth. For depth much larger than the distance between the camera and the light projector, a small angular error on light projection could cause a significant measurement error. A very precise and reliable measurement of the projection angle can be difficult while the light projector is being rotated.

A. Sanfeliu et al. (Eds.): CIARP 2004, LNCS 3287, pp. 108–115, 2004.

In this paper, a setup with the use of a rotational mirror is presented. This system is composed of a single camera, a laser light projector and a rotating mirror. The striped laser light is projected toward the rotational axis of the mirror, and reflected to the surface to be measured. The camera detects the striped light on object surfaces through the same mirror. This arrangement creates several advantages. The first is that potential problems from image blur are eliminated. One special characteristic of this new system is that the light projected to any point (at any direction) at the same horizontal level with the same distance to the mirror axis always forms an image at the same pixel on the camera. Consequently, unless the depth changes over the scanned width, the image of the projected light will not get blurred. This sharp image of the striped light makes necessary image processing easier and measured results more reliable. A blurred image indicates that there is a gradual or abrupt change in depth within the scanned width during one frame of capturing period. The second advantage is that the possible effect from the angular inaccuracy of the light scanning mechanism can be minimized. The only moving part is the mirror. However, the mirror angle is not involved in depth computation. Since the light projector is fixed, only one time of precise calibration for its orientation is required.

2 The New Depth Measurement System with Striped Lighting

The new depth measurement system has the single vertical laser light stripe projected to the rotating mirror, and reflected to the scene. The image formed by the same mirror is acquired by the CCD camera. Figure 1 shows the picture of the developed measurement device and the triangulation geometry for the single point projection. Without losing the generality, we focus on the image formation of a single light point. Figure 1(b) shows that the light is reflected by the mirror and projected to an object surface. Note that the mirror can be rotated.

Let the angle between the vertical line and the light source be ζ, and the angle of the mirror from the horizontal axis be θ. Also, let the distance between the camera axis and the rotating axis of the mirror be δ_o, the distance between the focal point of the camera and the horizontal axis be d_m, and the focal distance of the camera be f.

The laser light is reflected onto the object at point T with the mirrored image at T'. When the mirror angle is θ, $\angle SOT$, which is the angle between the projected light and the reflected light, equals $2(\theta-\zeta)$ and the angle $\angle TOM$ equals $(90^o-\theta+\zeta)$. Since T' is the mirrored image of T, we have $\angle T'OM = \angle TOM = 90^o-\theta+\zeta$.

Consequently, $\angle SOT' = 2(\theta-\zeta) + (90^o-\theta+\zeta) + (90^o-\theta+\zeta) = 180^o$. This shows that T' will always be on the line along the laser beam, at a distance R from the point O. This characteristic indicates that if the depth of the scanned points during one frame of capturing period is not changed, the image of laser light will remain sharp. Figure 2 illustrates the effect; the projected light point (near the center of the image) is clear while the background gets blurred due to mirror rotation. In image processing, the blurred background actually makes the light point (or stripe) stand out and easy to detect. Note that the part of clear picture at the right is from the scene outside of the mirror.

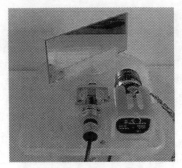

(a) The measurement system

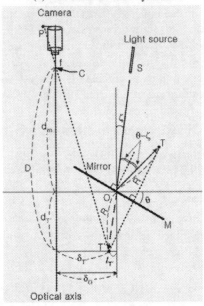

(b) Triangulation geometry for a single point projection

Fig. 1. Depth measurement with light projection and mirror reflection

To derive equations for projection in 3-dimensional space, let's use the cylindrical coordinate system with the mirror axis as the Z-axis. Assume that the light point T with coordinates (R, ϕ, Z) has its image on the CCD sensor at $p = (p_x, p_z)$ in the coordinates of image plan. Figure 1(b) shows the projection of a point on x-y plane. In this figure, p_x is the distance from P to the camera optical axis. Using the property of similar triangles, one obtains

$$p_x : f = \delta_{T'} : D, \quad \text{where} \quad D = d_m + d_{T'} \tag{1}$$

or

$$p_x (d_m + d_{T'}) = f \delta_{T'}. \tag{2}$$

Note that $d_{T'} = R\cos\zeta$, $\delta_{T'} = \delta_O - l_{T'}$ and $l_{T'} = R\sin\zeta$. Thus

$$p_x(d_m + R\cos\zeta) = f(\delta_0 - R\sin\zeta). \tag{3}$$

Solving the above equation for R gives

$$R = \frac{f\delta_0 - p_x d_m}{f\sin\zeta + p_x\cos\zeta}. \tag{4}$$

The angle for the observed point T is ϕ, which is defined as the angle measured clockwise from the vertical axis to the line OT. This angle is determined by the laser light direction and the mirror angle as

$$\phi = 2(\theta\text{-}\zeta) + \zeta = 2\theta - \zeta. \tag{5}$$

For the value Z, the triangular similarity will give

$$p_z : f = Z : D \tag{6}$$

or

$$p_z(d_m + d_{T'}) = fZ. \tag{7}$$

Dividing (7) by (2), one obtains

$$p_z / p_x = Z / \delta_{T'} = Z /(\delta_0 - R\sin\zeta). \tag{8}$$

Solving the above equation for Z gives

$$Z = \frac{p_z(\delta_0 - R\sin\zeta)}{p_x}. \tag{9}$$

As a summary, R, ϕ, and Z can be computed by

$$R = \frac{f\delta_0 - p_x d_m}{f\sin\zeta + p_x\cos\zeta}. \tag{4}$$

$$\phi = 2\theta - \zeta. \tag{5}$$

and

$$Z = \frac{p_z(\delta_0 - R\sin\zeta)}{p_x}. \tag{9}$$

Note that the mirror angle is not involved in equation (4) for depth computation. Only the fixed angle ζ is included and needs to be carefully calibrated. Conceptually, one can consider the 3-D measurement problem as one to determine the position of T', which is the intersection of lines SO and PC (see Figure 1(b)); an error arises when either of those two lines is inaccurately determined. In this setup, the error from inaccurate SO can be minimized by calibrating the angle ζ. Note that for a setup with its laser projector rotated, a measurement error of the projection angle is harder to prevent; so is the depth error. The error from inaccurate PC is caused by inaccurate position of P. Since P is the pixel position of the light point, a sharper image tends to provide a more precise and reliable result. The characteristic of sharp image illustrated in Figure 2 helps minimize the error from this factor.

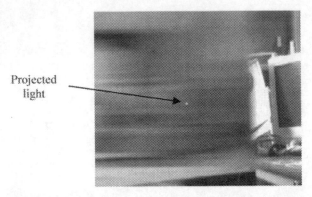

Fig. 2. Laser light point (near the image center) remains sharp while the background is blurred due to mirror rotation

3 Calibration and Depth Computation

To use equations (4) to determine the range R, system parameters must be either measured or calibrated. In our experiments, δ_0 and d_m are measured and known parameters. Other parameters needed include f, inter-cell distance δ_{cell} on the CCD sensor and the angle ζ. Since the measurement precision is very sensitive to the error of ζ, it is impractical to measure ζ directly. This parameter must be determined through careful calibration. Precise values of internal parameters of camera such as the inter-cell distance on the CCD plane and the focal length f may not be available and need to be obtained through calibration too.

It is noted that equation (4) can be rewritten such that only the ratio $k=f/\delta_{cell}$ needs to be calibrated. Let the integer n_x be the pixel number corresponding to p_x, which is the distance from the center of image plane to P. Then p_x can be expressed as

$$p_x = \delta_{cell}\, n_x \tag{10}$$

Plugging (10) into (4) gives

$$R = \frac{f\delta_0 - \delta_{cell} n_x d_m}{f \sin \zeta + \delta_{cell} n_x \cos \zeta} = \frac{\dfrac{f}{\delta_{cell}}\delta_0 - n_x d_m}{\dfrac{f}{\delta_{cell}}\sin \zeta + n_x \cos \zeta} \tag{11}$$

Replacing $\dfrac{f}{\delta_{cell}}$ by k in (11) results in

$$R = \frac{k\delta_0 - n_x d_m}{k \sin \zeta + n_x \cos \zeta} \tag{12}$$

Depth can be computed using equation (12) after the calibrated values of k and ζ have been obtained.

3.1 Calibration of the Internal Parameter $k = \dfrac{f}{\delta_{cell}}$

The camera and the projector can be set up in parallel, *i.e.*, with $\zeta = 0$. This is achieved by adjusting the laser light source orientation so that the distance between the laser beam and the camera optical axis at a long distance (*e.g.*, longer than 5 meters) equals δ_0. Upon having ζ set to 0, experiments can be performed to obtain n_x's for different known ranges of R. The collected pairs of R and n_x can be plugged into (12) to obtain the estimated values of parameter k; the average of these estimated values is used. This parameter needs to be calibrated only once.

3.2 Calibration of the External Parameter ζ

For a system with unknown ζ, equation (12) can be used for calibration. One can set up the system to measure a known distance R. The value n_x can be obtained from image. Values of δo and d_m are known and k has been calibrated. As a result, the only unknown in (12) is ζ, which can be solved. Since the value of depth is sensitive to the error of angle ζ, recalibration is recommended if the angle is possibly changed.

4 Experimental Results

In this section, experimental results are reported. A CCD camera (with 512×480 8-bit pixels) has been used in this study. The distances d_m and δ_0 were set to 15cm and 8cm, respectively.

4.1 Calibration of k and ζ

The method described in Section 3 has been used to determine the constant k. The average value of k evaluated at different distances with ζ set to $0°$ is 1377.56. For depth measurement experiments, ζ was set approximately to $4°$. It was difficult to have ζ equal exactly to $4°$. The precise value had to be obtained from calibration. The system was set up at a distance of 500cm from an upright planar surface. The value of n_x for the projected light point was obtained. The actual ζ was solved from (12) to be $3.869°$.

4.2 Experimental Results on Depth Measurement

Performance was evaluated for objects at different distances. Figure 3 shows the results for calculations with $\zeta = 3.869°$ and $\zeta = 4°$. The result for $\zeta = 4°$ is provided to show the sensitivity of the precision to ζ and the importance of good calibration. The mirror angle for this experiment was set to 40°. Measurements have also been performed at different directions including 30°, 40° and 50°. Figure 4 shows that the precision is quite consistent for different directions. Note that pixel numbers can only be integer. The quantization seems to be one major factor affecting the precision.

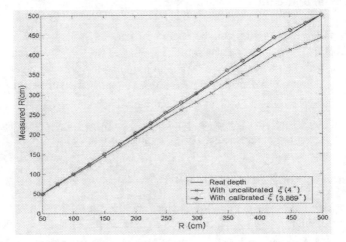

Fig. 3. Results with and without having ζ calibrated

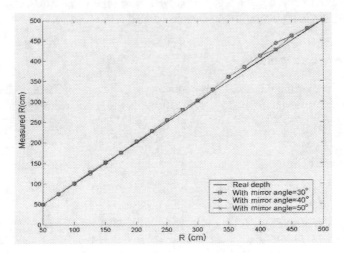

Fig. 4. Plots for measurement at different directions

5   Conclusions

A new depth measurement system that consists of a single camera, a laser light stripe projector and a rotating mirror has been investigated. Error analysis provides an idea on the magnitude of expected measurement error. For the distance 400-500cm, a 20cm depth error is expected to be from one-pixel error. Experimental results show a similar magnitude. This arrangement creates several advantages. The first one is that the image of the light stripe won't become blurred due to the mirror rotation. The sharpness of the image of light makes necessary image processing easier and measured results more reliable. The second advantage is that the imprecision caused by the inaccurate angle measurement of a laser projector is eliminated with this setup because the light source is not rotated and its angle can be carefully calibrated.

Acknowledgement

This work has been supported by KESRI(04502), which is funded by MOCIE (Ministry of commerce, industry and energy), and the Korea Institute of Information Technology Assessment.

References

1. T. Tsukiyama, "Measuring the distance and orientation of a planar surface using nonstructured lighting - 3D measurement system for indoor mobile robots," IEEE Tr. on Instrumentation and Measurement, vol. 45, no. 5, Oct. 1996.
2. V. Srinivasan and R. Lumia, "A pseudo-interferometric laser range finder for robot applications," IEEE Tr. on Robotics and Automation, vol. 5, no. 1, Feb. 1989.
3. M. Baba and T. Konishi, "Range imaging system with multiplexed structured light by direct space encoding," Proceedings of the 16th IEEE Instrumentation and Measurement Technology Conference, vol. 3, pp. 1437-1442, May 24-26, 1999.
4. P. M. Will and K. S. Pennington, "Grid coding: A preprocessing technique for robot and machine vision," Artificial Intelligence, vol. 2, pp. 319-329, 1971.
5. Y. Shirai and M. Suwa, "Recognition of polyhedrons with a rangefinder," in Proc. 2nd Int. Joint Conf. on Artificial Intelligence, pp.80-87, 1971.
6. T. C. Strand, "Optical three-dimensional sensing for machine vision," Optical Engineering, vol. 24, no.1, pp. 33-40, 1985.
7. R. Jain, R. Kasturi and B. G. Schunck, Machine Vision, McGraw-Hill Inc., 1995.

Fast Noncontinuous Path Phase-Unwrapping Algorithm Based on Gradients and Mask

Carlos Díaz and Leopoldo Altamirano Robles

National Institute of Astrophysics, Optics and Electronics, Luis Enrique Erro # 1,
Santa Maria Tonantzintla, Puebla, 72840, Mexico
{cdiaz,robles}@inaoep.mx

Abstract. Various algorithms based on unwrapping first the most-reliable pixels have been proposed. These were restricted to continuous path and were subject to troubles on defining an initial pixel. The technique proposed uses a reliability function that helps us to define starting points, it does not follow a continuous path to perform the unwrapping operation, and it uses a mask to pick out invalid pixels. The technique is explained with all the specifics and exemplify with some examples.

1   Introduction

Optical techniques such as 3D profilometry, photoelasticity, and interferometry have the advantage of being noncontact, fast, and capable of providing whole-field information. They have already been developed for measuring a wide range of physical parameters such as stress, vibration, displacement, and surface profile. In all these techniques, the measured parameters are modulated in the form of a 2D fringe pattern. Demodulation by the use of fringe pattern processing is thus an essential and important procedure.

First a wrapped phase map whose principal values range from $-\pi$ to π is calculated from the fringe pattern. Phase unwrapping is then carried out to restore the unknown multiple of 2π to each pixel. When the recorded images satisfy the Nyquist criteria, the phase unwrapping process is straightforward. If the phase difference calculated for two adjacent points is equal to 2π, then 2π or multiples of 2π must be added to or subtracted from the calculated value of the second pixel. The entire phase map is obtained by working outward from the starting location.

The diagram can explain the whole idea. Figure 1 shows the phase values calculated by arctangent at each pixel. Figure 2 shows the true phase values that are found by adding the correct number of 2π's to each of these values. The above process only shows how to do 1D unwrapping. However, it is very easy to extend the 1D process to unwrap a 2D map.

When phase wrap is getting by phase shifting interferometry there are additional information as data modulation that can aid in phase unwrap process.

The paper includes four sections: section 1 provides an overview of some existing phase-unwrapping algorithms, section 2 presents our proposal, section 3 gives experimental results of our algorithm, and finally, section 4 are conclusions.

A. Sanfeliu et al. (Eds.): CIARP 2004, LNCS 3287, pp. 116–123, 2004.
© Springer-Verlag Berlin Heidelberg 2004

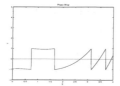

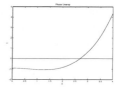

Fig. 1. 1D phase wrap distribution.   **Fig. 2.** 1D phase unwrap distribution.

2   Existing Phase-Unwrapping Algorithms

The phase unwrapping process is like a simple connect-the-dots game. However, things can be very complicated because of all kinds of error sources, especially when an automated phase unwrapping process is required. The error sources that arise most frequently in a fringe pattern are as follows:

1. Background noise or electronic noise produced during data acquisition.
2. Low data modulation points due to low surface reflectivity.
3. Abrupt phase changes due to surface discontinuities or shadows.
4. Violation of the sampling theorem (less than two sampling points per fringe). This error can cause the images to be totally unusable.

Most phase unwrapping algorithms can handle (1) and (2). (4) can be avoided by changing system setup. For error source (3), one needs to have a priori knowledge of the object or to use special techniques. Otherwise (3) will result in path-dependent phase unwrapping which is unacceptable.

A major goal of fringe analysis is to automate the phase unwrapping process. Automatic techniques are essential if systems are in a unsupervised way or high speed processing is in demand. Extensive research has been done in the development of phase unwrapping algorithms. However, a general approach to the problem of automated phase unwrapping in fringe analysis has been lacking. The following sections briefly review some of the representative phase unwrapping techniques.

2.1   Phase Fringe Scanning Method

Greivenkamp proposed this method in [7]. A horizontal line of the phase image is unwrapped first. Then starting at each point on this line, the whole phase map is unwrapped vertically. This is the most straightforward method of phase unwrapping and therefore is the fastest one among all phase unwrapping techniques. Unfortunately, this method can not handle phase images of objects with areas of low surface reflectivity.

2.2   Phase Unwrapping by Sections

Arevallilo and Burton developed this algorithm [1, 3]. An image can be subdivided into four sections. If a section is larger than 2×2 pixels, this section is further subdivided into four sections. It is easy to unwrap a 2×2 area (4 pixels) and two areas can be connected by checking their common edge. After sub-areas have been unwrapped, they are joined together. Points on the edge are traced to judge if a shift should be made, up by 2π, down by 2π, or no shift according to certain weighted criterion. This method tends to provide global unwrapping optima but has the complexity to deal with error source areas. The weighted criterion for connecting sections is also difficult to be used as a general criterion.

2.3   Phase Unwrapping by Using Gradient

This method was proposed by Huntley [8] in an attempt to solve the problem of surface discontinuity. Since a large phase difference between any two adjacent pixels increments the possibility of a discontinuous phase change, this algorithm always tries to choose the direction of the smallest gradient to unwrap phase. The phase at each pixel is compared with its 8 neighboring pixels. The direction in which the phase difference is the smallest is taken to unwrap the phase.

The drawback of this algorithm is that invalid pixels are phase unwrapped eventually, which introduce phase unwrapping errors. One solution to this problem is to set a threshold phase difference to reject invalid pixels due to noise or phase discontinuity. The threshold has to be flexible in order to adapt to different circumstances, which makes automatic phase unwrapping difficult. Using the first phase difference may result in misjudgment in choosing the right unwrapping direction. In [2, 4] is proposed the second order difference method which is used to improve the performance. Phase unwrapping based on least gradient does provide the most logic way for phase unwrapping. However, the method may not be able to unwrap all the pixels of interest automatically and to handle zones of high curvature of phase map.

3   Our Phase Unwrapping Algorithm Proposal

The phase unwrapping by using gradients approach provides the most logic way for phase unwrapping. The algorithm proposed in this research takes advantage of this approach and uses additional information obtained in data modulation to eliminate errors in the phase image. First of all, part of the fringe images may be saturated due to specular reflection. These pixels have to be excluded from the phase unwrapping process because they do not provide correct phase information. Also, the object may not fill the entire image and it may also have holes on its surface. This often results in a phase image with substantial background noise. All the pixels representing the background should also be excluded from the phase unwrapping process. These saturated pixels and background pixels are identified by calculating the data modulation at each pixel. Assigning a threshold value to the data modulation, a generated mask defines the areas of valid and invalid pixels. Phase unwrapping is done only at valid pixels.

The whole procedure can be summarized as the following steps:

1. *Generate Mask.* To generate a mask image M based on the data modulation calculation. This mask image indicates whether a pixel is valid or not. Only valid pixels are processed in the automatic unwrapping procedure. In figure 3, the black area represents an area of invalid pixels of the phase wrap distribution shown in figure 8.

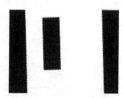

Fig. 3. Binary mask, black area represents invalid pixels.

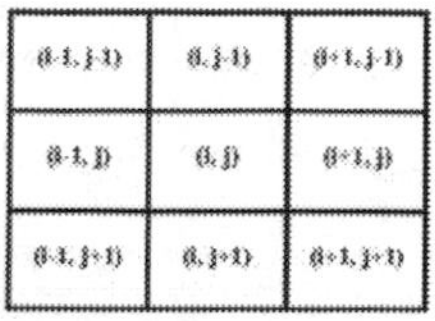

Fig. 4. Calculation of the second derivative in an image.

2. *Calculate Reliability Values.* In this step, we based upon the gradients. Those points with the lowest module 2π gradients with respect to their neighbors are determined to be the best points, therefore, these points are processed first.

   Second derivative would provide a measurement for the degree of concavity/convexity of the phase function. By use of second derivative a better detection of possible inconsistencies in the phase map is provided. The calculation of second derivative for pixels in an image can be explained with the aid of figure 4. To calculate the second difference for a pixel in an image, the values of its orthogonal and diagonal neighbors in a 3×3 window are required. The pixels $(i, j-1)$, $(i, j+1)$, $(i-1, j)$, and $(i+1, j)$ that are neighbors to the (i, j) pixels are called orthogonal neighboring pixels. Whereas $(i-1, j-1)$, $(i+1, j-1)$, $(i-1, j+1)$, and $(i+1, j+1)$ pixels are called diagonal neighboring pixels. The second difference D of an (i, j) pixel can be calculated by the equation:

$$D(i, j) = \sqrt{H^2(i, j) + V^2(i, j) + D_1^2(i, j) + D_2^2(i, j)}. \tag{1}$$

$H(i, j) = \gamma[\phi(i-1, j) - \phi(i, j)] - \gamma[\phi(i, j) - \phi(i+1, j)]$,
$V(i, j) = \gamma[\phi(i, j-1) - \phi(i, j)] - \gamma[\phi(i, j) - \phi(i, j+1)]$,
$D_1(i, j) = \gamma[\phi(i-1, j-1) - \phi(i, j)] - \gamma[\phi(i, j) - \phi(i+1, j+1)]$,
$D_2(i, j) = \gamma[\phi(i-1, j+1) - \phi(i, j)] - \gamma[\phi(i, j) - \phi(i+1, j-1)]$.

where $\gamma[(.)]$ is a simple unwrapping operation to remove any 2π steps between two consecutive pixels. The second derivative should be calculated for all valid pixels in M. The reliability R of a pixel is defined as:

$$R(i, j) = \frac{1}{D(i, j)}. \tag{2}$$

Consequently, pixels are more reliable if their second derivatives are lower.

3. *Edge Computation.* For this research an edge is considered an intersection of two pixels that are connected horizontally or vertically. Any pixel with its left hand side, right hand side, upper, or lower neighboring pixel can construct an edge. Every two orthogonal neighboring pixels can produce an edge.

   We only compute edges of valid pixels in M. An unwrapping path cannot be defined relative to the reliability of the pixels. Instead, it is defined by looking at the value of the reliability of the edges. We define edge reliability as the summation of the reliabilities of the two pixels that the edge connects:

$$R_{e_{k,l}} = R_k + R_l .\tag{3}$$

   where $R_{e_{k,l}}$ is the edge's reliability defined by k and l pixels.

4. *Initialize Groups.* Initially all valid pixels are considered not belonging to any group. Not valid pixels are considered belonging to group 0, that it won't be considered in automatic phase unwrap process.

5. *Unwrapping Path.* In unwrapping path those valid edges with higher reliability are unwrapped first. The edges are stored in an array and sorted by value of reliability. The edges with a higher reliability are resolved first. When the process is performed, pixels form groups of pixels. When is analyzed an edge in the unwrapping process, three cases are possible:

   (a) Both pixels have not been unwrapped before. The pixels are unwrapped with respect to each other and gathered into a single group of unwrapped pixels.

   (b) One of the pixels has been processed before, P_1 but the other has not, P_2. P_2 is unwrapped with respect to P_1 and added to the P_1's group.

   (c) Both pixels have been processed before. If they do not belong to the same group, the two groups need to be unwrapped with respect to each other. The smallest group is unwrapped with respect to the largest group.

If the wrapped phase map is composed of disconnected valid parts, the above steps finish all parts without depending on where the starting point is located. Certain relationships among these separate parts have to be predetermined in order to connect the whole surface.

4   Simulated and Experimental Results

The proposed algorithm has been tested using simulated and experimental images. All images depicting phase distribution are scaled between black and white for display.

Simulated Results. Figure 5(a) shows a simulated wrapped phase distribution with no noise and no physical discontinuities present. This image has been used to test the proposed algorithm under ideal conditions. Figure 5(b) shows the simulated unwrapped phase.

   Figure 5(c) shows a simulated wrapped phase distribution in which there is no noise in the body of the phase, but there is a small central area that contains only random noise. The purpose of this data set is to test the unwrapper's ability to isolate this noise and to prevent it from corrupting the unwrapping of the good data. Figure 5(d) shows the simulated unwrapped phase map.

We make a comparison between unwrapped phase simulated depicted in figures 5(b) and 5(d), and unwrapped phase obtained by algorithms show in figures 6 and 7, and we obtain a consistent in pixels values of 93%, see table 2. We compute percent of phase consistency by subtracting the phase unwrap obtained by any method from the reference phase unwrap distribution.

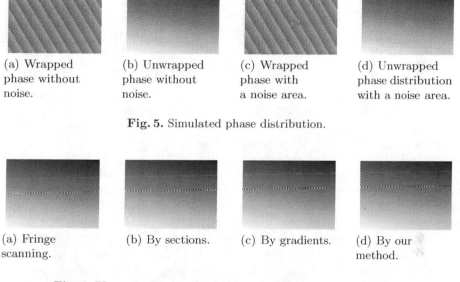

(a) Wrapped phase without noise.

(b) Unwrapped phase without noise.

(c) Wrapped phase with a noise area.

(d) Unwrapped phase distribution with a noise area.

Fig. 5. Simulated phase distribution.

(a) Fringe scanning.

(b) By sections.

(c) By gradients.

(d) By our method.

Fig. 6. Phase unwrap results of phase wrap show in figure 5(a).

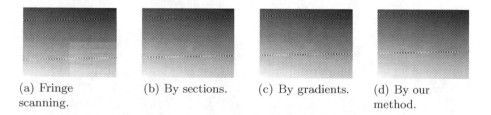

(a) Fringe scanning.

(b) By sections.

(c) By gradients.

(d) By our method.

Fig. 7. Phase unwrap results of phase wrap show in figure 5(c).

Experimental Results. Figure 8 shows a wrapped phase map resulting from the analysis of a real fringe pattern. The wrapped phase map contains corrupted areas that result from a shadow of the projected fringes. The wrapped phase map has been unwrapped using the proposed algorithm. The unwrapped phase

Table 1. Percent of phase unwrap distribution consistent between simulated and obtained phase unwrap without noise (see table 2).

Method	Percent of consistency	Time (in seconds)
Fringe scanning	99%	0.32
Sections	96%	1.85
Gradients only	95%	1.91
Our proposal	96%	1.71

Table 2. Percent of phase unwrap distribution consistent between simulated and obtained phase unwrap with noise.

Method	Percent of consistency	Time (in seconds)
Fringe scanning	78%	0.35
Sections	89%	2.30
Gradients only	91%	2.11
Our proposal	93%	1.82

map is shown in figure 9, which indicates that the algorithm was capable of unwrapping the unreliable regions last to prevent error propagation. The algorithm copes well with these problems and successfully unwraps the image. A 3D representation of the unwrapped phase map is shown in figure 10. The dynamic range of the unwrapped phase map can be more larger than the dynamic range of the wrapped phase map. The displaying of the unwrapped phase map by scaling it between black and white is not always indicative of the unwrapping process being performed correctly. Therefore following Ghiglia and Romero's method [6], we rewrapped the unwrapped phase map to permit a direct comparison with the wrapped image. This rewrapping is visually convincing that the unwrapping is qualitatively correct. Figure 11 shows the rewrapped phase map of the unwrapped phase map shown in figure 9. Figures 8 and 11 show a good agreement between the wrapped and the rewrapped phase maps, which demonstrates that the proposed algorithm unwrapped the wrapped phase map successfully.

Fig. 8. Wrapped phase distribution.

Fig. 9. Unwrapped phase distribution.

Fig. 10. 3D representation of the resulting phase.

Fig. 11. Rewrapped phase map.

The execution time of the proposed algorithm varies from image to image and depends on the particular phase distribution being analyzed. The tested images are 640 × 480 pixels in size. The proposed algorithm has been executed on a PC system. The PC contains a Pentium 4 processor that runs at 2.0 GHz clock speed. The memory on this PC is 256 MB RAM. The execution time is in the order of two seconds on average. The execution time to unwrap the image shown in figure 8 was 1.8 seconds.

5 Conclusions

A fast, reliable 2D unwrapper has been proposed, described, and tested. The algorithm that follows a noncontinuous path and, is based on unwrapping points with higher reliability values, it produces consistent results when discontinuities or noisy areas are presented.

The above algorithm works closely with the masking technique based on data modulation to provide a fast and reliable phase unwrapping method. Compared to the previously developed algorithms reviewed in the previous section, this new algorithm is simple and fast yet produces comparable good results.

References

1. M. Arevallilo Herraéz, D. R. Burton, and D. B. Clegg, "Robust, Simple, and Fast Algorithm for Phase Unwrapping", Applied Optics, 1996, Vol. 35, 5847-5852.
2. M. Arevallilo Herraéz, D. R. Burton, M. J. Lalor, and M. A. Gdeisat, "Fast Two-Dimensional Automatic Phase Unwrapping Algorithm Based on Sorting by Reliability Following a Noncontinuous Path", Applied Optics, 2002, Vol. 41, No. 35, 7437-7444.
3. M. Arevallilo Herraéz, M. A. Gdeisat, D. R. Burton, and M. J. Lalor, "Robust, Fast, and Effective Two-Dimensional Automatic Phase Unwrapping Algorithm Based on Image Decomposition", Applied Optics, 2002, 41, 35, 7445-7455.
4. R. Cusack, J. M. Huntley, and H. T. Goldrein, "Improved Noise-Immune Phase-Unwrapping Algorithm", in Applied Optics, Vol. 34, No. 5, 781-789, 1995.
5. D. C. Ghiglia, G. A. Masting, and L. A. Romero, "Cellular-Automation Method for Phase Unwrapping", in Journal of Optical Society of America, Vol. 4, No. 5. 267-280, 1987.
6. D. C. Ghiglia, and L. A. Romero, "Robust Two-Dimensional Weighted Phase Unwrapping that Uses Fast Transforms and Iterative Methods", in Journal of Optical Society of America, Vol. 11, No. 1. 107-117, 1994.
7. J. E. Greivenkamp and J. H. Bruning, "Phase Shifting Interferometers", in Optical Shop Testing, D. Malacara, 2nd Ed. 501-598, Wiley, New York, 1992.
8. J. M. Huntley and H. O. Saldner, "Error Reduction Methods for Shape Measurement by Temporal Phase Unwrapping", in Journal of Optical Society of America, Vol. 14, No. 2. 3188-3196, 1997.

Color Active Contours for Tracking Roads in Natural Environments

Antonio Marín-Hernández[1], Michel Devy[2], and Gabriel Aviña-Cervantes[2]

[1] Facultad de Física e Inteligencia Artificial, Universidad Veracruzana,
Sebastián Camacho No. 5, Centro, 91000, Xalapa, Mexico
anmarin@uv.mx

[2] LAAS – CNRS, 7 avenue Colonel Roche
31077 Toulouse, Cedex 04, France
{michel,gavina}@laas.fr

Abstract. Scene interpretation and feature tracking in natural environments are very complex perceptual functions. Complexity lies on several factors, for example: the lack of control on illumination conditions and the presence of different textures in the environment. This paper presents a real-time method to track roads in natural environments. The scene is previously characterized and classified in different regions by a combined ICA and color segmentation method (not described in this paper). This method is not so fast to track desired features in real time. The region tracking is executed on color active contours. New color potential fields are proposed: a) one to attract active contours depending on the selected region color, and b) the second one to repulse active contours when it is inside the region. Two potential fields are defined from the results of the initial characterization process and are updated by the same process at a given constant frequency, to avoid errors mainly due to global changes in illumination conditions or to local changes on the characteristics of the selected region. This approach has been evaluated on image sequences, acquired in natural environments.

1 Introduction

In natural environments, objects can be characterized by their color or texture. It compensates the lack of structure in order to extract, localize and recognize objects. However, segmentation and real-time tracking of objects or features in such environments are very hard and complex tasks. The complexity lies on several factors like, lack of control in illumination conditions, not structured images, and a great scene variability, making difficult the region interpretation and classification.

This work concerns the navigation of autonomous vehicles in agricultural environments. The principal task is to detect and track roads in real-time, in order to guide an autonomous machine, for example to go from a farm to a given field.

The task of road extraction and tracking in an image sequence acquired on natural environments can be considered as the segmentation and tracking of a deformable object that grows or shrinks in the image with unpredicted directions. This task could be solved by the active contour method (*snakes*) proposed by Kass et al. [1]. An active contour is a deformable curve, which is deformed by internal and external forces, to fit desired features along an image sequence. The main problems of active contours

A. Sanfeliu et al. (Eds.): CIARP 2004, LNCS 3287, pp. 124–131, 2004.

are well known: a) they need to be initialized close to the object to be tracked in order to get a good convergence, and b) they could be trapped by objects in their neighborhood with higher gradient zones.

This paper presents a tracking method for roads in natural environments; roads are previously characterized by an ICA and color segmentation algorithm [2]. Classification results allow (1) to initialize an active contour on a region boundary and (2) to define two external potentials in the image. The active contour is attracted by the first potential towards a selected color gradients; the second potential works as a repulsive field, when the active contour is over the selected region. The definitions of these new potential fields add robustness to active contour fitting in such complex environments. Color gradients for snake segmentation or tracking have been studied in different papers. However, more of them restrict the complexity to track matte or saturated colors as in [3].

The paper structure is as follows. Section 2 describes the classic approach of active contour methods. Section 3 develops the new potential fields required for real-time tracking and defined from the region characterization process. In section 4, our approach is compared with others works. Section 5 describes results obtained on several image sequences acquired in natural environments, and finally section 6 gives our conclusions.

2   Active Contours

Snakes or active contours have been extensively used for object segmentation and tracking. This method is based on the minimization of an energy function (equation 1) along a continuous curve subject to internal and external forces. These forces are defined by the desired curve and image properties, respectively.

The total energy for an active contour $\mathbf{v}$ described with a parametric representation $\mathbf{v} = (x(s), y(s))$ can be written as:

$$E_{tot}(\mathbf{v}) = \int E_{\text{int}}(\mathbf{v}(s)) + E_{ext}(\mathbf{v}(s)) \, ds \qquad (1)$$

where subscripts on E represent the internal and external energy terms.

Internal energy is commonly defined by:

$$E_{\text{int}}(\mathbf{v}) = \int_0^1 \omega_1(s)\mathbf{v}_s^2 + \omega_2(s)\mathbf{v}_{ss}^2 \, ds \qquad (2)$$

where subscripts on $\mathbf{v}$ denote differentiation, $\omega_1(s)$ and $\omega_2(s)$ are weights given to the elasticity and the smoothness energy terms.

In order to reduce complexity, the control points that define the deformable curve can be restricted to move to preferential directions (i.e. perpendicular lines to the curve). However, if there is no a priori knowledge about the possible curve shapes or about the directions of future deformations (as in our case), the contour could not fit with the boundary of the desired region, here the road region. Some problems can be solved, as in [4], where the contour is considered as an electric conductor that is charged by a constant electric charge Q. This charge generates a new repulsive force that distributes the control points along a curve according to its curvature [5].

Taking into account this new repulsive force, the internal energy (equation 2) can be written as:

$$E_{int}(\mathbf{v}) = \int \omega_1(s)\mathbf{v}_s^2 + \omega_2(s)\mathbf{v}_{ss}^2 + k\frac{\sigma^2}{\mathbf{v}_s^2} ds \qquad (3)$$

where k is a constant coefficient, and σ is the electrical charge density. Once the electric charge is given $k\sigma^2$ can be see as a constant coefficient.

Classic active contours move to the desired characteristics under the influence of external energy currently defined as:

$$E_{ext}(\mathbf{v}) = \int_0^1 P(\mathbf{v}(s))ds \qquad (4)$$

where commonly $P(\mathbf{v}(s))$ is the image gradient intensity.

Due to the intrinsic complexity of natural environments, the image gradient provides many contours. In addition, the lack of control on illumination conditions could create very poor gradients. These gradient difficulties could perturb the fitting of active contour to the desired characteristics. Such problems could be solved adding information to the image gradient, as multi-spectral images, in order to focalize the tracking to the desired color combination, as it will be develop ed in the next section.

3 Color Active Contours

Some works have been proposed to deal with multi-spectral information in order to get invariant color snakes. In [3], Gevers and al have analyzed the following color features derived from *RGB*: a) Intensity $I=(R+G+B)/3$, b) normalized colors, $r = \dfrac{R}{R+G+B}$, $g = \dfrac{G}{R+G+B}$, $b = \dfrac{B}{R+G+B}$, and c) Hue, $H = \arctan\left(\dfrac{\sqrt{3}(G-B)}{(R-G)+(R-B)}\right)$.

They define different color gradients for these spaces showing that Hue gradient and the normalized color gradients are the best in order to get color invariance. However, they only have studied matte and shiny objects, under controlled illumination conditions.

In [6], Ivins and al have defined an active region model. They replace the external energy of the active contour by a region force, defined as multi-spectral goodness function. Considering that tracking needs to be made in real time, they choose to use normalized colors. However, they also use controlled illumination conditions as well as a matte color.

Our main problem is that in natural environments it is quite difficult to have regions with a matte color or a plain texture. So it is not easy, to find a good region attribute, to characterize it. A suitable color space must be found in order to easily filter a specific region by its color characteristics in real time. This information should be incorporated in a region color gradient, in order to avoid noise from other features or objects. However, as we can see in figure 1, neither intensity gradient, nor color gradients tested in different color spaces are enough to guarantee good stability and convergence on the desired features, here the road boundary.

Moreover, in complex environments, any of these color spaces are enough robust to characterize regions features. So for tracking initialization, a region will be charac-

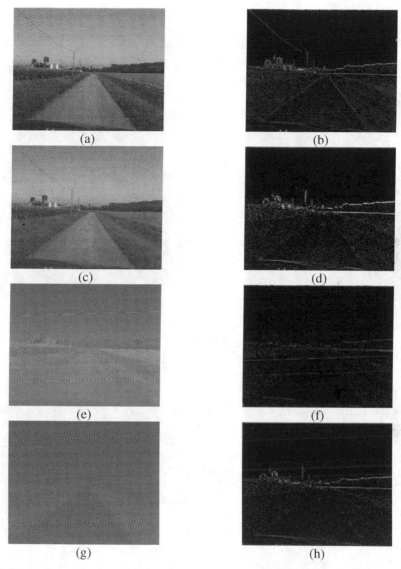

Fig. 1. Image features and gradients. In a), c), e) and g) are shown, Intensity, *RGB*, Ohta, and normalized color spaces respectively, and b), d), f), and h) are single or multi-spectral gradients of left images.

terized by the method described in [2], which will be also used on line to adapt the region attributes in order to avoid error accumulation. In [2] it is proposed to add extra features based on texture operators in order to get a good region characterization. This method uses Ohta color space, in the first step of the segmentation process; so, region characteristics in this space have been calculated previously and can be incorporated easily, in the tracking process. However, this color space is not the optimum to characterize the region, as we will see on next section.

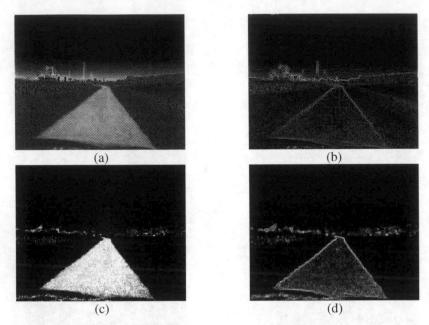

Fig. 2. Region characterization for different color spaces and gradient images. a) and b) respectively are region detection and gradient for Ohta color space and, c) and d) for normalized color space.

3.1   Color and Region Potentials

To track the desired region in real-time, it is important to characterize it by a reduced set of color features in some color space. This information will be introduced on external potentials. It is very important to compute external potentials easily, in order to get the required real-time performance. These potentials are defined from the results of the previous region classification, to get the color mean and variance on the selected region, using different color spaces. As we can see in figure 2, the selected region is very well characterized on both, Ohta and normalized color spaces. The specific textures of a natural environment make the region characterization more difficult on other spaces as HSV. The strongest image potential from gradient images is the one resulting from normalized color space (fig. 2d), because texture is almost erased on this color space.

In order to incorporate previous color space characterization, two external potentials are defined: a) one to attract active contour to desired characterized features and b) the second to make a repulsive force when the active contour is inside the region. Then external energy will be described as:

$$E_{ext}(\mathbf{v}) = \int P_G(\mathbf{v}(s))ds + \int P_R(\mathbf{v}(s))ds \tag{5}$$

where subscripts on P denotes, the *gradient* potential field G which generates attractive forces (figure 2d), and the *region* potential field R, which generates repulsive forces (figure 2c).

As we have described on previous sections, the region classification method is used at a constant frequency, in order to correct errors, and to reinitialize the active contour adapting the number of control points, depending on the size of the tracked surface. Consequently, variations of the mean and variance due to illumination changes can be incorporated.

Our implementation for specific region potentials could be seen as a combination of a multi-spectral band pass filter, and a color gradient function.

4 Discussion

Recently, it has been proposed similar methods to deal with active contours in color images. In [7] is proposed to use the HSV color space: the external potential field given by the image gradient, is replaced by a statistical pressure term. However, initially, they suppose that HSV color space is enough to characterize regions, which is not always true. As we can see in their examples, where two adjacent blocks are fused, nonetheless they have different textures. Moreover, the pressure term is redundant, because when the active contour is not on the statistical region, the attractive force made by the statistical term could be replaced by doubling the weight of tension term on internal forces.

In [8], Seo and al have proposed an adaptive color snake model, adding a new energy term to the original active contour model. This term acts in an opposite way depending if the snake is inside or outside the region. The region is defined by its color distribution on normalized color space. However, the use of normalized color space is not justified, and they left the external potential field without any change. As we can see in figure 1, color gradient computed on different color spaces does not assure that active contour will evolve to the desired features. Moreover, the color value manually assigned to the tracked region is adapted, only by some scale factors without knowing how this color changes with respect to the environment.

As we have described, our method initializes active contours and makes color adaptation automatically using previous region classification results. It is important to note that the chosen color space is the best adapted to our conditions; for different conditions or for a different task, it could be different.

5 Results

Our approach has been evaluated on several image sequences acquired on natural environments. The region characterization and classification have been automatically processed by the method described in [2]. The contour of the region to be tracked has been sampled at a given frequency (approximately each 20 pixels) to initialize our active contour. The same region is used to find the mean and variance color using a normalized color space as described above. This first process takes about 80 ms on a Sun Blade 100.

The tracking method uses this information to attract active contour to the desired object boundary. The method processes an average of 14 images per second (on the same computer); the performance depends strongly on the number of control points, but not from the results of the image region gradient. The minimization problem is solved by a dynamic programming method proposed by Amini et al. [9] and it is accelerated applying it with a multi-scale neighborhood.

The process runs in double loop, in order to reinitialize active contours, with a different number of control points and different regions features, depending on the region size and on illumination conditions.

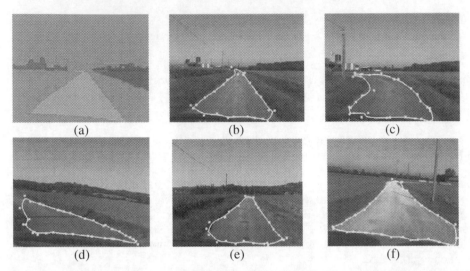

(a)   (b)   (c)

(d)   (e)   (f)

Fig. 3. Tracking results: a) segmented image use for the initialization and characterization, and from b) to f) results from the tracking sequence (Because color is important in this work, color images can be see on http://www.uv.mx/anmarin/CIARP04.html).

The first image in figure 3 shows the characterization and classification process; the central grey zone, classified as a road, defines the region to be tracked; its boundary is used to initialize an active contour. The next five images show different tracking steps on the same sequence; as we can see, the method works in spite of some changes in the road color, caused principally by illumination variations.

6 Conclusion

This paper has proposed two new external potential fields for use in real time tracking on natural environments These new external potentials combine region and contour features to attract active contours on specific zones along an image sequence. The features are defined by an initialization process, consisting in a region segmentation and classification function described in [2]. Different color gradients have been tested using different color spaces, on which individual pixels could be easily expressed. Nevertheless, as is show in this paper they do not contain enough information to assure active contour convergence on the selected region. The statistical region segmentation has been made for Ohta color space, as well as, for normalized color space. Despite the characteristics for Ohta color space have been calculated in classification process, they shows that are not enough to assure convergence. Normalized color regions features are calculated for the desired region using a previous classification process.

Normalized color space is better suitable for region description because it erase the texture, in the selected region. Tracking has been achieved at a very good frame frequency; the tracker is updated on line by the classification process to deal with convergence errors or illumination changes.

References

1. Kass, M., A. Wirkin, and D. Terzopoulous, "Snakes: Active Contours Models," *Int'l J. Computer Vision*, vol. 1, pp. 321-331, 1988.
2. Aviña-Cervantes, J. G. and M. Devy, "Scene Modeling by ICA and Color Segmentation", in Proc. of MICAI 2004: LNIA vol. 2972, pp. 574-583, April, 2004.
3. Gevers, T., S. Ghebreab, A. Smeulders, "Color Invariant Snakes", In *Proceedings of the Ninth British Machine Vision Conference*, pp. 578-588, Southampton, UK, 1998.
4. Marin-Hernandez, A., H.V. Rios-Figueroa, "Eels: Electric Snakes", *Computación y Sistemas*, vol. 2, no. 2-3 pp. 87-94, 1999.
5. Weidner R.T. and R.L. Sells, *Elementary Classical Physics*. Allyn and Bacon, USA, Vol. 2, pp. 692-696, 1971.
6. Ivins, J. and J. Porrill, "Constrained Active Region Models for Fast Tracking in Color Image Sequences", *Computer Vision and Image Understanding*, vol. 72, No. 1, pp. 54-71, Oct, 1998.
7. Schaub H. and C. E. Smith, "Color Snakes for Dynamic Light Conditions on Mobile Manipulation Platforms", in Proc. of Intl. Conference on Intelligent Robots and Systems, Las Vegas, USA, pp. 1272-1277, October 2003.
8. Seo K., T. Choi, and J. Lee, "Adaptive Color Snake Model for Real-Time Object Tracking", in Proc. of Intl. *Conference on Robotics and Automation* 2004 (ICRA'04), New Orleans, USA, pp. 122-127, April, 2004.
9. Amini, A.A., T.E. Weymouth, R.C. Jain, "Using Dynamic Programming for Solving Variational Problems in Vision," *IEEE. Trans. on Pattern Analysis and Machine Intelligence*, vol. 12, no. 9, Sep. 1990.

Generation of N-Parametric Appearance-Based Models Through Non-uniform Sampling

Luis Carlos Altamirano[1], Leopoldo Altamirano Robles[2], and Matías Alvarado[1]

[1] Instituto Mexicano del Petróleo, PIMAyC, Eje Central Lázaro Cárdenas 152,
San Bartolo Atepehuacán, C.P. 07730, México, DF
(laltamir,matiasa)@imp.mx
[2] Instituto Nacional de Astrofísica, Óptica y Electrónica
Luis Enrique Erro No. 1, C.P. 7200, Puebla, Pue., México
robles@inaoep.mx

Abstract. In this work, a generalization of non-uniform sampling technique to construct appearance-based models is proposed. This technique analyses the object appearance defined by several parameters of variability, determining how many and which images are required to model appearance, with a given precision ε. Throughout non-uniform sampling, we obtain a guideline to spend less time on model construction and to diminish storage, when pose estimation no matters. The proposed technique is based on a scheme of N-linear interpolation and SSD (Sum-of-Squared-Difference) distance, and it is used in conjunction with the eigenspaces method for object recognition. Experimental results showing the advantages are exposed.

1 Introduction

Appearance-based approaches were proposed as an alternative to the geometrical ones for object recognition. They use the image data, i.e., the pixel intensities, directly without previous segmentation process. Several appearance-based methods have been proposed in the literature [1], [2], [3], [4], [5].

So far in the current literature, efforts to determine characteristic views under illumination changes have been made [6, 7]. However, if viewing position (instead of illumination) is changing, no characterization of the image set is done. To work on viewing position changes, diverse techniques on image synthesis have been introduced [8, 9]. However, there are several differences between the appearance-based approach and image synthesis [10]. Usually, appearance-based approaches require a big quantity of images in order to build object models. For this reason, several techniques for modeling objects with fewer views have been introduced, for example, aspect graphs [11] or eigenspaces [1]. However, calculating these characteristic views is an expensive computational process. Recently, some works to determine how many and which images are necessary to model an object have been presented. However, their application is restricted to specific objects as faces [12], or they only work with the object shape [13].

Non-uniform sampling was introduced in [14] as an alternative for reducing the quantity of necessary images for object modeling and object recognition. Experimen-

A. Sanfeliu et al. (Eds.): CIARP 2004, LNCS 3287, pp. 132–139, 2004.
© Springer-Verlag Berlin Heidelberg 2004

tal results showed that a reduction in the quantity of required views is possible, if the behavior of the object appearance is taken into count, and no pose estimation is necessary. If pose estimation is required, reduction is also possible but it could be not significant.

However, non-uniform sampling cannot model objects under more than one parameter. For this reason, in this work, a generalization to N parameters of the basic technique proposed in [14] is developed. This generalized technique allows determining the strictly necessary images for modeling any object, under N parameters and for a precision ε. Image election is guided by N-linear interpolation and SSD (Sum-of-Squared-Difference) criterion. We show how this technique can be jointed to eigenspaces one to support object recognition.

2 Preliminaries

2.1 Eigenspaces Overview

By using Principal Component Analysis, the eigenspaces technique [1] comprises a set I of training images into a compact representation which can be used for object recognition. This compression process is computationally intensive, and its complexity depends upon the size of I (if the size of I is smaller than the number of pixels that constitutes the images; otherwise, depends upon the number of pixels). For this reason, reducing the size of I is desired.

2.2 Interpolation and SSD Distance

Definition 1: A parameterized surface is a function ϕ: $D \subset R^N \to R^M$, where D is any domain in R^N [15]. Notice that a parameterized surface is a generalization of a parameterized trajectory, because if N=1 the surface becomes a trajectory.

Definition 2: Let ϕ_1: $D \subset R^N \to R^M$ be a parameterized surface. Let $C=\{(x_1,y_1), (x_2,y_2),...,(x_m,y_m)\}$ be such that $\phi_1(x_i)=y_i$, for i=1,...,m. A parameterized surface ϕ_2: $D \subset R^N \to R^M$ interpolates $\phi_1(x)$ on points x_i in C, if $\phi_2(x_i)=y_i$, for i=1,...,m. Because $\phi_2(x)$ is not determined uniquely, for an ε given, $\phi_2(x)$ is usually selected such that $|\phi_1(x) - \phi_2(x)| < \varepsilon$, for all x in D. Such ε is named the associate interpolation error.

Sometimes, it is impossible to find a parameterized surface $\phi_2(x)$ such that it meets the error criterion inside the interval. In this case, the interpolation problem of $\phi_1(x)$ is changed for the $\phi_1(x)$ *piecewise interpolation problem*: it is necessary to find a set of m-1 parameterized surfaces $\phi_2(x)$, $\phi_3(x)$,..., $\phi_m(x)$, such that interpolate $\phi_1(x)$, respectively, in a partition of D, within the tolerance ε.

Definition 3: Let $X = (x_1, x_2, ..., x_n)$ and $Y = (y_1, y_2, ..., y_n)$ be two vectors in R^n. The SSD distance (Sum-of-Squared-Difference) between X and Y is defined by:

$$\| X - Y \|^2 = \sum_1^n (x_i - y_i)^2$$

A detailed explanation of the properties of SSD distance on appearance-based models can be founded in [16].

3   Generalized Image Acquisition

In order to build the appearance-based model of an object, it should be in the turntable's center, and rotates in front of the camera. The camera is in a fixed position respect to turntable, and it cannot move. Finally, the illumination source is fixed with respect to the camera and the turntable. Under these conditions, images taken around the object belong to a trajectory, which is parameterized for the angle θ of the object rotation in front of the sensor; this trajectory is called in the literature the trajectory determined by object appearance, or simply, the object appearance. The object model is constructed by sampling this trajectory. Notice that the sampling can be uniform or non-uniform, but uniform sampling requires a lot of space and time for building models. Non-uniform sampling was introduced for reducing space and time requirements. However, the object appearance would be defined by several parameters. For example, if we let illumination source moves or camera moves. In this case, the technique exposed in [15] is no more applicable.

Then, we extend the previous non-uniform sampling technique to work with several parameters. Some parameters that we could consider are: turntable angle, camera elevation angle, position of illumination source, position of any part of an articulated object, etc. To experiment with the proposed technique, in this work we will use only two parameters of those: turntable angle and camera elevation angle, but we emphasize that the same technique can work with whichever number of parameters, as explained below.

3.1   Generalized Uniform Image Acquisition

If we use uniform sampling to acquire images for building the model of an object defined by N parameters, we need sampling on the whole workspace determined by N parameters. One image parameterized with N parameters, i.e., $I(p_1, p_2, ..., p_n)$, is obtained for each point of this sampling. Whenever all images acquired in this manner are represented as $n \times m$ matrixes, and matrix's columns are stacked to form vectors $v \in R^{nm}$, looking at Definition 1, we can see that such vectors belong to a surface $\phi: D \subset R^N \rightarrow R^{nm}$ defined by N parameters. This parameterized surface is called in the literature the surface determined by object appearance, or simply, object appearance. However, as mentioned before, uniform sampling implies to use a big quantity of images and spend too much computing time. To avoid these problems, the usage of non-uniform sampling is proposed.

3.2   Non-uniform Image Acquisition

The basic non-uniform sampling technique is based on the observation that object appearance can be approximated by means of piecewise linear interpolation. In this work, the use of linear interpolation to approximate the object's appearance is also proposed. Of course, because we are considering N parameters, we need to approximate a parameterized surface (see Definition 2) instead of a trajectory. For this reason, we propose to approximate the parameterized surface with N-linear interpolation, instead of linear interpolation.

N-linear interpolation is the straight generalization of linear interpolation, because if N=1, we obtain linear interpolation (1-linear interpolation). Linear interpolation interpolates between points b_0 and b_1 by means of the straight line (simplest curve) between them:

$$g(t_1) = (1-t_1)b_0 + t_1 b_1 \;\; ; \;\; 0 \le t_1 \le 1 . \tag{1}$$

In bi-dimensional case, bilinear interpolation interpolates between four points b_{00}, b_{01}, b_{10} and b_{11} by means of the simplest surface between these points (a hyperbolic paraboloid); it is obtained by the following expressions [17]:

$$\mathbf{B}_{00}^{10} = (1-t_1)b_{00} + t_1 b_{10} \;\; ; \;\; 0 \le t_1 \le 1$$

$$\mathbf{B}_{01}^{11} = (1-t_1)b_{01} + t_1 b_{11} \;\; ; \;\; 0 \le t_1 \le 1 \tag{2}$$

$$g(t_1, t_2) = (1-t_2)\,\mathbf{B}_{00}^{10} + t_2 \,\mathbf{B}_{01}^{11} \;\; ; \;\; 0 \le t_1 \le 1 ; 0 \le t_2 \le 1$$

We can observe that it is possible to obtain the generalized expression for N-linear interpolation between 2^N points. Those expressions are obtained easily by means of an algorithmic procedure [17]. So, we do not show it here.

As we can observe, N-linear interpolation can be used to approximate parameterized surfaces inside an error ε, according to Definition 2. So, N-linear interpolation can be used in the basic non-uniform sampling technique for obtaining a generalized technique.

To clarify these ideas, in Algorithm 1 the generalized algorithm to determine the necessary images to build the model of an object is given; this is defined by several parameters. The algorithm uses N-lineal interpolation to determine when a new image should be added as a part of the object model. A new image is added if the current model cannot interpolate this image appropriately (inside the error ε). Notice that the technique just guarantees good approximation on the middle point of interval analyzed. Some technical details are beyond the scope of this work, for example, for acquiring an image just once, we need to have special data structures and extra code.

An important aspect to be considered occurs in step 6 of the Algorithm 1. Here, split can be done homogeneously or heterogeneously. Homogeneously split is desired if all parameters are defined initially with the same bounds and the mechanical system has the same resolution for all parameters. If it is not the case, heterogeneous split is desired and it is necessary to prove the correct interpolation in each parameter. It can be done with N linear interpolations, one for each parameter. Throughout the following experiments, heterogeneous split is used.

```
Algorithm 1:
    0. Set ε to the desired precision. Set low and high
       bounds for each one of N parameters.
    1. Acquire 2ᴺ images, one for each vertex of the zone
       to analyze.
```

2. Compute middle point of the zone to analyze (Lm).
3. Acquire image for position Lm.
4. Interpolate N-linearly between 2^N images acquired in step 3 using expression(1), (2), or the appropriate expression to obtain: $g(t_1, t_2, ..., t_N)$; $0 \leq t_i \leq 1$.
5. If it is possible to interpolate image Lm with $g(0.5, 0.5, ..., 0.5)$ within error ε, using sum-of-squared-difference (Definition 3) as criterion to compare Lm and $g(0.5, 0.5, ..., 0.5)$, i.e., $|| Lm - g(0.5, 0.5, ..., 0.5) ||^2 \leq \varepsilon$ then go to step 8.
6. Split zone in 2^N sub-zones. Push in the stack these 2^N sub-zones.
7. Go to 9.
8. Keep images acquired in step 3, as necessary images to build object's model.
9. If stack is not empty, then pop a zone to analyze and go to step 2.
10. END.

4 Experiments

The software system that acquires the necessary images for modeling the object appearance defined by several parameters was developed. The software was coupled to a mechanical system (turntable) that rotates the object. Additionally, for this work, the mechanical system was able to elevate and descend the camera over turntable plane. The software system determined how many and which images are required to satisfy the precision criterion ε, for each object studied, respectively, for 1 (rotation) and 2 (rotation, elevation) parameters. For this work, we use the proposed generalized technique to analyze the objects showed in Fig. 1.

4.1 One Parameter

In this case, just one parameter (rotation) was used. Results about this case were reported in [14] over the Columbia Object Image Library [16], and the number of images founded by the proposed algorithm represented a significant reduction with respect to traditional approaches. Also, results about object recognition rate were typically very good because model precision was improved.

Fig. 1. Objects used to test the proposed technique

4.2 Generalized Case

In this case, the mechanical system was enabled with the capacity of ascending and descending the camera over the turntable plane. This extra capacity implies that the software system was required to analyze the appearance of the objects on 2 parameters: turntable rotation and camera elevation. In these experiments, the turntable rotation covered all 360° but camera elevation was limited to 0°-20° range.

Table 1. Results obtained to objects in Fig. 1, applying the proposed technique using two parameters (turntable rotation and camera elevation)

		OBJECT									
		1	2	3	4	5	6	7	8	9	10
	$\varepsilon = 2000$	+	+	+	+	+	+	+	+	+	+
	$\varepsilon = 2500$	+	+	8	8	+	+	+	+	+	+
P	$\varepsilon = 3000$	+	+	8	8	+	+	+	+	+	+
R	$\varepsilon = 3500$	+	15	6	6	+	92	64	81	+	+
E	$\varepsilon = 4000$	+	8	6	6	+	64	50	64	+	+
C	$\varepsilon = 4500$	+	8	6	6	+	55	46	50	+	+
I	$\varepsilon = 5000$	+	6	6	6	69	46	37	43	+	+
S	$\varepsilon = 5500$	+	6	6	6	63	40	30	35	+	6
I	$\varepsilon = 6000$	+	6	6	6	55	32	29	32	48	6
O	$\varepsilon = 6500$	+	6	6	6	41	29	29	31	34	6
N	$\varepsilon = 7000$	54	6	6	6	38	24	24	27	26	6
	$\varepsilon = 7500$	44	6	6	6	29	24	21	24	23	6
	$\varepsilon = 8000$	38	6	6	6	22	21	15	17	21	6

We applied the generalized technique over 50 objects, but we just documented results for objects in Fig. 1. We obtain the results shown in Table 1. The algorithm determined the strictly necessary images for modeling each object to specified precision ε, shown in column 1 of Table 1. In these experiments, we restricted our system to rotate or descend/elevate the camera more than 5° between consecutive images. For this reason, in Table 1, a + symbol means that to obtain the required precision ε, the system needed to rotate, descend or elevate the camera less than 5° between consecutive images (in the literature are reported precisions between 10° - 12°, typically). Notice the important reduction on the image quantity respect to a uniform sampling (36×3=108 images, 10° between consecutive images).

Finally, the precision of the models generated with the proposed technique was tested, by comparing the interpolated images obtained from the model, with real images obtained on corresponding positions. We show results in Fig. 2 for the model of object 1 in Fig. 1. The SSD between real and synthetic images is usually less than ε, showing that the estimated model is typically a good approximation of the object appearance (see definition 3), as reported in [14].

5 Non-uniform Sampling and Eigenspaces

The eigenspaces technique can be faster if it uses the images determined by the proposed algorithm as its training set of images, instead of the larger number used cur-

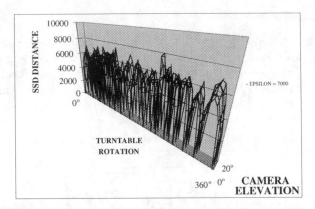

Fig. 2. Testing a 2-parametric model

rently, and it can be safety done, because both measure of model precision and criterion to select the strictly necessary object images for a given precision ε, are preserved in eigenspace [14]. Notice that the generalized proposed technique should be
used in applications where pose estimation no matters, because the computation of
eigenspaces will be faster using non-uniform sampling.

6   Conclusions

Non-uniform sampling to build N-parametric appearance-based models was presented. The method determines the strictly necessary images to capture the object
appearance defined by N parameters, within a precision ε. With this technique, more
complete object models are obtained than 1 parameter, and reduction of image quantity to build object models is achieved by eliminating unnecessary images.

References

1. Murase, H., Nayar, S.K.: Visual learning and recognition of 3-D objects from appearance.
   International Journal of Computer Vision. Vol. 14 No. 1 (1995) 5-24
2. Nelson, R. C., Selinger, A.: Experiments on (Intelligent) Brute Force Methods for Appearance-Based Object Recognition. DARPA Image Unders. Worksh. (1997) 1197-1205
3. Pauli, J., Benkwitz, M., Sommer, G.: RBF Networks Appearance-Based Object Detection.
   Proceedings of ICANN, Paris, Vol. 1 (1995) 359-364
4. Poggio, T., Beymer, D.: Regularization Networks for Visual Learning. In Early Visual
   Learning, Oxford University Press (1996)
5. Moghaddam, B., Pentland, A.: Probabilistic visual learning for object representation. In
   Early Visual Learning, Oxford University Press (1996)
6. Belhumeur, P. N., Kriegman, D. J.: What is the Set of Images of an Object Under All Possible Ilumination Conditions?. Int. J. C. Vision. Vol. 28, Issue 3 (1998) 245-260
7. Epstein, R., Hallinan, P., Yuille, A.: 5±2 Eigenimages suffice: An empirical investigation of
   low-dimensional lighting models. Proc. IEEE Worksh. on physics-based modeling in computer vision (1995)

8. Glassner, A.S.: Principles of digital image synthesis. Morgan-Kaufmann Pub. (2000)
9. Seitz, S.M., Dyer, C.R.: Photorealistic Scene Reconstruction by Voxel Coloring. Int. Journal of Computer Vision, 35(2) (1999)
10. Epstein, R., Yuille, A.L., Belhumeur, P.N.: Learning Object Representations from Lighting Variations. Object Representation in Computer Vision Vol. II. In Proceedings of ECCV'96 International Workshop, Cambridge, U.K. (1996)
11. Koenderink, J.J., Van Doorn, A.J.: The internal representation of solid shape with respect to vision. Biological Cybernetics, Vol. 32, (1979)
12. Cootes, T.F., Wheeler, G.V., Walker, K.N., Taylor, C.J.: Coupled-View Active Appearance Models. The Eleventh British Mach. Vis. Conf. U. of Bristol (2000)
13. Mokhtarian, F., and Abbasi, S.: Automatic Selection of Optimal Views in Multi-view Object Recognition. The Eleventh British Mach. Vis. Conf., U. of Bristol (2000)
14. Altamirano, L.C., Altamirano, L., Alvarado, M.: Non-Uniform Sampling For Improved Appearance-Based Models. Pattern Rec. Letters, V. 24, Issue 1-3, (2003) 529-543
15. Marsden, J.E., Tromba, A.J.: Vector Calculus. W.H. Freeman and Co., Eds. (1976)
16. Nayar, S., Murase, H., Nene, S.: Parametric Appearance Representation. In Early Visual Learning, New York Oxford, Oxford University Press (1996)
17. Farin, G.: Curves and Surfaces for Computer Aided Geometric Design. A. Press, Inc, (1988)

Gaze Detection by Wide and Narrow View Stereo Camera

Kang Ryoung Park

Division of Media Technology, SangMyung University, 7 Hongji-Dong, JongRo-Gu, Seoul, Republic of Korea

Abstract. Human gaze is very important information for the interaction with the computer. In this paper, we propose the new gaze detection system with a wide and a narrow view stereo camera. In order to locate the user's eye position accurately, the narrow-view camera has the functionalities of auto P/T/Z/F based on the detected 3D eye positions from the wide view camera. In addition, we use the IR-LED illuminators for wide and narrow view camera, which can ease the detecting of facial features, pupil and iris position. The eye gaze position on a monitor is computed by a multi-layered perceptron with a limited logarithm function. Experimental results show that the gaze detection error between the computed positions and the real ones is about 2.89 cm of RMS error.

Keywords: Gaze Detection, Dual Cameras, Dual IR-LED Illuminators

1 Introduction

Human gaze is very important information for the interaction with the computer including many applications such as the view control in 3D simulation programs, virtual reality and video conferencing. In addition, they can help the handicapped to use computers and are also useful for those whose hands are busy controlling other menus on the monitor[19]. Most Previous studies were focused on 2D/3D head rotation/translation estimation[2][15], the facial gaze detection[3-9][16][17][19][23] and the eye gaze detection[10-14][18][24-29]. Recently, the gaze detection considering both head and eye movement has been researched. Rikert et al.[9]'s method has the constraints that the Z distance between a face and the monitor must be maintained unchanged during training and testing procedures, which can give much inconvenience to user. In the methods of [11][13][14][16][17], a pair of glasses having marking points is required to detect facial features, which can be also inconvenient to a user. The researches of [3][4][20] show the gaze detection methods only considering head movements and have the limits that the gaze errors are increased in case that the eye movements happen. To overcome such problems, the research of [21] shows the gaze detection considering both head and eye movements, but uses only one wide view camera, which can capture the whole face of user. In such case, the eye image resolution is too low and the fine movements of user's eye cannot be exactly detected. To overcome above problems, we propose the new method of computing

A. Sanfeliu et al. (Eds.): CIARP 2004, LNCS 3287, pp. 140–147, 2004.

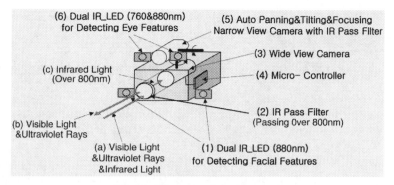

Fig. 1. The gaze detecting system

gaze position. In order to implement practical gaze system based on our method, we use dual cameras (a wide view and a narrow view camera). In order to track the positions of user's eye changed by head movements, the narrow view camera has the functionalities of auto focusing/panning/tilting based on the detected 3D eye positions from the wide view camera. In addition, we use IR-LED illuminators for wide and narrow view camera, which can ease the detecting of facial features, pupil and iris position. To overcome the problem of specular reflection on glasses by illuminator, we use dual IR-LED illuminators for wide and narrow view camera.

2   Localization of Facial Features in Wide View Image

In order to detect gaze position on a monitor, we first locate facial features (both eye centers, eye corners, nostrils) in wide view images. There have been many researches for detecting facial features. One of them is to use facial skin color[22], but their performance can be affected by the environmental light or race, etc. To overcome such problems and detect the facial features robustly in any environment, we use the method of detecting specular reflection on the eyes. For that, we implement the gaze detection system as shown in Fig. 1.

As shown in Fig. 1, the IR-LED(1) is used to make the specular reflections on eyes. The IR pass filter(2) in front of camera lens can only pass the infrared light (over 800 nm) and the brightness of input image is only affected by the IR-LED(1) excluding external illumination. We use a wide view(3) and a narrow view(5) CCD camera (interlaced scan mode). The reason of using IR-LED(1) of 880nm is that human eye can only perceive the visible and the near infrared light (below about 880nm) and our illuminators do not make dazzling to user's eye, consequently. When a user starts our gaze detection S/W in PC, the starting signal is transmitted to the micro-controller(4) in camera via the RS-232C. Then, the micro-controller turns on the illuminator(1) synchronized with the even field of CCD signal and turns off it synchronized with the next odd field of CCD signal, successively[21]. From that, we can get a difference image between the even and the odd image and the specular reflection points on both eyes can be easily detected because their image gray level are higher than other regions[21]. Around the detected corneal specular reflection points, we determine the eye candidate region of 30*30 pixels and locate the accurate eye (iris) center by the circular edge detection method[30]. Because the eye localization is performed in the restricted region, it can be done in real-time (below 3 ms in Pentium-III 866MHz). After locating the eye center, we detect the eye corner by using eye corner shape template and SVM (Support Vector Machine)[21]. We get 2000 successive image frames (100 frames × 20 persons in various sitting positions) for SVM training. From that, 8000 eye corner data (4 eye corners × 2000 images) are obtained and additional 1000 (50 frames × 20 persons in various sitting positions) images are used for testing. Experimental results show the classification error for training data is 0.11% (9/8000) and that for testing data is 0.2% (8/4000) and our algorithm is also valid for the users with glasses or contact lens. In comparing experiments, MLP (Multi-Layered Perceptron) shows the worse performance (the error of 1.58% for training data and 3.1% for testing data). The classification time of SVM is so small as like 8 ms in Pentium-III 866MHz. After locating eye centers and eye corners, the positions of nostrils can be detected by anthropometric constraints in a face and SVM. In order to reduce the effect by the facial expression change, we do not use the lip corners for gaze detection. Experimental results show that RMS error between the detected feature positions and the actual positions (manually detected positions) are 1 pixel (of both eye centers), 2 pixels (of both eye corners) and 4 pixels (of both nostrils) in 640×480 pixels image. From them, we use 5 feature points (left/right eye corners of left eye, left/right eye corners of right eye, nostril center) in order to detect facial gaze position.

3   4 Steps for Computing Facial Gaze Position

After feature detection, we take 4 steps in order to compute a gaze position on a monitor[3][4][21]. At the 1st step, when a user gazes at 5 known positions on a monitor, the 3D positions (X, Y, Z) of initial 5 feature points (detected in the section 2) are computed automatically[3][4]. At the 2nd step and 3rd step, when the user rotates/translates his head in order to gaze at one position on a monitor, the new (changed) 3D positions of those 5 features can be computed from 3D motion estimation. Considering many limitations of previous motion estimation researches, we use the EKF (Extended Kalman Filtering)[2] for 3D motion estimation and the new 3D positions of those features can be computed by the EKF and affine transform[3][21]. The estimation accuracy of the EKF is compared with 3D position tracking sensor[32]. Experimental results show the RMS errors are about 1.4 cm and 2.98° in translation and rotation. In addition, the experimental results show that the RMS error of between the changed(estimated) 3D positions of 5 features and the actual ones (measured by 3D position tracking sensor) is 1.15 cm (0.64cm in X axis, 0.5cm in Y axis, 0.81cm in Z axis) for 20 person data which were used for testing the feature detection performance. At the 4th step, one facial plane is determined from the new (changed) 3D positions of the 5 features and the normal vector (whose origin exists in the middle of the forehead) of the plane shows a gaze vector by head (facial) movements. The gaze position on a monitor is the intersection position between a monitor and the gaze vector[3][4] as shown in Fig. 2(b).

4 Auto Panning/Tilting/Focusing of Narrow View Camera

Based on the new (changed) 3D positions of the 5 feature points (which are computed at the 2nd and 3rd step as mentioned in section 3), we can pan and tilt the narrow view camera in order to capture the eye image. For that, we also perform the coordinate conversion between monitor and narrow view camera using the internal/external camera parameters, which are obtained at initial calibration stage. Such calibration method is same to that between the wide view camera and the monitor. Detail accounts can be referred in [3]. When the user rotates his head severely, one of his eyes may disappear in camera view. So, we track only one visible eye with auto panning/tilting narrow view camera. Conventional narrow view camera has small DOF (Depth of Field) and there is the limitation of increasing the DOF with the fixed focal camera. So, we use the auto focusing narrow view camera in order to capture clear eye image. For auto focusing, the Z distance between the eye and the camera is required and we can obtain the Z distance at the 2nd and 3rd step (as mentioned in section 3). In order to compensate the focusing error due to the inaccurate Z distance measure, we use an additional focus quality checking algorithm. That is, the auto focusing for eye image is accomplished based on the computed Z distance and the captured eye image is transmitted to PC. With that, the focus quality checking algorithm computes the focus quality. If the quality does not meet our threshold (70 of the range (0 ~ 100)), then we perform additional focusing process by sending the moving command of focus lens to camera micro-controller. In this stage, we should consider the specular reflection on glasses. The surface of glasses can make the specular reflection, which can hide the whole eye image. In such case, the eye region is not detected and we cannot compute the eye gaze position. So, we use dual IR-LED illuminators like Fig. 1(6). When the large specular reflection happens from one illuminator (right or left illuminator), then it can be detected from image. As mentioned in section 2, the NTSC analog level of specular reflection region is higher than any other region and they can be detected by changing decoder brightness setting. When the large specular region proves to exist with the changed decoder brightness value, then our gaze detection system change the illuminator (from left to right or right to left) and the specular reflection on glasses does not happen, consequently.

5 Localization of Eye Features in Narrow View Image

After we get the focused eye image, we perform the localization of eye features. We detect $P_1 \sim P_4'$ in right eye image and also detect $P_5 \sim P_8'$ in left eye image for computing eye gaze detection. Here, the P_1 and P_1' show the pupil center and the P_2 and P_2' does the iris center. J. Wang et al.[1] uses the method that detects the iris outer boundary by vertical edge operator, morphological "open" operation and elliptical fitting. However, the upper and lower region of iris outer boundary tend to be covered by eyelid and inaccurate iris elliptical fitting happens due to the lack of iris boundary pixels. In addition, their method computes eye gaze position by checking the shape change of iris when a user gazes at monitor positions. However, our experimental results show that the shape change amount of iris is very small and it is difficult to detect the accurate eye gaze position only by that information. So, we use the positional information of both pupil and iris. Also, we use the information of shape change of pupil, which does not tend to be covered by eyelid. In general, the IR-LED of short wavelength (700nm $\sim$ 800nm) makes the high contrast between iris and sclera. On the other hand, that of long wavelength (800nm $\sim$ 900nm) makes the high contrast between pupil and iris. Based on that, we use the IR-LED illuminator of multi-wavelength (760nm and 880nm) as shown in Fig. 1(6). The shapes of iris and pupil are almost ellipse, when the user gazes at a side position of monitor. So, the method of circular edge detection[30] cannot be used. Instead, we use the canny edge operator to extract edge components and a 2D edge-based elliptical Hough transform[31]. From that, we can get the center positions and the major/minor axes of iris/pupil ellipses. In order to detect the eye corner position, we detect the eyelid. That is because the upper and lower eyelids meet on two eye corner positions. To extract the eyelid region, we use the region-based template deformation and masking method. In detail, we make the eyelid edge image with canny edge operator and apply the deformable template as the eyelid mask. Here, we use 2 deformable templates (parabolic shape) for upper and lower eyelid detection. From that, we can detect the accurate eye corners. Experimental results show that RMS errors between the detected eye feature positions and the actual ones (manually detected) are 2 pixels (of iris center), 1 pixel (of pupil center), 4 pixels (of left eye corner) and 4 pixels (of right eye corner). Based on the detected eye features, we select the 22 feature values ($f_1 \sim f_{11}$ are used in case that right eye image can be captured by narrow view camera and $f_{12} \sim f_{22}$ are used in case that left eye image can be captured). With those feature values, we can compute eye gaze position on a monitor as shown in Fig. 2(a). Detail accounts are shown in section 6.

6   Detecting the Gaze Position on a Monitor

In section 3, we explain the gaze detection method only considering head movement. As mentioned before, when a user gazes at a monitor position, both the head and eyes tend to be moved simultaneously. So, we compute the additional eye gaze position with the detected 22 feature values (as mentioned in section 5) and a neural network (multi-layered perceptron) as shown in Fig. 2(a). Here, the input values for neural network are normalized by the distance between the iris/pupil center and the eye corner, which are obtained in case of gazing at monitor center. That is because we do not use a zoom lens in our camera. That

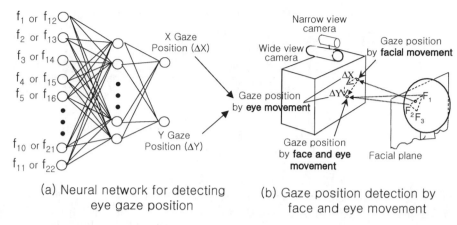

(a) Neural network for detecting
eye gaze position

(b) Gaze position detection by
face and eye movement

Fig. 2. The neural network for eye gaze detection and gaze position detection by face and eye movement

is, the more the user approaches the monitor (camera), the larger the eye size becomes and the farther the distance between the pupil/iris and the eye corner becomes, consequently. After detecting eye gaze position based on the neural network, we can determine a final gaze position on a monitor by head and eye movements based on the vector summation of each gaze position (face and eye gaze) as shown in Fig. 2(b).

7   Performance Evaluations

The gaze detection error of the proposed method is compared to that of our previous methods[3][4][19][21] as shown in Table 1. The researches[3][4] compute facial gaze position not considering the eye movements. The research[19] calculates the gaze position by mapping the 2D facial feature position into the monitor gaze position by linear interpolation or neural network without 3D computation and considering eye movements. The method[21] computes the gaze positions considering both head and eye movements, but uses only one wide view camera. The test data are acquired when 10 users gaze at 23 gaze positions on a 19" monitor. Here, the gaze error is the RMS error between the actual gaze positions and the computed ones. Shown in Table 1, the gaze errors are calculated in two cases. The case I shows that gaze error about test data including only head movements and the case II does that the gaze error including head and eye movements.

Shown in Table 1, the gaze error of the proposed method is the smallest in any case. At the 2nd experiment, the points of radius 5 pixels are spaced vertically and horizontally at 1.5" intervals on a 19" monitor with the screen resolution of 1280×1024 pixels as such Rikert's research[9]. The RMS error between the real and calculated gaze position is 2.85 cm and it is much superior to Rikert's method (almost 5.08 cm). Our gaze error is correspondent to the angular error of

Table 1. Gaze error about test data (cm)

Method	Linear interpol.[19]	Single neural net[19]	Combined neural nets[19]	[3] method	[4] method	[21] method	Proposed method
case I	5.1	4.23	4.48	5.35	5.21	3.40	2.24
case II	11.8	11.32	8.87	7.45	6.29	4.8	2.89

2.29 degrees on X axis and 2.31 degrees on Y axis. In addition, we tested the gaze errors according to the Z distance (55, 60, 65cm). The RMS errors are 2.81cm at 55cm, 2.85cm at 60cm, 2.92cm at 65cm. It shows that the performance of our method is not affected by the user's Z position. Last experiment for processing time shows that our gaze detection process takes about 500ms in Pentium-III 866MHz and it is much smaller than Rikert's method (1 minute in alphastation 333MHz). Our system only requires the user to gaze at 5 known monitor positions at the initial calibration stage (as shown in the section 3) and can track/compute the user's gaze position without any user's intervention at real-time speed. The research[1] shows the angular error of below 1 degree, but their method supposes that they know the 3D distance between two eyes and that between both lip corners and there is no individual variation for the 3D distances. In addition, they suppose that they know the 3D diameter of eye ball and there is no individual variation for that. However, our preliminary experiments show that there are much individual variations for the 3D distances/3D diameter and such cases can increase much gaze errors (the angular error of more than 4 degree).

8 Conclusions

This paper describes a new gaze detecting method. In future works, we have plans to research the method of capturing higher resolution eye image with zoom lens and it will increase the accuracy of final gaze detection. In addition, the method to increase the auto panning/tilting/focusing speed of narrow view camera should be researched to decrease total processing time.

References

1. J. Wang and E. Sung, 2002. Study on Eye Gaze Estimation, IEEE Trans. on SMC, Vol. 32, No. 3, pp.332-350
2. A. Azarbayejani., 1993, Visually Controlled Graphics. IEEE Trans. PAMI, Vol. 15, No. 6, pp. 602-605
3. K. R. Park et al., Apr 2000, Gaze Point Detection by Computing the 3D Positions and 3D Motions of Face, IEICE Trans. Inf.&Syst.,Vol. E.83-D, No.4, pp.884-894
4. K. R. Park et al., Oct 1999, Gaze Detection by Estimating the Depth and 3D Motions of Facial Features in Monocular Images, IEICE Trans. Fundamentals, Vol. E.82-A, No. 10, pp. 2274-2284
5. K. OHMURA et al., 1989. Pointing Operation Using Detection of Face Direction from a Single View. IEICE Trans. Inf.&Syst., Vol. J72-D-II, No.9, pp. 1441-1447

6. P. Ballard et al., 1995. Controlling a Computer via Facial Aspect. IEEE Trans. on SMC, Vol. 25, No. 4, pp. 669-677
7. A. Gee et al., 1996. Fast visual tracking by temporal consensus, Image and Vision Computing. Vol. 14, pp. 105-114
8. J. Heinzmann et al., 1998. 3D Facial Pose and Gaze Point Estimation using a Robust Real-Time Tracking Paradigm. Proceedings of ICAFGR, pp. 142-147
9. T. Rikert, 1998. Gaze Estimation using Morphable Models. ICAFGR, pp.436-441
10. A.Ali-A-L et al., 1997, Man-machine Interface through Eyeball Direction of Gaze. Proc. of the Southeastern Symposium on System Theory, pp. 478-82
11. A. Tomono et al., 1994. Eye Tracking Method Using an Image Pickup Apparatus. European Patent Specification-94101635
12. Eyemark Recorder Model EMR-NC, NAC Image Technology Cooperation
13. Porrill-J et al., Jan 1999, Robust and Optimal Use of Information in Stereo Vision. Nature. vol.397, no.6714, pp.63-6
14. Varchmin-AC et al., 1998, Image based Recognition of Gaze Direction Using Adaptive Methods. Gesture and Sign Language in Human-Computer Interaction. Int. Gesture Workshop Proc. Berlin, Germany, pp. 245-57.
15. J. Heinzmann et al., 1997. Robust Real-time Face Tracking and Gesture Recognition. Proc. of the IJCAI, Vol. 2, pp. 1525-1530
16. Matsumoto-Y, et al., 2000, An Algorithm for Real-time Stereo Vision Implementation of Head Pose and Gaze Direction Measurement. Proc. the ICAFGR. pp. 499-504
17. Newman-R et al., 2000, Real-time Stereo Tracking for Head Pose and Gaze Estimation. Proceedings the 4th ICAFGR 2000. pp. 122-8
18. Betke-M et al., 1999, Gaze Detection via Self-organizing Gray-scale Units. Proc. Int. Workshop on Recog., Analy., and Tracking of Faces and Gestures in Real-Time System. pp. 70-6
19. K. R. Park et al., 2000. Intelligent Process Control via Gaze Detection Technology. EAAI, Vol. 13, No. 5, pp. 577-587
20. K. R. Park et al., 2002. Gaze Position Detection by Computing the 3 Dimensional Facial Positions and Motions. Pattern Recognition, Vol. 35, No.11, pp. 2559-2569
21. K. R. Park et al., 2002, Facial and Eye Gaze detection. LNCS, Vol.2525, pp. 368-376
22. Jie Yang and Alex Waibel, A Real-time Face Tracker, Proceedings of WACV'96, pp. 142-147
23. Y. Matsumoto, 2000. An Algorithm for Real-time Stereo Vision Implementation of Head Pose and Gaze Direction Measurement, ICFGR, pp.499-505
24. http://www.iscaninc.com
25. http://www.seeingmachines.com
26. B Wolfe, D. Eichmann, 1997. A Neural Network Approach to Tracking Eye Position, International Journal Human Computer Interaction, Vol. 9, No.1, pp. 59-79
27. David Beymer and Myron Flickner, 2003. Eye Gaze Tracking Using an Active Stereo Head, IEEE Computer Vision and Pattern Recognition
28. J. Zhu et al., 2002. Subpixel Eye Gaze Tracking, International Conference on Face and Gesture Recognition
29. R. Stiefelhagen, J. Yang, and A. Waibel, 1997. Tracking Eyes and Monitoring Eye Gaze, Proceedings of Workshop on Perceptual User Interfaces, pp. 98-100
30. J. Daugman, 2003. The Importance of Being Random: Statistical Principles of Iris Recognition, Pattern Recognition, vol. 36, no. 2, pp. 279-291
31. Ramesh Jain, 1995, Machine Vision, McGraw-Hill International Edition
32. http://www.polhemus.com

A New Auto-associative Memory
Based on Lattice Algebra

Gerhard X. Ritter, Laurentiu Iancu, and Mark S. Schmalz

CISE Department, University of Florida, Gainesville, FL 32611-6120, USA
{ritter,liancu,mssz}@cise.ufl.edu

Abstract. This paper presents a novel, three-stage, auto-associative memory based on lattice algebra. The first two stages of this memory consist of correlation matrix memories within the lattice domain. The third and final stage is a two-layer feed-forward network based on dendritic computing. The output nodes of this feed-forward network yield the desired pattern vector association. The computations performed by each stage are all lattice based and, thus, provide for fast computation and avoidance of convergence problems. Additionally, the proposed model is extremely robust in the presence of noise. Bounds of allowable noise that guarantees perfect output are also discussed.

1 Introduction

The computational framework of morphological associative memories involves lattice algebraic operations, such as dilation, erosion, and max and min product. Using these operations, two associative memories can be defined. These memories can be either hetero-associative or auto-associative, depending on the pattern associations they store. The morphological auto-associative memories are known to be robust in the presence of certain types of noise, but also rather vulnerable to random noise [1–4].

The kernel method described in [1, 3, 5] allows the construction of auto-associative memories with improved robustness to random noise. However, even with the kernel method, complete reconstruction of exemplar patterns that have undergone only minute distortions is not guaranteed. In this paper we present a new method of creating an auto-associative memory that takes into account the kernel method discussed in [1, 3] as well as a two-layer morphological feed-forward network based on neurons with dendritic structures [6–8].

2 Auto-associative Memories in the Lattice Domain

The lattice algebra in which our memories operate is discussed in detail in [1]. In this algebraic system, which consists of the set of extended real numbers $\mathbb{R}_{\pm\infty}$ and the operations $+$, $\vee$ and $\wedge$, we define two matrix operations called *max product* and *min product*, denoted by the symbols $\boxed{\vee}$ and $\boxed{\wedge}$, respectively. For an $m \times p$ matrix A and a $p \times n$ matrix B with entries from $\mathbb{R}$, the $m \times n$ matrix

A. Sanfeliu et al. (Eds.): CIARP 2004, LNCS 3287, pp. 148–155, 2004.

Fig. 1. Images $\mathbf{p}^1, \ldots, \mathbf{p}^6$, converted into column vectors $\mathbf{x}^1, \ldots, \mathbf{x}^6$, and stored in the morphological auto-associative memories W_{XX} and M_{XX}.

$C = A \boxtimes B$ has the i, jth entry $c_{ij} = \bigvee_{k=1}^{p}(a_{ik} + b_{kj})$. Likewise, the i, jth entry of matrix $C = A \boxtimes B$ is $c_{ij} = \bigwedge_{k=1}^{p}(a_{ik} + b_{kj})$.

For a set of pattern vectors $X = \{\mathbf{x}^1, \ldots, \mathbf{x}^k\} \subset \mathbb{R}^n$ we construct two natural auto-associative memories W_{XX} and M_{XX} of size $n \times n$ defined by $W_{XX} = \bigwedge_{\xi=1}^{k} \left[\mathbf{x}^\xi \times (-\mathbf{x}^\xi)' \right]$ and $M_{XX} = \bigvee_{\xi=1}^{k} \left[\mathbf{x}^\xi \times (-\mathbf{x}^\xi)' \right]$. Here the symbol $\times$ denotes the *morphological outer product* of two vectors, such that $\mathbf{x} \times \mathbf{x}' = \mathbf{x} \boxtimes \mathbf{x}' = \mathbf{x} \boxtimes \mathbf{x}'$. In [1] we proved that

$$W_{XX} \boxtimes X = X = M_{XX} \boxtimes X , \tag{1}$$

where X can consist of any arbitrarily large number of pattern vectors. In other words, morphological auto-associative memories have infinite capacity and perfect recall of undistorted patterns.

Example 1. For a visual example, consider the six pattern images $\mathbf{p}^1, \ldots, \mathbf{p}^6$ shown in Fig. 1. Each $\mathbf{p}^\xi$, $\xi = 1, \ldots, 6$, is a 50×50 pixel 256 gray scale image. For uncorrupted input, perfect recall is guaranteed by Eq. (1) if we use the memory W_{XX} or M_{XX}. Using the standard row-scan method, each pattern image $\mathbf{p}^\xi$ can be converted into a pattern vector $\mathbf{x}^\xi = \left(x_1^\xi, \ldots, x_{2500}^\xi \right)'$ by defining $x_{50(r-1)+c}^\xi = p^\xi(r, c)$ for $r, c = 1, \ldots, 50$.

Morphological associative memories are extremely robust in the presence of certain types of noise, missing data, or occlusions. We say that a distorted version $\tilde{\mathbf{x}}^\xi$ of the pattern $\mathbf{x}^\xi$ has undergone an *erosive change* whenever $\tilde{\mathbf{x}}^\xi \leq \mathbf{x}^\xi$ and a *dilative change* whenever $\tilde{\mathbf{x}}^\xi \geq \mathbf{x}^\xi$. The morphological memory W_{XX} is a memory of dilative type (patterns are recalled using the max product) and thus is extremely robust in the presence of erosive noise. Conversely, the memory M_{XX}, of erosive type, is particularly robust to dilative noise.

Several mathematical results proved in [1] provide necessary and sufficient conditions for the maximum amount of distortion of a pattern that still guarantees perfect recall. In spite of being robust to the specific type of noise they tolerate, the morphological memories W_{XX} and M_{XX} can fail to recognize patterns that are affected by a different type of noise, even in a minute amount. Thus, W_{XX} fails rather easily in the presence of dilative noise, while M_{XX} fails in the presence of erosive noise. Additionally, both types of morphological memories are vulnerable to random noise, i.e. noise that is both dilative and erosive in nature.

The following experiment illustrates this behavior of the lattice auto-associative memories. Figure 2 shows the images $\mathbf{p}^1, \ldots, \mathbf{p}^6$ in which 75% of the pixels

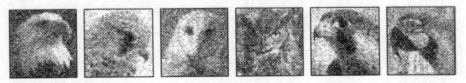

Fig. 2. Images corrupted with 75% random noise (both dilative and erosive) in the range $[-72, 72]$. Pixel values are in the range $[0, 255]$.

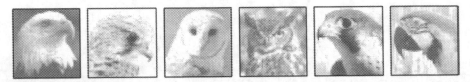

Fig. 3. Incorrect recall of memory W_{XX} when presented with the noisy input images from Fig. 2. The output appears shifted towards white pixel values.

have been corrupted by random noise. The noise has uniform distribution and is in the range $[-72, 72]$. When the pixel values affected by noise become less than 0 or greater than 255, the result is clamped at 0 and 255, respectively. The range of noise has been chosen by calculation, in order to compare the memories W_{XX} and M_{XX} to the ones based on the dendritic model, as discussed in the subsequent sections of this paper.

The output of the memory W_{XX} when presented with the patterns corrupted with random noise is illustrated in Fig. 3. When compared to the original images from Fig. 1 stored in the memory, the patterns recalled by W_{XX} appear to be different from the original $\mathbf{p}^\xi$, $\xi = 1, \ldots, 6$. The output of W_{XX} is offset toward white (high pixel values), as W_{XX} is applied dilatively via the max product. A similar experiment will show that the output of M_{XX} will be shifted toward black (low pixel values), as M_{XX} is a memory of erosive type, used in conjunction with the min product.

Because of this failure of the memories W_{XX} and M_{XX}, we developed the method of *kernels* to treat random noise. This method is discussed in detail in [3]. Basically, a *kernel* for X is a set of vectors $Z = \{\mathbf{z}^1, \ldots, \mathbf{z}^k\} \subset \mathbb{R}^n$ such that $\forall \gamma = 1, \ldots, k$,

1. $\mathbf{z}^\gamma \wedge \mathbf{z}^\xi = 0 \ \forall \xi \neq \gamma$,
2. $\mathbf{z}^\gamma$ contains exactly one non-zero entry, and
3. $W_{XX} \boxtimes \mathbf{z}^\gamma = \mathbf{x}^\gamma$.
4. If z_i^γ denotes the non-zero entry of $\mathbf{z}^\gamma$, then $z_i^\gamma = x_i^\gamma$.

Now if Z satisfies the above conditions and $\tilde{\mathbf{x}}^\gamma$ denotes a distorted version of $\mathbf{x}^\gamma$ such that $\tilde{x}_i^\gamma = z_i^\gamma$, where z_i^γ denotes the non-zero entry of $\mathbf{z}^\gamma$, then $W_{XX} \boxtimes (M_{ZZ} \boxtimes \tilde{\mathbf{x}}^\gamma) = \mathbf{x}^\gamma$. Here we assume that the set X of exemplar patterns have non-negative coordinates, which is generally the case in pattern recognition problems. If, however, $\tilde{x}_i^\gamma \neq z_i^\gamma$, then perfect recall cannot be achieved. To overcome this shortcoming, we developed an extended model that takes into account dendritic neural structures.

3   The Dendritic Model

The artificial neural model that employs dendritic computation has been motivated by the fact that several researchers have proposed that dendrites, and not the neurons, are the elementary computing devices of the brain, capable of implementing logical functions such as AND, OR, and NOT [9–14]. In the mammalian brain, dendrites span all cortical layers and account for the largest component in both surface and volume. Thus, dendrites cannot be omitted when attempting to build artificial neural models.

Inspired by the neurons of the biological brain, we developed a model of *morphological neuron* that possesses *dendritic structures*. A number of such neurons can then be arranged on one layer, similarly to the classical single layer perceptron (SLP), in order to build a single layer morphological perceptron with dendritic structures (SLMP). This artificial model is described in detail in [8, 15] and only briefly summarized below due to page limitation.

Let $N_1, \ldots, N_n$ denote a set of input neurons, which provide synaptic input to the main layer of neurons with dendritic structures, $M_1, \ldots, M_m$, which is also the output layer. The value of an input neuron N_i $(i = 1, \ldots, n)$ propagates through its axonal tree to the terminal branches that make contact with the neuron M_j $(j = 1, \ldots, m)$. The weight of an axonal branch of neuron N_i terminating on the kth dendrite of M_j is denoted by w_{ijk}^ℓ, where the superscript $\ell \in \{0, 1\}$ distinguishes between *excitatory* $(\ell = 1)$ and *inhibitory* $(\ell = 0)$ input to the dendrite. The kth dendrite of M_j will respond to the total input received from the neurons $N_1, \ldots, N_n$ and will either accept or inhibit the received input. The computation of the kth dendrite of M_j is given by

$$\tau_k^j(\mathbf{x}) = p_{jk} \bigwedge_{i \in I(k)} \bigwedge_{\ell \in L(i)} (-1)^{1-\ell} \left(x_i + w_{ijk}^\ell \right) , \tag{2}$$

where $\mathbf{x} = (x_1, \ldots, x_n)'$ denotes the input value of the neurons $N_1, \ldots, N_n$ with x_i representing the value of N_i; $I(k) \subseteq \{1, \ldots, n\}$ corresponds to the set of all input neurons with terminal fibers that synapse on the kth dendrite of M_j; $L(i) \subseteq \{0, 1\}$ corresponds to the set of terminal fibers of N_i that synapse on the kth dendrite of M_j; and $p_{jk} \in \{-1, 1\}$ denotes the excitatory $(p_{jk} = 1)$ or inhibitory $(p_{jk} = -1)$ response of the kth dendrite of M_j to the received input.

It follows from the formulation $L(i) \subseteq \{0, 1\}$ that the ith neuron N_i can have at most two synapses on a given dendrite k. Also, if the value $\ell = 1$, then the input $\left(x_i + w_{ijk}^1 \right)$ is excitatory, and inhibitory for $\ell = 0$ since in this case we have $-\left(x_i + w_{ijk}^0 \right)$.

The value $\tau_k^j(\mathbf{x})$ is passed to the cell body and the state of M_j is a function of the input received from all its dendrites. The total value received by M_j is given by $\tau^j(\mathbf{x}) = p_j \bigwedge_{k=1}^{K_j} \tau_k^j(\mathbf{x})$, where K_j denotes the total number of dendrites of M_j

and $p_j = \pm 1$ denotes the response of the cell body to the received dendritic input. Here again, $p_j = 1$ means that the input is accepted, whereas $p_j = -1$ means that the cell rejects the received input. The *next* state of M_j is then determined by an activation function f, namely $y_j = f(\tau^j(\mathbf{x}))$. Typical activation functions used with the dendritic model include the hard-limiter and the pure linear identity function. The single layer morphological perceptron usually employs the former.

For a more thorough understanding of this model as well as its computational performance, we refer the reader to examples and theorems given in [7, 8, 15].

4   An Auto-associative Memory Based on the Dendritic Model

Based on the dendritic model described in the previous section, we construct an auto-associative memory that can store a set of patterns $X = \{\mathbf{x}^1, \ldots, \mathbf{x}^k\} \subset \mathbb{R}^n$ and can also cope with random noise. The memory we are about to describe will consist of n input neurons $N_1, \ldots, N_n$, k neurons in the hidden layer, which we denote by $H_1, \ldots, H_k$, and n output neurons $M_1, \ldots, M_n$. Let $\mathrm{d}(\mathbf{x}^\xi, \mathbf{x}^\gamma) = \max\{|x_i^\xi - x_i^\gamma| : i = 1, \ldots, n\}$ and choose an allowable noise parameter α with α satisfying

$$\alpha < \frac{1}{2} \min\{\mathrm{d}(\mathbf{x}^\xi, \mathbf{x}^\gamma) : \xi < \gamma,\ \xi, \gamma \in \{1, \ldots, k\}\} . \tag{3}$$

For $\mathbf{x} \in \mathbb{R}^n$, the input for N_i will be the ith coordinate of $\mathbf{x}$. Each neuron H_j in the hidden layer has exactly one dendrite, which contains the synaptic sites of the terminal axonal fibers of N_i for $i = 1, \ldots, n$. The weights of the terminal fibers of N_i terminating on the dendrite of H_j are given by

$$w_{ij}^\ell = \begin{cases} -\left(x_i^j - \alpha\right) & \text{if } \ell = 1 \\ -\left(x_i^j + \alpha\right) & \text{if } \ell = 0 \end{cases},$$

where $i = 1, \ldots, n$ and $j = 1, \ldots, k$. For a given input $\mathbf{x} \in \mathbb{R}^n$, the dendrite of H_j computes $\tau^j(\mathbf{x}) = \bigwedge_{i=1}^n \bigwedge_{\ell=0}^1 (-1)^{1-\ell}(x_i + w_{ij}^\ell)$. The state of the neuron H_j is determined by the hard-limiter activation function

$$f(z) = \begin{cases} 0 & \text{if } z \geq 0 \\ -\infty & \text{if } z < 0 \end{cases} .$$

Thus, the output of H_j is given by $f[\tau^j(\mathbf{x})]$ and is passed along its axon and axonal fibers to the output neurons $M_1, \ldots, M_n$.

Similar to the hidden layer neurons, each output neuron M_h, $h = 1, \ldots, n$, has one dendrite. However, each hidden neuron H_j has exactly one excitatory axonal fiber and no inhibitory fibers terminating on the dendrite of M_h. Figure 4 illustrates this dendritic network model. The excitatory fiber of M_j terminating on M_h has synaptic weight $v_{jh} = x_h^j$. The computation performed by M_h is

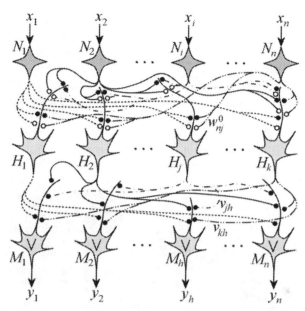

Fig. 4. The topology of the morphological auto-associative memory based on the dendritic model. The network is fully connected; all axonal branches from input neurons synapse via two fibers on all hidden neurons, which in turn connect to all output nodes via excitatory fibers.

given by $\tau^h(\mathbf{q}) = \bigvee_{j=1}^{k} (q_j + v_{jh})$, where q_j denotes the output of H_j, namely $q_j = f\left[\tau^j(\mathbf{x})\right]$. The activation function for each output neuron M_h is the simple linear identity function $f(z) = z$.

Each neuron H_j will have output value $f(q_j) = 0$ if and only if $\mathbf{x}$ is an element of the hypercube $B^j = \left\{ (x_1, \ldots, x_n) \in \mathbb{R}^n : x_i^j - \alpha \leq x_i \leq x_i^j + \alpha, \; i = 1, \ldots, n \right\}$ and $f(q_j) = -\infty$ whenever $\mathbf{x} \in \mathbb{R}^n \setminus B^j$. Thus, the output of this network will be $\mathbf{y} = (y_1, \ldots, y_n) = \left(x_1^j, \ldots, x_n^j\right) = \mathbf{x}^j$ if and only if $\mathbf{x} \in B^j$. That is, whenever $\mathbf{x}$ is a corrupted version of $\mathbf{x}^j$ with each coordinate of $\mathbf{x}$ not exceeding the allowable noise level α, then $\mathbf{x}$ will be identified as $\mathbf{x}^j$.

If $\mathbf{x}$ does not fall within the allowable noise level α specified by Eq. (3), then the output will not be $\mathbf{x}^j$. We can, however, increase the geometric territory for distorted versions of $\mathbf{x}^j$ by first employing the kernel method. In particular, suppose that X is strongly lattice independent and Z is a kernel for X satisfying properties 1–4 specified earlier. Then, for each pattern $\mathbf{x}^j$, the user can add the noise parameter α about $\mathbf{z}^j$ as well, as shown in Fig. 5. This increases the allowable range of noise. In particular, if $|z_i^j - x_i| > \alpha \; \forall i$, then $\mathbf{x}$ is rejected as an input vector. However, if $\mathbf{x}$ falls within any of the shaded regions illustrated in Fig. 5, then the memory flow diagram $\mathbf{x} \to M_{ZZ} \to W_{XX} \to M \to \mathbf{x}^j$, where M denotes the two-layer feed-forward dendritic network, provides perfect recall output. That is, we first compute $\mathbf{y} = W_{XX} \boxtimes (M_{ZZ} \boxtimes \mathbf{x})$ and then use $\mathbf{y}$ as the input vector to the feed-forward network M. For purpose of illustration, we

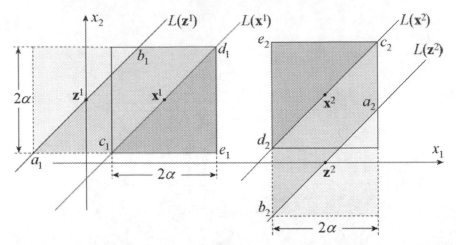

Fig. 5. The two patterns $\mathbf{x}^1, \mathbf{x}^2$ with corresponding kernel vectors $\mathbf{z}^1, \mathbf{z}^2$. The non-zero entries of $\mathbf{z}^1$ and $\mathbf{z}^2$ are z_2^1 and z_1^2, respectively. Every point on and between the lines $L(\mathbf{x}^1)$ and $L(\mathbf{x}^2)$ is a fixed point of W_{XX}. Similarly, every point on and between $L(\mathbf{z}^1)$ and $L(\mathbf{z}^2)$ is a fixed point of M_{ZZ}.

used two independent vectors in $\mathbb{R}^2$. The corresponding kernel vectors lie on the coordinate axes. Observe that if $\mathbf{x}$ lies in the lightly shaded area above the line $L(\mathbf{z}^1)$, then $M_{ZZ} \boxtimes \mathbf{x}$ lies on the segment $[a_1, b_1] \subset L(\mathbf{z}^1)$. If $\mathbf{x}$ lies within the other shaded regions, then $M_{ZZ} \boxtimes \mathbf{x} = \mathbf{x}$. Everything within the parallelogram $\langle a_1, b_1, d_1, c_1 \rangle$ (including $[a_1, b_1]$) will be mapped under W_{XX} onto the segment $[c_1, d_1] \subset L(\mathbf{x}^1)$ and any point within the triangle specified by $\langle c_1, d_1, e_1 \rangle$ will be mapped by M to $\mathbf{x}^1$. This schema can be easily extended to any dimension.

Example 2. To illustrate the performance of this auto-associative memory, we stored the same exemplar patterns $\mathbf{x}^1, \mathbf{x}^2, \ldots, \mathbf{x}^6 \in \mathbb{R}^{2500}$ used in Example 1 and shown in Fig. 1. The images were then distorted by randomly corrupting 75% of the coordinates within a noise level α, chosen to satisfy the inequality in (3). Letting $\alpha = \frac{2}{5} \min \left\{ \mathrm{d} \left(\mathbf{x}^\xi, \mathbf{x}^\gamma \right) : 1 \leq \xi < \gamma \leq 6 \right\}$ we obtain $\alpha = \frac{2}{5} \cdot 180 = 72$. This is how the allowable amount of distortion $[-72, 72]$ was chosen in Example 1, and applied to the images resulted in the noisy patterns of Fig. 2. Using the same corrupted patterns as input to the memory based on the model described here, we obtain perfect recall, i.e. patterns identical to the input patterns in Fig 1.

5 Conclusions

We presented a new paradigm for an auto-associative memory based on lattice algebra that combines correlation matrix memories and a dendritic feed-forward network. We gave a brief overview of correlation matrix memories in the lattice domain as well as single layer morphological perceptrons with dendritic structures, whose computational capability exceeds that of the classical single layer perceptrons. Using a two-layer dendritic model, we defined an auto-associative memory that is able to store and recall any finite collection of n-dimensional pattern vectors. We showed by example that this memory is robust in the presence of noise where the allowable noise level depends only on the minimum Chebyshev distance between the patterns.

The allowable noise level can be increased dramatically if the set of patterns is strongly lattice independent. It follows from the description of this model that recognition does not involve any lengthy training sessions but only straightforward computation of weights in terms of pattern distances. Convergence problems are non-existent as recognition is achieved in one step in terms of information feed-forward flow through the network.

References

1. Ritter, G.X., Sussner, P., Diaz de Leon, J.L.: Morphological Associative Memories. IEEE Trans. on Neural Networks **9**(2) (March 1998) 281–293
2. Ritter, G.X., Diaz de Leon, J.L., Sussner, P.: Morphological Bidirectional Associative Memories. Neural Networks **12** (March 1999) 851–867
3. Ritter, G.X., Urcid, G., Iancu, L.: Reconstruction of Noisy Patterns Using Morphological Associative Memories. J. of Mathematical Imaging and Vision **19**(2) (2003) 95–111
4. Urcid, G., Ritter, G.X., Iancu, L.: Kernel Computation in Morphological Bidirectional Associative Memories. Proc. 8th Iberoamerican Congress on Pattern Recognition CIARP'03. Havana, Cuba (November 2003) 552–559
5. Sussner, P.: Observations on Morphological Associative Memories and the Kernel Method. Neurocomputing **31** (2000) 167–183
6. Ritter, G.X., Iancu, L., Urcid, G.: Neurons, Dendrites, and Pattern Classification. Proc. 8th Iberoamerican Congress on Pattern Recognition CIARP'03. Havana, Cuba (November 2003) 1–16
7. Ritter, G.X., Iancu, L.: Lattice Algebra Approach to Neural Networks and Pattern Classification. Pattern Recognition and Image Analysis **14**(2) (2004) 190–197
8. Ritter, G.X., Iancu, L.: Morphological Perceptrons. Preprint submitted to IEEE Trans. on Neural Networks.
9. Eccles, J.C.: The Understanding of the Brain. McGraw-Hill, New York (1977)
10. Koch, C., Segev, I. (eds.): Methods in Neuronal Modeling: From Synapses to Networks. MIT Press, Boston (1989)
11. McKenna, T., Davis, J., Zornetzer, S.F. (eds.): Single Neuron Computation. Academic Press, San Diego (1992)
12. Mel, B.W.: Synaptic Integration in Excitable Dendritic Trees. J. of Neurophysiology **70** (1993) 1086–1101
13. Rall, W., Segev, I.: Functional Possibilities for Synapses on Dendrites and Dendritic Spines. In: Edelman, G.M., Gall, E.E., Cowan, W.M. (eds.): Synaptic Function. Wiley, New York (1987) 605–636
14. Segev, I.: Dendritic Processing. In: Arbib, M. (ed.): The Handbook of Brain Theory and Neural Networks. MIT Press, Boston (1998) 282–289
15. Ritter, G.X., Urcid, G.: Lattice Algebra Approach to Single Neuron Computation. IEEE Trans. on Neural Networks **14**(2) (March 2003) 282–295

Image Segmentation
Using Morphological Watershed Applied to Cartography

Nilcilene das Graças Medeiros, Erivaldo Antonio da Silva,
Danilo Aparecido Rodrigues, and José Roberto Nogueira

Unesp, Faculdade de Ciências e Tecnologia – Rua Roberto Simonsen, 305 – Presidente
Prudente – SP, CEP 19060 – 900 – Brasil
{medeiros,erivaldo}@prudente.unesp.br

Abstract. Image segmentation is a process frequently used in several different
areas including Cartography. Feature extraction is a very troublesome task, and
successful results require more complex techniques and good quality data. The
aims of this paper is to study Digital Image Processing techniques, with emphasis in Mathematical Morphology, to use Remote Sensing imagery, making image segmentation, using morphological operators, mainly the multi-scale morphological gradient operator. In the segmentation process, pre-processing
operators of Mathematical Morphology were used, and the multi-scales gradient
was implemented to create one of the images used as marker image. Orbital image of the Landsat satellite, sensor TM was used. The MATLAB software was
used in the implementation of the routines. With the accomplishment of tests,
the performance of the implemented operators was verified and carried through
the analysis of the results. The extration of linear feature, using mathematical
morphology techniques, can contribute in cartographic applications, as cartographic products updating. The comparison to the best result obtained was performed by means of the morphology with conventional techniques of features
extraction.

1 Introduction

Effective procedures on images segmentation are required for the successful
achievement of the features extraction stage, which are of great interest of several
areas, but in the specific case of the cartography area, for features identification and
updating.

This work assembles the use of Remote Sensing data and Image Digital Processing
techniques, especially the Mathematical Morphological toolbox in the features semi-
automatic extration.

The features extraction process is, in this case, established with the use of morphological operators for the images segmentation. The main morphological segmentation
tool is based on the transformation that defines the waters divisor line (WDL) or watershed of a function [1][2].

The use of the watershed operator in orbital images generates results with
oversegmentation, mainly coming from textures existing in such images.

In order to attenuate the excess of segments, a technique used on the generation of
marker images, which is one of the input parameters in the used watershed function,
was studied, implemented and used in this work. The technique used was the multi-
scale morphological gradient.

A. Sanfeliu et al. (Eds.): CIARP 2004, LNCS 3287, pp. 156–162, 2004.

2 Mathematical Morphology

According to [3], the mathematical morphology includes the area that deals with structural and topological properties of objects from their images. This way, the several techniques employed in this area, especially when the image continuous domain is concerned, are similar to some of the techniques employed for geometric modeling.

This study is performed from the structuring element, which is characterized as a completely known and defined set (shape, size). Such set is compared, from a transformation, to the image unknown set.

The mathematical morphology is composed of two basic operators: erosion and dilatation. Both operators, once applied separately, are transformations not always enhancing the images characteristics. Anyway, they allow us to construct some very interesting functions, as an example, the morphological gradient, the opening, the closing, the segmentation and others.

2.1 Morphological Segmentation

The current methods for image segmentation basically use two ideas: One of them is finding the contour of objects in the image. The other is assembling points with similar characteristics so that the object of interest is fully reconstructed. The problem of contour identification may be solved with the use of the watershed operator, which is the main morphological segmentation tool, also known as water line.

An intuitive idea of the watershed notion may be composed considering the gray levels image as a topographic surface and assuming that holes have been perforated in each regional minimum of the surface. The surface is then slowly immerged into water. Starting from the minimum at the lowest altitude, the water will progressively flood the retention basins of the image. In addition, dams are raised at the places where the waters coming from two different minimums would emerge. At the end of this flooding procedure, each minimum is surrounded by dams delineating its associated retention basin. The whole set of dams correspond to the watersheds. They provide us with a partition of the input image into its different retention basins [2].

According to [4], watershed associated to the regional minimums set $M = \bigcup_{i \in \Re} m_i$ of an image S may be defined as the union complement of all retention basins $C_f(m_i)$, and it is expressed through the following equation:

$$\text{WL } (f) = [\bigcup_{i \in \Re} C_f(m_i)]^c \tag{1}$$

where: m_i: regional minimum and $C_f(m_i)$: retention basin.

2.2 Morphological Multi-scale Gradient

According to [2], if the size of the structuring element is greater than 1 (mask 3x3), the morphological gradients are defined as thick gradients, which may be expressed through the equation 2:

$$\rho_{nB} = \delta_{nB} - \varepsilon_{nB} \tag{2}$$

where: δ_{nB} represents the dilation operator, with structuring element of size n;

ε_{nB} represents the erosion operator, with structuring element of size n.

The thick gradients are recommended when transitions between objects are smooth. However, such gradients establish thick edges, this way loosing the original location of such edges.

Besides, when the distance between two boudaries of a region is shorter than the width of the structuring element, the resulting edges become one. Both problems can be avoided with the use of the morphological multi-scale gradient.

The thickess of the edges obtained from a thick gradient of size n can be reduced by an erosion ε with element of size "n-1".

According to [2], when thick gradients are originated from two different united edges, the resulting thickness is greater than the concerned structuring element width. Those regions may be removed through the use of the white top-hat *(WTH)* operator by size n, which is then followed by an erosion of size n-1 to output a thin edge at scale n.

The magnitude of the resulting edges is smaller than the magnitude corresponding to the edge's size morphological gradient. The solution is found by adjusting pixels different from zero from the eroded white top-hat for their original value in the thick gradient image. This way, the morphological gradient is defined for the scale n, which is by $\rho^{*}{}_{nB}$ [2], given by the expression 3:

$$\rho^{*}{}_{nB} = \rho_{nB} * T_{[1,t_{max}]}\varepsilon_{(n-1)B}WTH_{nB}\rho_{nB} \tag{3}$$

where ρ_{nB} is conventional morphologic gradient and $T_{[1,tmax]}$ is the threshold.

The edges map for all scales is obtained by calculating the maximum between $\rho^{*}{}_{nB}$ for all n, which is expressed through the equation 4.

$$\rho^{*} = \bigvee_{nB} \rho^{*}_{nB} \tag{4}$$

where $\bigvee_{nB}$ represents the maximum operation for all n.

So we call ρ^{*} the non-parametric multi-scale morphological gradient. Figure 1 illustrates an example of a multi-scale gradient.

Fig. 1. Orbital image (a), multi-scale morphological gradient obtained through the maximum calculation of all multi-scale morphological gradiente $\rho^{*}{}_{nB}$ (b)

The multi-scale gradient allows us to enhance edges of each scale, comparing edges only belonging to a certain scale; in other words, such tool evidences the edges belonging to the original image. This way, the information of interest is better evidenced.

3   Methodology

For the development and achievemet of routines concerning the watershed segmentation, was used the image corresponding to the track of the international airport Antonio Carlos Jobim (Galeão), on 8/1/1987 (path 271, Row 76) from Landsat/TM satellite.

The treatment of the input image in the watershed function was performed in this work through morphological filters. In order to generate the markers images, the achievement of the multi-scale morphological gradient technique, in the MATLAB software environment was performed.

Besides the dilation and erosion operators, white top-hat and threshold were used for the development of the multi-scale gradient, also achieved. Such operator's implemented function requires four parameters, which are the input image, the number of scales, the threshold value and the struturing element.

The perfomed processing sequence began with the input image filtering through the morphological operators, progressively employing the implemented operator for the marker image generation, and the watershed segmentation function was applied.

4   Results

The used watershed segmentation operator has as input parameters, the raw or treated original images, the markers image and the structuring element.

The inlet image used in tests is shown in Figure 2. Figure 3a presents the result of the marker image generated through the multi-scale gradient, processed with 10 scales, threshold 10 and isotropic structuring element. Now figure 3b shows the marker image generated through simple morphologic gradient.

Figures 4a and 4b respectively shows the result from the watershed morphological segmentation with multi-scale gradient marker image and the result from the watershed morphological segmentation with the simple morphologic gradient as marker image.

Fig. 2. Original image

The images presented in 3a and 3b were used as marker images and the results obtained are presented in figures 4a and 4b.

Figure 4a presents less segmentation when compared to the result obtained in 4b. When the result obtained in 4a is analyzed, it is clearly observed that the features of interest are preserved in 4a; the same does not occur in 4b.

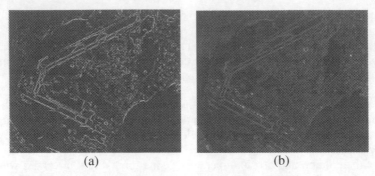

(a)   (b)

Fig. 3. Image resulting from the multi-scale gradient (a), image resulting from simple morphological gradient technique (b)

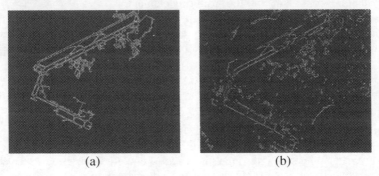

(a)   (b)

Fig. 4. Image resulting from the watershed operator with multi-scale gradient (a), image resulting from the watershed operator with simple morphological gradient (b)

In another test, the markers image generated after the original image passed through a pre-processing stage was used. In this stage, morphological operators with the function of removing contrast peaks higher than the stipulated, removing areas smaller than the stipulated and reconstructing the image with infinite interactions of the contrasted image dilation operator in relation to the inlet image were used. Such result is presented in figure 5.

Fig. 5. Image resulting from the watershed operator with pre-process image original as marker

Comparing the results obtained in figures 4a and 5, one concludes that the result obtained in 4a remains to be the one presenting the best result of all morphological processing used. Such comparison is corroborated when we observe the large amount of segmentation presented in figure 5.

With regard to the application of morphological operators, the work could be considered as concluded, presenting as the best result, as already explained, the result obtained in figure 4a.

In order for this work to emphasize even more the positive contribution of the use of morphological operators aiming at the extraction of linear features of interest from digital images, a comparison between the best result obtained by means of the morphology to conventional techniques of features extraction was performed.

For this, the Sobel operator was applied to the original image with the purpose of obtaining the markers image in order for the conventional Watershed operator to be applied. The results obtained in this processing are presented in figure 6.

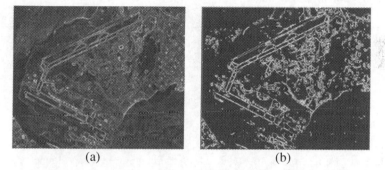

(a)   (b)

Fig. 6. Image resulting from the Sobel detector (a), image resulting from the conventional watershed detector with Sobel detector as marker (b)

The Sobel operator was applied with 3x3 size mask and the conventional watershed operator that best result presented was with initial value of 50.

As final analysis, the comparison between the best result obtained by means of the morphology (figure 4a) to the result obtained through conventional technique (figure 6b) was then performed. From this analysis, it is concluded that the use of the morphology operators presented better result if compared to conventional technique, what corroborates the potential use of the Mathematical morphology in processes of features extraction from digital images.

It is worth emphasizing that in the segmentation process, the treatment performed with the morphological pre-processing operators has fairly improved the final results for the use of the inlet image in the watershed operator, reinforcing the importance of such treatment for the images visual improvement.

5   Conclusions

As conclusion for the tests performed, the result obtained with the application of the morphological watershed using as markers image, the result obtained by means of the multi-scale gradient technique was the best in all analyses and comparisons conducted.

Thus, the use of morphological operators showed to be effective for the task of extracting features from digital images.

It is important emphasizing that the improvement on the results obtained was achieved partly by the treatment performed in the raw image from the pre-processing for the inlet image in the watershed operator process, improving such information may bring on significant results.

The objective of this paper, which was to search for better results with the multi-scale gradient approach, was achieved, bringing positive contributions for the segmentation processes, where watershed is employed.

From all tests performed, even results not presented, but still supporting the analysis, we conclude that the results of applications with the implemented morphological operators were better.

Thus, the morphological segmentation will be able to be employed as an semi-automatic alternative method in features extractions for targets identification tasks or in the cartographic products updating.

Acknowledgements

This work was subsidized by the CNPq and FAPESP, both Brazilian Foundations to Research.

References

1. Meyer, F., Beucher, S.: The morphological approach to segmentation: the watershed transformation. In Dougherty, E. R. Mathematical Morphology in Image Processing. Marcel Dekker, New York. (1993) 433-481
2. Soille, P.: Morphological Image Analysis - Principles and Applications. In Springer-Verlag Berlin Heidelberg (1999) 316
3. Gomes, J., Velho, L.: Computação Gráfica: Imagem. Série de Computação e Matemática, SBM/IMPA (1995)
4. Préteux, F.: On a distance function approach for grey-level mathematical morphology. In Dougherty E.R. Mathematical Morphology in Image Processing. Marcel Dekker, New York (1993) 323-351

3D Object Surface Reconstruction Using Growing Self-organised Networks

Carmen Alonso-Montes and Manuel Francisco González Penedo

Dpto. de Computación, Universidade da Coruña, 15071 A Coruña, Spain
{carmen,cipenedo}@dc.fi.udc.es

Abstract. This paper studies the adaptation of growing self-organised neural networks for 3D object surface reconstruction. Nowadays, input devices and filtering techniques obtain 3D point positions from the object surface without connectivity information. Growing self-organised networks can obtain the implicit surface mesh by means of a clustering process over the input data space maintaining at the same time the spatial-topology relations. The influence of using additional point features (e.g. gradient direction) as well as the methodology characterized in this paper have been studied to improve the obtained surface mesh.

Keywords: Neural networks, Self-organised networks, Growing cell structures, Growing neural gas, 3D surface reconstruction, Gradient direction

1 Introduction

The study of 3D surface reconstruction techniques has become an important aspect of different applications in a variety of scientific areas, such as medicine, mechanical fluids, robotics or virtual reality. The main issue in 3D surface reconstruction is to obtain the mesh which defines the object surface, which is used as a basic 3D model by different applications. Input devices or filtering techniques obtain the 3D scene composed by isolated 3D points without connectivity information. This set of points is usually called unorganised cloud of points. The main step previous to the reconstruction process is to obtain the surface mesh which is defined by the connectivity among the points.

Several studies have focused on developing different algorithms to deal with point connectivity, like is shown in [1], where a new surface reconstruction algorithm is proposed. Obtaining the implicit mesh of the object surface has been tackled by different traditional techniques such as *Marching Cubes* [2] and *Voronoi filtering* [3]. The surface mesh is defined by representative elements and their spatial-topological relations. One disadvantage of using this kind of techniques is the impossibility of unifying the stages of obtaining the representative elements and their spatial-topological relations, which maintain a continuous surface. A further argument against these techniques is that only a point feature can be used. The results obtained are also dependent on the unorganised cloud of points. These techniques cannot deal properly with mesh surface continuity.

A. Sanfeliu et al. (Eds.): CIARP 2004, LNCS 3287, pp. 163–170, 2004.

The research has tended to focus on algorithm improvement rather than studying the influence of using new point features [1]. However, few studies have considered the neural networks for the surface reconstruction problem [4]. The aim of this paper is to characterize a methodology to deal with the 3D surface reconstruction problem by means of growing self-organised networks in order to avoid the disadvantages of traditional techniques and improve previous results of self-organised networks using aditional point features.

2   Growing Self-organised Networks

Self-organised networks are a flexible alternative to deal with the problem of obtaining the implicit surface mesh, since they perform a clustering of the input data space maintaining, at the same time, the spatial-topological relations by means of neurons. The most representative network in this area is the *Self-Organised Map (SOM)*, proposed by Kohonen [5]. This network, whose size and structure are fixed, adjusts itself the values associated with each neuron by means of a cyclic process of comparing input data patterns and weight vectors, learning gradually the input data space. Nevertheless, *SOM* are limited to obtain a true fitted surface mesh because of the fixed topology and size, being necessary the introduction of a *growing* stage [6, 7]. This issue, within this area, can be addressed by means of two main approaches: *Growing Neural Gas (GNG)* [8] and *Growing Cell Structures (GCS)* [9], whose behaviours are based on *SOM*.

   GCS adds new neurons maintaining network topology. In the initialisation stage, it is established a k-dimensional structure of $k+1$ neurons and $(k+1)k/2$ connections, the learning rate for the winning neuron (ε_b), the learning rate for its direct neighbours (ε_n), and the resource values (τ_i) and weights (w_i) for each neuron i (n_i). In the training stage, P input patterns are presented to the net A in groups of λ, called adaptation step, until the stop criterion is satisfied. For each input pattern (ξ), a winning neuron $(\phi_w(\xi))$ is determined by means of the distance between its weight and the input pattern

$$\|w_{\phi_w(\xi)} - \xi\| = \min_{r \in A} \|w_r - \xi\| \tag{1}$$

where $\|.\|$ is the normal Euclidean vector. The weights associated with the winning neuron j and with its direct neighbours (N_j) are updated by means of

$$\begin{aligned} w_j &= w_j + \varepsilon_b(\xi - w_j) \\ w_c &= w_c + \varepsilon_n(\xi - w_c) \ \forall c \in N_j \end{aligned} \tag{2}$$

and the resource value for the winning neuron is updated as

$$\tau_j = \tau_j + \|\xi - w_j\|^2 \tag{3}$$

Every λ patterns a new neuron is added between the neuron (n_i) with the highest resource value and its direct neighbour (n_j) whose resource value is the highest among the direct neighbours (N_i). Their weights and their resource values are updated.

GNG not only allows insertion of new neurons, but also modification and elimination of neurons and connections. In the initialisation stage weights, their resource values, the age parameter for each connection and the learning rates (ε_b and ε_n) are established. In the training stage, P input patterns are presented to the net in groups of λ, until one of the stop criteria is satisfied. For each input pattern (ξ), two winning neurons (n_1, n_2) are determined in the net A

$$n_1 = \min \|\xi - w_c\|, \ \forall c \in A$$
$$n_2 = \min \|\xi - w_c\|, \ \forall c \in A - \{n_1\}$$
$$(4)$$

If these neurons are connected, the resource value (τ_{n_1}) and the weights of both n_1 and its direct neighbours (N_{n_1}) are updated like in *GCS*. The age for each connection of n_1 is increased. Otherwise, a new connection is established between them, initialising its age to 0. After this, the connections whose age parameter is higher than a certain threshold T as well as isolated neurons are removed. Every λ patterns a new neuron is added in a similar way than *GCS*.

3   3D Object Surface Reconstruction Methodology

The methodology proposed in order to deal with 3D object surface reconstruction problem defines several stages (Fig. 1): obtaining the edge points, training the growing self-organised networks, obtaining the surface mesh and finally surface reconstruction.

Fig. 1. Methodology steps

In the first step, 3D images are processed by means of the edge filters. We have used both *Canny edge detector* [10] and *lineal multi-scale filter* [11, 12]. The aim of this step is to obtain the set of surface edges which defines the 3D object surface. Each edge point is defined both by its 3D position (v_x, v_y, v_z) and by its 3D weighted gradient direction (α', β'), which are obtained during the filtering process. The 3D weighted gradient direction is calculated as

$$\alpha' = R \ \sin\left(\arctan\left(G_x/G_y\right)\right) + R, \quad \alpha' \in [0, 2R]$$
$$\beta' = R \ \sin\left(\arctan\left(G_z/G_y\right)\right) + R, \quad \beta' \in [0, 2R]$$
$$(5)$$

where G_i is the gradient in the axis i, $\arctan(G_i/G_j)$ is the direction of the gradient vector measured with respect to the j axis, *sin* function allows to obtain continuous gradient values and R is a scale factor which weights the influence of the feature with respect to the 3D position. This is the main feature to guide the following reconstruction stage. 3D weighted gradient direction feature is used to make a distinction between close point positions. Using this feature, neighbour points belong to different surfaces if they have opposite gradient directions.

The set of edge points, previously obtained, is used for making two different sets of input patterns, used to train GCS and GNG in order to study the influence of using 3D gradient direction feature. In the first set, each input pattern is only represented by its 3D position (v_x, v_y, v_z), and in the second, each of them is represented both by its 3D position and by its weighted gradient direction $(v_x, v_y, v_z, \alpha', \beta')$.

GCS nets can only add new neurons. During the training stage, neighbour neurons can move to distant positions. In such case, connections become inappropriate due to the fact that deletion of connections is not allowed, which also prevents the proper processing of scenes with several objects. A heuristic way is proposed to avoid inappropriate connections. Our approach consists of splitting the training stage into two steps: first, a fast training in order to avoid inappropriate connections and second, a slow training to fit the object surface. The main parameters which have influence on GCS behaviour are ε_b, ε_n and λ. In the first step, a fast training is necessary to adjust the net to the object shape. This is achieved by means of high values for ε_b and ε_n which obtain a fast movement of of the winning neuron and its direct neighbours to the input patterns, and a low value for λ which implies that new neurons are added quickly between far neurons breaking inappropriate connections. The object shape is fitted without regarding the surface adjustment. In the second step, the surface is fitted by the mesh by means of a slow training with low values for ε_b and ε_n and a high value for λ. The training stops when the final size of the network is reached.

GNG nets resolve the previous GCS problems by means of addition, modification and deletion of neurons and connections. Besides the number of neurons, also used in GCS training, a new stop criterion, the global error measure, is employed. The training process stops when the resource value of each neuron of the net is below the global error measure parameter. The influence of both ε_b and ε_n parameters is less outstanding in the training process than in GCS net. The obtained surface mesh, composed by neurons and spatial-topological relations, is used as a basic 3D model by different applications.

4   Results

Two kinds of 3D input images have been employed: synthetic tubular images built up from a serie of fifteen 2D slices and anatomical images based on 64 computed tomography *(CT)* slices from the *Visual Human Project*. The images used for the filtering process (Fig. 2(b) and 3(b)) belong to the 3D scenes in Fig. 2(a) and 3(a), respectively. The synthetic images have been filtered by means of the lineal multi-scale filter obtaining the edge points of the object surface (Fig. 2(c) and 3(c)), whereas anatomical images have been processed by means of the Canny edge detector. The most suitable filter was chosen in each case. The input pattern sets employed in the next stage to train each net have been obtained from these edge points.

Initially, GCS net has been trained using only 3D position feature. As it can be seen from Fig. 2(d), a lot of inappropriate connections appear linking distant neurons due to the fact that the net has been trained in a classical way [9]. However, following the heuristic approach proposed in the previous section these connections have been avoided (Fig. 2(e)). During the fast training stage (Table 1), the 150-neuron net fits the object shape and the slow training, adjusts the mesh to the object surface (Fig. 2(e)), where the final number of neurons fitted to the surface are 905. *GNG* net has been trained with the same input pattern set as in *GCS* case and it has obtained a more accurate surface mesh and a better adjustment (Fig. 2(g)) than *GCS*, specially regarding the original surface continuity (see both mesh details in Fig. 2(f)). The object surface (Fig. 2(h)) has been obtained from the previous obtained mesh.

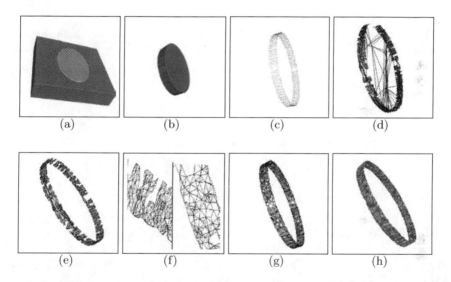

Fig. 2. 2(a) 3D scene. 2(b) 3D object. 2(c) Obtained edge points. 2(d) *GCS* Surface mesh obtained using only 3D positions trained in a classical way. 2(e) Like in 2(d) but with our heuristic approach. 2(f) mesh detail (left) from 2(e) and (right) from the *GNG* mesh surface 2(g). 2(h) Surface reconstruction from 2(g)

From Fig. 3(c) two different input pattern sets have been constructed, one considering only 3D point position feature, and the other considering both 3D position and 3D weighted gradient direction features. In order to guide neuron movement properly, 3D position is approximately four times as important as 3D weighted gradient direction, using a scale factor $R = 32$ (Eq. 5) for 256x256 slices. It has been experimental checked that this weighting maximises the adjustment of the net. However, although the use of our heuristic approach and both features improve the obtained mesh, *GCS* net cannot deal in a proper way with several objects (Fig. 3(d) and 3(e)). *GNG* net has not been able to distinguish close object surfaces employing only 3D position feature (Fig. 3(f) and 3(g)). This problem has been avoided using both 3D position and 3D weighted gradient direction features (Fig. 3(h)) without changing the main training parameters (Table 2).

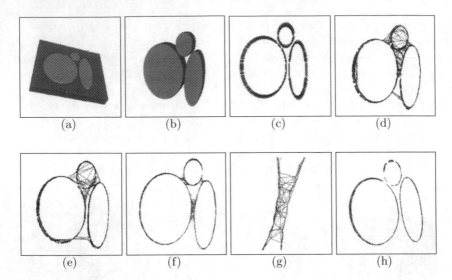

Fig. 3. 3(a) 3D scene. 3(b) 3D object. 3(c) Obtained edge points. 3(d) and 3(e) *GCS* Surface mesh obtained using our heuristic considering respectively, only 3D position feature and both 3D position and 3D gradient direction features. 3(f) *GNG* Surface mesh obtained using only 3D positions. 3(g) Mesh detail from 3(f). 3(h) Like in 3(f) but considering both 3D position and 3D weighted gradient direction features

For anatomical images, *GNG* net has been trained using both 3D position and 3D weighted gradient direction features (Fig. 4(b) and 4(c)). Discarding gradients, surfaces cannot be accurately distinguished (Fig. 4(a)).

The runtime needed for the training stage for each net, measured in seconds (*s.*), and the main training parameters used for each net are shown in Tables 1 and 2. The training stage has been processed in an Athlon XP at 1.667 GHz processor running Linux.

5 Summary and Conclusions

In this paper, self-organised networks are shown as a good choice for 3D surface reconstruction. 3D scenes with several objects cannot be processed properly by

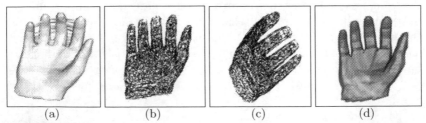

Fig. 4. 4(a) *GNG* mesh surface using only 3D position. 4(b) and 4(c) different views of *GNG* surface mesh using 3D gradient direction 4(d) Surface obtained from 4(b)

Table 1. *GCS* training parameters

Figure		λ	ε_b	ε_n	Input Patterns	Neurons	Runtime
2(d)		150	0.05	0.008	16560	905	7231 s.
2(e)	fast training	6	0.3	0.09	16560	150	1289 s.
	slow training	150	0.05	0.008	16560	905	5923 s.
3(d)	fast training	10	0.2	0.09	22200	50	583 s.
	slow training	150	0.05	0.008	22200	3000	16806 s.
3(e)	fast training	5	0.2	0.09	22200	50	452 s.
	slow training	150	0.05	0.008	22200	3000	17105 s.

Table 2. *GNG* training parameters

Figure	λ	ε_b	ε_n	*Error*	Input Patterns	Neurons	Runtime
2(g)	150	0.05	0.005	0.995	16560	1700	2527 s.
3(f)	150	0.05	0.005	0.995	22200	700	978 s.
3(h)	150	0.05	0.005	0.995	22200	800	1239 s.
4(b) & 4(c)	150	0.05	0.008	0.05	20000	8000	345601 s.

GCS net due to the impossibility of deletion of connections. Distant neurons linked by connections which do not belong to the object surface, appear during early steps of the training process of *GCS* net. The heuristic approach proposed in this paper avoids these connections improving the obtained surface mesh. However, the obtained surface mesh is non-uniform with a lot of broken areas due to the inability to create new connections. *GNG* nets can deal with several objects in a more proper way than *GCS* because the deletion and the establishment of new connections is allowed. Surface mesh obtained by means of *GNG* is more accurate to the original object surface with less time effort than with *GCS*. However, when only 3D point position feature is involved, several close surfaces cannot be distinguished. In this sense, 3D weighted gradient direction feature allows the net to distinguish each surface using the same training parameters. Finally, it can be said that the runtime needed in order to complete the training process (Tables 1 and 2), is lower for *GNG* net than for *GCS* with the same input set. In conclusion, *GNG* net is more suitable than *GCS* for obtaining the surface mesh.

The obtained neurons and their neighbourhood relations are suitable to reconstruct the object surface, being needed far less neurons than input patterns used in other techniques [1]. Therefore, several point features can be used in an easy way in both *GCS* and *GNG* nets improving the obtained surface mesh. In conclusion it can be said that using the methodology characterized in this paper and taking into account new features related to the geometry of the object (like gradient), *GCS* and *GNG* improve the obtained surface mesh.

Acknowledgements

This work has been partly supported by Ministerio de Ciencia y Tecnología (TIC2003-04649-C02-01) and Xunta de Galicia (PGIDIT03TIC10503PR).

References

1. Hoppe, H., DeRose, T., Duchamp, T., McDonald, J., Stuetzle, W.: Surface Reconstruction from Unorganized Points. ACM SIGGRAPH Computer Graphics **26** (1992) 71–78
2. Lorensen, W.E., Cline, H.E.: Marching Cubes: A High Resolution 3D Surface Construction Algorithm. ACM SIGGRAPH Computer Graphics **21** (1987) 163–169
3. Amenta, N., Bern, M.: Surface Reconstruction by Voronoi filtering. In: Proceedings of the 14th Annual Symposium on Computational Geometry. (1998) 39–48
4. Ivrissimtzis, I.P., Jeong, W.K., Seidel, H.P.: Using Growing Cell Structures for Surface Reconstruction. In: Proceedings of the Shape Modeling International 2003, IEEE Computer Society (2003) 78–86
5. Kohonen, T.: The Self-organizing Map. In: Proceedings of the IEEE. Volume 78(9). (1990) 1464–1480
6. Fritzke, B.: Kohonen Feature Maps and Growing Cell Structures–a Performance Comparison. In Hanson, S.J., Cowan, J.D., Giles, C.L., eds.: Advances in Neural Information Processing Systems 5, NIPS 1992, Denver. Volume 5. (1993) 115–122
7. Fritzke, B.: Growing Self-organizing Networks – Why? In: ESANN'96, European Symposium on Artificial Neural Networks. (1996) 61–72
8. Fritzke, B.: A Growing Neural Gas Network Learns Topology. In: Advances in Neural Information Processing Systems. Volume 7. (1995) 864–869
9. Fritzke, B.: Growing Cell Structures – a Self-organizing Network for Unsupervised and Supervised Learning. Neural Networks **7** (1994) 1441–1460
10. Trucco, E., Verri, A.: Introductory Techniques for 3-D Computer Vision. 1 edn. Prentice Hall (1998)
11. Sato, Y., Nakajima, S., Nobuyuki, S., Atsumi, H., Yoshida, S., Koller, T., Gerig, G., Kikinis, R.: Three-dimensional Multi-scale Line Filter for Segmentation and Visualization of Curvilinear Structures in Medical Images. Medical Image Analysis **2** (1998) 143–168
12. Koller, M., Gerig, G., Székely, G., Dettwiler, D.: Multiscale Detection of Curvilinear Structures in 2-D and 3-D Image Data. In: 5th International Conference on Computer Vision. (1995) 864–869

Single Layer Morphological Perceptron Solution to the N-Bit Parity Problem

Gonzalo Urcid[1,*], Gerhard X. Ritter[2], and Laurentiu Iancu[2]

[1] Optics Department, INAOE, Tonantzintla, Pue. 72000, Mexico
gurcid@inaoep.mx
[2] CISE Department, University of Florida, Gainesville, FL 32611–6120, USA
ritter,liancu@cise.ufl.edu

Abstract. Morphological perceptrons use a lattice algebra approach to learn and classify a set of patterns. Dendritic structure combined with lattice algebra operations have properties that are completely different than those of traditional perceptron models. In the present paper, we focus our attention in *single layer morphological perceptrons* that classify correctly the parity of all bit strings of length n, as a *one-class* pattern recognition problem. The n-bit parity problem is the n-dimensional extension of the classic XOR problem in the Euclidean plane and is commonly used as a difficult benchmark to test the performance of training algorithms in artificial neural networks. We present results for values of n up to 10, obtained with a training algorithm based on elimination.

1 Introduction

The n-bit *parity problem* is defined as follows, given a binary n-dimensional input vector, $x = (x_1, \ldots, x_n)$, the parity is 1 if the number of 1's in x is *odd*, otherwise the parity is 0. Arithmetically, the parity equals $(x_1 + \cdots + x_n) \mod 2$. The parity problem, categorized as a statistical neutral problem [1], is known to be a "hard" learning benchmark for neural network classifiers and has been the subject of considerable research and experimentation [2–4]. In [4], a single hidden layer feedforward neural network with $(n/2) + 1$ hidden units for even n, or $(n+1)/2$ hidden units for odd n, without direct connections, and sigmoids for hidden and output units, correctly classifies all 2^n input patterns. The weights of the network are explicitly computed, e.g., the weights between the hidden and output layers are found by solving a system of $h \times h$ linear equations where h is the number of hidden units. For $n \in \{3, \ldots, 7\}$, training experiments by gradient type algorithms using a single or two hidden layer topology with a variable number of hidden units in each layer are reported in [5–7]. Another network architecture based on the majority algorithm [8], solves the parity problem with a $n : n : 1$ topology for n odd, or a $(n + 1) : n : 1$ topology for n even. The network weights equal ± 1 only, it has no direct connections between the input and output layers, and requires n^2 connections from the input layer to the hidden

---

* Corresponding author. Fax: +52 (222) 247-2940; Tel.: +52 (222) 266-3100 Ext.8205

A. Sanfeliu et al. (Eds.): CIARP 2004, LNCS 3287, pp. 171–178, 2004.
© Springer-Verlag Berlin Heidelberg 2004

layer. Stacked vs. cross-validation generalization performance of classifiers have been addressed in [9]; for $n = 9, 13$, generalization accuracy improves rapidly if the number of training exemplars exceeds one third of the entire class, and $\sin(x)$ is used as the activation function for the nodes in the hidden layers. In [10], a reduced number of iterations during the training phase is accomplished by modifying the performance index or the activation function slope used in the Levenberg-Marquardt (LM) optimization technique; a comparison against LM is made for $n = 2, 3, 4$ with $2, \{2, 3\}, 6$ hidden units respectively. A different approach used for 3–8 bit parity problems [11], uses a network that adds a hidden neuron to its hidden layer when several consecutive attempts failed to escape from a local minimum using standard LM. Therefore, neural networks with the least number of hidden units are constructed in agreement with the theoretical results stated in [2, 4].

Recently, the foundation of *morphological perceptrons* (MPs) with dendritic structure was established in [12–16] as a new paradigm in machine learning. It was proved that a single layer morphological perceptron (SLMP) with one output neuron can approximate, to any desired degree of accuracy, any compact set of points in pattern space, whether it is convex or non-convex, connected or not connected, or contains a finite or infinite number of points [13]. Specifically, SLMPs were built to solve the parity problem for $n = 2$ (XOR) and $n = 3$; this paper gives the solution to the general case using SLMPs training by elimination [13, 14].

Our work is organized as follows: Section 2 gives a brief background of single neuron computation based on lattice algebra and describes the basic architecture of an SLMP. Section 3 outlines the SLMP training algorithm based on elimination and Section 4 presents numerical results obtained for values of n up to 10, as well as comments about the neural architecture and its performance. Finally, in Section 5 we give our conclusion to the research presented here.

2   Morphological Perceptrons with Dendrites

Computation at a neurode M in the classical theory of artificial neural networks (ANNs) is performed within the *ring* of real numbers $(\mathbb{R}, +.\times)$, by adding the products of neural values and connection weights from all input neurons connected to M, followed by the application of a nonlinear activation function. Morphological neurocomputation is performed using the *bounded lattice group* $(\mathbb{R}_{\pm\infty}, \wedge, \vee, +)$ where $\mathbb{R}_{\pm\infty}$ is the extended real number system, $\wedge = \min$, $\vee = \max$, and $+$ is addition. Therefore, the output from neuron M is computed as the minimum or maximum of the sums of neural values and corresponding synaptic weights, and it is nonlinear before application of an activation function. To bear a closer resemblance with biological neurons and their processes, *artificial dendrites* with excitatory and inhibitory responses are incorporated in morphological neurons to perform logical computations as suggested by recent research in the biophysics of real neurons (see References in [13]).

Let $N_1, \ldots, N_n$ denote a set of input neurons with dendrites. Assume these neurons provide synaptic input at an output neuron M also with dendrites. The value of the neuron N_i travels along its axonal tree until it reaches the synaptic knobs that make contact with the dendrites of neuron M. The weight w_{ik}^λ is associated to the axonal branch of the neuron N_i terminating on the kth dendrite of M; $\lambda = 0$ represents *inhibitory* input, and $\lambda = 1$ represents *excitatory* input to the dendrite. The kth dendrite of M will respond to the total input received from the neurons $N_1, \ldots, N_n$ and will either reject or pass the input. The value computed at the kth dendrite of M, for input $\boldsymbol{x} \in \mathbb{R}^n$ is given by

$$\tau_k(\boldsymbol{x}) = p_k \bigwedge_{i \in I(k)} \bigwedge_{\lambda \in L(i)} (-1)^{(1-\lambda)}(x_i + w_{ik}^\lambda), \tag{1}$$

where x_i is the value of neuron N_i, $I(k) \subseteq \{1, \ldots, n\}$ is the index set of input neurons with terminal knobs that synapse on the kth dendrite of M, $L_i \subseteq \{0, 1\}$ denotes the two only possible types of synapses the input N_i may have on dendrite k of M, and $p_k \in \{-1, 1\}$ signals if the kth dendrite of M, inhibits ($p_k = -1$) or accepts ($p_k = 1$) the received input. In (1), note that, if $\lambda = 0$, then the input $-(x_i + w_{ik}^0)$ is inhibitory, and excitatory for $\lambda = 1$ since in this case we have $(x_i + w_{ik}^1)$.

The total value received by M is computed as the minimum of $\tau_k(\boldsymbol{x})$ for all $k = 1, \ldots, K$ where K denotes the total number of dendrites of M and its next state is determined by a Heaviside type hard limiter f. Before application of the activation function f, neuron M has its own inhibitory ($p = -1$), or excitatory response ($p = 1$). The final output value of the morphological neuron M is therefore given by

$$y(\boldsymbol{x}) = f\left(p \bigwedge_{k=1}^{K} \left[p_k \bigwedge_{i \in I(k)} \bigwedge_{\lambda \in L(i)} (-1)^{(1-\lambda)}(x_i + w_{ik}^\lambda) \right] \right). \tag{2}$$

A *single layer morphological perceptron* (SLMP) with one output neuron, depicted in Fig. 1, is a morphological neuron endowed with a finite number of dendrites and n input neurons that follows the propagation rule (2). For the n parity problem, we restrict the pattern space to the discrete boolean space $\{0, 1\}^n$ of n-dimensional binary vectors.

3   SLMP Training Algorithm

The architecture of an SLMP is *not* predetermined beforehand. It is during the training phase that the morphological neuron grows new dendrites while the input neurons expand their axonal branches to synapse on the new dendrites to learn the training patterns. The algorithm proposed in [13] is based on elimination of misclassified patterns; basically, an initial hyperbox containing all patterns is reduced through elimination of foreign patterns and smaller regions that enclose them. Training ends when all foreign patterns in the training set have been removed. Removal is performed by computing the intersection of the regions recognized by the grown dendrites, as expressed by the total input value to neuron M, i.e., by $\tau(\boldsymbol{x}) = p_k \bigwedge_{k=1}^{K} \tau_k(\boldsymbol{x})$.

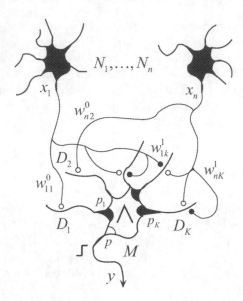

Fig. 1. SLMP with n input neurons N_i and one output neuron M

The SLMP training by elimination algorithm is outlined below and its mathematical description with more detailed steps can be found in [13]. The algorithm builds and trains an SLMP to recognize the training patterns as either belonging to class C_1 (odd parity) or not belonging to it. Hence it solves a *one-class* problem, where the class of interest is denoted by C_1 and the rest of points in pattern space by C_0 (even parity). In the present study, $C_1 \cup C_0 = \{0, 1\}^n$.

Algorithm 3.1. (SLMP training by elimination [17].)

STEP 1. Grow a first dendrite, D_1, that recognizes the hyperbox enclosing all patterns labeled class C_1. This dendrite is excitatory. Initialize the dendrite counter $K = 1$.

STEP 2. Using the K dendrites grown thus far, $D_1, \ldots, D_k$, use (2) to compute the output of the perceptron for each pattern in the training set.

STEP 3. If all training patterns are correctly classified, STOP. Otherwise, increment K and grow another dendrite, D_k. This dendrite will be inhibitory.

STEP 4. Select a pattern in class C_0 that is erroneously classified as belonging to class C_1.

STEP 5. Find a region enclosing the pattern selected in STEP 4 such that this region may also contain other patterns from C_0 but not from C_1.

STEP 6. Assign weights and responses to make dendrite D_K recognize the region determined in STEP 5.

STEP 7. Repeat from STEP 2.

The separation surfaces drawn in pattern space during training are always closed and the trained SLMP will always correctly recognize 100% of the patterns in the training set. Thus, the SLMP procedure based on lattice computation with dendrites provides a competitive learning alternative compared with other multilayer perceptron architectures mentioned in the Introduction [4, 8, 11].

4 Numerical Results and Performance

Each training pattern set for the n parity problem was formed as an augmented matrix T with 2^n rows and $n + 1$ columns, by adjoining the class vector C to the binary matrix B of patterns using the following expressions

$$B_{ij} = \mod (\lfloor (i - 1)2^{j-n} \rfloor, 2), \qquad (3)$$
$$C_i = \mod (B_{i1} + \cdots + B_{in}, 2), \qquad (4)$$

where $i = 1, \ldots, 2^n$ and $j = 1, \ldots, n$. The training algorithm described in 3.1 was applied to each matrix T to generate the corresponding dendritic structure as well as compute the weights and responses of the SLMP that solves the parity problem for $n = 1$ to 10. For example, Table 1 shows the network parameters for $n = 4$.

Table 1. Weights and responses of the SLMP that solves the 4-parity problem

D_k	w^1_{1k}	w^1_{2k}	w^1_{3k}	w^1_{4k}	w^0_{1k}	w^0_{2k}	w^0_{3k}	w^0_{4k}	p_k
1	0	0	0	0	-1	-1	-1	-1	$+1$
2	∞	∞	∞	∞	-1	-1	-1	-1	-1
3	∞	∞	0	0	-1	-1	$-\infty$	$-\infty$	-1
4	∞	0	∞	0	-1	$-\infty$	-1	$-\infty$	-1
5	∞	0	0	∞	-1	$-\infty$	$-\infty$	-1	-1
6	0	∞	∞	0	$-\infty$	-1	-1	$-\infty$	-1
7	0	∞	0	∞	$-\infty$	-1	$-\infty$	-1	-1
8	0	0	∞	∞	$-\infty$	$-\infty$	-1	-1	-1
9	0	0	0	0	$-\infty$	$-\infty$	$-\infty$	$-\infty$	-1

Entries in Table 1 marked with $\pm\infty$ mean that no excitatory/inhibitory connection exists between the input neurons $N_1, \ldots, N_4$, and the dendrites $D_1, \ldots, D_9$ of the output neuron M. Inspection of the parameters for each trained SLMP using Algorithm 3.1 reveals that the *number of dendrites* $K(n)$, and the *number of weights* $w(n)$ (both excitatory and inhibitory) necessary to solve the n-bit parity problem are given by

$$K(n) = 2^{n-1} + 1, \qquad (5)$$
$$w(n) = n(K(n) + 1). \qquad (6)$$

In addition, we observe that the SLMP weight assignments for n-bit parity contains all the weights for $(n - m)$-bit parity for $m = 1, \ldots, n - 2$. For example, the weights for $n = 3$ are embedded in Table 1 and can be extracted by considering the subtable formed by rows $D_1, \ldots, D_5$ and columns $w_{2k}^\lambda, w_{3k}^\lambda, w_{4k}^\lambda$. Similarly, the weights for $n = 2$ (XOR) are obtained as the submatrix from Table 1 with rows D_1, D_2, D_3 and columns $w_{3k}^\lambda, w_{4k}^\lambda$. Therefore, once an SLMP is trained for n-bit parity, the SLMP for $(n - m)$-bit parity can readily be obtained with *no* training; in this case, the weights correspond to the submatrix formed with rows $D_1, \ldots, D_{2^{(n-m)}+1}$ and columns $w_{(1+m)k}^\lambda, \ldots, w_{nk}^\lambda$. The diagram shown in Fig. 2 illustrates the *morphological neural structure* that corresponds to Table 1.

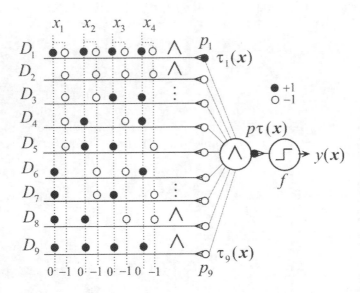

Fig. 2. SLMP structure for 4-parity; 0,-1 at the bottom are weight values

Table 2 displays the number of patterns, the number of dendrites, the number of weights, the *learning time* (LT) needed to find the network parameters (including I/O file operations on data and result sets), and the *recognition time* (RT) spent to classify correctly all patterns in boolean space for $n = 1, \ldots, 10$. We remark that the training phase for each SLMP takes only *one* iteration to complete without any convergence problems. The computer used was a Pentium 4 processor running at 1.2 GHz with 512 Mb main memory.

It is important to remark that direct comparison of the SLMP performance against known *numerical* solutions to the n-bit parity problem, proposed by several researchers, would be difficult since in each reported study different goals and performance measures have been used. For example, in [7], the goal was to compare the average number of epochs between a single hidden layer and a two hidden layer network topology trained by backpropagation. On the other hand, the results presented in [18, 19], were focused to find the minimum number of hidden units in a single hidden layer topology together with the number

Table 2. SLMP performance parameters for the n-bit parity problem

n	2^n	$K(n)$	$\omega(n)$	LT	RT
1	2	1	2	200 ms	20 ms
2	4	3	8	310 ms	20 ms
3	8	5	18	420 ms	20 ms
4	16	9	40	550 ms	20 ms
5	32	17	90	760 ms	30 ms
6	64	33	204	1.71 sec	70 ms
7	128	65	462	8.75 sec	240 ms
8	256	129	1,040	1.13 min	1.01 sec
9	512	257	2,322	9.54 min	4.38 sec
10	1,024	513	5,140	1.4 hrs	19.05 sec

of iterations needed to converge, respectively, by a dynamic node creation or a feedforward neural network construction algorithm. Interested readers with the n-bit parity problem as a pattern recognition challenge, will find specific examples related to computer experiments and numerical results using a wide variety of learning algorithms in [5, 7, 10, 11, 18, 19].

5   Conclusion

The n-bit parity problem will remain a tough benchmark used to test the learning performance in artificial neural networks, as well as an interesting pattern recognition problem by itself. The lattice algebra approach, coupled with the novel idea of introducing dendrite computation in neurodes has conducted our research in different directions to tackle non-trivial classification problems. As demonstrated in this paper, trained SLMPs, configured with specific excitatory and inhibitory weights and responses in dendrites, imitate biological neurons more closely than their traditional artificial models. The SLMP learning algorithm "grows" dendrites as needed and the n-bit parity data set is an extreme case corresponding to a *worst* case situation. However, SLMPs offer complete recognition capability as well as competitive computational performance in comparison to other artificial neural network architectures and training algorithms. Future research with the SLMP training algorithm used here, will consider its computational complexity and its application to other benchmark problems.

References

1. Thornton, C.: Parity: the problem that won't go away. Proc. of Artificial Intelligence, Toronto, Canada (1996) 362–374.
2. Sontag, E. D.: Feedforward nets for interpolation and classification. Journal of Computer and System Sciences **45** (1992) 20–48.
3. Duch W.: Scaling properties of neural classifiers. Proc. 3rd Conf. on Neural Networks and their Applications, Kule, Poland (1997) 663–670.

4. Setiono, R.: On the solution of the parity problem by using a single hidden layer feedforward neural network. Neurocomputing **16**(3) (1997) 1059–1065.
5. Looney, C. G.: Pattern Recognition using Neural Networks. Theory and Algorithms for Engineers and Scientists. Oxford University Press, New York, USA (1997).
6. Setiono, R: Algorithmic techniques and their applications, in Neural Networks Systems, Techniques, and Applications, C. T. Leondes, Ed. Academic Press, San Diego, California, USA **5** (1998) 296–301.
7. Hjelmås, E.: A comment on the parity problem. Technical Report (7), Gjøvik University College, Norway (1999).
8. Park, C-Y., Nakajima K.: Majority algorithm: a formation for neural networks with the quantized connection weights. IEICE Trans. Fundamentals **E83-A**(6) (2000) 225–235.
9. Ghorbani, A. A., Owrangh K.: Stacked generalization in neural networks: generalization on statistically neutral problems. IEEE Proc. IJCNN, Washington, DC, USA (2001) 1715–1720.
10. Wilamowski, B. M. et al.: An algorithm for fast convergence in training neural networks. IEEE Proc. IJCNN, Washington, D.C., USA (2001) 1778–1782.
11. Liu, D., Chang T-S., Zhang Y.: A constructive algorithm for feedforward neural networks with incremental training. IEEE Trans. on Circuits and Systems **49**(12) (2002) 1876–1879.
12. Ritter, G. X., Urcid, G., Selfridge R.:Minimax dendrite computation. ASME Proc. ANNIE, St. Louis Missouri, USA **12**(2002) 75–80.
13. Ritter, G. X., Urcid G.: Lattice algebra approach to single neuron computation. IEEE Trans. on Neural Networks **14**(2) (2003) 282–295.
14. Ritter, G. X., Iancu, L., Urcid G.: Morphological perceptrons with dendritic structure. Proc. FUZZ-IEEE, St. Louis, Missouri, USA (2003) 1296–1301.
15. Ritter, G. X., Iancu, L.: Lattice algebra approach to neural networks and pattern classification. Proc. 6th Open German-Russian Workshop on Pattern Recognition and Image Understanding, Katun Village, Altai Region, Russian Federation (2003) 18–21.
16. Ritter, G. X., Iancu, L., Urcid G.: Neurons, dendrites, and pattern recognition. Proc. 8th Iberoamerican Congress on Pattern Recognition, Havana, Cuba (2003) 1296–1301.
17. Ritter, G. X., Iancu, L.: Lattice algebra, dendritic computing, and pattern recognition. Invited tutorial, 8th Iberoamerican Congress on Pattern Recognition, Havana, Cuba (2003) 16–24.
18. Ash, T.: Dynamic node creation in backpropagation networks. Connectionist Science **1** (1989) 365–375.
19. Setiono, R., Hui, L. C. K.: Use of quasi-Newton method in a feedforward neural network construction algorithm. IEEE Transactions on Neural Networks **6** (1995) 273–277.

Robust Self-organizing Maps*

Héctor Allende[1], Sebastián Moreno[1], Cristian Rogel[1], and Rodrigo Salas[1,2]

[1] Universidad Técnica Federico Santa María,
Dept. de Informática, Casilla 110-V, Valparaíso-Chile
{hallende,smoreno,crogel,rsalas}@inf.utfsm.cl
[2] Universidad de Valparaíso, Departamento de Computación
Rodrigo.Salas@uv.cl

Abstract. The Self Organizing Map (SOM) model is an unsupervised learning neural network that has been successfully applied as a data mining tool. The advantages of the SOMs are that they preserve the topology of the data space, they project high dimensional data to a lower dimension representation scheme, and are able to find similarities in the data.

However, the learning algorithm of the SOM is sensitive to the presence of noise and outliers as we will show in this paper. Due to the influence of the outliers in the learning process, some neurons (prototypes) of the ordered map get located far from the majority of data, and therefore, the network will not effectively represent the topological structure of the data under study.

In this paper, we propose a variant to the learning algorithm that is robust under the presence of outliers in the data by being resistant to these deviations. We call this algorithm Robust SOM (RSOM). We will illustrate our technique on synthetic and real data sets.

Keywords: Self Organizing Maps, Robust Learning Algorithm, Data Mining, Artificial Neural Networks.

1 Introduction

The Self-Organizing Map (SOM) was introduced by T. Kohonen [7] and is one of the most popular neural network models. The SOM has proven to be a valuable tool in data mining and in Knowledge Discovery Database (KDD) with various engineering applications in pattern recognition, image analysis, process monitoring and fault diagnosis.

The success of the SOM is due to its special property of effectively creating spatially organized *internal representations* of various features of input signals and their abstractions [6]. The SOM quantizes the data space formed by the training data and simultaneously performs a topology-preserving projection of the data onto a regular low-dimensional grid. The grid can be used efficiently in visualization. The SOM implements an ordered dimensionality-reducing map of the data and follows the probability density function of the data.

* This work was supported in part by Research Grant Fondecyt 1040365 and 7040051 and in part by Research Grant DGIP-UTFSM

A. Sanfeliu et al. (Eds.): CIARP 2004, LNCS 3287, pp. 179–186, 2004.

In real data there may exist outliers, data items lying very far from the main body of the data. Neural networks are not robust to the presence of outliers as we have shown in early work [1]. It is also possible that the outliers are not erroneous but that some data items really are strikingly different from the rest, for this reason it is not advisable to discard the outliers and instead special attention must be paid.

In this paper, we show that the SOM is not robust and we propose a variant to the learning algorithm that diminishes the influence of outliers, but still considers them during the training. We call this model RSOM (Robust Self Organizing Maps). The remainder of this paper is organized as follows. The next section briefly presents the Kohonen SOM algorithm. In the third section, we will give a detailed discussion on our method of generating a feature map that is robust to the presence of outliers in the data. Simulation results on synthetic and real data sets are provided in the fourth section. Conclusions and further work are given in the last section.

2 Self-organizing Maps

The SOM may be described formally as a nonlinear, ordered, smooth mapping of high-dimensional input data manifolds onto the elements of a regular, low-dimensional array.

The self-organizing maps (SOM) algorithm is an iterative procedure capable of representing the topological structure of the input space (discrete or continuous) by a discrete set of prototypes (*weight vectors*) which are associated to neurons of the network. The SOM maps the neighboring input patterns onto neighboring neurons.

The map is generated by establishing a correspondence between the input signals $\underline{x} \in \chi \subseteq \mathbb{R}^n$, $\underline{x} = [x_1, ..., x_n]^T$, and neurons located on a discrete lattice. The correspondence is obtained by a competitive learning algorithm consisting of a sequence of training steps that iteratively modifies the weight vector $\underline{m}_k \in \mathbb{R}^n$, $\underline{m}_k = (m_1^k, ..., m_n^k)$, of the neurons, where k is the location of the prototype in the lattice.

When a new signal $\underline{x}$ arrives every neuron competes to represent it. The best matching unit (bmu) is the neuron that wins the competition and with its neighbors on the lattice they are allowed to learn the signal. Neighboring neurons will gradually specialize to represent similar inputs, and the representations will become ordered on the map lattice.

The best matching unit is the reference vector c that is nearest to the input and is obtained by some metrics, $\|\underline{x} - \underline{m}_c\| = \min_i\{\|\underline{x} - \underline{m}_i\|\}$. In general, the Euclidean distance is used,

$$\|\underline{x} - \underline{m}_i\|_E = \sqrt{(\underline{x} - \underline{m}_i)^T(\underline{x} - \underline{m}_i)} = \sqrt{\sum_{j=1}^{n}(x_j - m_i^j)^2} \tag{1}$$

The winning unit and its neighbors adapt to represent the input by modifying their reference vectors towards the current input. The amount the units learn will be governed by a neighborhood kernel $h_c(j, t)$, which is a decreasing function of the distance between the unit j and the bmu c on the map lattice at time t. The kernel is usually given by a Gaussian function:

$$h_c(j, t) = \alpha(t) \exp\left(\frac{-\|\underline{r}_j - \underline{r}_c\|^2}{2\sigma(t)^2}\right) \tag{2}$$

where $\underline{r}_j$ and $\underline{r}_c$ denote the coordinates of the neurons c and i in the lattice, $\alpha(t)$ is the learning rate parameter and $\sigma(t)$ is the neighborhood range. In practice the neighborhood kernel is chosen to be wide in the beginning of the learning process to guarantee global ordering of the map, and both its width and height decrease slowly during learning.

The learning parameter function $\alpha(t)$ is a monotonically decreasing function with respect to time, for example this function could be linear $\alpha(t) = \alpha_0 + (\alpha_f - \alpha_0)t/t_\alpha$ or exponential $\alpha(t) = \alpha_0(\alpha_f/\alpha_0)^{t/t_\alpha}$, where α_0 is the initial learning rate (< 1.0), α_f is the final rate (≈ 0.01) and t_α is the maximum number of iteration steps to arrive α_f. The final result is not greatly affected by the selection of this function [10]

During the learning process at time t the reference vectors are changed iteratively according to the following adaptation rule,

$$\underline{m}_j(t+1) = \underline{m}_j(t) + h_c(j, t)[\underline{x}(t) - \underline{m}_j(t)] \qquad j = 1..M \tag{3}$$

where M is the number of prototypes that must be adjusted. If we consider the following neighborhood:

$$h_c^*(j, t) = \frac{h_c(j, t)}{\alpha(t)} = \exp\left(-\frac{\|\underline{r}_c - \underline{r}_j\|^2}{2\sigma^2(t)}\right) \tag{4}$$

with a discrete data set and a fixed neighborhood kernel $h_c^*(j, t)$, the quantization error or the distortion measure that is stochastically minimized by the SOM [9], is

$$E = \sum_{i=1}^{N}\sum_{j=1}^{M} h_c(j, t)^* \|\underline{x}_i - \underline{m}_j\|^2 \tag{5}$$

where N is the number or training samples, and M is the number of map units. Some properties of the SOM can be found in [3].

Besides the classical SOM, there exist some variants to this algorithm, but we will not treat them here. For example, we can mention the K-means, Learning Vector Quantization and Neural Gas (see [7]).

3   Robust Self-organizing Map (RSOM)

Most data mining applications involve data that is contaminated by outliers. The identification of outliers can lead to the discovery of truly unexpected knowledge in areas such as electronic commerce exceptions, bankruptcy, credit card fraud. One approach to identifying outliers is to assume that the outliers have a different distribution with respect to the remaining observations.

As we mention before, real data are not free of outlying observations and special care should be taken in the learning process to preserve the most important topological and metric relationships of the primary data items. In such cases it would be desirable that the outliers would not affect the result of the analysis. Each outlier affects only one map unit and its neighborhood.

First we will show that the learning algorithm given by equation (3) is not robust in the sense of Hampel criterion [4] when an outliying observation is presented. Suppose that an observation $\underline{x}$ is very distant from the majority of the data and therefore from the map. The distance from the best matching unit to the outlier has big magnitude and the learning step of this unit and its neighbors neurons moves the map towards the outlier and apart from the remaining observations. To measure this impact we used the supremum of the learning step over the whole input space

$$\sup_{\underline{x} \in \chi} \left(h_c^*(j)[\underline{x} - \underline{m}_j] \right) = \infty \tag{6}$$

i.e., the learning step is not bounded and indeed not B-robust [4], and the parameter estimation process is badly affected. To overcome this problem we propose to diminish the influence of the outliers by introducing a robust $\psi(\cdot)$ function, $\psi : \chi \times \mathcal{M} \to \mathbb{R}^n$, $\underline{m}_i \in \mathcal{M} \subseteq \mathbb{R}^n$, in the update rule as follows:

$$\underline{m}_i(t+1) = \underline{m}_i(t) + h_c(i,t)\psi \left(\frac{\underline{x}(t) - \underline{m}_i(t)}{s_i(t)} \right) \tag{7}$$

where $s_i(t)$ is a robust estimation of the variance of the data modelled by the neuron i. To estimate $s_i(t)$ we use a variant of the MEDA function given by:

$$s_i(t) = 1.483 \; median \left\{ |h_c^*(i,t)[\underline{x} - \underline{m}_i] - median(h_c^*(i,t)[\underline{x} - \underline{m}_i]|)\right\} \tag{8}$$

For example the Huber function could be used, which is given by $\psi_H(\underline{x}, \underline{m}_i) = sgn(\underline{r}_i)min\{|\underline{r}_i|, \delta\}$, $\delta \in \mathbb{R}^+$, $\underline{r}_i = (\underline{x} - \underline{m}_i)/s_i$

The quantization error that the robust learning algorithm (7) stochastically minimized is given by the following expression:

$$E = \sum_{i=1}^{N} \sum_{j=1}^{M} h_c^*(j,t)\rho \left(\frac{x_i - m_j}{s_j} \right) \tag{9}$$

where $\rho : \chi \times \mathcal{M} \to \mathbb{R}$ is a convex, symmetric with derivative $\psi(\underline{x}, \underline{m}) = \frac{\partial \rho(\underline{x}, \underline{m})}{\partial m}$. The conditions that the function $\rho(\underline{x}, \underline{m})$ and $\psi(\underline{x}, \underline{m})$ must fulfill can be found in [5].

4   Simulation Results

4.1   Experiment #1: Computer Generated Data

In order to see how the RSOM algorithm performs under a synthetic situation, the process was affected by an outlier generating process. Two clusters of spherical Gaussian distribution in 2 dimensions were constructed. A total of 500 training samples were drawn, where the expected size of each cluster was 250. In addition additive outliers were introduced.

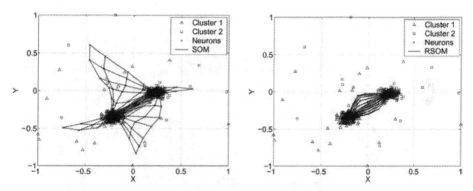

Fig. 1. Synthetic data results: Computer generated data with 5% outliers. (Left) Classical SOM modelling the data, the map is affected by the outliers as can be noted by the wings created in the map. (Right) Robust SOM modelling the data, the map is less affected and does not open towards the outliers.

Let $\chi_N = \{(x_1^i, x_2^i)\}_{i=1..N}$ be the independent sampled data from the gaussian distribution $\underline{X} = (X_1, X_2) \sim \mathcal{N}(\mu_k, \Sigma_k)$, $k = 1, 2$, where μ_k and Σ_k are the mean and the covariance matrix of the cluster k, and $\mathcal{N}(\mu_k, \Sigma_k)$ a two-dimensional gaussian distribution.

The observational process $\underline{z} = (z_1, z_2)$ is obtained by adding additive outliers: $\underline{Z} = \underline{X} + V\,U$, where V is zero-one process with $P(V \neq 0) = \gamma$, $0 < \gamma \ll 1$ and U has distribution $\mathcal{N}(\underline{0}, \Sigma_U)$ with $|\Sigma_U| \gg |\Sigma_k|, k = 1, 2$.

For the simulations we consider the following values for the data generation: $\mu_1 = [6, 4]^T$, $\Sigma_1 = 0.9 * I_2$, $\mu_2 = [-2, -3]^T$, $\Sigma_2 = 0.9 * I_2$, $\Sigma_U = 9 * I_2$ where I_2 is the identity matrix of size 2. The generating process was affected with $\gamma = 0\%, 1\%, 5\%, 10\%$ and 20% of outliers. To model this data we construct a SOM lattice with sizes 5×5 and 9×9.

In figure 1 synthetic data, the SOM model and the RSOM model are shown from left to right. The size of the map showed in the figure is 15×15. The Classical SOM is affected by outliers as can be noted by the wings created in the map, nevertheless the Robust SOM is less affected because it does not open towards the outliers. In table 1 the simulation results are shown.

In figure 2 a comparative study is shown, where in the left side the percentage of outliers in the data was fixed to 10%, and the graph of the Error v/s the

Table 1. Summary results showing the performance of the classical and robust learning methods with several sizes using the synthetic datasets. The column *Algorithm* is the type of learning algorithm, *Dim* gives the size of the map, *Neurons* gives the number of prototypes used, column $E1$ and $E2$ are the quantization error (9) of the test set consisting in 250 samples, $E1$ considers the data with outliers, $E2$ does not. Finally, columns $E3$ and $E4$ are the percentage of misclassification using the test set by considering and not considering the presence of outliers respectively.

Algorithm	Dim.	Neurons	% outliers	E1	E2	E3%	E4%
SOM	5X5	25	0	36.58	36.58	0.00	0.00
RSOM	5X5	25	0	76.77	76.77	0.00	0.00
SOM	9X9	81	0	15.58	15.58	0.00	0.00
RSOM	9X9	81	0	22.75	22.75	0.02	0.02
SOM	5X5	25	1	13.09	8.29	0.01	0.01
RSOM	5X5	25	1	22.37	16.76	0.00	0.00
SOM	9X9	81	1	8.04	4.13	0.00	0.00
RSOM	9X9	81	1	10.32	5.22	0.00	0.00
SOM	5X5	25	5	10.58	6.19	0.02	0.00
RSOM	5X5	25	5	16.05	10.32	0.02	0.00
SOM	9X9	81	5	7.28	4.33	0.02	0.01
RSOM	9X9	81	5	10.17	4.30	0.04	0.02
SOM	5X5	25	10	12.56	7.46	0.03	0.00
RSOM	5X5	25	10	15.59	9.55	0.03	0.00
SOM	9X9	81	10	9.16	9.16	0.07	0.02
RSOM	9X9	81	10	11.72	5.97	0.05	0.00
SOM	5X5	25	20	14.05	7.03	0.08	0.01
RSOM	5X5	25	20	19.28	7.20	0.05	0.00
SOM	9X9	81	20	7.66	10.20	0.10	0.02
RSOM	9X9	81	20	16.30	4.56	0.09	0.02

number of neurons for the SOM and RSOM are shown. In the right side the number of neurons was fixed to 81 and the graph of the Error v/s the percentage of outliers for the SOM and RSOM are shown and the evaluation of the test error by considering the outliers ($E1$) and without considering them ($E2$). As can be noted in the figure, the RSOM evaluated without outliers outperforms the other methods with increasing number of neurons or percentage of outliers. The SOM with bigger number of neurons tends to approximate the outliers and a poor performance is obtained if they are not considered. The quantization error $E1$ of the RSOM is worst than in the other cases with an increasing percentage of outliers implying that this is not a good performance measure when the data has outliers. When there are no outliers the classical method obtained better performance, but most real data are contaminated with outliers.

4.2   Experiment #2: Real Datasets

The second application consists of a real dataset known as the *Wisconsin Breast Cancer Database* obtained from the UCI Machine Learning repository [2] and

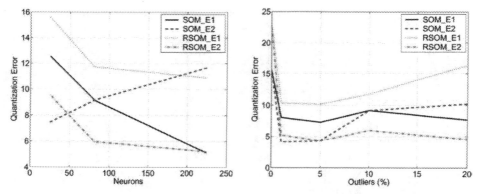

Fig. 2. Comparative Graph: (Left) The percentage of outliers in the data was fixed to 10%, and the graph of the Error v/s the number of neurons for the SOM and RSOM are shown. (Right) The number of neurons was fixed to 81 and the graph of the Error v/s the percentage of outliers for the SOM and RSOM are shown.

was collected by Dr. Wolberg, N. Street and O. Mangasarian at the University of Wisconsin [8]. The samples consist of visually assessed nuclear features of fine needle aspirates (FNAs) taken from patients' breasts. Each sample describes characteristics of the cell nuclei present in the image. It consist in 569 instances, with 30 real-valued input features and a diagnosis (M = malignant, B = benign) for each patient. Malignancy is determined by taking a sample tissue from the patient's breast and performing a biopsy on it. A benign diagnosis is confirmed either by biopsy or by periodic examination, depending on the patient's choice.

To model this data we construct a SOM lattice with sizes 3×3, 5×5, 7×7 and 9×9. In table 2 the performance of the classical and robust learning methods with several sizes are shown. The $E1$ column gives the quantization error and the $E3$ column the percentage of misclassification. The RSOM has worst performance in the quantization error $E1$, because, as shown in the previous example, the measure used considers only the global behavior. For these reason the classical SOM tends to approximate the outliers, and the quantization error is better than the RSOM. But, if the misclassification error is observed (column $E3$), the RSOM shows better results than the SOM.

5   Concluding Remarks

In this paper we introduce a Robust Self Organizing Map (RSOM) for modelling data that were affected by outliers. We apply a robust learning algorithm to the classical SOM to diminish the influence of the outlier in the learning process. We demonstrate that the classical update rule used to learn the data is not robust when there are samples that are very different (far) from the majority.

The performance of our algorithm shows better results in the simulation study in both the synthetic and real data sets. In the synthetic data set we study several degree of contamination and different networks sizes and we made

Table 2. Summary results showing the performance of the classical and robust learning methods with several sizes using the Wisconsin Breast Cancer Database.

Algorithm	Dim.	Neurons	Quantization Error (**E1**)	Misclassification Error (**E3** %)
SOM	3X3	9	565.14	0.0710
RSOM	3X3	9	559.74	0.1183
SOM	5X5	25	473.19	0.0888
RSOM	5X5	25	475.54	0.0296
SOM	7X7	49	417.59	0.1006
RSOM	7X7	49	448.50	0.0769
SOM	9X9	81	389.14	0.1420
RSOM	9X9	81	421.12	0.0947

a comparative analysis showing that the RSOM outperforms the SOM. In the real case, we investigate a benchmark named Wisconsin Breast Cancer Database that were studied by several researches. The RSOM shows better topology representation than the SOM obtaining better classification performance of the patients.

We also present our concern about the need of an error measure that considers the local behavior, because the quantization error given in equation (9) is global, and does not show the quality of the topology representation. Further studies are needed in order to analyze the convergence, the ordering properties together with the stationary states, metastability and convergence rate of the RSOM.

References

1. H. Allende, C. Moraga, and R. Salas, *Robust estimator for the learning process in neural networks applied in time series*, ICANN. LNCS **2415** (2002), 1080–1086.
2. C.L. Blake and C.J. Merz, *UCI repository of machine learning databases*, 1998.
3. E. Erwin, K. Obermayer, and K. Schulten, *Self-organizing maps: ordering, convergence properties and energy functions*, Biological Cybernetics **67** (1992), 47–55.
4. F.R. Hampel, E.M. Ronchetti, P.J. Rousseeuw, and W.A. Stahel, *Robust statistics*, Wiley Series in Probability and Mathematical Statistics, 1986.
5. Peter J. Huber, *Robust statistics*, Wiley Series in probability and mathematical statistics, 1981.
6. T. Kohonen, *The self-organizing map*, Proceedings of the IEEE, vol. 78, 1990, pp. 1464–1480.
7. _____, *Self-Organizing Maps*, vol. 30, Springer Verlag, 2001.
8. O. Mangasarian, W. Street, and W. Wolberg, *Breast cancer diagnosis and prognosis via linear programming*, Operations Research **43** (1995), no. 4, 570–577.
9. H. Ritter and K. Schulten, *Kohonen's self organizing maps: Exploring their computational capabilities*, IEEE ICNN 88 **I** (1988), 109–116.
10. M. Su and H. Chang, *Fast self-organizing feature map algorithm*, IEEE Trans. on Neural Networks **11** (2000), no. 3, 721–733.

Extended Associative Memories
for Recalling Gray Level Patterns

Humberto Sossa[1], Ricardo Barrón[1], Francisco Cuevas[2],
Carlos Aguilar[1], and Héctor Cortés[1]

[1] Centro de Investigación en Computación - IPN
Av. Juan de Dios Bátiz s/n, Esquina con Miguel Othón de Mendizábal
Colonia Nueva Industrial Vallejo, C. P. 07700, México, D. F. Mexico
[2] Centro de Investigaciones en Óptica, A. C.
Apdo. Postal 1-948, León, Guanajuato, México

Abstract. We show how the binary $\alpha\beta$ associative memories recently proposed by Yáñez in [1] can be extended to work now in the gray-level case. To get the desired extension we take the operators α and β, foundation of the $\alpha\beta$ memories, and propose a more general family of operators among them the original operators α and β are a subset. For this we formulate a set of functional equations, solve this system and find a family of solutions. We show that the α and β originally proposed in [1] are just a particular case of this new family. We give the properties of the new operators. We then use these operators to build the extended memories. We provide the conditions under which the proposed extended memories are able to recall a pattern either from the pattern's fundamental set or from altered versions of them. We provide real examples with images where the proposed memories show their efficiency.

1 Introduction

An associative memory $\mathbf{M}$ is a system that relates input vectors, and outputs vectors as follows: $\mathbf{x} \to \mathbf{M} \to \mathbf{y}$ with $\mathbf{x}$ and $\mathbf{y}$, respectively the input and output patterns vectors. Each input vector forms an association with a corresponding output vector.

An associative memory, $\mathbf{M}$ is represented by a matrix whose ij-th component is m_{ij}. $\mathbf{M}$ is generated from a finite a priori set of known associations, known as the *fundamental set of associations*, or simply the *fundamental set* (FS). If ξ is an index, the fundamental set is represented as: $\left\{ \left(\mathbf{x}^\xi, \mathbf{y}^\xi \right) \mid \xi = 1, 2, \dots, p \right\}$ with p the cardinality of the set. The patterns that form the fundamental set are called *fundamental patterns*.

If it holds that $\mathbf{x}^\xi = \mathbf{y}^\xi \ \forall \ \xi \in \{1, 2, \dots p\}$, $\mathbf{M}$ is auto-associative, otherwise it is hetero-associative. A distorted version of a pattern x to be recuperated will be denoted as $\tilde{\mathbf{x}}$. If when feeding a distorted version of $\mathbf{x}^w$ with $w \in \{1, 2, \dots, p\}$ to an associative memory $\mathbf{M}$, it happens that the output corresponds exactly to the associated pattern $\mathbf{y}^w$, we say that recuperation is perfect.

Many ways to build an associative memory have been reported in the literature. Recently, Yáñez in [1], the authors describe a new class of associative memories, the so-called $\alpha\beta$ memories. Their functioning is founded in two binary operators: α and

A. Sanfeliu et al. (Eds.): CIARP 2004, LNCS 3287, pp. 187–194, 2004.
© Springer-Verlag Berlin Heidelberg 2004

β. In the properties of these two important operators lays the power of the above-mentioned memories. These memories work very well in the presence of additive or subtractive noise; its domain is however restricted to the binary one. In this work we extend this class of associative memories to work but with gray-level patterns. For this we solve a systems of functional equations by using some of the central properties of the original α and β.

2   Development of the Extended Memories

In this section the extended memories are developed. First we derive the extended operators **A** and **B** operators. The new memories are then developed. We also investigate the conditions under which the extended memories are able to recall patterns either from the fundamental set or from altered versions of them. Due to space limitations we only memories of type **M** are described.

2.1   Operators A and B

When the $\alpha\beta$ memories make use of the α and β operators described in [10] its range of usability is $[0,1]$; when they make use of the extended operators A and B, introduced in this section, its range as we will see is the gray-level: $[0, L-1]$, with L the number of gray levels. We will use the symbols, A and B to denote the extended operators, the capitals of α and β. Taking into account the properties of the original binary operators α and β described in Section 2.1, one way to find a generalization consists on formulating a system of functional equations [7]. It can be shown that in this case the system should have the following form:

$$B(A(x,y),y)= x$$
$$B((x \vee y),z)= B(x,z)\vee B(y,z) \tag{1}$$

As we will later see, these two properties of A and B are all that we need to characterize most of the solutions of interest. Once a family of solutions is found, one should show that the α and β originally proposed in [6] are just a particular case of this new family. By taking into account Cauchy's functional equation [8], we propose as initial solution the following:

$$A(x,y)= f(x)+g(y)$$
$$B(x,y)= p(x)+q(y) \tag{2}$$

If A and B have this form, the matter of being increasing or decreasing with respect to x or y reduces to the fact that f, g, p, q, be also increasing or decreasing. As we will also see, distributivity by the left with respect to the **max** operator is equivalent to the fact that B is increasing with respect to its first element. As can be seen, the problem is already solved by means of the second equation. With this, we can see that we only need to focus on the inverse left relation between A and B . By taking into account the proposed structure for A and B we have:

$$B(\alpha(x,y))= p(f(x)+g(y))+q(y)= x \tag{3}$$

p distributes in its argument only if it is a solution of Cauchy's equation [8], this is p is a homotecy of the form $p(x) = cx$ where c is an arbitrary constant. Then

$$pf(x)+ pg(y)+q(y)= x. \tag{4}$$

This implies that

$$pf(x)= x,(pg +q)(y)= 0. \tag{5}$$

Thus, $p = f^{-1}$, $q = -f^{-1}g$

As a first observation, we have that once established the parameters of A, those of B are determined. Also as p is a homotecy, f, its inverse, also is. Taking f as the most simple homotecy (the identity) we have:

$$f(x)= x, p(x)= x, q =-g . \tag{6}$$

If also g is minus the identity, A and B are as follows:

$$A(x,y)= x- y \tag{7}$$
$$B(x, y)= x+ y$$

On the other hand, it can be shown that when adding a constant, let say k to A, generates a non-linearity on B, this is:

$$A(x,y)= x- y+k . \tag{8}$$

This implies that $B(x, y)= \phi(x+ y)$ where ϕ is non-linear function.

The family of binary operators generated this way allows us to obtain, on the one hand, the expression for binary operators α and β, where ϕ (Figure 1) is the sep function centered on 1:

$$\alpha(x,y)= x- y+1 \tag{9}$$
$$\beta(x,y)= \phi(x+ y)$$

$$\phi(x)= \begin{cases} 0 & x \le 1 \\ 1 & x > 1 \end{cases}. \tag{10}$$

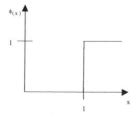

Fig. 1. Graph of ϕ.

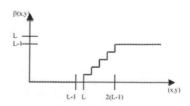

Fig. 2. Graph of B.

On the other hand, the same family of operators allows us to obtain an expression for patterns with L gray levels, whose discrete domain is, for example $A = \{0,1,2,\ldots,L-1\}$, in this case A and B take the form

$$
\begin{aligned}
\mathrm{A}(x,y) &= x - y + L - 1 \\
\mathrm{B}(x,y) &= \phi(x+y)
\end{aligned}
\tag{11}
$$

where now ϕ is in this case the staircase function (Figure 2) defined as follows:

$$
\mathrm{B}(x,y) = \begin{cases} 0 & \text{if } (x+y) \leq L-1 \\ x+y-(L-1) & \text{if } L \leq x+y < 2(L-1) \\ L-1 & \text{if } (x+y) \geq 2(L-1) \end{cases}
\tag{12}
$$

Functions A and B have the same form as in the binary case, this is: $A : A \times A \to B$ and $B : B \times A \to A$ where now $A = \{0,1,2,\ldots,L-1\}$ and $B = \{0,1,2,\ldots,2(L-1)\}$. The properties of these two important operations are much alike those of the binary operators. They are not here enlisted due to space limitations.

2.2 Extended AB Memories

In this section we introduce the extended memories able to recall gray-level patterns. The proposed memories have the same structure as the $\alpha\beta$ memories presented in [10]. The difference between the extended memories and the standard $\alpha\beta$ memories is of course the use of operators A and B instead of operators α and β. We provide the conditions under which the extended memories are able to recall patterns either from the fundamental set or from altered versions of them. Due to space limitations we only analyze extended auto-associative memories of type $\mathbf{M}$ (EAS $\mathbf{M}$ memories). We provide several examples to better illustrate the ideas here presented. To operate an EAS $\mathbf{M}$ memory we again first use the operator $\otimes$, then the **max** operator $\vee$. During training equation (**4**) changes as follows:

$$
m_{ij} = \bigvee_{\xi=1}^{p} \mathrm{A}\left(x_i^{\xi}, x_j^{\xi}\right).
\tag{13}
$$

In the same way, during recuperation, equations (**5**) and (**6**) change to:

$$
\left(\mathbf{M} \wedge_{\mathrm{B}} \mathbf{x}^{\omega}\right)_i = \bigwedge_{j=1}^{n} \mathrm{B}\left(m_{ij}, x_j^{\omega}\right).
\tag{14}
$$

$$
\left(\mathbf{M} \wedge_{\mathrm{B}} \tilde{\mathbf{x}}\right)_i = \bigwedge_{j=1}^{n} \mathrm{B}\left(m_{ij}, \tilde{x}_j\right).
\tag{15}
$$

Next we give the conditions under which an EAS $\mathbf{M}$ memory provides perfect recall. We first give the results concerning the perfect recall of a pattern of the fundamental set. We do then the same thing but an altered version of a pattern of the fundamental set is presented to the memory. The results here presented are essentially the same as given in [10]. Instead of using operators α and β, they take into account operators A and B. Their proof is not included due to space limitations.

Example 3.1. *Suppose we want to first memorize and then recuperate the following fundamental set, with L=8:*

$$\mathbf{x}^1 = \begin{pmatrix} 1 \\ 0 \\ 1 \end{pmatrix}, \ \mathbf{x}^2 = \begin{pmatrix} 4 \\ 2 \\ 3 \end{pmatrix} \text{ and } \mathbf{x}^3 = \begin{pmatrix} 6 \\ 5 \\ 5 \end{pmatrix}.$$

TRAINING PHASE:

$$\mathbf{x}^1 \vee_A \left(\mathbf{x}^1\right)^T = \begin{pmatrix} 7 & 8 & 7 \\ 6 & 7 & 6 \\ 7 & 8 & 7 \end{pmatrix}, \ \mathbf{x}^2 \vee_A \left(\mathbf{x}^2\right)^T = \begin{pmatrix} 7 & 9 & 8 \\ 5 & 7 & 6 \\ 6 & 8 & 7 \end{pmatrix}, \ \mathbf{x}^3 \vee_A \left(\mathbf{x}^3\right)^T = \begin{pmatrix} 7 & 8 & 8 \\ 6 & 7 & 7 \\ 6 & 7 & 7 \end{pmatrix}.$$

Thus

$$\mathbf{M} = \begin{pmatrix} 7 & 9 & 8 \\ 6 & 7 & 6 \\ 7 & 8 & 7 \end{pmatrix}.$$

RECALLING PHASE:

$$\mathbf{M} \wedge_B \mathbf{x}^1 = \begin{pmatrix} 7 & 9 & 8 \\ 6 & 7 & 6 \\ 7 & 8 & 7 \end{pmatrix} \wedge_B \begin{pmatrix} 1 \\ 0 \\ 1 \end{pmatrix} = \begin{pmatrix} B(7,1) \wedge B(9,0) \wedge B(8,1) \\ B(6,1) \wedge B(7,0) \wedge B(6,1) \\ B(7,1) \wedge B(8,0) \wedge B(7,1) \end{pmatrix} = \begin{pmatrix} 1 \wedge 2 \wedge 2 \\ 0 \wedge 0 \wedge 0 \\ 1 \wedge 1 \wedge 1 \end{pmatrix} = \begin{pmatrix} 1 \\ 0 \\ 1 \end{pmatrix}.$$

You can easily verify that the other two patterns are also perfectly recalled.

The following proposition provides conditions for perfect recall of a pattern of the fundamental set when an altered version of it is presented to EAS $\mathbf{M}$ memory.

Theorem 3.2. *Let* $\left\{\left(\mathbf{x}^\xi, \mathbf{x}^\xi\right) \mid \xi = 1,2,\ldots,p\right\}$ *the fundamental set of an EAS $\mathbf{M}$ memory and L the number of levels the elements of each* $\mathbf{x}^\xi$ *can take. Let* $\tilde{\mathbf{X}}$ *an altered version with additive noise. If* $\tilde{\mathbf{X}}$ *is presented as input to the EAS $\mathbf{M}$ memory and if besides for each* $i \in \{1,\ldots,n\}$ *it holds that* $\exists j = j_0 \in \{1,\ldots,n\}$, *which depends on w and i such as* $m_{ij_0} \le A\left(x_i^\omega, \tilde{x}_{j_0}\right)$, *then we have perfect recall, this is* $\mathbf{M} \wedge_B \tilde{\mathbf{X}} = \mathbf{x}^w$.

Example 3.3. *Let us take an altered version by additive noise of pattern* $\mathbf{x}^2 = \begin{pmatrix} 4 \\ 2 \\ 3 \end{pmatrix}$,

for example $\tilde{\mathbf{x}}^2 = \begin{pmatrix} 4 \\ 3 \\ 3 \end{pmatrix}$:

$$\mathbf{M}_{\wedge_B}\, \tilde{\mathbf{x}}^2 = \begin{pmatrix} 7 & 9 & 8 \\ 6 & 7 & 6 \\ 7 & 8 & 7 \end{pmatrix} \wedge_B \begin{pmatrix} 4 \\ 3 \\ 3 \end{pmatrix} = \begin{pmatrix} B(7,4) \wedge B(9,3) \wedge B(8,3) \\ B(6,4) \wedge B(7,3) \wedge B(6,3) \\ B(7,4) \wedge B(8,3) \wedge B(7,3) \end{pmatrix} = \begin{pmatrix} 4 \wedge 5 \wedge 4 \\ 3 \wedge 3 \wedge 2 \\ 4 \wedge 4 \wedge 3 \end{pmatrix} = \begin{pmatrix} 4 \\ 2 \\ 3 \end{pmatrix}.$$

The reader can easily verify that this example satisfies the conditions given by Theorem 3.2 for perfect recall in the presence of additive noise.

3 Experimental Results

In this section the proposed extended associative memories are tested with more realistic patterns. Images of five well-known personalities (Descarte, Einstein, Euler, Galileo and Newton) were used are shown in Figure 3. The images are 32 by 29 pixels and 256 gray levels. Only EAS associative memories of type $\mathbf{M}$ were tested.

3.1 Construction of the Association Matrix

The images shown in Figure 3 were first converted to vectors of 968 elements (32 times 29) each one. These vectors were then used to construct the corresponding $\mathbf{M}$ matrices, by using the techniques described in Section 3.

Fig. 3. Images of the five objects used in to test the proposed associative memories.

3.2 Recalling of the Fundamental Set

In this first experiment, the five images were fed to $\mathbf{M}$ matrices already built. To all of them, the procedures described in Section 3 were applied. In all cases, of course, the five patterns were perfectly recalled.

3.3 Recalling of a Pattern by a Corrupted Version of It

Three groups of images were generated: The first one with additive noise, the second one with saturated noise of type salt, and the third one with manually added saturated noise. In the first case, to the gray-value $f(x, y)$ of pixel with coordinates (x, y), an integer v was added, such that $f(x, y) + v \leq (L-1)$. In the second case, again to the gray-value of a pixel an integer v was added, such that $f(x, y) + v = (L-1)$. The value $f(x, y)$ of the gray-level of the pixel was changed if $s < t$. $s \in [0,1]$ is an uniformly randomly distributed random variable, t is the parameter controlling how much of the image is corrupted. In the third case Microsoft PAINT utility was used. Due to space, only the result for the first set are presented.

Case of additive noise. Twenty five images were obtained as explained. Parameter s was varied form 0.99 to 0.95 in steps of 0.01. Figure 4(a) shows the obtained images. In some cases the original images were perfectly recalled, in others they were not. The recalled versions are shown in Figure 4(b). Under each recalled image it is indicated if it matches the original image or not. Notice how despite the level of noise introduced, recalled versions match very well with the originals.

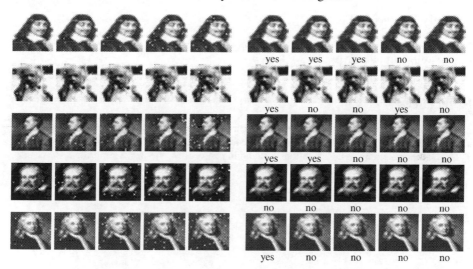

Fig. 4. (a) Altered versions with additive noise. (b) Recalled versions.

We want it to investigate the performance of the proposed model in the presence of huge quantities of additive noise. For this all the pixels of the five images of Fig. 3 were contaminated with additive noise. Figure 5(a) shows the obtained altered versions. Figure 5(b) shows the recalled images. Notice how despite the level of noise introduced, recalled versions match very well with the originals.

Fig. 5. (a) Completely altered versions of the original images. (b) Recalled versions.

It is worth mentioning that the average time to recall an image in all cases, when using the proposed model, is 0.4 seconds in a Pentium 4 at 1.3 GHz.

4 Conclusions

We have proposed a new set of associative memories able to work with gray-level patterns as an extension of the associative binary $\alpha\beta$ memories recently introduced in [10]. To derive the set of extended memories, we first we take operators α and β, and solve a set of functional equations to get the extended operators, **A** and **B**. It is shown that the operators α and β are a special case if the general operators **A** and **B**. We give conditions under which the proposed set of memories is able to recall first the fundamental set of patterns, and second a pattern from an altered version of it when additive or subtractive noise is added to the pattern.

The proposed extension was tested with several real patterns (images of five famous people) with very satisfactory results. Even in the case of severe noise, the proposed extended memories are able to recall patterns from distorted versions of them.

Acknowledgements

This work was supported by CIC-IPN, COFAA-IPN, CONACYT under grants 41529 and 40114Y and CGPI-IPN under grant 20020658.

References

1. C. Yáñez, Associative Memories based on Order Relations and Binary Operators (In Spanish), PhD Thesis, Center for Computing Research, February of 2002.
2. A. Dhombres, Functional Equations Containing Several Variables, Cambridge University Press, 1991.
3. J. Aczel, Functional Equations: History, Applications and Theory, Kluwer Academic Pub. Group, 1984.

New Associative Memories
to Recall Real-Valued Patterns

Humberto Sossa, Ricardo Barrón, and Roberto A. Vázquez

Centro de Investigación en Computación-IPN
Av. Juan de Dios Bátiz, esquina con Miguel Othón de Mendizábal
Mexico City, 07738, Mexico
hsossa@cic.ipn.mx

Abstract. In this note we describe a new set of associative memories able to re-call patterns in the presence of mixed noise. Conditions are given under which the proposed memories are able to recall patterns either from the fundamental set of patterns and from distorted versions of them. Numerical and real examples are also provided to show the efficiency of the proposal.

1 Introduction

An associative memory is a device designed to recall patterns. These patterns might appear altered by noise. An associative memory $\mathbf{M}$ can be viewed as an input-output system as follows: $\mathbf{x} \rightarrow \mathbf{M} \rightarrow \mathbf{y}$, with $\mathbf{x}$ and $\mathbf{y}$, respectively the input and output patterns vectors. Each input vector forms an association with a corresponding output vector. The associative memory $\mathbf{M}$ is represented by a matrix whose ij-th component is m_{ij}. $\mathbf{M}$ is generated from a finite a priori set of known associations, known as the *fundamental set of associations*, or simply the *fundamental set* (FS). If ξ is an index, the fundamental set is represented as: $\left\{ \left(\mathbf{x}^{\xi}, \mathbf{y}^{\xi} \right) \mid \xi = 1, 2, \ldots, p \right\}$ with p the cardinality of the set. The patterns that form the fundamental set are called *fundamental patterns*. If it holds that $\mathbf{x}^{\xi} = \mathbf{y}^{\xi} \ \forall \xi \in \{1, 2, \ldots p\}$, then $\mathbf{M}$ is auto-associative, otherwise it is hetero-associative. A distorted version of a pattern $\mathbf{x}$ to be recuperated will be denoted as $\tilde{\mathbf{x}}$. If when feeding a distorted version of $\mathbf{x}^{w}$ with $w \in \{1, 2, \ldots, p\}$ to an associative memory $\mathbf{M}$, then it happens that the output corresponds exactly to the associated pattern $\mathbf{y}^{w}$, we say that recalling is perfect. Several models for associative memories have emerged in the last 40 years. Refer for example to [1-4].

2 Foundations of the Proposed Memories

Let $P = \left\lfloor p_{ij} \right\rfloor_{m \times r}$ and $Q = \left\lfloor q_{ij} \right\rfloor_{r \times n}$ two matrices.

Definition 1. *The following two matrix operations are defined to recall integer-valued patterns:*

1. Operation $\lozenge_A$: $P_{m \times r} \lozenge_A Q_{r \times n} = \left\lfloor f_{ij}^A \right\rfloor_{m \times n}$ where $f_{ij}^A = \overset{r}{\underset{k=1}{\otimes}} A\left(p_{ik}, q_{kj} \right)$.

A. Sanfeliu et al. (Eds.): CIARP 2004, LNCS 3287, pp. 195–202, 2004.

2. Operation $\lozenge_B$: $P_{m\times r}\lozenge_B Q_{r\times n} = \left\lfloor f_{ij}^B \right\rfloor_{m\times n}$ where $f_{ij}^B = \overset{r}{\underset{k=1}{\otimes}} B\left(p_{ik}, q_{kj}\right)$.

According to the operators $\otimes$, A and B used different results can be obtained. If we want, for example, to compensate for additive or subtractive noise, operator $\otimes$ should be replaced either by **max** ($\vee$) or **min** ($\wedge$) as in [4]. Median operator (**med**), should be adopted in the case of mixed noise. In this paper we use **med** operator because as we will show, it provides excellent results in the presence of mixed noise. It can be easily shown that if $\mathbf{x} \in \mathbf{Z}^n$ and $\mathbf{y} \in \mathbf{Z}^m$, then $\mathbf{y}\lozenge_A\mathbf{x}^t$ is a matrix of dimensions $m \times n$.

Relevant simplifications are obtained when operations $\lozenge_A$ and $\lozenge_B$ are applied between vectors:

1. If $\mathbf{x} \in \mathbf{Z}^n$ and $\mathbf{y} \in \mathbf{Z}^m$, then $\mathbf{y}\lozenge_A\mathbf{x}^t$ is a matrix of dimensions $m\times n$, and also it holds that

$$\mathbf{y}\lozenge_A\mathbf{x}^t = \begin{pmatrix} A(y_1,x_1) & A(y_1,x_2) & \cdots & A(y_1,x_n) \\ A(y_2,x_1) & A(y_2,x_2) & \cdots & A(y_2,x_n) \\ \vdots & \vdots & \ddots & \vdots \\ A(y_m,x_1) & A(y_m,x_2) & \cdots & A(y_m,x_n) \end{pmatrix}_{m\times n}.$$

2. If $\mathbf{x} \in \mathbf{Z}^n$ and P a matrix of dimensions $m\times n$, operations $P_{m\times n}\lozenge_B\mathbf{x}$ gives as a result one vector with dimension m, with i-th component given as

$$\left(P_{m\times r}\lozenge_B\mathbf{x}\right)_i = \overset{n}{\underset{j=1}{\mathbf{med}}} B\left(p_{ij}, x_j\right).$$

If $\mathbf{x} \in \mathbf{Z}^n$ and P a matrix of dimensions $m \times n$ then operation $\mathbf{M}_{m\times n}\lozenge_B\mathbf{x}$ outputs an m-dimensional column vector, with i-th component given as:

$$\left(\mathbf{M}_{m\times n}\lozenge_B\mathbf{x}\right)_i = \overset{n}{\underset{j=1}{\mathbf{med}}} B\left(m_{ij}, x_j\right).$$

Operators A and B might be chosen among those already proposed in the literature. In this paper we use operators A and B proposed in [4]. Operators A and B are defined as follows:

$$A(x,y) = x - y \qquad\qquad (1.a)$$
$$B(x,y) = x + y \qquad\qquad (1.b)$$

3   Kinds of Noises

The proposed memories can cope with several kinds of noises. Among them: additive, subtractive and mixed. In this paper, we are interested in leading with mixed noise. Let $\mathbf{x} \in \mathbf{R}^n$ be an input fundamental pattern to an associative memory. Pattern $\mathbf{x}$ can be altered or corrupted by mixed noise to produce a vector $\widetilde{\mathbf{x}}$ by adding or subtracting at random to each component of $\mathbf{x}$, x_i a real c, $\widetilde{x}_i = x_i + c$ (additive noise), and $\widetilde{x}_i = x_i - c$ (subtractive noise).

4   The New Memories

Two kind of associative memories are proposed, hetero-associative and auto-associative. Due to space, in this paper only hetero-associative memories are described. One hetero-associative memory is described: HS-memory of type **M**.

TRAINING PHASE:

Step 1:   For each $\xi = 1, 2, \cdots, p$, from each couple $\left(\mathbf{x}^{\xi}, \mathbf{y}^{\xi}\right)$ build matrix:

$$\left[\mathbf{y}^{\xi} \Diamond_{A} \left(\mathbf{x}^{\xi}\right)^{t}\right]_{m \times n}.$$

Step 2:   Apply the median operator to the matrices obtained in Step 1 to get matrix **M** as follows:

$$\mathbf{M} = \underset{\xi=1}{\overset{p}{\mathbf{med}}}\left[\mathbf{y}^{\xi} \Diamond_{A} \left(\mathbf{x}^{\xi}\right)^{t}\right]. \tag{2}$$

The ij-th component **M** is given as follows:

$$m_{ij} = \underset{\xi=1}{\overset{p}{\mathbf{med}}}\, A\left(y_{i}^{\xi}, x_{j}^{\xi}\right). \tag{3}$$

RECALLING PHASE:
We have two cases, i.e.:

Case 1: Recall of a fundamental pattern. A pattern $\mathbf{x}^{w}$, with $w \in \{1, 2, \cdots, p\}$ is presented to the memory **M** and the following operation is done:

$$\mathbf{M} \Diamond_{B} x^{w}. \tag{4}$$

The result is a column vector of dimension n, with i-th component given as:

$$\left(\mathbf{M} \Diamond_{B} x^{w}\right)_{i} = \underset{j=1}{\overset{n}{\mathbf{med}}}\, B\left(m_{ij}, x_{j}^{w}\right). \tag{5}$$

Case 2: Recalling of a pattern from an altered version of it. A pattern $\tilde{\mathbf{x}}$ (altered version of a pattern $\mathbf{x}^{w}$ is presented to the hetero-associative memory **M** and the following operation is done:

$$\mathbf{M} \Diamond_{B} \tilde{\mathbf{x}}. \tag{6}$$

Again, the result is a column vector of dimension n, with i-th component given as:

$$\left(\mathbf{M} \Diamond_{B} \tilde{\mathbf{x}}\right)_{i} = \underset{j=1}{\overset{n}{\mathbf{med}}}\, B\left(m_{ij}, \tilde{x}_{j}\right). \tag{7}$$

Conditions, not proved here due to space, for perfect recall of a pattern of the FS or from altered version of them follow:

Theorem 1. Let $\left\{\left(\mathbf{x}^{\alpha}, \mathbf{y}^{\alpha}\right) \mid \alpha = 1, 2, \ldots, p\right\}$ with $\mathbf{x}^{\alpha} \in \mathbf{R}^{n}$, $\mathbf{y}^{\alpha} \in \mathbf{R}^{m}$ the fundamental set of an HS-memory **M** and let $\left(\mathbf{x}^{\gamma}, \mathbf{y}^{\gamma}\right)$ an arbitrary fundamental couple with $\gamma \in \{1, \cdots, p\}$. If $\underset{j=1}{\overset{n}{\mathrm{med}}}\, \varepsilon_{ij} = 0$, $i = 1, \cdots, m$, $\varepsilon_{ij} = m_{ij} - A(y_i^{\gamma}, x_j^{\gamma})$ then $(M \Diamond_B x^{\gamma})_i = y_i^{\gamma}, i = 1 \ldots m$.

More restricted conditions are given by the following:

Corollary 1. Let $\{(x^{\alpha}, y^{\alpha}) | \alpha = 1, 2, \ldots, p\}$, $x^{\alpha} \in \mathbf{R}^n$, $y^{\alpha} \in \mathbf{R}^m$. A HA-median memory $\mathbf{M}$ has perfect recall if for all $\alpha = 1, \cdots, p$, $\mathbf{M}^{\alpha} = \mathbf{M}$ where $\mathbf{M} = y^{\xi} \Diamond_A (x^{\xi})^t$ is the associated partial matrix to the fundamental couple (x^{α}, y^{α}) and p is the number of couples.

Theorem 2. Let $\{(x^{\alpha}, y^{\alpha}) | \alpha = 1, 2, \ldots, p\}$, $x^{\alpha} \in \mathbf{R}^n$, $y^{\alpha} \in \mathbf{R}^m$ a FS with perfect recall. Let $\eta^{\alpha} \in \mathbf{R}^n$ a pattern of mixed noise. A HA-median memory $\mathbf{M}$ has perfect recall in the presence of mixed noise if this noise is of median zero, this is if $\underset{j=1}{\overset{n}{\mathrm{med}}}\, \eta_j^{\alpha} = 0, \forall \alpha$.

Example 1. The reader can easily verify that for the following set of patterns satisfies the conditions given by Theorem 1 and Corollary 1:

$$x^1 = \begin{pmatrix} 0.1 \\ 0.0 \\ 0.2 \end{pmatrix}, \; y^1 = \begin{pmatrix} 0.2 \\ 0.3 \\ 0.3 \\ 0.4 \end{pmatrix}; \; x^2 = \begin{pmatrix} 0.4 \\ 0.3 \\ 0.5 \end{pmatrix}, \; y^2 = \begin{pmatrix} 0.5 \\ 0.6 \\ 0.6 \\ 0.7 \end{pmatrix} \text{ and } x^3 = \begin{pmatrix} 0.7 \\ 0.6 \\ 0.8 \end{pmatrix}, \; y^3 = \begin{pmatrix} 0.8 \\ 0.9 \\ 0.9 \\ 1.0 \end{pmatrix}.$$

If a FS satisfies the conditions imposed by Theorem 1, and the noise added to a pattern x^{α} of this FS satisfies Theorem 2, then no matter the level of noise added, the pattern is perfectly recalled. If this is the case you can easily prove that a given pattern x^{α} is recalled through the information of the associated column of matrix $M \Diamond_B \tilde{x}^{\alpha}$ of an element x_i^{α} of x^{α} not affected by noise. Let us verify this with an example.

Example 2. Suppose we want to recall the first fundamental pattern from Example 1 given the following distorted version of its key:

$$\tilde{x}^1 = \begin{pmatrix} 0.3 \\ 0.0 \\ -0.2 \end{pmatrix}.$$

As you can appreciate for the distorted pattern, the median of the noise added to x equals 0: $\mathbf{med}(0.2, 0.0, -0.4) = 0.0$. Also element number two of x^1 is not affected by the added noise. Pattern x^1 is thus recalled through the information of column two (underlined) associated to x_2^1 of $M \Diamond_B \tilde{x}^1$. Let us verify this.

RECALLING PHASE:

$$M\lozenge_B x^1 = \begin{pmatrix} 0.1 & 0.2 & 0.0 \\ 0.2 & 0.3 & 0.1 \\ 0.2 & 0.3 & 0.1 \\ 0.3 & 0.4 & 0.2 \end{pmatrix} \lozenge_B \begin{pmatrix} 0.3 \\ 0.0 \\ -0.2 \end{pmatrix} = \begin{pmatrix} \text{med}[B(0.1,0.3),B(0.2,0.0),B(0.0,-0.2)] \\ \text{med}[B(0.2,0.3),B(0.3,0.0),B(0.1,-0.2)] \\ \text{med}[B(0.2,0.3),B(0.3,0.0),B(0.1,-0.2)] \\ \text{med}[B(0.3,0.3),B(0.4,0.0),B(0.2,-0.2)] \end{pmatrix} = \begin{pmatrix} \text{med}(0.4,\underline{0.2},-0.2) \\ \text{med}(0.5,\underline{0.3},-0.1) \\ \text{med}(0.5,\underline{0.3},-0.1) \\ \text{med}(0.6,\underline{0.4},0.0) \end{pmatrix} = \begin{pmatrix} 0.2 \\ 0.3 \\ 0.3 \\ 0.4 \end{pmatrix}$$

5   Case of a General Fundamental Set

In practice most of the fundamental sets of patterns do not satisfy the restricted conditions imposed by Theorem 1 and its Corollary. If this not the case, we propose the
following procedure to perfectly recall a general FS. Given a FS not satisfying Theorem 1:

TRAINING PHASE:
Step 1. Transform the FS into an auxiliary fundamental set (FS') satisfying Theorem 1:

1) Make $d = cont$.
2) Make $(x^1, y^1) = (x^1, y^1)$.
3) For the remaining couples do {
   For $\xi = 2$ to p {
      For $i=1$ to n {
         $$\bar{x}_i^\xi = \bar{x}_i^{\xi-1} + d \; ; \; \hat{x}_i^\xi = \bar{x}_i^\xi - x_i^\xi \; ;$$
         $$\bar{y}_i^\xi = \bar{y}_i^{\xi-1} + d \; ; \; \hat{y}_i^\xi = \bar{x}_i^\xi - x_i^\xi \; .$$
      }
   }
}

Step 2. Build matrix **M** in terms of set FS': Apply to FS' steps 1 and 2 of the training
procedure described at the beginning of Section 2.3.

Remark 1. We can use any d. In this work we decided to use however the difference
between the first components.

RECALLING PHASE:
We have also two cases, i.e.:

Case 1: Recalling of a fundamental pattern of FS:

1) Transform x^ξ to $\bar{x}^\xi$ by applying the following transformation: $\bar{x}^\xi = x^\xi + \hat{x}^\xi$.
2) Apply equations (4) and (5) to each $\bar{x}^\xi$ of FS' to recall $\bar{y}^\xi$.
3) Recall each y^ξ by applying the following inverse transformation:
   $$y^\xi = \bar{y}^\xi - \hat{y}^\xi .$$

Case 2: Recalling of a pattern y^ξ from an altered version of its key $\tilde{x}^\xi$:

1) Transform $\tilde{x}^\xi$ to x^ξ by applying the following transformation: $\bar{x}^\xi = \tilde{x}^\xi + \hat{x}^\xi$.

2) Apply equations (6) and (7) to $\mathbf{x}^\xi$ to get $\mathbf{y}^\xi$, and

3) Anti-transform $\mathbf{y}^\xi$ as $\mathbf{y}^\xi = \overline{\mathbf{y}}^\xi - \hat{\mathbf{y}}^\xi$ to get $\mathbf{y}^\xi$.

Example 3. Suppose we want to first memorize and then recall the following general fundamental set:

$$\mathbf{x}^1 = \begin{pmatrix} 0.1 \\ 0.0 \\ 0.2 \end{pmatrix}, \ \mathbf{y}^1 = \begin{pmatrix} 1 \\ 0 \\ 0 \end{pmatrix}; \ \mathbf{x}^2 = \begin{pmatrix} 0.4 \\ 0.2 \\ 0.5 \end{pmatrix}, \ \mathbf{y}^2 = \begin{pmatrix} 0 \\ 1 \\ 0 \end{pmatrix} \text{ and } \mathbf{x}^3 = \begin{pmatrix} 0.6 \\ 0.6 \\ 0.8 \end{pmatrix}, \ \mathbf{y}^3 = \begin{pmatrix} 0 \\ 0 \\ 1 \end{pmatrix}.$$

TRAINING:

1) $d = x_1^2 - x_1^1 = 0.4 - 0.1 = 0.3$.

2) $\overline{\mathbf{x}}^1 = \begin{pmatrix} 0.1 & 0.0 & 0.2 \end{pmatrix}^T$ and $\overline{\mathbf{y}}^1 = \begin{pmatrix} 1 & 0 & 0 \end{pmatrix}^T$.

3) $\overline{\mathbf{x}}^2 = \begin{pmatrix} 0.4 \\ 0.3 \\ 0.5 \end{pmatrix}, \ \hat{\mathbf{x}}^2 = \begin{pmatrix} 0.0 \\ 0.1 \\ 0.0 \end{pmatrix}, \ \overline{\mathbf{y}}^2 = \begin{pmatrix} 1.3 \\ 0.3 \\ 0.3 \end{pmatrix}, \ \hat{\mathbf{y}}^2 = \begin{pmatrix} 1.3 \\ -0.7 \\ 0.3 \end{pmatrix};$

$\mathbf{x}^3 = \begin{pmatrix} 0.7 \\ 0.6 \\ 0.8 \end{pmatrix}, \ \hat{\mathbf{x}}^3 = \begin{pmatrix} 0.1 \\ 0.0 \\ 0.0 \end{pmatrix}, \ \overline{\mathbf{y}}^3 = \begin{pmatrix} 1.6 \\ 0.6 \\ 0.6 \end{pmatrix}, \ \hat{\mathbf{y}}^3 = \begin{pmatrix} 1.6 \\ 0.6 \\ -0.4 \end{pmatrix}.$

You can easily show that: $\mathbf{M} = \mathbf{M}^1 = \mathbf{M}^2 = \mathbf{M}^3 = \begin{pmatrix} 0.9 & 1.0 & 0.8 \\ -0.1 & 0.0 & -0.2 \\ -0.1 & 0.0 & -0.2 \end{pmatrix}.$

RECALLING PHASE:
Let us consider only Case 2, which is of more interest. Suppose we want to recall pattern $\mathbf{y}^2$ from its following distorted key: $\tilde{\mathbf{x}}^2 = \begin{pmatrix} 0.6 & 0.2 & 0.1 \end{pmatrix}^T$.

1) As discussed: $\overline{\mathbf{x}}^2 = \tilde{\mathbf{x}}^2 + \hat{\mathbf{x}}^2 = \begin{pmatrix} 0.6 & 0.3 & 0.1 \end{pmatrix}^T$.

2) $\mathbf{M} \Diamond_B \overline{\mathbf{x}}^2 = \begin{pmatrix} 0.9 & 1.0 & 0.8 \\ -0.1 & 0.0 & -0.2 \\ -0.1 & 0.0 & -0.2 \end{pmatrix} \Diamond_B \begin{pmatrix} 0.6 \\ 0.3 \\ 0.1 \end{pmatrix} = \begin{pmatrix} \text{med}(1.5,1.3,0.9) \\ \text{med}(0.5,0.3,-0.1) \\ \text{med}(0.5,0.3,-0.1) \end{pmatrix} = \begin{pmatrix} 1.3 \\ 0.3 \\ 0.3 \end{pmatrix}.$

Finally, $\mathbf{y}^2 = \overline{\mathbf{y}}^2 - \hat{\mathbf{y}}^2 = \begin{pmatrix} 1.3 \\ 0.3 \\ 0.3 \end{pmatrix} - \begin{pmatrix} 1.3 \\ -0.7 \\ 0.3 \end{pmatrix} = \begin{pmatrix} 0 \\ 1 \\ 0 \end{pmatrix}.$

6   Experiments with Real Patterns

The proposed associative memories were also tested with real patterns. We used the objects shown in Fig. 1.

Fig. 1. The five objects used in the experiments. (a) A bolt. (b) A washer. (c) An eyebolt. (d) A hook. (e) A dovetail.

6.1 Construction of the Association Matrix

We did not directly recognize the objects by their images. We preferred to do it indirectly by invariant descriptions of each of them. For this, ninety images of each object in different positions, rotations and scale changes were captured. To each image a standard thresholder [5] was applied to get its binary version. Small spurious regions, due to bas thresholding, were eliminated form each image by means of a size filter [6, pp.47-48]. To each of the 19 images of each object (class) the first three Hu geometric invariants, to translations, rotations and scale changes were computed [7]. The five associations were built as:

$$\mathbf{x}^1 = \begin{pmatrix} 0.4429 \\ 0.1594 \\ 0.0058 \end{pmatrix}, \; \mathbf{y}^1 = \begin{pmatrix} 1 \\ 0 \\ 0 \\ 0 \\ 0 \end{pmatrix}; \; \mathbf{x}^2 = \begin{pmatrix} 0.1896 \\ 5.78E-5 \\ 4.14E-6 \end{pmatrix}, \; \mathbf{y}^2 = \begin{pmatrix} 0 \\ 1 \\ 0 \\ 0 \\ 0 \end{pmatrix}; \; \mathbf{x}^3 = \begin{pmatrix} 0.7038 \\ 0.2911 \\ 0.1825 \end{pmatrix}, \; \mathbf{y}^3 = \begin{pmatrix} 0 \\ 0 \\ 1 \\ 0 \\ 0 \end{pmatrix};$$

$$\mathbf{x}^4 = \begin{pmatrix} 1.1421 \\ 1.5517 \\ 0.8467 \end{pmatrix}, \; \mathbf{y}^4 = \begin{pmatrix} 0 \\ 0 \\ 0 \\ 1 \\ 0 \end{pmatrix}; \; \mathbf{x}^5 = \begin{pmatrix} 0.2491 \\ 0.0195 \\ 2.41E-5 \end{pmatrix}, \; \mathbf{y}^5 = \begin{pmatrix} 0 \\ 0 \\ 0 \\ 0 \\ 1 \end{pmatrix};$$

The three real numbers for each $\mathbf{x}^\alpha$ are the average values of the four Hu invariants computed with each set of 19 images of each object. The "1" at each $\mathbf{y}$ represents the index of the class of each object. After applying the methodology described in Section 4, matrix $\mathbf{M}$ is:

$$\mathbf{M} = \begin{pmatrix} 0.5571 & 0.8406 & 0.9942 \\ -0.4429 & -0.1594 & -0.0058 \\ -0.4429 & -0.1594 & -0.0058 \\ -0.4429 & -0.1594 & -0.0058 \\ -0.4429 & -0.1594 & -0.0058 \end{pmatrix}.$$

6.2 Recalling of a Pattern by a Corrupted Version of Its Key

In practical applications the noise added to the values of the patters rarely satisfies Theorem 2. To cope with this situation, we propose the following strategy: Once a general FS has been processed as described in Section 5, one of its patterns is classified in terms of a possible altered version of its key as follows:

$$\mathbf{y}^j, j = \arg\min_i\left(\min_{k=1}^m\left(y_k - y_k^i\right)\right) \tag{8}$$

Table 1. Percentage of classification for the test set.

	Bolt	Washer	Eyebolt	Hook	Dovetail
Bolt	100%	0	0	0	0
Washer	0	100%	0	0	0
Eyebolt	10%	0	90%	0	0
Hook	0	0	0	100%	0
Dovetail	0	15%	0	0	85%

Fifty images (10 for each object), and different from those used to build matrix **M** were used to measure the efficiency of the proposal. Of course the values of the invariants change. Table 1 shows the recalling results. As you can appreciate in 10% of the cases the eyebolt is classified as a bolt, and in 15% of the cases a dovetail is classified as a washer. In remaining cases the objects were correctly classified.

7 Conclusions

We have described a set of associative memories able to recall patterns altered by mixed noise. The proposed memories are based on the median operation. Numerical and real examples with images of real objects have been provided showing the performance of these memories. We gave the necessary and sufficient conditions under which the proposed memories are able to recall patterns either from the fundamental set of from altered versions of them. In this paper we show for the first time that associative memories combined with invariant features can be used to recognize objects in the presence of image transformations. Actually, we are investigating how to bypass the restricted conditions imposed by theorem 2, and to avoid using equation (8).

Acknowledgements

This work was supported by CIC-IPN, COFAA-IPN, CONACYT under grants 41529 and 40114Y and CGPI-IPN under grant 20020658. We thank the reviewers for its comments for the improvement of this paper.

References

1. K. Steinbuch, Die Lernmatrix, *Kybernetik*, 1(1):26-45, 1961.
2. J. A. Anderson, A simple neural network generating an interactive memory, *Mathematical Biosciences*, 14:197-220, 1972.
3. J. J. Hopfield, Neural networks and physical systems with emergent collective computational abilities, *Proceedings of the National Academy of Sciences*, 79: 2554-2558, 1982.
4. G. X. Ritter el al. Morphological associative memories, *IEEE Transactions on Neural Networks*, 9:281-293, 1998.
5. N. Otsu, A threshold selection method from gray-level histograms, *IEEE Transactions on SMC*, 9(1): 62-66, 1979.
6. R. Jain et al. *Machine Vision*, McGraw-Hill, 1995.
7. M. K. Hu, Visual pattern recognition by moment invariants, IRE Transactions on Information Theory, 8: 179-187, 1962.

Feature Maps for Non-supervised Classification of Low-Uniform Patterns of Handwritten Letters

Pilar Gómez-Gil, Guillermo de-los-Santos-Torres, and Manuel Ramírez-Cortés

Department of Computer Science and CENTIA
Universidad de las Américas, Puebla
Santa Catarina M. Cholula Puebla, 72820, México
pgomez@mail.udlap.mx

Abstract. When input data is noisy and with a lack of uniformity, classification is a very difficult problem, because decision regions are hard to define in an optimal way. This is the case of recognition of old handwritten manuscript characters, where patterns of the same class may be very different from each other, and patterns of different classes may be similar in terms of Euclidian distances between their feature vectors. In this paper we present the results obtained when a non-supervised method is used to create feature maps of possible classes in handwriting letters. The prototypes generated in the map present a topological relationship; therefore similar prototypes are near each other. This organization helps to solve the problem of variance in the patterns, allowing a better classification when compared with other supervised classification method, a nearest-neighbor algorithm. The feature map was built using a Self-organized Feature Map (SOFM) neural network.

1 Introduction

Today the use of OCR´s is very common for printed documents. However, the automatic transcription of handwritten documents is still a challenge. In the other hand, there is a huge amount of old handwritten documents with valuable information that need to be digitized and translated in order to preserve them and make them available to a large community of historians. Currently this task is made by expert humans, making it expensive and slow.

The problems found when building an OCR that work for handwritten old documents are several: cleaning the digitized image, segmentation of words, segmentation of characters, recognition of characters and recognition of words. In this paper only the problem of recognition of handwritten characters is addressed, looking it as a classification of ill-defined patterns. We understand by ill-defined patterns those that:

- do not show an evident prototype to represent each class,
- the variance among all members of one class is greater than a threshold,
- a metric of similarity over the patters, such as Euclidian distance, may be greater among members of two different classes than members of the same class,
- noise in the patterns is high.

It is clear that these characteristics make the solution space of classification difficult to be defined using any classifier. A classifier for this type of patterns should be able to represent, in some way, the ambiguity imbedded in the training data. One possibility is that the classifier defines by itself the prototypes and number of classes.

A. Sanfeliu et al. (Eds.): CIARP 2004, LNCS 3287, pp. 203–207, 2004.

2 SOFM Network

There is evidence that cerebral cortex of the human brain is organized in computational maps [1]. This organization provides, among other benefits, efficient information processing and simplicity of access to processed information. Inspired on this property, in 1982 T. Kohonen developed the self organizing feature mapping algorithm (SOFM) [2]. The goal of SOFM algorithm is to store a set of input patterns $\mathbf{x} \in X$ by finding a set of prototypes $\{\mathbf{w}j \mid j = 1, 2...N\}$ that represent the best feature map Φ, following some topological fashion. The map is formed by the weights connection $\mathbf{w}_j$ of a one or two-dimensional lattice of neurons, where the neurons are also related each other in a competitive way.

This learning process is stochastic and off-line; that is, two possible stages are distinguished for the net: learning and evaluation. It is important to notice that the success of map forming is highly dependent on the learning parameters and the neighborhood function defined in the model. The map is defined by the weights connecting the output neurons to the input neurons. The learning SOFM algorithm is: [1]

1. Initialize the weights with random values:

$$\mathbf{w}_j(0) = \text{random}() \ , j = 1..N \text{ (number of neurons)} \tag{1}$$

2. Choose randomly a pattern $\mathbf{x}(t)$ from the training set X at iteration t.
3. For each neuron i in the map feature map Φ calculate the similarity among its corresponding weight set $\mathbf{w}_i$ and $\mathbf{x}$. The Euclidian distance may be used:

$$d^2(\mathbf{w}_i, \mathbf{x}) = \sum_{k=1}^{n} (w_{ik} - x_k)^2 \ i = 1..N \tag{2}$$

4. Find a wining neuron $i*$ which is the one with maximum similarity (minimum distance).
5. Update the weights of winning neuron $i*$ and their neighbors as:

$$\mathbf{w}_j(t+1) = \mathbf{w}_j(t) + \alpha(t)(\mathbf{x}(t) - \mathbf{w}_i(t)) \text{ for } j \in \Lambda_{i*}(t) \tag{3}$$

Where $\Lambda_{i*}(t)$ corresponds to a neighborhood function centered on the winning neuron. For this problem, we choose a neighborhood distance of 0 neurons. $\alpha(t)$ is a learning rate function depending on time. We choose: $\alpha(t) = 1/t$.

6. Go to step 2 until no more changes in the feature map are observed or a maximum number of iterations is reached.

3 Characteristics of the Patterns

This algorithm was tested with an ill-defined set of patterns: manuscript characters extracted from a collection of telegrams written by a famous person, Gral. Porfirio Díaz, at the beginning of 20th century in México. Figure 1 shows an example of one of these telegrams. Figure 2 shows some examples of words taken from such documents. Notice that the same class of letter looks very different when it appears in different positions of the word or in different words, as in the first and third word in the figure. Also notice that different classes of letters may look very similar.

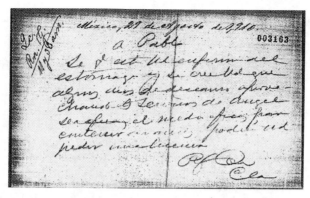

Fig. 1. A telegram written at the beginning of 20th century by Porfirio Díaz.

Fig. 2. Some examples of manuscript words written by Díaz.

To build the data set, words were manually extracted from the telegrams and their characters segmented also by a person. After that, character images were represented as bit maps, normalized with respect to a fixed number of rows and columns, and cleaned out of any blank rows or columns in their binary representation. The resulting patterns have 12 rows and 18 columns giving a total of 216 pixels. Figure 3 shows an example of the output of the software used to generate the patterns.

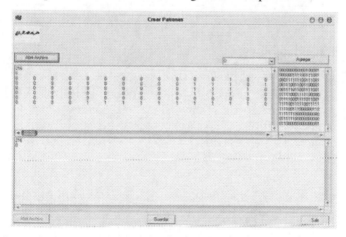

Fig. 3. Building patters from .gif files. In the top left the original word is shown; the map bit at the right shows the normalized pattern of the first character.

4   Building Feature Maps for Manuscript Letters

We used a 2-dimensional SOFM network. The formation of a feature map in a SOFM is stochastic, therefore several trails of learning using different sets of initial weights, with different topologies in the output layer (feature map) need to be tested in order to find good results. Up today, there is no a formal way to find the best architecture of a network for a specific problem.

To analyze the behavior of SOFM network for the problem described in this article, we followed the next strategies:

1. We created several sub-sets of the problem, going from a simple problem with only 3 classes (instead of whole alphabet) up to 21 classes. It must be pointed out that, for the time of implementation of these experiments, we did not count with enough processed data to test the 27 classes forming the Spanish alphabet.
2. We compared the results obtained by SOFM network with a supervised classification algorithm, the nearest-neighbor, using a K-means algorithm to find the prototypes required, both as described at [3].

Table 1 shows a summary of the best results found during our experiments for 3, 5, and 21 classes. The numbers in parenthesis following the word "Kohonen" at column 3 represent the topology of the feature map tested in that case. For example (2x30) represents a feature map with 2 rows and 30 columns.

Table 1. Some results of Classification

Number of Classes	Number of training patterns	Type of Recognizer	Recognition rate
3	13	Nearest neighbor	84%
		Kohonen (3x3)	**92%**
5	56	Nearest neighbor	58%
		Kohonen (5x1)	58%
		Kohonen (5x2)	71%
		Kohonen (5x5)	**73%**
21	86	Nearest neighbor	6%
		Kohonen (5x12)	63%
		Kohonen (2x30)	**70%**

Notice that for all cases, particularly with the most difficult case (21 classes), SOFM performs much better than Nearest algorithm. Figures 4 and 5 show the 2 feature maps formed for the two Kohonen experiments performed with 21 classes. As expected, both maps follow a topological order, locating similar prototypes near each other. More details may be found at [4].

Fig. 4. Feature map with 5 rows and 12 columns generated for 21 classes.

Fig. 5. Feature map with 2 rows and 20 columns generated for 21 classes.

5   Conclusions and Perspectives

The advantages on the use of non-supervised generation of feature maps for an ill-defined set of patterns have been shown in these results. The behavior of SOFM network for the experiments executed in this research was as expected, creating well defined prototypes, and being able to classify better than a popular supervised algorithm. Future research work may include the determination of heuristics to help with the definition of the best topology of the feature maps, and the inclusion of weights in the feature maps marking the importance of each feature prototype, based on the frequency of patterns in the training set.

References

1. Haykin S.: Neural Networks: a Comprehensive Foundation. Macmillan College Publishing Company. New York. (1994).
2. Kohonen, T.: Self-Organized formation of topologically correct feature maps. Biological Cybernetics, 43, (1982) 59-69.
3. Tao, J.T. and Gonzalez, R.C. Pattern Recognition Principles. Addison-Wesley (1974)
4. De-los-Santos-Torres, G.: Reconocedor de Caracteres Manuscritos. Master thesis. Departamento de Ingeniería en Sistemas Computacionales. Universidad de las Américas, Puebla. (2003).

Learning Through the KRKa2 Chess Ending

Alejandro González Romero and René Alquézar

Departament de Llenguatges I Sistemes Informàtics, Universitat Politècnica de Catalunya,
Jordi Girona Salgado 1-3, Mòdul C6, 08034 Barcelona, Spain
{aromero,alquezar}@lsi.upc.es

Abstract. The chess ending (KRKa2) has been studied using decision trees, neural networks and human reasoning to build a classifier for this ending, and for the discovery of convenient chess attributes. These chess attributes will serve for testing new ideas in planning. The idea is to investigate whether good automatically learnt policies for a planning problem can be generated using training examples along with evolutionary algorithms. The training examples, used as input to the learning algorithm, describe specific descriptions of a number of solved instances in one domain; then to improve the learnt policies obtained from the training examples, the policies should evolve. We believe that the domain of games is well-suited for testing these new ideas in planning.

1 Introduction

Chess skill requires an ability to form plans, generalise from examples, learn from experience and to recognise the important features of a position such as a "strong" square or weak pawn structure ([1], [2]). The fact that attempts to incorporate, say, planning into chess-playing programs have only been partially successful so far is an indication that the game of chess provides a serious and complex, yet well-defined and self-contained testbed for Artificial Intelligence theories and techniques ([3], [4]).

A classifier for the ending KRKa2 (King and Rook vs. King and pawn on a2) has been built with the aid of neural networks, decision trees and human reasoning. For space reasons, only the problem of deciding whether Black wins or not is presented, although we have solved also the problem of deciding whether White wins or not. The previous three techniques also allowed the discovery of a set of useful short predicates. They will serve to construct training examples for an evolutionary learning algorithm [5] that will learn a policy set to solve this domain.

2 The KRKa2 Chess Ending Domain

The ending KRKa2 (King and Rook against King and pawn on a2) was first studied by Alen Shapiro in 1983 [6]. Given a legal position with Black (the pawn's side) to play, Shapiro considers the problem of deciding whether Black wins or not. The problem of deciding whether the rook's side wins or draws is not treated in his work. We consider the same ending with significant modifications: It's White's (the rook's side) turn to play and is determined if White wins, Black wins or it's a draw. See diagram 1.

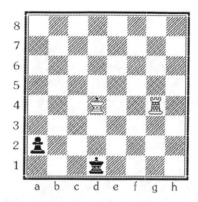

Diagram 1. Comparison between the two works: In Shapiro's work it's Black's turn; Black wins by queening the pawn and thus checking the white King. In the present work it is White's turn; White wins but the process is not trivial: *1. Kc4! Kc2(1... Kc1 2. Kb3 a1+(Knight promotion) 3. Kc3 Kb14.Rg2+ –) 2. Rg2+ Kb1 3. Kb3 a1+(Knight promotion) 4. Kc3 and White wins since Black's knight is trapped*

Another important difference between the present work and Shapiro's work is that in our case besides building a classifier we started to work in the construction of automatically built policy sets [5]. To this end, a set of short predicates is needed to conform the LHS (left hand side) and RHS (right hand side) of our rules. To increment substantially the learning chances of our learning system, it is very important that these short predicates be as good as possible. Thus to deduce them we used neural networks, decision trees and human reasoning.

As in Shapiro(1987) [7] the problem has been tackled using decision trees, but neural networks have also been employed. In both techniques a training set, consisting of a subset of chess positions, has been used to induce the classification rules. Then another subset of chess positions (the test set) has been classified with the learned rules (or the learned function in case of NN). The results were compared with the true classification giving an average accuracy of the rules.

2.1 Some Definitions and Useful Notation

For convenience some chess concepts will be mentioned, they serve to build be attributes for the construction of training and test examples.

Hidden check: It consists of just one move; for our purposes it will be moving the WK permitting with this move a check by the rook.

Horizontal check: It is a check given along a row by the rook, it can be a rook move or a king move in case of a hidden check.

Vertical check: It is a check given along a column by the rook, it can be a rook move or a king move in case of a hidden check.

The *distance function* is calculated by the minimal number of king moves that takes to go from one square to another.

Let us introduce some useful notation:

U: set of squares different from a2.

x: cartesian product. Thus $AxC=\{ (a,c): a \in A$ and $c \in C \}$.

+: union.

-: difference of sets. Thus $A-C= \{ x \in A : x \notin C \}$

A symbol as $\{defgh\}$ means the set of squares of U on columns d, e, f, g, h.

$A'=U-A$, that is, the complement of the set A in U.

The symbols i, j, k denote numbers between 1 and 8; the symbols α, β, γ will denote letters between a and h. Let us define $n(a)=1$, $n(b)=2$, $n(c)=3$, $n(d)=4$, $n(e)=5$, $n(f)=6$, $n(g)=7$, $n(h)=8$; $\beta - \alpha=n(\beta) - n(\alpha)$; $\alpha<\beta$ if $n(\alpha)<n(\beta)$. We will denote by $\beta-1$ the letter preceding β and by $\beta-2$ the letter preceding $\beta-1$. The distance between two squares αi and βj is given by $d(\alpha i, \beta j)=\max\{|j - i|, |\beta - \alpha|\}$, which is the number of king moves needed to go from αi to βj.

We define the segments $[\alpha i, \beta i]=\{(\gamma i): \alpha \leq \gamma \leq \beta\}$ and $[\alpha i,\alpha j]=\{(\alpha k): i \leq k \leq j\}$ that refer respectively to row and column segments. Also [d4,h8] will denote the diagonal segment $\{(\alpha k): 4 \leq n(\alpha)=k\}$.

It is assumed that (*) different pieces occupy different squares, the black king is not in check and the distance between the kings is greater than one ($d(WK,BK) > 1$). One must eliminate from the positions specified below those that do not satisfy (*).

3   Results

3.1   Classifying Positions and Choosing Attributes Using NN and DT

There were several tries of sets of attributes in order to find the attributes that are more useful to the learning algorithm. A first try consisting of 21 attributes had the following results.

Using 21 attributes, 80 training examples and a program that induces decision trees, a decision tree was obtained. The tree was tested using 150 test examples; its percentage of right answers was 71.6%. In the same set of 80 training examples, a feed-forward neural network was employed. A 10-fold cross-validation was utilised, each fold contained 80 training examples and 15 test examples, and the network had one hidden layer of 15 units. The right hit performance was 63.75%; using sequential backward feature selection (*backselection*) the percentage of right answers increased to 65.75% and five attributes remained in the best line.

More training examples were added, up to 140, and using 150 test examples, the decision tree method had a performance of 75% correct answers, while the neural network scored 71.33%, using 15 hidden units, 10-fold cross-validation, each fold composed with 140 training examples and 15 test examples, and backselection. Again five attributes remained in the best line, two of them coincide with those obtained using the 80 training examples.

To improve classification results the number of attributes was reduced to eleven, although the attributes had to be more complicated. In this case, we obtained the following results. Using 140 training examples and 150 test examples, the decision tree method had a performance of 92% correct answers. The feed-forward neural network scored 85%, using 15 hidden units, 10-fold cross-validation, each fold composed with 140 training examples and 15 test examples. After using backselection the NN method reached 90%. The best line of attributes was: 1), 2), 3), 5), 6) and 10). Those attributes were:

1. White can win in one or two moves:
   a) Checkmating in the next move.
   b) Capturing the pawn in the next move.
   c) Giving a *skewer* in the next move. (A *skewer* will be defined as a check followed by a safe pawn capture with the rook).
   d) Giving checkmate in two moves.
   e) Threatening the pawn in the first move and capturing it in the 2nd move.
2. White can draw in any of the following cases:
   a) The WK is in check, the rook is threatened and is not attacking the pawn.
   b) The BK is in a stalemate position and it is not possible to make a move that changes the "state" of the position, that is, no matter what White moves, the BK will remain in a stalemate position.
   c) There is a *pseudoskewer position*. This is a position such that it is possible to move a *pseudoskewer* (a check with the rook, followed by an exchange of the rook for the pawn. In diagram 2, Re2+ followed by Rxa2 is a pseudoskewer).
   d) There is an *A position*. (an *A position* is one in which the rook or the WK can be moved threatening a pseudoskewer). Diagram 3, illustrates an A position, for example, Rh4 would threaten the pseudoskewer (Rh2+ followed by Rxa2).

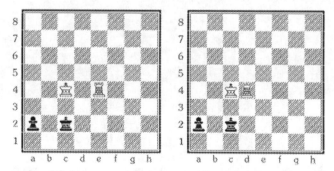

Diagrams 2 and 3. Show a *pseudoskewer position* and an *A position* respectively

   e) The rook can check the BK creating an A position; we could name it as an almost A position. See diagram 3.
   f) It is possible to give perpetual check.
3. The rook can guard the promotion square.
   a) And at the same time threaten the pawn. (The rook can be moved to column "a" and nothing interferes between it and the pawn).
   b) Without threatening the pawn. (The rook can be moved to row "1" and nothing interferes between it and the pawn).

5. The rook or the King can be moved threatening mate or skewer. It is possible to check BK and then give a skewer or threaten mate or skewer.
6. The rook can check (horizontally or vertically) and afterwards protect the promotion square.
10. d(WK,a2) ≤ 2.

These results confirm certain key concepts to build proper attributes, such as: giving a vertical check with the rook and the distance between the white king and the pawn. Other useful concepts were found, for example what Shapiro calls a delay skewer, i.e. moving the rook or the white king threatening skewer in the next move.

3.2 Position Classifier

Another approach to tackle the main problem is to divide the main problem into two smaller problems. The first one consists of deciding if in the chess position given, Black (the pawn's side) wins or not. If Black does not win, the second problem would arise, which consist of deciding when White (the rook's side) wins or draws. The advantage of this strategy is that it reduces the size of the tree, and increases the accuracy of the classification.

An important result of our research is the position classifier that can serve to classify random positions for the learning algorithm. Unfortunately, due to space reasons, we only present part of the classifier, which determines for every legal position of the KRKa2 ending with White to play, whether Black wins or not. This part was obtained using human reasoning for the construction of the attributes and a decision tree program for the tree construction.

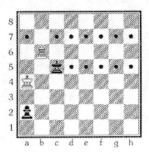

Diagram 4. Some ab positions (won by Black). The black dot denotes Black king positions

Eight attributes (to determine whether Black wins or not):

1. (ab position)
    (BK, WK, R) belongs to $\{(\gamma k,ai,bj) : 4 \le i \le 6,\ i \le j,\ i \le k,\ |j\text{-}k|=1\} - \{(ak,ai,bj) : j=i+1\}$
2. (WK against the ropes)
    (BK, WK, R) belongs to $\{(ci,ai,aj) :\ 4 \le i,\ j=i+1\} + \{(\alpha 3,\alpha 1,\beta 1) :\ d \le \alpha,\ \beta=\alpha+1\}$
3. (BK in northwest)   BK=γk γ=a or b k=6, 7 or 8
    (WK,R) belongs to $\{(\alpha i,\alpha j) : 2 \le i < j,\ e \le \alpha \le h,\ |j\text{-}k|=1\} + \{(di,dj) : 4 \le i < j,\ i \ne 5,\ |j\text{-}k|=1\}$
    $+ \{(ci,cj) : 4 \le i < j,\ |j\text{-}k|=1\}\ + (\ \{defgh\}+[c4,c6]\ )x\{bj : |j\text{-}k|=1\} + \{(a5,a8)\}$

4. (BK in southeast)   BK=γk γ=f,g or h   k=1 or 2
   (WK,R) belongs to   {(ei, hi) : i=3-k} + {(α3,β3) : d$\leq\alpha<\beta$+(1-k), $\alpha\neq$f, |β-γ|=1|}
   +{(α4,β4) : d$\leq\alpha<\beta$, $\alpha\neq$e, |β-γ|=1} + {(αi,βi) : 5$\leq$ i, b$\leq\alpha<\beta$, |β-γ|=1}

 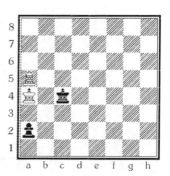

Diagrams 5 and 6. Two "against the ropes" positions (won by Black)

5. (BK on row 2)   BK=γ2
   (WK,R) belongs to {(αi, βi) : 5$\leq$i, b$\leq\alpha<\beta$, |β-γ|=1}
6. (BK in south)   BK=γk γ=d or e   k=1 or 2
   (WK,R) belongs to {(αi,βi) : d$\leq\alpha<\beta$, i=n(α), |β-γ|=1}
7. (BK on column a)   BK=ak
   (WK,R) belongs to {(αi,bj) : αi $\in$ [d1,h1]+[d4,h8], |j-k|=1, 3$\leq$j}
   +{(αi,αj) : 4$\leq$n(α)=i<j, |j-k|=1}
8. (BK on column b)   BK=bk
   (WK,R) belongs to {(αi,αj) : e$\leq\alpha\leq$h, 2$\leq$i<j, |j-k|=1} + {(d4,dj) : 4<j, |j-k|=1)}

Using the above eight attributes, seventeen examples (not stated for space reasons) and the decision tree induction program, a decision tree was obtained that can determine whether a position is won by Black or not. The resulting decision tree is functionally equivalent to the following If statement:

If (ab position) or (against the ropes WK) or (BK in northwest) or (BK in southeast) or (BK on row 2) or (BK in south) or (BK in column a) or (BK in column b) then Black wins; if not then Black does not win.

3.3 Discovery of Attributes for Learning Policy Sets

Finally with the aid of neural networks, decision trees, and human reasoning a set of useful short predicates was discovered. They will serve to construct training examples that are used as an input to an evolutionary learning algorithm which will learn a policy set that solves this domain. Although much work remains to be done, we believe that this method to automatically construct plans [5] will work for many domains.

Let WK=αi, R=βj, and BK=γk. Then:

|β-γ|=1: Rook and black king are on adjacent columns (and therefore a horizontal (=lateral) check at βk is not possible unless it is supported by the white king, that is, d(WK,βk)=1).

|j-k|=1: Rook and black king are on adjacent rows (and therefore a vertical check at γj is not possible unless it is supported by the white king, that is, d(WK,γj)=1).

i=j and α < β (i can be 1, 2, ...or 8): Rook on the right of the white king on row i.

α=β and i < j (α can be a, b, ...or h): Rook above the white king on column α.

β=b: Rook on column b (so it cannot move to b1 which is protected by the pawn).

Concepts regarding distance: d(WK,p)>n, d(BK,p)>n (n=1,2,...). Note, for example, that d(WK,p)=1 is equivalent to NOT (d(WK,p)>1) which is the negation of a concept.

a=γ<β and i<=j: (WK a-blocks the rook), 1=i<j and γ<β: (WK 1-blocks the rook).

R ∈ {2}+{a} and WK ∉ [p,R]: Rook attacks pawn.

i=1 or i=n(α): The white King would be in check if Black could queen.

These short predicates would serve as primitive predicates to the learning algorithm. To be precise the above short predicates would play the role of concepts that would be placed in the left hand side of the rule.

A list of possible actions (the right hand side of the rule) would be: R x P (Capture the pawn with the Rook), WK x P (Capture the pawn with the King), *Rook to a* (move the rook to column a), *Rook to 1* (move the rook to row 1), *Rook to 2* (move the rook to row 2), give a horizontal check, give a vertical check, etc.

An example of a policy set for the KRKa2 domain would be:

$$\pi_1 = \quad (R \in \{2\}+\{a\} \text{ and } WK \notin [p,R]) \wedge d(BK,P) > 1 \rightarrow R \times P$$

$$\pi_2 = \quad \neg\ d(WK,P) > 1 \wedge d(BK,P) > 1 \rightarrow WK \times P$$

Rule π_1 says: if the Rook is attacking the pawn and BK's distance to the pawn is greater than 1 then capture the pawn with the Rook. Rule π_2 says: if the WK's distance to the pawn is NOT greater than 1 (d(WK,P) = 1) and BK's distance to the pawn is greater than one then capture the pawn with the white king.

4 Conclusions

In [3] Fürnkranz states: "A significant body of research has gone into the task of learning to classify positions from a given chess endgame as wins or no wins. Endgame databases for KPK, KPa7KR, or KRKN have become standard benchmark problems for induction algorithms. Research in this area is also important for computer chess, because if endgame positions could be correctly classified with a few rules, this would save many resources compared to the alternative of storing all positions of a variety of endgames. Besides, many of the endgame databases that are now available are not thoroughly understood by human experts". We believe that these ideas hold true for many domains.

In the KRKa2 ending when deciding whether a position is won by Black or not, using the eight attributes, we noticed that in order to obtain a perfect classifier (one that correctly classifies every position), it is convenient, whenever possible, to build attributes that are sufficient conditions, that is, those attributes that might classify by themselves. For example: 1) *If (ab position) then Black wins.*

In every planning domain it is necessary to have some human knowledge about it in order to build a solver, in our case conformed of policy sets. Unfortunately this was not the case for the KRKa2 domain. Shapiro (1987) [7] writes: "In relation to its complexity the textbook treatment of KPKR (King and Pawn vs. King and Rook) is even more sketchy than that of KPK. Indeed the particular subset of KPKR that was chosen for this experiment (Ka7KR) is not mentioned at all in any chess ending book". In our case the lack of chess literature for this ending increases even more the difficulty of the problem. Recall that it is harder to analyze the ending when it is the Rook's side turn (KRKa2). Therefore we had to deduce this knowledge using human reasoning, neural networks and decision trees.

From the results of the system that makes policy sets for the Blocks World [5] and the construction of the KRKa2 classifiers, we believe that it is possible to build a system that constructs good policy sets for the KRKa2 domain. Since the KRKa2 domain involves more attributes (chess concepts) and more actions than the Blocks World, it constitutes a much better testbed for the evolutionary learning algorithm [5]. In fact the main idea is to prove that the learning algorithm can serve for many domains, but it is convenient to pass the KRKa2 barrier first.

References

1. Bain, M.E.: Learning Logical Exceptions in Chess. Ph. D. thesis, Department of Statistics and Modelling Science, University of Strathclyde, Scotland (1994)
2. De Groot, A. and Gobet, F.: Perception and memory in chess. Heuristics of the professional eye. Assen: Van Gorcum, Assen, The Netherlands. (With R.W. Jongman) (1996)
3. Fürnkranz, J.: Machine learning in computer chess: The next generation. International Computer Chess Association Journal, 19(3), (1996)
4. Khardon, R.: Learning action strategies for planning domains. Artificial Intelligence, 113, (1999)
5. González, A.: Learning Policy Sets using Evolutionary Computation. http://www.lsi.upc.es/ ~alquezar/gonzalez2003 ps (2003)
6. Shapiro, A.D. and Niblett T.: Automatic induction of classification rules for a chess endgame. In M. R. B. Clarke (Ed.), Advances in Computer Chess 3, Oxford: Pergamon (1983) 73-92
7. Shapiro, A. D.: Structured Induction in Expert Systems. Turing Institute Press. Addison-Wesley (1987)

One-Class Support Vector Machines and Density Estimation: The Precise Relation

Alberto Muñoz[1] and Javier M. Moguerza[2]

[1] University Carlos III, c/ Madrid 126, 28903 Getafe, Spain
`alberto.munoz@uc3m.es`
[2] University Rey Juan Carlos, c/ Tulipán s/n, 28933 Móstoles, Spain
`j.moguerza@escet.urjc.es`

Abstract. One-Class Support Vector Machines (SVM) afford the problem of estimating high density regions from univariate or multivariate data samples. To be more precise, sets whose probability is specified in advance are estimated. In this paper the exact relation between One-Class SVM and density estimation is demonstrated. This relation provides theoretical background for the behaviour of One-Class SVM when the Gaussian kernel is used, the only case for which successful results are shown in the literature.

1 Introduction

Density estimation [14] arises explicitly in a number of pattern recognition tasks involving interesting problems such as outlier (novelty) detection [8, 11, 15] or cluster analysis (see for instance [10, 5]). The density estimation task can be regarded as a particular type of inverse problem. In this setting, we consider a mapping $H_1 \xrightarrow{A} H_2$, where H_1 represents a metric function space and H_2 represents a metric space in which the observed data (which could be functions) live. In the density estimation problem, H_1 and H_2 are both function spaces and A is a linear integral operator given by: $(Af)(x) = \int K(x,y)f(x)dx$, where K is a predetermined kernel function and f is the density function we are seeking. The problem to solve is $Af = F$, where F is the distribution function. As far as F is unknown, the empirical distribution function F_n is used instead, where n is the number of data points, and the inverse problem to solve is $Af = y$, with $y = F_n$. Within the framework of regularization theory [16], if H_1 is chosen as a reproducing kernel Hilbert space (RKHS) [2], by the representer theorem [9], the estimator $\hat{f}$ of f takes the form $\hat{f}(x) = \sum_{i=1}^{n} c_i K(x, x_i)$. Taking $K(x, x_i) = K_h(x, x_i) = e^{-\|x - x_i\|^2/h}$, we obtain the well-known kernel density estimator with Gaussian kernel (see [14]), where each $c_i = 1/nh^d$, $h > 0$ and d is the data dimension.

One-Class Support Vector Machines [13, 15] are designed to solve density estimation related problems with tractable computational complexity.

The concrete problem to solve is the estimation of minimum volume sets of the form $S_\alpha(f) = \{x | f(x) \geq \alpha\}$, such that $P(S_\alpha(f)) = 1 - \nu$, where f is the

A. Sanfeliu et al. (Eds.): CIARP 2004, LNCS 3287, pp. 216–223, 2004.

density function and $0 < \nu < 1$. These sets are known in the literature as density contour clusters at level α [4, 6]. One-Class SVMs deal with a problem related to that of estimating $S_\alpha(f)$. The method computes a binary function that takes the value $+1$ in 'small' regions containing most data points and -1 elsewhere.

The rest of the paper is organized as follows: in Section 2 One-Class SVMs are briefly described. Section 3 makes explicit the relation between One-Class SVMs and classic density estimation. In Section 4 experiments that corroborate the theoretical findings are shown. Section 5 concludes.

2 One-Class SVMs in a Nutshell

The strategy of One-Class support vector methods is to map the data points into the feature space determined by the kernel function, and to separate them from the origin with maximum margin. Thus, it follows the general scheme of SVMs.

In order to build a separating hyperplane between the origin and the mapped points $\{\Phi(x_i)\}$, the One-Class SVM method solves the following quadratic optimization problem:

$$
\begin{aligned}
\min_{w,\rho,\xi} \quad & \frac{1}{2}\|w\|^2 - \nu n\rho + \sum_{i=1}^{n} \xi_i \\
\text{s.t.} \quad & \langle w, \Phi(x_i)\rangle \geq \rho - \xi_i, \\
& \xi_i \geq 0, \qquad\qquad i = 1, \ldots, n,
\end{aligned}
\tag{1}
$$

where Φ is the mapping defining the kernel function, ξ_i are slack variables, $\nu \in [0, 1]$ is an a priori fixed constant which represents the fraction of outlying points, and ρ is the decision value which determines if a given point belongs to the estimated high density region. The decision function will take the form $h(x) = sign(w^{*T}\Phi(x) - \rho^*)$, where w^* and ρ^* are the values of w and ρ at the solution of problem (1).

In [13] the mapping induced by the exponential (Gaussian) kernel $K_c(x, y) = e^{-\|x-y\|^2/c}$ is used. This kernel maps the data onto the unit hypersphere within the positive orthant. Figure 1 illustrates the situation.

In the following we will refer to 'quadratic One-Class SVM' simply as 'One-Class SVM'. Notice the difference with linear One-Class SVM, which were stated in [12].

The dual problem of (1) (see [3] for details on the derivation of the dual formulation) is:

$$
\begin{aligned}
\max_{\alpha} \quad & -\frac{1}{2} \sum_{i=1}^{n} \sum_{j=1}^{n} \alpha_i \alpha_j K(x_i, x_j) \\
\text{s.t.} \quad & \sum_{i=1}^{n} \alpha_i = \nu n, \\
& 0 \leq \alpha_i \leq 1, \qquad\qquad i = 1, \ldots, n.
\end{aligned}
\tag{2}
$$

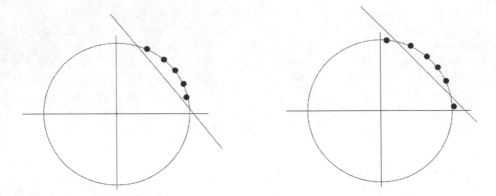

Fig. 1. Left: separating hyperplane in feature space. Right: the same for a percentage of points.

Points x_i such that at the solution of problem (2) satisfy $\alpha_i > 0$ are called *support vectors*. It can be shown that $h(x_i) > 0$ for the non-support vector points, that is, those points such that $\alpha_i = 0$ at the solution of problem (2).

The numerical results in [13] show that, for the exponential kernel, the performance of the method is similar to that of a kernel density estimator (Parzen windows).

3 Density Estimation and One-Class SVMs

In this section we show the strong relation that exists between One-Class SVM and kernel density estimation. This relation provides theoretical background for the behaviour of One-Class SVM with the exponential kernel (also known as Gaussian or RBF kernel), the only case illustrated with examples in [13]. In that work a relation in terms of (loose) probability bounds is given but, as stated by its authors, the relation is not conclusive.

The exponential kernel is a Mercer's kernel; therefore there exists a map $\phi : \mathbb{R}^d \longrightarrow \mathbb{R}^\infty$ such that $K(x, y) = \phi(x)^T \phi(y)$. Denote by d^* the distance induced by the kernel K in the feature space: $d_{ij}^* = d(\phi(x_i), \phi(x_j)) = \|\phi(x_i) - \phi(x_j)\|_K$. Considering that $d_{ij}^{*2} = K_{ii} + K_{jj} - 2K_{ij}$ and $K_{ii} = 1$ for the exponential kernel, a direct calculation shows that $K_{ij} = 1 - d_{ij}^{*2}/2$.

Hence, the One-Class SVM in its dual formulation (2) for the exponential kernel can be stated as the following equivalent optimization problem:

$$\min_{\alpha} \frac{1}{2}(\nu n)^2 - \frac{1}{4}\sum_{i=1}^{n}\sum_{j=1}^{n}\alpha_i\alpha_j d_{ij}^{*2}$$

$$\text{s.t. } \sum_{i=1}^{n}\alpha_i = \nu n,$$

$$0 \leq \alpha_i \leq 1, \quad i = 1, \ldots, n. \tag{3}$$

Note that in the One-Class SVM problem with exponential kernel ν represents the fraction of outlying points (see [13]).

In order to minimize the objective function of problem (3), the term $\sum_{i=1}^{n}\sum_{j=1}^{n}\alpha_i\alpha_j d_{ij}^{*2}$ has to be maximized. As a consequence of Proposition 4 in [13], as $n \to \infty$, the α_i's become 1 or 0. Thus, we have to choose a subset of νn points from the sample such that the sum of the distances among their images in the feature space is maximized. Equivalently, we can find the $(1-\nu)n$ points such that the sum of distances among their images in the feature space is minimized. For notational simplicity, assume these points are the first $(1-\nu)n$ in the sample.

Lemma 1. *Given n points x_i in a metric space, the following equality holds:* $\sum_i \sum_j d^2(x_i, x_j) = 2n \sum_i d^2(x_i, \bar{x})$, *where $\bar{x}$ stands for the sample mean.*

Proof. $\sum_i \sum_j d^2(x_i, x_j) = \sum_i \sum_j \|x_i - x_j\|^2 = \sum_i \sum_j \|x_i - \bar{x} + \bar{x} - x_j\|^2 = \sum_i \sum_j \left(\|x_i - \bar{x}\|^2 + \|x_j - \bar{x}\|^2 \right) - 2 \sum_i \sum_j (x_i - \bar{x})^T (x_j - \bar{x})$ and the last term becomes zero by definition of sample mean: $\sum_j (x_j - \bar{x}) = 0$. $\square$

By the preceding lemma and Proposition 4 in [13], as $n \to \infty$,

$$\sum_{i=1}^{(1-\nu)n} \sum_{j=1}^{(1-\nu)n} d_{ij}^{*2} = 2(1-\nu n) \sum_{i=1}^{(1-\nu)n} d^{*2}(\phi(x_i), \overline{\phi(x)}),$$

where $\overline{\phi(x)}$ stands for the average of the mapping $\psi(x_i)$ of the $(1-\nu)n$ points. This quantity will be minimized choosing the $(1-\nu)n$ points closest to their average.

Thus, we have proved the following theorem.

Theorem 1. *Consider the One-Class SVM with the exponential kernel. Asymptotically, the points obtained as non-support vectors correspond to those whose sum of distances to their mean in the feature space is minimum.*

The next theorem relates kernel density estimation with One-Class SVM.

Theorem 2. *Consider the One-Class SVM with the exponential kernel. Asymptotically, the points obtained as non-support vectors are those closest to the mode estimator calculated on this set of $(1-\nu)n$ non-support vectors, using a kernel density estimator with Gaussian kernel (Parzen windows).*

Proof. Again for notational simplicity, assume the non-support vector points are the first $(1-\nu)n$ points in the sample. Consider the kernel density estimator with exponential kernel $\hat{f}(x) = \frac{1}{(1-\nu)nh^d} \sum_{i=1}^{(1-\nu)n} K_h(x, x_i)$ where $K_{xx_i} = K_h(x, x_i) = e^{-\|x-x_i\|^2/h}$. Since $K_{xx_i} = 1 - 1/2d^{*2}(\phi(x), \phi(x_i))$, a simple calculation shows that $\hat{f}(x) = \frac{1}{h^d} - \frac{1}{2nh^d} \sum_{i=1}^{(1-\nu)n} d^{*2}(\phi(x), \phi(x_i))$.

Now consider the mean of the $(1-\nu)n$ non-support vector points, $\overline{\phi(x)}$.

Since $\frac{1}{h^d} - \frac{1}{2nh^d} \sum_{i=1}^{(1-\nu)n} d^{*2}(\overline{\phi(x)}, \phi(x_i))$ is maximum (see the proof of Theorem 1), Theorem 1 and standard continuity arguments guarantee that the points obtained as non-support vectors will be the points nearest to the maximum of $\hat{f}(x)$. $\square$

Statistical properties of the mode estimator using kernel density estimators have been studied in [7]. In particular, the estimator is consistent.

Remark 1. In case of existence of ϕ^{-1} (which is not guaranteed), the anti-image through ϕ, $x^* = \phi^{-1}(\overline{\phi(x)})$ would be the mode estimator. In fact, since $\hat{f}(x^*) = \frac{1}{h^d} - \frac{1}{2nh^d} \sum_{i=1}^{(1-\nu)n} d^{*2}(\overline{\phi(x)}, \phi(x_i))$ and by Theorem 2, the second term of $\hat{f}(x^*)$ is minimum; being the first term a constant, $\hat{f}(x^*)$ will be maximum.

Remark 2. The kernel density estimator $\hat{f}(x)$ relies critically on the value of the smoothing parameter h. Therefore the performance of the One-Class SVM will critically depend on a good choice of such parameter, and on the solution of the optimization problem itself.

4　Experiments

The main aim of the paper is to provide a deeper understanding of One-Class SVMs, by demonstrating its relation to already existing density estimation techniques. Anyhow, for the sake of completeness, next we show a couple of applications derived from the previous theoretical results.

4.1　An Example of Biased Behaviour

The asymptotical result in Theorem 1 suggests a suboptimal performance for One-Class SVM with asymmetrical data for non-huge data sets: for spherically symmetric distributions, asymptotically, the average of the whole set of points will converge to the true mean (which coincides with the mode) and so will happen with the $(1 - \nu)n$ points closest to their average. This can not be guaranteed for asymmetric distributions. To check the behaviour of One-Class SVM in this case, we have generated 2000 points from a gamma $\Gamma(\alpha, \beta)$ distribution, with $\alpha = 1.5$ and $\beta = 3$. Figure 2 shows the histogram, the gamma density curve, the true mode $(\alpha - 1)/\beta$ as a bold vertical line, and the One-Class SVM (five lines) estimations of the 50% highest density region. The parameters have been chosen applying the widely used rule $c = hd$ in $K_c(x, y)$, where $h \in \{0.1, 0.2, 0.5, 0.8, 1.0\}$ and d is the data dimension (see for instance [13]). The bias is apparent, since none of the five estimated support sets contains the true mode (and they should).

4.2　Improving One-Class SVM Performance

To illustrate a practical consecuence of Remark 2 next we show an example from the pattern recognition field, where the choice of the parameter c of kernel $K_c(x, y)$ is crucial. The database used contains nearly 4000 instances of handwritten digits from Alpaydin and Kaynak [1]. Each digit is represented by a

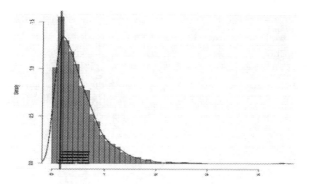

Fig. 2. Gamma sample with 2000 points. The figure shows the histogram, the density curve, a vertical line at the true mode, and One-Class SVM (five lines) estimations of the 50% highest density region.

vector in $\mathbb{R}^{64}$ constructed from a 32×32 bitmap image. Figure 3 shows a sample from the data base. The calligraphy of the digits in the database seems to be easily perceivable, which is supported by the high success rate of various classifiers. In particular, for each digit, nearest neighbour classifiers accuracy is always over 97% [1]. From this database we have selected a set of 409 data points made up by the 389 instances of digit '3' and the first 20 instances of digit '4' (approximattely 5% of the selected sample). The underlying hypothesis is that the support of the data is constituted by instances corresponding to digit '3', while the outlying points should correspond to instances of digit '4'.

We have run a set of experiments applying the rule for the choice of c described in the previous example. In the five experiments using this rule none of the outlying digits was detected by the One-Class SVM.

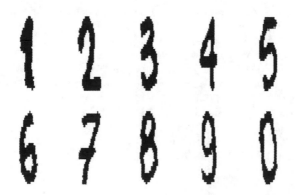

Fig. 3. A sample of the Alpaydin and Kaynak digit data base.

In order to improve this behaviour, and taking into account the result in Theorem 1, next we give a simple rule to choose the parameter c. This rule tries to minimize the numerical errors arising from the use of an exponential function. Thus we choose $c = \max\{d_{ij}^2\}$, where d_{ij} stands for the Euclidean distance between data points x_i and x_j. This value implies that the argument inside the exponent of $K_c(x_i, x_j)$ will be upper bounded for the data set, avoiding as far as possible numerical errors. Using this rule, 50% of the outlying instances were detected by the One-Class SVM, which certainly represents a remarkable improvement. The results were similar when different pair of digits were used for the experiments.

5   Conclusions

One-Class Support Vector Machines (SVM) afford the important task of estimating high density regions from data samples, a problem strongly related to the classical problem of density estimation. In this paper we have clearly stated the relation that exists between One-Class SVM and kernel density estimation. This relation provides theoretical background for the suboptimal behaviour of One-Class SVM when the Gaussian kernel is used, which is corroborated in the paper with some data examples. Finally, a simple rule to fix the parameter of the Gaussian kernel is given.

Acknowledgments

This work was partially supported by Spanish grants BEC2000-0167 (DGICYT), TIC2003-05982-C05-05 (MCyT) and PPR-2003-42 (URJC).

References

1. E. Alpaydin and C. Kaynak. *Cascading Classifiers*. Kybernetika, 34(4):369-374, 1998.
2. N. Aroszajn. *Theory of Reproducing Kernels*. Transactions of the American Mathematical Society, vol. 68, Issue 3, 1950, pp. 337-404.
3. M.S. Bazaraa, H.D. Sherali and C.M. Shetty. *Nonlinear Programming: Theory and Algorithms, 2nd Ed.* Wiley, New York, 1993.
4. S. Ben-David and M. Lindenbaum. *Learning distributions by their density levels: a paradigm for learning without a teacher.* Journal of Computer and System Sciences, 55:171-182, 1997.
5. A. Ben-Hur, D. Horn, H. Siegelmann and V. Vapnik. *Support Vector Clustering.* Journal of Machine Learning Research, 2:125-137, 2001.
6. A. Cuevas and R. Fraiman. *A plug-in approach to support estimation.* The Annals of Statistics, 25(6):2300-2312, 1997.
7. L. Devroye. *Recursive estimation of the mode of a multivariate density.* The Canadian Journal of Statistics, 7(2):159-167, 1979.
8. L. Devroye and Wise, G. *Detection of abnormal behavior via nonparametric estimation of the support.* SIAM J. Appl. Math., 38:480-488, 1980.

9. G.S. Kimeldorf and G. Wahba. *A Correspondence between Bayesian Estimation on Stochastic Processes and Smoothing by Splines.* Annals of Mathematical Statistics, 2:495-502, 1971.
10. J.M. Moguerza, A. Muñoz and M. Martin-Merino. *Detecting the Number of Clusters Using a Support Vector Machine Approach.* Proc. ICANN 2002, LNCS 2415:763-768, Springer, 2002.
11. A. Muñoz and J. Muruzabal. *Self-Organizing Maps for Outlier Detection.* Neurocomputing, 18:33-60, 1998.
12. G. Rätsch, S. Mika, B. Schölkopf and K.R. Müller. *Constructing Boosting Algorithms from SVMs: an Application to One-Class Classification.* IEEE Trans. on Pattern Analysis and Machine Intelligence, 24(9):1184-1199, 2002.
13. B. Schölkopf, J.C. Platt, J. Shawe-Taylor, A.J. Smola and R.C. Williamson. *Estimating the Support of a High Dimensional Distribution.* Neural Computation, 13(7):1443-1471 , 2001.
14. B.W. Silverman. *Density Estimation for Statistics and Data Analysis.* Chapman and Hall, 1990.
15. D.M.J. Tax and R.P.W. Duin. *Support Vector Domain Description.* Pattern Recognition Letters, 20:1991-1999, 1999.
16. A.N. Tikhonov and V.Y. Arsenin. *Solutions of ill-posed problems.* John Wiley & Sons, New York, 1977.

Fuzzy Model Based Control Applied
to Path Planning Visual Servoing

Paulo J. Sequeira Gonçalves[1], Luís F. Mendonça[2],
João Costa Sousa[2], and João Rogério Caldas Pinto[2]

[1] Instituto Politécnico de Castelo Branco
Escola Superior de Tecnologia
Dept. of Industrial Engineering
6000-767 Castelo Branco, Portugal
pgoncalves@est.ipcb.pt
[2] Technical University of Lisbon,
Instituto Superior Técnico
Dept. of Mechanical Engineering, GCAR/IDMEC
1049-001 Lisboa, Portugal
{mendonca,j.sousa,jcpinto}@dem.ist.utl.pt

Abstract. A new approach to eye-in-hand path planning image-based visual servoing based on fuzzy modeling and control is proposed in this paper. Fuzzy modeling is applied to obtain an inverse model of the mapping between image features velocities and joints velocities, avoiding the necessity of inverting the Jacobian. The inverse model is directly used as a controller. The control scheme is applied to a robotic manipulator performing visual servoing, for a given profile of planned image features velocities. The obtained results show the effectiveness of the proposed control scheme.

1 Introduction

In eye-in-hand image-based visual servoing, the Jacobian plays a decisive role in the convergence of the control, due to its analytical model dependency on the selected image features. Moreover, the Jacobian must be inverted on-line, at each iteration of the control scheme. Nowadays, the research community tries to find the right image features to obtain a diagonal Jacobian [10]. The obtained results only guarantee the decoupling from the position and the orientation of the velocity screw. This is still a hot research topic, as stated very recently in [10]. In this paper, the previous related problems in the Jacobian are addressed using fuzzy techniques, to obtain a controller capable to control the system. First, the desired trajectory is planned in the image space. Second, a fuzzy model to derive the inverse model of the robot is used to compute the joints and end-effector velocities in a straightforward manner. A two degrees of freedom planar robotic manipulator is controlled, based on eye-in-hand image-based visual servoing using fuzzy control systems. The paper starts by describing briefly the concept of image-based visual servoing and path planning. Fuzzy modeling and identification is described next. The obtained results and finally the conclusions and the possible future research are discussed.

A. Sanfeliu et al. (Eds.): CIARP 2004, LNCS 3287, pp. 224–231, 2004.

2   Image-Based Visual Servoing

In image-based visual servoing, the choice of different image features induces different control laws, and its number depends also on the number of degrees of freedom (DOF) of the robotic manipulator under control. The robotic manipulator used as test-bed in this paper is depicted in Fig. 1, and it has 2 DOF. Thus, the image features s consist of the coordinates x and y of one image point, which are needed to perform the control.

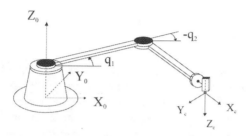

Fig. 1. Planar robotic manipulator with eye-in-hand looking down.

2.1   Modeling the Image-Based Visual Servoing System

Image-based visual servoing is used in an eye-in-hand system [6], where the camera is fixed at the robotic manipulator end-effector. The kinematic modeling of the transformation between the image features velocities and the joints velocities must be found. The kinematic modeling of the transformation between the image features velocities, $\dot{s}$, and the joints velocities $\dot{q}$ is defined as follows [4]:

$$\dot{s} = J(x, y, Z, q) \cdot \dot{q}, \tag{1}$$

where J is the total Jacobian, defined as:

$$J(x, y, Z, q) = J_i(x, y, Z) \cdot {}^c W_e \cdot {}^e J_R(q) \tag{2}$$

where Z is the depth between the camera and object frames; $J_i(x, y, Z)$ is the image Jacobian; ${}^c W_e$ is defined as the transformation between the camera and end-effector frames velocities and ${}^e J_R$ is the robot Jacobian for the planar robotic manipulator, [4].

2.2   Controlling the Image-Based Visual Servoing System

One of the classic control scheme of robotic manipulators using information from the vision system, is presented in [3]. The global control architecture is shown in Fig. 2, where the block *Robot inner loop* law is a PD control law, with sample time of 1 ms. The robot joint velocities $\dot{q}$ to move the robot to a predefined point in the image, s^* are derived using the *Visual control law*, [4], where an exponential decayment of the image features error is specified:

$$\dot{q} = -K_p \cdot \hat{J}^{-1}(x, y, Z, q) \cdot (s - s^*). \tag{3}$$

K_p is a positive gain, that is used to increase or decrease the decayment of the error velocity.

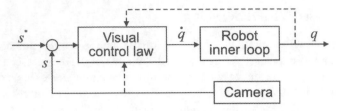

Fig. 2. Control loop of image-based visual servoing.

2.3   Visual Servoing by Path Planning

The path planning scheme presented follows the work in [7]. An image features trajectory is computed off-line, in order to be introduced on the visual control loop as
the reference to be followed. The method for obtaining the image features trajectory is
divided in three main parts. The first one is the data initialization, in which the initial
pose is obtained from the initial and desired robot position. The second part consists
of a iteration process in which the image features discrete path is composed. The third
part consists of obtaining the final trajectory of the image features over time. During
initialization, the image points corresponding to the image features as seen in the initial
and desired robot position are obtained. The translational vector and rotational matrix
between the object and the initial/desired position are computed using a pose estimation method [2]. The initialization ends with the computation of the initial pose relative
to the desired one, from the resulting data. The iteration process in which the image
features discrete path is composed begins with the estimation of the next pose, Υ_{k+1},
from the actual pose, Υ_k, and a composed force, F. The composed force is a sum of
two different forces, an attractive, F_a, and a repulsive, F_r. For details see [7].

$$
\begin{aligned}
\Upsilon_{k+1} &= \Upsilon_k + \varepsilon_k \cdot \frac{F(\Upsilon_k)}{\|F(\Upsilon_k)\|}, \varepsilon_k > 0 \\
F(\Upsilon_k) &= F_a(\Upsilon_k) + F_r(\Upsilon_k)
\end{aligned}
\tag{4}
$$

where ε_k is a positive scaling factor denoting the length of the kth increment. The attractive force minimizes the trajectory and the repulsive force is set to avoid, only, the physical image limits. All the remaining poses until the robot reaches the desired position
are estimated in a recursive process, which begins with the initial pose. The attractive
force is highest in the initial pose and it will diminish during the trajectory, tending to
zero at the final pose. The recursion ends when the attractive potential reaches a certain
value close to zero, meaning that the actual pose is close enough to the desired position. The result of the iteration process is a vector of image features which contains the
image variation of each image feature as the camera goes from the initial to the desired
position. The final trajectory of the image features over time, s^p, must be continuous
and differentiable, so was chosen a C^2 curve. It is computed from the vector obtained
during the iteration process, a pre-defined sample time - video rate $\Delta T = t_k - t_{k-1}$,
and the final time for the servoing, using a cubic spline.

$$
s^p(t) = A_k \cdot t^3 + B_k \cdot t^2 + C_k \cdot t + D_k
\tag{5}
$$

where: $(k-1) \cdot \Delta T \leq t \leq (k) \cdot \Delta T$. The control law used follows [7].

$$\dot{q} = -\lambda \cdot J^{-1} \cdot (e_p) + K_2 \cdot J^{-1} \cdot (e_{pp}) \tag{6}$$

where, $K_2 = \frac{\lambda}{\Delta T}$; $e_p = s_k - s_k^p$; $e_{pp} = s_k^p - s_{k-1}^p$.

2.4   Problem Statement

To derive an accurate global Jacobian, J, a perfect modeling of the camera, the image features, the position of the camera related to the end-effector, and the depth of the target related to the camera frame must be accurately determined. Even when a perfect model of the Jacobian is available, it can contain singularities, which hampers the application of a control law. To overcome these difficulties, a new type of differential relationship between the features and camera velocities was proposed in [9]. This approach estimates the variation of the image features, when an increment in the camera position ^cP is given, by using a relation G. This relation is divided into G_1 which relates the position of the camera to the image features, and F_1 which relates their respective variation:

$$s + \delta s = G(^cP + \delta^cP) = G_1(^cP) + F_1(^cP, \delta^cP). \tag{7}$$

Considering only the variations in (7):

$$\delta s = F_1(^cP, \delta^cP), \tag{8}$$

let the relation between the camera position variation δ^cP, the joint position variation, δq and the previous position of the robot q be given by:

$$\delta^cP = F_2(\delta q, q). \tag{9}$$

The two previous equations can be composed because the camera is rigidly attached to the robot end-effector, i.e., knowing q, ^cP can easily be obtained from the robot direct kinematics. Thus, an inverse function F^{-1} stating that the joint velocities depends on the image features velocities and the previous position of the robot manipulator can be obtained and discretized as follows:

$$\delta q(k) = F_k^{-1}(\delta s(k+1), q(k)). \tag{10}$$

In image-based visual servoing, the goal is to obtain a joint velocity, $\delta q(k)$, capable of driving the robot according to a desired image feature position, $s(k+1)$, with an also desired image feature velocity, $\delta s(k+1)$, from any position in the joint spaces. This goal can be accomplished by modeling the inverse function F_k^{-1}, using inverse fuzzy modeling as presented in Section 3. This new approach to image-based visual servoing allows to overcome the problems stated previously regarding the Jacobian inverse, the Jacobian singularities and the depth estimation, Z.

3   Fuzzy Control Strategies

3.1   Fuzzy Modeling

Fuzzy models can be identified based entirely on systems measurements. In the following, we consider data-driven modeling based on fuzzy clustering [1]. We consider rule-based models of the Takagi-Sugeno (TS) type. It consists of fuzzy rules which each describe a local input-output relation, typically in a linear form:

$$R_i : \text{If } x_1 \text{ is } A_{i1} \text{ and } \dots \text{ and } x_n \text{ is } A_{in} \text{ then } y_i = \mathbf{a}_i \mathbf{x} + b_i, \quad i = 1, 2, \dots, K.$$

Here R_i is the ith rule, $\mathbf{x} = [x_1, \dots, x_n]^T$ are the input (antecedent) variable, $A_{i1}, \dots$, A_{in} are fuzzy sets defined in the antecedent space, and y_i is the rule output variable. K denotes the number of rules in the rule base. The aggregated output of the model, $\hat{y}$, is calculated by taking the weighted average of the rule consequents: $\hat{y} = \sum_{i=1}^K \beta_i y_i / \sum_{i=1}^K \beta_i$, where β_i is the degree of activation of the ith rule: $\beta_i = \Pi_{j=1}^n \mu_{A_{ij}}(x_j)$, $i = 1, \dots, K$, and $\mu_{A_{ij}}(x_j) : \mathbb{R} \to [0, 1]$ is the membership function of the fuzzy set A_{ij} in the antecedent of R_i. To identify the model in (11), the regression matrix X and an output vector y are constructed from the available data: $X^T = [\mathbf{x}_1, \dots, \mathbf{x}_N]$, $\mathbf{y}^T = [y_1, \dots, y_N]$, where $N \gg n$ is the number of samples used for identification. The number of rules, K, the antecedent fuzzy sets, A_{ij}, and the consequent parameters, $\mathbf{a}_i, b_i$ are determined by means of fuzzy clustering in the product space of the inputs and the outputs [1]. Given the data set and an estimated number of clusters K, the Gustafson-Kessel fuzzy clustering algorithm [5] is applied to compute the fuzzy partition matrix U. The fuzzy sets in the antecedent of the rules A_{ij} are obtained from the partition matrix U, whose ikth element $\mu_{ik} \in [0, 1]$ is the membership degree of the data object $\mathbf{z}_k$ in cluster i. The consequent parameters for each rule are obtained as a weighted ordinary least-square estimate. Let $\theta_i^T = [\mathbf{a}_i^T; b_i]$, let X_e denote the matrix $[X; \mathbf{1}]$ and let W_i denote a diagonal matrix in $\mathbb{R}^{N \times N}$ having the degree of activation, $\beta_i(\mathbf{x}_k)$, as its kth diagonal element. Assuming that the columns of X_e are linearly independent and $\beta_i(\mathbf{x}_k) > 0$ for $1 \leq k \leq N$, the weighted least-squares solution of $\mathbf{y} = X_e \theta$ becomes $\theta_i = [X_e^T W_i X_e]^{-1} X_e^T W_i \mathbf{y}$. For the robotic application in this paper, the inverse model is identified using input-output data from the inputs $\dot{q}(k)$, outputs $\delta s(k+1)$ and the state of the system $q(k)$. A commonly used procedure in robotics is to learn the trajectory that must be followed by the robot. From an initial position, defined by the joint positions, the robotic manipulator moves to the predefined end position, following an also predefined trajectory, by means of a PID joint position controller. This specialized procedure has the drawback of requiring the identification of a new model for each new trajectory. However, this procedure revealed to be quite simple and fast. Moreover, this specialized identification procedure is able to alleviate in a large scale the problems derived from the close-loop identification procedure.

4   Results

This section presents the simulation results obtained for the robotic manipulator. First, the identification of the inverse fuzzy model of the robot is described. Then, the control results using the fuzzy model based controller introduced in this paper are presented.

4.1 Inverse Fuzzy Modeling

In order to apply the controller described in this paper, first an inverse fuzzy controller must be identified. Recall that a model must be identified for each trajectory. The profile chosen for the image features velocity was derived for the planned features path, that moves the robot from the initial joints position $q = [-1.5; 0.3]$ to the final position $q = [-1.51; 1.52]$, in one second, starting and ending with zero velocity. An inverse fuzzy model (10) for this trajectory is identified using the fuzzy modeling procedure described in Section 3.1. The measurements data is obtained from a simulation of the planar robotic manipulator eye-in-hand system. The set of identification data used to build the inverse fuzzy model contains 250 samples, with a sample time of 20ms. Figure 3a presents the input data, which are the joint positions $q_1(k)$ and $q_2(k)$, and the image features velocities $\delta s_x(k)$ and $\delta s_y(k)$, used for identification. Note that to iden-

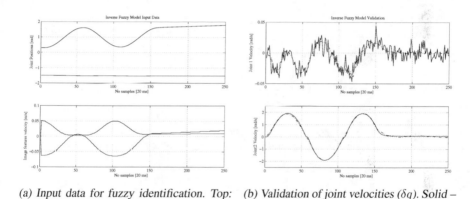

(a) Input data for fuzzy identification. Top: joint positions, q. Bottom: image feature velocity, δs.

(b) Validation of joint velocities (δq). Solid – real output data, and dash-dotted – output of the inverse fuzzy model.

Fig. 3. Input data for fuzzy modeling and validation of the obtained inverse fuzzy model.

tify the inverse model, one cannot simply feed the inputs as outputs and the outputs as inputs. Since the inverse model (10) is a non-causal model, the output of the inverse model must be shifted one step, see [8]. The validation of the inverse fuzzy model is shown in Fig. 3b, where the joint velocities δq are depicted. Note that two fuzzy models are identified, one for each velocity. It is clear that the model is quite good. Considering, e.g. the performance criteria *variance accounted for* (VAF), the models have the VAFs of 70.2% and 99.7%. When a perfect match occur, this measure has the value of 100%. Then, the inverse model for the joint velocity δq_2 is very accurate, but the inverse model for δq_1 is not so good. This was expectable as the joint velocity δq_1 varies much more than δq_2. However, this model will be sufficient to obtain an accurate controller, as is shown in Section 4.2. In terms of parameters, four rules (clusters) revealed to be sufficient for each output, and thus the inverse fuzzy model has 8 rules, 4 for each output, δq_1 and δq_2. The clusters are projected into the product-space of the space variables and the fuzzy sets A_{ij} are determined.

4.2   Control Results

This section presents the obtained control results, using the classical image-based path planning visual servoing presented in Section 2, and the inverse fuzzy model-based control scheme presented in Section 3. The implementation was developed in a simulation of the planar robotic manipulator eye-in-hand system. This simulation was developed and validated in real experiments, using classic visual servoing techniques, by the authors.

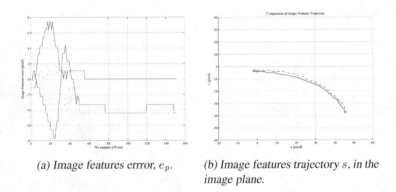

(a) Image features errror, e_p.

(b) Image features trajectory s, in the image plane.

Fig. 4. Comparison between fuzzy and classical path planning visual servoing, image errors and trajectories. Solid – inverse fuzzy model control, and dash-dotted – classical visual servo control.

The comparison of the image features trajectory for both the classic and the fuzzy visual servoing controllers is presented in Fig. 4a. In this figure, it is shown that the classical controller follows the trajectory with a better accuracy than the fuzzy controller. The image features trajectory in the image plane is presented in Fig. 4b, which shows that both controllers can achieve the goal position (the plus, +, sign in the image) with a very small error. This figure shows also that the trajectory obtained with the inverse fuzzy model controller is smoother. This fact is due to the high proportional gain that the classical controller must have to follow the trajectory, which demands higher velocities. This effect is easily removed by slowing down the classical controller. But in this case, the fuzzy controller clearly outperforms the classical controller. The classical controller can only follow the trajectory without oscillations in the joint velocities if the robot takes 1.5s to move from one point to the other. In this case, the classical controller is about 50% slower than the fuzzy model-based controller proposed in this paper.

5   Conclusions

This paper introduces an eye-in-hand path planning image-based visual servoing scheme based on fuzzy modeling and control. The fuzzy modeling approach was applied to obtain an inverse model of the mapping between image features velocities and joints velocities. This inverse model is directly used as controller of a robotic manipulator performing path planning visual servoing, for a given image features velocity profile. The obtained results showed that both the classical and the fuzzy controllers can follow the image features velocity profile. However, the proportional gain of the classic visual servoing must be very high. This fact justifies the more smooth trajectory in the image plane for the fuzzy controller. For that reason, the inverse fuzzy control proposed in this paper performs better. As future work, the proposed fuzzy model based control scheme will be implemented in the experimental test-bed. Note that an off-line identification of the inverse fuzzy model must first be performed. The complete automation of this identification step is also under study.

Acknowledgement

This work is supported by the "Programa de Financiamento Plurianual de Unidades de I&D (POCTI) do Quadro Comunitário de Apoio III", by program FEDER, by the FCT project POCTI/ EME/39946/2001, and by the "Programa do FSE-UE, PRODEP III, acção 5.3, no âmbito do III Quadro Comunitário de apoio".

References

1. R. Babuška. *Fuzzy Modeling for Control*. Kluwer Academic Publishers, Boston, 1998.
2. D. Dementhon and L. Davis. Model-based object pose in 25 lines of code. *International Journal of Computer Vision*, 15(1/2):123–141, 1995.
3. B. Espiau, F. Chaumette, and P. Rives. A new approach to visual servoing in robotics. *IEEE Transactions on Robotics and Automation*, 8(3):313–326, 1992.
4. P. S. Gonçalves and J. C. Pinto. Camera configurations of a visual servoing setup, for a 2 dof planar robot. In *Proceedings of the 7th International IFAC Symposium on Robot Control, Wroclaw, Poland.*, pages 181–187, Wroclaw, Poland, Sept. 2003.
5. D. E. Gustafson and W. C. Kessel. Fuzzy clustering with a fuzzy covariance matrix. In *Proceedings IEEE CDC*, pages 761–766, San Diego, USA, 1979.
6. S. Hutchinson, G. Hager, and P. Corke. A tutorial on visual servo control. *IEEE Transactions on Robotics and Automation*, 12(5):651–670, 1996.
7. Y. Mezouar and F. Chaumette. Path planning for robust image-based control. *IEEE Transactions on Robotics and Automation*, 18(4):534–549, 2002.
8. J. Sousa, C. Silva, and J. S. da Costa. Fuzzy active noise modeling and control. *International Journal of Approximate Reasoning*, 33:51–70, April 2003.
9. I. Suh and T. Kim. Fuzzy membership function based neural networks with applications to the visual servoing of robot manipulators. *IEEE Trans. on Fuzzy Systems*, 2(3):203–220, 1994.
10. O. Tahri and F. Chaumette. Application of moment invariants to visual servoing. In *Proc. of the IEEE Int. Conf. on Robotics and Automation*, pages 4276–4281, Taipeh, Taiwan, 2003.

A Color Constancy Algorithm
for the Robust Description
of Images Collected from a Mobile Robot*

Jaume Vergés-Llahí and Alberto Sanfeliu

Institut de Robòtica i Informàtica Industrial
Technological Park of Barcelona, U Building
Llorens i Artigas 4-6, 08028 Barcelona, Catalonia
{jverges,asanfeliu}@iri.upc.es

Abstract. In mobile robotics, it is necessary to have a robust and efficient way of describing the visual stream provided by a vision system to be used afterwards in tasks such as object recognition. Color histograms are a useful tool to capture and represent color properties of sets of images taken from a certain position. Since those images were obtained at different time and light conditions, their appearance have greatly changed, reducing the performance of the color descriptor. In this work, we develop a color constancy algorithm that copes with the color variation among sets of images taken from nearly the same place. We show that the performance of the color histogram descriptor rises after color constancy, becoming a more robust and useful color descriptor. In the results section, we support that claim with several sets of images of scenes belonging to different positions.

Keywords: color histograms, color constancy, mobile robots

1 Introduction

Suppose a mobile robot equipped with a camera which is moving about an area in a way that is able to take images of the environment and associate them to a pose $\mathbf{p}$ consisting in a position $(x, y) \in \mathbf{R}^2$ and an orientation $\theta \in [0, 2\pi)$, expressed in a chosen framework $\mathcal{O}$.

Consequently, after some time of moving, the robot will have provided a huge database of images of such area indexed through the pose $\mathbf{p}$. Any time a query is carried out to know what the robot is likely to see when located at a pose $\mathbf{p}$, given an uncertainty ϵ, the system answer will be a set of images $\mathcal{I}_{\mathbf{p}} = \{I_{\mathbf{p}_1}, \cdots, I_{\mathbf{p}_M}$ such that $\|\mathbf{p} - \mathbf{p}_i\| < \epsilon\}$.

The set $\mathcal{I}_{\mathbf{p}}$ encompasses the whole visual knowledge of the system at a certain pose which can be useful in a number of tasks in mobile robotics, such as recognition of an object or person in the scene. Furthermore, if the set were stable and distinctive enough it could be used in the reversed way. Once in an

* Part. funded by the Gov. of Catalonia and the CICYT DPI2001-2223.

A. Sanfeliu et al. (Eds.): CIARP 2004, LNCS 3287, pp. 232–240, 2004.

unknown position, identify where the robot is located matching what it sees with the descriptors of different locations in a database previously gathered.

Aforementioned tasks require that any set $\mathcal{I}_\mathbf{p}$ should be described in a simple, generic and computationally inexpensive way. Additionally, the images in $\mathcal{I}_\mathbf{p}$ must be mutually comparable, i.e., look similar at close poses, and so their descriptors. In other words, any descriptor accounting for the visual information of $\mathcal{I}_\mathbf{p}$ should be representative of the actual content of the scene at $\mathbf{p}$ and be unaffected by the presence of variations.

There are three main sources of variation in $\mathcal{I}_\mathbf{p}$. First, $\|\mathbf{p}_i - \mathbf{p}_j\| < \epsilon$ implies the points of view where the images were taken from are not exactly the same, so are not the images $I_{\mathbf{p}_i}$ and $I_{\mathbf{p}_j}$. Secondly, some objects may have appeared, disappeared or just changed their relative position in images taken at different times due to independent movement or mutual occlusions. Third, objects can look differently due to changes in the position relative to light sources, but also to a variation through time of those lights.

This paper focuses on a framework to describe sets of images in a simple, generic and compact way coping with the previous sources of variation. First, we employ the α–trimmed average histogram to integrate the images in one descriptor by analogy to the problem of representing a group of frames in a video by their color histograms [1]. Since our images have greater color variation, we apply a color constancy technique to improve the descriptor stability. At the end, we show the performance of the descriptor and its improvement after using the color constancy step. This way, we get a robust representation of an area build up by different color histograms reduced to a canonic light conditions and combined in a way that outliers and light variation have been greatly reduced.

2   Descriptor of a Set of Images (SoI)

Our problem is close to that of finding a general framework for an efficient representation of video sequences, where the goal is usually to develop fast and robust algorithms for the identification of the video segment to which a query belongs [2]. In both cases, there is a set of images to be reduced to an efficient, robust and stable descriptor which can be used in a content-based query.

A generic mechanism to describe the content in a video sequence is the shot-based representation model. Once the shot is selected, it is customary to describe the visual and color content of shots using key frames and key frame histograms, respectively. Another framework is the groups of frames that are collections of frames selected according to a certain criterion. It is more flexible and general than the shot-based approach and well-suited for representing the sequential and hierarchical nature of video data.

Although the key frame histogram is a very simple descriptor of the color content of a shot, it is highly dependent on the selection criterion of the representative frame(s) and may lead to unreliable results. A more favourable approach is to consider the color content of *all* frames within a shot. Considering different strategies to get this *cumulative* color histogram, the simplest approach is the mean histogram, though potential problems with its sensitivity to outliers may make advisable the use of the median [1].

An alternative approach for computing the histogram of a set of images (SoI) is to define a family of α-trimmed average histograms [1], obtained by sorting the set of image histogram values for each bin in ascending order and averaging only the central $M - 2\lfloor \alpha M \rfloor$ elements of the ordered array, where M is the number of images in the SoI. Then, each bin j is computed as

$$\alpha TrimHist(j, \alpha) = \frac{1}{M - 2\lfloor \alpha M \rfloor} \sum_{i=\lfloor \alpha M \rfloor + 1}^{M - \lfloor \alpha M \rfloor} \tilde{\mathcal{H}}_i(j) \tag{1}$$

where $\{\tilde{\mathcal{H}}_1(j), \ldots, \tilde{\mathcal{H}}_M(j)\}$ is the sorted array of image histogram values for the jth bin, i.e., $\{\mathcal{H}_1(j), \ldots, \mathcal{H}_M(j)\}$. The trimming parameter $\alpha \in [0, \frac{1}{2}]$, controls the number of data points excluded from the average computation. While $\alpha = 0$ corresponds to the mean histogram, $\alpha = \frac{1}{2}$ computes the median one.

The interest of the above aggregation scheme is that of reducing the effect of outliers such as those belonging to objects that appear or disappear in the frames embodied in a SoI while easily encompassing either the mean or the median by tuning the α parameter. Additionally, the use of histograms minimizes the importance of relative positions of the objects in the scene. This way, two out of three main variation sources are reduced using those descriptors.

The third source of variability, illumination, needs special consideration. The kind of sequences in video data [1] have a relatively small light variation within a shot since a great effort in the visual uniformity of sequences has been put during the shooting and post-production. Nevertheless, in the case of images taken from a mobile robot, no control on the illumination can be done and the images belonging to the same SoI may have been taken at different times implying greater light variations which affect the color of the objects in the scene, as appreciated in Fig. (1).

3   Color Constancy in a Set of Images

Images in a SoI may present some degree of color variation due to changing light conditions. Our approach consists in reducing this variation before aggregating their color histograms using Eq. (1). On that purpose, we compute for every image in a SoI the set of all feasible color mappings rendering the image back to a canonical illumination – corresponding to a canonical image selected from the SoI – and selecting one mapping afterwards based on a measure of its likelihood.

More precisely, let I_c and I_a be the *canonic* and the *actual* images, respectively, picturing pretty much a similar scene since they are taken at nearly the same pose under two different illuminations. Our aim is to find the most likely color transformation T which maps the pixel colors of image I_a as close to those of image I_c as possible, hence reducing the color variation in the SoI. We now sketch the basis of our color constancy algorithm.

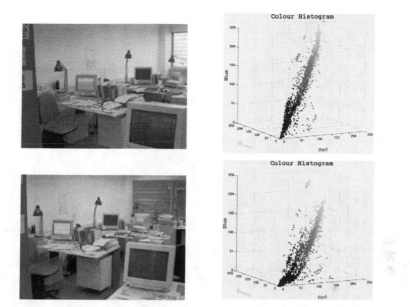

Fig. 1. Images taken nearly at the same a pose.

3.1   Likelihood Function

First, we introduce some notation and definitions. We note as $\mathcal{I} \subset \mathbf{R}^n$ a certain set of colors. Those colors can come from a specified color gamut or an image I. We also get the color histogram $\mathcal{H}(\mathcal{I})$ from $\mathcal{I}$. If the mapping $T \in \mathcal{T}$ is applied to every color in $\mathcal{I}$, the transformed set $T(\mathcal{I})$ is obtained. $\mathcal{T}$ is the set of all feasible color mappings.

In general, given two color sets, $\mathcal{I}_a$ and $\mathcal{I}_c$, a model of color change is a mapping $T \in \mathcal{T}$ so that $T(\mathbf{s}) = \mathbf{q}$, where $\mathbf{s} \in \mathcal{I}_a$ and $\mathbf{q} \in \mathcal{I}_c$ are corresponding colors. Finally, the set of feasible mappings can be defined as $\mathcal{T} = \{T = G(\mathbf{s}, \mathbf{q}) \mid \forall \mathbf{s} \in \mathcal{I}_a$ and $\forall \mathbf{q} \in \mathcal{I}_c\}$, where G is a *recovery scheme* (a function or an algorithm) computing one single mapping T out of two colors $\mathbf{s}$ and $\mathbf{q}$.

The color constancy algorithm will select the most likely transformation $\hat{T}$ from the set $\mathcal{T}$. Therefore, if $\mathcal{L}_G(T|\mathcal{I}_a, \mathcal{I}_c)$ is a function computing the likelihood for every mapping $T \in \mathcal{T}$, the algorithm finds the mapping that

$$\hat{T} = \operatorname{argmax}\{\,\mathcal{L}_{\mathbf{G}}\,(T|\mathcal{I}_a, \mathcal{I}_c)\,,\,T \in \mathcal{T}\} \tag{2}$$

A likelihood function $\mathcal{L}_G$ can be related to a probability function $\Pr$ in the way $\mathcal{L}_G(T|\mathcal{I}_a, \mathcal{I}_c) = log(\Pr(T|\mathcal{I}_a, \mathcal{I}_c))$. So, first we must get a value for the probability $\Pr$ of a certain mapping T. As an estimate of $\Pr(T|\mathcal{I}_a, \mathcal{I}_c)$ we use the histogram of the set of feasible mappings, $\mathcal{H}(\mathcal{T})$, computed from the sets $\mathcal{I}_a$ and $\mathcal{I}_c$ and the recovery scheme G. *The key idea is that the more likely a mapping is, the more frequent it should be in the histogram $\mathcal{H}(\mathcal{T})$.*

Let $G^{-1}(T) = \{(\mathbf{s}, \mathbf{q}) \in \mathcal{I}_a \times \mathcal{I}_c \mid G(\mathbf{s}, \mathbf{q}) = T\}$ be the set of all pairs $(\mathbf{s}, \mathbf{q})$ giving rise to a certain mapping T using the recovery scheme G. The set $G^{-1}(T)$ can be taken instead of T since $G^{-1}(T) = G^{-1}(T') \Leftrightarrow T = T'$. Hence, $\Pr(T|\mathcal{I}_a, \mathcal{I}_c)$) is estimated as $\Pr(G^{-1}(T)|\mathcal{I}_a, \mathcal{I}_c)$).

In addition, since our color sets are discrete, $G^{-1}(T)$ can be thought as a finite disjoint union of singletons $\{(\mathbf{s}, \mathbf{q})\}$. Each singleton $\{(\mathbf{s}, \mathbf{q})\} \in \mathcal{I}_a \times \mathcal{I}_c$ can be further divided in two different pieces, namely, $\{\mathbf{s}\} \in \mathcal{I}_a$ and $\{\mathbf{q}\} \in \mathcal{I}_c$, which can be assumed to be independent. Therefore,

$$\Pr((\mathbf{s}, \mathbf{q})|\mathcal{I}_a, \mathcal{I}_c) = \Pr(\mathbf{s}|\mathcal{I}_a) \cdot \Pr(\mathbf{q}|\mathcal{I}_c) \qquad (3)$$

where $\Pr(\mathbf{s}|\mathcal{I}_a)$ and $\Pr(\mathbf{q}|\mathcal{I}_c)$ estimates come from their corresponding bins in histograms $\mathcal{H}(\mathcal{I}_a)$ and $\mathcal{H}(\mathcal{I}_c)$, respectively. Then,

$$\Pr(T|\mathcal{I}_a, \mathcal{I}_c)) = \sum_{\forall(\mathbf{s}, \mathbf{q}) \in G^{-1}(T)} \Pr(\mathbf{s}|\mathcal{I}_a) \cdot \Pr(\mathbf{q}|\mathcal{I}_c) \qquad (4)$$

That is, the frequency of the bin corresponding to a mapping T in the histogram of feasible mappings $\mathcal{H}(\mathcal{T})$ can be computed adding the product of frequencies of the two bins in $\mathcal{H}(\mathcal{I}_a)$ and $\mathcal{H}(\mathcal{I}_c)$ corresponding to all the color pairs giving rise to the mapping T by means of the recovery scheme G.

In order to improve the robustness of Eq. (4), a measure of similarity between the transformed set $T(\mathcal{I}_a)$ and the canonical set $\mathcal{I}_c$ is taken into account which evaluates the performance of a particular mapping. We use the Swain&Ballard intersection measure [3] defined as $\cap(\mathcal{H}, \mathcal{M}) = \sum_k \min\{H_k, M_k\} \in [0, 1]$ for its computational simplicity. This measure is helpful in practice to eliminate outlier mappings among the set of candidates.

Finally, we joint the probability and performance of a mapping in a single likelihood function as follows

$$\mathcal{L}_G(T|\mathcal{I}_a, \mathcal{I}_c) = log(\cap(T(\mathcal{H}_a), \mathcal{H}_c)) \cdot \Pr(T|\mathcal{I}_a, \mathcal{I}_c) \qquad (5)$$

where $\mathcal{H}_a = \mathcal{H}(\mathcal{I}_a)$, $\mathcal{H}_c = \mathcal{H}(\mathcal{I}_c)$ and $\Pr(T|\mathcal{I}_a, \mathcal{I}_c)$) is as in Eq. (4). Furthermore, $T(\mathcal{H})$ is the transformation of a histogram $\mathcal{H}$ by T.

3.2   Color Change Model and Recovery Scheme

To complete the previous scheme, the kind of color coordinates and the model of color change T as well as the recovery function G must be explicitly stated.

First, colors are vectors in $\mathbf{R}^n$, where $n = 3$ in a (R, G, B) color space or $n = 2$ in a *chromaticity space*. In our case, to alleviate problems found in images with specularities or shades, and to reduce at the same time the computational burden, we use the *perspective color coordinates* $(r, g) = (R/B, G/B)$ defined by Finlayson in [4] which discard intensity. Finlayson and Hordley proved in [5] that the set of feasible mappings computed in a $3D$ space and projected into a $2D$ space afterward is the same as the set computed directly in a $2D$ space.

A general lineal color change model can be mathematically describe as $T(\mathbf{s}) = T \cdot \mathbf{s} = \mathbf{q}$, where $T \in \mathcal{M}_n(\mathbf{R})$ is a square matrix encompassing a particular color change between two different lights [6]. A reasonable tradeoff between simplicity and performance can be attained employing a diagonal model [6, 7, 4]. This model assumes color sensors are completely uncorrelated and any change in the light arriving to them equates to independently scaling each channel value, that is, $T = diag(t_1, \ldots, t_n)$. Equivalently, T can be also expressed as a vector $\mathbf{t} = (t_1, \ldots, t_n) \in \mathbf{R}^n$. Therefore, for any pair $(\mathbf{s}, \mathbf{q}) \in \mathcal{I}_a \times \mathcal{I}_c$, the color change model we use is

$$T: \mathcal{I}_a \longrightarrow \mathcal{I}_c$$
$$\mathbf{s} \longmapsto T(\mathbf{s}) = T \cdot \mathbf{s} = \mathbf{q} \tag{6}$$

and the recovery scheme is

$$G: \mathcal{I}_a \times \mathcal{I}_c \longrightarrow \mathcal{T} \subset \mathbf{R}^n$$
$$(\mathbf{s}, \mathbf{q}) \longmapsto G(\mathbf{s}, \mathbf{q}) = (\tfrac{q_1}{s_1}, \ldots, \tfrac{q_n}{s_n}) = \mathbf{t} \tag{7}$$

where $\mathcal{T} = \{(\tfrac{q_1}{s_1}, \ldots, \tfrac{q_n}{s_n}) \,|\, \forall\, (\mathbf{s}, \mathbf{q}) \in \mathcal{I}_a \times \mathcal{I}_c\}$.

3.3   A Color Constant Set of Images

Once a *canonical* image $I_c \in \mathcal{I}$ is selected, we apply the previous color constancy to the set $\{I_1, \ldots, I_M\}$ employing their color histograms $\{\mathcal{H}_1, \ldots, \mathcal{H}_M\}$ and the canonical $\mathcal{H}_c$. Afterward, the set $\{T_1(\mathcal{H}_1), \ldots, T_M(\mathcal{H}_M)\}$ of transformed histograms can be used to generate the α-trimmed average histogram defined in Eq. (1) representing the whole SoI, noted as $\mathcal{H}_{SoI}$.

4   Results

We want to show how the performance of the scene description $\mathcal{H}_{SoI}$ improves after using our color constancy algorithm. A natural way to measure the fidelity of these descriptors is in terms of the average error $E_{\mathcal{H}_{SoI}}$ within a set of images defined in [1] as the average of the accumulated distance between each image histogram $\mathcal{H}_i$ in the SoI and the SoI histogram $\mathcal{H}_{SoI}$,

$$E_{\mathcal{H}_{SoI}} = \frac{1}{M} \sum_{i=1}^{M} \sum_{j=1}^{N} |\mathcal{H}_i(j) - \mathcal{H}_{SoI}(j)| \tag{8}$$

where N and M are the number of bins and that of images, respectively. This error provides a consistent way to assess the performance of the proposed descriptor. The less representative of the color content of the SoI the descriptor is, the greater the error measure is.

Our database consist in a set of 21 images at five different poses and with very different light conditions picturing a regular office environment. The canonical image of these scenes can be seen in the leftmost column of Fig. (2). The first four scenes have 3 images each, while the last one has 9. Besides, images belonging to the same scene have appreciable variations in the point of view and light conditions, as depicted in Fig. (1). The group with a greater variation is the last one, where there are occlusions and some objects have appeared or disappeared.

The rightmost column in Fig. (2) shows the error $E_{\mathcal{H}_{SoI}}$ as a function of the trimming parameter α. The results obtained if no color constancy step – No CC

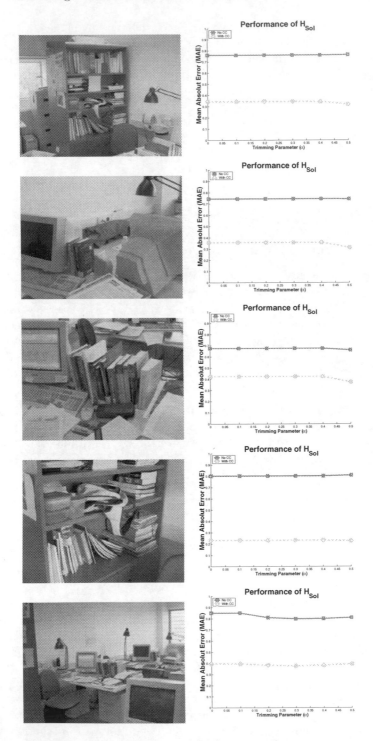

Fig. 2. Scenes and Performance plots.

Table 1. No Color Constancy Step.

Scene	Mean	Std	Max	Min
No.1	0.760	0.001	0.763	0.760
No.2	0.744	0.000	0.744	0.743
No.3	0.673	0.006	0.676	0.661
No.4	0.804	0.003	0.809	0.802
No.5	0.820	0.024	0.851	0.799

Table 2. With Color Constancy Step.

Scene	Mean	Std	Max	Min	% Red.
No.1	0.341	0.010	0.345	0.320	55.13
No.2	0.350	0.018	0.358	0.313	52.96
No.3	0.415	0.020	0.424	0.374	38.34
No.4	0.232	0.002	0.233	0.227	71.14
No.5	0.389	0.008	0.396	0.378	52.56

– is applied are plotted with a red solid line with squares, while those obtained after the color constancy step – With CC – are depicted with a green dashed line with circles. To clarify numerically those results, we have expressed the mean, standard deviation, maximum and minimum values of these plots in Table 1 and 2, as well as the error reduction in the last column in Table 2.

The results clearly show there has been a reduction (54% in average) of the error $E_{\mathcal{H}_{SoI}}$ between the image histograms $\mathcal{H}_i$ and the scene descriptor $\mathcal{H}_{SoI}$ after the color constancy step, which means a decrease of the internal image variation and an improvement for representativeness of SoI by the proposed scene descriptor. Furthermore, the obtained error reduction is far greater than that achieved by only tuning the trimming parameter, which means that a simpler descriptor could be used instead, for example, by only employing the mean ($\alpha = 0$) or the median ($\alpha = 1/2$) to compute $\mathcal{H}_{SoI}$.

5   Conclusions

This paper has exposed the problem of obtaining a global color-based description of a set of images captured from a mobile robot picturing a particular location. Our main concern has been to generate a kind of descriptors robust to a certain number of sources of variation, being color variation due to illumination changes the most important one to cope with among images taken from a mobile platform. As a result, we have shown that a reduction in the average error between the histograms of the set images and the histogram describing the whole set can be attained by applying a color constancy step. The color descriptor is then more robust and representative of the set since its color variation has been greatly reduced. A future work would be the extension of these descriptors to the task of robot localization only by means of the set of captured images.

References

1. Ferman, A.M., Tekalp, A.M., Mehrotra, R.: Robust color histogram descriptors for video segment retrieval and identification. IEEE Trans. on Image Processing **11** (2002) 497–508
2. Idris, F., Panchanathan, S.: Review of image and video indexing techniques. Journal of Visual Communication and Image Representation **8** (1997) 146–166
3. Swain, M., Ballard, D.: Indexing via color histograms. In: Proc. Int. Conf. on Computer Vision. (1990) 390–393

4. Finlayson, G.: Color in perspective. IEEE Trans. on Pattern Analysis and Machine Intelligence **18** (1996) 1034–1038
5. Finlayson, G., Hordley, S.: Improving gamut mapping color constancy. IEEE Trans. on Image Processing **9** (2000) 1774–1783
6. Forsyth, D.: A novel algorithm for color constancy. Int. Journal of Computer Vision **5** (1990) 5–36
7. Finlayson, G., Hordley, S., Hubel, P.: Colour by correlation: A simple, unifying framework for colour constancy. IEEE Trans. on Pattern Analysis and Machine Intelligence **23** (2001) 1209–1221

Unconstrained 3D-Mesh Generation Applied to Map Building

Diego Viejo and Miguel Cazorla

Robot Vision Group
Departamento de Ciencia de la Computación e Inteligencia Artificial
Universidad de Alicante
E-03690, Alicante, Spain
Phone +34 96 590 39 00, Fax +34 96590 39 02
{dviejo,miguel}@dccia.ua.es

Abstract. 3D map building is a complex robotics task which needs mathematical robust models. From a 3D point cloud, we can use the normal vectors to these points to do feature extraction. In this paper, we will present a robust method for normal estimation and unconstrained 3D-mesh generation from a not-uniformly distributed point cloud.

1 Introduction

Map building is a main task in robotics. This task estimates a map from sensor data (sonar, laser, 3D data, ...). Our work is focused in 3D map building. We use data from a stereo camera and our goal is to obtain geometric primitives (such as planes, cylinders, and so on) from this data.

Some previous approaches has been proposed to 3D map building. Some of them ([1], [2]) use a laser pointing upwards and taking data every small interval of time. The triangulation between points turns out fast and easy. In [3] an additional step is applied in order to reduce the error between two consecutive steps. However, our main problem is the use of a stereo camera. In environments with low texture the camera does not provide points and the point set is not uniform. So, we have to address the "holes" inside data. We propose to use a (robust) triangulation algorithm which takes into account these holes from data.

Our work will be guided from some assumptions. We assume that our robot will work in a indoor (structured) environment. For this reason, we can guess that the environment is formed from geometric primitives, like (mainly) planes or cylinders. Extracting these primitives might help in the overall process. In order to obtain these primitives we propose to use the normals obtained from a triangulation of the point set. First, we apply a 3D pose registration method, so that the odometry error is reduced. Then, with the rectified point set, we triangulate it taking into account the limitations of our sensor, which is our main contribution. Finally, we calculate the normals from the triangulation in a robust way.

The rest of the paper is organized as follows: In Section 2, we describe the experiment set, the hardware used and the method for pose registration. Section 3

A. Sanfeliu et al. (Eds.): CIARP 2004, LNCS 3287, pp. 241–248, 2004.

describes the method developed for the estimation of normals. Section 4 introduces the triangulation method which takes into account the non-uniformity of data and, finally, some conclusions are drawn in Section 5.

2   Obtaining a 3D Point Set from a Stereo Camera

The experiment was realized in the faculty of Economics Sciences at the University of Alicante. In Figure 1 (right) we show the building plant and the approximate path performed by our robot. Our robot Frodo (see Figure 1 left) is a Magellan Pro from RWI with a tri-stereo Digiclops camera (see [4] for more details).

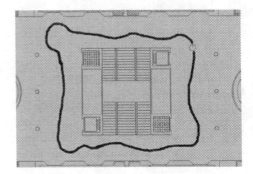

Fig. 1. Left: Robot and stereo camera used in the experiment. Right: Building plant where the experiment was realized and path followed by the robot.

The camera provides us a 3D point set and the intensity value at each point. While the robot is moving it takes 3D images approximately every 1 meter or 15 degrees. We have the odometry information provided by the encoders of the robot. This information yields an approximation of the actions realized by the robot $A = \{a_1, a_2, \ldots, a_n\}$, where each action $a_i = (x_i, y_i, \theta_i)$. We can obtain a reconstruction of the environment (map building) using this odometry information. To do that, provided that the coordinates of the points are local to every position of the robot, we must apply a transformation to the coordinates of the points using such information.

Figure 2 (left) shows a zenithal view of the plant of this environment. Note that points both from the floor and the roof have been removed which allows to observe accurately the reconstruction. We can observe that certain problems existing in the reconstruction come from odometry errors. In order to minimize this we can use a pose registration method applied to two consecutive point sets. The classic algorithm for 3D pose registration is ICP: Iterative Closest Point [5]. ICP calculates, iteratively, the best transformation between two point sets in two steps. The first one, given an initial transformation, it calculates correspondences between points using a distance criterion after applying the transformation. In the second one, the latter correspondences are used to estimate the best transformation in terms of minimum squares. The latter transformation is retained for a new first step. ICP ensures convergence to a local minimum. A modified algorithm [6] provides better results in terms of efficiency and it reduces the odometry error. This algorithm rather than determining the correspondences by one-way form, it uses random variables to estimate the probability that a given point in one set matches another one in the other set. Figure 2 (right) shows the result of applying such algorithm.

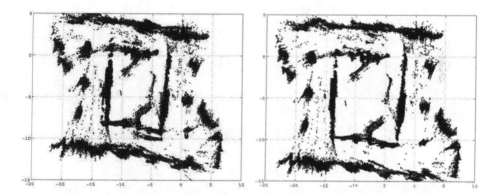

Fig. 2. Zenithal view of the floor of the reconstructed environment. Left: using odometry. Right: Using ICP-EM.

3 Normal Classification

The aim of this work is to extract geometric primitives from a cloud of 3D points, which have been obtained from the environment in the latter step. As we set before, we assume that our environment can be described from planar surfaces. We estimate the normal vectors of the underlying surfaces on each of the 3D points extracted from the environment. A later geometric primitive recognition will depend on the robustness of this normal estimation step.

Normal estimation relies on the method described in [7]: given a triangle mesh it returns the normal at each vertex of this mesh. The basic idea is to select a region from the mesh around a vertex. This region is specified in terms of geodesic neighborhood of the vertex. Each triangle T_i in this neighborhood casts a vote N_i which depends on the normal vector of the plane that contains the triangle. To avoid the problem that normals with opposite orientation annihilate each other, N_i is represented as a covariance matrix $V_i = N_i N_i^t$. Votes are collected as a weighted matrix sum $\mathbf{V}_v$ with

$$\mathbf{V}_v = \sum w_i V_i = \sum w_i N_i N_i^t \tag{1}$$

$$w_i = \frac{A_i}{A_{max}} \exp(-\frac{g_i}{\sigma}) \qquad (2)$$

where A_i is the area of T_i, A_{max} is the area of the largest triangle in the entire mesh, g_i is the geodesic distance of T_i from v, and σ controls the rate of decay. Figure 3 shows the effects of the rate of decay. The lower σ the higher the smoothness of the normals obtained.

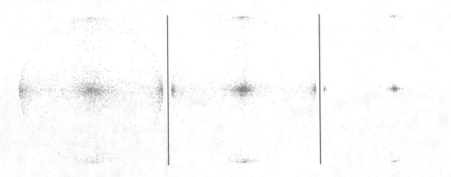

Fig. 3. Normals projection on a semi-sphere using several rates of decay, from left to right: $\sigma = 5/3cm, \sigma = 5/9cm$ and $\sigma = 5/15cm$.

With these equations we obtain knowledge about the variance instead of loosing information about normal sign orientation. This knowledge allows us to draw conclusions about the relative orientation of the vertex. So, we can decompose $\mathbf{V}_v$ using eigen-analysis and then classify vertex v. Since $\mathbf{V}_v$ is a symmetric semidefinite matrix, eigen-decomposition generates real eigenvalues $\lambda_1 \geq \lambda_2 \geq \lambda_3 \geq 0$ with corresponding eigenvectors E_1, E_2, end E_3. With this information we can define the saliency map [8] as:

$$S_s = \lambda_1 - \lambda_2,$$
$$S_c = \lambda_2 - \lambda_3,$$
$$S_n = \lambda_3 \qquad (3)$$

And so, we propose the following vertex classification scheme for the eigenvalues of $\mathbf{V}_v$ at each vertex:

$$\max S_s, \varepsilon S_c, \varepsilon\eta S_n = \begin{cases} S_s : \text{surface matches with normal } N_v = E_1; \\ \epsilon S_c : \text{crease junction with tangent } T_v = E_3; \\ \epsilon\eta S_n : \text{no preferred orientation} \end{cases} \qquad (4)$$

where $0 \leq \varepsilon \leq \infty$ and $0 \leq \eta \leq \infty$ are constants that control the relative significance of the saliency measures. Given such a classification we are interested in vertices $N_v = E_1$, and we can filter the rest. Using vector voting, we can calculate the normal of a 3D point from a triangle mesh. However, prior to obtain normals we must compute the triangulation. Our approach is addressed to generate a Delaunay triangulation from 3D points, which is explained in the next section.

4   Triangle Mesh Generation

The Delaunay triangulation of a set of 3D points is a well-known topic in the literature. Many of these methods [9, 10] obtain the triangulation for a 3D solid. Nevertheless, our problem cannot be solved by these approaches since we cannot assume that our set of points comes from a 3D solid. Mainly, our data comes from walls of corridors and rooms where the robot moves. Walls are, in fact, 2D surfaces in a 3D space. Others approaches [12, 13] are used to build topographic maps from a piece of terrain. These methods also build a mesh from a 2D surface in a 3D space, but really what they do is to project the 3D points over a horizontal plane, and so, final calculation is a 2D Delaunay triangulation.

Our approach wants to resolve a Delaunay triangulation of clouds of 3D points without either any consideration about sensor geometry or data coming from a closed volume. On the other hand, due to the nature of the problem that we want to solve, we introduce a constraint about the maximum size of the triangles in the mesh in order to maintain openings between walls or between a wall and any nearby objects from the environment. To solve this, we use a *divide & conquer* (D&C) schema that is based on the recursive partition and local triangulation of the point set, follow by a merging phase where the resulting triangulations are joined.

In general, D&C methods work well in 2D spaces, but nevertheless, to do the same in 3D space is not a simple task because merging is simple in 2D [11] but hard to design in more than two dimensions. DeWall [14] proposed an interesting triangulation method that uses a D&C strategy by reversing the order between the solutions of sub-problems and the merging phase. Instead of merging partial results, it applies a more complex dividing phase which partitions a set and builds, as first step, the merging triangulation.

In order to build our mesh (see figure 4), we use this idea and then we incorporate the constraints imposed by the problem. First, DeWall uses a tetrahedron as geometric basic entity to build a mesh from a set of 3D points that form a closed volume. The supposition of closed volume is not fulfilled in our case and it would be a source of problems due to the high noise that we must handle. For this, we are going to use the triangle as geometric basic entity to calculate the triangulation, in spite of the tetrahedron. This idea arises from the fact that we are triangulating points from 2D planes inside a 3D environment and, in general, to build a triangulation from 2D points the geometric basic entity is the triangle. In addition, we have to consider the fact that the triangle size constraint has a consequence: it might happen that certain parts of the space remain unconnected and, therefore, not be triangulated. For this reason, before the triangulation process, we compute clusters of connected points which will be the input to this triangulation process.

Our mesh generation approach is as follows: First, we use a plane α to split the space in two half spaces. Then, we compute the merging triangulation Σ_α using the splitting plane α. The technique used to build the Σ_α is a slight variation on an incremental construction algorithm: a starting triangle is founded and then Σ_α is built by adding a new triangle at each step. To find the first triangle we

```
function Triange_Builder (P: point_set, Lα: side_list): triangle_list
    var f: side; , Ll, Lr: side_list;
        t: triangle; Σ: triangle_list; α: splitting_plane;
    begin
        if Lα = ∅ then
            t:=FindFisrtTriangle(P, α);
            Σ := Σ ∪ t;
            for each f': f'∈ Sides(t) do
                if IsIntersected(f', α) then Insert(f', Lα);
                if InHalfSpaceL(f', α) then Insert(f', Ll);
                if InHalfSpaceR(f', α) then Insert(f', Lr);
        while Lα! = ∅
            f:=Extract(Lα);
            t:=FindTriangle(f, P);
            if t ≠ null then
                Σ := Σ ∪ t;
                for each f': f'∈ Sides(t) AND f' ≠ f do
                    if IsIntersected(f', α) then Insert(f', Lα);
                    if InHalfSpaceL(f', α) then Insert(f', Ll);
                    if InHalfSpaceR(f', α) then Insert(f', Lr);
        /*Recursive Triangulation*/
        if Ll ≠ ∅ then Σ := Σ ∪ Triangulator(P, Ll);
        if Lr ≠ ∅ then Σ := Σ ∪ Triangulator(P, Lr);
        Triange_Builder:=Σ;
    end.
```

Fig. 4. Algorithm Triange_Builder computes 3D Delaunay triangulation.

select the nearest point p_1 to plane α. Then, we select a second point p_2 such that it is the nearest point to p_1 on the other side of α. From p_1 and p_2 we search the point p_3 such that the *circum-circle* around p_1, p_2 and p_3 has the minimum radius r_i. The center of the *circum-circle* are extracted and we can compute a sphere with center c_i and radius r_i. Finally, to accept p_3 as the point which complete the triangle, it has to fulfill a pair of conditions. First, the Delaunay condition: no one point is inside the sphere; second, point p_3 is near enough from p_1 and p_2 to accomplish the triangle size constraint.

The rest of Σ_α is built from the first triangle. We label each triangle side as it lies completely contained in one of the two half-spaces (left or right) defined by α or it is intersected by the plane. We use three lists L_l, L_r and L_α to insert the triangles sides depending on their label. We extract a side from L_α and search for a new triangle, but now we must consider that this side comes from an exiting triangle. Each side of a triangle has a plane β which is perpendicular to the triangle. β divides the space into two half-spaces, therefore, we just search the next triangle in the valid half-space. The sides of the new triangle are now inserted in the corresponding list.

In Figure 5(left) we show a detail of a 3D point set. Figure 5(Center) shows the result of applying our proposed algorithm to generate the triangulation of the points: unconnected zones appear due to the absence of information and the constraint of the maximum size of triangle imposed. In Figure 5 (right) normal vectors calculated from the triangle mesh are shown.

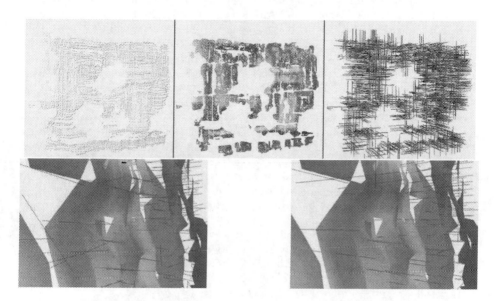

Fig. 5. Detail of normal estimation process. Top: Left: source 3D points. Center: triangle mesh. Right: resulting normals. Bottom: Left: normals before normalization. Right: normals after normalization.

5   Conclusions and Future Work

The line of work that we are following tries to obtain a 3D map of an environment. In this paper we improved the method of normals estimation, endowing it with higher robustness. For this, it has been necessary to develop a method to build a mesh of triangles from the point set. The method proposed obtains a triangulation from the point set, taking into account that our data are not uniformly distributed. The work is completed by the previous phase of reconstruction of the environment.

As continuation of this work we try to address the SLAM problem in order to improve the reconstruction of the 3D map. In addition we want to build a robust system of constraints that allows us to obtain geometric primitives (planes, cylinders, boxes, and so on) from the normals obtained.

Acknowledgments

This work has been supported by grant TIC2002-02792 funded by *Ministerio de Ciencia y Tecnología* and FEDER.

References

1. S. Thrun, W. Burgard, and D. Fox: A real-time algorithm for mobile robot mapping with applications to multi-robot and 3D mapping. In Proc. of the IEEE International Conference on Robotics and Automation (ICRA) (2000)
2. S. Thrun and D. Hähnel and D. Ferguson and M. Montemerlo and R. Triebel and W. Burgard and C. Baker and Z. Omohundro and S. Thayer and W. Whittaker: A System for Volumetric Robotic Mapping of Abandoned Mines. In Proceedings of the IEEE International Conference on Robotics and Automation (ICRA) (2003)
3. H. Surmann and A. Nuchter and J. Hertzberg: An autonomous mobile robot with a 3D laser range finder for 3D exploration and digitalization of indoor environments. Robotics and Autonomous Systems. **45** (2003) 181-198
4. J.M. Saez and F. Escolano: A Global 3D Map-Building Approach Using Stereo Vision. In Proceedings of IEEE International Conference on Robotics and Automation (ICRA) (2004)
5. P. Besl and N. McKay: A method for registration of 3-d shapes. IEEE Trans. On Pattern Analysis and Machine Intelligence, **14** (1992) 239-256
6. M. Cazorla and B. Fisher: Characterizing local minima in 3d registration methods. Not yet published, (2004)
7. D. L. Page, Y. Sun, A. F. Koschan, J. Paik and M. A. Abidi: Normal vector voting: crease detection and curvature estimation on large, noisy meshes. Graphical Models, Special Issue on Larte Triangle Mesh Models, **64** (2002) 199-229
8. G. Medioni, M. Lee, and C. K. Tang. A Computational Framework for Segmentation and Grouping, Elsevier Science Ltd., Amsterdam (2000)
9. E. Mücke: A Robust Implementation for Three-dimensional Delaunay Triangulations. In Proceedings of the 1st International Computational Geometry Software Workshop (1995)
10. K. Hormann and M. Reimers: Triangulating Point Clouds with Spherical Topology. Curve and Surface Design (2003) 215-224
11. D. T. Lee and B.J. Schchter: Two algorithms for constructing a Delaunay triangulation. Int. J. of Computer and Information Science, **9** (1980) 219-242
12. M. de Berg, M. van Kreveld, M. Overmars and O. Schwarzkopf: Computational Geometry, Algoritms and Applications. Ed. Springer (1991) 181-183.
13. G. Petrie and T.J.M Kennie: Terrain modelling in Survey and Civil Engineering. Computer Aided Design, **19**, number 4 (1987).
14. P. Cignoni, C. Montani and R. Scopigno: DeWall: a fast divide and conquer Delaunay triangulation algorithm. Ed. Computer-Aided Design **30** (1998) 333-341

A Model of Desertification Process in a Semi-arid Environment Employing Multi-spectral Images

Jorge Lira

Instituto de Geofísica-UNAM,
Circuito Institutos, Cd. Universitaria
04510 México DF, México
lira@geofisica.unam.mx

Abstract. A model of desertification in semi-arid environment employing satellite multi-spectral images is presented. The variables proposed to characterize desertification are: texture of terrain, vegetation index for semi-arid terrain, and albedo of terrain. The texture is derived from a divergence operator applied upon the vector field formed by the first three principal components of the image. The vegetation index selected is the TSAVI, suitable for semi-arid environment where vegetation is scarce. The albedo is calculated from the first principal component obtained from the bands of the multi-spectral image. These three variables are input into a clustering algorithm resulting in six desertification grades. These grades are ordered from no-desertification to severe desertification. Details are provided for the computer calculation of the desertification variables, and the parameters employed in the clustering algorithm. A multi-spectral Landsat TM image is selected for this research. A thematic map of desertification is then generated with the support of ancillary data related to the study area.

1 Introduction

The process of desertification is affecting large areas of the Earth surface with social and economic consequences. There is no consensus on a definition of desertification applicable in all regions and accepted by researchers of all concerned disciplines. Hence, a model that quantifies the surface manifestations of desertification from the remote sensing point of view may help to understand such definition. In addition to this, a model is useful to derive quantitative conclusions, such as: i) to determine the degree and extension of desertification, ii) to monitor the desertification over the years, and iii) to simulate various scenarios of desertification.

The causes of desertification are divided in two broad categories: natural and anthropogenic. A climate change producing dry atmospheric conditions brings drought leading to a decline in biological productivity. The origin of anthropogenic causes is related to cultivation practices, rangeland use, and fire ignition of vegetation species. The origin of natural causes is climate change, whether long term or indefinite. Both, the climate and the anthropogenic causes produce a reduction of the quantity and diversity of natural vegetation [1], [2], [3], [4]. In addition to this, the consequences

A. Sanfeliu et al. (Eds.): CIARP 2004, LNCS 3287, pp. 249–258, 2004.

of climate change and anthropogenic activities upon soil and vegetation degradation, and upon erosion processes, may be observed by means of satellite data [5], [6], [7]. The main ecological conditions characterizing desertification may be resumed as follows: increase of aridity, irregular but intense precipitation leading to irregular runoff, extreme events such as droughts causing soil erosion, desiccation and salinization of soils, and decline of vegetation. The main physical aspects characterizing desertification are: displacement of desert-like conditions, change of vegetation cover types, change of vegetation density, increase in albedo, and smoothness of terrain roughness.

In one of the earliest works related to desertification, Robinove and co-workers [8] uses differencing registered images of albedo to measure general conditions of an arid land. These workers determined that albedo is correlated with: erosion, increases or decreases in soil moisture, and increases or decreases in vegetation density. They concluded that decrease of albedo implies an improvement of land quality, and that increase of albedo implies a degradation of land quality. Albedo is therefore an indicator to measure desert-like conditions. In brief, in desertification processes, a change of vegetation cover types and a change of vegetation density results in an increase of albedo due to the exposure of soil.

Desertification results in changes of the quantity and composition of vegetation: a vegetation dynamics that results in a decline of plant cover and biological productivity [9], [10]. On the other hand, semi-arid areas comprise a series of vegetation complexes with various canopy closures over a variety of soils. To measure the vegetation dynamics in desertification processes for semi-arid environments a number of authors have used vegetation indices [10], [11].

Ecological circumstances and anthropogenic activities combine to generate conditions of physical land degradation. This leads to a change of texture of terrain surface, the stronger the desertification the smoothness the texture [12]. Non-desertified areas show homogeneous vegetation cover with a certain texture. When a desertification process develops, low-variability areas are decreased and replaced by higher variance areas [13]. Hence, environmental heterogeneity increases as a result of desertification processes. Increased spatial heterogeneity is an indicator of desertification [14]. As the desertification further proceeds, the spatial heterogeneity decreases reaching a limit - in desert-like conditions - when terrain surface appears smooth. From space, spatial heterogeneity may be observed as terrain texture. Therefore, under desertification processes, texture varies from a certain roughness to the limit, in desert-like conditions, when texture is smooth.

On the grounds of the above discussion, three variables may be considered to characterize desertification processes from the remote sensing standpoint: albedo of terrain, vegetation strength, and terrain texture. These variables have been considered independently by previous works, however, they must be considered concurrently to provide full, quantitative description of desertification conditions. Based on the above discussion, the following objectives are set: i) to define the variables that characterize desertification processes from a remote sensing view point, ii) to establish a model based on these variables, and iii) to produce a thematic map of desertification strength in semi-arid environment.

2 Area Description, Methods and Materials

2.1 Study Site

An area of northern Mexico, where semi-arid conditions prevail, was selected to test the desertification model proposed in this research. From the Landsat image given by path/row = 29/41, a sub image was extracted from certain pixel coordinates. This sub image is geocoded to UTM projection with a pixels size of 28.5 x 28.5 m^2. The size of this sub image is: 1700 pixels x 2048 lines. The acquisition date is: July 29, 1996. The geographic coordinates are: northwest corner: 27° 30′ 39.36″ W, 101° 39′ 33.36" N, southeast corner: 26° 59′ 34.22″ W, 101° 9′ 32.47″ N.

The elevation in this area ranges between 450 and 1400 meters above sea level. Sedimentary rocks form the dominant lithologic unit of the area. The climatic conditions prevailing for till-plains and high lands, for elevations ranging between 1,000 and 1400 meters, determine a dry and semi-dry atmosphere. In areas with till-plains and hills, for elevations ranging between 500 y 1000 meters, the climatic conditions are warm temperatures and dry atmosphere. The predominant climate types are BSohw and BS1kw, semiarid temperate [15]. The average annual temperature is 22° C. The annual average precipitation is between 300 and 400 mm.

Climatological conditions prevailing in the area support the presence of a widely spread halophilous vegetation in the highs of the mountains. Areas with shrubbery, grass/herbage and agriculture fields are present in plains and till-plains. Other areas with soil and soil/herbage correspond to zones of exposed soil with a certain degree of erosion and spare vegetation. Overgrazing, pasture, and agriculture not suited for the area occur as well. Natural conditions determine a dry temperate climate with low precipitation, whereas anthropogenic activities impose stressing conditions to vegetation cover types. These two conditions are driving the selected study area towards a desertification process.

2.2 Desertification from Space

Viewed from space, desertification manifests itself as variations of spatial heterogeneity, vegetation strength and albedo. As the desertification process develops, the spatial heterogeneity of the spectral cover types varies from a certain value up to some maximum of spatial heterogeneity. If the desertification further proceeds, the number of cover types diminishes leading to a scene of homogeneous appearance. Spatial heterogeneity varies from a certain roughness up to a certain maximum value diminishing consecutively to smooth roughness. On the other hand, the albedo of the scene increases from some value up to a maximum when vegetation is scarce or nil. In addition to this, salinization of the soil further increases the value of albedo. When biological productivity is completely lost in a certain area, vegetation cover types are absent so the soil is fully exposed leading to high values of albedo. Furthermore, the density and strength of vegetation decreases as desertification processes develops. Therefore, we propose that desertification, as observed from space, can be modeled by measurement of three variables: texture, albedo and vegetation strength. None of these variables by themselves can account to characterize the strength and variability of desertification. These variables must be taken concurrently, measured from the same image, and used to describe the spatial distribution of desertification in a given area. The set of such variables may be used to write an expansion of the image to describe desertification processes; details of this are given in the next section.

Desertification is a process that may take a long time to develop. To study in time such process, a series of images of the same scene for different dates would be required. The analysis of many images for a long period is costly and time consuming. Therefore, ergodicity must be assumed. Physically, ergodicity is satisfied whenever the observation, in different times, of n-copies of a system is equivalent to the observation in time of a single system. This means that from a single image different stages of desertification may be observed. The image must cover an area embracing a set of zones where desertification is present in different stages of development. In the present research, it is sufficient to assume ergodicity with respect to the first two statistical moments: the mean and the autocorrelation. To satisfy this statistical condition, the random field formed by the three variables characterizing desertification processes must be stationary or homogeneous. On the other hand, published research reveals the existence of a second order stationarity of the data used to study desertification processes [13]. In addition to this, second order stationarity implies the ergodicity for the first two statistical moments [16]. On the grounds of these results, ergodicity for the mean and autocorrelation is assumed. This assumption is sufficient for the purposes of this research, i.e., preparing a thematic map where several levels of desertification strength may be appreciated from a single image.

2.3 Desertification Model

A representation of a multi-spectral image **g** is expressed by the following equation

$$g_i(k,l) = \mu_i^g + \sum_{j=1}^{m} a_{ij} X_j(k,l), \; \forall \, i = 1, 2, \ldots n, \text{ and } k, l = 1, 2, \ldots M, N. \quad (1)$$

The vector $\mu^g = \{ \mu_1^g, \mu_2^g, \ldots \mu_n^g \}$ represents the mean of the multi-spectral image **g** = $\{g_1, g_2, \ldots g_n\}$ composed by n bands. The size of the image is M x N pixels. The bi-dimensional functions $X_1, X_2, \ldots X_m$, with $m \le n$, are zero-mean random variables with a certain correlation among them. When the set of X_j are zero-mean non-correlated random functions, they are named canonical bands in terms of which the image **g** is represented [17]. The variables X_i are named the functions. The quantities a_{ij} are deterministic functions named the coeficientes. The indices (k,l) are the coordinates of a pixel in the image. When zero-mean random functions are used in equation (1), useful representation of the image **g** may follow; even when some correlation may exists among the functions X_i [17]. Hence, a suitable set of X_i variables shall represent the key factors that provide a characterization of desertification. The variables X_1, X_2 and X_3 are in general not zero-mean; therefore the mean must be subtracted.

On the grounds of the discussion provided in section one and section 2.2, the following bands to model desertification processes are proposed: X_1 - First desertification band: albedo; X_2 - Second desertification band: texture:X_3 - Third desertification band: vegetation index.

In the present research, the functions a_{ij} are set to one; however, these functions may be used to introduce different weights to the X_i. The bands X_1, X_2 and X_3 are the variables that characterize desertification processes from the remote sensing standpoint. In this sense, a multi-spectral image is expanded in terms of the variables: albedo, texture and vegetation strength. This expansion allows the characterization of desertification processes from the remote sensing standpoint. The following section shows the necessary background to compute these variables.

2.4 Calculation of Desertification Bands

Albedo is an indicator of desertification condition. Albedo is defined as the ratio: total scattered power/incident power, integrated over the wavelength range of the multi-spectral image. On the other hand, the first principal component is directly proportional to the albedo of the cover types of terrain [18]. Therefore, to calculate the albedo, the principal components decomposition was applied to the bands of the multi-spectral image; the infrared band was not included due to a different pixel size. Hence, the first principal component is the first desertification band.

Texture is defined as a spatial organization of pixels in a certain region of the image and is directly associated to the roughness of terrain [19]. Desertification processes transform the roughness of landscape terrain. The calculation of texture is based on a vector field model for the multi-spectral image. The vector field is constructed in an n-dimensional space defined by the ensemble of multi-spectral image bands. The pixels form the vectors of this field. Upon this field, a divergence operator is applied to produce a map of texture variation in the image. The vector field flux derived by the divergence operator is directly related to terrain texture [20]. Hence, the divergence operator upon the image produces the second desertification band.

Vegetation cover types change both in density and in diversity as a consequence of desertification processes. To quantify vegetation change in semiarid environments a proper vegetation index must be used. The transformed soil adjusted vegetation index (TSAVI) shows a good behaviour to account for vegetation changes for such environments [21]. The TSAVI takes into account the reflectivity of soils that may be exposed in a semi-arid land. Hence, the TSAVI is the third desertification band. Figure 1 show a color composite of desertification bands. To complete the computation of desertification bands, and taking into account that $a_{ij} = 1$ for all desertification bands in equation (1), a linear stretch was applied to cover the range of: $[0 - 255]$.

2.5 Classification of Desertification Bands

To prepare a thematic map of desertification grades, a non-supervised classification was applied to X_1, X_2 and X_3. The algorithm selected for this task is the ISODATA clustering procedure. The parameters used in this algorithm are the default values of the PCI Geomatica module. On the grounds of field data consisting of topographic, vegetation and soil maps, six grades of desertification were established. The resulting classification was edited to merge clusters into one desertification grade. Depending on variations of topography, soil and vegetation, one or more clusters were needed to form one desertification grade class. The merging of clusters was done using the field data and table 1 as a general rationale to define desertification grades.

Table 1. General conditions of study site for desertification grades

Grade	Texture roughness	Albedo	Vegetation density	Topography
Nil	Various	Very low	Very high	Various elevations
Minimum	Various	Low	High	Various elevations
Low	Medium	Medium	Medium	Till-plains and low lands
Medium	Smooth	High	Low	Till plains and low lands
High	Smooth	High	Very low	Low lands
Very High	Very smooth	Very high	Soil fully exposed	Low lands

Fig. 1. Color composite of desertification bands: [RGB] = [Albedo, Texture, TSAVI]

3   Results and Analysis

The thematic map depicting six grades of desertification is shown in figure 2. There is no quantitative definition of desertification grades; therefore, on the grounds of a comparison of field data with results shown in the thematic map (Table 1), the following classification is adopted: Nil desertification – No disturbance of vegetation is appreciated. Minimum desertification – Some disturbance of vegetation is observed.

Low desertification – Moderate disturbance of vegetation is present. Medium desertification – Vegetation partially covers the soil. High desertification – Scarce vegetation is observed, soil is partially exposed. Very high desertification – No vegetation is observed, soil is fully exposed.

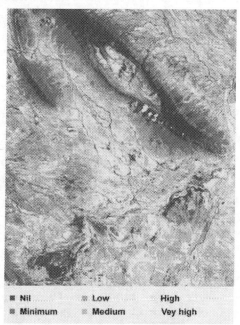

Fig. 2. Thematic map with six grades of desertification

As a rule in the above classification, the albedo steadily increases as desertification strength increases. On other hand, vegetation density strength diminishes as desertification strength increases. None the less, various texture roughnesses may be present in nil, minimum and low desertification grades. This is particularly true for agriculture fields where texture is smooth. However, medium, high and very high desertification grades always occur in areas of smooth or very smooth texture roughness. This means that vegetation density and albedo may contribute more to the determination of desertification grades. This might lead to the conclusion that different weights in equation (1) may be needed for the variables characterizing desertification processes. The ensuing discussion confirms this asseveration. Digital counts observed in desertification bands, for a selected area, confirm the above classification rationale (Table 2). An explanation of the general conditions where these grades take place follows.

Nil desertification occurs in high lands where vegetation is dense and unaltered, and texture is rough. However, this desertification grade may occur as well in low lands in areas of dense vegetation with smooth roughness; this is the case of fully developed agriculture fields (Table 3). In both situations, the albedo values are very low.

Table 2. Digital counts for nil, medium, and very high desertification grades

Desertification grade	Albedo	Texture	TSAVI
Nil	0 – 25	180 – 255	233 – 255
Medium	74 – 133	23 – 144	90 – 166
Very high	240 – 255	0 – 24	0 – 24

Table 3. Various desertification levels for selected spots

Coordinates	Altitude (m)	Vegetation	Grade
27°31' N, 101°31' W	1,050	Shrubbery, high density	Nil
27°26' N, 101°42' W	750	Shrubbery, low density	Low
27°20' N, 101°33' W	550	Grass/herbage	High
27°12' N, 101°21' W	550	Agriculture, medium density	Low
27°14' N, 101°32' W	500	Exposed soil	Very high
27°09' N, 101°11' W	500	Agriculture, high density	Nil

Minimum desertification is present in medium elevation lands with high-density vegetation and low albedo values. In this grade, the vegetation presents some disturbance: this disturbance appears as terrain areas containing some patches with low-density vegetation. None the less, this desertification grade may occur as well in low lands, in particular, for well developed agriculture fields (Table 3). Texture roughness may be medium for high elevation lands and till-plains.

A low desertification grade is associated to areas with emerging agriculture fields. This desertification grade occurs as well in till-plains with moderate disturbance of vegetation and medium albedo values. Areas of moderate disturbance of vegetation show a homogenous distribution of patches with low-density vegetation.

A medium desertification grade is associated to low vegetation density and high albedo values. The texture in this grade is always smooth. These desertification grades always occur in low lands and till-plains.

High desertification is observed in very low-density vegetation where soil is partially exposed. The texture is smooth or very smooth and albedo values are high due to the contribution of soil to the reflectance of terrain. These desertification grades always occur in low lands.

Very high desertification grade is present when vegetation is absent and highly reflected soil is fully exposed. The medium, high and very high desertification grades always take place in low lands with smooth texture roughness. The very high desertification grade is always associated to very high albedo values. These desertification grades always occur in low lands. In addition to the above, some scattered clouds are visible in the upper right quadrant of the image. As expected, clouds produce a very high desertification grade; this is a confirmation of the desertification model. On the other hand, cloud shadows modify the desertification grade on the ground.

Ergodicity is an important element in the interpretation of the desertification map. Under this assumption, the evolution of desertification may be observed in a single image. The conditions for this evolution can also be drawn as well from the desertification model. The evolution to high grades of desertification implies the smoothing of terrain jointly followed by a decrease in vegetation strength and exposure of soil. An increase of albedo is also involved in this evolution. From a single image, it is possible to appreciate the spatial and spectral change experienced by an ecosystem when drifting from one desertification grade to some other grade. General conditions when this evolution takes place are shown in table 3. In this framework, it is expected that, in desertification processes, an area of a certain desertification grade may drift to a higher grade when natural and anthropogenic forces are set for this change.

4 Conclusion

A desertification model to describe desertification processes in a semi-arid environment from the remote sensing standpoint has been established. This model is written as an expansion of a multi-spectral image in terms of a number of bands named desertification bands. These bands represent a set of variables that characterize desertification processes in a semi-arid environment: texture roughness of terrain, vegetation density strength, and albedo of terrain surface. The model expressed in equation (1) allows the introduction of a set of coefficients a_{ij}. These coefficients may be used as weighting factors to provide different weights to each desertification band. The assumption of ergodicity in desertification processes permits the observation of the evolution from nil desertification to a high desertification grade from a single image. In addition to this, with a set of images in different times, a time series of the spatial evolution of desertification classes may be prepared. Even though the classification of desertification grades provided in this work is qualitative, digital counts in desertification bands may help to quantify these grades. Human made areas such as agriculture fields may show low or nil desertification grades even though the texture is smooth. This might lead to the conclusion that the variables X_i do not equally contribute to the characterization of desertification. However, agriculture fields are not natural spectral objects in a scene. None the less, the model proposed in this research produces a low or nil desertification grades for fully developed agriculture fields, as expected, since the biological productivity is maintained in this case.

References

1. Fredrickson, E., Havstad, K.M., Estell, R., Hyder, P.: Perspectives on Desertification: South-Western United States. J. of Arid Env. 39 (1998) 191–207
2. Rubio, J.I.., Bochet, E.: Desertification Indicators as Diagnosis Criteria for Desertification Risk Assesment in Europe. J. of Arid Env. 39 (1998) 111–120
3. Puigdefábregas, J., Mendizabal, T.: Perspectives on Desertification: Western Mediterranean. J. of Arid Env. 39 (1998) 209–224
4. Barth, H.J.: Desertification in the Eastern Province of Saudi Arabia. J. of Arid Env. 43 (1999) 399–410
5. Hill, J., Sommer, S., Mehl, W., Megier, J.: Use of Earth Observation Satellite for Land Degradation Mapping and Monitoring in Mediterranean Ecosystems: Towards a Satellite-Observatory. Environ. Monitor. and Asses. 37 (1995) 143-158
6. Grigorev, A.A., Kondratev, K.Y.: Satellite Monitoring of Natural and Anthropogenic Disasters. Earth Observ. and Rem. Sens. 14 (1997) 433-448

7. Witt, R.G.: GIS and Remote Sensing Applications for Environmental Assesment. Earth Observ. and Rem. Sens. 16 (2000) 179-192
8. Robinove, C.J., Chavez, P.S., Gehring, D., Holmgren, R.: Arid Land Monitoring Using Landsat Albedo Difference Images. Rem. Sens. of Env. 11 (1981) 133-156
9. de Soyza, A.G., Whitford, W.G., Herrick, J.E., Van Zee, J.W., Havstad, K.M..: Early Warning Indicators of Desertification: Examples of Tests in the Chihuahuan Desert. J. of Arid Env. 39 (1988) 101-112
10. Xu, X.K., Lin, Z.H., Li, J.P., Zeng, Q.C.: Temporal-Spatial Characteristics of Vegetation Cover and Desertification of China Using Remote Sensing Data. Progr. in Nat. Sci. 12 (2002) 45-49
11. Palmer, A.R., van Rooyen, A.F.: Detecting Vegetation Change in the Southern Kalahari Using Landsat TM Data. J. of Arid Env. 39 (1998) 143-153
12. Tripathy, G.K., Ghosh, T.K., Shah, S.D.: Monitoring Desertification Process in Kamataka State of India Using Multi-Temporal Remote Sensing and Ancillary Information Using GIS. Inter. J. of Rem. Sens. 17 1996) 2243-2257
13. Seixas, J.: Assesing Heterogeneity From Remote Sensing Images: The Case of Desertification in Southern Portugal. Inter. J. of Rem. Sens. 21 (2000) 2645-2663
14. Schlesinger, W.H., Raikes, J.A., Hartley, A.E., Cross, A.F.: On the Spatial Patterns of Soil Nutrients in Desert Ecosystems. Ecology 77 (1996) 364-374
15. García, E.: Modificaciones al Sistema de Clasificación Climática de Kopen, Para Adaptarlo a las Condiciones de la República Mexicana. Reporte Técnico, Universidad Nacional Autónoma de México, México.
16. Papoulis, A.: Probability, Random Variables, and Stochastic Processes. McGraw-Hill, Boston (1991)
17. Dougherty, E.R.: Random Processes for Image and Signal Processing. SPIE/IEEE Press, Bellingham (1999)
18. Galvão, L.S., Vitorello, I., Paradella, W.R.: Spectroradiometric Discrimination of Laterites With Principal Components Analysis and Additive Modelling. Rem. Sens. of Env. 53 (1995) 70-75
19. Lira, J., Frulla, L.: An Automated Region Growing Algorithm for Segmentation of Texture Regions in SAR Images. Inter. J. of Rem. Sens. 19 (1998) 3595-3606
20. Lira, J.: A Divergence Operator to Segment Urban Texture. IEEE/ISPRS Joint Workshop on Remote Sensing and Data Fusion Over Urban Areas (2001) 159-163. November 8-9, Rome.
21. Baret, F., Guyot, G.: Potentials and Limits of Vegetation Indices for LAI and APAR Assesment. Rem. Sens. of Env. 39 (1991) 161-173

A Gesture-Based Control for Handheld Devices Using Accelerometer

Ikjin Jang and Wonbae Park

Dept. of Information & Communication, Kyungpook National University,
Daegu 702-701, Republic of Korea
frog30@korea.com, wbpark@ee.knu.ac.kr

Abstract. The current paper presents how the signals from an accelerometer can be processed to accurately recognize user gestures after applying a small accelerometer to a handheld device. For gesture-based control to be effective in handheld devices, the overheads involved in recognizing gestures should be minimal and the gestures accurately recognized in real operational environments. Therefore, the signals detected from accelerometers were classified into acceleration and dynamic acceleration, then the signal patterns of the accelerometers in relation to simple gestures were analyzed. A device control module was created and its operating process compared to that of a normal control device to evaluate the usability of gesture recognition. As a result, gesture-based control was found to be easy to use, reduced the preparation process, a produced a rapid system reaction. Accordingly, gesture-based control would seem to be an effective user interface for handheld devices primarily used in mobile environments.

1 Introduction

For mobile convenience, handheld devices do not provide the user interfaces included in notebooks, such as a keyboard and mouse. Instead, they use a keypad, stylus pen, and/or input-panel as the input device, and a small LCD device to output several lines of text or simple images. However, these input devices are time-consuming and difficult to use, as the small buttons on the display need to be manipulated several times. Extensive research has already been conducted on new input/output methods to solve this problem, particularly in relation to voice recognition and gesture recognition [1,3,5,6,9,10]. Yet, proper sensors are necessary to detect user actions or recognize gestures in the case of handheld devices, plus the processing capacity and mobile convenience should also be considered when applying sensors. Small accelerometers, the most appropriate sensors for handheld devices, measure mobility and actions through acceleration, thus the size and moving directions detected by the sensors can be used to classify simple user gestures. Accordingly, the current paper investigates the application of small accelerometers to handheld devices, and describes the gesture-based interactions required to replace a keypad or stylus pen operation.

A. Sanfeliu et al. (Eds.): CIARP 2004, LNCS 3287, pp. 259–266, 2004.

2   Related Works

Accelerometers are used in various fields and have been extensively studied in the context of gesture recognition In particular, Ken Hinckley studied how to recognize various user gestures using several sensors altogether (Tilt Sensor, Touch Sensor and Proximity Sensor) [4]. In addition, accelerometers have also been used in pointing devices, where finger movements are detected based on attaching accelerometers to the finger parts and hand of a glove[8], and in handwriting-recognition, where pen movements are detected based on attaching a pair of accelerometers to a pen [7]. When applying these case studies to the user interfaces of handheld devices, the operational environment and capacity of handheld devices must be considered, plus the overheads due to the inclusion of accelerometers must be minimized. Therefore, it is necessary to study how to recognize simple gestures efficiently, while also minimizing the number of accelerometers. In this paper, signal patterns make for gestures easily expressed in a real operational environment, and its usability be evaluated by simple examples.

3   Signal Processing of the Accelerometer for Gesture Awareness

The signal which is detected from the Accelerometers is divided with static acceleration and dynamic acceleration. Static acceleration is like tilt or gravity, and dynamic acceleration is like shock and vibration.

3.1   Static Acceleration (e.g., Gravity)

An accelerometer can detect gesture changes based on its horizontal status[2]. When an accelerometer is in a perfect horizontal status and there is no movement at all, the detected values for the dual axis are all zeros. If the position is then changed in a specific direction, the detected value will differ from that of the horizontal status even if there is no movement at all, and this value is sustained until the horizontal status is recovered. Fig. 1 shows the signal type detected when an accelerometer changes its position and produces signals for one-axis.

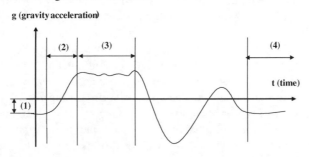

Fig. 1. Signal type of static acceleration

In Fig.1, the differences in section (1) mean that the signals detected from the accelerometer differed from those in the horizontal status, because the display of the handheld device used was tilted in the user direction. Meanwhile, the signals in section (2) are the signals detected when the position of the handheld device was change and those in section (3) were detected when a specific position was sustained for a while. Finally, the signals in section (4) were those detected when the handheld device returned to its original position. As such, static acceleration can detect a position change from the original status and determine which direction the position is changed in relation to the original position if the changed status is sustained for a while. The steps shown in Fig.2 are necessary to recognize gestures from static acceleration signals detected by an accelerometer.

The signals detected from an accelerometer are processed for each dual-axis, as shown in Fig.2, to grasp a change in the position of the accelerometer in one or two directions. The processes performed in each step of Fig.2 are outlined below.

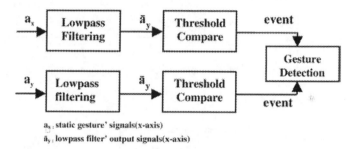

a_x: static gesture' signals(x-axis)

$\hat{a}_y$: lowpass filter' output signals(x-axis)

Fig. 2. The steps to recognize gestures from static acceleration

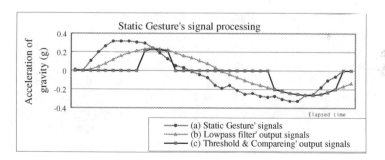

Fig. 3. Signal processing about Static gesture (1-axis' signal)

Low Pass Filtering

This makes signal changes consecutive by processing a trivial movement. The current study used a first-order Butterworth filter, as a simple filter is preferable considering the capacity of handheld devices. Fig. 3 shows the output signals at each step in the signal processing, where (a) shows the signals detected from the accelerometer and (b) shows the output signals of the lowpass filter.

Thresholding and Comparing

If the detected signals are lower than a threshold value, they are ignored. As such, Fig. 3 (c) shows the status of trivial movements that are eliminated at the Threshold

& Comparing step (which ignores signals where the gravity acceleration is smaller than 0.2g)

3.2 Dynamic Acceleration (e.g., Vibration)

Dynamic acceleration occurs when a sudden movement or short shock is transmitted to the accelerometer, resulting in short-term peaks in the detected signals. These kinds of signals happen when user gestures are not consecutive or from slight knocking or sudden shocks. Fig.4 shows an example of dynamic acceleration, based on signals from knocking gestures.

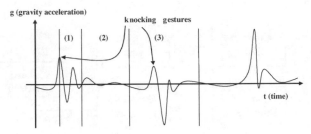

Fig. 4. Knocking Gesture's signal form

In Fig.4, section (1) shows several peaks generated by one knocking gesture. Although knocking gestures can occur for various reasons (bag, pocket, or hand etc.), the peak duration is normally within 100 ms(milliseconds). Therefore, the problem of 'multiple peaks' can be solved by debouncing, i.e. the identification of section (1) as a 'dead period', because users cannot generate knocking gestures within intervals of 100 ms. If knocking gestures occur while a user is moving, multiple peaks and consecutive vibrations can happen simultaneously. Therefore, a silent period, as marked in section (2), needs to be set to identify regular knocking signals, as distinct from vibration due to user movements. In addition, a subsequent signal needs to be detected some time after the former signal is detected. That is, another knocking gesture needs to exist in section (3) to be effective. Fig.5 shows the processes necessary to recognize user gestures using dynamic acceleration signals, and the output signals from each step ((a)~(d)) are shown in Fig.6.

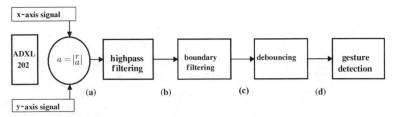

Fig. 5. Dynamic Acceleration's signal processing step

In Fig.5, the first step marked by a circle is the process used to obtain the amplitude from the dual-axis signals, and the content of each step is outlined below.

Highpass Filtering

When handheld devices are not used horizontally, the accelerometer is under the influence of gravity acceleration. Therefore, changing the position of the accelerometer also changes the detected signals. Fig.6 (a) shows the signal detected from an accelerometer in the case of a knocking gesture, i.e. seizing the handheld device. Because this signal is detected as the accelerometer is tilted in a random direction, the x-axis signal and y-axis signal sustain random values. Therefore, when considering various operational environments, the DC components should be eliminated first in order to process the detected signals in the same way, regardless of the tilt direction of the accelerometer. Fig.6 (b) shows the signals after eliminating the DC components using a highpass filter.

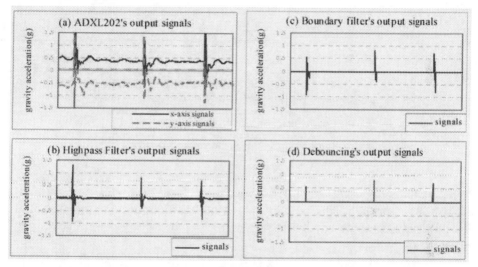

Fig. 6. Output signals about Fig.5 (Dynamic Acceleration's processing step)

Boundary Filtering

This process eliminates trivial signals to prevent the transmission of unwanted gestures arising from slight vibrations or movements. It removed signals that below 0.2g by the experimentation. Fig.6 (c) shows the output signal of the boundary-filtering step.

Debouncing

In the case of several peaks generated by one gesture, debouncing avoids recognizing such peaks as different gestures. As such, the multiple peaks shown in Fig.4 (1) are ignored. Fig.6 (d) shows the elimination of multiple peaks through debouncing.

4   Examples of Gesture-Based Control

4.1   Example 1: Bell and Sound Control

This is the function of stopping the bell using a knocking gesture without withdrawing the handheld device when it rings. Bell control is difficult in places such as convention halls or public meetings, thus rapid control through gestures is desirable. To control a bell using a knocking gesture, it is important that other gestures are not be wrongfully recognized. Therefore, regular knocking gestures more than 3 times are necessary, plus a state machine is needed to detect regular knocking gestures more than 3 times, as shown in Fig.7.

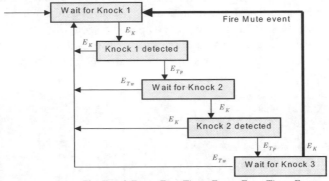

Ek : Knock Event, Etp : Timer Event, Etw : Timer Event
Tp : Minimum interval between two knocking events
Tw : Maximum waiting interval for a knocking event

Fig. 7. State machine for knocking gesture awareness

For effective knocking gesture detection, the Tp and Tw need to be properly selected. In the current experiment, Tp was 200 milliseconds, while Tw was 500 milliseconds. This should be adjustable by users. Fig 8 shows an example of bell control using knocking gestures, which demonstrates the step-by-step process of recognizing knocking gestures.

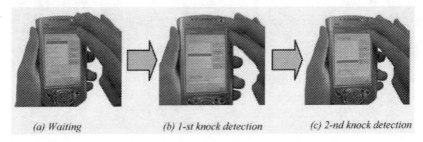

(a) Waiting   *(b) 1-st knock detection*   *(c) 2-nd knock detection*

Fig. 8. Bell Control Application

4.2 Example 2: Scrolling

To scroll a handheld device, a small button must be clicked using a stylus pen. However, it is not easy to click the scroll button on a small display panel. To scroll using gestures, information about the direction of the user gestures should be included. An example of gestures including information about the user direction is the tilt method. In the case of an accelerometer, if a one-axis signal is changed, this indicates a tilt in the related direction, while if both dual axes change, this indicates a complex tilt in two directions. When using tilting gestures to scroll, there can be a slight movement or vibration, because handheld devices are not fixed. Therefore, a dead zone should be set, and signals from the dead zone should not impact the scrolling. In the current experiments, a 0.2g dead zone was applied. Furthermore, since there is no signal larger than 2g from a tilting gesture, any signal larger than 2g was ignored. Fig.9 shows an example of Tilt & Scroll.

Fig. 9. Scrolling Application

4.3 Example 3: Display Mode Alteration (Pivot)

Handheld devices use rectangular display panels, and the display modes change according to the content and user preference. Sensor detection of axis-rotation is necessary to change display modes, yet the signals detected from dual axes are not changed if there is an axis-rotation when the accelerometer is in a horizontal status. However, if the display status tilted in the user direction is set as the original status, then a display rotation can be easily determined, because the signals detected from the dual axes will differ from the original signals if axis-rotation occurs. Fig.10 shows an example of realizing 'display mode alteration' based on detecting axis-rotation in a handheld device.

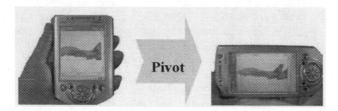

Fig. 10. Display Mode Alteration

5 Conclusions

The use of a keyboard or mouse as a user interface for handheld devices is awkward and impractical, therefore, the current study designed and realized a system that uses gesture-based interactions as user interfaces after applying accelerometers to handheld devices. As such, the signal features of accelerometers towards gestures that can easily be used in the real operational environments of handheld devices were surveyed, plus the signals detected from accelerometers were processed after classifying them according to the kind of gesture. To recognize the signals detected from accelerometers as user gestures, the signal pattern of each gesture was analyzed and recognized as a valid gesture only when a signal pattern matched a gesture pattern. In the current research, only one accelerometer was used based on the capacity of handheld devices and their mobile convenience. In addition, simple filters were used for the signal-processing step. Further research on using multiple sensors, designing precise filters, and algorithms that can exactly distinguish various gestures is necessary to identify various user gestures.

References

1. Bartlett, J.F., "Rock 'n' Scroll Is Here to Stay", IEEE Computer Graphics and Applications, 2000.
2. Analog Devices, "ADXL202E: Low-Cost ?2g Dual-Axis Accelerometer With Duty Cycle Output Data Sheet (Rev. A, 10/00)",
   http://www.analog.com/UploadedFiles/Datasheets/567227477ADXL202E_a.pdf
3. Ehreumann, M.; Lutticke, T.; Dillmann, R., "Dynamic gestures as an input device for directing a mobile platform", Robotics and Automation, 2001. Proceedings 2001 ICRA. IEEE International Conference on , vol.3 , 2001, pp: 2596-2601.
4. Ken Hinckley.; Jeff Pierce.; Mike Sinclair.; Eric Horvitz, "Sensing techniques for mobile interaction", Symposium on User Interface Software and Technology, CHI Letters 2, 2000, pp: 91-100.
5. Mantyla, V-M,; Mantyjarvi, J.; Seppanen, T.; Tuulari, E., "Hand gesture recognition of a mobile device user", ICME 2000. 2000 IEEE International Conference on Multimedia and Expo, 2000. vol. 1, 2000, pp: 281 -284
6. Matthieu, B.; Hedvig, S.;Jan-Olof, E., "Recognition of gestures in the context of speech", Pattern Recognition, 2002. Proceedings. 16th International Conference on, vol. 1, 2002, pp: 356 –359.
7. Milner, B., "Handwriting recognition using acceleration-based motion detection", IEE Colloquium on Document Image Processing and Multimedia, 1999.
8. Perng, J. K.; Fisher, B.; Hollar, S.; Pister, K. S. J., "Acceleration sensing glove(ASG)", The Third International Symposium on Wearable Computers, 1999, pp: 178 – 180.
9. Randell, C.; Muller, H., "Context awareness by analyzing accelerometer data", The Fourth International Symposium on Wearable Computers(ISWC00), 2000, pp: 175-176.
10. Sawada, H.; Hata, S.; Hashimoto, S., "Gesture recognition for human-friendly interface in designer-consumer cooperate design system", Robot and Human Interaction, 1999. RO-MAN '99. 8th IEEE International Workshop on, 1999, pp: 400 –405.

A Method for Re-illuminating Faces from a Single Image

Mario Castelán* and Edwin R. Hancock

Dept. of Computer Science, University of York, York YO10 5DD, UK
{mario,erh}@cs.york.ac.uk

Abstract. In this paper we propose a local-shape based method for correcting shape-from-shading information for raw surface height recovery of faces aiming to generate differently illuminated versions of a face. The underpinning idea comes from the observation that subtle changes in the elements of a gradient field can cause notable changes in its integrated surface. A new gradient field is calculated by modifying its orientations in accordance with critical points on the surface and local shape indicators. A raw height map is then calculated by integrating such field. Experiments show that altering the directions of a surface normal field of a face can be enough to generate differently illuminated fixed-pose versions of a face from a single image.

1 Introduction

The problem of acquiring surface models of faces is an important one with potentially important applications in biometrics, computer games and production graphics. There are many ways in which surface models can be acquired, and these include the use of range-scanners, stereoscopic cameras and structured light sensors. However, one of the most appealing methods is to use shape-from-shading (SFS), since this is a non-invasive process which mimics the capabilities of the human vision system. Unfortunately, the use of SFS for face analysis has proved to be an elusive task, since the concave-convex ambiguity can result in the inversion of prominent features such as the nose. To overcome this problem, domain specific constraints must be used. For instance Zhao and Chellappa [9] have exploited facial symmetry to overcome the problem.

In general, though, SFS is an under-constrained problem since the two degrees of freedom for surface orientation (slant and tilt), must be recovered from a single measured intensity value. Hence, it is frequently posed as that of minimizing cost functionals that capture constraints on the gradient field. This is usually carried out through iterative schemes in the discrete domain. Despite sustained research activity in the field for some three decades[7, 10], no SFS scheme has been demonstrated to work as accurately as the *specially* constrained SFS

---

* Supported by National Council of Science and Technology (CONACYT), Mexico, under grant No. 141485.

A. Sanfeliu et al. (Eds.): CIARP 2004, LNCS 3287, pp. 267–274, 2004.

cases of photometric stereo[3,5] and statistical SFS[1]. The first of these methods requires at least three images of the same object illuminated from different view-points, while the second uses a database of accurate surface information (height or gradient) belonging to objects of the same class, i.e. faces. When it comes to the original single-image SFS problem, the resulting data is seriously affected by the noise caused by factors such as inaccurately calculated illumination direction and unknown reflectance properties, and both of these are difficult to obtain from a single image. The restrictions imposed by most SFS schemes on the gradient field (smoothness, irradiance, integrability, unit length) are insufficient to overcome with these problems. Moreover, if misused, they may result in either oversmoothing of the gradient field, loss of fine surface detail, or over-dependence on the intensity information. As a result, the recovered height surface may represent an oversmoothed reconstruction of the object under study.

However, although a precise height map is difficult to obtain by integration of the field of surface normals delivered by SFS, due to local errors in direction, this does not imply that the entire field of surface normals is in error. In fact, some regions on the image do provide surface normal information that is sufficiently faithful for good surface reconstruction. The problem originates from those locations where the combined effects of image noise, and overreliance on the consistency constraints, results in effects such as inversion of the surface convexity or concavity. When applied to the problem of face reconstruction, for instance, the effect can be to cause high curvature features such as the nose to become imploded with respect to the remainder of the surface. If such regions can be identified and the surface normal directions corrected, then the result is improved overall surface topography.

The outline of the this paper is as follows. We commence with a brief overview of the Frankot and Chellappa's global surface integration method and local shape indicators, then we develop a method that can be used to reassign the surface gradient orientations. We provide experiments to evaluate the method on a human face. Finally, we present some conclusions and identify directions for future work.

2   Integrating a Gradient Field

The integrability condition in SFS ensures that the recovered surface satisfies the following condition on the partial derivatives of the height function: $Z_{xy} = Z_{yx}$. In [4] Frankot and Chellappa proposed a method to project a gradient field to the nearest integrable solution. They suggested to use a set of integrable basis functions to represent the surface slopes so as to minimize the distance between an ideally integrable gradient field and a non integrable one.

Following [4], if the surface Z is given by

$$\tilde{Z}(x,y) = \sum_{\omega \in \Omega} \tilde{C}(\omega)\phi(x,y,\omega)$$

where ω is a two dimensional index belonging to a domain Ω, and $\phi(x,y,\omega)$ is a set of basis functions which are not necessarily mutually orthogonal, the partial derivatives of $\tilde{Z}$ can also be expressed in terms of this set of basis functions using the formulae

$$\tilde{Z}_x(x,y) = \sum_{w \in \Omega} \tilde{C}(w)\phi_x(x,y,w) \quad \text{and} \quad \tilde{Z}_y(x,y) = \sum_{w \in \Omega} \tilde{C}(w)\phi_y(x,y,w)$$

Given that $\phi_x(x,y,w)$ and $\phi_y(x,y,w)$ are integrable, then so are the mixed partial derivatives of $\tilde{Z}(x,y)$.

In the same way, the possibly non integrable gradient field (which, indeed, is the only information we have) can be represented as

$$\hat{Z}_x(x,y) = \sum_{w \in \Omega} \hat{C}_1(w)\phi_x(x,y,w) \quad \text{and} \quad \hat{Z}_y(x,y) = \sum_{w \in \Omega} \hat{C}_2(w)\phi_y(x,y,w)$$

Note that, as $\hat{C}_1 \neq \hat{C}_2$, then $\hat{Z}_{xy} \neq \hat{Z}_{yx}$.

The goal then is to find the set of coefficients that minimize the quantity

$$d\left\{(\hat{Z}_x, \hat{Z}_y), (\tilde{Z}_x, \tilde{Z}_y)\right\} = \int\int \left\|\tilde{Z}_x - \hat{Z}_x\right\|^2 + \left\|\tilde{Z}_y - \hat{Z}_y\right\|^2 dx dy$$

In [4], details are given about how to solve this equation globally, in the Fourier domain.

3   Local Shape Indicators

A local shape indicator is a scalar that gives information about the local to-pography of a surface using its principal curvatures. The principal curvatures may be estimated using the surface normal directions to compute the Hessian matrix. They may also be estimated by fitting a local quadric surface patch $P(u,v) = \frac{1}{2}(\kappa_1 u^2, \kappa_2 v^2)$ having κ_1 and κ_2 as the principal curvatures with directions u and v respectively. κ_1 and κ_2 are the calculated eigenvalues of the Hessian matrix.

Local shape indicators are usually coupled. For instance, the HK classification[2] uses the Gaussian and mean curvatures $H = \frac{(\kappa_1 + \kappa_2)}{2}$ and $K = \kappa_1 * \kappa_2$ respectively. By distinguishing between the cases in which H and K are individually negative, zero or positive, it is possible on the basis of the joint behavior to assign topographic labels to points on a surface.

A different and slightly more convenient set of attributes is the shape-index and curvedness representation developed by Koenderink and Von Doorn SC[8]. Here the principal curvatures are used to compute the shape index $S = -\frac{2}{\pi} * arctan(\frac{\kappa_1 + \kappa_2}{\kappa_1 - \kappa_2})$ for $\kappa_1 \geq \kappa_2$; and the curvedness, $C = (\frac{\kappa_1^2 + \kappa_2^2}{2})^{1/2}$. The shape index is an angular variable that relates to the local surface topography. It varies continuously from -1 to $+1$ as the surface changes through cup, rut, saddle-rut, saddle, saddle-ridge, ridge and dome, and cup again. The curvedness relates to the degree of curvature of the surface.

4   Using the Curvedness Indicator to Redirect SFS Gradient Fields

Inevitably, any surface gradient field delivered by SFS will be inaccurate due to noise or albedo changes which cause variations in the intensities of the input image. SFS works well for objects that are uniformly concave or convex. However, if the object under study is more complex, with both concave and convex regions, then SFS can fail. In these situations although the recovered surface normal direction is consistent with the measured image brightness, the recovered surface does not reflect the structure of the object under study. In particular, there may be inversions of the sign of the surface curvature with convex regions appearing concave and vice-versa. However, in the case of faces (and many other objects) the surface under study is largely convex.

Based on this above observation, in this paper we present a method for enforcing the convexity of the integrated surface while ensuring a global maximum on a particular position of it.

Formally stated, suppose S is a smooth surface immersed in $\mathbb{R}^3$. Let p and U_p be a critical point of S and a neighborhood of p respectively. Suppose that S is locally concave over U_p. Then, the new surface $\widetilde{S}$ constructed from S by reversing the sign of all its partial derivatives, S_x and S_y, is locally convex in U_p. Besides, a local maximum on $\widetilde{S}$ will be located on that point where the function stops increasing and starts decreasing[1]; if all the partial derivatives of $\widetilde{S}$ with respect to x, $\widetilde{S}_x$, have negative sign before reaching the position of the critical point p in the x axis and have positive sign after reaching it, and the same occurs for $\widetilde{S}_y$, then the critical point p on U_p will be the position of the global maximum[2] of $\widetilde{S}$.

The main idea underlying this paper is to enforce the condition that the integrated surface has a global height maximum where it is suitable for our problem, i.e. the tip of the nose. Such a point will serve as a division for the positive and negatively signed areas of the needle map. To enforce this condition we follow the simple rule:

$$\breve{Z}_x(x,y) = \begin{cases} abs(\hat{Z}_x(x,y)) & \text{if } x \leq a \text{ and } C(x,y) \geq \tau_x \\ -abs(\hat{Z}_x(x,y)) & \text{if } x > a \text{ and } C(x,y) \geq \tau_x \\ \hat{Z}_x(x,y) & \text{otherwise} \end{cases}$$

$$\breve{Z}_y(x,y) = \begin{cases} abs(\hat{Z}_y(x,y)) & \text{if } y \leq b \text{ and } C(x,y) \geq \tau_y \\ abs(\hat{Z}_y(x,y)) & \text{if } y > b \text{ and } C(x,y) \geq \tau_y \\ \hat{Z}_y(x,y) & \text{otherwise} \end{cases}$$

---

[1] Of course, $\widetilde{S}$ will present many local maxima for a face-like surface.
[2] It might be a maximum or a minimum depending on the integration method.

where $\check{Z}_x$ and $\check{Z}_y$ are the updated gradients, $\hat{Z}_x$ and $\hat{Z}_y$ are the original gradients, a and b are the coordinates for the position of the desired global height maximum, on the x and y axis respectively. $C(x,y)$ is the curvedness indicator which is compared to the thresholds τ_x and τ_y for deciding whether the element of the gradient field at the location (x,y) will be altered or not.

To illustrate the global height maximum enforcement procedure, Figure 1 (left) shows the results of applying the method to the derivatives of a sphere with radius 75 units. From left to right, transversal plots of the recovered surface on the x axis are shown. The peak coordinates (a,b) are both set to 75, 50 and 20 respectively, and τ_x and τ_y are set to zero: all the derivatives are taken into account to expose the extreme case. The convexity strengthening is clearer in Figure 1 (right), where the method is applied to the Mexican hat function. Cross sections of the recovered surface are shown, and from left to right they show the original surface and recovered surface after applying the method taking as a peak point the center of the surface with $\tau_x = \tau_y = 0$. Note how the concave parts of the hat become convex.

Fig. 1. Applying the method to a sphere and mexican hat.

It is evident that the peak-enforcement procedure will segment the recovered surface into four quadrants. As a result the curvedness of the recovered surface will be reduced. This is not desirable from the point of view of surface recovery from a face. The net effect will be to make the surface structure pyramidal. This problem is overcome by using the thresholding procedure to either force the normals to change direction or to allow them to remain unchanged.

In the following section some experiments will be presented in order to illustrate these points on an application involving raw face reconstruction using SFS and its use for calculating differently illuminated images of a face.

5 Experiments

The tests were carried out on the image shown in Figure 3(top row - left)[3]. To compute the surface gradients from the raw image brightness we followed a geometric method. The method involves first computing the image gradient. The surface normals are positioned on a cone whose axis is in the light source direction and whose opening angle is given by $\theta = \arccos E$. The position of the

---

[3] The face database was provided by the Max-Planck Institute for Biological Cybernetics in Tuebingen, Germany.

surface normal on the cone is such at its projection onto the image plane is the same as the direction of the measured image gradient. This construction ensures the image irradiance equation to be satisfied. For the surface integration step we used the global method proposed in [4] which recovers surface height using the inverse Fourier transform of the field of surface normal directions.

The first analysis is shown in figure 2. From left to right: curvedness, first partial derivative with respect to x, first partial derivative with respect to y, $[0, 0, 1]$ re-illumination of the gradient field and recovered height map. The first row corresponds to the originally obtained needle map whilst the second row shows the case for the modified gradient field with $\tau_x = 0.4$ and $\tau_y = 0.3$. It is important to mention that a post-processing step of smoothing was realized in order to soften the recovered surface for better illumination effects. Note how the curvedness (first column) is diminished in the second row, as a consequence of the convexity enforcement, which becomes evident when analyzing the partial derivatives of each case (second and third columns), when the imploded regions of the face seem to emerge for the modified case. The perpendicular re-illumination of the needle maps (fourth column) also shows the convexity enforcement effect, since the second row case seems to naturally fit the illumination of the *surface* of a face rather than the re-illumination of the *image* of a face. The fifth column makes evident the improvement in the recovered height map, showing a profile plot of the surface. Note how the formerly imploded features of the face (first row) become salient (second row). Special comment deserves the choice of an appropriate threshold, since we are able to enhance the salient features of a particular face while maintaining the overall face composition.

It is important to remark that, if considerable, the improvement of the recovered height map depends on the accuracy of the input data, therefore the obtained raw height information still lacks the preciseness of that delivered by invasive methods. However, our method could be used for tasks such as generation of unseen illuminated views with fixed pose, as suggested by the following set of experiments.

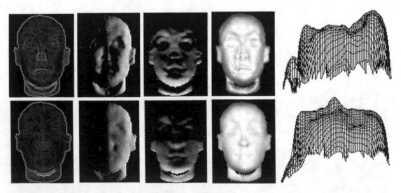

Fig. 2. Curvedness, gradient and surface recovery analysis (see text).

Figure 3 presents re-illumination experiments for a couple of images of faces. The first column corresponds to the input image. The next columns show the generated re-illuminations after applying the method. The light source vector is nearly parallel to the x axis in both negative in positive directions, for the second and third columns, while nearly parallel to the y axis, for the fourth and fifth columns. The input images were assumed to be the albedo maps, and negative values for the re-illuminations (zero values under the lambertian model) were forced to be positive for illustrative clarity.

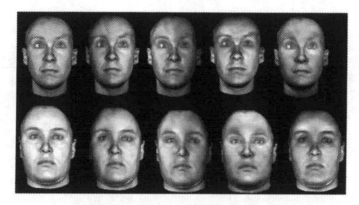

Fig. 3. Re-illumination tests for two different images (see text).

A further analysis is shown in figure 4, where an unprocessed image of a face (first column, middle of the rows) was used for the experiments. The first row presents the results for the modified gradient field with both $\tau_x = \tau_y = 0.3$. The second row exhibits the case for the original gradient field. Note how in the top row the quality of the re-illuminations is improved, contrasting the evidently imploded features presented in the second row case. It is necessary mentioning, however, that some incorrectness appears in some areas of the face, i.e. those

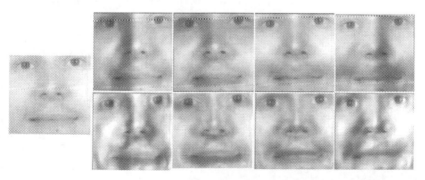

Fig. 4. Comparison of re-illuminations (see text).

surrounding the mouth. This can be explained as the consequence of the change in reflectance properties on the lips. Of course, the eyes and the mustache area also present different reflectance properties. This suggests that more attention should be paid on the reflectance model for the re-illumination, and also for the recovery of the gradient field.

6   Conclusions

We have proposed an algorithm for correcting a gradient field of a face aiming to generate a height map with a global maximum on a critical point and whose concave regions are constrained to become convex in accordance with curvedness indicators. The recovered height maps from the new gradient fields can be used to generate re-illuminated versions of the face in a straightforward way. Future lines of work are proposed towards the use of a special reflectance model for the skin as well as taking into account face-symmetry constraints for the recovery of a better height map.

References

1. Atick, J., Griffin, P. and Redlich, N. (1996), Statistical Approach to Shape from Shading: Reconstruction of Three-Dimensional Face Surfaces from Single Two-Dimensional Images, *Neural Computation*, Vol. 8, pp. 1321-1340.
2. Besl, P.J. and Jain, R.C. (1986) Invariant surface characteristics for 3-d object recognition in range images, *Comput. Vision Graphics Image Proc.*, Vol. 33,pp. 33-80.
3. Forsythe, D. and Ponce, J. (2001), Computer Vision: a Modern Approach, Prentice-Hall.
4. Frankot, R.T. and Chellapa, R. (1988), A Method for Enforcing Integrability in Shape from Shading Algorithms, *IEEE Trans. Pattern Analysis and Machine Intelligence*, Vol. 10, No. 4, pp. 438-451.
5. Georghiades, A., Belhumeur, D. and Kriegman, D. (2001), From Few to Many: Illumination Cone Models fro Face Recognition under Variable Lighting and Pose, *IEEE Trans. Pattern Analysis and Machine Intelligence*, pp. 643-660.
6. Horn, B.K.P. (1977), Understanding Image Intensities, *Artificial Intelligence*, Vol. 8, pp. 201-231.
7. B.K.P. Horn and M.J. Brooks (1989), Shape from Shading.*MIT Press, Cambridge, MA*.
8. Koenderink, J.J., and Van Doorn, A.J. (1992), Surface Shape and Curvature Scales, *Image en Vision Computing*, Vol. 10,pp. 557-565.
9. Zhao, W. and Chellapa, R. (2000), Illumination-insensitive Face Recognition Using Symmetric Shape-from-Shading. *Conference on Computer Vision and Pattern Recognition*, pp. 286-293.
10. R. Zhang, P.S. Tsai, J.E. Cryer and M. Shah (1999), Shape from Shading: A Survey, *IEEE Trans. on Pattern Analysis and Machine Intelligence*, 21(8):690–706.

Unsupervised Font Clustering Using Stochastic Versio of the EM Algorithm and Global Texture Analysis

Carlos Avilés-Cruz, Juan Villegas,
René Arechiga-Martínez, and Rafael Escarela-Perez

Universidad Autónoma Metropolitana - Azcapotzalco, Departamento de Electrónica,
Av. San Pablo 180 Col. Reynosa, C. P. 02200,
Distrito Federal, México
caviles@correo.azc.uam.mx

Abstract. An Unsupervised Font clustering technique is proposed in this work. The new approach is based on global texture analysis, using high order statistic features, Gaussian classifier and a stochastic version of the EM algorithm. The font recognition is performed by taking the document as a simple image, where one or several types of fonts are present. The identification is not performed letter by letter as with conventional approaches. In the proposed method a window analysis is employed to obtain the features of the document, using fourth and third order moments. The new technique does not involve a study of local typography; therefore, it is content independent. A detailed study was performed with 8 types of fonts commonly used in the Spanish language. Each type of font can have four styles that lead, to 32 font combinations. The font recognition with clean images is 100% accurate.

1 Introduction

Font recognition is a fundamental issue in the identification and analysis of documents. Khoubybari and Hull [2] took a document as an image, where clusters of word images were located within a reference word function base. The base font was chosen as the font that is more similar to the one being analyzed. In reference [3] a set of local detectors were employed to identify individual features of each font, such as height, width, thickness, base line, etc. Shi and Pavlidis [4] made recognition of fonts based on histogram properties of words, where inclination properties, histogram densities, etc. were measured. Zramdini and Ingold [5] show a statistical approach for the recognition of fonts based on their local topographic aspects. A similar approach was taken by Schreyer [6], where local attributes of textons were used (see [7] for the definition of textons and [8] as an alternate approach to textons). It can be seen that all these works are based on typographic aspects that were extracted with very local analysis instead of a global analysis. Only one author [9] was found to make use of global texture analysis. Gabor filters were tuned at different frequencies and orientations, leading to recognition results that are a function of pepper noise (degradation of recognition as a function of additive noise). Although the results given in [9] are good, there is room for substantial improvements. Experience shows that a global analysis may lead to good results in pattern recognition.

A. Sanfeliu et al. (Eds.): CIARP 2004, LNCS 3287, pp. 275–286, 2004.

In this paper, the global analysis approach was followed. The use of high-order statistical moments (third and fourth order) and a principal-component analysis were proposed to characterize the textures of documents (fonts). As a method is unsupervised, the maximum of likelihood was used as a way to find the number of fonts. The likelihood was found via the expectation maximization algorithm (EM-algorithm). Once the mean value and variance/covariance matrix were estimated, those values are then passed to a standard statistical classifier, such as Bayes [10]. The purpose of this paper was to determine if the use of the method described here would result in better unsupervised font recognition. The approach followed is independent of document content and it is based on global texture analysis. The font identification process proposed in this work is summarized in the flow chart of fig. 1. The original image is pre-processed so as to create a uniform text block, which, in turn, is used to extract high-order statistical attributes. An analysis of principal components is then applied to eliminate linear redundancies, leading to a reduced number of features. Finally, the stochastic EM-algorithm get the number of different fonts and their parameters. For the identification task, the document (only test) is scanned window by window and estimated their high order features (third and fourth order moments); The features can now be categorized using a Bayes classifier. The structure of the paper is organized as follows. Section 2 gives details of the pre-processing stage, whereas the features used during the clustering process and the way to extract them are given in section 3. The definition and implementation of third and fourth order moments are included in section 4. The unsupervised classification method is discussed in section 5 and section 6 shows the efficacy of the proposed approach. Finally, future work and conclusions are presented in section 7.

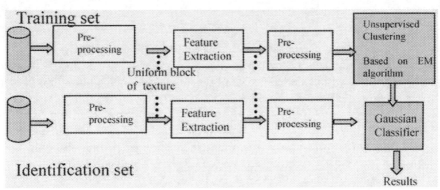

Fig. 1. General scheme for font identification system

2   Pre-processing: Creation of a Uniform Block of Text

The text to be analyzed is contained within a JPG format file (the jpg format is converted to gray level image), which was used for the learning and identification stages. The text can include space characters or spaces between words, letters or lines. It is assumed that the document to be analyzed only contains text information, that is, no pictures or figures are in the document. In addition, characters may have different sizes between words or lines. There can be two types of spaces within a line: a) spaces between characters, which are characteristic and unalterable of each type of font and b) spaces between words, which are irrelevant, as they do not provide any information about the type of font. The font information is extracted by going through the words in order to obtain a uniform block of text. The same procedure is applied to spaces between lines in order to eliminate them. The pre-processing stage is divided in four stages that are described in the following subsections.

2.1 Locating Text Lines

The location of a text line was made by calculating the horizontal projection profile (HPP) of the whole text, which was determined by adding over each line the intensity of the pixels that belong to it (gray levels). The values are then normalized with respect to the maximum value found. Figure (2b) shows an example of this procedure. The valleys between peaks correspond to blank spaces between text lines. The distance between two valleys gives the height of each text line. As a result, it is possible to locate and to determine the height of each text line (see fig. 2).

The printing area is 122 mm × 193 mm. The text should be justified to occupy the full line width, so that the right margin is not ragged, with words hyphenated as appropriate. Please fill pages so that the length of the text is no less than 180 mm.

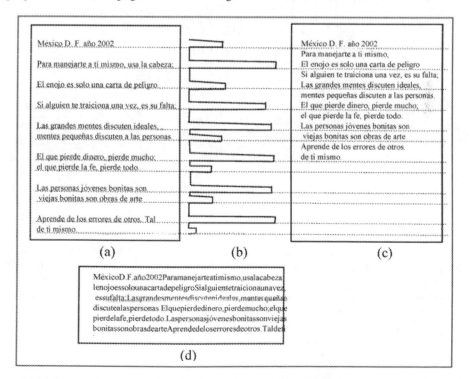

Fig. 2. Example of pre-processing. (a) Original image, (b) HPP of the image, (c) image after line normalization, and (d) uniform text block after pre-processing

2.2 Text Line Normalization

A text can contain several types of fonts and different sizes for them. Therefore, it is necessary to normalize letters and words of different sizes to a standard one. Once a text line was located (see previous section), fonts were easily normalized to have them all to be of the same size. However, it is worth to mention that small font deformations could lead to small mistakes when the normalization stage was applied, for example an original letter "i" could appear as "l" or "1".

2.3 Spacing Normalization

The normalization of vertical spacing was used to reduce the undesired influence of spaces on each line. In other words, it was used to eliminate spaces between words. The vertical projection profile (VPP) was calculated for each line, a valley between peaks corresponds to the width of each character or word. The normalization is used to obtain a predefined constant width. Figure 3 shows an example of this procedure.

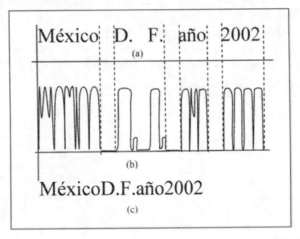

Fig. 3. Example of spacing normalization. (a) Original text line, (b) VPP of line text, and (c) normalized line text

2.4 Text Padding

Since the text may not be justified, refilling of blank spaces was performed (at this stage) when the text did not ended with the rest of the lines. The option followed consisted on copying parts of the text of the preceding (or following) line, as there is a bigger probability that words be of the same type when they are close to each other. Figure 2d shows an example of a completely pre-processed text.

3 Feature Extraction

The uniform text obtained in the previous section, could be analyzed with any texture technique, evidently each technique is well adapted for texture type (i.e. fine grain texture, coarse grain texture, etc). As it is remarked in the introduction section, only one paper using "global texture analysis"[9] was found and it is based on Gabor filters. In our project, we proposed to use high order statistics (third and fourth order moments) since in [8] Julesz is shown that when only first and second order moments are used it is not always possible to distinguish two textures. In the literature, there are techniques to analyze textures (in general texture not text [25],[26],[27] and [28]): Gabor filters [9],[11], co-occurrence matrices [12], [13],[29],[31], principal component analysis [14], [10], low-order statistical moments (mean value, standard deviation, correlation, etc.) [4], [14], [15], [24],[30], high-order statistical moments [16], [17], [15] and analysis with wavelet transforms [18], [19]. A method is given in reference [19] for the recognition of characters, but the recognition of the type of fonts is disregarded. In this project, statistical moments were used since it has been found that they have a very good performance with non-structured random textures [16], [17], [1], [15]. The goal of this paper is to report an other methodology to the optical font recognition problem based on high order statistics showing that our scheme improve the results obtained in [9]. The following subsections describe the theoretical and estimation aspects involved with third and fourth order moments.

Fourth and third order moments

Statistical moments represent an averaging process of the values (powered to order n) when a random variable is involved. Here, the original and pre-processed images were considered as two-dimensional arrays of a random variable of dimension $N \times N$. The random variable takes values from level 0 to 255, as the images were considered in gray levels quantized in 8 bits (gray levels are obtained from the jpg format). The images were obtained directly from a scanner or were digitally obtained from word processors or image converters.

Moments were calculated for the random variable X, which was identified with the image block. In addition, X is a vector obtained through matrix line linking. The definition of third-order central moments is given by:

$$m_3(i,j) = E[(X - \overline{X})_n * (X - \overline{X})_{n+i} * (X - \overline{X})_{n+j}]$$ (1)

where $E[\cdot]$ is the mathematical expectation or statistical average, $\overline{X}$ is the average value of the block to be processed, n is the central pixel whereas (i,j) represents the spaces between values of the random variable.

The estimator of (1) can be expressed as:

$$m_3(i,j) = \frac{1}{N} \sum_{n=1}^{N} ((x - \overline{x})_n * (x - \overline{x})_{n+i} * (x - \overline{x})_{n+j})$$ (2)

where N is the total number of image pixels. It is worth mentioning that this estimator is biased. The values that (i,j) may get are [0,1,2], such a small neighbor is chosen in order to reduce the huge number of possible combinations. When small neighborhoods are taken around the central pixel n. different combinations of eq. (1) can be developed by taking into consideration these small regions. For third order moments and taking into account all possible combinations, only six estimation are the most significant (between 9) when considering the non-redundant ones (m3(0,0), m3(0,1), m3(0,2), m3(1,1), m3(1,2) and m3(2,2)).

Fourth-order central moments of a random variable X can be obtained from:

$$m_4(i,j,k) = E[(X-\overline{X})_n * (X-\overline{X})_{n+i} * (X-\overline{X})_{n+j} * (X-\overline{X})_{n+k})] \qquad (3)$$

The average value of four pixels is taken in this case. The estimator of eq. (4) is given by:

$$m_4(i,j,k) = \frac{1}{N}\sum_{n=1}^{N}((x-\overline{x})_n * (x-\overline{x})_{n+i} * (x-\overline{x})_{n+j} * (x-\overline{x})_{n+k}) \qquad (4)$$

If small regions are considered around the central pixel n, the values that (i,j,k) may take in this case are [0,1,2]. As a result, ten non-redundant estimator expressions (the most significant ones) can be obtained[1]: (m4(0,0,0), m4(0,0,1), m4(0,0,2), m4(0,1,1), m4(0,1,2), m(02,2), m4(1,1,1,), m4(1,1,2), m4(1,2,2) and m4(2,2,2)).

The estimations were performed with four orientations (0, 45, 90 and 135 degrees) in order to take into account the non-isotropic characteristics of the different font types (see fig. 4). Hence, 24 third-order moments result (4 orientations multiplied by 6 features per orientation). 40 moments were obtained for the fourth-order case (4 orientations multiplied by 10 features per orientation). The total number of estimated moments was 64 per window, which were obviously linearly redundant and excessive. A principal component analysis was applied to each moment in order to reduce attributes and linear relationships. The dimensions that retain the 99.99% of inertia were hold.

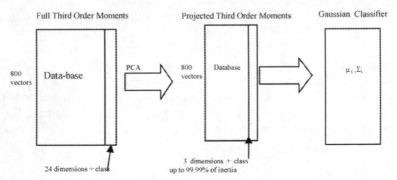

Fig. 4. Feature reduction by Principal Components Analysis (PCA) in order to withdraw linear redundancies. This scheme is also valid for fourth order moments

4 Font Clustering

The methodology applied in our processing image algorithm was based on to estimate features not over full image, instead of this, feature estimation was done over regions of images called "sub-image". The estimated attribute arrays of each sub-image were the reference database to clustering font process (100 windows are taken randomly over full text). Fig. 5 depicts the principal component analysis of the high-order moments (third or fourth order) from their features, where the number of dimensions taken keeps 99.99% of inertia. This lead to a matrix composed of 800 vectors of dimension 24 for third-order moments, whereas 800 vectors of dimension 40 were

---

[1] Remarking that $m_4(0,0,1) = m_4(0,1,0) = m_4(1,0,0)$, $m_4(0,0,2) = m_4(0,2,0) = m_4(2,0,0)$ and so on.

obtained for fourth-order moments. 99.99% of inertia was achieved with three dimensions for both cases. As a result, a learning database, with 800 vectors of dimension 3 for each moment, results after post-processing. Unsupervised technique was used in order to determine the number of fonts and their parameters (mean value and variance/covarianza matrix). The stochastic EM algorithm was initialized to 32 functions (searching up to 32 different fonts types and styles), of course, if the fonts number is less than that, several functions will have the same parameters and as result only one is taken. Once parameters determined, a Bayes classifier was chosen to fulfill the classifications task.

Unsupervised Technique

The unsupervised technique is based in the likelihood theory, the foundation is to say, *a priori*, the data model is gaussian, so the total model is a mix of gaussian functions.

$$f\ (\ \overline{x}\ /\ \Theta\ )\ =\ \sum_{k\ =\ 1}^{K}\ P_k\ f_k\ (\ \overline{x}\ /\ \theta\ ) \tag{5}$$

Where

$$f_k(\overline{x}/\theta)\ =\ \frac{1}{(2\pi)^{d/2}|\Sigma_k|^{1/2}}\ e^{-\frac{1}{2}(\overline{x}-\overline{\mu_k})^T\Sigma_k^{-1}(\overline{x}-\overline{\mu_k})} \tag{6}$$

P_k is the factor of mixing of model k $(0 < P_k < 1)$ and $\sum_{k=1}^{K} P_k = 1$, θ_k is the vector of parameters $[\overline{\mu}_k, \Sigma_k]$ and Θ is the vector of global parameters $[P_1, P_2, ... P_K; \theta_1, \theta_2, ... \theta_K]$ and d is the dimension of the sample $\overline{x}$.

For this model, two parameters will be calculated, the first one is the mean value and the second one is the variance. The "EM" ("Expectation-Maximization") algorithm is a general technique for the estimation of those parameters. In this paper, the stochastic version of the EM algorithm was used [30],[31].

5   Results

Several tests were performed to validate the method proposed in the project. Eight different types of fonts were chosen: a) Arial, b) Bookman, c) Century Gothic, d) Courier, e) Comic Sans MS, f) Impact, g) Modern and h) Times New Roman, see figure 8. In addition, four different styles for each font were employed: a) Regular, b) Bold, c) Italic and d) Bold Italic, see figure 9. A total of 32 combinations of styles and fonts were considered. This particular set of fonts and styles was chosen in order to compare the results with those produced in reference [9]. It is interesting to mention that the fonts considered here were those given by the Microsoft Word Processor.

The images considered in this work were digitally generated by the Microsoft Word Processor and then converted to images. This way, it is possible to control all the fonts and their sizes accurately. A text was written using fonts of 12 point size at 300 dpi. Each image is 640×640 pixels in size for each type of font.

Finding the right size of each window is essential to make a good estimation, that is, the number of pixels that are necessary to reach convergence with the high-order moments considered. This task was performed by making estimations of fourth and third order moments with different window sizes, starting from a 2×2 pixel size and ending with the maximum image size (640×640 pixel size in this work). If the whole image, the estimation was taken as the reference value, estimation errors can be calculated for smaller windows. Fig. 6 shows the estimation errors, where it can be seen that for a 32×32 window size, the error was less than 5%. Due to space constrains, Fig. 6 shows only up to 64x64 window size because, and however the error estimation remained on zero for the windows of size 64x64 to 640x640.

Once defined the size of the estimation (32x32 pixels, allowing an error less than 5% on convergence), the methodology described on Fig. 1 and Fig. 5 was applied. In order to find the mean values and variance/covariance matrices, the Expectation Maximization algorithm was used starting with 32 functions, as an example, Fig. 7 shows in the feature domain (after principal components analysis) five classes, corresponding to 5 fonts type. After have been found mean values and variance/covariance matrices, a Gaussian classifier was used to classifier any text having the fonts used in the learning phase. Table I shows the obtained confusion matrix. It can be observed that 8 types of fonts are 100% identified. Also, four different styles were 100% identified, as shown in table II. These results can be compared with those given in reference [9], where an average recognition of 99.1% is obtained with maximum and minimum intervals of recognition of 97.2% for Regular Arial and 100% for Times New Roman. It must be emphasized that 100% recognition of the type of font and style is achieved with the method proposed in this project. An average recognition value of 96.91% is obtained in reference [5] using a typographic approach, a value which is considerably lower than the obtained in this project.

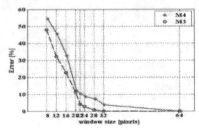

Fig. 5. Analysis of estimation convergence (window size estimation): Third order moments $M_3(0,0)$ and Fourth order moments $M_4(0,0,0)$

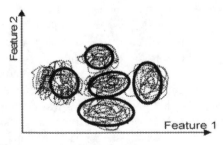

Fig. 6. Maximum likelihood estimation by EM-Algorithm, this example shows only 5 different classes

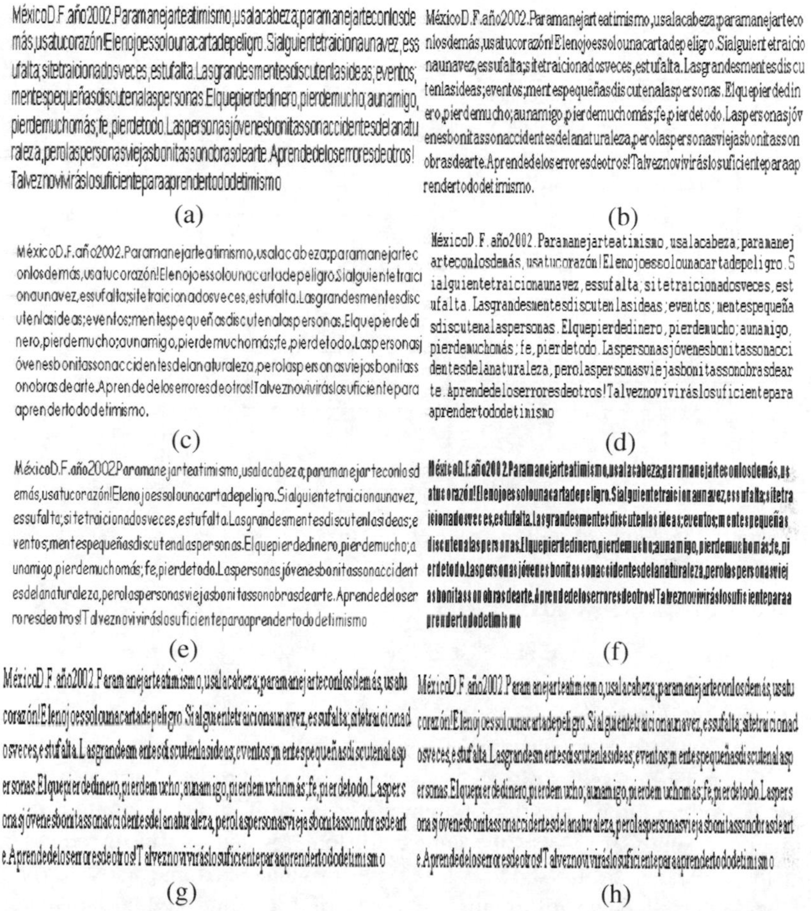

(a)

(b)

(c)

(d)

(e)

(f)

(g)

(h)

Fig. 7. Fonts used during the recognitions (in regular style), (a)Arial, (b)Bookman, (c)Century Gothic, (d) Courier, (e)Comic Sans MS, (f)Impact, (g)Modern y (h)Times New Roman

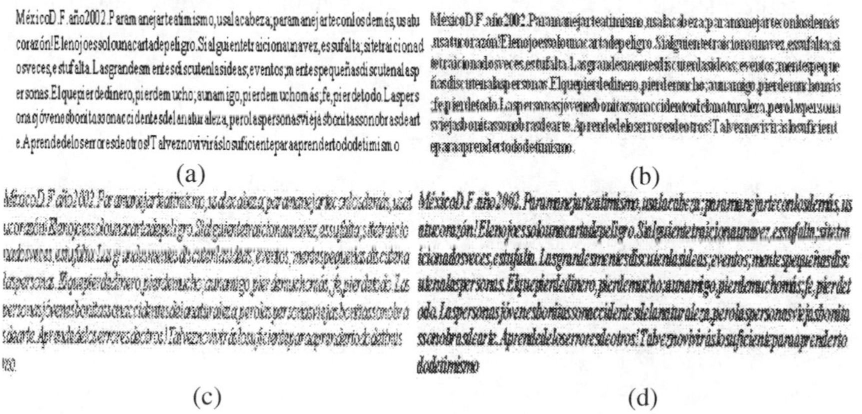

(a)

(b)

(c)

(d)

Fig. 8. Of four styles, Times New Roman font, (a) regular, (b) bold, (c) italic y (d) italic -bold

Table 1. Confusion matrix for eight fonts in regular style, using a cross-validation method (50%) and a Bayes classifier

	Arial	Bookman	Century Gothic	Courier	Comic San MS	Impact	Modern	New Times Roman
Arial	100	0	0	0	0	0	0	0
Bookman	0	100	0	0	0	0	0	0
Century Gothic	0	0	100	0	0	0	0	0
Courier	0	0	0	100	0	0	0	0
Comic San MS	0	0	0	0	100	0	0	0
Impact	0	0	0	0	0	100	0	0
Modern	0	0	0	0	0	0	100	0
New Times Roman	0	0	0	0	0	0	0	100

Concerning the style recognition, it was recognized at 100%.

6 Conclusions and Future Works

A new approach was proposed and tested for font clustering. The method was based on the use of high-order central moments (third and fourth order), using a stochastic version of EM-algorithm in order to determine the number of different fonts and the function parameters (mean values and variance/covariance matrices). For classification task, a standard classifier (Bayes) was used. Non-isotropic characteristics were taken into consideration by making estimations in four different orientations. A principal component analysis reduces the number of features and the linear redundancies between them. Thus, results show a 100% performance, that is, a 0% error. The method worked well when differentiating types of fonts and styles. However, the method cannot identify the size of a letter, since the pre-processing stage of the method homogenizes every character to the same pre-established size. Future work involves the development of a technique where the size of fonts can be distinguished. This goal can be achieved by combining the text-independent technique proposed in this project with typographic and local approaches.

Acknowledgment

This work was partially supported by The Mexican National Council of Science and Technology (CONACYT) under project J31916.

References

1. G. Nagy, "Twenty Years of Document Image Analysis in PAMI", *IEEE Trans. Pattern Analysis and Machine Intelligence,* vol. 22, no. 1, pp. 38-62, Jan 2000.
2. S. Khoubyari and J.J. Hull, "Font and function word identification in Document Recognition", *Computer Vision and Image Understanding,* vol. 63, no. 1, pp. 66-74, 1996.

3. R. Cooperman, "Producing Good Font Attribute Determination Using Error-Prone Information", *Int. Society for Optical Eng. J.,* vol. 3027, pp. 50-57, 1997.
4. H. Shi and T Pavlidis, "Font Recognition and Contextual Processing for More Accurate Text Recognition", *Proc. Fourth Int. Conference Document Analysis and Recognition, (ICDAR'97)* pp. 39-44, Aug 1997.
5. A. Zramdini and R. Ingold, "Optical Font Recognition Using Typographical Features", *IEEE Trans. Pattern Analysis and Machine Intelligence,* vol. 20, no. 8, pp. 877-882, Aug. 1998.
6. A. Schreyer, P. Suda, and G. Maderlechner, "Font Style Detection in Document Using Textons", *Proc. Third Document Analysis Systems Work-Shop, Assoc. for Pattern Recognition Int.,* 1998.
7. B. Julesz and J. R. Bergen, "Textons, the Fundamental Elements in Preattentive Vision and Perception of Textures", The Bell System Technical J., Vol. 62, no. 6, pp. 1619-1645,July/August 1983.
8. J. Malik, S. Belongie, J. Shi and T. Leung, "Textons, Contours and Regions: Cue Integration in Image Segmentation", *IEEE International Conference on Computer Vision, Corfu, Greece, September 1999.*
9. Yong Zhu, Tieniu Tan and Yunhong Wang, "Font Recognition Based on Global Texture Analysis", *IEEE Trans. Pattern Analysis and Machine Intelligence,* vol. 23, no. 10, pp. 1192-1200, October 2001.
10. Fukunaga K., "Introduction to Statistical Pattern Recognition", Academic press 1990. United Kingdom, 591 páginas.
11. A.C. Bovik, M. Clark, and W.B. Geisler, "Multichannel Texture Analysis Using Localized Spatial Filters", *IEEE Trans. Pattern Analysis and Machine Intelligence,* vol. 12, no. 1, pp. 55-73, Jan 1990.
12. Haralick R. M., "Texture Feature for Image Classification", IEEE Trans. On SMC, 3(1):610-621,1973.
13. Haralick R. M., "Statistical and Structural approaches to texture", IEEE TPAMI 67(5):786-804,1979.
14. David H. Evans, "Probability and its Applications for Engineers", Prentice Hall, 2000, ISBN/Part Number: 0824786564.
15. Jain A. K. et al. "Statistical Pattern Recognition: a Review", IEEE Transactions on Pattern Analysis and Machine Intelligence, Vol. 22, No. 1, January 2000, 4-37.
16. Avilés-Cruz, "Texture recognition by high order statistics: characterization and performance", PhD Thesis, Institute National Polytechnic of Grenoble L.T.I.R.F. Grenoble, France. 1997.
17. Avilés-Cruz, "Unsupervised texture segmentation using stochastic version of the EM algorithm and data fusion", Proceedings International Conference on Pattern Recognition ICPR 98, Vol. 2, pp. 1005-1009, Brisbane-Australia, August 1998.
18. T. Reed and J.M. Hans De Buf, "A Review of Recent Texture Segmentation and Feature Extraction Techniques", *CVGIP: Image understanding ,* vol. 57, pp. 359-372, 1993.
19. Iftekharuddin K. M., Jemili K and Karim, M.A , "A feature-based neural wavelet optical character recognition system", Aerospace and Electronics Conference, 1995. NAECON 1995., Volume: 2, pp 621-628.
20. González R., "Digital Image Processing", Prentice Hall 1990.
21. G. S. Peake and T. N. Tan, "Script and Language Identification from Document Images", *Proc. BMVC'97,* vol. 2, pp. 169-184, Sept. 1997.

22. T.N. Tan, "Rotation Invariant Texture Features and their Use in Automatic Script Identification", *IEEE Trans. Pattern Analysis and Machine Intelligence,* vol. 20, no. 7, pp. 751-756, July 1998.
23. G. R. Cross and A. K. Jain, 1983. Markov random field texture models. *IEEE Trans. Pattern Analysis and Machine Intelligence,* PAMI vol. 5 pp. 25-39.
24. R. M. Haralick, K. Shanmugam, and I. Dinstein. 1973. Textural features for image classification. *IEEE Trans. Systems, Man, and Cybernetics,* vol. 3, no.6, pp. 610-621.
25. B. Julesz. 1975 Experiments in the visual perception of texture. *Scientific American,* no. 232, pp. 34- 43.
26. K.L Laws, 1980 Rapid texture identification, *SPIE: Image processing for missile guidance,* vol. 238, pp. 376-380.
27. T. Leung and J. Malik. 1999 Recognizing surfaces using three-dimensional textons. *IEEE International Conference on Computer Vision,* pp. 1010-1017.
28. H. Tamura, S. Mori, and T. Yamawaki, 1978, Textural features corresponding to visual perception, *IEEE Trans. on Systems., Man and Cybernetics,* SMC - 8, no. 6, pp. 460 – 472.
29. Tomita, Y. Shirai and S. Tsuji, 1982, Description of textures by a structural analysis, *IEEE Transactions on Pattern Analysis and Machine Intelligence,* vol. 4, no. 2, pp. 183-191.
30. L. Wang and D.C. He, 1990, Texture classification using texture spectrum, *Pattern Recognition,* vol. 23, pp. 905-910, 1990.
31. Zucker, S. W. and D. Terzopoulos, 1980, Finding Structure in Co-Occurrence Matrices for Texture Analysis, *Computer Graphics and Image Processing,* vol 2, pp 286-308.
32. L. Xu and M. I. Jordan, On Convergence Properties of the EM Algorithm for Gaussian Mixtures. C.B.C.L. paper No. 111, A.I. Memo No. 1520, Massachusetts Institute of Technology, July 1995.
33. J. Zhang and W. J. Modestino, Maximum Likelihood Parameter Estimation for Unsupervised Stochastic Model_Base Image Segmentation. IEEE Trans. on Image Processing, 3(4):404-420, July 1994.

Structural Pattern Recognition for Industrial Machine Sounds Based on Frequency Spectrum Analysis

Yolanda Bolea[1], Antoni Grau[1], Arthur Pelissier[1], and Alberto Sanfeliu[2]

[1] Automatic Control Dept, Technical University of Catalonia UPC, Barcelona, Spain
{yolanda.bolea,antoni.grau}@upc.es
[2] Institute of Robotics, IRI, UPC, Barcelona, Spain

Abstract. In order to discriminate different industrial machine sounds contaminated with perturbations (high noise, speech, etc.), a spectral analysis based on a structural pattern recognition technique is proposed. This approach consists of three steps: 1) to de-noise the machine sounds using the Morlet wavelet transform, 2) to calculate the frequency spectrums for these purified signals, and 3) to convert these spectrums into strings, and use an approximated string matching technique, finding a distance measure (the Levenshtein distance) to discriminate the sounds. This method has been tested in artificial signals as well as in real sounds from industrial machines.

1 Introduction

A common problem encountered in industrial environments is that the electric machine sounds are often contaminated by interferences such as speech signals, environmental noise, background noise, etc. Consequently, pure machine sounds may be difficult to identify using conventional frequency domain analysis techniques. For example, the effectiveness of the Fourier transform relies on the signals containing distinct characteristic frequency components of sufficient energy content, within a limited frequency band. If however the feature components spread over a wide spectrum, it can be difficult to differentiate them from other disturbing or masking components, especially when the feature components are weak in amplitude. This has been shown in various situations involving machine systems with incipient defects [1][2].

It is generally difficult to extract hidden features from the data measured using conventional spectral techniques because of the weak amplitude and short duration of structural electric machine signals, and very often the feature sound of the machine is immersed in heavy perturbations producing hard changes in the original sound. For these reasons, the wavelet transform has attracted increasing attention in recent years for its ability in signal features extraction [3][4], and noise elimination [5]. While in many mechanical dynamic signals, such as the acoustical signals of an engine, Donoho's method seems rather ineffective, the reason for their inefficiency is that the feature of the mechanical signals is not considered. Therefore, when the idea of Donoho's method and the sound feature are combined, and a de-noising method based on the Morlet wavelet is added, this methodology becomes very effective when applied to an engine sound detection [6].

A. Sanfeliu et al. (Eds.): CIARP 2004, LNCS 3287, pp. 287–295, 2004.

In this work, we propose a new approach in order to discriminate among different industrial machine sounds, which can be affected by noise of various sources. We use the Morlet wavelet to de-noise the machine sounds, before frequency spectrums are extracted. These purified spectrums are the bases for a comparison between sound signals and a further discrimination step among sounds. A structural pattern recognition technique is used to compare the signal spectrums, because we convert each spectrum into a string, and a distance is found between strings. Since frequency spectrum does not follow a perfect pattern repeated along signals, it is not possible to use an exact matching algorithm to compare spectrums. To perform such comparison an approximated matching is used and the Levenshtein distance between spectrums is found. If the distance is short enough, these spectrums correspond to similar sounds. The use of string-to-string correction problem applied to pattern recognition is deeply treated in [7] and [8]. In order to check our approach, firstly we use some artificial signals with added gaussian noise, and the results are promising enough as to be used with real sounds.

This paper is organized as follows. In Section 2 the Morlet wavelet transform for de-noising the acoustical signals is explained. In Section 3 the approximated string matching is shown. Simulation and experimental results are presented in Section 4 and Section 5.

2   Wavelet and Its Application for Feature Extraction

2.1   Review of Wavelet Transform

The wavelet was originally introduced by Goupilland et al. in 1984 [9]. Let $\psi(t)$ be the basic wavelet function or the mother wavelet, then the corresponding family of daughter wavelets consists of

$$\psi_{a,b}(t) = |a|^{-1/2} \psi\left(\frac{t-b}{a}\right) \tag{1}$$

where a is the scale factor and b the time location, and the factor $|a|^{-1/2}$ is used to ensure energy preservation.

The wavelet transform of signal $x(t)$ is defined as the inner product in the Hilbert space of the L^2 norm, as shown in the following equation

$$W(a,b) = \langle \psi_{a,b}(t), x(t) \rangle = |a|^{-1/2} \int x(t)\psi_{a,b}^* dt \tag{2}$$

Here the asterisk stands for complex conjugate. Time parameter b and scale parameter a vary continuously, so that transform defined by Eq. (2) is also called a continuous wavelet transform, or CWT. The wavelet transform coefficients $W(a,b)$ can be considered as functions of translation b for each fixed scale a, which give the information of $x(t)$ at different levels of resolution. The wavelet coefficients $W(a,b)$ also measure the similarity between the signal $x(t)$ and each daughter wavelet $\psi_{a,b}(t)$. This implies that wavelets can be used for feature discovery if the wavelet used is close enough to the feature components hidden in the signal.

For many mechanical acoustic signals impulse components often correspond to the feature sound. Thus, the basic wavelet used for feature extraction should be similar to an impulse. The Morlet wavelet is such a wavelet defined as

$$\psi(t) = \exp(-\beta^2 t^2 / 2)\cos(\pi t) \tag{3}$$

2.2 Feature Extraction Using the Morlet Wavelet

The most popular algorithm of wavelet transform is the Mallat algorithm. Though this algorithm can save a lot of computations, it demands that the basic wavelet is orthogonal. The Morlet wavelet is not orthogonal. Thus, the wavelet transform of the Morlet wavelet has to be computed by the original definition, as shown in Eq. (2). Although the CWT brings about redundancy in the representation of the signal (a one-dimensional signal is mapped to a two-dimensional signal), it provides the possibility of reconstructing a signal. A classical inversion formula is

$$x(t) = C_\psi^{-1} \int \int W(a,b)\psi_{a,b}(t)\frac{da}{a^2}db \tag{4}$$

Another simple inverse way is to use the Morlet's formula, which only requires a single integration. The formula is:

$$x(t) = C_\psi^{-1} \int W(a,b)\frac{da}{a^{3/2}} \tag{5}$$

where

$$C_{1\psi} = \int_{-\infty}^{\infty} \hat{\psi}^*(\omega)/|\omega|d\omega \tag{6}$$

It is valid when $x(t)$ is real and either $\psi(t)$ is analytic or $\hat{\psi}(\omega)$ is real. The condition is satisfied by the Morlet wavelet. If the wavelet coefficients $W(a,b)$, corresponding to feature components, could be acquired, we could obtain the feature components just by reconstructing these coefficients. In calculations, the feature coefficients should be reserved and the irrelevant ones set to zero, then the signal can be purified by using formula Eq. (5). Thus, the key to obtaining the purified signal is how to obtain these feature coefficients.

Wavelet coefficients measure the similarity of the signal and each daughter wavelet. The more the daughter wavelet is similar to the feature component, the larger is the corresponding wavelet coefficient. So these large wavelet coefficients are mainly produced by the impulse components in the signal if the signal is transformed by the Morlet wavelet. We can get the impulse components in the signal reconstructing these large coefficients. Usually a threshold T_w should be set in advance, but it is not evident to choose it properly. The basic rule for threshold choice is that the higher the correlation between the random variables, the larger the threshold; and the higher the signal-noise ratio (SNR), the lower the threshold. In practice, the choice of the threshold T_w mainly depends on experience and knowledge about the signal. In fact, the quantitative relation between the threshold T_w and the SNR still remains an open question.

3 Approximated Matching of Strings

Since we propose a structural approach, two purified frequency spectrum can be represented by R_p and R_q, the discrimination step is defined as follows: two sounds p and q are similar iif their purified frequency spectrum R_p and R_q approximate match.

The problem of string-matching can generally be classified into exact matching and approximate matching. For exact matching, a single string is matched against a set of strings and this is not the purpose of our work. For approximate string matching, given a string v of some set V of possible strings, we want to know if a string u approximately matches this string, where u belongs to a subset U of V. In our case, V is the global set of purified frequency spectrums and u and v are purified frequency spectrums obtained from different sounds. Approximate string matching is based on the string distances that are computed by using the editing operations: substitution, insertion and deletion [10].

Let Σ be a set of symbols and let Σ^* be the set of all finite strings over Σ. Let Λ denote the *null string*. For a string $A = a_1 a_2 ... a_n \in \Sigma^*$, and for all $i, j \in \{1, 2,..., n\}$, let $A<i, j>$ denote the string $a_i a_{i+1} ... a_j$, where, by convention $A<i, j> = \Lambda$ if $i > j$.

An *edit operation* s is an ordered pair $(a, b) \neq (\Lambda,\Lambda)$ of strings, each of length less than or equal to 1, denoted by $a \rightarrow b$. An edit operation $a \rightarrow b$ will be called an *insert* operation if $a = \Lambda$, a *delete* operation if $b = \Lambda$, and a substitution operation otherwise.

We say that a string B results from a string A by the edit operation $s = (a \rightarrow b)$, denoted by $A \rightarrow B$ via s, if there are strings C and D such that $A = CaD$ and $B = CbD$. An *edit sequence* $S:= s_1 s_2 ... s_k$ is a sequence of edit operations. We say that S *takes* A *to* B if there are strings $A_0, A_1, ..., A_k$ such that $A_0 = A$, $A_k = B$ and $A_{i-1} \rightarrow A_i$ via s_i for all $i \in \{1, 2, ..., k\}$.

Now let γ be a cost function that assigns a nonnegative real number $\gamma(s)$ to each edit operation s. For an edit sequence S as above, we define the cost $\gamma(S)$ by $\gamma(S):= \Sigma_{i=1,...,k} \gamma(s_i)$. The *edit distance* $\delta(A, B)$ from string A to string B is now defined by $\delta(A, B):= \min\{\gamma(S) \mid S$ is an edit sequence taking A to $B\}$. We will assume that $\gamma(a \rightarrow b)= \delta(A, B)$ for all edit operations $a \rightarrow b$. The key operation for string matching is the computation of edit distance. Let A and B be strings, and $D(i,j)= \delta(A(1, i), B(1, j))$, $0 \leq i \leq m$, $0 \leq j \leq n$, where m and n are the lengths of A and B respectively, then:

$$D(i,j)= \min\{ D(i-1,j-1) + \gamma(A(i) \rightarrow B(j)), D(i-1,j) + \gamma(A(i) \rightarrow \Lambda), D(i,j-1) + \gamma(\Lambda \rightarrow B(j)) \} \tag{7}$$

for all $1 \leq i \leq m$, $1 \leq j \leq n$. Determining $\delta(A, B)$ in this way can in fact be seen as determining a minimum weighted path in a weighted directed graph. Note that the arcs of the graph correspond to insertions, deletions and substitutions. The Levenshtein distance (metric) is the minimum-cost edit sequence taking A to B from vertices $v(0,0)$ to $v(n,m)$. In our case both strings have the same length (N) and the algorithm used is $O(N^2)$ [7].

4 Discrimination of Artificial Signals

In order to test the capacity of analysis, feature extraction, and discrimination of the above proposed method, eight artificial signals have been taken. The first set of signals are two sinusoidal signals with the equation $S_i(t)=A_i\cos(2\pi f_i t)$ (with $i=1,2$, and $A_1=0.2$, $f_1=0.002$Hz, and $A_2=0.1$, $f_2=0.01$Hz) and two signals described by the following expressions:

$$S_3(t) = 0.75\big(\exp(-(t-200)^2/2400)\cos(\pi t/6) + \exp(-(t-400)^2/3000)\cos(\pi t/5.4)$$
$$+ \exp(-(t-600)^2/2700)\cos(\pi t/7)\exp(-(t-800)^2/3200)\cos(\pi t/4.7)\big)$$
$$S_4(t) = \exp(-(t-200)^2/80)\cos(\pi t/15) + \exp(-(t-400)^2/70)\cos(\pi t/18)$$
$$+ \exp(-(t-600)^2/90)\cos(\pi t/14)\exp(-(t-800)^2/60)\cos(\pi t/16)$$

The other set of signals are the contaminated first set of signals, with additive white noise, which has a normal distribution with variance $\sigma^2 = 0.2$ and zero mean. The SNR for these signals is 0.09677, 0.02471, 0.36153 and 0.11263, respectively.

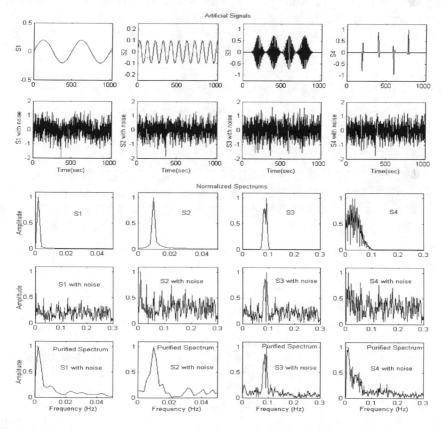

Fig. 1. Artificial signals; top to bottom: signals, signals with noise, frequency spectrum of the clean signals, frequency spectrum of contaminated signals, and frequency spectrum of the purified noisy signals.

Fig. 1 shows the two sets of artificial signals. In the first rows, the clean signals S_1, S_2, S_3 and S_4 as well as their contaminated versions can be seen. The next row contains the frequency spectrum from the clean signals, while the fourth row contains the spectrum of the signals with noise. It is important to note that there exists a huge difference between the signal spectrum with noise respect the spectrum of its clean signal.

In order to remove the maximum added noise to the signals, the contaminated signals are transformed with the Morlet wavelet, filtered (that is, removing the coefficients lower that a prefixed threshold) and reconstructed again. The frequency spectrum for these purified signals can be seen in the fifth row, and now, it is easy to observe that they are quite similar to these spectrums of the clean signals. The threshold T_w values are set to one-third of the maximum wavelet coefficients of the clean signals, fulfilling the basic rule stated in Section 2.2.

In order to quantify the similarity between signals, these spectrums are treated as strings, where each position is the amplitude of the spectrum. As the match will not be perfect, we use an approximate string matching technique and the Levenshtein distance (metric) is calculated, see Table 1. The distance is normalized respect the maximum distance, and the higher the distance, the more unlikely the signals is the same.

Table 1. Normalized distance from the artificial clean signals to the contaminated signals.

	Distance, using $T_s = 0$			
Clean signals	Signals with noise			
	S_1	S_2	S_3	S_4
S_1	0.32	0.60	0.68	0.92
S_2	0.39	0.56	0.68	0.88
S_3	0.54	0.69	0.40	1.00
S_4	0.58	0.71	0.81	0.64

The study and analysis of the discrimination algorithm are performed setting three threshold values T_s. This threshold T_s serves to eliminate all the amplitudes in the frequency spectrum above its value. Initially, we do not use any threshold ($T_s = 0$), and we use all the amplitudes in the spectrum; second, we use a value of $T_s = 0.2$ in order to remove the spurious frequencies; and finally, the threshold is set to $T_s = 0.5$ to capture the fundamental frequency and the most important harmonics in the signal.

In this study, we have realized that a similar distance i) between a clean signal and its contaminated version and ii) between this clean signal and another contaminated signal, can be discriminant enough if the distance between the clean signals is close. For this reason, it is important to check all the distances among the clean and contaminated signals. This effect can be observed in Table 1. The distance between S_1 and S_1 with noise ($d = 0.32$) and S_2 and S_1 with noise ($d = 0.39$) is enough to think that S_1 with noise is a contaminated version of S_1, because the distance between S_1 and S_2 is only

$d=0.09$. The same reasoning is applied to S_2 with noise respect S_1 and S_2, obviously. In the other contamined signals (S_3 and S_4) their distance to their clean signals is short enough to perform a good discrimination ($d=0.40$ and $d=0.64$).

5   Discrimination of Real Sounds

For testing the proposed method with real sounds we have been working with 4 machine sounds: mill sound (S_{l1}), drill sound (S_{l2}), mill sound contamined with vibrations and speech (S_{r1}), drill sound contamined with speech (S_{r2}). The two former signals are considered the clean sounds. The latter are their contaminated version. The frequency sample is 22,050Hz, 16-bit, mono.

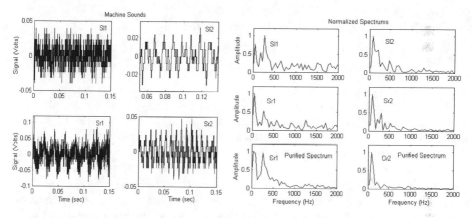

Fig. 2. (Left) Machine sounds; (right) first and second row: spectrums of machine sounds; third row: purified spectrums of the contaminated signals S_{r1} and S_{r2}.

As it can be seen in Fig.2. (1st and 2nd row right), the spectrum of clean signals (S_{l1} and S_{l2}) have two distinct features: i) S_{l1} has two important frequency peaks and S_{l2} has only one; ii) the fundamental frequencies of each signal are located at different spectrum positions. Taking into account these features and the low SNR of contaminated signals, the threshold T_w values are set to one-fourth of the maximum wavelet coefficient.

Table 2. Normalized distance among the real sounds and their contaminated versions

Clean signals	Distance	
	Signals with noise	
	S_{r1}	S_{r2}
S_{l1}	0.58	0.64
S_{l2}	0.83	0.35

When the drill sound is contamined with vibrations and speech, the signal becomes stronger and there is a shift in the fundamental frequency from 258.7 Hz to 44.5 Hz due to: i) the vibrations reduce the fundamental frequency; and ii) the pitch in adult male speakers is between 50 Hz and 250 Hz. On the other hand, when the mill signal is contaminated with speech, the fundamental frequency does not vary because the clean signal fundamental frequency is already in this range (about 86.1 Hz).

In Fig.2 (3rd row right), the purified spectrum (with Morlet wavelet transform) captures very well the most important frequency peaks of the clean signals.

When these spectrums are converted into strings, if the frequency peaks between signals are closely located, the distance will also be close, and then the discrimination will be effective.

Many experiments have done with different parameters, $T_s = 0.2$ and $T_s = 0.6$, considering all the frequencies or discretizing them (the X-axis of the spectrums) when the string is generated. In all the cases the results (see Table 2) show that the proposed method can be used to discriminate real sounds.

6 Conclusions

Machine sound varies depending on the factors as background noise, failures of their mechanisms, environmental aspects (speech, noise, ...), etc. Besides, when the feature sound is immersed in heavy perturbations as the previously cited is hard to capture. CWT can be used to discover the relevant signal components respect the selected wavelet bases. Then, using a proper basic wavelet, we can obtain the feature components of a signal by reconstructing the wavelet coefficients. The machine sound can be purified following this procedure. Together with an approximated matching technique, the original source of real contaminated sounds can be effectively detected.

References

1. Mori, K., Kasashima, N., Yoshioha, T. and Ueno, Y, "Prediction of Spalling on a Ball Bearing by Applying the Discrete Wavelet Transform to Vibration Signals", Wear, vol.195, no.1-2, pp. 162-168, 1996.
2. Liu, H.-C. and Srinath, M.D., "Classification of partial shapes using string-to-string matching", *Intell. Robots and Comput. Vision, SPIE Proc.*, vol. 1002, pp. 92-98, 1989.
3. Bolea, Y., Grau, A. and Sanfeliu, A., "Non-speech Sound Feature Extraction based on Model Identification for Robot Navigation", *8th Iberoamerican Congress on Pattern Recognition*, CIARP 2003, Lectures Notes in Computer Science, LNCS 2905, pp. 221-228, Havana, Cuba, November 2003.
4. Mallat, S. and Zhang, Z., "Matching pursuits with time-frequency dictionaries", *IEEE Trans. on Signal Processing*, vol.45, no.12, pp. 3397-3415, 1993.
5. Donoho, D.-L., "De-noising by soft-thresholding", *IEEE Trans. on Information Theory*, vol.33, no.7, pp. 2183-2191, 1999.
6. Lin, J., "Feature Extraction of Machine Sound using Wavelet and its Application in Fault Diagnosis", NTD&E International, vol.34, pp.25-30, 2001.

7. Sankoff, D. and Kruskal, J.B. eds, *Time Warps, String Edit and Macromolecules: The Theory and Practice of Sequence Comparison*, Addison-Wesley, Reading, MA, 1983.
8. Bunke, H. and Sanfeliu, A., *Syntactic and Structural Pattern Recognition Theory and Applications*, Series in Computer Science, vol.7, World Scientific Publ., 1990.
9. Goupilland, P., Grossmann, A. and Morlet, J., "Cycle octave and related transforms in seismic signal analysis", *Geoexploration*, vol.23, pp.85-102, 1984.
10. Wagner, R.A. et al., "The string-to-string correction problem", *J. Ass. Comput. Mach.*, vol.21, no.1, pp. 168-173, 1974.

An Extended Speech De-noising Method
Using GGM-Based ICA Feature Extraction

Wei Kong, Yue Zhou, and Jie Yang

Institute of Image Processing & Pattern Recognition, Shanghai Jiaotong University,
Shanghai 200030, China
{kongwei,zhouyue,jieyang}@sjtu.edu.cn

Abstract. ICA (independent component analysis) feature extraction is an efficient sparse coding method for noise reduction. In many ICA-based de-noising
processing, however, they need noise-free source data to train the basis vectors
as a priori knowledge. The noise-free data is always not acquirable in practice.
In this paper, the generalized Gaussian model (GGM) is proposed as the p.d.f.
estimator in ICA to extract the basis vectors directly from the noisy observation,
since GGM can easily characterize a wide class of non-Gaussian statistical distributions. Simultaneously, the distribution of the coefficients learned by GGM
is benefit for obtaining the shrinkage functions. The de-nosing experiments of
noisy speech signals show that the proposed method is more efficient than conventional methods in the environment of additive white Gaussian noise. It demonstrates that the proposed method offer an efficient approach for detecting
weak signals from the noise environment.

1 Introduction

Sparse coding is a method for fining a representation of data in which only a small
number of the components are significantly non-zero. Because of this one may assume that the activities of components with small absolute values are noise or redundancy information and set them to zero, retaining just a few components with large
activities. So such a representation is benefit for redundancy reduction and de-noising.
In the work of [2]-[5], ICA has been successfully applied in extracting efficient
speech features since it can extract statistical independent vectors based on the higher
order statistics from data, and it was proved an efficient sparse coding method.

In many ICA-based speech de-noising works, however, the de-noising process of
noisy speech signals needs noise-free source data to train the ICA basis vectors as a
priori knowledge. Unfortunately, the noise-free speech signal is always not acquirable
in practice. In this paper, the generalized Gaussian model (GGM) was introduced in
ICA algorithm to estimate the p.d.f. of coefficients. By inferring only one parameter
q, ICA algorithm can extract the efficient basis vectors directly from the noisy signals
since GGM provide a general method for modeling non-Gaussian distribution. At the
same time the shrinkage function can be obtained from the p.d.f. of each coefficient.
Then using the maximum likelihood (ML) method on the non-Gaussian variables
corrupted by additive white Gaussian noise, we show how to apply the shrinkage
method on the coefficients to reduce noise. Experiments of noisy male and female
speech signals show that even in the intensive noise environment, our method shows
much improvement on the signal to noise ratio (SNR) after de-noising.

A. Sanfeliu et al. (Eds.): CIARP 2004, LNCS 3287, pp. 296–302, 2004.

2 ICA Feature Extraction Using GGM

The success of the ICA learning algorithm depends highly on how well it can model the underlying statistical distribution of data. Therefore in this paper the GGM proposed by Miller J. H. et al [6] is introduced in ICA algorithm as the model for non-Gaussian coefficients. It can give different distribution models for different variables, so it is more accurate than the ICA algorithms with fixed model. Using this model in ICA, It shows that the estimation of the density of the independent coefficients is conveniently and accurately.

2.1 The Generalized Gaussian Model

The GGM models a family of density functions that is peaked and symmetric at the mean, with a varying degree of normality in the following general form [7]

$$p_g(s \mid \theta) = \frac{\omega(q)}{\sigma} \exp[-c(q) \mid \frac{s - \mu}{\sigma} \mid^q], \quad \theta = \{\mu, \theta, q\} \tag{1}$$

where

$$c(q) = [\frac{\Gamma[3/q]}{\Gamma[1/q]}]^{q/2} \tag{2}$$

and

$$\omega(q) = \frac{\Gamma[3/q]^{\frac{1}{2}}}{(2/q)\Gamma[1/q]^{\frac{3}{2}}} \tag{3}$$

$\mu = E[s], \sigma = \sqrt{E[(s - \mu)^2]}$ are the mean and standard deviation of the data respectively, and $\Gamma[\cdot]$ is the Gamma function. By inferring q, a wide class of statistical distributions can be characterized. The Gaussian, Laplacian, and strong Laplacian (such as speech signal) distributions can be modeled by putting $q = 2$, $q = 1$, and $q < 1$ respectively. The exponent q controls the distribution's deviation from normal. When $q=2$, the distribution is the standard normal fig. 1 gives the examples of the exponential power distribution for various values of q.

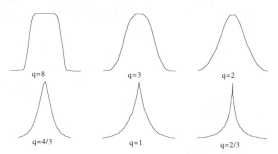

Fig. 1. Generalized Gaussian model for various exponent q

For the purposes of finding the basis functions and the parameter q in ICA, zero mean and unit variance is assumed. The problem then becomes to estimate the value

of q from the data. This can be accomplished by simply finding the maximum posteriori value q. The posterior distribution of q given the observations $x=\{x_1,...,x_n\}$ is

$$p(q\,|\,x) \propto p(x\,|\,q)\,p(q) \tag{4}$$

where the data likelihood is

$$p(x\,|\,q) = \prod_n \omega(q)\,\exp[\,-c(q)\,|\,x_n\,|^q\,] \tag{5}$$

and $p(q)$ defines the prior distribution for q. Gamma function $\Gamma[\cdot]$ is used as $p(q)$
here. More details can be seen in the work of Box and Tiao (1973) [8] on inference
with the exponential power distribution.

   Fig. 2. shows some estimation examples of the values of q in GGM for different
distributions by the maximum posterior.

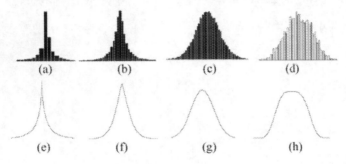

Fig. 2. (a)-(d) histogram of the distribution of s1, s2, s3 and s4 respectively, (e) $q=2/3$, (f)
$q=4/3$, (g) $q=2$, (h) $q=7/2$

2.2   ICA Feature Extraction Using GGM

To extract basis functions from speech signals, ICA algorithm is applied to a number
of speech segments

$$x = As = \sum_{i=1}^{N} a_i s_i \tag{6}$$

   ICA algorithm is performed to obtain the estimation of independent components s
from speech segments x by the un-mixing matrix W

$$u = Wx \tag{7}$$

where u is the estimation of independent components s. Basis functions A can be
calculated from the ICA algorithm by the relation $A= W^{-1}$.

   By maximizing the log likelihood of the separated signals, both the independent
coefficients and the unknown basis functions can be inferred. The learning rules is
represented as

$$\Delta W \propto \frac{\partial \log\,p(s)}{\partial W} W^T W = \eta[I - \varphi(s)s^T\,]W \tag{8}$$

here W^TW is used to perform the natural gradient, it simplifies the learning rules and
speeds convergence considerably. The vector $\varphi(s)$ is a function of the prior and is

defined by $\varphi(s) = \frac{\partial \log p(s)}{\partial s}$. In the case of the generalized Gaussian distribution (eq. 1),

the vector $\varphi(s)$ can be derived as

$$\varphi_i(s_i) = -qc\sigma_i^{-q} |s_i - \mu_i|^{q-1} sign(s_i - \mu_i)$$ (9)

where $\mu_i = E[s_i], \sigma_i = \sqrt{E[(s_i - \mu_i)^2]}$ are the mean and standard deviation of the data respectively. Using the learning rule (8) the un-mixing matrix W is iterated by the natural gradient until convergence is achieved.

3 Speech De-noising Based on Maximum Likelihood Estimation

The GGM-based ICA algorithm in section 2.2 has been used to extract the basis vectors of noisy speech when the noise-free speech cannot be obtained, and the p.d.f. of the coefficients $p(s)$ learned by the GGM are got simultaneously. In the noise environment, denote y as the noisy coefficient of a basis vector, s as the original noise-free version of coefficient of basis vector, and v as a Gaussian noise with zero mean and variance σ^2. Then the variable y can be describe as

$$y = s + v$$ (10)

We want to estimate s from the only observed noisy coefficient y. Denote p as the probability of s, and $f = -\log p$ as its negative log-density, the estimator of s can be obtained by the maximum likelihood (ML) method

$$\hat{s} = \arg\min_s \frac{1}{2\sigma^2}(y - s)^2 + f(s)$$ (11)

Assuming $f(\cdot)$ to be strictly convex and differentiable, the ML estimation gives the equation

$$\hat{s} = h(y)$$ (12)

where the nonlinear function $h(\cdot)$ is called as *shrinkage* function, and the inverse is given by

$$h^{-1}(s) = s + \sigma^2 f'(s)$$ (13)

Thus, the estimation of s is obtained by inverting a certain function involving $f'(\cdot)$. Since $f(\cdot)$ is a function of p, the probability of s has been obtained by GGM in ICA feature extraction, the shrinkage function can be obtained easily.

To recover the de-noised speech signal from the noisy source three steps are needed. Firstly, By using GGM-based ICA, we can obtain the un-mixing matrix W and the p.d.f. of the corresponding coefficients $p(s)$ at the same time. From the experiments, it shows that the coefficients of the basis vectors extracted from noisy speech have sparse distributions. Secondly, the shrinkage functions can be estimated by $p(s)$ by eq. (13), and the de-noised coefficients can be calculated by $\hat{s} = h(y)$. Finally, recover the de-noised speech signal by $\hat{x} = W^{-1}\hat{s} = A\hat{s}$.

This method is closed related to the wavelet shrinkage method. However, the sparse coding based on ICA may be viewed as a way for determining the basis and corresponding shrinkage functions base on the data themselves. Our method use the transformation based on the statistical properties of the data, whereas the wavelet shrinkage method chooses a predetermined wavelet transform. And the second difference is that we estimate the shrinkage nonlinearities by the ML estimation, again adapting to the data themselves, whereas the wavelet shrinkage method use fixed threshold derived by the mini-max principle.

4 Experiments

Noisy male speech and noisy female speech signals mixed with white Gaussian noise were used to test the performance of the proposed method. The sampling rates are both 8kHz and 20000 samples of each noisy speech signal is used. The first step is the feature extraction of the noisy signals using the GGM-based ICA algorithm described in section 2. For each noisy speech signal, the mean was subtracted (eq.14) and then 500 vectors of length 40 (5ms) were generated, and each segment was pre-whitened to improve the convergence speed (eq.15).

$$x = x - E\{x\} \tag{14}$$

$$v = E\{x\,x^T\,\}^{-1/2}\,x \tag{15}$$

This pre-processing removes both first- and second-order statistics from the input data, and makes the covariance matrix of x equal to the identity matrix, where x denoted as the observed noisy signals. The adaptation of the un-mixing matrix W started from the 40×40 identity matrix and trained through the 500 vectors. The learning rate was gradually decreased from 0.2 to 0.05 during the iteration. Then the un-mixing matrix W was extracted by the learning rule (8), and it was used as the filter in the de-noising processing. To judge the results of the de-noising, the signal-to-noise ratio (SNR) is used

$$SNR_i = 10\log\left|\frac{\sum_{t=1}^{N} Signal(t)^2}{\sum_{t=1}^{N} Noise(t)^2}\right| \tag{16}$$

In the first experiment, the noisy male speech signals corrupted by four different intensity of additive white Gaussian noise were used to test the de-noising method. Their SNR of the input noisy signals are 4.8004, 0.4854, -5.0242 and -12.6541dB respectively. The output SNR results of the de-noised speech signals are 8.0815, 6.0971, 3.4017 and -0.2596dB respectively, it can be seen that the SNR have much improvement. Fig. 3 shows the de-noising results of the noisy male speech with the input SNR of −5.0242dB and it was compared to the median filter and the wavelet filter method.

The de-noising results of these four noisy male speech signals with different intensity Gaussian noise are shown in table 1. Where SNR_{in} denotes the input SNR of the noisy male speech signals and SNR_{out} denotes the output SNR of the de-noised male speech signals.

And the de-noising results of these four noisy female speech signals with different intensity Gaussian noise are shown in table 2.

Fig. 5 shows the SNRs in different intensities of the additive white Gaussian noise for male speech experiments and female speech experiments respectively. It shows that our method of extracting basis vectors directly from the noisy signals based on GGM is efficient and always better than conventional methods.

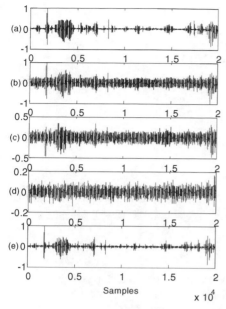

Fig. 3. (a) noisy-free male speech signals, (b) noisy male speech signals with input SNR of – 5.0242dB, (c) de-noising result of median filter with n=3, output SNR is -4.8481dB, (d) de-noising result of wavelet filter with db3 and n=3, output SNR of this method is -1.8335dB, (e) de-noising result of our method, output SNR is 3.4017 dB

Fig. 4. (a)noisy-free female speech signals, (b)noisy female speech signals with input SNR of -7.0775dB, (c) de-noising result of median filter with n=3, output SNR is -4.6386dB, (d) de-noising result of wavelet filter with db3 and n=3, output SNR of this method is -2.2646dB, (e) de-noising result of our method, output SNR is 4.7150 dB

Table 1. Signal-to-noise ratio (SNR) of the de-noised male speech signals

SNR$_{in}$ of noisy male speech (dB)	SNR$_{out}$ of median filter (dB)		SNR$_{out}$ of wavelet filter,db3,n=3 (dB)	SNR$_{out}$ of our method (dB)
	n=3	n=5		
4.8004	-1.7077	-2.7722	-0.6592	8.0815
0.4854	-2.8087	-3.4863	-1.0537	6.0971
-5.0242	-4.8481	-4.8504	-1.8335	3.4017
-12.6541	-8.9528	-7.7528	-3.6795	-0.2596

Table 2. Signal-to-noise ratio (SNR) of the de-noised female speech signals

SNR$_{in}$ of noisy female speech (dB)	SNR$_{out}$ of median filter (dB)		SNR$_{out}$ of wavelet filter,db3,n=3 (dB)	SNR$_{out}$ of our method (dB)
	n=3	n=5		
2.6087	-0.0310	-4.4573	-0.8806	6.5623
-1.6538	-1.7842	-5.1106	-1.3522	5.8288
-7.0775	-4.6386	-6.3778	-2.2646	4.7150
-14.5406	-9.6556	-9.2051	-4.3425	0.7533

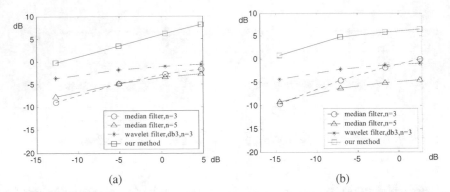

Fig. 5. (a) the SNR comparison of several de-noising method on noisy male speech signals, (b) the SNR comparison of several de-noising method on noisy female speech signals

5   Conclusions

How to extract efficient basis vectors directly from the observed noisy speech signals is the key objective of noisy speech de-noising since the corresponding noise-free signal is always not acquirable in practice. So in this paper, ICA feature extraction using generalized Gaussian model (GGM) is proposed to extract basis vectors directly from noisy data. By inferring only one parameter, different kinds of non-Gaussian distributions of coefficients can be characterized. Sparse coding is achieved by ICA feature extraction. And the ICA features and the shrinkage functions can be obtained at the same time. By shrinkage the absolute values of the sparse components to wards zero, noise can be reduced. Experiments on noisy male and female speech signals show that the proposed method can efficiently remove the additive white Gaussian noise.

References

1. A. Hyvärinen, Sparse code shrinkage: Denoising of nongaussian data by maximum likeli-hood estimation. Technical Report A51, Helsinki University of Technology, Laboratory of Computer and Information Science, 1998
2. Te-Won Lee, Gil-Jin Jang, The Statistical Structures of Male and Female Speech Signals, in Proc. ICASSP, (Salt Lack City, Utah), May 2001
3. Jong-Hawn Lee, Ho-Young Jung, Speech Feature Extraction Using Independent Component Analysis, in Proc. ICASP, Istanbul, Turkey, June, 2000,Vol. 3, pp: 1631-1634
4. Anthony J Bell, Terrence J Sejnowski, Learning the Higher-order structure of a nature sound, Network: Computation in Neural System 7 (1996), 261-266
5. Gil-Jin Jang, Te-won Lee, Learning statistically efficient features for speaker recognition, Neurocomputing, 49 (2002): 329-348
6. Miller J. H. & Thomas J. B., Detectors for Discrete-Time Signals in Non-Gaussian noise, IEEE Transactions on Information Theory, Vol IT-18, no. 2, March 1972. Page(s) 241-250
7. Te-Won Lee, Michael S. Lewicki, The Generalized Gaussian Mixture Model Using ICA, in international workshop on Independent Component Analysis (ICA'00), Helsinki, Finland, June 2000, pp: 239-244

Spanning Tree Recovery via Random Walks in a Riemannian Manifold

Antonio Robles-Kelly and Edwin R. Hancock

Department of Computer Science,
University of York, York YO1 5DD, UK
{arobkell,erh}@cs.york.ac.uk

Abstract. In this paper, we describe the use of Riemannian geometry and graph-spectral methods for purposes of minimum spanning tree recovery. We commence by showing how the sectional curvature can be used to model the edge-weights of the graph as a dynamic system in a manifold governed by a Jacobi field. With this characterisation of the edge-weights at hand, we proceed to recover an approximation for the minimum spanning tree. To do this, we present a random walk approach which makes use of a probability matrix equivalent, by row-normalisation, to the matrix of edge-weights. We show the solution to be equivalent, up to scaling, to the leading eigenvector of the edge-weight matrix. We approximate the minimum spanning tree making use of a brushfire search method based upon the rank-order of the eigenvector coefficients and the set of first-order neighbourhoods for the nodes in the graph. We illustrate the utility of the method for purposes of network optimisation.

1   Introduction

The recovery of the minimum spanning tree is a classical problem in pattern recognition. For a weighted graph, the minimum spanning tree is the set of edges that connects all its vertices without cycles and with minimum total length. The minimum spanning tree finds application in a number of areas such as network optimisation, database indexing and logistic planning. The problem is clearly one of optimisation, which is traditionally solved using greedy algorithms [1, 2].

However, one of the methods that has received little attention is that of posing the problem in an energy minimisation setting and using graph-spectral techniques to recover the solution. To cast the problem in such way has a number of advantages. Firstly, it would allow the modeling of processes that occur in arbitrary dimension under non-linear constraints. It also allows the problem to be modeled as a conservative process in a manifold. Viewed in this manner, the edge-weight then becomes the energy required to move between a pair of adjacent nodes in the graph. Once the edge-weights are at hand, the apparatus of graph-spectral theory can be used to recover the tree whose cost is optimum.

Graph-spectral methods have recently proved highly effective in image processing and computer vision. By computing the eigenvalues and eigenvectors of

A. Sanfeliu et al. (Eds.): CIARP 2004, LNCS 3287, pp. 303–311, 2004.

the weight matrix, it is possible to find groups or clusters of entities. Perhaps the best known method is that of Shi and Malik [3] which has shown how to locate image regions by recursively locating the eigenvector associated with the second smallest eigenvalue of the Laplacian matrix, i.e. the degree matrix minus the affinity weight matrix. Although it is convenient to work with the Laplacian, since it is positive semi-definite, grouping and segmentation can also be performed using an edge-weight or affinity matrix. For instance, both Sarkar and Boyer [4] and Perona and Freeman [5] have developed matrix factorisation methods for line-segment grouping that use eigenvectors of an affinity matrix rather than the associated Laplacian. The Sarkar and Boyer [4] method can be understood as that which maximises the total edge weight of the clusters.

The methods described above all share the feature of using the eigenvectors of a Laplacian or an affinity matrix to define groups or clusters or objects. However, graph-spectral methods can also be used for path analysis tasks on graphs. For instance, it is well known that the path length distribution can be computed from the spectrum of eigenvalues of the adjacency matrix [6]. Ideas from spectral-graph theory have also been used to analyse the behaviour of random walks in graphs [7–9]. In addition, there are important relationships between the eigenvectors of the edge weight matrix and other quantities related to random walks. Further, the relationship between the leading eigenvector of the edge weight matrix and the steady state random walk has been exploited in a number of areas including routeing theory and information retrieval [10, 11].

The advantage of graph-spectral methods is that they can be used to find approximate or relaxed solutions without the need for parallel iterative updates at the vertex level. The method also obviates the need for complex search algorithms. However, although they have been applied to region segmentation and grouping problems, graph-spectral methods have not been applied to curve detection problems of the sort that arise in the determination of the optimal spanning tree.

2 Riemannian Geometry and Markovian Processes

In this section, we provide the theoretical basis for our minimum spanning tree approximation algorithm. We commence by showing how Riemannian geometry invariants can be used to model the edge-weights of the graph as the energy of a particle moving along a geodesic between a pair of points in a Riemannian manifold. There are clearly a number of ways in which the energy of such dynamic system can be minimised. Here, we have chosen to present a random walk approach that makes use of the apparatus of Markov chains to approximate the tree whose cost is minimum.

2.1 Riemannian Manifolds

In this section, we aim at providing a means of characterising the step between two adjacent nodes in the graph as a geodesic in a Riemannian manifold. To do this, we pose the problem in a graph-based setting. Let $G = (V, E, W)$ denote a weighted graph with index-set V, edge-set $E = \{(i, j) | (i, j) \in V \times V, i \neq j\}$ and edge-weight set $W = \{W(i, j) | (i, j) \in V \times V \wedge W(i, j) \in [0, 1]\}$. If the nodes in the graph are viewed as points on the manifold, the edge weight between a pair of nodes can then be interpreted as the energy of a particle moving along the geodesic under the influence of a vector field. With these ingredients, the energy $\mathcal{E}_{p_i, p_j}$ of the dynamic system can be used to define the elements of the edge-weight matrix such that $W(i, j) = \exp[-\mathcal{E}_{p_i, p_j}]$.

To express the energy $\mathcal{E}_{p_i, p_j}$ in terms of geometric invariants, we employ the theory of Jacobi vector fields and their relation to the curvature tensor to characterise the sectional curvature of the manifold. The reasons for using the curvature tensor are twofold. Firstly, the curvature tensor is natural, i.e. invariant under isometries. Secondly, the curvature tensor can be defined intrinsically through coordinate changes and it appears as the second differential form of the metric. Hence, the curvature tensor is one of the main invariants in Riemannian geometry. Here, unless noted otherwise, we use tensor notation in order to provide a framework which is both, consistent with the material available from mathematics and compatible with concepts drawn from physics. We consider a function f to be differentiable if it is of class C^∞, i.e. all its partial derivatives, of all orders, exist and are continuous.

Consider a n-dimensional differentiable manifold M. For any point $p \in M$, let M_p denote the tangent space of M at p. Further, let Y be a differentiable vector field in $\Re^n$ such that $Y = \sum_{i=1}^{n} \eta^i \partial_i$, where η^i is the ith coordinate of the vector $\eta = \sum_{i=1}^{n} \eta^i \partial_{i|_p}$ and $e = \{e_1, e_2, \ldots, e_n\}$ is the natural basis $(\Re^n)_p$, i.e. the natural basis of $\Re^n$ at $p \in M$. In the equations above, the symbol ∂_i has been defined so as to be consistent with both, the notion of chart in Riemannian geometry and the natural basis e. To provide a definition of ∂_i, we turn our attention to the natural identification $\Im_p : \Re^n \mapsto (\Re^n)_p$ of the tangent space at p, i.e. $(\Re^n)_p$, onto $\Re^n$. For the natural basis, the chart is then given by the identity map such that $\partial_{i|p} = \Im_p e_i$.

In order to take our analysis further, we require a well-defined method for differentiating vector fields. Hence, for a collection of vector fields $\wp^1$ of class C^1 and a differentiable vector $\xi \in M_p$, the connection $\nabla : M_p \times \wp^1(M_p) \mapsto M_p$ is given by $\nabla_\xi Y = \sum_{i=1}^{n} (\xi \eta^i) \partial_i$. This definition implies that the vector $\nabla_\xi Y$ is in the same tangent space as ξ. Furthermore, the connection expresses the covariant derivatives of the vector field Y in terms of the vector ξ. This is, $\nabla_\xi Y$ describes the rate of change of the vector field Y in the direction ξ in terms of ξ itself.

In this section, we aim to characterise the transition between two nodes in the graph as a dynamic system in a manifold. To provide a characterisation invariant over isometric transformations, we use the notion of connection provided above to define the curvature tensor. Consider the vector fields Y, X and Z to be extensions in a neighbourhood of p of the vectors $\eta, \xi, \zeta \in M_p$. The curvature tensor, which is quadrilinear in nature [12], is then denoted by $R(\xi, \eta)\zeta$. Here, we are interested in the sectional curvature, which is bilinear in nature. To obtain a bilinear form, i.e. the sectional curvature, from the curvature tensor we use two linearly independent vectors $\eta, \xi \in M_p$ and write

$$\mathcal{K}(\xi, \eta) = \frac{\langle R(\xi, \eta)\xi, \eta \rangle}{|\xi|^2 |\eta|^2 - \langle \xi, \eta \rangle} \tag{1}$$

As mentioned earlier, we are interested in modeling the edges in the graph as geodesics in a manifold. Consider the parameterised curve $\gamma : t \in [\alpha, \beta] \mapsto M$. From Riemannian geometry, we know that for γ to be a geodesic, it must satisfy the condition $\nabla_{\gamma'}\gamma' = 0$. It can be shown that the connection ∇ for geodesics is, in fact, a Levi-Civita connection [12]. Further, Levi-Civita connections are metric preserving, unique and are guaranteed to exist.

To take our analysis further, we define the Jacobi field along γ as the differentiable vector field $Y \in M_p$, orthogonal to γ, satisfying Jacobi's equation $\nabla_t^2 Y + R(\gamma', Y)\gamma' = 0$, where ∇ is a Levi-Civita connection.

With this ingredients, we can substitute ξ and η with γ' and Y in Equation 1 and write $\mathcal{K}(\gamma', Y) = \frac{\langle R(\gamma', Y)\gamma', Y \rangle}{|\gamma'|^2 |Y|^2 - \langle \gamma', Y \rangle}$. But, because Y is orthogonal to γ', the equation above becomes

$$\mathcal{K}(\gamma', Y) = \frac{\langle R(\gamma', Y)\gamma', Y \rangle}{|\gamma'|^2 |Y|^2} \tag{2}$$

To simplify the expression for the sectional curvature further, we make use of the fact that, since Y is a Jacobi field, it must satisfy the condition $\nabla_t^2 Y = -R(\gamma', Y)\gamma'$. Hence, we write $\mathcal{K}(\gamma', Y) = \frac{\langle -\nabla_t^2 Y, Y \rangle}{\langle Y, Y \rangle}$, where we have substituted $|Y|^2$ with $\langle Y, Y \rangle$ and set $|\gamma'| = 1$. As a result, it follows that $\nabla_t^2 Y = -\mathcal{K}(\gamma', Y)Y$.

This suggests a way of formulating the energy along the geodesic $\gamma \in M$ connecting the pair of points indexed i and j. Consider a particle of mass ρ moving along the geodesic γ subject to the Jacobi field Y. The energy of the particle can be expressed making use of the equations above as

$$\mathcal{E}_{p_i, p_j} = \rho\left(\int_\gamma |\gamma' + \nabla_t^2 Y|^2 \, dt\right) = \rho\left(\int_\gamma |\gamma' - \mathcal{K}(\gamma', Y)Y|^2 \, dt\right) \tag{3}$$

where p_i is the point indexed i in M. This is, we have expressed the energy of the particle moving from the point indexed i to the point indexed j as the sum of its kinetic energy and the potential contributed by the Jacobi field along γ. Hence, the edge-weight is small if a pair of points are far from each other or the curvature along the geodesic between them is large.

2.2   Random Walks

To take our analysis further and make the relationship to the sectional curvature more explicit, we cast the problem into a random walk setting. In order to profit from a Markov chain approach to the problem, we commence by row-normalising the weight matrix W so its rows sum to unity. To do this, we compute the degree of each node $deg(i) = \sum_{j=1}^{|V|} W(i,j)$. With the diagonal degree matrix $D = diag(deg(1), deg(2), \ldots, deg(|V|))$ at hand, the transition probability matrix is given by $P = D^{-1}W$. The elements of the transition matrix are hence given by $P_{i,j} = \frac{1}{deg(i)}W_{i,j}$. It is interesting to note that the transition matrix P is a row stochastic matrix. Moreover, it is related to the normalised symmetric positive definite matrix $\hat{W} = D^{-\frac{1}{2}}WD^{-\frac{1}{2}} = D^{\frac{1}{2}}PD^{-\frac{1}{2}}$. As a result, we can write $P = D^{-\frac{1}{2}}\hat{W}D^{\frac{1}{2}}$. It is worth noting in passing that the matrix $\hat{W}$ is related to the normalised Laplacian $L = D^{-\frac{1}{2}}(D-W)D^{-\frac{1}{2}} = I - D^{-\frac{1}{2}}WD^{-\frac{1}{2}} = I - \hat{W}$.

Our aim is to use the steady state random walk on the graph G for purposes of recovering the spanning tree whose cost is minimum. The walk commences at the node j_1 and proceeds via the sequence of nodes $\Upsilon = \{j_1, j_2, j_3, \ldots\}$. If the random walk can be represented by a Markov chain with transition matrix P, then the probability of visiting the nodes in the sequence above is

$$P_\Upsilon = P(j_1) \prod_{l \in \Upsilon} P_{j_{l+1}, j_l} = \prod_{l \in \Upsilon} \frac{W_{j_{l+1}, j_l}}{deg(l)} \tag{4}$$

Substituting for the path energy, we have that

$$P_\Upsilon = \frac{\exp\left[-\rho \sum_{l \in \Upsilon} \left(\int_\gamma | \gamma' - \mathcal{K}(\gamma', Y)Y |^2 \, dt\right)\right]}{\prod_{l \in \Upsilon} deg(l)} = \frac{1}{Z_\Upsilon} \exp[-\mathcal{E}_\Upsilon] \tag{5}$$

where $\mathcal{E}_\Upsilon = \rho \sum_{l \in \Upsilon} \left(\int_\gamma | \gamma' - \mathcal{K}(\gamma', Y)Y |^2 \, dt\right)$ and $Z_\Upsilon = \prod_{l \in \Upsilon} deg(l)$.

Hence, the path is a Markov chain with energy function $\mathcal{E}_\Upsilon$ and partition function Z_Υ. Further, let $Q_k(i)$ be the probability of visiting the node indexed i after k-steps of the random walk and let $Q_k = [Q_k(1), Q_k(2), \ldots]^T$ be the vector whose components are the probabilities of visiting the nodes at step k. After k steps we have that $Q_k = P^k Q_0$. If $\hat{W}^k$ is the result of multiplying the symmetric positive definite matrix $\hat{W}$ by itself k times, then $P^k = D^{-\frac{1}{2}}\hat{W}^k D^{\frac{1}{2}}$.

To develop a spectral method for locating the steady state random walk, we turn to the spectral decomposition of the normalised affinity matrix $\hat{W}$ $\hat{W} = D^{-\frac{1}{2}}WD^{-\frac{1}{2}} = \sum_{i=1}^{|V|} \lambda_i \phi_i \phi_i^T$, where the λ_i are the eigenvalues of $\hat{W}$ and the ϕ_i are the corresponding eigenvectors. By constructing the matrix $\Phi = (\phi_1|\phi_2|\ldots|\phi_{|V|})$ with the eigenvectors of $\hat{W}$ as columns and the matrix $\Lambda = diag(\lambda_1, \lambda_2, \ldots, \lambda_{|V|})$ with the eigenvalues as diagonal elements, we can write the spectral decomposition in the more compact form $\hat{W} = \Phi\Lambda\Phi^T$. Since, the eigenvectors of $\hat{W}$ are orthonormal, i.e. $\Phi\Phi^T = I$, we have that $\hat{W}^k = \Phi\Lambda^k\Phi^T$.

Recall that the leading eigenvalue of $\hat{W}$ is unity. Furthermore, from spectral graph theory [8], provided that the graph G is not a bipartite graph, then the smallest eigenvalue $\lambda_{|V|} > -1$. As a result, when the Markov chain approaches its steady state, i.e. $k \to \infty$, then all but the first term in the above series become negligible. Hence, the steady state random walk is given by $Q_s = \lim_{k \to \infty} Q_k = D^{\frac{1}{2}}\phi_* \phi_*^T D^{-\frac{1}{2}}Q_0$. This establishes that the leading eigenvector of the normalised affinity matrix $\hat{W}$ determines the steady state of the random walk. It is also important to note that the equilibrium equation for the Markov process is $Q_s = PQ_s$, where Q_s is the vector of steady-state site visitation probabilities. Hence, since the leading eigenvalue of P is unity, then it follows that Q_s is the leading eigenvector of P. For a more complete proof of this result see the book by Varga [13] or the review of Lovasz [7].

We aim to visit the points in the manifold in the order of their steady-state state probabilities. Suppose that the initial state vector for the sites is uniform, i.e. $Q_0 = (\frac{1}{|V|}, \ldots, \frac{1}{|V|})^T$. As a result, the steady-state probability of visiting the node indexed i is

$$Q_s(i) = \frac{1}{|V|} \sum_{j=1}^{|V|} \sqrt{\frac{deg(j)}{deg(i)}} \phi_*(i)\phi_*(j) = \frac{1}{|V|} \frac{\phi_*(i)}{\sqrt{deg(i)}} \sum_{j=1}^{|V|} \sqrt{deg(j)}\phi_*(j) \qquad (6)$$

Since the summation appearing above is the same for all the vertices in the graph, the probability rank order is determined by the quantity $\psi_*(i) = \frac{\phi_*(i)}{\sqrt{deg(i)}}$.

We can make the relationship to the energy of the path more explicit by expanding the expressions above and substituting the energy functional for every element of the matrix W. Further, if the mass of the particle is small, we can make use of the Maclaurin expansion for the exponential weighting function and write $\hat{W}(i,j) \simeq \frac{1}{\sqrt{deg(i)deg(j)}}(1 - \rho[\int_\gamma |\gamma' - \mathcal{K}(\gamma',Y)Y|^2 \, dt])$. Hence, the path can be shown to be the one that satisfies the condition

$$\phi_* = \arg\min_\Phi \sum_{i=1}^{|V|} \sum_{j=1}^{|V|} \left(\frac{\phi(i)\phi(j)}{\sqrt{deg(i)deg(j)}} \int_\gamma |\gamma' - \mathcal{K}(\gamma',Y)Y|^2 \, dt \right) \qquad (7)$$

As a result, the integration path will minimise both, the sectional curvature along the geodesic and the length of the geodesic itself.

Our aim is to use the probability rank order to recover the spanning tree for which the cost of traversing its branches is minimum. If we visit the nodes in the order defined by the magnitudes of the coefficients of the leading eigenvector of the normalised affinity matrix, then the path is the steady state of the Markov chain. Unfortunately, the path followed by the steady state random walk is not edge-connected. Hence, we need a means of placing the nodes in an order in which neighbourhood connectivity constraints are preserved using the elements of the scaled leading eigenvector ψ_*.

3   Recovering the Spanning Tree

The idea underpinning our spanning tree recovery algorithm is to use the rank-order provided by the components of the leading eigenvector to locate those graph-edges that correspond to branches of the spanning tree. We pose this as a brushfire search which is driven from the rank order of the nodes in the data. In a nutshell, the idea is to traverse the rank-ordered list of graph nodes, commencing with the node of largest coefficient and terminating with the node of

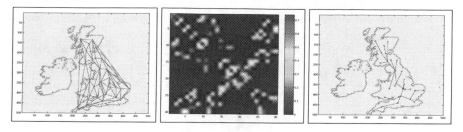

Fig. 1. From left-to-right: Delaunay triangulation corresponding to 30 cities in the UK; Corresponding matrix W; Approximation to the minimum spanning tree delivered by our algorithm.

smallest coefficient. To do this, we use the rank-order of the nodes in the graph, which is given by the list of sorted node-indices $O_D = (j_1, j_2, j_3, ..., j_{|V_D|})$ where $\psi_*(1) > \psi_*(2) > \psi_*(3) > ... > \psi_*(|V|)$. The subscript i of the node-index $j_i \in V$ is hence the rank-order of the coefficient $\psi_*(i)$.

We commence by placing the first ranked node as the root of the spanning tree, which we label j_1. We proceed with our brush-fire search by considering the list of first-neighbours $\mathcal{N}_{j_1}$ for the root node j_1. The candidates which may be assigned to the node j_1 must satisfy the edge-connectivity constraints provided by the graph-edges. These candidates are the first-neighbours of the root j_1. We rank the nodes in the list $\mathcal{N}_{j_1}$ according to the coefficients of the vector ϕ_* and propagate this procedure by visiting each node in the graph in the order specified by the ranked-list O_D. This is an iterative process which spreads like a brush-fire from the root node j_1.

To keep track of the nodes visited we maintain a list L of the nodes that have already been assigned to a branch of the tree. Suppose that we have reached the nth ranked node which is not in the list L, i.e. $j_n \notin L$, such that $L \cap \mathcal{N}_{j_n} \neq \emptyset$. The algorithm proceeds as follows. We find the set of first-neighbours of the node j_n which are in the list L. We would like to preserve edge-connectivity constraints while assigning the node ranked n as a leaf of the node $j_i \in L$ on the basis of the rank-order of the coefficients of the scaled leading eigenvector ψ_*. Hence, we assign the node j_n as a leaf of the node j_i so as to satisfy the condition $j_i = \{j_l \mid \psi_*(l) = \max_{j_l \in \{\mathcal{N}_{j_n} \cap L\}} \{\psi_*(l)\}\}$. This process is repeated until all of the nodes in the graph have been assigned to a branch of the spanning tree, i.e. $L = V$.

4 Experiments

In this section, we illustrate the utility of our method for purposes of network optimisation. Our experimental vehicle is a distribution network in the United Kingdom (UK). For this purpose, we have used a set of 30 points drawn from city locations in the UK. We do this by making use of the postcodes for 30 cities to locate points, by longitude and latitude, on a map of the UK. Our graph is then given by the Delaunay triangulation of these points.

To compute the edge-weights, we have done the following. Since the earth can be considered to be a sphere, we have set the sectional curvature to the constant κ, i.e. $\mathcal{K}(\gamma', Y) \equiv \kappa$. It can be shown that, for the special case of constant, positive sectional curvature, Jacobi's equation becomes $\nabla_t^2 Y = -\kappa Y$ and its solution, given $Y(0) = 0$ and $| \nabla_t Y(0) |= 1$, is $Y(t) = \frac{\sin(\sqrt{\kappa}t)}{\sqrt{\kappa}}\eta$, where the vector η is in the tangent space of M at p_i and is orthogonal to γ' at the point indexed i, i.e. $\eta \in M_{p_i}$ and $\langle \eta, \gamma' |_{p_i} \rangle = 0$.

With these ingredients, and by rescaling the parameter t so that $| \gamma' |= \tau$, we can express the cost of the step between nodes indexed i and j as follows

$$\mathcal{E}_{p_i, p_j} = \int_0^a \left((\tau)^2 + \kappa \left(\sin(\sqrt{\kappa}t) \right)^2 \right) dt \tag{8}$$

In our experiments, we have set κ to unity and rescaled τ so as to take into account the circumference of the earth and satisfy the condition $| \gamma' |= \tau$. As a result, the value of a is given by the arc length of the geodesic between the points p_i and p_j.

In Figure 1, we show the results obtained by our algorithm. In the left-hand panel, we show the Delaunay graph for the 30 cities used in our experiments. The middle panel shows the edge-weight matrix, i.e. the matrix W for the Delaunay graph in the left-hand panel. Finally, the right-hand panel shows the spanning tree recovered by our algorithm. Here, we have indicated the root of the tree with a circle, while the rest of the points have been plotted using asterisks.

5   Conclusions

In this paper, we have described how geometric invariants and random walks can be used to pose the recovery of the minimum spanning tree in an energy minimisation setting. The work described here can be further extended and improved in a number of different ways. Firstly, there is clearly scope for developing a more sophisticated method for the brushfire search process. It may also be interesting to investigate whether the ideas presented here can be applied to 2D curve enhancement problems.

References

1. J. B. Kruskal. On the shortest spanning subtree of a graph and the travelling salesman problem. *Prof. of the American Mathematical Society*, 7:48–50, 1956.
2. R. C. Prim. Shortest connection networks and some generalizations. *Bell System Technical Journal*, 36:1389–1401, 1957.
3. J. Shi and J. Malik. Normalized cuts and image segmentation. *IEEE Transactions on Pattern Analysis and Machine Intelligence*, 22(8):888–905, 2000.
4. S. Sarkar and K. L. Boyer. Quantitative measures of change based on feature organization: Eigenvalues and eigenvectors. *Computer Vision and Image Understanding*, 71(1):110–136, 1998.

5. P. Perona and W. T. Freeman. Factorization approach to grouping. In *Proc. ECCV*, pages 655–670, 1998.
6. N. L. Biggs. *Algebraic Graph Theory*. Cambridge University Press, 1993.
7. L. Lovász. Random walks on graphs: a survey. *Bolyai Society Mathematical Studies*, 2(2):1–46, 1993.
8. Fan R. K. Chung. *Spectral Graph Theory*. American Mathematical Society, 1997.
9. D. Cvetković, M. Doob, and H. Sachs. *Spectra of Graphs:Theory and Application*. Academic Press, 1980.
10. Y. Azar, A. Fiat, A. R. Karlin, F. McSherry, and J. Saia. Spectral analysis of data. In *ACM Symposium on Theory of Computing*, pages 619–626, 2000.
11. J. Kleinberg. Authoritative sources in a hyperlinked environment. In *Proc. ACM-SIAM symposium on discrete algorithms*, pages 668–677, 1998.
12. I. Chavel. *Riemannian Geometry: A Modern Introduction*. Cambridge University Press, 1995.
13. R. S. Varga. *Matrix Iterative Analysis*. Springer, second edition, 2000.

Discriminant Projections Embedding for Nearest Neighbor Classification

Petia Radeva and Jordi Vitrià

Computer Vision Centre and Dept. Informàtica
Universitat Autònoma de Barcelona
08193 Bellaterra (Barcelona), Spain
{petia,jordi}@cvc.uab.es

Abstract. In this paper we introduce a new embedding technique to linearly project labeled data samples into a new space where the performance of a Nearest Neighbor classifier is improved. The approach is based on considering a large set of simple discriminant projections and finding the subset with higher classification performance. In order to implement the feature selection process we propose the use of the adaboost algorithm. The performance of this technique is tested in a multiclass classification problem related to the production of cork stoppers for wine bottles.

1 Introduction

One of the most common steps when designing a classifier system is to transform the original data representation to a new representation that is built by combining the original data features. This is called the feature extraction process. We can use different criteria to build this process. One of such criteria is the level of compactness that we get with the new input data representation, that leads to different dimensionality reduction techniques. In our case we focus in a different kind of criterium: discriminability. In this case the feature extraction process takes into account class membership of the input data to learn invariant data features that increase the classification ratios of the system.

Our objective is to find an embedding from the original data representation space to a new one that is specially designed to increase the performance of the nearest neighbor classification rule. We have not made assumptions on the data distribution, and we don't force our projection to be orthogonal [2]. The only assumption we impose is that our embedding must be based on a set of simple 1D projections, which can complement each other to achieve better classification results. We have made use of Adaboost algorithm [9] as a natural way to select feature extractors, and the coefficients that can rank the importance of each projection.

1.1 Discriminant Analysis

Discriminant analysis is a feature extraction tool based on a criterion J and two square matrices S_b and S_w. These matrices generally represent the scatter of

A. Sanfeliu et al. (Eds.): CIARP 2004, LNCS 3287, pp. 312–319, 2004.

sample vectors between different classes for S_b, and within a class for S_w. The most frequently used criterion is to choose $J = trace(S_w^{-1}S_b)$.

It can be seen that, maximization of J is equivalent to finding the $D \times M$ linear transformation W such that

$$\hat{W} = \arg \max_{W^T S_w W = I} trace(W^T S_b W) \qquad (1)$$

where I is the identity matrix. It can be proven that, given N samples of D dimensional data X and discriminant space dimensionality M, there is general method to solve the optimization problem given in equation (1) [5].

1.2   Fisher Discriminant Analysis

The most widely spread approach for discriminant analysis is the one that makes use of only up to second order statistics of the data. This was done in a classic paper by Fisher [1], and it is called Fisher Discriminant Analysis (FDA). In FDA the within class scatter matrix is usually computed as a weighted sum of the class-conditional sample covariance matrices where the weights are given by the class prior probabilities,

$$S_w = \sum_{k=1}^{K} P(C^k) \Sigma^k \qquad (2)$$

where Σ^k is the class-conditional covariance matrix, estimated from the sample set. On the other side, the most common way of defining the between class-scatter matrix is as,

$$S_b = \sum_{k=1}^{K} P(C^k)(\mu^k - \mu^0)(\mu^k - \mu^0)^T \qquad (3)$$

where μ^k is the class-conditional sample mean and μ^0 is the unconditional (global) sample mean. Many other less spread out forms, always based on sample means and class-conditional covariance matrices are also available for these two scatter matrices [5]. The two main drawbacks of FLD are: Gaussian assumption over the class distribution of the data samples; and the dimensionality of the subspaces obtained is limited by the number of classes.

1.3   Nonparametric Discriminant Analysis

In [3] Fukunaga and Mantock present a linear and nonparametric method for discriminant analysis in an attempt to overcome the limitations present in (FDA) [1], and name the technique Nonparametric Discriminant Analysis (NDA).

In NDA we define a between-class matrix as the scatter matrix obtained from vectors locally pointing to another class. This is done as follows: Given a norm $\|\|$ in the metric space where the samples are defined, the extraclass nearest neighbor for a sample $x \in C^k$ is defined as

$$x^E = \{x' \in \overline{C^k} / \|x' - x\| \le \|z - x\|, \forall z \in \overline{C^k}\} \qquad (4)$$

where $\overline{C^k}$ notes the complement set of C^k. In the same fashion we can define the intraclass nearest neighbor as

$$x^I = \{x' \in C^k / \|x' - x\| \le \|z - x\|, \forall z \in C^k\} \tag{5}$$

Both definitions (4) and (5) can be extended to the K nearest neighbors case by defining x^E and x^I as the mean of the K nearest extra or intra-class samples. From these neighbors or neighbor averages, the extraclass differences are defined as $\mathbf{\Delta}^E = x - x^E$ and the intraclass differences as $\mathbf{\Delta}^I = x - x^I$. Notice that $\mathbf{\Delta}^E$ points locally to the nearest class (or classes) that does not contain the sample. The nonparametric between-class scatter matrix is then defined as

$$S_b = \frac{1}{N} \sum_{n=1}^{N} w_n (\mathbf{\Delta}_n^E)(\mathbf{\Delta}_n^E)^T \tag{6}$$

where $\mathbf{\Delta}_n^E$ is the extraclass distance for sample x_n, w_n a sample weight defined as

$$w_n = \frac{\min\{\|\mathbf{\Delta}^E\|^\alpha, \|\mathbf{\Delta}^I\|^\alpha\}}{\|\mathbf{\Delta}^E\|^\alpha + \|\mathbf{\Delta}^I\|^\alpha} \tag{7}$$

and α is a control parameter between zero and infinity. The within-class scatter matrix is defined in the same way as FDA (eq.2).

Figure (1) shows the FDA and NDA solutions for two artificial datasets. For this example a single nearest neighbor was used in the computation of the between-class scatter matrix and uniform sample weights were considered. Particularly interesting is the case illustrated in fig. (1.b). Though both within-class scatter matrices are equal, the bimodality of one of the classes displaces the estimate of the class mean used in the computation of the parametric between-class scatter matrix. This is the main source of error for FDA.

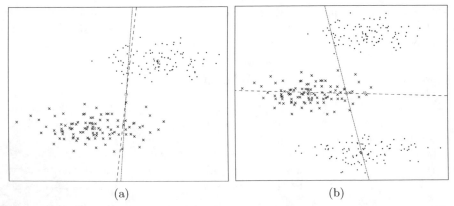

(a)   (b)

Fig. 1. First direction of nonparametric discriminant projection space on two artificial datasets. Dashed line: FDA direction. Solid line: NDA direction.

NDA and Nearest Neighbors. Making use of the introduced notation we can examine the relationship between NN and NDA. Given a training sample x, the accuracy of the 1-NN rule can be directly computed by examining the ratio $\|\Delta^E\|/\|\Delta^I\|$. If this ratio is more than one, x will be correctly classified.

Given a $M \times D$ linear transform W, the projected distances are defined as $\Delta_W^{E,I} = Wx - Wx^{E,I}$ Notice that this definition does not exactly agree with the extra and intraclass distances in projection space since, except for the orthonormal transformation case, we have no warranty on distance preservation. Equivalence of both definitions is asymptotically true on the number of samples. By the above remarks it is expected, that optimization of the following objective function should improve or, at least not downgrade NN performance,

$$\hat{W} = \arg\max_{W} \frac{E\{\|\Delta_W^E\|^2\}}{E\{\|\Delta_W^I\|^2\}} \tag{8}$$

Considering that [5], we have that

$$E\{\|\Delta_W^{E,I}\|^2\} = trace(W^T S_{b,w} W) \tag{9}$$

where, in this case, S_b (the between-class scatter matrix) agrees with (6), but the within-class scatter matrix is now defined in a nonparametric fashion [6],

$$S_w = \frac{1}{N} \sum_{n=1}^{N} \Delta_n^I \Delta_n^{I^T} \tag{10}$$

The same methodlogy that can be used to solve (1) can also be applied to the optimization of this objective function (8). This method has showed a good performance for standard data sets as well as for practical applications [6], but presents some problems when intraclass (or extraclass) diferences are not normally distributed around a direction.

2   A New Embedding Technique

In this section we propose the construction of a global discriminant embedding using discriminant projections that can be seen as the combination of multiple NDA projections. We are interested in a combination of one-dimensional projections that can yield a strong nearest neighbor classifier.

The main idea can be stated as follows: if we push the NDA approach to its limits, we can consider that every point x^j in the sample has associated *its most discriminant 1D-projection* W^j, that is, the 1D projection that simultaneously minimizes the norm of the vectors that point to the nearest neighbor of its class and to the nearest neighbor of the other class[1]. Thus, given a learning problem,

---

[1] Observe that this concept can be easily defined to a m-class setting by considering the $m-1$ nearest neighbors in its class and the nearest neighbor in each one of the other classes.

we can get as much 1-D NDA projections as examples we have in the learning set. Our hypothesis is that a careful selection of a subset of these 1D-projections can define an embedding (where each new dimension is defined by a 1D projection) of the original data that outperforms the other discriminant methods when using the nearest neighbour classifier.

Our scheme takes benefit of a very known algorithm in machine learning, Adaboost ([8]), for selecting the best 1D NDA projections. The use of boosting in our scheme is specially justified, because our 1D projections perform always as weak classifiers (In fact, see figure 3, these classifiers have a similar performace to the nearest neighbor classifier in the original space), and we can exploit the sample weight actualization intrinsic in the boosting scheme to focus the selection of the next feature axis to the examples that are more difficult to classify.

Let x^k be a data point, x^i its nearest neighbor of the same class and x^e its nearest neighbor of the other class $(x^k, x^i, x^e \in X)$. We will define the vectors u and v which point to x^i and x^e from x^k. We need to find a linear projection $f(x) : X \to R$ that minimizes the distance between the point $f(x^k)$ to the points of its same class, and maximizes the distance to the points of the other class. In the case we are dealing with the projection matrix will be a simple vector that can be computed using simple vector operations.

2.1   AdaBoost

We have followed a boosting implementation similar to the one proposed by Viola et al. [7]. Given a training set of n points $x^{1 \cdots n}$ belonging to k different classes ($\frac{n}{k}$ points for each class), the algorithm performs as follows:

1. First we define a set of weights $W^{1 \cdots n}$ (each weight assigned to one vector). The weights are initialized to $\frac{1}{n}$. We also build the set of partial classifiers as 1D projections as defined above, so each sample x^i generates a projection to a 1D dimensional space.
2. Then a fixed number of boosting steps are generated. At each boosting step s:
   - The whole set of classifiers is tested using the training points $W^{1 \cdots n}$. We project each data point in the 1D space generated by each feature extraction and classify it according to it's nearest neighbor. For each different projection, we evaluate its classification error as:

$$Error_j = \sum_{i=1}^{n} W_{s,i} \cdot l_{i,j} \tag{11}$$

   where $l_{i,j}$ is set to 0 if the point x_i has been correctly classified by the classifier j and to 1 otherwise. Finally we select the classifier c with minimum $Error_{1..n}$
   - Using the classification results of the classifier c, the set of weights W is actualized as:

$$W^{s+1,i} = W^{s,i} \cdot \beta^{1-l_{i,c}} \tag{12}$$

where

$$\beta = \frac{Error_c}{1 - Error_c} \tag{13}$$

– The coefficient α_s corresponding to the classifier at the step s is computed as:

$$\alpha = log\frac{1}{\beta} \tag{14}$$

– Finally the weights are normalized, $\boldsymbol{W}^{s+1,i} = \frac{\boldsymbol{W}^{s,i}}{\sum_j^n \boldsymbol{W}^{s,j}}$.

3. The output of the algorithm is a projection matrix, where we place at each column i_s the 1-D projection corresponding to the best classifier at the step s of the Adaboost algorithm. In addition the $\alpha_{1,...,s}$ coefficients can be used to rank the importance of the features extracted for each 1-D projection.

3   Application and Results

Cork inspection is the least automated task in the production cycle of the cork stopper. Due to the inspection difficulty of the natural cork material and the high production rates even the most experienced quality inspection operators frequently make mistakes. In addition, human inspection leads to a lack of objectivity and uniform rules applied by different people at different time. As a result, there is a urgent need to modernize the cork industry in this direction. In this paper, we consider a real industrial computer vision application of classification of natural (cork) products.

During its production, cork stoppers must be classified in five different classes that correspond to different quality groups (see fig. 2). When human operators perform this classification on-line, they rely on a set of visual characteristics that are far from being objective and that present a large variation among different operators. In order to develop an automatic system, a large set of carefully classified stoppers have been selected (more than one thousand examples per class). Next, we have got an image from every stopper that represents its surface, and this image has been segmented using a fixed threshold. Cork stopper classification will be based on a set of visual features that are related to the blobs resulting from this segmentation.

We have extracted from the image of each stopper a set of global as well local features [10]. Global features are: the total number of blobs, the total area of blobs, the mean of grey-level appearance of blobs, the average blob area, the average blob elongation, the average blob compactness, and the average blob roughness. Local stopper features refer to the first and second largest blobs of the cor stopper and particularly: area, length, width, perimeter, convex perimeter, compactness, roughness, elongation, average blob grey-level, and position with respect to the centre of the stopper. Following this strategy we defined a set of 43 features for every cork stopper.

Next, we have used this learning set for constructing a discriminant embedding as described in the last section. Figure (3) shows the result of the learning

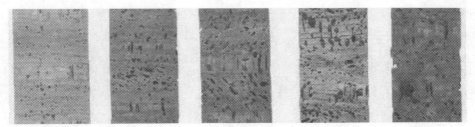

Fig. 2. Surfaces of cork stoppers of 5 quality groups ordered from best to worst quality (from left to right).

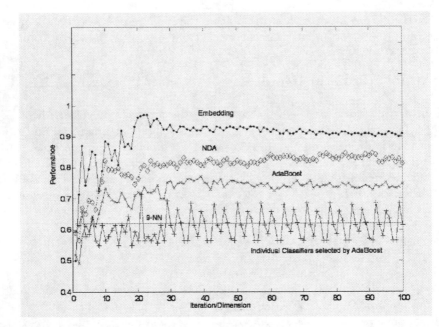

Fig. 3. Results: the horizontal line (solid line) represents the performance of a 9-nearest neighbor classifier in the original space, the + line represents the performace of every individual 1D classifier that is computed at every step of the algorithm, the x line corresponds to classifier that would be produced by the Adaboost combination, the ◇ line represents the NDA performance for different dimensionalities, and finally, the ● line represents the performance of the nearest neighbor classifier in the embedding space.

method. Results have been computed with a 10-fold cross-validation, using a data set of 1000 samples per class. As can been seen, classifiying a stopper using the nearest neighbor in the embedded space shows the best performance when compared to the other methods: nearest neighbor in the original space, NDA of different dimensions, Adaboost classifier stopped at different iteration steps, and the set of 1D classifiers that are computed at every step of the Adaboost algorithm.The embedding approach converges, with respect to dimension, to a

90 per cent of correct classification, while all the other methods are all under or around 80 per cent.

4 Conclusions

We have presented a new method for learning a linear embedding for labeled data that is specially designed to be used with the nearest neighbor classifier. Every embedding dimension is defined by a linear projection that corresponds to the optimal projection of a given point. This projection is selected in a sound way by using the Adaboost algorithm. We have shown the performance of this method in a real industrial application: the quality classification of cork stoppers.

Acknowledgments

This work is supported by MCYT grant TIC2003-00654, Ministerio de Ciencia y Tecnologia, Spain.

References

1. R. Fisher: On subharmonic solutions of a Hamiltonian system. The use of multiple measurements in taxonomic problems, Ann. Eugenics 7 (1936) 179–188.
2. M. Aladjem: Linear discriminant analysis for two classes via removal of classification structure, IEEE Trans. Pattern Anal. Machine Intell. 19 (2) (1997) 187–192.
3. K. Fukunaga, J. Mantock: Nonparametric discriminant analysis, IEEE Trans. Pattern Anal. Machine Intell. 5 (6) (1983) 671–678. 11
4. P. Devijver, J. Kittler: Pattern Recognition: A Statistical Approach, Prentice Hall, London, UK, 1982.
5. K. Fukunaga: Introduction to Statistical Pattern Recognition, 2nd Edition, Academic Press, Boston, MA, 1990.
6. M. Bressan, J. Vitria: Nonparametric discriminant analysis and nearest neighbor classification, Pattern Recognition Letters 24 (15) (2003) 2743–2749.
7. P. Viola, M. Jones: Rapid object detection using a boosted cascade of simple features, in: IEEE Conference on CVPR, Kauai, Hawaii, 2001, pp. 511–518.
8. Y. Freund, R. E. Schapire: Experiments with a new boosting algorithm, in: International Conference on Machine Learning, 1996, pp. 148–156.
9. R. E. Schapire: A brief introduction to boosting, in: IJCAI, 1999, pp. 1401–1406.
10. P. Radeva, M. Bressan, A. Tobar, J. Vitrià: Bayesian Classification for Inspection of Industrial Products, in M.T. Escrig Monferrer, F. Toledo, E. Golobardes (Eds.), Topics in Artificial Intelligence, Sringer Verlag Series: Lecture Notes in Computer Science. Volume. 2504, 2002, pp. 399–407.

Regularization Kernels and Softassign

Miguel Angel Lozano and Francisco Escolano

Robot Vision Group,
Departamento de Ciencia de la Computación e Inteligencia Artificial,
Universidad de Alicante, Spain
{malozano,sco}@dccia.ua.es
http://rvg.ua.es

Abstract. In this paper we analyze the use of regularization kernels on graphs to weight the quadratic cost function used in the Softassign graph-matching algorithm. In a previous work, we have showed that when using diffusion kernels on graphs such a weighting improves significantly the matching performance yielding a slow decay with increasing noise. Weights, relying on the entropies of the probability distributions associated to the vertices after diffusion kernel computation, transform the original unweighted matching problem into a weighted one. In this regard, as diffusion kernels are a particular case of regularization kernels it is interesting to study the utility of this family of kernels for matching purposes. We have designed an experimental set for discovering the optimal performance for each regularization kernel. Our results suggest that kernel combination could be a key point to address in the future.

1 Introduction

The Softassign algorithm [4] is a typical energy minimization approach for graph matching that relies on transforming the discrete search space into a continuous one and then optimizing a quadratic cost function through a polynomial computational complexity process in order to find a, typically approximate, solution. It has been reported [5] that the use of an alternative non-quadratic energy function complemented by a continuous editing process yields a slow decay of matching performance with increasing graph corruption (noise). However, in a recent paper [7] we report a similar decay with a simpler strategy consisting on computing structural attributes for the vertices of the original unweighted graph and then use these attributes to weight the quadratic function. Such good results are due to the fact that these attributes encode the structural similarities between each vertex and the rest of vertices of the graph, and such information is key to choose the proper attractor in contexts of high matching ambiguities where the classical Softassign fails, specially at higher levels of distortion.

Kernels on graphs provide a natural way of computing similarities between the vertices of the same graph. In the case of the diffusion kernel, the one we used in our initial experiments, Kondor and Lafferty [6] (see also [3] for a survey on kernels for structures like strings, trees and graphs) transferred to the domain

A. Sanfeliu et al. (Eds.): CIARP 2004, LNCS 3287, pp. 320–327, 2004.

of graphs the well-known concept of *kernel* defined for the domain of vectors [2][10][8]. Diffusion kernels on graphs are positive semi-definite matrices (it is necessary to be a kernel or Gram matrix) having as many rows and columns as the number of vertices in the graph (like the adjacency matrix) where the value of each entry defines the similarity between two vertices and such a similarity decays exponentially with the *distance* between the vertices that we are comparing. The similarity can be interpreted as the probability of reaching one vertex from another by following a *lazy* random walk (a random walk with a given probability of remaining at each visited vertex). Given such a probabilistic interpretation, we retain as attribute for a given vertex the entropy of the probability distribution arising from considering the probability of reaching the rest of the nodes and the probability of resting. This approach is closely related to the use of distance matrices in matching and tests for isomorphism [9], and, more recently, to the use of powers of the adjacency matrix [13].

Although understanding the role of the diffusion kernel in graphs is intuitive because these kernels are the discrete version of continuous Gaussian kernels, this is not the case for the regularization kernels recently proposed by Smola and Kondor [12]. These latter kernels are derived from studying the usefulness of the Laplacian of a graph (and its normalized version) as a smoothing operator (section 2). Considering smoothing operators from a spectral point of view, it results that a family of kernels emerges from considering different penalization functions. It can be proved that the inverse of the so called *regularization matrix* for each element of the family yields a kernel (actually, the diffusion kernel belongs to this family). In (section 3) we review the weighted energy function and its minimization through the Softassign continuation process. In order to build the attributes of the vertices we consider that the similarities defined by each kernel induce a probability distribution and, in order to characterize such a distribution, we use its entropy. In (section 4) we evaluate the matching performance of each kernel in different conditions of noise and edge connectivity.

2   Regularization Kernels on Graphs

Given a undirected and unweighted graph $G = (V, E)$ with vertex-set V of size m, and edge-set $E = \{(i, j) | (i, j) \in V \times V, i \neq j\}$, its adjacency matrix and degree matrix are respectively defined as

$$A_{ij} = \begin{cases} 1 & \text{if } (i,j) \in E \\ 0 & \text{otherwise} \end{cases} \quad \text{and} \quad D_{ij} = \begin{cases} \sum_{j=1}^{m} A_{ij} & \text{if } i = j \\ 0 & \text{otherwise}. \end{cases}$$

Then, the Laplacian of G, $L = D - A$, and its degree-normalized version, $\tilde{L} = D^{-\frac{1}{2}} L D^{-\frac{1}{2}} = I - D^{-\frac{1}{2}} A D^{-\frac{1}{2}}$ or Normalized Laplacian [1], are defined as

$$L_{ij} = \begin{cases} -1 & \text{if } (i,j) \in E \\ D_{ii} & \text{if } i = j \\ 0 & \text{otherwise} \end{cases} \quad \text{and} \quad \tilde{L}_{ij} = \begin{cases} -D_{ii}^{-\frac{1}{2}} D_{jj}^{-\frac{1}{2}} & \text{if } (i,j) \in E \\ 1 & \text{if } i = j \text{ and } D_{ii} \neq 0 \\ 0 & \text{otherwise}. \end{cases}$$

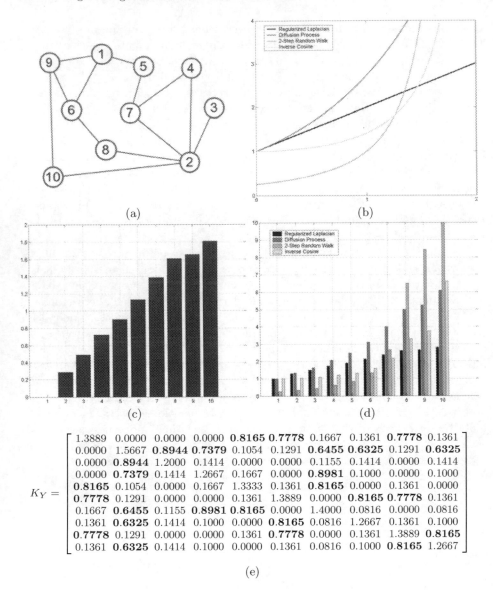

$$
K_Y =
\begin{bmatrix}
1.3889 & 0.0000 & 0.0000 & 0.0000 & \mathbf{0.8165} & \mathbf{0.7778} & 0.1667 & 0.1361 & \mathbf{0.7778} & 0.1361 \\
0.0000 & 1.5667 & \mathbf{0.8944} & \mathbf{0.7379} & 0.1054 & 0.1291 & \mathbf{0.6455} & \mathbf{0.6325} & 0.1291 & \mathbf{0.6325} \\
0.0000 & \mathbf{0.8944} & 1.2000 & 0.1414 & 0.0000 & 0.0000 & 0.1155 & 0.1414 & 0.0000 & 0.1414 \\
0.0000 & \mathbf{0.7379} & 0.1414 & 1.2667 & 0.1667 & 0.0000 & \mathbf{0.8981} & 0.1000 & 0.0000 & 0.1000 \\
\mathbf{0.8165} & 0.1054 & 0.0000 & 0.1667 & 1.3333 & 0.1361 & \mathbf{0.8165} & 0.0000 & 0.1361 & 0.0000 \\
\mathbf{0.7778} & 0.1291 & 0.0000 & 0.0000 & 0.1361 & 1.3889 & 0.0000 & \mathbf{0.8165} & \mathbf{0.7778} & 0.1361 \\
0.1667 & \mathbf{0.6455} & 0.1155 & \mathbf{0.8981} & \mathbf{0.8165} & 0.0000 & 1.4000 & 0.0816 & 0.0000 & 0.0816 \\
0.1361 & \mathbf{0.6325} & 0.1414 & 0.1000 & 0.0000 & \mathbf{0.8165} & 0.0816 & 1.2667 & 0.1361 & 0.1000 \\
\mathbf{0.7778} & 0.1291 & 0.0000 & 0.0000 & 0.1361 & \mathbf{0.7778} & 0.0000 & 0.1361 & 1.3889 & \mathbf{0.8165} \\
0.1361 & \mathbf{0.6325} & 0.1414 & 0.1000 & 0.0000 & 0.1361 & 0.0816 & 0.1000 & \mathbf{0.8165} & 1.2667
\end{bmatrix}
$$

(e)

Fig. 1. Illustrating regularization kernel computation. (a) Graph with $m = 10$ nodes. (b) Penalizing functions corresponding to Table 1. (c) Eigenvalues of the Normalized Laplacian sorted in ascending order and contained in $[0, 2]$. (d) Result of applying the penalizing functions on the graph spectrum. (e) Resulting *p-step kernel* with $a = 2$ and $p = 2$.

The connection of the latter Laplacian matrices with regularization theory stands from the fact that given a real-valued function f defined over the vertices of G, that is, $f : V \to \mathbb{R}$ both, L and $\tilde{L}$ can be seen as discrete differential operators which tend to penalize changes of f between adjacent edges. Considering now f a column vector, that is $f \in \mathbb{R}^m$, the following inner product is a measure of the smoothness of f over the graph G:

$$\langle f, Lf \rangle = f^T L f = \sum_{i=1}^{m} f_i^2 D_{ii} - \sum_{(i,j) \in E} 2 f_i f_j = \sum_{(i,j) \in E} (f_i - f_j)^2 \ ,$$

and the result is called the Dirichlet sum of G. Furthermore, given $g = D^{\frac{1}{2}} f$ the Dirichlet sums associated to L and $\tilde{L}$ are related by:

$$\langle f, Lf \rangle = (D^{-\frac{1}{2}}g)^T L (D^{-\frac{1}{2}}g) = g^T \underbrace{D^{-\frac{1}{2}} L D^{-\frac{1}{2}}}_{\tilde{L}} g = \left\langle g, D^{-\frac{1}{2}} L D^{-\frac{1}{2}} g \right\rangle = \left\langle g, \tilde{L} g \right\rangle$$

An alternative way of formulating regularization is through spectral analysis. In [11], Smola et al stablished the connection between regularization, Fourier analysis and kernels in continuous spaces. A smoothness operator in Fourier space can be built by multiplying the Fourier transform by a penalizing function increasing in frequency. As such a multiplication in Fourier space becomes the application of the latter function on the continuous Laplacian operator, an spectral-based regularization operator in graphs comes from

$$\langle f, r(\mathcal{L})f \rangle = f^T \underbrace{\left[\sum_{i=1}^{m} r(\lambda_i) \phi_i \phi_i^T \right]}_{r(\mathcal{L})} f = \sum_{i=1}^{m} \langle f, \phi_i \rangle \, r(\lambda_i) \, \langle \phi_i, f \rangle \ ,$$

where $\mathcal{L}$ denotes both L and $\tilde{L}$, $\{\lambda_i, \phi_i\}$ are the eigenvalues and eigenvectors of $\mathcal{L}$, and $r(\lambda_i)$ is a monotone increasing function. Actually, $r^{-1}(\lambda)$, the inverse of such a function is the Fourier transform of the associated kernel in the continuous case, and the discrete regularization kernel K is the inverse (or the pseudo-inverse if necessary) of the so called *regularization matrix* $r(\mathcal{L})$. Then we have that

$$K = r^{-1}(\mathcal{L}) \quad \text{where} \quad r^{-1}(\mathcal{L}) = \sum_{i=1}^{m} r^{-1}(\lambda_i) \phi_i \phi_i^T \ , \tag{1}$$

and $0^{-1} = 0$. For instance, in the particular case of the diffusion kernel, which relies on *matrix exponentiation* but not on componentwise exponentiation, we have that

$$K = e^{-\beta \mathcal{L}} = (\sum_{i=1}^{m} e^{\beta \lambda} \phi_i \phi_i^T)^{-1} = \sum_{i=1}^{m} e^{-\beta \lambda} \phi_i \phi_i^T \ .$$

In the general case, the relation $K = r^{-1}(\mathcal{L})$ is derived from the fact that given a regularization operator, for instance $M = r(\mathcal{L})$, the matrix K must satisfy the *self-consistency condition* $KMK = K$ to be a kernel, and therefore $K = M^{-1}$ or equal to the pseudo-inverse if M is not invertible. Furthermore, it can be proved [12] that such regularization operator defines a reproducing kernel Hilbert space whose kernel is $K = M^{-1}$. In table 1 we show several penalization functions and their associated regularization kernels. The process of obtaining a regularization kernel is summarized in Fig. 1. As it can be seen, choosing $\tilde{L}$ yields and spectrum contained in $[0, 2]$.

3   Kernelizing Softassign

A feasible solution to the graph matching problem between G_X and G_Y, with adjacency matrices X_{ab}, and Y_{ij}, is encoded by a matrix M of size $m \times n$, being $m = |V_X|$ and $n = |V_Y|$. Following the Gold and Rangarajan formulation we are interested in finding the feasible solution M that minimizes the following cost function,

$$F(M) = -\frac{1}{2} \sum_{a=1}^{m} \sum_{i=1}^{n} \sum_{b=1}^{m} \sum_{j=1}^{n} M_{ai} M_{bj} C_{aibj} , \qquad (2)$$

where typically $C_{aibj} = X_{ab}Y_{ij}$. Furthermore, considering the entropies defined in the previous section a simple way of *kernelizing* the latter energy function is to redefine C_{aibj} as

$$C_{aibj}^K = X_{ab}Y_{ij} \exp -[(H_a^{K_X} - H_i^{K_Y})^2 + (H_b^{K_X} - H_j^{K_Y})^2] , \qquad (3)$$

where H^{K_X} and H^{K_Y} are the entropies of the probability distributions associated to the vertices of the graph and induced respectively by K_X and K_Y. Given a pair of vertices, for instance a, b of graph G_X the kernel K^X induces the following probability distribution

$$p_{ab}^X = K_{ab}^X (\sum_{c=1}^{m} K_{ac}^X)^{-1} \text{ and } H_a^{K_X} = \sum_{b=1}^{m} p_{ab}^X \log p_{ab}^X ,$$

and the same holds for p_{ij}^Y and $H_i^{K_Y}$ in case of vertices i, j of G_Y. We use entropy because building attributes in the properties of distributions yields more robustness than building them in the crude values of the kernels.

The latter definition of C_{aibj}^K ensures that $C_{aibj}^K \leq C_{aibj}$, and the equality is only verified when nodes a and i have similar entropies, and the same for nodes b and j. In practice, this weights the rectangles in such a way that rectangles with compatible entropies in their opposite vertices are preferred, and otherwise they are underweighted and do not attract the continuation process.

To see intuitively the difference between two kernels in Fig. 2 we show the results obtained both for the cosine and the p-step kernel. We show the matching strength prior to performing clean-up. Cosine kernel is very ambiguous (similar to the classical Softassign) whereas the p-step one finds the most coherent subgraph in terms of structural similarity.

Table 1. Penalization Functions and Regularization Kernels.

$r(\lambda)$	$K = r^{-1}(\mathcal{L})$	Name
$1 + \beta\lambda$	$(I + \beta\mathcal{L})^{-1}$	Regularized Laplacian
$e^{\beta\lambda}$	$e^{-\beta\mathcal{L}}$	Diffusion Process
$(a - \lambda)^{-p}$	$(aI - \mathcal{L})^p$	p−step Random Walk
$(\cos \lambda\pi/4)^{-1}$	$\cos \mathcal{L}\pi/4$	Inverse Cosine

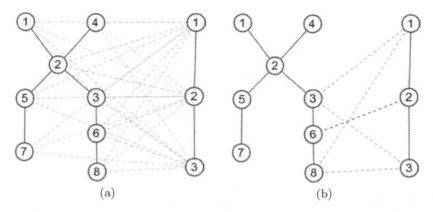

(a)   (b)

Fig. 2. Illustrating matching differences between the cosine kernel (a) and the p-step one (b).

4 Experiments

We have performed several matching experiments with graphs of 30 nodes, considering three levels of edge density (10%, 30% and 50%), and six different noise levels (0% or isomorphism, 10%, 20%, 30%, 40%, and 50%). We have also considered both the Laplacian L and the Normalized Laplacian $\tilde{L}$ for kernel computation. In all cases $\beta = 1$ unless we specify that β is normalized by the number of nodes of the graph. In all experiments we compare kernels with the classical Softassign driven by degree similarity. Furthermore, in the plots (see Fig. 3) each point corresponds to the averaged result for 100 graphs randomly generated. We have registered the fraction of complete graphs successfully matched.

Analyzing the obtained results, at low edge densities (10%) we observe that cardinality outperforms all kernels at zero noise (isomorphism). However, kernels, specially p-step with $\tilde{L}$, yield slower decays as the noise increases. P-step has a similar behavior at 30% edge density, although the diffusion kernel with L and normalized β is the best choice even at isomorphism. This latter kernel yields the slower decay for a density of 50% although p-step with $\tilde{L}$ is only acceptable for a corruption percentage greater than 30%. We conclude that p-step is a good choice for low densities, whereas the diffusion one with L and normalized β is preferable for higher densities.

5 Conclusions and Future Work

In this paper we have analyzed the use of regularization kernels in the context of graph matching, particularly in the Softassign algorithm. We have studied the performance of several kernels in different noise and edge-density conditions and we conclude that p-step is good for low densities and diffusion is good for higher densities. This is why in the future we will develop an strategy for combining them. Another question in which we are currently working is how to formulate a pure kernelized energy function and its associated matching algorithm.

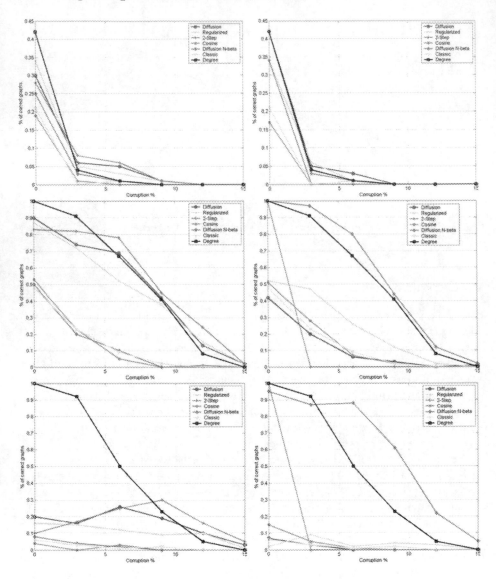

Fig. 3. Matching results. Graphs successfully matched. Left column: results with the Normalized Laplacian $\tilde{L}$. Right column: results with the classical Laplacian L. Each row corresponds to a different edge density: 10%, 30% and 50%.

Acknowledgements

This work was partially supported by grant $TIC2002 - 02792$ funded by *Ministerio de Ciencia y Tecnología* of the Spanish Government and by *FEDER*.

References

1. Chung, F.R.K.: Spectral Graph Theory. Conference Board of the Mathematical Sciences (CBMS) **92**. American Mathematical Society (1997)
2. Cristianini, N., Shawe-Taylor, J.: An Introduction to Support Vector Machines Cambridge University Press (2000)
3. Gärtner: A Survey of Kernels for Structured Data. ACM SIGKDD Explorations Newsletter **5**(1) (2003) 49–58
4. Gold, S., Rangarajan, A.: A Graduated Assignment Algorithm for Graph Matching. IEEE Transactions on Pattern Analysis and Machine Intelligence **18** (4) (1996) 377-388
5. Finch, A.M., Wilson, R.C., Hancock, E.: An Energy Function and Continuous Edit Process for Graph Matching. Neural Computation, **10** (7) (1998) 1873-1894
6. Kondor, R.I., Lafferty, J.: Diffusion Kernels on Graphs and other Discrete Input Spaces. In: Sammut, C., and Hoffmann, A. G. (eds) Machine Learning, Proceedings of the Nineteenth International Conference (ICML 2002). Morgan Kaufmann (2002) 315–322
7. Lozano, M.A., Escolano, F.: A Significant Improvement of Softassing with Diffusion Kernels. In Proceedings of the IAPR International Workshop on Syntactical and Structural Pattern Recognition SSPR 2004. Lecture Notes in Computer Science (2004)(accepted for publication)
8. Müller, K.-R., Mika, S., Räshc, Tsuda, K., Schölkopf, B.: An Introduction to Kernel-based Learning Algorithms. IEEE Transactions on Neural Networks, **12**(2) (2001) 181–201.
9. Schmidt, D.C., Druffel, L.E. : A Fast Backtracking Algorithm to Test Direct Graphs for Isomorphism Using Distance Matrices. Journal of the ACM **23** (3) (1976) 433-445
10. Schölkopf, B., Smola, A.: Learning with Kernels. MIT Press (2002).
11. Smola, A., Schölkopf, B., Müller, K.-R.: The Connection between Regularization Operators and Support Vector Kernels. Neural Networks **11** (1998) 637–649
12. Smola, A., Kondor, R.I.: Kernels and Regularization on Graphs. In: Schölkopf,B., and Warmuth, M. K. (eds) Computational Learning Theory and Kernel Machines, 16th Annual Conference on Computational Learning Theory and 7th Kernel Workshop, COLT/Kernel 2003. Lecture Notes in Computer Science. Springer. Vol. **2777** (2003) 144–158
13. DePiero, F.W., Trivedi, M., Serbin, S.: Graph Matching Using a Direct Classification of Node Attendance. Pattern Recognition, Vol. **29**(6) (1996) 1031–1048
14. Ozer, B., Wolf, W., Akansu, A.N.: A Graph Based Object Description for Information Retrieval in Digital Image and Video Libraries. In: Proceedings of the IEEE Workshop on Content-Based Access of Image and Video Libraries (1999) 79–83

Pattern Recognition via Vasconcelos' Genetic Algorithm

Angel Kuri-Morales

Instituto Tecnológico Autónomo de México
Río Hondo No.1, Tizapán San Angel, C.P. 01000, México
akuri@itam.mx

Abstract. In this paper we describe a heuristic approach to the problem of identifying a pattern embedded within a figure from a predefined set of patterns via
the utilization of a genetic algorithm (GA). By applying this GA we are able to
recognize a set of simple figures independently of scale, translation and rotation. We discuss the fact that this GA is, purportedly, the best among a set of alternatives; a fact which was previously proven appealing to statistical techniques. We describe the general process, the special type of genetic algorithm
utilized, report some results obtained from a test set and we discuss the aforementioned results and we comment on these. We also point out some possible
extensions and future directions.

1 Introduction

In [1] we reported on the application of the so-called *Eclectic* Genetic Algorithms
applied to the problem of pattern recognition. In this paper we offer new insights via
the so-called Vasconcelos' GA. The problem of pattern recognition has long been
considered to be a topic of particular interest in many areas of Computer Science. It
has been tackled in many ways throughout a considerably large span of time and, as
of today, it remains a subject of continuous study.

In this paper we report yet another method to solve a particular problem of pattern
recognition. This problem may be described as follows:

a) We are given a certain graphical figure, possibly composed of an unknown non-
linear combination of simpler (component) graphical figures. For our discussion
we shall call this figure the master figure or, simply, the master.

b) We are given a set of "candidate" figures, which we are interested to discover
within the master if any of these does indeed "lie" within it. What we mean when
we say that a figure lies within another figure is, in fact, central to our method and
we shall dwell upon this matter in what follows. We shall call these possibly embedded figures the *patterns*.

c) We would like to ascertain, with a given degree of certainty, whether one or several of the patterns lie within the master.

1.1 General Process

In figure 1, a set of patterns is shown surrounding a master. The main problem of
defining when a pattern lies within a master is interesting only when such relation is
not direct. That is, it is relatively simple to find, say, a square within a master if such a

A. Sanfeliu et al. (Eds.): CIARP 2004, LNCS 3287, pp. 328–335, 2004.

square is one of the patterns on a 1 to 1 scale, in the same position and with the same inclination. Here, however, we are looking for a much more general case. Namely, we impose upon our method, the task of identifying a pattern in the master even if the pattern is found on a different scale, a different position and a different inclination than the ones in the pattern. We shall define, therefore, three operators on the pattern:

1. A scale operator, which we denote by $\sigma(s, f)$, where **s** is the scale factor and **f** is the figure being scaled.

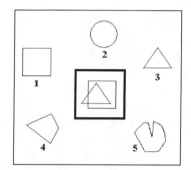

Fig. 1. A Set of Patterns and a Master.

2. A rotation operator, which we denote by $\rho(r, f)$, where **r** is the rotation angle, and **f** is the figure being rotated.
3. A translation operator which we denote by $\tau(t_1, t_2, f)$, where $\mathbf{t_1}$, $\mathbf{t_2}$ are the translations on the x and y axis respectively and **f** is the figure being translated.

Henceforth, a pattern is mapped an arbitrarily selected number of times under scaling, rotation and translation into a *derived pattern* or *descendant*. That is, from every pattern we extract a family of descendants which arise from a process of repeated application of σ, ρ and τ.

The i-th descendant ($\delta_i(f)$) is denoted by

$$\delta_i(f) = \sigma_i \{s_i, \rho_i [r_i, \tau_i (t_{i1}, t_{i2}, f)]\} \tag{1}$$

where the operators are successively applied to a figure *f*.

The rationale behind this strategy is simple: under the assumption that the possible number of configurations is sufficiently large, we settle with a sample of the configuration space in the hope of capturing the essence of the pattern in all its possible states where by "state" we mean any one of the possible combinations of s, r, t_1, t_2. Clearly the number of possible states is sufficiently large so that an exhaustive enumeration of these is impractical. The size of the sample is largely determined, therefore, by practical considerations such as the amount of information contained in the figure, the speed of the computer where the process of identification is performed and the amount of memory at our disposal. We denote the family of descendants for a given figure **f** by $\phi(f)$.

Once the samples (one per pattern) are obtained, we attempt to characterize the relationship between the i-th pattern and the master by minimizing a norm which should reflect the distance between the master and the pattern. If the said distance is minimum we shall accept the fact that the pattern is embedded within the master. This is what we mean when we say that a pattern *lies* within a figure. We shall accept that pattern **f** is found in the master **m** if the distance between **f** and **m** is relatively small. We could have, of course, attempted to minimize such distance from a "traditional" norm such as L_1, L_2 of L_∞. Indeed, such a scheme was applied in [2] where we attempted to minimize the said distance in L_∞. There we recognized a set of fuzzy alphabetic (i.e. A, B, ..., Z, ...) characters with a neural network and with a scheme similar to the one reported here. There, however, the patterns were unique. That is, the master consisted of only one of the fuzzified characters and the method performed unsatisfactorily when several patterns were put together. Our conclusion was that the problem lied in the fact that $\phi(f)$ was not sufficiently rich and/or the master was too complex.

In order to overcome the limitations outlined above we felt it necessary to enrich ϕ and to adopt an ad hoc distance norm. To achieve these two goals while retaining the essence of the method we appealed to a genetic algorithm.

In the algorithm a set of random patterns (each of which will act as a probe π) is generated. Thus, information is maximized to begin with. That is, in terms of a Fourier decomposition no harmonics of the pattern are left out. Then the distance between the test pattern and **both** ϕ and the master is minimized **simultaneously**. To do this:

a) The average distance $\overline{\Delta_\delta}$ between the probe (π) and each of the δ_i is calculated from $\overline{\Delta\delta} = \dfrac{1}{N}\sum_1 (\pi - \delta_i)$.

b) The distance Δ_m between π and the master is calculated from $\Delta_m = \pi - m$.

c) A mutual distance $\Delta_{\delta m}$ is derived from $\Delta_{\delta m} = \dfrac{1}{2}(\overline{\Delta_\delta} + \Delta_m)$.

The genetic algorithm receives as its initial population, therefore, a set of random patterns. Its fitness function is then the mutual distance $\Delta_{\delta m}$, which it tries to minimize. The population, thereafter, evolves to a fittest individual, which is constantly closer to both the set of descendants and the master, thereby establishing an informational meaningful link between the particular sample from which $\phi(f)$ originally arose and the master. In order to calculate the above mentioned distances the system is fed a set of figures in compressed (PCX) format. This set comprises both the master and the patterns. As a second step, the δ_i are generated. Once having these samples (the arguments of the operators are generated randomly) the genetic string of the master and the descendants is composed of the a concatenation of the rows of the pattern (1 bit per pixel). The distance between probe and descendants, on the one hand, and probe and master, on the other, is trivially calculated by counting those positions where the values agree. In our test we only considered black and white images. Therefore, an empty space is a "1", whereas a filled space is a "0". It should be clear that the genetic algorithm is basically measuring the information content coincidence in the probe vs. the descendants and vs. the master. It should also be clear that the fact that pattern information is state independent given a properly selected size of the sample. That is, regardless of where the pattern may be within the space of the master and regardless of its position and/or angle of inclination relative to the master, as long as the information of the pattern remains a match will be found, that is, as long as the pattern is not deformed.

2 Genetic Algorithm

For those familiar with the methodology of genetic algorithms it should come as no surprise that a number of questions relative to the best operation of the algorithm immediately arose. The Simple Genetic Algorithm frequently mentioned in the literature leaves open the optimal values of, at least, the following parameters:

a) Probability of crossover (P_c).
b) Probability of mutation (P_m).
c) Population size.

Additionally, premature and/or slow convergence are also of prime importance [3].

In the past we have conducted experiments [4] which led us to take the following decisions:

a) We utilize Vasconcelos' scheme, i.e. selection is deterministic on an extreme crossover schedule with N-elitism.
b) Crossover is annular.
c) Mutation is uniform.

In what follows we describe in more detail the points just outlined.

2.1 The "Best" Genetic Algorithm

Optimality in GA's depends on the model chosen. For reasons beyond the scope of this paper (but see reference [5]) we have chosen to incorporate in our model the following features:

2.1.1 Initial Population
It was randomly generated. We decided not to bias the initial population in any sense for the reasons outlined above. For these work we selected initial populations of size 50.

2.1.2 Elitism
All of the individuals stemming from the genetic process are rated according to their performance. It has been repeatedly shown that elitism leads to faster convergence. Furthermore, simple elitism (and stronger versions) guarantee that the algorithm converges to a global optimum (although time is not bounded, in general). In figure 2 we show the kind of elitism implemented. This is called "full" elitism, where the best N individuals of *all* populations (up to iteration *t*) are kept as those of the initial population of iteration *t+1*.

2.1.3 Selection

The individuals are selected deterministically. The best (overall) N individuals are considered. The best and worst individuals (1-N) are selected; then the second best and next-to-the-worst individuals (2-[N-1]) are selected, etc.

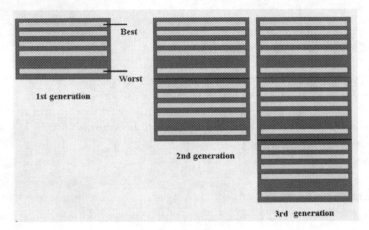

Fig. 2. Full Elitism.

This is known as Vasconcelos' model of GA's. Vasconcelos' model has shown to guarantee that there is no premature convergence and that, as a consequence, it reaches generally better results than other models. Vasconcelos' coupling scheme is illustrated in figure 3.

2.1.4 Crossover

It is performed with a probability P_c. In our GA $P_c = 0.9$. Further, we adopted annular crossover. Annular crossover makes this operation position independent. In the past several authors [6] have attempted to achieve position independence in the genome. Annular crossover allows for unbiased building block search, a central feature to GA's strength. Two randomly selected individuals are represented as two rings (the parent individuals). Semi-rings of equal size are selected and interchanged to yield a set of offspring. Each parent contributes the same amount of information to their descendants.

2.1.5 Mutation

Mutation is performed with probability $P_m = 0.005$. Mutation is uniform and, thus, is kept at very low levels. For efficiency purposes, we do not work with mutation probabilities for every independent bit. Rather, we work with the *expected number of mutations*, which, statistically is equivalent to calculating mutation probabilities for every bit. Hence, the expected number of mutations $E(m)$ is calculated from $E(m) = P_m \times l \times N$, where l is the length of the genome in bits and N is the number of individuals in the population. Since the pattern representation consisted, in our case, of a 5625 bit long binary string($l = 5625$), $P_m = 0.005$ and N=50 we have that $E(m) = 1,406$, i.e. in every generation 1,406 (out of 281,250) bits are randomly selected and complemented ($0 \rightarrow 1$ and $1 \rightarrow 0$).

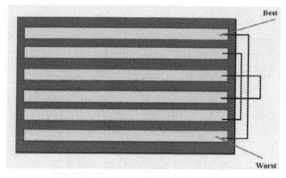

Fig. 3. Deterministic Coupling.

3   Experiments

We performed an initial set of experiments to test the scheme we have described. We designed 5 sets of 10 descendants each: $\Phi_1(f_1), \Phi_1(f_2), \Phi_1(f_3), \Phi_1(f_4), \Phi_1(f_5)$ and 5 sets of 25 descendants each: $\Phi_2(f_1), \Phi_2(f_2), \Phi_2(f_3), \Phi_2(f_4), \Phi_2(f_5)$. The descendants were obtained by applying operators σ and τ as described above. These we matched vs. a master figure (the patterns and the master figure correspond to the ones shown in Figure 1.). The two following tables show the results for these experiments. The selection criterion is actually very simple: accept as an embedded pattern the one which shows the smallest $\Delta_{\delta m}$.

In tables 1 and 2, the smallest $\Delta_{\delta m}$ correspond to patterns 1 and 3, which are shown in Figure 1. The patterns not recognized are shown in the same figure. The master figure is shown in Figure 4. As seen, in this simple trial the correlation between the matches and what our intuition would dictate is accurate. This results are encouraging on two accounts: First, it would seem that

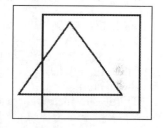

Fig. 4. Master Figure.

the method, in general, should be expected to yield reasonably good results. Second, from the tables, it seems that whenever $\phi(f)$ is enriched, the precision is enhanced.

Table 1. Results for Φ_1.

Pattern	Maximum	Average	Standard Deviation	Selected Pattern
1	170.70	169.60	.37	YES
2	140.90	139.39	.39	NO
3	173.8	172.889	.35	YES
4	150.70	150.24	.09	NO
5	136.40	135.29	.36	NO

Table 2. Results for Φ_2.

Pattern	Maximum	Average	Standard Deviation	Selected Pattern
1	180.17	179.50	.35	YES
2	150.90	148.39	.42	NO
3	185.7	187.32	.35	YES
4	156.70	155.00	.12	NO
5	137.44	136.79	.38	NO

4   Conclusions

In the method described above the genetic algorithm, by its own definition evolves under supervision of the environment [7], via the fitness function. However, the fitness function itself has been determined by a random sampling of the possible space of solutions. In that sense the search is unsupervised, in as much as the way the spectrum of the restricted sample space is "blind". Although we have proven that Vasconcelos' model is superior to alternative ones [8] still much work remains to be done. In the first place, the patterns and the master were specifically selected to validate the model in first instance. The figures that we attempted to recognize were directly embedded in the master. What would happen if the sought for relationship were not so straightforward? We intend to pursue further investigation along these lines. Secondly, although the results of the model, as reported, correspond to intuition, it is not clear that this intuition could be substantiated in general. For example, are we sure that the figure in pattern 4, for instance, is not informationally contained in the master? Thirdly, the measure that we used is amenable to reconsideration and enrichment. Do we have certainty that this direct difference is the best norm? We remarked earlier that a way to ensure that this norm is adequate is that the algorithm itself selects it. This is true in the sense that the genetic methodology assigns a certain degree of fuzziness to the measure. For example, the random walk implicit in the GA translates into the fact that the distance being minimized is adaptive. Similar distances (but not identical) would have been obtained by slight changes in the initial conditions set in the GA.

Finally, the technical details were quite interesting in themselves. The mere process of applying the defined operators ρ, σ and τ became an interesting matter. The figures were to remain within the boundaries of the master's environment; the discreetness of the binary mapping disallowed certain arguments s, r and t1, t2; the repeated comparison of the probe vs. the patterns in implied vast amounts of computation. In view of the technical shortcomings of the method, it remains to generalize it and prove its universality before attempting to solve large practical problems with it. We hope to report on the (successful) completion of the investigation shortly.

References

1. Kuri, A., "Pattern Recognition via a Genetic Algorithm", II Taller Iberoamericano de Reconocimiento de Patrones, La Habana, Cuba, pp. 127-133, Mayo, 1997.
2. Fernández-Ayala, A., Implementación de una Red Neuronal Multi-Capa para el Reconocimiento de Patrones, Tesis de Maestría, Instituto de Investigaciones Matemáticas Aplicadas y Sistemas, 1991.
3. Mühlenbein, Gorges-Schleuter & Krämer: Evolution Algorithms in combinatorial optimization, Parallel Computing, Vol. 7, pp. 65-85, 1988.
4. Kuri, A., "Penalty Function Methods for Constrained Optimization with Genetic Algorithms: a Statistical Analysis", Lectures Notes in Artificial Intelligence No. 2313, pp. 108-117, Coello, C., Albornoz, A., Sucar, L., Cairó, O., (eds.), Springer Verlag, April 2002.
5. Goldberg, D., Genetic Algorithms in Search, Optimization and Machine Learning, Addison-Wesley Publishing Company, 1989.
6. Vose, M., Generalizing the notion of schema in genetic algorithms, Artificial Intelligence, 50, (1991), 385-396.
7. Tsypkin, Ya. Z., Neural Networks and Fuzzy Systems, p. 179, Prentice-Hall, 1993.
8. Kuri, A., "A Methodology for the Statistical Characterization of Genetic Algorithms", Lectures Notes in Artificial Intelligence No 2313, pp. 79-89, Coello, C., Albornoz, A., Sucar, L., Cairó, O., (eds.), Springer Verlag, April 2000.

Statistical Pattern Recognition Problems and the Multiple Classes Random Neural Network Model

Jose Aguilar

CEMISID, Dpto. de Computación, Facultad de Ingeniería, Av. Tulio Febres,
Universidad de los Andes, Mérida 5101, Venezuela
aguilar@ing.ula.ve

Abstract. The purpose of this paper is to describe the use of the multiple classes random neural network model to learn various statistical patterns. We propose a pattern recognition algorithm for the recognition of statistical patterns based upon the non-linear equations of the multiple classes random neural network model using gradient descent of a quadratic error function. In this case the classification errors are considered.

1 Introduction

The Random Neural Network (RNN) has been proposed by Gelenbe in 1989 [6], [7], [8]. This model calculates the probability of activation of the neurons in the network. Signals in this model take the form of impulses which mimic what is presently known of inter-neural signals in biophysical neural networks. The RNN has been used to solve optimization [1], [2], [3] and pattern recognition problems [4], [5]. Fourneau and Gelenbe have proposed an extension of the RNN, Multiple Classes Random Neural Network (MCRNN) [9]. The problem addressed in this paper concerns the proposition of a pattern recognition algorithm for the recognition of statistical patterns, using MCRNN. In statistical pattern recognition a pattern is represented by a set of attributes, viewed like a d-dimensional feature vector [11], [12]. We present a back-propagation type learning algorithm for the MCRNN, using gradient descent of a quadratic error function when a set of input-output pairs is presented to the network. This work is organized as follows, in section 2 the theoretical bases of MCRN are reviewed. Section 3 presents our pattern recognition algorithm for MCRNN. In section 4, we present the statistical pattern recognition problem and some comparisons. Remarks concerning future work and conclusions are provided in section 5.

2 The Multiple Classes Random Neural Model

The MCRNN is composed of n neurons and receives exogenous positive (excitatory) and negative (inhibitory) signals as well as endogenous signals exchanged by the neurons. Excitatory and inhibitory signals are sent by neurons when they fire, to other neurons in the network or to outside world. In this model, positive signals may belong to several classes and the potential at a neuron is represented by the vector $\underline{K_i}$ = $(K_{i1}, ..., K_{iC})$, where K_{ic} is the value of the "class c potential" of neuron i, or its

A. Sanfeliu et al. (Eds.): CIARP 2004, LNCS 3287, pp. 336–341, 2004.

"excitation level in terms of class c signals", and negative signals only belong to a single class. The total potential of neuron i is $K_i = \Sigma_{c=1}^{C} K_{ic}$. When a positive signal of class c arrives at a neuron, it merely increases K_{ic} by 1, and when a negative signals arrives at it, if $K_i > 0$, the potential is reduced by 1, and the class of the potential to be reduced is chosen randomly with probability K_{ic}/K_i for any $c = 1, ..., C$. Exogenous positive signals of class c arrive at neuron i in a Poisson stream of rate $\Lambda(i, c)$, while exogenous negative signals arrive at it according to a Poisson process of rate $\lambda(i)$. A neuron is excited if its potential is positive ($K_i > 0$). It then fires, at exponentially distributed intervals, sends excitatory signals of different classes, or inhibitory signals, to other neurons or to the outside of the network. The neuron i sends excitatory signals of class c at rate $r(i, c) > 0$, with probability K_{ic}/K_i. When the neuron fires at rate $r(i, c)$, deletes by 1 its class c potential and sends to neuron j a class φ positive signal with probability $p^+(i, c; j, \varphi)$, or a negative signal with probability $p^-(i, c; j)$. On the other hand, the probability that the deleted signal is sent out of the network is $d(i, c)$. Let $q(i, c)$ with $0 < q(i, c) < 1$ be the solution of the system of non-linear equations:

$$q(i,c) = \lambda^+(i, c)/(r(i, c)+\lambda^-(i))$$ (1)

where, $\lambda^+(i, c) = \Sigma_{(j, \varphi)} q(j, \varphi) r(j, \varphi) p^+(j, \varphi ; i, c) + \Lambda(i, c)$

$\lambda^-(i) = \Sigma_{(j, \varphi)} q(j, \varphi) r(j, \varphi) p^-(j, \varphi; i) + \lambda(i)$

The synaptic weights for positive ($w^+(j, \varphi; i, c)$) and negative ($w^-(j, \varphi; i)$) signals are defined as:

$$w^+(j, \varphi; i, c) = r(j, \varphi) p^+(j, \varphi; i, c) \qquad w^-(j, \varphi; i) = r(j, \varphi) p^-(j, \varphi; i)$$

and, $r(j, \varphi) = [\Sigma_{(i, c)} w^+(j, \varphi; i, c) + \Sigma_{(i, c)} w^-(j, \varphi; i)]$

3 Pattern Recognition Algorithm

We propose a gradient descent learning algorithm for choosing the set of network parameters $w^+(j, z; i, c)$ and $w^-(j, z; i)$ in order to learn a given set of m input-output pairs (X, Y) where the set of successive inputs is denoted by:

$$X = \{X_1, ..., X_m\} \qquad X_k = \{X_k(1,1), ..., X_k(n, C)\}$$

where, $X_k(i, c)$ is the cth class on the neuron i for the patron k

$X_k(i, c) = \{\Lambda_k(i, c), \lambda_k(i)\}$

and the successive desired outputs are the vector
$$Y = \{Y_1, ..., Y_m\}$$
where, $Y_k = \{Y_k(1,1), ..., Y_k(n, C)\}$,   and $Y_k(1,1) = \{0, 0.5, 1\}$

The values $\Lambda_k(i, c)$ and $\lambda_k(i)$ provide the network stability. Particularly, in our model $\Lambda(i, c)=Lic$ and $\lambda(i)=0$, where Lic is a constant for the class c of the neuron i. $X_k(i, c)$ are initialized as follows:

$$Y_k(i, c) > 0 \Rightarrow X_k(i, c) = (\Lambda_k(i, c), \lambda_k(i)) = (Lic, 0)$$

$$Y_{ik}(i, c) = 0 \Rightarrow X_k(i, c) = (\Lambda_k(i, c), \lambda_k(i)) = (0, 0)$$

The rule to update the weights may be written as:

$$w_k^+(u,p; v,z) = w_{k-1}^+(u,p; v,c) - \mu\Sigma^n_{i=1} \Sigma^C_{c=1} (q_k(i,c) - y_k(i,c))[\delta q(i,c) / \delta w^+(u,p; v,z)]_k$$

$$w_k^-(u,p; v) = w_{k-1}^-(u,p; v) - \mu\Sigma^n_{i=1} \Sigma^C_{c=1} (q_k(i,c) - y_k(i,c))[\delta q(i,c) / \delta w^-(u,p; v)]_k$$

(2)

where, $\mu > 0$ is the learning rate (some constant).

$q_k(i)$ is calculated using X_k, $w^+_k(u, p; v, z) = w^+_{k-1}(u, p; v, z)$ and

$w^-_k(u, p; v) = w^-_{k-1}(u, p; v)$ in (1)

$[\delta q(i,c) / \delta w^+(u,p;v,z)]_k$ and $[\delta q(i,c) / \delta w^-(u,p;v)]_k$ are evaluated

using the values $q(i,c) = q_k(i,c)$, $w^+_k(u, p; v, z) = w^+_{k-1}(u, p; v, z)$

and $w^-_k(u, p; v) = w^-_{k-1}(u, p; v)$ in (2)

and, $\delta q(i, c)/ \delta W^+(u,p;v,z) = \gamma^+(u,p;v,z)/q(u,p) [I-W]^{-1}$

$\delta q(i, c)/ \delta W^-(u,p;v) = \gamma^-(u,p;v)/q(u,p) [I-W]^{-1}$

if (u=i) and (v≠i) then   if (u≠i) and (v=i) then

$\gamma^+(u,p;v,z) = -1/D(i,c)$ $\gamma^+(u,p;v,z) = 1/D(i,c)$

$\gamma^-(u,p;v) = -1/D(i,c)$ $\gamma^-(u,p;v) = -q(i,c)/D(i,c)$

if (u=i) and (v=i) then   if (u≠i) and (v≠i) then

$\gamma^+(u,p;v,z) = 0$ $\gamma^+(u,p;v,z) = 0$

$\gamma^-(u,p;v) = -(1+ q(i,c))/D(i,c)$ $\gamma^-(u,p;v) = 0$

finally, $D(i,c) = r(i, c) + \Sigma^n_{j=1} \Sigma^C_{z=1} q(j, z) w^-(j, z; i)]$

$$W = \Sigma^n_{j=1} \Sigma^C_{z=1} [w^+(j, z; i, c) + w^-(j, z; i)q(j,z)]/D(j,z)$$

The complete learning algorithm for the network is:

– *Initiate the matrices W_0^+ and W_0^- in some appropriate manner. Choose a value of μ in (2).*
– *For each successive value of m:*
   – *Set the input-output pair (X_k, Y_k)*
   – *Repeat*
      – *Solve the equation (1) with these values*
      – *Using (2) and the previous results update the matrices W_k^+ and W_k^-*

Until the change in the new values of the weights is smaller than some predetermined valued.

Once the learning phase is completed, the network must perform as well as possible the completion of noisy versions of the training vectors. In this case, we propose a progressive retrieval process with adaptive threshold value. Let $X' = \{X'(1, 1), ..., X'(n, C)\}$ be any input vector with values equal to 0, 0.5 or 1, for each $X'(i, c)$, $i=1, ..., n$ and $c=1, ..., C$. In order to determine the corresponding output vector $Y = \{Y(1,1), ..., Y(n, C)\}$, we first compute the vector of probabilities $Q=(q(1, 1), ..., q(n, C))$. We consider that $q(i, c)$ values such that $1-T < q(i, c) < T/2$ or $1-T/2 < q(i, c) < T$, with for instance $T=0.8$, belong to the uncertainty interval Z. When the network stabilizes to an attractor state, the number NB_Z of neurons whose $q(i, c) \in Z$ is equal to 0. Hence, we first treat the neurons whose state is considered certain to obtain the output vector $Y^{(1)} = (Y^{(1)}(1,1), ..., Y^{(1)}(n,C))$, with:

$$Y^{(1)}(i, c) = Fz(q(i, c)) = \begin{cases} 1 & \text{if } q(i, c) > T \\ 0 & \text{if } q(i, c) < 1-T \\ 0.5 & \text{if } T/2 <= q(i, c) <= 1-T/2 \\ x'_i & \text{otherwise} \end{cases}$$

where Fz is the thresholding function by intervals. If NB_Z=0, this phase is terminated and the output vector is $Y=Y^{(1)}$. Otherwise, Y is obtained after applying the thresholding function $f\beta$ as follows:

$$Y(i, c) = f\beta (q(i, c)) = \begin{cases} 1 & \text{if } q(i, c) > \beta \\ 0.5 & \text{if } \beta/2 < q(i, c) < \beta \\ 0 & \text{otherwise} \end{cases}$$

where β is the selected threshold. Each value $q(i, c) \in Z$ is considered as potential thresholds. That is, for each $q(i, c) \in Z$:

$$\beta = \begin{cases} q(i, c) & \text{if } q(i, c) > 0.666 \\ 1-q(i, c) & \text{otherwise} \end{cases}$$

Eventually, Z can be reduced by decreasing T (for $T > 0.666$). For each potential value of β, we present to the network the vector $X'^{(1)}(\beta) = f\beta(Q)$. Then, we compute the new vector of probabilities $Q^{(1)}(\beta)$ and the output vector $Y^{(2)}(\beta) = Fz(Q^{(1)}(\beta))$. We keep the cases where NB_Z=0 and $X'^{(1)}(\beta) = Y^{(2)}(\beta)$. If these two conditions are never satisfied, the initial X' is considered too much different of any training vector. If several thresholds are candidate, we choose the one which provides the minimal error (difference between $q(i, c)$ and $Y(i, c)$, for $i=1, n$ and $c=1, ..., C$):

$$E(\beta) = 1/2 \sum_{i=1}^{n} [q(i, c)^{(1)}(\beta) - Y(i, c)^{(1)}(\alpha)]^2$$

4 Statistical Pattern Recognition Problem

We test our approach in statistical pattern recognition problems [11]. In statistical pattern recognition a pattern is represented by a set of attributes, viewed like a d-dimensional feature vector [11], [12]. Well-known concepts from statistical decision theory are used to establish decision boundaries between pattern classes. The decision making process in statistical pattern recognition can be summarized as follow: A given pattern is to be assigned to one of c categories w_1, ..., w_c based on a vector of d attributes values $x=\{x_1, ..., x_d\}$. The attributes are assumed to have a probability density or mass function condition on the pattern class (depending on whether the attributes are continuous or discrete). A number of well-known decision rules are available to define the decision boundary (Bayes decision rule, maximum likelihood rule, etc.) [11]. Various strategies are utilized to design a classifier in statistical pattern recognition according to: the kind of information available about class-conditional densities, supervised learning versus unsupervised learning, whether the decision boundaries are obtained directly (geometric approach) or indirectly (probabilistic approach). We compare our approach with several classifier systems for the recognition of a digit dataset that consists of handwritten numeral ("0"..."9") extracted from a collection of Dutch utility maps [10], [12]. Two hundred patterns per class (for a total of 2000 patterns) are available in the form of 30*48 binary images. These characters are represented in terms of the following six attributes: 76 Fourier coefficients of the character shapes, 216 profiles correlations, 64 Karhunen-Loeve coefficients, 240 pixel averages, in 2*3 windows, 47 Zernike moments, 6 morphological attributes. The following classifiers are used to compare with our approach [11]: the bayes-plug-in rule assuming normal distributions (BP), the Nearest Mean rule (NM), the Parzen technique, a feed-forward neural networks (based on the Matlab Neural Network Toolbox), with a hidden layer consisting of 20 neurons (NN), and the quadratic Support Vector classifier (SV). The classifiers were trained on the same patterns from each of the six attribute sets and tested on the same patterns. The resulting classification errors (in percentage) are reported in table 1.

Table 1. Error rate (in percentage) of different classifiers.

Classifiers	Attribute Sets					
	1	2	3	4	5	6
BP	21.3	3.4	5.7	9.9	18.9	29.1
NM	19.8	3.7	4.6	7.3	18.7	26.6
Parzen	17.1	7.9	3.7	3.7	18.5	52.1
NN	18.6	3.7	4.6	7.3	18.1	26.6
SV	21.2	5.4	4.8	6	19.3	81.1
Mult	18.2	3.5	4.2	6.2	18.6	28.2

Some of the classifiers, for example, the SV, do not perform well on this data. Some of the classifiers such as the Parzen and BP give good results. The performances of different classifiers vary substantially over different attribute sets. Only with our approach, we obtain good performances (it is not the best one) for all the attribute sets.

5   Conclusions

In this paper, we have proposed a learning algorithm based on the Multiple Classes Random Neural Model for the statistical pattern recognition problem. We have shown that this model can efficiently work as associative memory. We can learn arbitrary statistical patterns with this algorithm. During the learning phase, we have met classical problems like the existence of local minimal and large learning times. However, most of the computations are intrinsically parallel and can be implemented on SIMD or MIMD architectures. Next work will study a new retrieval algorithm adapted to these types of figures.

References

1. Aguilar, J. Evolutionary Learning on Recurrent Random Neural Network. Proc. of the World Congress on Neural Networks, International Neural Network Society (1995) 232-236.
2. Aguilar, J. An Energy Function for the Random Neural Networks. Neural Processing Letters, Vol. 4 (1996) 17-27.
3. Aguilar, J. Definition of an Energy Function for the Random Neural to solve Optimization Problems. Neural Networks, Vol. 11 (1998) 731-738.
4. Aguilar, J., Colmenares A. Resolution of Pattern Recognition Problems using a Hybrid Genetic/Random Neural Network Learning Algorithm. Pattern Analysis and Applications, Vol. 1 (1998) 52-61.
5. Atalay, V., Gelenbe, E., Yalabik, N. The random neural network model for texture generation. Intl. Journal of Pattern Recognition and Artificial Intelligence, Vol. 6 (1992) 131-141.
6. Gelenbe, E. Random neural networks with positive and negative signals and product form solution. Neural Computation, Vol. 1 (1989) 502-511.
7. Gelenbe, E.: Stability of the random neural networks. Neural Computation, Vol. 2 (1990) 239-247.
8. Gelenbe, E.: Learning in the recurrent random neural network. Neural Computation, Vol. 5 (1993) 325-333.
9. Fourneau, M., Gelenbe, E., Suros, R.: G-networks with Multiple classes of negative and positive customers. Theoretical Computer Science, Vol. 155 (1996) 141-156.
10. Machine Learning Repository, University of California, Irvine (www.ics.ucl.edu./~mlearn/MLRepository.html)
11. Jain A., Duin R., Man J.: Statistical Pattern Recognition: A Review. IEEE Transactions on Pattern Analysis and Machine Learning, Vol. 22 (2000), 4-37.
12. Van Breukelen M., Duin R, Tax D., Den Harlog J.: Handwritten Digit Recognition by Combined Classifiers, Kybernetika, Vol. 34 (1998), 381-386.

New Bounds and Approximations
for the Error of Linear Classifiers

Luis Rueda

School of Computer Science, University of Windsor
401 Sunset Avenue, Windsor, ON, N9B 3P4, Canada
lrueda@uwindsor.ca

Abstract. In this paper, we derive lower and upper bounds for the probability of error for a linear classifier, where the random vectors representing the underlying classes obey the *multivariate* normal distribution. The expression of the error is derived in the *one-dimensional space, independently of the dimensionality of the original problem*. Based on the two bounds, we propose an approximating expression for the error of a generic linear classifier. In particular, we derive the corresponding bounds and the expression for approximating the error of Fisher's classifier. Our empirical results on synthetic data, including up to five-hundred-dimensional featured samples, show that the computations for the error are extremely fast and quite accurate; the approximation differs from the *actual* error by at most $\varepsilon = 0.0184340683$.

1 Introduction

Assessing the performance of classifiers is a fundamental problem is pattern recognition, for which various approaches have been proposed in the literature. The main idea is to measure the discriminabilty of the classifier by means of its *misclassification rate* or *error rate*. The error rate or classification error, in general, measured as the *probability of error*, provides a quite useful insight about the quality of a classifier. We consider the classical problem of deriving the *true* error rate for a linear classifier, which we presently refer to as the *classification error* or *probability of error*. We deal with two classes, ω_1 and ω_2, whose *a priori* probabilities are $P(\omega_1)$ and $P(\omega_2)$ respectively, and which are represented by two normally distributed d-dimensional random vectors, $\mathbf{x}_1 \sim N(\boldsymbol{\mu}_1, \boldsymbol{\Sigma}_1)$ and $\mathbf{x}_2 \sim N(\boldsymbol{\mu}_2, \boldsymbol{\Sigma}_2)$, respectively. In order to derive a linear classification scheme, the aim is to find a linear function of the form:

$$g(\mathbf{x}) = \mathbf{w}^t \mathbf{x} + w_0 = 0, \tag{1}$$

that classifies an unknown object, represented by a real-valued feature vector, $\mathbf{x} = [x_1, \ldots, x_d]^t$, into the respective class, where $\mathbf{w}$ is a d-dimensional *weight* vector, such that $\mathbf{w} \neq \mathbf{0}_d$, and w_0 is a *threshold* weight.

    The problem of estimating the classification error has been studied for various cases, including an asymptotic formula for the expected error of the pseudo-Fisher classifier for the case in which the dimensionality of the problem is relatively larger than the size of the training dataset [8]. Bounds for more generic scenarios have been derived for

A. Sanfeliu et al. (Eds.): CIARP 2004, LNCS 3287, pp. 342–349, 2004.

linear classifiers that use kernel functions [5]. In the case of the Bayesian (quadratic) classifier for normal distributions, it is well-known that bounds on the classification exist, namely Chernoff's and Battacharyya's bounds [3, 4, 12], and the approximation method introduced by Lee *et al.* [7]. These bounds are applicable to the *optimal* classifier, which is linear only for equal covariance matrices, and that they are not tight enough for the majority of the cases.

2   Bounds and Approximations for the Error

We assume that we are dealing with the case in which μ_1 is on the "negative side" of the classifier, i.e. $g(\mu_1) < 0$, which implies that $g(\mu_2) > 0$. It is, thus, easy to see that to evaluate the opposite case, i.e. when $g(\mu_1) > 0$ and $g(\mu_2) < 0$, it suffices to rename the classes in such a way that the new class ω_1 satisfies $g(\mu_1) < 0$.

Given a linear classifier of the form of (1), and assuming that the space is divided into two regions, $\mathcal{R}_1$ and $\mathcal{R}_2$, which represent the areas in which an object is assigned to ω_1 and ω_2 respectively, the probability of error, Pr[error], is calculated as follows [3]:

$$\text{Pr[error]} = \int_{\mathcal{R}_2} p_{x_1}(\mathbf{x}|\omega_1)P(\omega_1)d\mathbf{x} + \int_{\mathcal{R}_1} p_{x_2}(\mathbf{x}|\omega_2)P(\omega_2)d\mathbf{x}, \tag{2}$$

where $p_{x_i}(\mathbf{x}|\omega_i)$ is the probability of $\mathbf{x}$ given ω_i, $\mathcal{R}_1$ is the region determined by $g(\mathbf{x}) < 0$, and $\mathcal{R}_2$ is the region determined by $g(\mathbf{x}) > 0$. Note that $g(\mathbf{x}) = 0$ is excluded from (2) since $\int_{g(\mathbf{x})=0} p_{x_i}(\mathbf{x}|\omega_i) = 0$.

The expression given in (2) is quite involved due to the fact that it invokes integrating multivariate normal distributions. Fortunately, when dealing with normal distributions, simpler expressions that involve $N(0, 1)$ random variables can be used (see [11]). An elegant way of writing the integrals of (2) in terms of an $N(0, 1)$ random variable, x, is as follows [4]:

$$\text{Pr[error]} = P(\omega_1) \int_{-\infty}^{a_1} \frac{1}{\sqrt{2\pi}} e^{-\frac{x^2}{2}} dx + P(\omega_2) \int_{-\infty}^{a_2} \frac{1}{\sqrt{2\pi}} e^{-\frac{x^2}{2}} dx, \tag{3}$$

where x is an $N(0, 1)$ random variable, and

$$a_1 = (\mathbf{w}^t \boldsymbol{\Sigma}_1 \mathbf{w})^{-\frac{1}{2}} (w_0 + \mathbf{w}^t \boldsymbol{\mu}_1), \text{ and} \tag{4}$$

$$a_2 = -(\mathbf{w}^t \boldsymbol{\Sigma}_2 \mathbf{w})^{-\frac{1}{2}} (w_0 + \mathbf{w}^t \boldsymbol{\mu}_2). \tag{5}$$

Although the multi-dimensional problem is reduced to its equivalent in the one-dimensional space, the analytic form of the integral for the univariate normal distribution density function is still not possible, and thus an algebraic analysis is only possible by means of bounds. To derive the expressions for the lower and upper bounds, we use a well-known inequality for the cumulative normal distribution function [6].

We know that $a_1 = (\mathbf{w}^t \boldsymbol{\Sigma}_1 \mathbf{w})^{-\frac{1}{2}} (w_0 + \mathbf{w}^t \boldsymbol{\mu}_1)$. Since $g(\mu_1) < 0$, it then follows that $\mathbf{w}^t \boldsymbol{\mu}_1 + w_0 < 0$. Also, $\boldsymbol{\Sigma}_1$ is positive definite, which implies that $(\mathbf{w}^t \boldsymbol{\Sigma}_1 \mathbf{w})^{-\frac{1}{2}} > 0$. Thus, it follows that $a_1 < 0$. Also, we know that $a_2 = -(\mathbf{w}^t \boldsymbol{\Sigma}_2 \mathbf{w})^{-\frac{1}{2}} (w_0 + \mathbf{w}^t \boldsymbol{\mu}_2)$.

Since $g(\mu_2) = \mathbf{w}^t\mu_2 + w_0 > 0$, and Σ_1 is positive definite, which implies that $(\mathbf{w}^t\Sigma_2\mathbf{w})^{-\frac{1}{2}} > 0$, it follows that $a_2 < 0$.

Since $a_i < 0$ for $a = 1, 2$, the inequality given in [6] can be expressed, in terms of a_i, as follows:

$$\frac{2e^{-\frac{a_i^2}{2}}}{\left(-a_i + \sqrt{a_i^2 + 4}\right)\sqrt{2\pi}} \le \int_{-\infty}^{a_i} \frac{1}{\sqrt{2\pi}} e^{-\frac{x^2}{2}} dx \le \frac{2e^{-\frac{a_i^2}{2}}}{\left(-a_i + \sqrt{a_i^2 + 2}\right)\sqrt{2\pi}}. \quad (6)$$

Pre-multiplying by $P(\omega_i)$, and adding the corresponding terms of (6) for $i = 1, 2$, we obtain the following inequality:

$$\sqrt{\frac{2}{\pi}}\left(\frac{P(\omega_1)e^{-\frac{a_1^2}{2}}}{-a_1 + \sqrt{a_1^2 + 4}} + \frac{P(\omega_2)e^{-\frac{a_2^2}{2}}}{-a_2 + \sqrt{a_2^2 + 4}}\right) \le \Pr[\text{error}] \le$$

$$\sqrt{\frac{2}{\pi}}\left(\frac{P(\omega_1)e^{-\frac{a_1^2}{2}}}{-a_1 + \sqrt{a_1^2 + 2}} + \frac{P(\omega_2)e^{-\frac{a_2^2}{2}}}{-a_2 + \sqrt{a_2^2 + 2}}\right), \quad (7)$$

where a_1 and a_2 are obtained as in (4) and (5) respectively.

The bounds for the classification error are important to obtain a fair assessment about the classifier, without computing the error using numeric integration methods. One should note, however, that these bounds are not tight enough for values of a_i close to 0, while being asymptotically accurate for $a_i < -1$. An alternative for this is to use the following approximating function for the probability of error:

$$\Pr[\text{error}] \cong \frac{1}{\sqrt{2\pi}}\left[P(\omega_1)e^{-\frac{a_1^2}{2}}\left(\frac{1}{-a_1 + \sqrt{a_1^2 + 4}} + \frac{1}{-a_1 + \sqrt{a_1^2 + 2}}\right)\right.$$

$$\left. + P(\omega_2)e^{-\frac{a_2^2}{2}}\left(\frac{1}{-a_2 + \sqrt{a_2^2 + 4}} + \frac{1}{-a_2 + \sqrt{a_2^2 + 2}}\right)\right]. \quad (8)$$

Thus, taking the average between the lower and the upper bounds as in (8) appears to be a very good approximation for the actual probability of error. To assess this, we first analyze the relationship between the integral and the average of the two bounds in (6). We are tempted to call the result given below *Lemma*, but unfortunately, one of the steps cannot be proved algebraically, and hence we leave it as a proposition. The complete proof of this result can be found in [9].

Proposition 1. *For all $a_i < 0$*

$$|g(a_i)| = \left|\int_{-\infty}^{a_i} \frac{1}{\sqrt{2\pi}} e^{-\frac{x^2}{2}} dx - \frac{e^{-\frac{a_i^2}{2}}}{\sqrt{2\pi}}\left(\frac{1}{-a_i + \sqrt{a_i^2 + 4}} + \frac{1}{-a_i + \sqrt{a_i^2 + 2}}\right)\right| \le \varepsilon,$$

$$(9)$$

where $\varepsilon = 0.0184340683$. $\qquad\qquad\qquad\square$

Using this result, we now state the relationship between the approximation function in (8) and the actual probability of error, which is computed as in (3).

Theorem 1. *The approximation given in (8) differs from the actual error in (3) in at most* $\varepsilon = 0.0184340683$.

Proof (Sketch). Since $P(\omega_1) \geq 0$ and $P(\omega_2) \geq 0$, using the inequality given in (9), we can write:

$$|P(\omega_1)g(a_i)| \leq P(\omega_1)\varepsilon, \text{ and} \tag{10}$$
$$|P(\omega_2)g(a_i)| \leq P(\omega_2)\varepsilon = [1 - P(\omega_1)]\,\varepsilon. \tag{11}$$

Adding (10) and (11), and rearranging, the result follows. The complete proof can be found in [9]. □

The result of Theorem 1 is quite important in our analysis, since it shows that the approximation for the error is very accurate, e.g. it differs from the actual error in at most two digits. This relationship is corroborated in the empirical results discussed in Section 4.

3   Error Analysis for Fisher's Classifier

We consider the two-class case for Fisher's classifier – for the general case see [3, 13]. Suppose then that we deal with two classes, ω_1 and ω_2, which are represented by two normally distributed d-dimensional random vectors, $\mathbf{x}_1 \sim N(\boldsymbol{\mu}_1, \boldsymbol{\Sigma}_1)$ and $\mathbf{x}_2 \sim N(\boldsymbol{\mu}_2, \boldsymbol{\Sigma}_2)$ respectively, where $\boldsymbol{\mu}_1 \neq \boldsymbol{\mu}_2$, and whose *a priori* probabilities are $P(\omega_1)$ and $P(\omega_2)$ respectively. The solution for the vector $\mathbf{w}$ that maximizes the *class separability* is given by:

$$\mathbf{w} = \mathbf{S}_W^{-1}(\boldsymbol{\mu}_2 - \boldsymbol{\mu}_1), \tag{12}$$

where $\mathbf{S}_W = \frac{1}{2}(\boldsymbol{\Sigma}_1 + \boldsymbol{\Sigma}_2)$.

To complete the linear classifier, the threshold w_0 has to be obtained. A simple approach (suggested in [12]) is to assume that the distributions in the original space have identical covariance matrices, and take the independent term of the optimal quadratic or Bayesian classifier, which results in:

$$w_0 = -\frac{1}{2}(\boldsymbol{\mu}_2 - \boldsymbol{\mu}_1)^t \mathbf{S}_W^{-1}(\boldsymbol{\mu}_1 + \boldsymbol{\mu}_2) - \log\frac{P(\omega_1)}{P(\omega_2)}. \tag{13}$$

Once we have derived the corresponding linear classifier by means of vector $\mathbf{w}$ and the corresponding threshold, we obtain the boundaries for the integrals in (3). The algebraic expression for the error is stated in the following theorem, whose proof can be found in [9]. A special condition is shown in the corollary given thereafter.

Theorem 2. *Let* $\mathbf{x}_1 \sim N(\boldsymbol{\mu}_1, \boldsymbol{\Sigma}_1)$ *and* $\mathbf{x}_2 \sim N(\boldsymbol{\mu}_2, \boldsymbol{\Sigma}_2)$ *be two normally distributed random vectors representing two classes,* ω_1 *and* ω_2, *whose a priori probabilities are* $P(\omega_1)$ *and* $P(\omega_2)$ *respectively, and* $g(\mathbf{x}) = \mathbf{w}^t\mathbf{x} + w_0$ *be Fisher's classifier, where* $\mathbf{w}$ *and* w_0 *are obtained as in (12) and (13) respectively.*

If $r^2 = (\boldsymbol{\mu}_1 - \boldsymbol{\mu}_2)^t \, (\boldsymbol{\Sigma}_1 + \boldsymbol{\Sigma}_2)^{-1} \, (\boldsymbol{\mu}_1 - \boldsymbol{\mu}_2) > \max \left\{ \log \frac{P(\omega_1)}{P(\omega_2)}, \log \frac{P(\omega_2)}{P(\omega_1)} \right\}$, *then:*

$$Pr[error(F)] = P(\omega_1) \int_{-\infty}^{b_1} \frac{1}{\sqrt{2\pi}} e^{-\frac{x^2}{2}} \, dx + P(\omega_2) \int_{-\infty}^{b_2} \frac{1}{\sqrt{2\pi}} e^{-\frac{x^2}{2}} \, dx \,, \quad (14)$$

where x is an $N(0,1)$ random variable, and

$$b_1 = \frac{1}{2} \left[(\boldsymbol{\mu}_2 - \boldsymbol{\mu}_1)^t \, (\boldsymbol{\Sigma}_1 + \boldsymbol{\Sigma}_2)^{-1} \, \boldsymbol{\Sigma}_1 \, (\boldsymbol{\Sigma}_1 + \boldsymbol{\Sigma}_2)^{-1} \, (\boldsymbol{\mu}_2 - \boldsymbol{\mu}_1) \right]^{-\frac{1}{2}}$$
$$\left[-(\boldsymbol{\mu}_2 - \boldsymbol{\mu}_1)^t \, (\boldsymbol{\Sigma}_1 + \boldsymbol{\Sigma}_2)^{-1} \, (\boldsymbol{\mu}_2 - \boldsymbol{\mu}_1) - \log \frac{P(\omega_1)}{P(\omega_2)} \right] \,, \quad (15)$$

$$b_2 = -\frac{1}{2} \left[(\boldsymbol{\mu}_2 - \boldsymbol{\mu}_1)^t \, (\boldsymbol{\Sigma}_1 + \boldsymbol{\Sigma}_2)^{-1} \, \boldsymbol{\Sigma}_2 \, (\boldsymbol{\Sigma}_1 + \boldsymbol{\Sigma}_2)^{-1} \, (\boldsymbol{\mu}_2 - \boldsymbol{\mu}_1) \right]^{-\frac{1}{2}}$$
$$\left[(\boldsymbol{\mu}_2 - \boldsymbol{\mu}_1)^t \, (\boldsymbol{\Sigma}_1 + \boldsymbol{\Sigma}_2)^{-1} \, (\boldsymbol{\mu}_2 - \boldsymbol{\mu}_1) - \log \frac{P(\omega_1)}{P(\omega_2)} \right] \,. \quad (16)$$

$\square$

Corollary 1. *Under the conditions of Theorem 2, and assuming that $P(\omega_1){=}P(\omega_2){=}$ 0.5, the probability of error of Fisher's classifier can always be computed as in (14).* $\square$

The algebraic expression for the error given in Theorem 2 shows that the classification error for Fisher's classifier can be derived directly from the parameters of the distributions, i.e. without finding the corresponding classifier. It is important to note, however, that the threshold in Fisher's classifier, and in general, for any classifier, can be obtained in other ways too (see [10]). Also, using the algebraic analysis of the probability of error discussed in the previous subsection, bounds and approximations for the error for Fisher's classifier can be found (see [9]).

4   Empirical Analysis

To test the accuracy and computational efficiency of the error analysis discussed in this paper, we performed a few simulations on synthetic data, which involve two normally distributed classes and a linear classifier. The two classes, ω_1 and ω_2, are then fully specified by their parameters, $\boldsymbol{\mu}_1, \boldsymbol{\mu}_2, \boldsymbol{\Sigma}_1$ and $\boldsymbol{\Sigma}_2$. We assume that the *a priori* probabilities for the two classes are equal, i.e. $P(\omega_1) = P(\omega_2) = 0.5$.

One of the tests involves the analysis of the *actual* classification error, as well as the bounds and the approximation introduced in this paper. To conduct the test, we generated random parameters for d-dimensional classes, where $d = 20, 40, \ldots, 200$. The linear classifier used to test our method is the traditional Fisher's classifier, where the threshold is obtained as in (13). The mean vectors for the two classes were generated randomly from a uniform distribution specified by the intervals $[0, 0.2]$ for $\boldsymbol{\mu}_1$, and $[0.2, 0.4]$ for $\boldsymbol{\mu}_2$. The covariance matrices were generated by invoking the *random correlation* method for generating *positive semidefinite* matrices [2]. The empirical results

Table 1. Comparison of the actual value, bounds and approximation for the error.

Dim.	a_1	a_2	Pr[error]	Lower bnd.	Upper bnd.	Approx.	Difference
20	-0.42678	-0.48947	0.32351	0.28622	0.36949	0.32785	0.00434
40	-0.81392	-0.78878	0.21148	0.19581	0.23851	0.21716	0.00567
60	-1.07009	-0.88201	0.16559	0.15554	0.18523	0.17039	0.00480
80	-1.14236	-1.04401	0.13745	0.13039	0.15274	0.14157	0.00412
100	-1.39993	-1.48340	0.07488	0.07240	0.08175	0.07707	0.00220
120	-1.97384	-1.89796	0.02653	0.02604	0.02836	0.02720	0.00068
140	-2.12477	-2.02669	0.01908	0.01878	0.02030	0.01954	0.00046
160	-2.34827	-2.17967	0.01204	0.01188	0.01274	0.01231	0.00027
180	-3.04408	-2.50596	0.00364	0.00360	0.00381	0.00371	0.00007
200	-3.46395	-2.99247	0.00083	0.00082	0.00086	0.00084	0.00001

obtained from our simulations are shown in Table 1. The second and third columns contain the boundaries for the two integrals, computed as in (4) and (5) respectively. The fourth column corresponds to the probability of error for Fisher's classifier, obtained as in (3), where the integrals were computed numerically by invoking the near-minimax Chebyschev approximations for the error function [1]. The fifth and sixth columns contain the lower and upper bounds for the classification error, which were computed as in (7). The seventh column represents the approximation of the classification error, obtained as in (8), and the last column corresponds to the difference (in absolute value) between the *actual* probability of error, the fourth column, and the *approximation* of the error, the seventh column. The results from the table show that the lower and upper bounds for the error are quite *loose* for large values of the classification error. Conversely, they are very *tight* for small values of the classification error. This is observed in the last row for dimension 200, in which the bounds are found to be very close to each other. A similar behavior is observed when analyzing the difference between the actual error and the approximation. The approximation differs from the actual error in nearly 10^{-5} for dimensions 180 and 200. Observe also, that in all cases, even in the case of dimension 20 in which the error is large, the approximation of the error differs from the actual value in less than $\varepsilon = 0.0184340683$, and hence achieving at least *two digits* of precision.

To experimentally analyze the computational efficiency for computing the classification error, we conducted simulations on test suites involving dimensions $d = 50, 100, \ldots, 500$. The results obtained are depicted in Table 2. The second and third columns contain the average for the probability of error, and the average of the difference between the actual value and the approximation. The fourth column contains the CPU time (in seconds) for computing the actual probability of error, the bounds, and the approximation for each of the experiments. The methods were tested using Matlab in an Intel 2.0Ghz workstation running Windows XP.

The results in the table show that our computational method is extremely fast for dimension 50, performing the computations in less than *a tenth* of a second. As the dimension of the feature space increases, the running times also increase. We also observe that the average differences between the actual error and the approximation are very small, e.g. below $\varepsilon = 0.0184340683$.

Table 2. Results for the running times and probabilities of error for different simulations on normally distributed classes whose dimensions range from 20 to 200.

Dim.	Avg. error	Avg. Diff.	Time
50	0.195821	0.005383	0.052680
100	0.114588	0.003450	0.157020
150	0.068887	0.002006	0.622500
200	0.044076	0.001213	1.411930
250	0.027769	0.000714	2.664730
300	0.017695	0.000424	5.195770
350	0.012043	0.000271	8.302140
400	0.008192	0.000174	13.113550
450	0.005368	0.000108	18.286700
500	0.003665	0.000070	26.335270

5   Conclusions

In this paper, we derive lower and upper bounds, and an expression that approximates the probability of error, which are obtained from the parameters of the distributions. The result can be used for *any* linear classifier, even though the underlying distributions are not normal. We have shown that the approximations differ from the *actual* error in at most $\varepsilon = 0.0184340683$.

Our empirical results on synthetic, *higher*-dimensional data, show that the bounds are very tight for small values of the classification error. Also, the approximation has been empirically shown to be very precise in the estimation of the error, which is approximated by a factor of at most $\varepsilon = 0.0184340683$. It has been shown to work efficiently for spaces involving up to *five hundred* features.

Many directions for future work exist, including the generalization of this model for more than two classes, the generalization of the model for piecewise linear classifiers that deals with more than one hyperplane. The latter is a difficult problem, since the linear transformations have to be applied simultaneously for all hyperplanes, leading a yet multivariate integration problem. Another problem that we are investigating is that of comparing the classification error for linear classifiers that use different thresholding methods.

Acknowledgments

The author's research is partially supported by NSERC, the Natural Sciences and Engineering Council of Canada.

References

1. W. Cody. A Portable FORTRAN Package of Special Function Routines and Test Drivers. *ACM Transactions on Mathematical Software*, 19:22–32, 1993.
2. P. Davies and N. Higham. Numerically Stable Generation of Correlation Matrices and their Factors. Technical Report 354, Manchester, England, 1999.
3. R. Duda, P. Hart, and D. Stork. *Pattern Classification*. John Wiley and Sons, Inc., New York, NY, 2nd edition, 2000.
4. K. Fukunaga. *Introduction to Statistical Pattern Recognition*. Academic Press, 1990.
5. R. Herbrich and T. Graepel. A PAC-Bayesian Margin Bound for Linear Classifiers. *IEEE Transactions on Information Theory*, 48(12):3140–3150, 2002.
6. M. Kendall and A. Stuart. *Kendall's Advanced Theory of Statistics, Volume I: Distribution Theory*. Edward Arnold, sixth edition, 1998.
7. C. Lee and E. Choi. Bayes Error Evaluation of the Gaussian ML Classifier. *IEEE Transactions on Geoscience and Remote Sensing*, 38(3):1471–1475, May 2000.
8. S. Raudys and R. Duin. Expected Classification Error of the Fisher Linear Classifier with Pseudo-inverse Covariance Matrix. *Pattern Recognition Letters*, 19:385–392, 1999.
9. L. Rueda. A One-dimensional Analysis for the Probability of Error of Linear Classifiers for Normally Distributed Classes. *Submitted for Publication*, 2004. Electronically available at http://davinci.newcs.uwindsor.ca/~lrueda/papers/ErrorEstJnl.pdf.
10. L. Rueda. An Efficient Approach to Compute the Threshold for Multi-dimensional Linear Classifiers. *Pattern Recognition*, 37(4):811–826, April 2004.
11. N. Vaswani. A Linear Classifier for Gaussian Class Conditional Distributions with Unequal Covariance Matrices. In *Proceedings of the 16th International Conference on Pattern Recognition*, volume 2, pages 60–63, Quebec, Canada, 2002.
12. A. Webb. *Statistical Pattern Recognition*. John Wiley & Sons, N. York, second edition, 2002.
13. Y. Xu, Y. Yang, and Z. Jin. A Novel Method for Fisher Discriminant Analysis. *Pattern Recognition*, 37(2):381–384, February 2004.

A Graphical Model
for Human Activity Recognition

Rocío Díaz de León[1] and Luis Enrique Sucar[2]

[1] IPICyT, Camino a la Presa San Jose 2025
San Luis Potosí, S.L.P. 78216, México
rdiaz@ipicyt.edu.mx
[2] ITESM Cuernavaca, Reforma 182-A, Colonia Palmira
Cuernavaca, Morelos 62589, México
esucar@itesm.mx

Abstract. We propose a general model for visual recognition of human activities, based on a probabilistic graphical framework. The motion of each limb and the coordination between them is considered in a layered network that can represent and recognize a wide range of human activities. By using this model and a sliding window, we can recognize simultaneous activities in a continuous way. We explore two inference methods for obtaining the most probable set of activities per window: probability propagation and abduction. In contrast with the standard approach that uses several models, we use a single classifier for multiple activity recognition. We evaluated the model with real image sequences of 6 different activities performed continuously by different people. The experiments show high recall and recognition rates.

1 Introduction

The recognition of human activities from video sequences is an important problem with many applications, such as surveillance, human–computer interaction, sports training, and rehabilitation. Recently there has been an increasing amount of work in this area, but there are still several outstanding issues to be solved: (i) continuous recognition, (ii) simultaneous activities, (iii) occlusions, (iv) scale and view variations. Existing models are targeted for certain types of activities or specific applications, so there is no general, high–level model for activity representation and recognition. The main hypothesis of this work is that most human activities can be recognized based on the motion of the limbs, and the relations between them.

We propose a general model to represent and recognize human activities, based on a layered, probabilistic graphical network, that considers the motion of the limbs' and their dependencies. The top layer represents the different activities, and the bottom layer the motion of each limb. The intermediate layer considers a classification of the limbs' motions, so these can be interpreted as different modalities for an activity. The structure of the model reflects the dependencies of each activity on the limbs' motions, and their coordination. The

A. Sanfeliu et al. (Eds.): CIARP 2004, LNCS 3287, pp. 350–357, 2004.

model includes several outstanding aspects: (i) representation of different activities using one model, (ii) recognition of simultaneous activities, (iii) recognition of activities performed on a continuous way. Using this model we can represent and recognize a wide range of human activities.

A Bayesian network based on the general model was implemented and tested with real image sequences of different activities: (i) activities performed with all limbs (arms and legs) at the same time like *aerobics*; (ii) activities performed with just one limb (right arm) like *goodbye* and *right*; and (iii) activities performed with two limbs at the same time like *attracting the attention* (both arms), and *jump and walk* (both legs). In some test sequences several activities were performed at the same time, for example, *jump* and *attracting the attention*. Recognition was performed using two alternative inference methods: likelihood weighting and total abduction. The model was tested with video sequences of different people, with a high recall-precision for both inference schemes.

2 Related Work

Several computational models for human activity recognition have been proposed, including neural networks [3], hidden Markov models [10], Bayesian networks [2], scale-space curve analysis [9], spatio-temporal models [8, 12] and exemplars based on principal components [11].

Vogler and Metaxas [10] use parallel hidden Markov models to recognize American sign language. They consider signs that are performed with one or both hands. They assume that the motion of each limb evolves independently, while we consider activities that require coordination. [2] use DBNs for hand gesture recognition. With dynamic models, such as HMMs and DBNs, it is difficult to perform temporal segmentation for continuous recognition.

[9] present a view invariant representation using the spatio-temporal curvature of the trajectory of the hand. This model is restricted to activities performed with one limb. [8] describes a system that uses periodicity measures of the image sequences for recognizing periodic activities; it requires at least 4 repetitions for recognition. A model based on parameterized exemplars was developed by [11], and recognition involves matching the observation against the exemplars using principal component analysis. The previous models assume a previous segmentation of the activities, so they can not recognize continuous activities.

There are very few systems that can recognize activities performed in a continuous way. [1] describes a model to represent and recognize continuous activities. Their model represents 7 activities performed with the legs and the torso. They use a nearest neighbor classifier obtaining an average recognition rate of 77%. They comment that tracking the trajectory of other parts of the body along with the leg components could make the system more robust, and this would help in recognizing more complex actions taken from different views. [12] constructs an event based representation of a video sequence using spatio-temporal templates at different scales, and use a sliding temporal window for continuous recognition. However, this approach recognizes activities based on the global motion, so it can not differentiate *similar* or simultaneous activities.

3   Recognition Process

Our recognition process involves the following stages:

VIDEO → partition → feature extraction → recognition → ACTIVITIES

The video sequence is partitioned in a series of overlapping windows, with N frames per window, and an overlap of $N - 3$ frames. For each consecutive image pair in a window, we obtain the motion parameters of each limb (arms and legs), which are transformed into a discretized representation which we call *displacement directions*. The displacement directions are reduced to consider only a fixed number of *different* displacement directions in a window, and these constitute the feature set per limb, in each window, that is fed to the recognition network. Based on these features, the recognition process determines the most probable activities in each window via probability propagation.

3.1   Feature Extraction

The first step in the recognition process is to obtain the motion features of the different parts of the body. Although there could be global motion of the person or other parts of the body, we consider that the motions of the limbs are the most relevant features for human activities. The global trajectory of a limb is its position sequence (X, Y, Z) when the activity is performed. Given that our current focus is on the high-level recognition model, we simplify the feature extraction process by using color landmarks on the wrists and the ankles. We apply a color detection process to get each landmark based on a Bayesian classifier [4]. We segment the landmarks using 8-connectivity and we extract their center of mass (we initially consider only X, Y) to get the wrist and the ankle positions in each frame; these are tracked in the image sequence.

Working with the absolute X, Y positions of the landmarks' centroids is very susceptible to the distance between the person and the camera, and her way of performing the activity. The angular velocity of each limb is a more robust feature for recognition. Therefore, we estimate the angular velocity by obtaining the displacement direction (dd), for each limb, between two consecutive frames as: $dd(i) = arctan((y2 - y1)/(x2 - x1))$; where $x1, y1$ are centroid coordinates for limb(i) in frame t, and $x2, y2$ for limb(i) in frame $t + 1$. The displacement directions are discretized in eight 45 degree intervals (8 values). When there is no movement between frames we assign a value of zero. Although we are currently using markers, the estimate of the angular motion of each limb can be obtained using low–level vision techniques, for instance motion [11] or color [9].

The problem is how to determine how many frames are required to represent an activity. For this we consider that most human activities are periodic, such as walking, running, waving the hand, etc. So an activity can be characterized by a basic *pattern* that is repeated. In many activities, this basic pattern has a relative short duration, usually less than a second. Thus, we use a one second window, with 15 images per window (frame rate is 15 images per second). In principle, we can have 15 displacement directions in a window. However, we notice that many times the *dd* is the same for several consecutive frames. So instead of using all the *dd* in a window, we only use the *different displacement directions* (ddd). Based on statistics from different activities performed by different people, we obtained that in a sequence of 15 frames, 5 different displacement directions are enough to represent the basic pattern of an activity. So we look for at most 5 different displacement directions per window. If more than 5 different directions are detected in the window, we only consider the first five; and if there are less than 5, the rest are set to zero. These features are used in the recognition network. The observation window is continuously taken from the image sequence by displacing the window 3 frames each step, until the complete sequence is scanned. Key frames from a video are shown in figure 1.

Fig. 1. Part of the image sequence for two simultaneous activities, *jump* and *attract the attention*. Top row: original images. Middle row: landmarks. Bottom row: frame number. There are 5 landmarks, we only use 4 (ankles and wrists) for the experiments.

4   Recognition Model

Our recognition model is based on the assumption that many human activities can be recognized by the motion of the limbs. It considers that several activities can be executed simultaneously. It also takes into account the inherent uncertainty in the model due to variations in activity execution and to the feature extraction process.

We propose a model to represent human activities based on a Bayesian network classifier. The model represents each activity and each limb as a variable. Each activity variable is related to the limbs' variables that are relevant for this activity. Each limb variable is related to the motion features (ddd) for that limb, and to other limbs, taking into account the dependencies between limbs' motions. The Bayesian network model (fig. 2) includes 3 layers:

- Top layer (root nodes): a binary node for each activity, A_i
- Middle layer: a multivalued node for each limb, L_i
- Bottom layer (leaf nodes): motion information for each limb (m node, one for each *ddd* in a window), D_i.

The model considers that each activity is recognized by combining the motion features of the limbs. Depending on the activity, different limbs are considered.

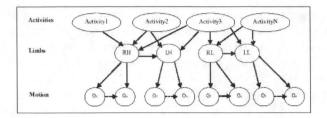

Fig. 2. General recognition model. The top layer nodes correspond to activities, A_i, the middle to limbs, L_i, and the bottom to observations. The observations, $O_{1:n}$, per limb, are the *ddd*, D_i, obtained in the feature extraction process.

The nodes in the middle level give information about the type of movement of each limb. The coordination between limb motions is considered in this case by the link between hand nodes (LH-RH) and the leg nodes (LL-RL). However, it is possible to consider also the dependencies between hands and legs. The leaf nodes are linked in a dynamic chain, so that each *ddd* depends on the previous one (except the first one in the window). Thus, the network can be used to complete the trajectory in case there is missing information (occlusion), providing the most probable trajectory.

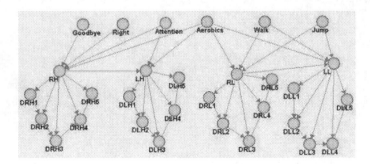

Fig. 3. Recognition network used in the experiments.

The BN in figure 3 represents a particular case of the general model which was used in the experiments. This network considers 6 activities: *goodbye, move right, attracting the attention, walk, jump and aerobics*; and 5 direction changes per window. The intermediate or limb nodes (RH,LH,RL,LL) are used to represent the type of motion performed by each limb. Each limb node has several possible values, associated to different activities, so we can have different descriptions for each activity. In our test network, the activity *walk*, has two subtypes, *walk in front of, walk in profile*, that are expressed by the intermediate nodes; so these can also be recognized.

4.1   Learning

Learning a Bayesian network can be divided into structure learning and parameter learning. The structure of the BN is derived from the general model for the particular set of activities to be recognized, by:

1. Adding a link from each activity node, to the the limb nodes that are *relevant*.
2. Adding links between the limb nodes which require coordination.
3. Adding a link from each limb node to the corresponding motion nodes (ddd).
4. Adding a link from each motion node to the next (in time).

Given the structure, the parameters can be estimated from training data. We consider a supervised learning scheme in which the parameters are obtained from a set of video sequences for each activity. There are 3 set of parameters: (i) prior probabilities for each activity, $P(A_i)$; (ii) probability of a limb node given the related activities and limbs, $P(L_i \mid A_{1:n_i}, L_{1:m_i})$; and (iii) probability of each motion node given the corresponding limb and previous motion node, $P(D_i \mid L_j, D_{i-1})$. Where: $A_{1:n_i}$, is set of n_i activities that influence a limb variable; $L_{1:m_i}$, is the set of m_i limb nodes that influence a limb node. Parameter learning was done using a MAP estimator with uniform Dirichlet priors.

4.2   Recognition

Recognition consists in obtaining the most probable activities given the motion data. We consider two alternative schemes. In the first scheme we obtain the posterior probability of each activity given the motion information: $P(A_i \mid D_{1:k,1:m})$, where $D_{1:k,1:m}$ represents the set of m motion variables for each of the k limbs. These probabilities are obtained via probability propagation in the BN. The activities whose posterior probability is above certain threshold, T, are the recognized set, R:

$$R = \{A_i\}, \leftrightarrow P(A_i \mid D_{1:k,1:m}) > T \qquad (1)$$

By changing this threshold, we can make a trade off between recall (fraction of labeled activities) vs. precision (fraction of windows that are labeled correctly). For the second scheme, we obtain the *most probable explanation* (MPE) set given the evidence. This corresponds to total abduction in BNs, the configuration(s) of maximum probability containing all the unobserved variables. That is:

$$MPE = argmax_{\mathbf{A},\mathbf{L}} P(\mathbf{A}, \mathbf{L} \mid D_{1:k,1:m}) \qquad (2)$$

where $\mathbf{A}, \mathbf{L}$ denotes the set of activity and limb nodes in the network. So in this way we obtain the set of activities which have a higher probability given the data. Thus, the recognized set, R, consists of all the activities that have value "yes" in the MPE set:

$$R = \{A_i\}, \leftrightarrow A_i = yes \in MPE \qquad (3)$$

The inference mechanism is applied to each window in the sequence, obtaining R. For the experiments, we used a stochastic simulation algorithm [5] for probability propagation, and Nilsson's algorithm [7] for total abduction.

5   Experimental Results

To test the proposed methodology for activity recognition, we considered the 6 types of activities previously described, using the recognition network shown in figure 3. We used videos with a black background and with people wearing color landmarks. The camera is fixed and captures the persons facing the camera or in profile. We trained the network with 175 samples of 7 persons performing 6 types of activities. The test activities were selected to include different conditions. The sampling rate was 15 images per second, with 15 frames per window and an overlap of 12 frames. We tested both inference schemes for recognition, with a set of 50 different sequences. In the test set, 5 of the sequences consisted of two activities that were performed simultaneously. Recognition was performed continuously, so each sequence is part of a video in which a person can change activity at any time.

We used the precision–recall rates for quantitative evaluation. There is a trade off between recall and precision that depends on the recognition threshold. If we set the threshold to 0.6, the results are summarized in table 1 for both inference schemes. We notice a better recall using abduction, and similar precisions with both schemes. For the cases that were labeled incorrectly, only 2 (for both schemes) were labeled with a different activity, the other were partial matches (of two simultaneous activities, one was recognized).

We used the precision–recall framework to assess the performance with respect to the recognition threshold for probability propagation. We obtain a high recognition rate, above 93%, for a wide range of different tresholds (the recall varies from 0.4 to 1). In general, the model correctly recognizes the activities or it is indecisive; in very few cases it confuses the activities. The misclassified sequences occur mainly when there is a transition between different activities in the continuous sequence. Some of the unlabeled windows are between correctly labeled ones, so by taking into account the labels from neighbor windows, the problem could be reduced.

6   Conclusions and Future Work

We have developed a general model for human activity recognition. The motion of each limb and the coordination between them is considered in a layered Bayesian network that can represent and recognize a wide range of human activities. It can recognize continuous and simultaneous activities, as well as handle occlusions and missing data. We explore two inference methods: probability

Table 1. Precision–recall for probability propagation (PP) and total abduction (TA).

	No. of seqs.	Recall	Precision
Test set (PP)	50	84%	93%
Test set (TA)	50	94%	91.5%

propagation and abduction. The model was tested with video sequences of different people performing 6 activities. The recall-precision rate was evaluated with good results for both inference schemes. In the future, we plan to avoid the use of markers on the limbs. We will also take into account the information from previous windows, by building a dynamical model on top of the classifier.

References

1. Ali, A. and Aggarwal J. K., Segmentation and Recognition of Continuous Human Activity, Proceedings of the IEEE Workshop on Detection and Recognition of Events in Video (2001)
2. Aviles-Arriaga, H., Sucar, L.E. Dynamical Bayesian Networks for Visual Recognition of Dynamic Gestures, Journal of Intelligent and Fuzzy Systems, Vol. 12 (2002) 243–250.
3. Bohm, K., Broll, W., Sokolewicz, M. Dynamic Gesture Recognition Using Neural Networks; A Fundament for Advanced Interaction Construction, SPIE Conference on Electronic Imaging, Science and Technology, San Jose California, USA (1994)
4. Jones, M.J. and Rehg, J.M. Statistical Color Models with Application to Skin Detection, Computer Vision and Pattern Recognition (1999) 274–280
5. Kanazawa, J., Koller, D. and Russell, S. Stochastic Simulation Algorithms for Dynamic Probabilistic Networks, Proceedings of the 11th Annual Conference on Uncertainty in Artificial Intelligence (1995)
6. Kjaerulff, U. A Computational Scheme for Dynamic Bayesian Networks, Department of Mathematics and Computer Science, Institute for Electronic Systems, Aalborg University. Denmark (1993)
7. Nilsson, D. An Efficient Algorithm for Finding the M Most Probable Configurations in Bayesian Networks. Statistics and Computing, Vol. 9 (1998) 159–173.
8. Polana, R., Nelson, R. Detection and Recognition of Periodic, Nonrigid Motion. International Journal of Computer Vision, Vol. 23 (1997) 261–282.
9. Rao, C., Shah, M. View-Invariance in Action Recognition. IEEE Computer Vision and Pattern Recognition (2001) 316–321.
10. Vogler, C. and Metaxas, D. Parallel Hidden Markov Models for American Sign Language Recognition. Proceedings of the International Conference on Computer Vision (1999)
11. Yaacoob, Y., Black, M.J. Parameterized Modeling and Recognition of Activities. Computer Vision and Image Understanding, Vol. 73 (1999) 232–247.
12. Zelnik-Manor, L. Irani, M. Event-Based Analysis of Video. IEEE Computer Vision and Pattern Recognition (2001)

A Fuzzy Relational Neural Network
for Pattern Classification

Israel Suaste-Rivas[1], Orion F. Reyes-Galaviz[2],
Alejandro Diaz-Mendez[1], and Carlos A. Reyes-Garcia[1]

[1] Instituto Nacional de Astrofisica Optica y Electronica (INAOE), Mexico
isuaste@susu.inaoep.mx, ajdiaz@inaoep.mx, kargaxxi@inaoep.mx
[2] Instituto Tecnologico de Apizaco, Mexico
orionfrg@yahoo.com

Abstract. In this paper we describe the implementation of a fuzzy relational neural network model. In the model, the input features are represented by fuzzy membership, the weights are described in terms of fuzzy relations. The output values are obtained with the max-min composition, and are given in terms of fuzzy class membership values. The learning algorithm is a modified version of back-propagation. The system is tested on an infant cry classification problem, in which the objective is to identify pathologies in recently born babies.

1 Introduction

In this paper we describe the implementation of a general pattern classifier based on a neural network architecture which uses fuzzy sets for both input/output data and the structure of the classifier itself. The general system architecture was inspired by the work presented by Pal in [1, 2]. The idea of using a relational neural network was taken from the general classifier presented by Pedrycz in [3]. The implemented system has been tested on an infant cry recognition problem. The pathological diseases in infants are commonly detected several months, and often times, years, after the infant is born. If any of these diseases would have been detected earlier, they could have been attended and maybe avoided by the opportune application of treatments and therapies. It has been found that the infant's cry has much information on its sound wave. Based on the information contained inside the cry's wave, it can be determined the infant's physical state; and even detect physical pathologies in very early phases [4].

2 The Infant Cry Recognition Process

The Automatic Infant Cry Recognition (AICR) process is similar to Automatic Speech Recognition (ASR). In AICR the goal is to take the crying wave as the input pattern, and at the end to obtain the class of cry the vector corresponds to. Generally, the whole process can be divided into two phases. The first phase is known as *signal processing* or *acoustic feature extraction* and the second is known as *pattern classification*.

A. Sanfeliu et al. (Eds.): CIARP 2004, LNCS 3287, pp. 358–365, 2004.

2.1   Signal Processing

The analysis of the raw cry waveform provides the information needed for its recognition. Acoustic feature extraction is a transformation of measured data into pattern data. The features may be spectral coefficients, linear prediction coefficients (LPC), or Mel frequency cepstral coefficients (MFCC) among others [5]. The set of values for n features may be represented by a vector in an n-dimensional space. Each vector represents a pattern.

2.2   Pattern Classification

During the second phase of the infant cry recognition process, the goal is usually to determine the class or category of each pattern. In this work we classify the patterns by means of a hybrid connectionist model.

3   The Fuzzy Neural Network Model

The system proposed in this work is based upon fuzzy set operations in both the structure of the neural network and in the learning process. Following Pal's idea of a general recognizer [2], the model is divided in two main parts, one for learning and another for processing, as shown in figure 1.

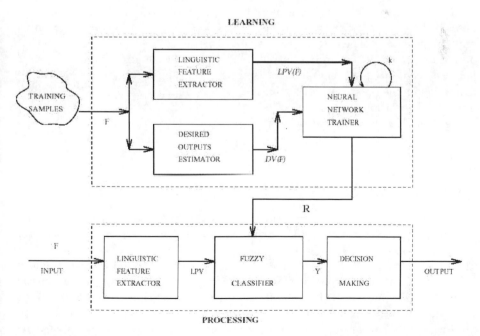

Fig. 1. General Automatic Infant Cry Recognition System

3.1   Fuzzy Learning

The fuzzy learning section is composed by three modules, namely the Linguistic Feature Extractor (LFE), the Desired Output Estimator (DOE), and the Neural Network Trainer (NNT). The Linguistic Feature Extractor takes training samples in the form of n-dimensional vectors containing n features, and converts them to a Nn-dimensional form vectors, where N is the number of linguistic properties. In case the linguistic properties are *low, medium,* and *high,* the resulting $3n$-dimensional vector is called Linguistic Properties Vector (LPV). In this way an input pattern $\mathbf{F}_i = [F_{i1}, F_{i2}, ..., F_{in}]$ containing n features, may be represented as [2]:

$$\mathbf{F}_i = [\mu_{low(F_{i1})}(\mathbf{F}_i), \mu_{med(F_{i1})}(\mathbf{F}_i), \tag{1}$$
$$\mu_{high(Fi1)}(\mathbf{F}_i), \ldots, \mu_{high(F_{in})}(\mathbf{F}_i)]$$

The DOE takes each vector from the training samples and calculates its membership to class k, in an l-class problem domain. The vector containing the class membership values is called the Desired Vector (DV). Both LPV and DV vectors are used by the neural Network Trainer (NNT), which takes them as the bases for training the network.

The neural network consists of only two layers. The input layer is formed by a set of Nn neurons, with each of them corresponding to one of the linguistic properties assigned to the n input features. In the output layer there are l neurons, where each node corresponds to one of the l classes; in this implementation, each class represents one type of crying. There is a link from every node in the input layer to every node in the output layer. All the connections are described by means of fuzzy relations $R : X \times Y \longrightarrow [0, 1]$ between the input and output nodes. The error is represented by the distance between the actual ouput and the target or desired output. During each learning step, once the error has been computed, the trainer adjusts the relationship values or weights of the corresponding connections, either until a minimum error is obtained or a given number of iterations is completed. The output of the NNT, after the learning process, is a fuzzy relational matrix (R in Figure 1) containing the knowledge needed to further map the unknown input vectors to their corresponding class during the classification process.

3.2   Fuzzy Processing

The fuzzy processing section is formed by three different modules, namely the Linguistic Feature Extractor (LFE), the Fuzzy Classifier (FC), and the Decision Making Module (DMM). The LFE works in exactly the same way as the one in the learning phase. It is used to calculate the corresponding membership value of each input feature in the classifying vector to each of the linguistic properties. The output of this module is an LPV vector. The LPV vector, along with the fuzzy relational matrix R, are used by the Fuzzy Classifier, which obtains the actual outputs from the neural network. The classifier applies the max-min composition to calculate the output. The ouput of this module is an output vector containing the membership values of the input vector to each of the classes. Finally, the Decision Making module takes the values coming from the classifier, and after applying some decision criteria assigns the corresponding class to the testing vector. The assigned class, in this implementation, represents one kind of infant cry.

3.3   Membership Functions

A fuzzy set is defined by a function that maps objects in a domain to their membership value in the set. Such a function is called the *membership function*. In many cases it is recomended to use standard functions whose parameters may be adjusted to fit a specified membership function in an approximate fashion. In the reported experiment the triangular membership function was used. There is some evidence that shows that the use of more linguistic properties to describe a pattern point makes a model more accurate [6]. One possibility is the use of seven linguistic properties: *very low, low, more or less low, medium, more or less high, high, very high.*

3.4   Desired Membership Values

Before defining the output membership function, we define the equation to calculate the weighted distance of the training pattern $\mathbf{F}_j$ to the kth class in an l-class problem domain as in [1]

$$z_{ik} = \sqrt{\sum_{j=1}^{n} \left[\frac{F_{ij} - o_{kj}}{v_{kj}} \right]^2} ,: for\ k = 1, \ldots, l \qquad (2)$$

where F_{ij} is the jth feature of the ith pattern vector, o_{kj} denotes the mean, and v_{kj} denotes the standard deviation of the jth feature for the kth class. The membership value of the ith pattern to class k is defined as follows

$$\mu_k(\mathbf{F}_i) = \frac{1}{1 + (\frac{z_{ik}}{f_d})f_e} ,: \mu_k(\mathbf{F}_i) \in [0, 1] \qquad (3)$$

where f_e is the exponential fuzzy generator, and f_d is the denominational fuzzy generator controlling the amount of fuzzines in this class-membership set. In this case, the higher the distance of the pattern from a class, the lower its membership to that class. Since the training data have fuzzy class boundaries, a pattern point may belong to one or more classes in the input feature space.

3.5   The Neural Network Trainer

The neural network model discussed here is based on the fuzzy neural structure proposed by Pedrycz in [3].

The Relational Neural Network. Let $\mathbf{X} = \{x_1, x_2, \ldots, x_n\}$ be a finite set of input nodes and let $\mathbf{Y} = \{y_1, y_2, \ldots, y_l\}$ represent the set of output nodes in an l-class problem domain. When the max-min composition operator denoted $X \circ R$ is applied to a fuzzy set X and a fuzzy relation R, the output is a new fuzzy set Y, we have

$$Y = X \circ R \tag{4}$$

$$Y(y_j) = max_{x_i}(min(X(x_i), R(x_i, y_j)))$$

where X is a fuzzy set, Y is the resulting fuzzy set and R is a fuzzy relation $R : X \times Y \longrightarrow [0, 1]$ describing all relationships between input and output nodes.

We will take the whole neural network represented by expression (4) as a collection of l separate n-input single-output cells.

Learning in a Fuzzy Neural Network. If the actual response from the network does not matches the target pattern, the network is corrected by modifying the link weights to reduce the difference between the observed and target patterns. For the relational neural network Pedrycz [3] defines a performance index called equality index, which is

$$T(y) \equiv Y(y) = \begin{cases} 1 + T(y) - Y(y), & \text{if } Y(y) > T(y) \\ 1 + Y(y) - T(y), & \text{if } Y(y) < T(y) \\ 1, & \text{if } Y(y) = T(y) \end{cases} \tag{5}$$

where $T(y)$ is the target output at node y, and $Y(y)$ is the actual output at the same node. $\overline{T}$ is the complement of T defined by $\overline{T}(y) = 1 - T(y)$. In a problem with n input patterns, there are n input-output pairs (x_{ij}, t_i) where t_i is the target value when the input is $\mathbf{X}_{ij}$.

Parameters Updating. In [3] Pedricz discusses the learning scheme for the structure of a neural network with n-inputs and single output, and proposes to complete the process of learning separately for each output node. The updating procedure is made independent of the size of the training set. The learning algorithm is a version of the gradient-descent-based backpropagation algorithm.

Lets consider an n-input-L-output neural network having the following form

$$y_i = f(\mathbf{x}_i; \mathbf{a}, \upsilon) = (\bigvee_{j=1}^{n} (a_j \wedge x_{ij}))$$

where $\mathbf{a} = [a_1, a_2, \ldots, a_L]$ is a vector containing all the weights or relations, $\mathbf{x}_i = [x_{i1}, x_{i2}, \ldots, x_{in}]$ is the vector with values observed in the input nodes. The parameters a and υ are updated iteratively by taking increments $\triangle a_m$ and $\triangle \upsilon_m$ resulting from deviations between all pairs y_i and t_i as follows

$$a(k+1) = a(k) + \tag{6}$$
$$\Psi_1(k) \left[\frac{\triangle a(k+1)}{Nn} + \eta \frac{\triangle a(k)}{Nn} \right]$$

where k is the iteration or learning step. Ψ_1 and Ψ_2 are non-increasing functions of k controlling the decreasing influence of increments $\triangle a_m$ and $\triangle v_m$. Ψ is the learning momentum specifying the level of modification of the learning parameters with regard to their values in the previous learning step k. A way of determining the increments $\triangle a_m$ and $\triangle v_m$ is with regard to the mth coordinates of a, $m = 1,2,...,L$. The computation of the overall performance index, and the derivatives to calculate the increments for each cordinate of a, and v are explained in detail in [7].

Once the training has been terminated, the output of the trainer is the updated relational matrix, which will contain the knowledge needed to map unknown patterns to their corresponding classes.

4   Implementation and Results

In the first place, the infant cries are collected by recordings obtained directly by medical doctors. Later, each signal wave is divided in segments of 1 second; each segment constitutes a sample. For the present experiments we have a corpus of 157 samples of normal infant cry, 879 of hypo acoustics, and 340 with asphyxia. At the following step the samples are processed extracting their MFCCs, by the use of the freeware program Praat 4.0 [8]. The acoustic characteristics are extracted as follows: every one second sample is windowed by 50-millisecond frames from which we extract 16 coefficients, generating vectors with 304 coefficients by sample. This vectors are further reduced, to a desired size, by the applicacion of PCA. The neural network and the training algorithm are implemented with Matlab. In order to make the training and recognition test, we select 157 samples randomly on each class. The number of normal cry samples available determines this number. From them, 107 samples of each class are randomly selected for training. The training is made up to 20 epochs. After the network is trained, we test it with the 50 samples of each class set apart from the original 157 samples. The recognition accuracy percentage, from each experiment, is presented in a confusion matrix. The best results at present have been obtained with the following parameters $\eta = 0.2$ and $k = 40$. The initial values for the relational matrix were set as 0.8. And the number of input features per vector, after the application of PCA, equal to 3. The feature space was divided in 7 linguistic terms, which makes the dimensionality of the input vector equal 21.

4.1   Preliminary Results

The results of the model when using the above mentioned set of values, triangular membership functions, and considering only the highest membership value of each input pattern in the output vector, are as given in the confusion matrix in Table 1

4.2   Performance Comparison with Other Models

Taco Ekkel [9] tried to classify sound of newborn cry in categories called normal and abnormal (hypoxia), and reports a result of correct classification of around

Table 1. Confusion Matrix.

Class	Samples	Normal	Deaf	Asphyxia	Accuracy
Normal	50	47	2	1	
Deaf	50	5	45		
Asphyxia	50	10		40	
Total	150				88 %

85% based on a neural network of radial base. In [10] Reyes and Orozco classify cry samples only from deaf and normal infants, obtaining recognition results that go from 79.05% up to 97.43%.

5   Further Work

One of the major proposed change is the automatic optimization of the required parameters, by the use of genetic algorithms. Another important addition is the use of the square relational product as in [11] besides the circlet product during the recognition phase to generate another criterion to help in the recognition decision.

6   Conclusions

Given the simplicity of the model implementation, the results obtained to date are very encouraging. Based on the observed results, we are convinced that by implementing the proposed changes the improved fuzzy relational neural network model can provide an effective, reliable and compact infant cry recognizer.

Acknowledgments

This work is part of a project that is being financed by CONACYT-Mexico (37914-A). We want to thank Dr. Edgar M. Garcia-Tamayo and Dr. Emilio Arch-Tirado for their invaluable collaboration when helping us to collect the crying samples, as well as for their wise advice.

References

1. Pal, S.K., "Multilayer Perceptron, Fuzzy Sets, and Classification," in *IEEE Trans. on Neural Networks*, vol 3, No 5, Sep 1992, pp 683-697.
2. Pal, S.K. and Mandal, D.P., "Linguistic Recognition Systems Based on Approximated Reasoning," in *Information Science*, vol 61, No 2, 1992, pp 135-161.
3. Pedrycz, W., "Neurocomputations in Relational Systems," in *IEEE Trans. on Pattern Analysis and Mach. Intelligence*, vol 13, No 3, Mar 91, pp 289-296.
4. O. Wasz-Hockert, J. Lind, V. Vuorenkoski, T. Partanen y E. Valanne, El Llanto en el Lactante y su Significación Diagnóstica, Cientifico-Medica, Barcelona, 1970.

5. Schafer, R.W., and Rabiner, L.R., "Digital Representations of Speech Signals," in *Readings in Speech Recognition*, Morgan Kauffmann Publishers Inc., San Mateo, Calif, 1990, pp 49–64.
6. Park, D., Cae, Z., and Kandel, A., "Investigations on the Applicability of Fuzzy Inference," in *Fuzzy Sets and Systems*, vol 49, 1992, pp 151-169.
7. Reyes, C.A., "On the Design of a Fuzzy Relational Neural Network for Automatic Speech Recognition", Doctoral Dissertation, The Florida State University , Tallahassee, Fl., Apr 94.
8. Boersma, P., Weenink, D. Praat v. 4.0.8. A system for doing phonetics by computer. In-stitute of Phonetic Sciences of the University of Amsterdam. February, 2002
9. Ekkel, T, *Neural Network-Based Classification of Cries from Infants Suffering from Hypoxia-Related CNS Damage*, Master Thesis. University of Twente, The Netherlands, 2002.
10. Orozco Garcia, J., Reyes Garcia, C.A. (2003), "Mel-Frequency Cepstrum Coeficients Extraction from Infant Cry for Classification of Normal and Pathological Cry with Feed-forward Neural Networks", in *proceedings of ESANN 2003*, Bruges, Belgium.
11. Bandler, W. and Kohout, L.J., "Fuzzy Relational Products as a tool for analysis and artificial systems," in P.P. Wang, and S.K. Chang, editors, *Fuzzy Sets: Theory and Applications to Policy Analysis and Information Systems*, Plenum Press, New York and London, 1980, pp 341-367.

Speaker Verification Using Coded Speech

Antonio Moreno-Daniel[1,2], Biing-Hwang Juang[1], and Juan A. Nolazco-Flores[2,*]

[1] Center for Signal and Image Processing, Georgia Institute of Technology,
Atlanta GA, USA
{antonio,juang}@ece.gatech.edu
[2] Departamento de Ciencias Computacionales, Instituto Tecnológico y de Estudios
Superiores de Monterrey, Monterrey NL, México
jnolazco@itesm.mx

Abstract. The implementation of a pseudo text-independent Speaker Verification system is described. This system was designed to use only information extracted directly from the coded parameters embedded in the ITU-T G.729 bitstream. Experiments were performed over the YOHO database [1]. The feature vector as a short-time representation of speech consists of 16 LPC-Cepstral coefficients, as well as residual information appended in the form of a pitch estimate and a measure of vocality of the speech. The robustness in verification accuracy is also studied. The results show that while speech coders, G.729 in particular, introduce coding distortions that lead to verification performance degradation, proper augmented use of unconventional information nevertheless leads to a competitive performance on par with that of a well-studied traditional system which does not involve signal coding and transmission. The result suggests that speaker verification over a cell phone connection remains feasible even though the signal has been encoded to 8 Kb/s.

1 Introduction

The objective of a Speaker Verification (SV) system is to correctly accept legitimate registered users and reject impostors, who falsely claim to be legitimate users, therefore protecting restricted information or privileges. The task of recognizing or verifying a person's identity has gained relevance and interest as the technology allows us to perform critical operations or receive services remotely, such as on-line or telephone banking, shopping, trading, etc. [2]. Among all biometrics, "voice" has the advantage [3] that it doesn't require any sophisticated apparatus; individuals can provide speech samples in a very natural way and most people are accustomed to speaking to a handset. Furthermore, the availability of cell phone services and Internet access (wired or wireless) makes this kind of operations simple and low-cost.

Speaker verification is a subject that has been rather well studied [2-3]. Many new advances have also been reported. For example, Ref. [4] proposed the use of general Gaussian mixture models which offer improved speech modeling resulting in better verification accuracy; Ref. [5] reported significant performance improvement using

* This work was supported by the ITESM Information Security Chair and CONACyT 2002-C01-41372

A. Sanfeliu et al. (Eds.): CIARP 2004, LNCS 3287, pp. 366–373, 2004.
© Springer-Verlag Berlin Heidelberg 2004

minimum verification error training; and Li et al. in [6] proposed the method of utterance verification embedded in a human-machine dialog which can be used for both automatic registration and speaker verification. In this work, we focus on the issue of speech coding and its impact on the performance of a speaker verification system due to the fact that nearly all telecommunication networks today are digital and thus speech signals that are being transmitted through the networks are all encoded into bit-streams at various bit rates. Since speech coding is in general of a lossy type, it thus will inevitably introduce distortion to the decoded signal. An assessment of the impact of signal distortion due to coding upon automatic speech recognition was provided by [7] for the purpose of evaluating the potential detriment that speech coding may bring upon voice-enabled services. Here we turn our attention to the application of speaker verification with a similar motivation. However, unlike the earlier report on speech recognition based on coded speech [8], our work here includes a novel use of additional information already existent in the output of the speech coder; our system thus can be considered a new design.

SV can be classified into a 'text-dependent' mode in which the SV system knows the transcription of the utterance pronounced by the claimant; or a 'text-independent' mode in which the transcription is unknown and the utterance may be arbitrary. In this work, a 'pseudo text-independent' SV system was built, where the system doesn't know the transcription of the input utterance, but it does know it is within a closed set (see Section 2.3).

This paper is organized as follows. First, background information is presented in Section 2, including details of interest about the encoder, the speaker verification database, and how they were used to build the SV system. Section 2.3 presents the basic configuration of the experiments, and Section 3 describes the proposed use of additional information which is derived from the encoded bit-stream; for brevity, we call the system a bit-stream level system. Finally, Section 4 presents a comparison of results obtained with our scheme against those with conventional SV systems.

2 Background

2.1 Database

Our evaluation uses the YOHO database [1], which consists of a series of lock-combination sentences pronounced in American English by 138 subjects (106 male and 32 female), having a wide range of ages, jobs and education, including at least 4 speakers with foreign mother tongue.

This database is originally divided into two main sets: the ENRollment set and the VERification set; furthermore, ENR has 4 sessions with 24 utterances each, and VER has 10 sessions with 4 utterances each; resulting in a total of 13,248 enrollment utterances and 5,520 verification utterances. Although the length of each wave file is around 3 to 4 seconds, only about 2.5 seconds is active speech, which yields to roughly 240 seconds of active speech for ENR per speaker.

2.2 ITU-T G.729

ITU-T G.729 [9] is a set of speech coding standards recommended for digital cellular phones, operating at the rate of 8 kb/s. The recommendation ITU-T G.729 describes a "toll quality" 8 kb/s Conjugate-Structure Algebraic-Code-Excited Linear-Prediction encoder (CS-ACELP), with a frame rate of 10ms at 80 bits/frame. The input speech waveform is sampled at 8 kHz with each sample represented in a 16-bit linear PCM (Pulse Code Modulation) format. A 10th order linear prediction analysis is performed on every frame of windowed speech generating parameters that characterize the signal production system. These parameters, sometimes referred to as short-term prediction or spectral envelope information, are transformed into Line Spectral Pairs (LSP) parameters for quantization. The residual or excitation information consists of two components: periodic and random. Table 1 illustrates how the 80 bits are allocated to the complete set of encoder parameters.

Table 1. Bit allocation for various parameters in G.729

Parameter		Codeword	Subframe 1	Subframe 2	Total per frame
Line Spectrum pairs		L0, L1, L2, L3	–	–	18
Periodic component	Pitch Delay index for Adaptive Codebook	P1, P2	8	5	13
	Pitch-Delay Parity	P0	1	–	1
	Gains (pitch) for Adaptive Codebook	Gp1, Gp2	3	3	6
Random component	Fixed Codebook Index	Ic1, Ic2	13	13	26
	Fixed Codebook Sign	S1	4	4	8
	Algebraic Codebook Gains	Ga1, Ga2	4	4	8
Total					80

As shown in the table, a total of 18 bits per frame are spent for the short-term predictor in the form of line spectral pair parameters, while 62 bits are used for the residual (20 for the periodic part and 42 for the random component).

The periodic part of the residual consists of pitch estimates **P**s, which provides an index pointer for a position in the adaptive codebook to facilitate "long-term" prediction spanning over a pitch period; and pitch gains **Gp**s, which is the corresponding scaling factor to produce the best match between the input speech and its delayed version as encapsulated in the adaptive codebook. Note that the gain is also a measure of correlation between the input and its delayed version; the magnitude of such a long-span correlation is nearly one for a periodic signal and nearly zero if the signal lacks periodicity. It can thus be considered a crude measure of vocality.

The random part consists of the algebraic codebook indices and signs (**Ic**s and **S**s) and the fixed (algebraic) codebook gain (**Ga**s). This component is related to the excitation function that cannot be properly represented with both the long and short-term predictors.

Figure 1 depicts how the decoded bit-stream is used in various components of the decoder/receiver for the reconstruction of speech waveform. Here we assume that the inner layer of information is available to the speaker verification system. We thus refer to such an SV system "the bit-stream level system" without ambiguity.

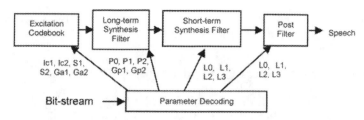

Fig. 1. Decoded parameters at the decoder for speech synthesis

Typical applications of G.729 speech coder include Voice over IP, satellite communications, and digital cellular phone service.

2.3 Experimental Setup

The application scenario considered consists of an individual requesting access to restricted information or privilege from a remote location (via a cellular phone or a Voice over IP connection) to a server, which has full access to the bit-stream transmitted (for example, an SV service provided by a cellular phone carrier, or an SV server connected to the Internet).

The SV system follows the Gaussian mixture universal background model (GMM-UBM) paradigm, also known as general or world background model [3]. There are 138 different models (one for each speaker) plus one speaker independent universal background model (UBM), a silence and a short pause. Although the transcriptions are unknown, it is known that the utterances have three words (lock combinations).

In order to build a UBM background model, the database was repartitioned into two sets: I and II, keeping half of the individuals on each set (53 male and 16 female per set). Each set has an ENR and VER subsets. Two separate runs of SV experiments were performed, where in one case, the entire set II was used to estimate (train) the background model, while in the other, only set I was used for registered users and verification attempts. By doing this, it is ensured that none of the individuals used to estimate the background model would be present during verification.

We use the tool kits of HTK [10] to train and test the models. Each individual's model and the UBM consist of Gaussian mixtures (single-state HMMs) with 40 mixture components, which attempt to model the different vocal tract configurations [4] as represented in the feature vectors.

We test the hypothesis {H_0: the claimant is indeed the registered user} against {H_1: the claimant is an impostor}, using the log likelihood ratio (LLR) computed as follows:

$$\textbf{Accept } H_0 \text{ if } \theta(\mathbf{O}) = \log \frac{P(\mathbf{O}|\lambda_c)}{P(\mathbf{O}|\lambda_{UBM})} \geq \tau \tag{1}$$

where λ_c is the claimed identity's model, λ_{UBM} is the universal background model, and $\mathbf{O}$ is the sequence of observed feature vectors. The decision whether to accept or reject the claimant depends on the threshold τ. For analysis purposes, results are presented using DET (Detection Error Tradeoff) plots, therefore leaving the choice of τ

open to suit a desired application. False-Alarm corresponds to False Acceptance (FA) and Miss corresponds to False Rejection (FR).

3   Bit-Stream Level Speaker Verification

As mentioned in Section 2.2, a quantized version of the spectral envelope information is available in the bit-stream from the 10 LSP parameters (Line Spectrum Pair frequencies). These parameters have a one-to-one correspondence to the LPC coefficients (Linear Prediction Coefficients), which can be further transformed to cepstral domain using the following recursion [11]:

$$c[n] = a_n + \sum_{k=1}^{n-1} \left(\frac{k}{n}\right) c[k] \, a_{n-k} \tag{2}$$

where we have used the convention of $1-A(z)$ for the inverse filter and $a_0=1$ and $a_n=0$ for $n>p$. It is clear that when p is known, $c[1] \ldots c[p]$ are sufficient to recover back the LPC coefficients. The effect of truncating the LPC-Cepstral coefficients (also called rec-cepstrum [12]), or multiplying the coefficients by a rectangular window, is a convolution of the log power spectrum with the Fourier transform of a rectangle window (i.e., a *sinc* function), causing smoothing of the power spectrum estimate from LPC coefficients, and reducing the sharpness of the formant peaks [13]. This smoothing effect is up to a point desirable, since sharp formant peaks are often artifact themselves.

Although spectral envelope conveys information that characterizes a person's identity, the residual carries another component (it is well known that it is still possible to guess the identity of the talker by simply listening to the LPC residual signal). Several techniques have been proposed to extract these characteristics from the residual, including LPC analysis over the residual [15] and appending the residual parameters [12] to the feature vector.

Our proposed feature vector appends residual information to the LPC-Cepstral coefficients, in the form of a fundamental frequency measure $(\log f_0)$ and a measure of vocality (mv_k) estimated by combining the pitch gain (**Gp**) and codebook gain (**Ga**) as follows:

$$\Gamma p_k = \text{median}\{Gp2_{k-2}, Gp1_{k-1}, Gp2_{k-1}, \\ Gp1_k, Gp2_k, Gp1_{k+1}, Gp2_{k+1}, Gp1_{k+2}\} \tag{3}$$

and similarly for Γa_k, to find:

$$mv_k = \ln(\frac{\Gamma p_k}{\Gamma a_k}) \tag{4}$$

where index k denotes the frame number, and Γs are results of a 40ms moving median, therefore removing spurious glitches.

The structure of our 54-dimensional feature vector is:

$$FV = \left[c_1, c_2, \ldots, c_{16}, \log(f_0), mv, [\Delta], [\Delta^2]\right]. \tag{5}$$

A baseline experimental setup 'A' consists of a conventional SV system applied to the original set of waveforms in YOHO. The SV system uses 12 MFCC (Mel-frequency cepstral coefficients) plus an energy term.

Additionally, Δ and Δ^2 are appended, resulting in a 39-dimensional feature vector.

Similarly, in order to illustrate the impact on SV performance using G.729 coded waveform, experimental setup 'B' applies the same scheme as in setup 'A' to a transcoded version of the database.

The performance of the proposed feature vector eq.(5) is tested in experimental setup 'C'.

For every experimental setup described above, robustness was tested in noisy conditions with SNR values of 20dB and 15dB. Noise level was adjusted using ITU-T P.56 recommendation software [14].

4   Experimental Results

As shown in Figure 2, a conventional SV system is capable of achieving an equal error rate (i.e., when %FA=%FR) of slightly more than 1.6% without obvious noise interference. When additive noise is present at 20dB SNR, the performance deteriorates to about 3.5% and to about 5% when SNR is 15dB.

When the speech signal undergoes G.729 coding and decoding, the SV system that takes the reconstructed waveform as input can only achieve roughly 2%, 4% and 5% equal error rate under clean, 20dB SNR and 15 dB SNR conditions, respectively, as shown in the second plot (Set B) of Figure 3. Note that the coder G.729 is generally considered toll quality at 8 kb/s. The result shows that while the distortion introduced by the coder may not be obvious to our perceptual apparatus, it is causing deterioration in the performance of a speaker verification system. The result is consistent with that of [7] and the recommendation is to avoid transcoding if possible.

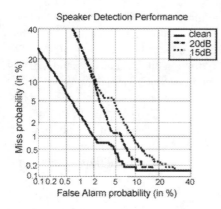

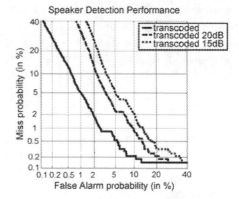

Fig. 2. Speaker Verification results from experimental setup A. Clean and noisy data with SNR values of 20 dB and 15 dB, using conventional MFCC features extracted from the waveform

Fig. 3. Speaker Verification results from experimental setup B. Transcoded waveforms and noise added before the codification for SNR values of 20 dB and 15 dB

When additional feature parameters are used as described in eq.(5), the performance is slightly better than experimental setup B, without having to synthesize the

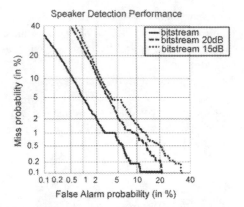

Fig. 4. Speaker Verification results from experimental setup C, using the proposed feature vector, extracted directly from the bit-stream (without synthesis)

quantized parameters into a waveform for preprocessing. Under a "clean" condition, use of the augmented feature vector is able to reduce the equal error rate to nearly 2%, as shown in Figure 4 (Set C). Even when noise is present, at 20dB and 15dB SNR, respectively, the equal error rates achieved by the new proposed system are approximately 4% and 4.8%. The augmented features show robustness comparable to MFCCs.

5   Conclusions and Future Work

Given the availability of mobile and telecommunication infrastructure that allows remote, ubiquitous access to critical service transactions, SV is an area that has gained attention recently. We have presented a bit-stream level SV system, that incorporates the residual in terms of an estimate of the log pitch frequency, and a measure of vocality, derived from G.729 pitch gains and codebook gains.

The experimental results show that this somewhat crude incorporation of the residual-derived (or excitation-derived) feature matches the performance of MFCCs extracted from transcoded speech; setting a baseline and leaving the opportunity to improve the performance by using the measure of vocality to distinguish the segments of speech that characterize the best the anatomic characteristics of the speakers.

References

1. Campbell, J.P., Jr.: Testing with the YOHO cd-rom voice verification corpus. Proc. ICASSP, (1995)
2. Furui A.: Recent Advances in Speaker Recognition. First Int. Conf. Audio- and Video-based Biometric Person Authentication. Switzerland, (1997) 237-252
3. Reynolds, D.A.: An Overview of Automatic Speaker Recognition Technology. Proc. ICASSP, (2002)
4. Reynolds, D.A., Rose R.: Robust Text-Independent Speaker Identification Using Gaussians Mixture Speaker Model. IEEE Transactions on Speech and Audio Processing, (1995)

5. Rosenberg, Aaron E., Siohan O., S. Parthasarathy: Speaker verification using minimum verification error training. Proc. ICASSP, (1998)
6. Li, Q., Juang, B.-H., Zhou, Q. and Lee, C.-H.: Automatic Verbal Information Verification for User Authentication. IEEE Transactions on Speech and Audio Processing, (2000) 585-596
7. Kim, H.K., and Cox, R.: Bitstream-based feature extraction for wireless speech recognition. Proc. ICASSP, (2000)
8. Zhong, X.: Speech coding and transmission for improved recognition in a communication network. PhD Dissertation, Georgia Institute of Technology, (2000)
9. ITU-T Recommendation G.729, Coding of speech at 8 kbit/s using conjugate-structure algebraic-code-excited linear-prediction (CS-ACELP), (1996)
10. Young S., et al.: The HTK Book, Cambridge University, Version 3.2 ed., (2002)
11. Huang X., Acero A., Hon H.W.: Spoken language processing, Prentice Hall, (2001)
12. Quatieri, T. F., et al: Speaker Recognition Using G.729 Speech Codec Parameters, Proc. ICASSP, (2000)
13. Rabiner L. and Juang B.H.: Fundamentals of Speech Recognition, Prentice Hall, (1993)
14. ITU-T Recommendation G.191, Software tool library 2000 user's manual, (2000)
15. Yu Eric W.M., Mak Man-Wai, Sit Chin-Hung and Kung Sun-Yuan: Speaker verification based on G.729 and G.723.1 coder parameters and handset mismatch compensation. Proc. of the 8th European Conference on Speech Communication and Technology, (2003)
16. Besacier L., Grassi S., Dufaux A., Ansorge M. and Pellandini F.: GSM Speech coding and Speaker Recognition. Proc. ICASSP, (2000)

A Radial Basis Function Network Oriented for Infant Cry Classification

Sergio D. Cano Ortiz[1], Daniel I. Escobedo Beceiro[1], and Taco Ekkel[2]

[1] Group of Voice Processing, Faculty of Electrical Engineering, University of Oriente,
Ave.Las Américas s/n, 90900 Santiago de Cuba, Cuba
{scano,daniele}@fie.uo.edu.cu
[2] Dept. of Computer Science, University of Twente, The Netherlands
taco@utwente.nl

Abstract. Several investigations around the world have been postulated that the infant cry can be utilized to asses the infant's status and the use of artificial neural networks (ANN) has been one of the recent alternatives to classify cry signals. A radial basis function (RBF) network is implemented for infant cry classification in order to find out relevant aspects concerned with the presence of CNS diseases. First, an intelligent searching algorithm combined with a fast non-linear classification procedure is implemented, establishing the cry parameters which better match the physiological status previously defined for the six control groups used as input data. Finally the optimal acoustic parameter set is chosen in order to implement a new non-linear classifier based on a radial basis function network, an ANN-based procedure which classifies the cry units into a 2 categories, normal-or abnormal case. All the experiments were based on the physioacoustic model for cry production and the Golub's muscle control model.

1 Introduction

Last research has reported the effectiveness of cry analysis for the study of infant's neurological status. Since this early work, there have been a number of advances that have broadened the potential application of cry analysis not only for cry generation area but also for cry perception. Some of them are: a better understanding of the mechanisms of cry production, getting factors that place the infant at risk for later handicap, such as prematurity, low birth weight, obstetrical complications [8], the cry as an evolutionary function of helping to ensure the survival of the infant [1], cry as a developmental function that make easy the development of social, perceptual, and cognitive skills [1,7], and so on. Recently the use of ANN has been one of the clue in the road mainly in the field of the Infant cry analysis oriented for diagnosis [4,9]. In this work, a RBF network is implemented and tested. Firstly the data acquisition and the structure of control groups are explained (see Section 2). Then the cry parameters which better matches the physiological status of the child are determined leading to the optimal acoustic parameter set (see Section 2). The RBF network performance and results are commented in Section 3. Finally, some concluding remarks and suggestions are also given in Section 4.

2 Materials and Methods

In this paper we address some general aspects concerned with the Golub's theory [6]. The Golub's hypothesis assumes that muscle control is accomplished within three

A. Sanfeliu et al. (Eds.): CIARP 2004, LNCS 3287, pp. 374–380, 2004.

levels of central nervous system processing as we see in Fig. 1. The *upper processor* is involved in choosing and modulating the state of action of the child and is probably where the more complex feedback from external and internal factors is collected and acted upon. Of course, during the neonatal period, this higher processor may be relatively unmature and precise control infrequent. As a result, at this stage of maturation, many activities occur in a reflexive manner. The *middle processor* encircles all vegetative states such as: swallowing, coughing, respiration, bowel movements, crying, etc. The stimuli that help the upper processor to choose the appropriate vegetative state include hunger, pain, hypoxemia, or hypercapnia, and a full bladder. The initiation of each of the previously mentioned vegetative states, in response to a stimulus, must result in the control of a large number of muscles.

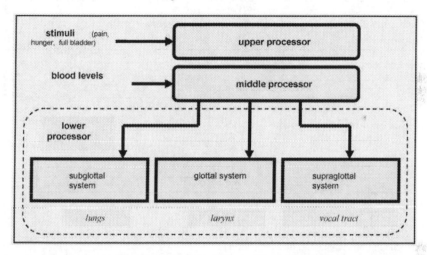

Fig. 1. The Golub's Muscle Control Model

Most likely, there exists some sort of "coordinative structure" that makes it unnecessary for higher processors to exert control of each individual muscle within a muscle group. For example, swallowing involves a well-defined control sequence that is kept relatively constant from one swallow to the next. Upper processor control of each muscle involved in swallowing would be that following the stimulus for swallowing the upper processor triggers the "swallow box" in the middle processor and the lower processor acts to control the muscular movements involved in swallowing. The newborn cry is envisioned as resembling the same type of process as the vegetative status mentioned above. Following the cry stimulus, the upper and/or middle processors for any production trigger the lower processor control of the relevant muscle groups.

Based on these muscle control hypothesis, we assume that each of the three muscle groups important for cry production are controlled independently. Then parameters that each are responsible for are likely to vary independently. Secondly, if we can pinpoint differences in the cry as caused by subglottal (respiratory), glottal (laryngeal), or supraglottal malfunctions, then we will be able to correlate the acoustic abnormality with specific physiological or anatomical abnormalities [6].

The cry recordings were made at the Eastern Maternity Hospital of Santiago de Cuba. A pain cry was induced by a standardized stimulus: a "heelstick", the infants were positional decubito supine and flat in open cribs and were not crying at the time of the cry stimulus. The digitization of the cry signals was made by an A/D acquisition system connected to an IBM-PC. The data set consists of a successive cry episodes in which the average values for one cry unit is considered as a single pattern, resulting in 187 patterns to be evaluated. The cry episodes were obtained from 35 neonates, nineteen healthy cases and sixteen sick neonates with hypoxia-based CNS diseases, considering six control groups of data (under the specialized criterion of physicians) as follow in Table 1:

Table 1. The control groups

Control Groups	
Normal Group 1:	normal transpelvian delivery
Normal Group 2:	cesarean dysthocic
Pathologic Group 3:	hypoxemia
Pathologic Group 4:	retarded intra-uterine growth
Pathologic Group 5:	hypoxemia with another risk
Pathologic Group 6:	hyperbilirrubin

Every pattern consists of 25 values as shown in Table 2,

Table 2. Example results from the feature extraction process

Feature	Parameters
F_0 (mean, min., max., std dev , variability)	5
F_1 (mean, min., max., standard deviation , variability)	5
Voicedness (mean, min., max., std dev , variability)	5
Energy (mean, min., max., std dev, variability)	5
First latency	1
Rising melody type	1
Stridor occurrences	1
Shift occurrences	1
Class	1

The goal of this research is to use crying features to automatically classify infant cries into those produced by children suffering from hypoxia-induced damage to the central nervous system, and those produced by children not suffering from this damage.

2.1 Pre-processing

A set of features of 25 different variables that could serve as input are quite available. The goal of *pre-processing* in general is to present and /or transform the input data in such a way that it can be optimally processed by a neural network (to reduce dimensionality). A process called *feature selection* was developed: to try every possible feature that can be constructed from the whole feature set and then selecting the subset yielding the best results. The feature selection process was then optimized in order to make it manageable in terms of available resources.

2.2 Feature Subset Testing Algorithm

Given the nonlinearity in the data set, we are forced to discard linear discriminant analysis as a viable option for producing a performance criterion for a data set, and must turn to non-linear methods such as neural networks [3,5]. When choosing a neural network model for testing subsets, it is important to choose one that has little manual parameters to be tuned. For example, some networks need a *learning rate* to be chosen when they are trained. This value can not or hardly be determined automatically, and therefore a number of different learning rates have to be tried to find the one yielding the best results. Obviously, this multiplies the total search time needed by the number of trials needed to find this optimal parameter. To counter this, we are looking for a fast, non-parametric, supervised network model with little or no parameters to tune.

This leads us to a class of neural networks known as *radial basis function networks*. These networks have their origin in a procedure known as the *exact interpolation procedure*.

Exact interpolation works as follows: consider a mapping from a d-dimensional input space x (consisting of N points) to a one-dimensional target space. An exact interpolation procedure introduces a set of *basis functions*, one for each data point x^n .The basis functions take the form of

$$\phi(\|x - x^n\|) \tag{1}$$

where ϕ is some non-linear function depending on the distance between x and x^n. Usually, the Euclidean distance metric is used. Then, the functional mapping $h(x)$ that is performed by the procedure is constructed by linearly combining the basis functions:

$$h(x) = \sum_n w_n \phi\left(\|x - x^n\|\right) \tag{2}$$

Usually, the basis function ϕ is chosen to be the Gaussian

$$\phi(x) = \exp\left[-\frac{x^n}{2\sigma^2}\right] \tag{3}$$

where σ is the 'width' of the basis function, a parameter controlling the smoothness of the total approximation $h(x)$.

Many basis functions, similar to the Gaussian, will in fact work more or less satisfactory. The Gaussian is often chosen because of its analogy to the normal distribution, on which the probability density functions of many natural processes are based [5]. The described exact interpolation procedure is known as a Probabilistic Neural Network (PNN) [3]. As you see in this algorithm the only parameter to be tuned is the width σ of the basis functions. In MATLAB, an algorithm was constructed for performing the search, using the classification rate of the accelerated PNN as criterion. The Table 3 shows the features that will be used according the feature search results:

Table 3. The best features

Feature	Appears in best feature set
First latency	71%
Voicedness mean	60%
F_1 minimum	59%
F_1 mean	52%
F_0 mean	51%
	41%
Voicedness variability	30%
Energy maximum	30%
Energy maximum	30%
F_0 maximum	26%
Energy mean	

F_1: First formant F_0 Fundamental frequency (pitch)

3 Results and Discussion

3.1 Building the Classificator

Normally, after the pre-processing stage, one would make the step to actual classification. In this case, classification has already been performed in the selection of the best feature set. However, as we optimized the classification algorithm for speed, there are probably some improvements that can be made in the classification stage. Apart from that, we should end up with an 'out-of-the-box'-classificator that can be used on new data, so this is the place to construct it.We already discussed exact interpolation as a powerful classification algorithm which has a flaw, namely that it tends to over-fit the data set. The interpolation function yielding the best generalization is the one which is typically much smoother than the one that is the result of exact interpolation. To achieve this smoothness, the algorithm is adjusted so that the complexity of the underlying function, rather than the size of the data set, determines the number of basis functions.

Using MATLAB neural network toolbox, a RBF network was constructed to classify the data set resulting from the feature search. The data sets maintain their respective sizes in terms of number of patterns; however, the dimensionality of the sets has been reduced to 10.

First a simple classification algorithm based on a single RBF network is constructed. As with the feature selector however, the resulting network is quite unstable, so, just as in the feature selection process, a kind of averaging mechanism is devised. This time however, it is not enough to simply average the classification rate since the output itself is of critical importance in this version of the classifier (as opposed to the feature search algorithm where it is the classification rate that is the only important parameter – the actual results did not yet). Instead, a mechanism called bagging-shorthand for bootstrap aggregation- is introduced [2].

3.2 Bootstrap Aggregation

Bootstrap aggregation is a form of *arcing:* adaptive re-weighting and combining. This general term refers to reusing or selecting data in order to improve classification [5].

In bagging, several versions of a training set, each creating by drawing samples with replacement from the data set, are created. Each training set is then used to train a classifier (RBF network). Then, in the classification stage, the outputs of all those networks are combined to form the final classification based on the vote of each individual network (also called component classifier).

In this multiclassifier system, all component classifiers are of the same type and share the same output format. The output of one component classifier may simply be seen as the probability that some case belongs in a certain class (or the probability that the case does not belong in the other class). We may therefore simply linearly add the probabilities provided by the component classifiers and average them. After this, rounding the average value directly provides us with the classification result.

A multiclassifier system of 10 networks was constructed. The performance on the data set was 85%. A confusion matrix is shown in Table 4, it shows a slight inclination towards type 1 errors ('false alarms') which is a 'good' thing (in medical terms, a false alarm could be considered less damaging than unjustly *not* reporting an abnormality). The resulting networks are 'fixed' by writing them to a MATLAB variable store so they can be used in real classification tasks.

The classifier's performance (correct classification rate) was 85% (with +/-5% on the confidence interval).

Table 4. Confusion matrix for the multiclassifier system

Actual class	Group size	Predicted class	
		0	1
0	15	79%	21%
1	21	12%	88%

(0: normal, 1: abnormal)

4 Conclusions

The extraction and classification system that was devised was capable of distinguishing between normal and abnormal cases with up to 85% (with +/-5% on the confidence interval). This result can be regarded as statistically significant when you compare with recent works [4,9]. The resulting cry feature selection is not a *generalized paradigm* that is just the result from a specific approach into the cry analysis: *the use of ANN for a cry unit classification.* However another approaches concerned with the best parameter selection should be developed in the future. The classification performances that were found quantify the network's ability to relate some examples of measured values to some examples of diagnosed classes.

Although the results presented here are preliminary in nature, more tests are currently ongoing. Different features for input into the neural network and other network architectures are currently being investigated so that it can be determined which features are the most suitable for correct classification of cry units.

References

1. Bell, R.Q.: Contributions of human infants to caregiving and social interaction. In M.Lewis & L.Rosenblum (Eds), The effect of the infant on its caregiver. New York: Wiley, (1974) pp 1-19

2. Breiman L., *Bagging Predictors,* Journal of Machine Learning, vol. 24 no. 2 (1996) pp123-140
3. Bishop C., *Neural Networks for Pattern Recognition,* Oxford University Press, (1995) , ISBN 0198538642
4. Cano S. D., Escobedo D. l., *El uso de los mapas auto-organizados de Kohonen en la clasificación de unidades de llanto infantil,* Proceedings of the *CYTED*-AIRENE Project Meeting, Universidad Católica del Norte, Antofagasta, Chile (1999) pp 24-29
5. Duda R., Hart Po, Stork D., *Pattern Classification, 2 nd edition,* John Wiley & Sons, Inc., ISBN 0-471-05669-3, (2001).
6. Golub H., Corwin M., *Infant cry: a clue to diagnosis,* Pediatrics, vol. 69 (1982), pp. 197-201.
7. Gustafson, G.E. & Green,J.A: On the importance of fundamental frequency in cry perception and infant development. Child Development, 60, Aug. (1989).
8. Lester, B.M.: A biosocial model of infant crying. In Leipsitt, L. & Rovee, C. (Eds.). Advances in Infancy Research. Norwood. N.Y. Ablex, (1984) pp 167-207
9. Schonweiler R., Kaese So,Mo1ler S., Rinscheid A., Ptok M., *Neuronal networks and self-organizing maps: new computer techniques in the acoustic evaluation of the infant* cry, International Journal of Pediatric Otorhinolaryngology 38 (1996) pp. 1-11
10. Wasz-Hockert O. Et al: *The infant cry: a spectrographic and auditory analysis,* Clin. Devo Med. 29 (1968) pp. 1-42.

On the Use of Automatic Speech Recognition for Spoken Information Retrieval from Video Databases

Luis R. Salgado-Garza and Juan A. Nolazco-Flores

Computer Science Department, ITESM, Campus Monterrey
Av. Eugenio Garza Sada 2501 Sur, Col. Tecnológico
Monterrey, N.L., México, C.P. 64849
{lsalgado,jnolazco}@itesm.mx

Abstract. This document describes the realization of a spoken information retrieval system and its application to words search in an indexed video database. The system uses an automatic speech recognition (ASR) software to convert the audio signal of a video file into a transcript file and then a document indexing tool to index this transcripted file. Then, a spoken query, uttered by any user, is presented to the ASR to decode the audio signal and propose a hypothesis that is later used to formulate a query to the indexed database. The final outcome of the system is a list of video frame tags containing the audio correspondent to the spoken query. The speech recognition system achieved less than 15% Word Error Rate (WER) and its combined operation with the document indexing system showed outstanding performance with spoken queries.

1 Introduction

The most natural way to transmit information among humans is by voice, unfortunately a permanent recording of such class of information has been less common than text archiving mainly because two reasons: the large amount of storage required for acoustics and its dificulties for indexing. Nowadays, massive storage technology is more affordable than ever, new algorithms for data compression permit to record several hours of video and audio in just only tenths or thousands of megabytes. The boost of broadcast communication via television, radio and Internet has promoted the use of digital audio and video (multimedia) recording as one of the fastest and most accessible resources for information transmission and storage [1]. Trends are that in the near future, due to the amount of information contained in multimedia documents, multimedia will surpass text based documents as the preferred archiving method for information storage [2].

In recent years, new techniques for text indexing and automatic information retrieval have been developed [3] and succesfully used over the Internet, focusing on digital documents containing text information. However, the future of these search engines requires its use on multimedia databases, if not, its application

A. Sanfeliu et al. (Eds.): CIARP 2004, LNCS 3287, pp. 381–385, 2004.

in mobile devices and hand-busy environments will be very limited. At present, several research groups have conducted efforts to develop search engines for multimedia repositories of information [4], commonly known as multimedia digital libraries. However, there is still much work to be done, particularly regarding speech information and spoken queries [5, 6].

This paper presents the architecture of a spoken information retrieval system and its application to video databases, using acoustic information for indexing. The system is structured using two main components: an automatic speech recogniton (ASR) system and a document indexing software. The input to the system is a speech signal, containing the words included in the video frames of interest to the user, the output is a sequence of indexes on the video for such frames. The system was trained in spanish and tested in the same language but using spontaneous speech and different speakers.

The organization of the document is the following, section 2 presents the general architecture and explanation of the modules of the system. Subsection 2.1 explains the acoustic and language models training procedure, subsection 2.2 presents the methodology used for the video database indexing while subsection 2.3 focuses in the spoken query procedure. Section 3 discuses the results and conclusions are presented in section 4.

2   System Architecture Description

Our system architecture is structured in three modules (Fig. 1), acoustic and language models training, video's acoustic information transcription and indexing and spoken query processing. A detailed description of each of these modules is presented in this section.

2.1   Acoustic and Language Models Training

In order to perform speech recognition we train triphone acoustic models using the CMU SPHINX-III system, that is a HMM-based automatic speech recognition environment for continuous speech and large vocabulary tasks. A speech database, containing several hours of audio, produced by different speakers, is used for training. First the analog signal, from each audio file in the database, is sampled and converted to MFCC coefficients, then the MFCC's first and second derivatives are concatenated [7], the number of MFCC is 13 then the total dimension of the feature vector accounts for 39.

The acoustic models are finally obtained using the SPHINX-III tools. This tools use a Baum-and-Welch algorithm to train this acoustic models [8]. The Baum-and-Welch algorithm needs the name of the word units to train as well at the label and feature vectors. The SPHINX-III system allows us to model either discrete, semicontinuous or continuos acoustic models. In SPHINX-III system tools allow to select as acoustic model either a phone set, a triphone set or a word set.

The language models (LM) are obtained using the CMU-Cambridge statistical language model toolkit version 2.0 [9]. The aim of the LM is to reduce

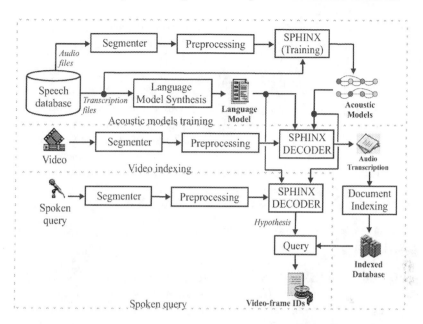

Fig. 1. Architecture of the spoken information retrieval system applied to video inexing

the perplexity of the task, by predicting the following word based in the words' history. Several techniques can be used to synthetize a LM [10], among them N-grams is the easiest technique with very good results. If all the n-grams are not contained in the language corpus, smoothing techniques need to be applied. In the CMU-Cambridge language model toolkit, unigram, bigrams or trigrams can be configured for this tool, as well as four types of discount model: Good Turing, Absolute, Linear and Witten-Bell.

2.2   Video Indexing

For our information retrieval system, the querable repository will be the audio into a video file. In order to build our indexed database we first need to get the transcript from the audio signal. The initial stage of video indexing deals with segment boundaries definition in the acoustic signals, for this we use the CMUseg [11] tool. Then, audio frames are preprocessed in order to calculate 13 MFCC coefficients, computing also first and second derivatives. The 39 sized feature vector for each frame is used as the input for the decoder. Each hypothesis from the decoder represents its best transcriptions for the audio signal, the whole set is stored as the audio transcription archive.

The transcription file is indexed using the MG [2] tools suite, that is a large scale inverted index based text retrieval system. The indexed database spans over the entire audio signal extracted from the video file, including every word detected by the speech recognizer. This database indexes the video in a frame-time bases and will be used for the queries of the next stage.

2.3   Spoken Information Retrieval

The spoken query module uses a close talk microphone to capture a query, composed by isolated words, uttered by a speaker. The audio signal is stored as a `wav` file. The acoustic stream is preprocessed to calculate MFCC coefficients and feeded into the speech recognition decoder. The best hypothesis is taken as the transcription for the query using the MG tools. The output from the system is a sequence of file tags, pointing to specific time of the video where each queried word appears.

3   Experiments

The configuration of the SPHINX-III system for our experiments used 13 mel-frequency cepstral coefficients (mfcc) and also their first and second deritatives, therefore the feature vector accounted for 39 elements. The speech lower and higher frequencies were stablished at 300 Hz and 7,000 Hz, respectively. The frame rate was set to 50 frames per second using a 30ms Hamming window. A 512 samples FFT length was used and the number of filterbans was set to 40. Five states continuous HMM was used as acoustic modeling technique with mixtures of 16 gaussians per state. The training data base for the speech recognition system had a vocabulary of 22,398 different words (409,927 words in 28,537 sentences). Triphones were used as the word unit and language modeling is based in word trigrams.

The baseline configuration of our speech recognition system was as reported in [10], for our latest experiments we used a new version of the SPHINX-III system leading us to the scores reported in table 1.

Table 1. Word Error Rates for the speech recognition system

Experiment	Language Weight	WER
Baseline	10.0	26.44%
Experiment 1	9.5	14.98%
Experiment 2	10.0	14.52%

With so emboldening results from the speech decoder, we were motivated to test the combined efficency with the MG indexing and retrieval system. For our experiments were performed spoken queries using single and multiple words, uttered by different speakers, independent form the ones in the training set for the ASR system. We found that the spoken query always performed correctly, reporting every video frame segment where the queried words were actually present.

4   Conclusions

As seen from the results, the overall performance of the system showed that the integration of a speech recognizer, a text based document indexing and retrieval tools comprise an effective architecture for a spoken query system on multimedia databases. However, more work is needed in order to increase the robustness of the system to OOV words and acoustic noise conditions. Worth to try is to use noise compensation methods, syntactically inspired language model techniques [10, 12] and n-Best list hypothesis from the decoder and evaluate the effect of these in the information retrieval cogency. We also propose the use of phonetic features into the document indexing algorithms (multifeatured information indexing), because the use of this kind of acoustic information could lead to more comprehensive classification system for spoken information retrieval.

The encoraging results shows the reliability of the system architecture and settles a testbed for future applications as Internet based user interface for spoken search engines and information storage and retrieval in mobile applications.

References

1. Chen, B., H.M. Wang, and L.S. Lee. "Retrieval of Broadcast News Speech in Mandarin Chinese Collected in Taiwan using Syllable-Level Statistical Characteristics", Proceedings of ICASSP-2000.
2. Witten, I.H., Moffat, A., and Bell, T.C. Managing gigabytes: compressing and indexing documents and images. Van Nostrand Reinhold, New York (1994).
3. D.R.H. Miller, T. Leek and R.M. Schwartz. "A hidden Markov model information retrieval system", In Proceedings of the 22nd ACM SIGIR Conference on Research and Development in Information Retrieval (SIGIR'99), pages 214-221, 1999.
4. Witten, I.H., Don, K.J., Dewsnip, M., and Tablan, V., "Text Mining in a digital library", Journal of Digital Libraries, 2003 (In Press).
5. Wolf, P.P.; Raj, B., "The MERL SpokenQuery Information Retrieval System: A System for Retrieving Pertinent Documents from a Spoken Query", IEEE International Conference on Multimedia and Expo (ICME), Vol. 2, 317-320, August 2002.
6. K. Spärck Jones, G. J. F. Jones, J. T. Foote, and S. J. Young. "Experiments in spoken document retrieval", Inf. Processing and Management, 32(4):399-417, 1996.
7. Deller, J.R., Proakis, J.G., Hansen, J.H.L., Discrete-Time Processing of Speech Signals, Prentice Hall, Sec. 6.2, 1993.
8. Dempster, A.P., Laird, N.M., Rubin, D.B., "Maximum likelehood for incomplete data via the EM algorithm", J. Roy. Stat. Soc., Vol. 39, No. 1, 1-38, 1977.
9. Clarkson, P., Rosenfeld, R., "Statistical Language Modelling using the CMU-Cambridge Toolkit", Proceedings of Eurospeech, Rodhes, Greece, 1997, 2707-2710.
10. Luis R. Salgado-Garza, Richard M. Stern, Juan Arturo Nolazco-Flores. "N-Best List Rescoring Using Syntactic Trigrams", Proceedings of MICAI 2004, Advances in Artificial Intelligence, Springer-Verlag (LNAI 2972:79-88)
11. M. Seigler, U. Jain, B. Raj, R. Stern. "Automatic segmentation, classification, and clustering of Broadcast news audio", Proc. Of the DARPA speech recognition workshop, February 1997.
12. Hsin-Min, W., Berlin, C., "Content-based Language Models for Spoken Document Retrieval", International Journal of Computer Processing of Oriental Languages (IJCPOL), Vol. 14, No.2, 2001.

Acoustical Analysis of Emotional Speech in Standard Basque for Emotions Recognition

Eva Navas, Inmaculada Hernáez, Amaia Castelruiz, Jon Sánchez, and Iker Luengo

Departamento de Electrónica y Telecomunicaciones, Escuela Técnica Superior de Ingeniería, University of the Basque Country, Alameda Urquijo s/n, 48013 Bilbao, Spain
{eva,inma,amaia,ion,ikerl}@bips.bi.ehu.es
http://bips.bi.ehu.es

Abstract. This paper presents the acoustical study of an emotional speech database in standard Basque to determine the set of parameters that can be used for the recognition of emotions. The database is divided into two parts, one with neutral texts and another one with texts semantically related with the emotion. The study is performed on both parts, in order to known whether the same criteria may be used to recognize emotions independently of the semantic content of the text. Mean F0, F0 range, maximum positive slope in F0 curve, mean phone duration and RMS energy are analyzed. The parameters selected can distinguish emotions in both corpora, so they are suitable for emotion recognition.

1 Introduction

With the progress of new technologies and the introduction of interactive systems, there has been a sudden increase in the demand for user friendly interfaces. For the correct development of such kind of interfaces, a high quality Text-to-Speech system and a system able to recognize the mood of the user are required. To build this kind of systems, a deeper research of the prosodic characteristics of emotional speech is necessary. To study the prosody of emotional speech in standard Basque, a new database that includes the six emotions considered the basic ones [1][2] (anger, disgust, fear, joy, sadness and surprise) was designed and recorded [3]. This set of basic emotions has been used in different studies related with speech, both for emotion recognition [4] and for emotion generation [5].

The corpus recorded in the database was divided into two parts: one part included emotion independent texts, which are common for all emotions. In this part neutral style has also been considered, to be used as a reference. The other part includes texts semantically related to each emotion, thus, this group is different for all the emotions. The acoustical analysis has been made separately for both parts of the database, to know whether the emotions were expressed in the same way independently of the semantic content of the text and as a result to determine the set of features that can be used for the recognition of emotions.

2 Subjective Evaluation of the Database

To prove the ability of the speaker to accurately simulate the emotions, assessing this way the validity of the database, we prepared a subjective test with the purpose of checking whether listeners could identify the intended emotion above chance level

A. Sanfeliu et al. (Eds.): CIARP 2004, LNCS 3287, pp. 386–393, 2004.
© Springer-Verlag Berlin Heidelberg 2004

(14%). A forced choice test was designed, where users had to select one of the seven proposed styles (six emotions plus neutral style). Sentences from both the common and specific corpora were selected for the test.

A total of 15 participants took part in the experiments. Fig. 1 shows the total recognition rate obtained for each emotion and the one obtained for the common and specific texts. Signals belonging to the specific corpus are better identified, but it is difficult to determine to what extent this is due to the semantic content of the stimulus, which helps the listener to decide, or to the better expression of the emotion.

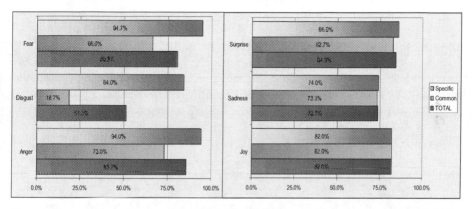

Fig. 1. Result of the subjective test, showing the recognition rate for each emotion separated by text type

Disgust is the emotion with worst recognition results. It has mainly been confused with neutral style. This emotion has also been the most difficult to identify in other works for different languages [6][7][8]. Recognition rates are similar in the common and specific corpus for surprise, sadness and joy. Anger and fear get poorer results for the common corpus, but still well above chance level. Therefore, subjective results for both corpora are good enough to use them to perform the acoustical analysis of the emotions.

3 Acoustic Analysis of the Database

Prosodic features are clearly related with emotion, but the nature of this relation has still to be determined. In this work, several acoustic parameters related with intonation, duration and energy have been automatically measured and analyzed to know how they change to express emotion. These features are mean F0 value (Hz), F0 range (Hz), maximum positive slope in F0 curve (Hz/ms), mean phone duration (ms), mean RMS (dB), mean RMS in low band, between 0 and 2000 Hz (dB) and mean RMS in high band from 2000 to 4000 Hz (dB). These values have been studied in the whole database, but also independently in the common and the specific corpora.

3.1 Comparison of the Distributions of Parameters Between Both Corpora

To know whether the speaker had expressed the emotions in the same way when reading texts related with emotion and texts with neutral content, an ANOVA test has been applied to each parameter with a confidence interval of 99%. Results of this analysis indicate that the parameter that has been more consistently applied by the speaker has been the maximum positive slope of the pitch curve, because none of the differences is significant. Besides, joy is the emotion that has been expressed more similarly in both corpora, because all the parameters studied, except for phone duration have differences not significant between both corpora. Anger and surprise have been expressed in a different way in the common and specific corpora, because most of the parameters have different distributions in both corpora.

When applying ANOVA to the values of the parameters measured in the common corpus, to determine whether differences among distributions were significant for different emotions, most of them were found significant (confidence interval of 95%). Some pairs were considered not significant in some parameters, but they were not the same pairs for every parameter, so a set of parameters that distinguish emotions can always been found in this corpus. The same analysis was applied to the values calculated from the specific corpus, and in this case, more pairs were found no significant, probably due to the fact that the speaker overacted in the common corpus to distinguish emotions that could not be differentiated by the content. In the specific corpus, as semantics indicated which one was the intended emotion, the speaker acted more naturally with less exaggerated emotions.

3.2 Analysis of the Pitch Features

The values of F0 curve were obtained from data provided by the laryngograph with a temporal resolution of 1 ms. Table 1 shows the mean values for the intonation related parameters and their related standard deviations separated by emotion. The first three columns list the values measured in the specific corpus and the rest of the columns have the values of the common corpus. Sadness is the emotion with lower values in all the parameters measured. Surprise is the one with wider pitch range. With regard to F0 maximum positive slope, anger has the larger one in the specific corpus and joy in the common corpus. The emotion with higher mean pitch value is fear.

Fig. 2 displays in the first graph the mean value of the parameters related with intonation for all emotions. Concerning the mean F0, the values corresponding to the specific texts are lower than those corresponding to the common texts for all emotions. This also happens with F0 range, as can be seen in the second graph of Fig. 2, but does not with maximum positive slope of pitch, as the third graph shows.

For all the parameters related with intonation, the emotions have the same relation with neutral style in both corpora: sadness is below neutral level in the three parameters, disgust is below for mean and F0 range and fear and surprise are below neutral level in maximum positive slope of F0.

Table 1. Values of the intonation parameters measured in the specific corpus (*first three columns*) and in the common corpus (*4th to 6th columns*), separated by emotion. Mean value and standard deviation are shown in the form mean ± standard deviation

Emotion	Mean F0	Range F0	MPS F0	Mean F0	Range F0	MPS F0
Anger	256.7±51.9	282.5±79.1	12.3±5.3	370.8±36.5	382.8±73.9	11.6±5.2
Disgust	206.8±33.7	201.4±59.7	9.5±3.9	217.8±28.7	190.3±53.4	8.8±4.0
Fear	322.2±44.2	265.6±104.6	5.5±1.3	379.2±36.3	302.2±112.4	5.6 ±1.5
Joy	306.6±32.1	320.0±80.0	10.9±4.4	314.1±30.8	327.5±87.9	12.3±4.4
Sadness	175.7±21.1	144.0±44.2	2.3±0.7	212.6±18.2	167.1±56.1	2.4±0.7
Surprise	280.0±33.9	371.8±52.3	5.6±1.3	339.0±35.8	398.4±61.8	5.4±1.5

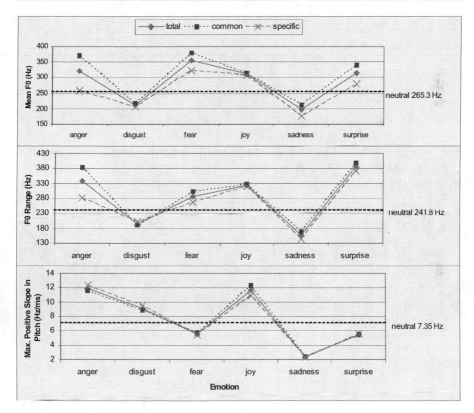

Fig. 2. Comparison of the mean pitch value in the entire database, in the part corresponding to the common texts and the specific texts

3.3 Analysis of the Duration

For the analysis of phone duration the sentences were automatically segmented using an algorithm based in Hidden Markov Models. No manual correction of the time labels was made. Duration of pauses was not considered because the database included only isolated sentences and the number of internal pauses was not sufficient for a statistical analysis.

Table 2 lists mean duration values measured in both corpora: first column has the values calculated from the specific texts and second column the values from the common texts. Sadness is the emotion with lower mean phone duration, therefore, it is the one with faster speaking rate. The emotions with slower speaking rate are fear and surprise.

Table 2. Mean value of phone duration for each emotion in the specific corpus (1st column) and in the common corpus (2nd column), expressed in ms Standard deviation is also shown in the form mean ± standard deviation

Emotion	Mean duration	Mean duration
Anger	88.5 ± 51.4	89.9 ± 52.0
Disgust	85.0 ± 45.3	84.4 ± 40.0
Fear	97.7 ± 61.1	92.2 ± 44.7
Joy	81.5 ± 46.7	78.4 ± 38.9
Sadness	78.8 ± 37.6	76.0 ± 31.9
Surprise	95.7 ± 61.1	99.5 ± 54.2

Fig. 3 shows a comparison of mean phone duration for all emotions in both corpora. Value measured for the neutral style in the common corpus is also displayed for reference: anger, fear and surprise have slower speaking rate than neutral style and joy and sadness have faster speaking rate. Disgust has a slightly faster speaker rate than neutral style.

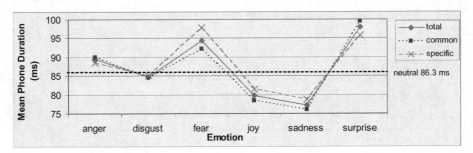

Fig. 3. Comparison of the mean phone duration in the entire database, in the part corresponding to the common texts and the specific texts

3.4 Analysis of the Power Features

For the analysis of the power features, the root mean square (RMS) energy of the signals was calculated. The spectral distribution of the energy has been considered important in other studies about emotional speech for other languages [4], so the RMS energy in the 0-2 KHz band (RMS LB) and in the 2-4 KHz band (RMS HB) have also been measured.

Table 3 lists the values related with energy measured for the specific corpus (columns 1 to 3) and the common corpus (columns 4 to 6). The emotions with more energy are anger and joy and sadness is the one with lower energy.

Table 3. Values related with energy measured in the specific corpus (*first three columns*) and in the common corpus (*4th to 6th columns*). All the parameters are expressed in dB. Mean values and standard deviation are shown in the form mean ± standard deviation

Emotion	RMS	RMS LB	RMS HB	RMS	RMS LB	RMS HB
Anger	20.5 ± 1.5	20.0 ± 1.7	15.6 ± 1.8	19.3 ± 1.5	18.0 ± 1.8	16.6 ± 1.9
Disgust	19.3 ± 2.1	19.0 ± 2.1	13.4 ± 2.9	18.4 ± 1.9	18.1 ± 1.9	13.3 ± 2.9
Fear	19.8 ± 1.3	19.5 ± 1.3	14.0 ± 2.4	16.1 ± 1.6	15.7 ± 1.6	12.2 ± 2.3
Joy	20.2 ± 1.3	19.6 ± 1.3	15.9 ± 1.7	19.8 ± 1.6	19.1 ± 1.8	15.6 ± 2.1
Sadness	16.0 ± 2.1	15.8 ± 2.1	8.2 ± 2.7	16.4 ± 2.2	16.3 ± 2.2	8.5 ± 2.7
Surprise	20.1 ± 1.6	19.7 ± 1.6	15.1 ± 1.9	16.7 ± 1.6	16.1 ± 1.6	13.3 ± 2.3

Fig. 4 shows the differences in RMS energy values in both parts of the database. In this case the values measured in the specific part are in general, higher than those of the common texts. This could be due to the fact that both parts of the database have been recorded in two different days, and no reference level was given to the speaker. RMS energy measured in low and high band have a similar behavior.

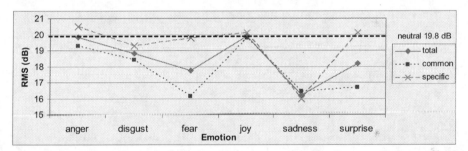

Fig. 4. Comparison of the RMS energy in the entire database, in the part corresponding to the common texts and the specific texts

3.5 Characterization of Emotions

Once the study of the acoustical correlates of emotion is performed, an analysis of their suitability to be used in the recognition of emotions is needed. Emotions are well separated, when representing the values of mean phone duration and RMS measured in both corpora, as Fig.5 shows. Fig. 6 shows the positions of different emotions when considering mean F0 and the maximum positive slope of F0 curve: emotions are also well separated according to these criteria in both corpora.

4 Conclusions

The acoustic correlates of emotion have been analysed in an emotional database for standard Basque. The analysis has been made independently for the part of the database that has common neutral texts and for the part that has specific texts related with emotions.

Subjective tests showed that both parts of the database were suitable for the study of the expression of emotions, because the recognition rates were well above chance

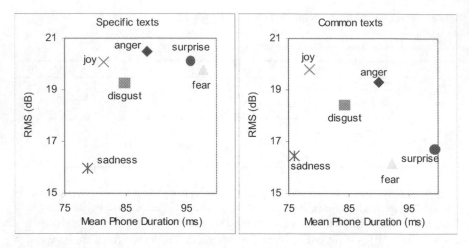

Fig. 5. Position of emotions in function of mean RMS energy and mean sound duration

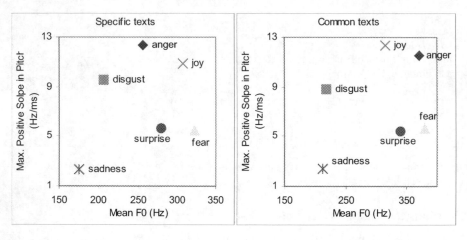

Fig. 6. Position of emotions in function of mean pitch range and maximum positive slope of pitch curve

level. Signals with text related with emotion were recognized with higher recognition rates, but signals with common texts also achieved good results.

Objective analysis of the prosodic features that characterize emotions has showed that mean F0, maximum positive slope in F0 curve, phone duration and RMS energy are suitable for emotion recognition.

Acknowledgements

This work has been partially funded by the Spanish Ministry of Science and Technology (TIC2000-1669-C04-03 and TIC2003-08382-C05-03) and by the University of the Basque Country (UPV-0147.345-E-14895/2002).

References

1. Scherrer, K.R.: Vocal Communication of Emotion: A Review of Research Paradigms. Speech Communication, Vol. 40. Elsevier, Amsterdam (2003) 227-256
2. Cowie, R., Cornelius, R.R.: Describing the Emotional States that Are Expressed in Speech. Speech Communication, Vol. 40(1,2). Elsevier, Amsterdam (2003) 2-32
3. Navas, E., Castelruiz, A., Luengo, I., Sánchez, J., Hernáez, I.: Designing and Recording an Audiovisual Database of Emotional Speech in Basque. Proc. LREC 2004. (2004)
4. Lay Nwe, T., Wei Foo, S., De Silva, L.: Speech Emotion Recognition Using Hidden Markov Models. Speech Communication, Vol. 41(4). Elsevier, Amsterdam (2003) 603-623
5. Boula de Mareüil, P., Célérier, P., Toen, J.: Generation of Emotions by a Morphing Technique in English, French and Spanish. Proc. Speech Prosody. Laboratoire Parole et Langage CNRS, Aix-en Provence (2002) 187-190
6. Iida, A., Campbell, N., Higuchi, F., Yasumura, M.: A Corpus-based Speech Synthesis System with Emotion. Speech Communication, Vol. 40(1,2). Elsevier, Amsterdam (2003) 161-187
7. Burkhardt, F., Sendlmeier, W.F.: Verification of Acoustical Correlates of Emotional Speech using Formant-Synthesis. Proc. ISCA Workshop on Speech and Emotion. ISCA Archive (2000) 151-156
8. Iriondo, I., Guaus, R., Rodríguez, A., Lázaro, P., Montoya, N., Blanco, J.M., Bernardas, D., Oliver, J.M., Tena, D., Ionghi, L.: Validation of an Acoustical Modelling of Emotional Expression in Spanish using Speech Synthesis Techniques. Proc. ISCA Workshop on Speech and Emotion. ISCA Archive (2000) 161-166

Scaling Acoustic and Language Model Probabilities in a CSR System*

Amparo Varona[1] and M. Inés Torres[1]

Departamento de Electricidad y Electrónica, Fac. de Ciencia y Tecnología,
UPV/EHU, Apartado 644, 48080 Bilbao, Spain
{amparo,manes}@we.lc.ehu.es

Abstract. It is well known that a direct integration of acoustic and language models (LM) into a Continuous Speech Recognition (CSR) system leads to low performances. This problem has been analyzed in this work as a practical numerical problem. There are two ways to get optimum system performances: scaling acoustic or language model probabilities. Both approaches have been analyzed from a numerical point of view. They have also been experimentally tested on a CSR system over two Spanish databases. These experiments show similar reductions in word recognition rates but very different computational cost behaviors. They also show that the values of scaling factors required to get optimum CSR systems performances are closely related to other heuristic parameters in the system like the beam search width.

1 Introduction

Integration of language and acoustic models in a Continuous Speech Recognition (CSR) system is invariably based on the well-known Bayes' rule, i.e., the recognizer must find the word sequence $\hat{\Omega}$ that satisfies:

$$\hat{\Omega} = \arg\max_{\Omega} P(\Omega)P(A/\Omega) \tag{1}$$

where $P(\Omega)$ is the probability that the word sequence $\Omega \equiv \omega_1\omega_2\ldots\omega_{|\Omega|}$ from some previously established finite vocabulary $\Sigma = \{\omega_j\}$, $j = 1\ldots|\Sigma|$, will be uttered and $P(A/\Omega)$ is the probability of the sequence of acoustic observations $A = a_1a_2\ldots a_{|A|}$ for a given sequence of words Ω. Probabilities $P(A/\Omega)$ are represented by acoustic models, usually Hidden Markov Models (HMM). The *a priori* probabilities $P(\Omega)$ are given by the Language Model (LM).

However, the combination of acoustic and LM probabilities obtained through Equation 1 usually leads to poor CSR system performances. In fact, it is well known that best performances of a CSR system are obtained when acoustic and language model probabilities in the Bayes' rule are modified by introducing exponential scaling factors [1] [2] [3].

---

* This work has been partially supported by the Spanish CICYT under grant TIC2002-04103-C03-02 and by the Basque Country University (00224.310-13566/2001)

A. Sanfeliu et al. (Eds.): CIARP 2004, LNCS 3287, pp. 394–401, 2004.

From a theoretical point of view, the scaling parameters are needed because acoustic and LM probability distributions are not real but approximations [1]. The two probability distributions are estimated independently using different stochastic models that model different knowledge sources. Moreover, the parameters of the acoustic and language models are estimated on the basis of speech and text data corpora, respectively. Thus, scaling parameters need to be applied to lessen these effects and then obtain good system performances.

In practice a numerical problem needs to be solved: the acoustic probabilities are normally much smaller than those of the LM. In addition, they appear more times. As a consequence, the contribution of LM probabilities could not be relevant [4] to obtain the most probable word sequence $\hat{\Omega}$. Therefore, low CSR system performances are usually obtained.

Section 2 illustrates this problem through an example of word sequence recognition. The usual way to get better system performances is to reduce the LM probabilities using a scaling factor $\alpha > 1$: $P(\Omega)^\alpha$. Alternatively, the acoustic probabilities can be increased by using a scaling factor $\gamma < 1$: $P(\Omega/A)^\gamma$. The effects of both scaling procedures are also analyzed in Section 2. Section 3 shows an experimental evaluation of both scaling procedures. The CSR system performance was measured in terms of both the Word Error Rate (WER) and the involved computational cost, which are also related with the heuristic beam-search applied. The experiments were carried out on two Spanish application tasks including read and spontaneous speech respectively. Therefore these databases represent two different levels of difficulty. Finally, some concluding remarks are given in Section 4.

2 Scaling Factors over Acoustic and LM Probability Distributions

Most of the current CSR systems use the one-pass Viterbi algorithm to obtain a sequence of decoded words given a sequence of acoustic observations according to Equation 1. The Viterbi-based search solves a maximization problem at each time t by choosing the higher accumulated probability for each node of the trellis. The argument of the maximization, i.e. the node at time $t - 1$ leading to maximum accumulated probability at time t, is also saved. Thus, finally the algorithm recovers in a backward step the most probable path of trellis nodes according to the whole acoustic observations sequence and, as a consequence, the most probable sequence of words uttered. Figure 1 shows this procedure for a small vocabulary of five words: $w_1, ... w_5$ at time t and time $t + 1$. $-log P_{w_i}$ [1] represents accumulated probabilities corresponding to partial paths ending at each word w_i, i.e. at trellis nodes that match the final state of word w_i at time t. For these nodes, the LM has to be checked to get the $-log P(w_i/w_j)$.

---

[1] In practice probabilities are managed as minus their logarithm to avoid numbers quickly falling to zero. We keep this representation in the example to better analyze differences among probability values. Thus lower values stand for higher probable paths.

Then, the accumulated probability $-logP_{w_i}$ at time $t+1$ is obtained through a new maximization procedure that includes this time combinations with LM probabilities. As a consequence of this maximization, a new word is added to the partial path under consideration.

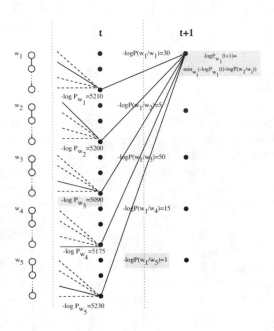

Fig. 1. The Viterbi based search choose at each time t the highest accumulated probability for each node of the trellis. $-logP_{w_i}$ represents accumulated probabilities for nodes matching the final state of a word model at time t. For these nodes, the language model has to be checked to get the $-logP(w_i/w_j)$. Then, the accumulated probability $-logP_{w_i}$ at time $t+1$ is obtained through a new maximization procedure that includes this time combinations with language model probabilities.

Figure 1 also shows the numerical problem previously discussed. The example in Figure 1 shows that the most probable partial path at time t ends at word w_3 and the less probable one ends at word w_5. According to the bigram model probabilities $P(w_1/w_j)$ the most probable word to be added at time t to the partial path is word w_5 and the less probable is w_3, when the word w_1 is considered at time $t+1$. Then, a new maximization has to be solved to estimate the accumulated probabilities at time $t+1$. For trellis node matching the initial state of word w_1:

$$P_{w_1}^{t+1} = \max_{w_i}(P_{w_i}^t P(w_1/w_i)) \rightarrow -log(P_{w_1}^{t+1}) = \min_{w_i}(-logP_{w_i}^t - logP(w_1/w_i)) \quad (2)$$

Table 1 shows the accumulated probabilities $-logP_{w_1/w_i}^{t+1}$ at time $t+1$ and initial state of word w_1 for all possible recognized word w_i at time t for the

Table 1. Accumulated probabilities $-logP_{w_1/w_i}^{t+1}$ at time $t+1$ and initial state of word w_1 for all possible recognized word w_i at time t for the example in Figure 1.

$-logP_{w_1/w_1}^{t+1}$	$-logP_{w_1/w_2}^{t+1}$	$-logP_{w_1/w_3}^{t+1}$	$-logP_{w_1/w_4}^{t+1}$	$-logP_{w_1/w_5}^{t+1}$
5249	5205	**5140**	5190	5231

example in Figure 1. Maximization in 2 is solved by choosing among values in Table 1. Thus word w_3 is selected to be added to this partial path, even if it is the less probable word according to the LM probabilities.

This example illustrates the numerical problem when Equation 1 is directly applied to decodeingan utterance without any scaling probabilities. Accumulated probabilities at the end of each partial sequence of words in the Viterbi trellis mainly depend on the values of acoustic $P(A/\Omega)$ probabilities because they are usually much smaller than those of the LM $P(\Omega)$. Moreover, acoustic probabilities appear, i.e. should be multiplied (or be summed their minus logarithm), at each node of the trellis whereas LM probabilities are only considered for trellis nodes matching final states of each word in the task lexicon. The gap among accumulated probabilities is therefore usually bigger than the gap among LM probabilities (see Figure 1). The immediate consequence is that LM probabilities are irrelevant in most situations when choosing the best, most probable, partial path [4]. The scarce contribution of the LM probabilities leads to low CSR system performances.

There are two easy ways to avoid this situation: to increase the gap among LM probabilities or to decrease the gap among accumulated probabilities. In the first case the LM probabilities are scaled by an exponential parameter $\alpha > 1 : (P(\omega))^\alpha$. In the second one the acoustic model probabilities are scaled by $\gamma < 1 : (P(A/\omega))^\gamma$ When LM probabilities are raised to a power $\alpha > 1 : (P(\omega))^\alpha$, all of them are attenuated, but this attenuation is higher for lower probability values. The gap between high and low probability values is now bigger. The LM probability values become more competitive with the increase of α values, up to a maximum where LM probabilities are overvalued. As a consequence, LM probabilities are now more relevant to choose the best partial path. Table 2 shows the accumulated probabilities at time $t + 1$ for the example in Figure 1 and Table 1 when LM probabilities have been scaled by different values of parameter α. This Table shows that word w_2 ($\alpha = 4$ and $\alpha = 6$) or w_4 ($\alpha = 8$) could now be selected to be added to partial path, even if they correspond to partial paths with low accumulated probabilities (see Figure 1). When acoustic probabilities are raised to a power $\gamma < 1 : (P(A/\omega))^\gamma$, all of them are increased but the increase is higher for lower probability values. The gap among accumulated probabilities is reduced in this case because accumulated probability values mainly depend on acoustic probabilities. The LM probabilities are also more and more competitive when γ decreases down to a minimum. As a consequence, LM probabilities are now also more relevant to choose the best partial path. Table 3 shows the accumulated probabilities at time $t + 1$ for example in Figure 1 and Table 1 when acoustic probabilities have been scaled by different values of parameter γ.

This Table shows that word w_2 ($\gamma = 0.4$), w_3 ($\gamma = 0.5$) or w_4 ($\gamma = 0.3$) could be now selected to be added to partial path, even if they correspond to partial paths with low accumulated probabilities at time t (see Figure 1).

Table 2. Accumulated probabilities $-log P^{t+1}_{w_1/w_i}$ at time $t+1$ and initial state of word w_1 for all possible recognized word w_i at time t for the example in Figure 1 and Table 1. LM probabilities have been scaled by $\alpha = 4, 6, 8$.

α	$-log P^{t+1}_{w_1/w_1}$	$-log P^{t+1}_{w_1/w_2}$	$-log P^{t+1}_{w_1/w_3}$	$-log P^{t+1}_{w_1/w_4}$	$-log P^{t+1}_{w_1/w_5}$
4	5330	**5220**	5340	5235	5234
6	5390	**5230**	5440	5265	5236
8	5450	5240	5540	5295	**5238**

Table 3. Accumulated probabilities $-log P^{t+1}_{w_1/w_i}$ at time $t+1$ and initial state of word w_1 for all possible recognized word w_i at time t for the example in Figure 1 and Table 1. Acoustic probabilities have been scaled by $\gamma = 0.5, 0.4, 0.3$.

γ	$-log P^{t+1}_{w_1/w_1}$	$-log P^{t+1}_{w_1/w_2}$	$-log P^{t+1}_{w_1/w_3}$	$-log P^{t+1}_{w_1/w_4}$	$-log P^{t+1}_{w_1/w_5}$
0.5	2635	2605	**2595**	2602	2616
0.4	2114	**2085**	2086	**2085**	2093
0.3	1593	1565	1577	**1555**	1570

When no scaling factors are applied ($\alpha = 1$ and $\gamma = 1$), the most probable partial path includes word w_3 (see Table 1). However, for $\alpha > 1$ (Table 2) and for $\gamma < 1$ (see Table 3) the most probable partial paths include word w_2. High values of α and low values of γ are not usually considered since LM probabilities are overvalued leading to low recognition rates.

CSR systems introduce a beam-search in order to reduce the computational cost of the search. The maximum probability of all trellis nodes, i.e. of all partial path is calculated at each time t, $1 \leq t \leq |A|$. Then, partial paths with accumulated probabilities under a percentage of this maximum are not considered any more. The value of an heuristic parameter $0 \leq bf \leq 1$ controls the number of partial paths considered. This parameter should be adjusted to reduce the computational cost without reducing the recognition rate. The number of partial paths to be evaluated mainly depends on the gap among accumulated probabilities corresponding to different partial paths at each time t. Both scaling factors modify partial path probabilities. However, scaling LM probabilities ($\alpha > 1$) increases the gap among accumulated probabilities whereas scaling acoustic probabilities ($\gamma < 1$) reduces it. As a consequence, the number of partial paths considered, and the involved computational cost, are expected to be very different for the two scaling procedures: higher for γ scaling than for α one.

3   Experimental Evaluation

The experimental evaluation was carried out on two Spanish databases with very different levels of difficulty: Bdgeo and Info_Tren.

Bdgeo is a task-oriented Spanish speech corpus [5] consisting of 82000 words and a vocabulary of 1208 words. This corpus represents a set of queries to a Spanish geography database. This is a specific task designed to test integrated systems for automatic speech understanding. Acoustic models were previously trained over a phonetic database consisting of 1530 sentences uttered by 47 speakers. The ML training corpus consisted of 9150 sentences. The test set consisted of 600 sentences uttered by 12 speakers in a laboratory environment at 16KHz. Perplexity values for this task were 13.1 for n=2, 7,53 for n=3 and 7,17 for n−4.

Info_Tren database was recorded as part of a Spanish project to develop a dialogue system. The task consisted of 227 Spanish dialogues on train information resulting in a vocabulary of around 2000 words. Info_tren is a difficult task since it was recorded through the telephone (8Khz), applying the well known *Wizard of Oz* mechanism. Thus, it is a spontaneous speech database were many different types of disfluencies are found: speaker and background noises, filled pauses, lengthenings, etc. [6]. Info_tren is the first spontaneous dialogue database recorded by Castilian Spanish speakers. The training corpus consisted of 191 dialogues uttered by 63 different speakers (1349 user turns resulting in 16500 words plus 5000 disfluencies). The test set consisted of 36 new dialogues uttered by 12 new speakers (308 user turns including 4000 words plus around 500 disfluencies). Perplexity values for this task were 36,8 for n=2, 34,8 for n=3 and 36,3 for n=4.

Uttered sentences were decoded by the time-synchronous Viterbi algorithm. In order to reduce the computational cost a beam-search algorithm was applied with different widths: high values of bf parameter for narrow beams and low values of bf for wide beams. The experiments were carried out using standard back-off n-gram models. Two series of experiments were carried out. In the first series LM probabilities were scaled by $|\alpha > 1$ $(P(\omega))^\alpha$. Table 4 shows the CSR system performance measured in terms of both, the Word Error Rate (WER) and the Average number of Active Nodes (AAN) in the lattice, including both acoustic and language model states. It shows WER and ANN for $\alpha=1\ldots7$ and $bf = 0.6, 0.5, 0.4$ values for three different n-gram ($n = 2, 3, 4$) models. Optimum performances are emphatized and underlined.

These experiments confirm that the scaling Language Model probabilities clearly leads to better CSR systems performances. Table 4 shows that both the word error rate and the average number of nodes in the lattice increased with α (up to a minimum), for any n-gram model and value of bf parameter. This Table also shows a relationship between the bf and α values required to get optimum performances: higher values of α are needed for wider beams search.

In the second series of experiments the acoustic probabilities have been scaled by $\gamma < 1$ $(P(A/\omega))^\gamma$. Table 5 shows the CSR system performances obtained through these experiments: the word error rate and the average number of active nodes in the lattice for three different n-gram ($n = 2, 3, 4$) models and different values of bf and γ parameters. Optimum performances are also emphatized and underlined.

These experiments confirm that the scaling acoustic model probabilities clearly leads to better CSR systems performances measured in terms of word

Table 4. CSR performance obtained using n-grams LMs with $n = 2\ldots 4$ for Bdgeo task and Info_tren task. Different values of the scaling factor over LM probabilities (α) and beam-search (bf) were applied.

α	BDGEO						Info_tren					
	bf=0.6		bf=0.5		bf=0.4		bf=0.6		bf=0.5		bf=0.4	
	WER	AAN	WER	AAN	WER	AAN	WER	AAN	WER	AAN	WER	AAN
						n=2						
1	41.89	1824	41.62	3964	41.87	6358	62.15	1363	61.69	3260	62.16	4798
2	26.43	781	25.8	2588	25.93	4843	51.12	751	50.23	2594	51.14	4038
3	21.65	280	20.22	1508	20.34	3456	**47.06**	**369**	43.83	1912	45.52	3217
4	**20.54**	**114**	16.99	764	16.72	2330	47.91	190	41.08	1291	43.95	2422
5	24.76	62	**15.80**	**380**	15.33	1441	51.50	97	**39.60**	**799**	42.56	1734
6	31.42	40	15.95	218	14.81	858	59.37	54	40.32	467	**42.29**	**1204**
7	40.39	28	17.01	143	**14.29**	**526**	66.61	36	41.75	294	42.34	855
						n=3						
1	44.18	2027	38.85	5189	38.85	9737	62.02	2011	58.69	6400	59.10	9998
2	22.43	746	21.86	2984	21.85	6659	51.30	1035	48.72	4668	53.08	5213
3	**17.19**	**238**	15.35	1529	15.18	4207	**47.31**	**488**	42.14	3172	47.10	3954
4	17.51	90	11.74	702	11.6	2526	47.68	240	38.72	1978	44.68	3112
5	21.79	48	10.85	328	10.32	1426	52.48	118	**38.01**	**1135**	42.73	2437
6	29.52	32	**10.82**	**179**	9.65	800	60.04	66	38.41	631	**41.13**	**1935**
7	36.81	23	13.04	114	**9.45**	**467**	68.43	41	41.58	378	43.01	968
						n=4						
1	38.75	2052	38.50	5374	38.51	9930	62.10	2122	58.80	6480	60.01	10112
2	21.77	746	21.86	3053	21.13	7041	51.40	1193	48.90	4720	53.10	5293
3	**16.41**	**235**	14.44	1544	14.35	4379	**47.48**	**593**	42.25	3286	47.30	4015
4	16.71	89	10.92	704	10.82	2593	47.96	310	38.83	2229	44.78	3210
5	21.11	47	10.24	328	9.45	1451	52.56	195	**37.84**	**1269**	42.96	2563
6	28.64	31	**10.22**	**177**	8.72	808	60.34	92	38.63	702	**41.20**	**2078**
7	35.84	23	12.48	113	**8.83**	**469**	67.13	68	42.31	415	43.60	1050

error rates. However, the reduction of word error rates is obtained along with important raises of the average number of active nodes in the lattice. Moreover, in this case a wide beam-search keeps a very high number of active hypotheses in the lattice increasing not only the involved computational cost but also the number of recognition errors. Table 5 also shows a relationship between the bf and γ values required to get optimum performances: lower values of γ are needed for wider beam search.

4   Concluding Remarks

In this work, we have experimentally analyzed the bad relationship between acoustic and LM probabilities when they are directly integrated using de Bayes' rule in CSR systems. A practical numerical problem arises since acoustic probabilities are much smaller than language ones. In addition they appear more times. As consequence, the contribution of LM probabilities could not be relevant when choosing the best path in the trellis. The gap among LM probabilities can be increased by scaling them by an exponential factor $\alpha > 1$ or the gap among accumulated probabilities can be reduced by scaling acoustic probabilities by an exponential factor $\gamma < 1$. Both possibilities have been analyzed and tested on a CSR system over two Spanish databases. Both scaling approaches clearly led to important reductions of word error rates. However, α scaling of LM probabilities

Table 5. CSR performance obtained using n-grams LMs with $n = 2 \ldots 4$ for Bdgeo and Info_tren task. Different values of the scaling factor over acoustic probabilities (γ) and beam-search (bf) were applied.

γ	BDGEO						Info_tren					
	bf=0.9		bf=0.8		bf=0.6		bf=0.8		bf=0.6		bf=0.5	
	WER	AAN	WER	AAN	WER	AAN	WER	AAN	WER	AAN	WER	AAN
					n=2							
1	68.58	20	46.91	243	41.89	1824	93.53	178	61.15	1363	61.69	3260
0.8	61.31	24	39.50	341	35.98	2484	92.06	350	58.03	2133	58.06	4334
0.5	44.34	39	27.15	708	25.60	4620	**51.45**	**793**	**43.92**	**4051**	**50.87**	**7247**
0.2	19.63	123	**15.13**	**2775**	**24.87**	**6538**	67.21	2987	67.21	9369	67.42	11610
0.1	**19.15**	**358**	17.45	7248	26.10	9361	91.48	6055	91.81	11455	91.99	12336
0.05	46.54	1076										
					n=3							
1	65.88	18	44.58	222	44.18	2027	93.82	204	60.02	2011	58.69	9980
0.8	60.34	20	37.24	315	33.12	2905	92.13	416	56.28	3364	**56.30**	**12415**
0.5	42.23	30	22.49	668	22.47	6402	**50.03**	**1024**	**41.77**	**5830**	59.77	18780
0.2	16.12	94	**10.4**	**3172**	**17.34**	**9000**	64.86	4010	53.60	12360		
0.1	**12.04**	**303**	10.95	12031	21.10	12314	80.04	8135				
0.05	44.85	1424										
					n=4							
1	65.23	18	44.36	221	38.75	2052	93.90	230	62.10	2122	58.80	6480
0.8	59.82	20	36.75	313	32.75	2961	92.23	426	55.35	3650	**54.30**	**13415**
0.5	42.12	30	21.89	668	21.26	6757	**49.92**	**1068**	**40.13**	**6930**	63.10	19565
0.2	16.63	93	**9.67**	**3313**	**17.10**	**9990**	63.10	4340	52.15	13360		
0.1	**11.74**	**308**	10.85	13730	20.90	12816	79.10	8240				
0.05	43.12	1472										

also led to important reductions of the computational costs whereas γ scaling of acoustic probabilities led to undesirable raises. It has also been shown that these effects are not independent of other heuristic phenomena in the system like the beam-search width. Thus, the values of scaling factors in CSR systems should be experimentally established along with other heuristic parameters.

References

1. Jelinek, F.: Five speculations (and a divertimento) on the themes of h. bourlard, h. hermansky and n. morgan. Speech Communication **18** (1996) 242–246
2. Rubio, J.A., Diaz-Verdejo, J.E., García, P., Segura, J.C.: On the influence of of frame-asynchronous grammar scoring in a csr system. In: Proc. IEEE International Conference on Acoustics, Speech, and Signal Processing. Volume II. (1997) 895–899
3. A.Ogawa, Takeda, K., Itakura, F.: Balancing acoustic and linguistic probabilities. In: Proc. IEEE International Conference on Acoustics, Speech, and Signal Processing. Volume II. (1998) 181–185
4. Varona, A., Torres, I.: High and low smoothed lms in a csr system. Progress in Pattern Recognition Speech and Image Analysis. Computer. LNCS **1** (2003) 236–243
5. Díaz, J., Rubio, A., Peinado, A., Segarra, E., Prieto, N., F.Casacuberta: Albayzin: a task-oriented spanish speech corpus. In: First Int. Conf. on language resources and evaluation. Volume II. (1998) 497–501
6. Rodríguez, L., Torres, I., Varona, A.: Evaluation of sublexical and lexical models of acoustic disfluencies for spontaneous speech recognition in spanish. In: Proc. of European Conference on Speech Technology. Volume 3. (2001) 1665–1668

Parallel Algorithm for Extended Star Clustering[*]

Reynaldo Gil-García[1], José M. Badía-Contelles[2], and Aurora Pons-Porrata[1]

[1] Universidad de Oriente, Santiago de Cuba, Cuba
{gil,aurora}@app.uo.edu.cu
[2] Universitat Jaume I, Castellón, Spain
badia@icc.uji.es

Abstract. In this paper we present a new parallel clustering algorithm based on the extended star clustering method. This algorithm can be used for example to cluster massive data sets of documents on distributed memory multiprocessors. The algorithm exploits the inherent data-parallelism in the extended star clustering algorithm. We implemented our algorithm on a cluster of personal computers connected through a Myrinet network. The code is portable to different architectures and it uses the MPI message-passing library. The experimental results show that the parallel algorithm clearly improves its sequential version with large data sets. We show that the speedup of our algorithm approaches the optimal as the number of objects increases.

1 Introduction

Clustering algorithms are widely used for document classification, clustering of genes and proteins with similar functions, event detection and tracking on a stream of news, image segmentation and so on. Given a collection of n objects characterized by m features, clustering algorithms try to construct partitions or covers of this collection. The similarity among the objects in the same cluster should be maximum, whereas the similarity among objects in different clusters should be minimum. The clustering algorithms involve three main elements, namely: the representation space, the similarity measure and the clustering criterion.

One of the most important problems in recent years is the enormous increase in the amount of unorganized data. Consider, for example, the web or the flow of news in newspapers. We need methods for organizing information in order to highlight the topic content of a collection, detect new topics and track them. The star clustering algorithm [1] was proposed for these tasks, and three scalable extensions of this algorithm can be found in [2]. The star method outperforms existing clustering algorithms such as single link, average link and k-means in the organizing information task, as it can be seen in [1]. However, the clusters obtained by this algorithm depend on the data order. In [3] we proposed a

[*] This work was partially supported by the Spanish CICYT projects TIC 2002-04400-C03-01 and TIC 2000-1683-C03-03.

A. Sanfeliu et al. (Eds.): CIARP 2004, LNCS 3287, pp. 402–409, 2004.

new clustering algorithm that outperforms the Aslam's algorithm and it is also independent of the data order.

Many recent applications involve huge data sets that cannot be clustered in a reasonable time using one processor. Moreover, in many cases the data cannot be stored in the main memory of the processor and it is necessary to access the much slower secondary memory. A solution to this problem is to use parallel computers that can deal with large data sets and reduce the time spent by the algorithms. Parallel versions of some clustering algorithms have been developed, such as *K-Means* [4], *MAFIA* [5], *GLC* [6] and the Incremental Compact Algorithm [7].

In this paper we present a new parallel algorithm that finds the clusters obtained by the Extended Star Clustering Algorithm [3]. This algorithm distributes the same number of objects to each processor and balances the workloads in average. The parallel algorithm was tested in a cluster of personal computers connected through a Myrinet network. Experimental results show a good behavior of the parallel algorithm that clearly reduces the sequential time. Moreover, we have achieved near linear speedups when the collection of objects and the number of features are large.

The remainder of the paper is organized as follows. Section 2 describes the main features of the sequential algorithm. Section 3 shows the parallel algorithm. Section 4 includes the experimental results. Finally, conclusions are presented in Section 5.

2   Extended Star Clustering Algorithm

Two objects are β_0-similar if their similarity is greater or equal to β_0, where β_0 is a user-defined parameter. We call β_0-similarity graph the undirected graph whose vertices are the objects to cluster and there is an edge from vertex o_i to vertex o_j, if o_j is β_0-similar to o_i. Finding the minimum vertex cover of a graph is a NP complete problem. This algorithm is based on a greedy cover of the β_0-similarity graph by star-shaped subgraphs. A star-shaped subgraph of $l + 1$ vertices consists of a single *star* and l *satellite vertices*, where there exist edges between the star and each of the satellite vertices.

On the other hand, we define the complement degree of an object o is the degree of o taking into account its neighbors not included yet in any cluster, namely:

$$CD(o) = |N(o) \setminus Clu|$$

where Clu is the set of objects already clustered and $N(o)$ is the set of neighbors of the object o in the β_0-similarity graph. As we can see, the complement degree of an object decreases during the clustering process as more objects are included in clusters.

In the extended star clustering algorithm the stars are the objects with highest complement degree. The isolated objects in the β_0-similarity graph are also stars. The algorithm guarantees a pairwise similarity of at least β_0 between the star and each of the satellite vertices, but such similarity is not guaranteed

---

Algorithm 1 Extended star clustering algorithm.

---

1. Calculate all the similarities between each pair of objects to build the β_0-similarity graph
2. Let $N(o)$ be the neighbors of each object o in the β_0-similarity graph
3. For each isolated object o ($|N(o)| = 0$): Create the singleton cluster $\{o\}$
4. Let L be the set of non-isolated objects
5. Calculate the complement degree of each object in L
6. While a non-clustered object exists:
    (a) Let M_0 be the subset of objects of L with maximum complement degree
    (b) Let M be the subset of objects of M_0 with maximum degree
    (c) For each object o in M:
        i. If $\{o\} \cup N(o)$ does not exist, create a cluster $\{o\} \cup N(o)$
    (d) $L = L \setminus M$
    (e) Update the complement degree of the objects in L

---

between satellite vertices. The main steps of our algorithm are shown in the Algorithm 1.

The complexity time of the algorithm is $O(n^2m)$ [3]. This algorithm creates overlapped clusters. Unlike the original star clustering algorithm, the obtained clusters are independent of the data order. Besides, the selection of stars using the complement degree allows the algorithm to cover quickly the data and it reduces the overlapping among the clusters.

In [3] we compare the extended star clustering algorithm with the original star algorithm in several subcollections of TREC data[1] using the F1 measure [8]. It obtains a better cluster quality in these subcollections in most cases.

3   Parallel Algorithm

Our parallel algorithm is based on the Single Program Multiple Data (SPMD) model using message passing, which is currently the most prevalent model on distributed memory multiprocessors. We assume that we have p processors each with a local memory. These processors are connected using a communication network. We do not assume a specific interconnection topology for the communication network, but the access time to the local memory of each processor must be cheaper than time to communicate the same data with other processor.

This algorithm uses a master-slaves model, where one of the processors acts as the master during some phases of the algorithm. The data is cyclically distributed among the processors, so that processor i owns the object j if $i = j \bmod p$. This data partition tries to balance the workload among the processors in order to improve the efficiency of the parallel algorithm. Each processor stores the indexes of the objects connected to its $\frac{n}{p}$ objects in the β_0-similarity graph.

Initially, the algorithm builds the β_0-similarity graph, and each processor creates the singleton clusters formed by its isolated objects. Then it spends most

---

[1] http://trec.nist.gov

Algorithm 2 Parallel algorithm.

1. Build_β_0-similarity_graph()
2. On each processor:
   (a) For each isolated object o: Create the singleton cluster $\{o\}$
   (b) Let L be the set of non isolated objects in this processor
3. Processor 0 gathers the singleton clusters
4. Processor 0 broadcasts the number of non-clustered objects
5. While there exist non-clustered objects
   (a) Find_stars()
   (b) Build_clusters()
   (c) Update_complement_degree()
   (d) On each processor: $L = L \setminus M$

Algorithm 3 Build_β_0-similarity_graph()

1. Processor 0 broadcasts the number of objects n
2. On each processor:
   (a) For $i = 1, ..., n$:
      i. If processor 0: read the object o_i and broadcast it
      ii. If processor owns o_i: store its description
      iii. Calculate the similarities of its objects with o_i to build the β_0-similarity subgraph
   (b) Let $N(o)$ be the neighbors of each object o in the β_0-similarity graph. The complement degree of o is $|N(o)|$

---

of the time of the algorithm to find the star shaped clusters. The algorithm terminates when all objects are clustered. The main steps of our parallel algorithm are shown in the Algorithm 2.

The parallel algorithm involves four major steps: building the β_0-similarity graph, finding of stars, constructing the clusters, and updating the complement degree. Each of the above four steps is carried out in parallel. The algorithms *Build_β_0-similarity_graph*, *Find_stars*, *Build_clusters* and *Update_complement_degree* describe each of these steps.

The *Build_β_0-similarity_graph()* algorithm is embarrassingly parallel. Observe that the similarity calculations are inherently data parallel, that is, they can be executed asynchronously and in parallel for each object. Therefore a perfect workload balance is achieved.

In the *Find_stars()* algorithm each processor starts by finding the candidate stars (step 1). Given the local maximum complement degree and the local maximum degree on each processor, the *Reduce* communication operation computes the global maxima and broadcasts them to all processors. For example, if $(2, 6)$, $(3, 4)$ and $(3, 5)$ are the maximum complement degrees and the maximum degrees calculated in the processors 0, 1 and 2 respectively, the obtained global maxima are $(3, 5)$. Notice that the global maximum degree is the maximum de-

---

Algorithm 4 Find_stars()

---

1. On each processor:
    (a) Let M_0 be the subset of objects of L with maximum complement degree
    (b) Let M be the subset of objects of M_0 with maximum degree
2. Reduce communication to get the global maximum complement degree and its corresponding global maximum degree
3. On each processor:
    (a) If its local maximum complement degree and its local maximum degree coincide with the global maxima, the stars are the objects of M. Else, $M = \varnothing$

Algorithm 5 Build_clusters()

---

1. On each processor:
    (a) For each star object o of M, build the cluster with o and its neighbors $N(o)$
    (b) Determine the number of non-clustered objects
2. Reduce communication to obtain the global clusters and the global number of non-clustered objects

---

gree corresponding to the global maximum complement degree. Finally, the stars are found by the processors whose maxima coincide with the global ones.

The algorithm 5 builds the clusters from the obtained stars. This process may lead to identical clusters being formed. We need to identify the repeated clusters and retain only one of them. Elimination of identical clusters is carried out on each processor and also on the *Reduce* communication operation. The elimination on each processor is not needed, but it decreases greatly the time during the *Reduce* operation. Finally, both the global clusters and the global number of non-clustered objects are broadcast to all processors.

The clusters built in this iteration, incorporate some objects that were not even clustered, that is, the objects that did not belong to any cluster built in previous iterations. The algorithm 6 firstly constructs the set of these objects.

Algorithm 6 Update_complement_degree()

---

1. On each processor:
    (a) Let C be the set of its objects clustered in this iteration
    (b) Build the set of pairs (o, v), where o is a neighbor of an object of C and v is the value in which its complement degree must be decreased. v is the number of objects of C that are neighbors of o.
2. Reduce communication to get the global set of pairs (o, v)
3. On each processor:
    (a) For each object o of the global set of pairs (o, v)
        i. If this processor owns o, decrease its complement degree in v

---

The neighbors of these objects change its complement degree and therefore we need update them. For this purpose, we build a data structure that contains these neighbors and the value in which its complement degree must be decreased. Since each processor only knows the complement degree decreases due to its objects clustered in this iteration, a *Reduce* communication operation is performed so that all processors have the global decreases. Finally, each processor updates the complement degree of its objects.

As we can see, the tasks are divided among the processors such that each processor gets approximately an equal amount of work when the number of objects is large. The description of objects and the β_0-similarity graph are fairly distributed among the processors. Thus the memory used by the parallel algorithm is similar in each processor. On the other hand, the overhead of communication is reduced by packing several informations in a single message.

4   Performance Evaluation

The target platform for our experimental analysis is a cluster of personal computer connected through a Myrinet network. The cluster consists of 34 Intel Pentium IV-2GHz processors, with 1 Gbyte of RAM each one. The algorithm has been implemented on a Linux operating system, and we have used a specific implementation of the MPI message-passing library that offers small latencies and high bandwidths on the Myrinet network. We have executed the parallel algorithm varying the number of processors from 1 to 32.

We used data (in Spanish) from the TREC-4 and TREC-5 conferences as our testing medium. The TREC-4 collection contains a set of "El Norte" newspaper articles in 1994. This collection has 5828 articles classified in 50 topics. The TREC-5 consists of articles from AFP agency in 1994-1996 years, classified in 25 topics. We only used the data from 1994, for a total of 695 classified articles. The TREC-4 document collection were partitioned in three subcollections to evaluate the performance of the parallel algorithm using data sets with different sizes. The documents are represented using the traditional vectorial model. Terms are statistically weighted using the normalized term frequency. Moreover, we use the traditional cosine measure to compare the documents. The obtained results are shown in table 1.

The clusters obtained with the parallel algorithm are independent of the number of processors involved. As we can see, the parallel algorithm clearly

Table 1. Experimental results.

Time (sec.)		Number of processors								
Collection	Size	1	2	4	8	12	16	20	24	28	32
afp	695	9.22	4.74	2.83	1.50	1.47	1.22	1.30	1.60	1.58	1.14
eln-1	1380	56.27	29.16	15.85	8.90	6.78	5.82	5.35	5.10	4.72	4.66
eln-2	2776	232.83	119.43	62.15	32.48	23.59	18.93	16.62	14.48	13.88	13.01
eln-3	5552	972.37	494.67	255.20	129.89	90.06	70.74	60.85	51.32	46.23	41.82

reduces the sequential time in all collections. The time reductions are larger as we increase the size of the data sets.

Figure 1 shows the speedups obtained with the parallel algorithm using different data sets. From the plot it can be seen that we have achieved near linear speedups for up to a certain number of processors depending on the data size. The computation time decreases almost linearly with the number of processors except in the smaller data (afp). Besides, when we deal with few objects, the number of stars and neighbors per processor could be quite different, and so the workload per processor could be unbalanced. However, with large data sets, all processor should have a similar number of stars, thus balancing the workload. On the other hand, the effect of the communication time is smaller as we increase the size of the data sets. Therefore, the higher the data size, the greater the speedup for the same number of processors.

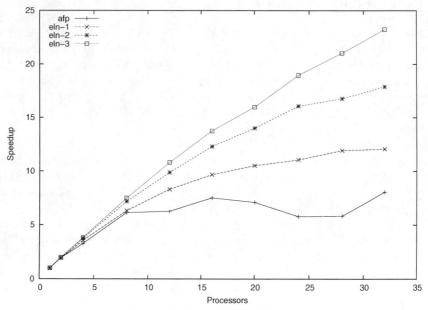

Fig. 1. Speedups on TREC data.

5   Conclusions

In this paper we present a parallel extended star clustering algorithm. The generated set of clusters is unique, independently of the arrival order of the objects. Another advantage of this algorithm is that it can deal with mixed incomplete object descriptions and it obtains overlapped clusters. On the other hand, the algorithm is not restricted to the use of metrics to compare the objects. The proposed parallel algorithm can be used in many applications such as information organization, browsing, filtering, routing and topic detection and tracking. Besides, the resulting parallel algorithm is portable, because it is based on standard tools, including the MPI message-passing library.

We have implemented and tested the parallel code in a cluster of personal computers. The experimental evaluations on TREC data show the gains in performance. The obtained results show a good behavior of the parallel algorithm that clearly reduces the sequential time. Moreover, we have achieved near linear speedups with large data sets. The main reason for this behavior is that we have tried to minimize the communications and to balance the load on the processors by carefully distributing the objects and the tasks that each processor performs during each step of the algorithm.

References

1. Aslam, J.; Pelekhov, K. and Rus, D.: Static and Dynamic Information Organization with Star Clusters. In *Proceedings of the 1998 Conference on Information Knowledge Management*, Baltimore, MD, 1998.
2. Aslam, J.; Pelekhov, K. and Rus, D.: Scalable Information Organization. In *Proceedings of RIAO*, 2000.
3. Gil-García, R. J.; Badía-Contelles, J. M. and Pons-Porrata, A.: Extended Star Clustering Algorithm. *In Proceedings of the 8th Iberoamerican Congress on Pattern Recognition*, LNCS 2905, Springer Verlag, pp. 480-487, 2003.
4. Dhillon, I. and Modha, B. A.: Data Clustering Algorithm on Distributed Memory Multiprocessor. *Workshop on Large-scale Parallel KDD Systems*, pp. 245-260, 2000.
5. Nagesh, H.; Goil, S. and Choudhary, A.: A Scalable Parallel Subspace Clustering Algorithm for Massive Data Sets. *International Conference on Parallel Processing*, pp. 447-454, 2000.
6. Gil-García, R. and Badía-Contelles, J.M.: GLC Parallel Clustering Algorithm. In *Pattern Recognition. Advances and Perspectives. Research on Computing Science* (In Spanish), pp. 383-394, 2002.
7. Gil-García, R. J.; Badía-Contelles, J. M. and Pons-Porrata, A.: A Parallel Algorithm for Incremental Compact Clustering. *In Proceedings of the Europar2003*, LNCS 2790, Springer-Verlag, pp. 310-317, 2003.
8. Larsen, B. and Aone, C.: Fast and Effective Text Mining Using Linear-time Document Clustering. In *KDD'99*, San Diego, California, pp. 16-22, 1999.

Hidden Markov Models for Understanding in a Dialogue System⋆

Fernando Blat, Sergio Grau, Emilio Sanchis, and María José Castro

Departament de Sistemes Informàtics i Computació
Universitat Politècnica de València
Camí de Vera s/n, 46022 València, Spain
{fblat,sgrau,esanchis,mcastro}@dsic.upv.es

Abstract. In this work, we present an approach to Automatic Speech Understanding based on stochastic models. In a first phase, the input sentence is transduced into a sequence of semantic units by using hidden Markov models. In a second phase, a semantic frame is obtained from this sequence of semantic units. We have studied some smoothing techniques in order to take into account the unseen events in the training corpus. We have also explored the possibility of using specific hidden Markov models, depending on the dialogue state. These techniques have been applied to the understanding module of a dialogue system of railway information in Spanish. Some experimental results with written and speech input are presented.

1 Introduction

Spoken dialogue systems are a natural human-machine interface within the framework of information systems. Due to advances in many areas, such as speech recognition, language modelling, speech understanding, or speech synthesis, it is possible to build prototypes of dialogue systems applied to restricted semantic domains, such as flight information (ATIS [1]), railway information (Basurde [2]), weather forecasts (Jupiter [3]), etc...

Dialogue systems are characterised by having a similar basic structure: an automatic speech recognition module, an understanding module, a dialogue module, an access module to the database and an answer generation module (usually, with speech synthesis). In this work, we will focus on the understanding module. There are two general ways to approach the understanding problem, one approach is based on rules and the other is based on stochastic models. *Rule-based understanding* is implemented through grammars defined from rules. In order to improve the behaviour of such systems, the human expert usually has to combine syntactic and semantic grammars to perform analyses at different levels. Examples of this approach are TINA [4], PHOENIX [5] and ARISE [6].

⋆ Thanks to the Spanish CICYT agency under contract TIC2002-04103-C03-03 for funding.

A. Sanfeliu et al. (Eds.): CIARP 2004, LNCS 3287, pp. 410–417, 2004.

Stochastic models are inductively trained in order to transduce the input sentences into sequences of semantic units. The most commonly used stochastic models are *n*-grams, stochastic grammars and hidden Markov models [7–9].

Independently of the approach to the understanding problem, we have to define a semantic model to represent the meaning of the user turns so that the computer can store such information. Semantic *frames* and their *attributes* [10] are the most widely used for this. A frame is a template that represents a given concept, and the information is complemented with a series of related attributes. Therefore, understanding can be viewed as a transduction process from the input (speech in natural language) into one or more semantic frames with their corresponding attributes.

Hidden Markov Models (HMMs) are known to perform well in speech recognition tasks, but they can also be used in understanding processes [8, 11]. We will use a HMM as a transducer from the natural language into an intermediate semantic language. Afterwards, the sequence of intermediate semantic units is converted into one or more semantic frames. The possibility of learning HMMs from samples, which makes it easy to change the tasks or language, makes this approach attractive.

One interesting way to improve the performance of the understanding process is to take advantage of the structure of the dialogue. Turns of the dialogues can be classified in terms of one or more dialogue acts. We have defined a set of three-level dialogue act labels that represents the general dialogue behaviour (first level) and specific semantic characteristics (second and third level). In our work, we study the use of specific stochastic models, that is, different models that depend on the dialogue acts.

In this work, we explore two approaches to stochastic language understanding in a dialogue system: the first is to infer a *global HMM* to extract the semantic information by segmenting the user turn into semantic units, and the second is to use *specific HMMs*, that is, different models that depend on the class of user turn. The results of the experiments with the correct transcriptions of the user turns (text data) and with the sequences of words obtained from the recognition process (speech data) are presented for these approaches.

2   The Dialogue Task

The final objective of this dialogue system is to build a prototype for information retrieval by telephone for a Spanish nation-wide train system. Queries about timetables, prices and services for long distance trains can be made to the dialogue system. Four types of scenarios were defined (departure/arrival time for a one-way trip, prices, services, and one free scenario). A total of 215 dialogues were acquired using the Wizard of Oz technique.

2.1   Labelling the Turns

The definition of dialogue acts is an important issue because they represent the successive states of the dialogue. The labels must be specific enough to show the different intentions of the turns in order to cover all the situations, and they must be general enough to be easily adapted to different tasks.

The main feature of the proposed labelling of our system is the division into three levels. The first level, called *speech act*, is general for all the possible tasks and it comprises the following labels: Opening, Closing, Undefined, Not_understood, Waiting, New_consult, Acceptance, Rejection, Question, Confirmation, Answer.

The second and third levels, called *frames* and *cases*, respectively, are specific to the working task and give the semantic representation. The frame labels defined for our task are: Affirmation, Departure_time, New_data, Price, Closing, Return_departure_time, Rejection, Arrival_time, Return_departure_time, Confirmation, Not_understood, Trip_length, Return_price, Return_train_type, Train_type. Each frame has a set of slots which have to be filled to make a query or which are filled by the retrieved data after the query. The specific data that fill in the slots are known as *cases*. Cases take into account the data given in the user turn to fill the slots. Examples of cases for this task are: origin_city, destination_city, departure_date, departure_time, train_type, price, . . .

2.2   Specific Classes of User Turns

User turns can be classified in accordance with the dialogue state defined from the speech act label of the previous computer turn. Only four speech acts have enough sentences to train relevant HMMs (see Table 1). These four classes are[1]:

Opening: user turns after the welcome message of the dialogue system.

Machine: *Welcome to the information system for nation-wide trains, what information would you like?*

User: *I would like to know the timetables of the Euromed train from Barcelona to Valencia.*

Confirmation: user turns after a confirmation question of the dialogue system.

Machine: *Do you wish to travel from Barcelona to Valencia?*
User: *Yes.*

New_consult: user turns after the question of the dialogue system *"Anything else?"*.

Machine: *Anything else?*
User: *How much is the one-way ticket?*

Question: the answers of the user after a question by the dialogue system.

Machine: *Which day do you want to travel?*
User: *Next Friday.*

2.3   Intermediate Semantic Language

The transduction of user turns into one or more semantic frames is not done directly, it is divided into two stages. In the first stage, the input sentence is

---

[1] An example of user turn from each class is given below (only the English translation).

Segmentation		Semantic frame
Can you tell me	query	
the railway timetable	<departure_time>	
from	origin_marker	
Valencia	origin_city	(Departure_time):
to	destination_marker	origin_city: valencia
Barcelona	destination_city	destination_city: barcelona
for	departure_marker	departure_date: 2004/May/21
Friday?	departure_weekday	

Fig. 1. An example of segmentation and final frame for the user turn *"Can you tell me the railway timetable from Valencia to Barcelona for Friday?"*. In the system, the user turn is first preprocessed using lemmas and categories. Only the English translation is given.

segmented and transduced into terms of a sentence from an intermediate semantic language using an HMM. In the second step, the result of the segmentation process will be the input of the translator which generates the semantic frame automatically. This step is quite simple, and it is performed by a rule-based approach. An example of segmentation and final frame is shown in Figure 1.

The intermediate semantic language we have defined for the task is composed by a set of semantic units which represents the meaning of words (or sequences of words) in the original sentences. For example, the semantic unit query can be associated to *"can you tell me"*, *"please tell me"*, *"what is"*, etc. In this way, an input sentence (sequence of words) has an associated semantic sentence (sequence of semantic units), and there is an inherent segmentation. A total of 64 semantic units have been defined in order to cover all the possible meanings of each user turn included in the corpus. Examples of semantic units are: courtesy, closing, query, confirmation, <departure_time>, etc.

3   Hidden Markov Models for Understanding

HMMs are known to perform well in speech recognition tasks, but they can also be used in understanding processes [8, 11]. We will use a HMM as a transducer from the natural language of the user turns into the intermediate semantic language described in section 2.3. This translation consists of a segmentation in which a semantic unit is assigned to one or more words.

Some advantages of these HMMs are the capability of automatic learning from training samples, the capability to represent the sequentiality of language in terms of sequence of states, and the representations of different observations (words) associated to each meaning (or semantic unit).

The transition probabilities between states are obtained in the learning process. These probabilities are the bigram probabilities of the semantic units in the training set. The observation probabilities of words in each state are obtained from the frequency of observations of each word in each state (see an example in Figure 2). Due to the lack of training samples, some observation probabilities

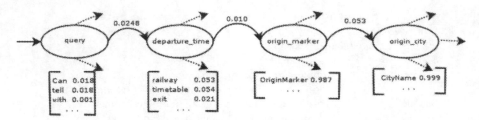

Fig. 2. Example of a fragment of a specific HMM of type New_consult.

Table 1. Characteristics of the Basurde corpus.

	Total	Opening	Confirmation	New_consult	Question
Total of turns	1,378	207	257	804	110
Total of words	16,219	5,034	1,371	9,228	586
Average of words by turn	11.7	24.3	5.3	11.5	5.3
Vocabulary size	635	410	214	483	163

are underestimated. Smoothing techniques can avoid this problem. In our case, we have implemented two different smoothing techniques: Laplace smoothing and back-off smoothing [12]. Once the model has been trained, the Viterbi algorithm [13] is used to determine the optimal segmentation of the user turns. Finally, a backtrace recovering algorithm determines the path followed by the model by extracting the maximum probability, that is, we obtain a segmentation of the sentence in terms of semantic units (see an example of segmentation from HMMs in Figure 1).

Afterwards, a simple translator based on manually defined rules converts the sequence of semantic units into one or more semantic frames with their attributes (see an example of the obtained frame in Figure 1).

4   The Basurde Corpus

For understanding purposes, we are only concerned with the semantics of the words present in the user turn of a dialogue. A total of 1,378 user turns were obtained from the 215 total dialogues of the task. Each of these turns can be composed of one or more sentences. The characteristics of the dataset are shown in Table 1, along with the distribution of each class of user turns[2].

4.1   Preprocessing

Problems of coverage and lack of training samples can occur when learning HMMs due to the fact that the number of instances of a word can be very low. We have to reduce the size of our lexicon by using lemmas and categories

---

[2] As a matter of fact, a total of 1,440 user turns were obtained from the dialogues, but some were discarded because their class frequency was very low.

[14]. Examples of lemmas are: substitution of any conjugated form of a verb with its corresponding infinitive form, plural words are substituted by singular words, etc. Examples of categories are: substitution of any instance of a city name with the category CityName, and the same for days, months, seasons, railway stations, etc.

In this way, we reduced the size of our lexicon from 635 to 386 different words. An example of a categorised and lemmatized sentence is:

Original user turn: *I would like to know the timetables of the Euromed train from Barcelona to Valencia.*

Preprocessed turn: want know timetable of TrainType train OriginMarker CityName DestinationMarker CityName

4.2   Speech Corpus

As mentioned above, 215 dialogues were acquired. The user turns were manually transcribed to have a correct written corpus. In addition, to emulate the real behaviour of the dialogue system, the user turns were processed using an automatic speech recognition system based on acoustic HMMs and bigrams as language model. The obtained Word Accuracy was 72%.

5   Experiments

Different measures were used to determine the correctness of the understanding models:

- **Correct semantic sequences (*css*):** percentage of semantic sentences that match up exactly with the reference sentences.
- **Correct semantic units (*csu*):** percentage of correct semantic units that match the reference sentences.
- **Correct frames (*cf*):** percentage of frames that match up exactly with the reference frames.
- **Correct frame units (*cfu*):** percentage of frame attributes that have the same value as the reference frames.

First of all, back-off and Laplace smoothing techniques were tested in order to decide which of the two smoothing techniques should be used. The results showed that back-off smoothing performed better. Thus, the rest of the tests were performed using back-off smoothing.

The categorised and lemmatized corpus was used for the experiments (some previous experiments were performed without lemmas or categories and the results were worse). First of all, a general HMM was trained using the whole training corpus. The final experiment envolved five runs using the Leaving-One-Out scheme: training the HMM with the data of four partitions and testing only with one partition[3]. Therefore, the measures obtained for the test set reported

---

[3] The corpus was homogeneously partitioned in five sets, using 80% of the corpus (4 partitions) for training and 20% of the corpus (1 partition) for testing.

Table 2. Performance of the general HMM and the specific HMMs.

	General HMM									
	Opening		Confirmation		New_consult		Question		Total	
	Text	Speech	Text	Speech	Text	Speech	Text	Speech	Text	Speech
css	30.8	3.4	72.2	55.0	51.4	25.0	67.6	24.2	53.5	27.2
csu	74.2	46.0	74.3	58.9	67.0	47.7	71.3	28.8	69.8	48.0
cf	66.0	23.6	82.0	71.0	72.4	52.4	79.2	46.4	73.8	51.0
cfu	87.4	75.0	90.3	80.6	85.0	74.6	91.0	62.0	86.8	74.8

	Specific HMMs									
	Opening		Confirmation		New_consult		Question		Total	
	Text	Speech	Text	Speech	Text	Speech	Text	Speech	Text	Speech
css	27.0	3.0	70.8	57.0	50.2	24.6	54.8	23.0	50.9	27.3
csu	71.5	43.0	63.9	52.5	65.7	46.0	45.5	17.3	64.6	44.4
cf	59.0	26.8	81.6	73.6	71.4	51.2	61.4	43.8	70.6	51.1
cfu	83.9	73.0	82.2	76.3	84.4	73.9	72.3	43.8	82.9	71.8

in Table 2 are the averaged results of the five runs of the experiment. Results are given for the entire test corpus (**Total** column of the table) and are also detailed for each class of user turn (Opening, Confirmation, New_consult and Question). Experiments were also performed with the correct transcriptions of the user turns (*Text* column in Table 2) and with the sequences of words obtained from the recognition process (*Speech* column).

Afterwards, we tested specific HMMs, that is, a different model for each class of the user turns. Experiments of this kind were performed to try to exploit the similarities of the user turns of each class in order to be able to better learn the structure of its class. The obtained results are also shown in Table 2 (as before, experiments with text and speech data were performed, and the averages of five runs of the experiments are given).

The results show that the understanding module is not capable of making a correct segmentation in many cases (*css* figures are very low for all cases, specially for speech input; only Confirmation turns can be segmented accurately). However, the number of correct semantic units (*csu*) and correct frames (*cf*) obtained are clearly much better than the correct segmentation sequences. This means that many segmentation errors are not semantically relevant and our model can recover from these errors.

If we compare the results obtained for the general HMM and the specific HMMs, it can be observed that general models are better than specific ones. One of the causes could be the lack of training samples for the classes of specific models, which makes it difficult to learn the structure of the classes they model.

6   Conclusions

We have presented the understanding process of a dialogue system as a transduction process from natural language into one or more semantic frames. In this process, we have seen the viability of using HMMs as transducers.

With this corpus we tested two types of HMMs: general and specific models for the different classes of user turns. The results show that the general model works better than the specific HMMs, because it is trained with more samples. It is necessary to use smoothing techniques in order to avoid the problem of underestimation and unseen words.

Other approaches to this same problem using grammatical inference techniques obtained similar results [15]. We can conclude that HMMs are a good approach as an understanding model in a dialogue system.

References

1. D. S. Pallet et al. The 1994 benchmark test for the ARPA spoken language program. In *Proceedings of ARPA Workshop on Spoken Language Technology*, 1995.
2. A. Bonafonte et al. Desarrollo de un sistema de diálogo oral en dominios restringidos. In *Primeras Jornadas de Tecnología del Habla*, Sevilla (Spain), 2000.
3. V. Zue et al. Jupiter: A telephone-based conversational interface for weather information. *IEEE Trans. on Speech and Audio Processing*, 8(1), 2000.
4. S. Seneff. TINA: A natural language system for spoken language applications. *Computational Linguistics*, 18(1):61–86, 1992.
5. W. Ward. Evaluation of the CMU ATIS system. In *Proc. of DARPA Speech and Natural Language Workshop*, pages 101–105, 1991.
6. L. Lamel et al. The LIMSI Arise system. *Speech Communication*, 31(4):339–354, 2000.
7. E. Levin and R. Pieraccini. Concept-Based Spontaneous Speech Understanding System. In *Proc. 4th Eurospeech'95*, pages 555–558, 1995.
8. H. Bonneau-Maynard and F. Lefèvre. Investigating stochastic speech understanding. In *Proc. of IEEE ASRU*, 2001.
9. Klaus Macherey, Franz Josef Och, and Hermann Ney. Natural Language Understanding Using Statistical Machine Translation. In *Proc. 7th Eurospeech'01*, pages 2205–2208, 2001.
10. C. J. Fillmore. The case for case. *Universals in Linguistic Theory*, pages 1–90, 1968.
11. Emilio Sanchis, Fernando García, Isabel Galiano, and Encarna Segarra. Applying dialogue constraints to the understanding process in a Dialogue System. In *Proc. of 5th TSD*, pages 389–395, 2002.
12. D. Vilar, M. J. Castro, and E. Sanchis. Connectionist classification and specific stochastic models in the understanding process of a dialogue system. In *Proc. Eurospeech'03*, pages 645–648, 2003.
13. Jr. G. D. Forney. The Viterbi algorithm. *Proc. IEEE*, pages 268–278, 1973.
14. E. Segarra and L. Hurtado. Construction of Language Models using Morfic Generator Grammatical Inference MGGI Methodology. In *Proc. Eurospeech'97*, pages 2695–2698, 1997.
15. E. Segarra et al. Extracting Semantic Information Through Automatic Learning Techniques. *IJPRAI*, 16(3):301–307, 2002.

Unsupervised Learning
of Ontology-Linked Selectional Preferences[*]

Hiram Calvo[1] and Alexander Gelbukh[1,2]

[1] Center for Computing Research, National Polytechnic Institute,
Av. Juan de Dios Bátiz s/n, esq. Av. Mendizábal, México, D.F., 07738, México
hcalvo@sagitario.cic.ipn.mx, gelbukh@gelbukh.com
www.gelbukh.com
[2] Department of Computer Science and Engineering, Chung-Ang University,
221 Huksuk-Dong, DongJak-Ku, Seoul, 156-756, Korea

Abstract. We present a method for extracting selectional preferences of verbs from unannotated text. These selectional preferences are linked to an ontology (e.g. the hypernym relations found in WordNet), which allows for extending the coverage for unseen valency fillers. For example, if *drink vodka* is found in the training corpus, a whole WordNet hierarchy is assigned to the verb *to drink* (*drink liquor*, *drink alcohol*, *drink beverage*, *drink substance*, etc.), so that when *drink gin* is seen in a later stage, it is possible to relate the selectional preference *drink vodka* with *drink gin* (as *gin* is a co-hyponym of *vodka*). This information can be used for word sense disambiguation, prepositional phrase attachment disambiguation, syntactic disambiguation, and other applications within the approach of pattern-based statistical methods combined with knowledge. As an example, we present an application to word sense disambiguation based on the Senseval-2 training text for Spanish. The results of this experiment are similar to those obtained by Resnik for English.

1 Introduction

Selectional Preferences are patterns that measure the degree of coupling of an argument (direct object, indirect object and prepositional complements) with a verb. For example, for the verb *to drink*, the direct objects *water*, *juice*, *vodka*, and *milk* are more probable than *bread*, *ideas*, or *grass*.

In order to have a wide coverage of possible complements for a verb, it is necessary to have a very big training corpus, so that every combination of a verb and a complement be found in such a training corpus. However, even for a corpus of hundreds of millions of words, there are word combinations that do not occur in it; sometimes these word combinations are not used very frequently, or sometimes they are used often but they are not seen in certain training corpora.

A solution for this problem is to use word classes. In this case, *water*, *juice*, *vodka* and *milk* belong to the class of *liquid* and can be associated with the verb *to drink*. However, not all verbs have a single class that is associated with them. For example the verb *to take* can have arguments of many different classes: *take a seat*, *take place*, *take time*, etc. On the other hand, each word can belong to more than one class. This

---

[*] Work done under partial support of Mexican Government (CONACyT, SNI, PIFI-IPN, CGEPI-IPN), Korean Government (KIPA), and RITOS-2. The second author is currently on Sabbatical leave at Chung-Ang University.

Table 1. Non-common usages (lower occurrence values) and common usages (higher occurrence values) of word combinations of verb + WordNet synset

verb	synset	Literal English gloss		Weighted occurrences
leer	*fauna*	'read	fauna'	0.17
leer	*comida*	'read	food'	0.20
leer	*mensaje*	'read	message'	27.13
leer	*escrito*	'read	writing'	28.03
leer	*objeto_inanimado*	'read	inanimate_object'	29.52
leer	*texto*	'read	text'	29.75
leer	*artículo*	'read	article'	37.20
leer	*libro*	'read	book'	41.00
leer	*comunicación*	'read	communication'	46.17
leer	*periódico*	'read	newspaper'	48.00
leer	*línea*	'read	line'	51.50
beber	*superficie*	'drink	surface'	0.20
beber	*vertebrado*	'drink	vertebrate'	0.20
beber	*lectura*	'drink	reading'	0.20
beber	*sustancia*	'drink	substance'	11.93
beber	*alcohol*	'drink	alcohol'	12.50
beber	*líquido*	'drink	liquid'	22.33
tomar	*artrópodo*	'take	arthropod'	0.20
tomar	*clase_alta*	'take	high_class'	0.20
tomar	*conformidad*	'take	conformity'	0.20
tomar	*postura*	'take	posture'	49.83
tomar	*resolución*	'take	resolution'	89.50
tomar	*control*	'take	control'	114.75
tomar	*acción*	'take	action'	190.18

depends not only on the sense of the word, but the main feature that has been taken into account when assigning it to a class. For example, if we consider the color of the objects, *milk* would belong to the class of white objects. If we consider physical properties, it may belong to the class of fluids or liquids. *Milk* can be *basic_food* too, for example. We can say then that the relevant classification for a word depends both on its use and the classification system being used.

To find a correlation between the usage of a noun, its sense, and the selectional preferences for the verbs, the following kind of information is needed: (1) Ontological information for a word – a word is not linked to a single class, but a whole hierarchy, and (2) information of the usage of the word in a sentences, given a verb and its specific position in the ontology.

In this paper we propose a method to extract selectional preferences that are linked to an ontology. This information is useful to solve several problems following the approach of pattern-based statistical methods combined with knowledge [1, 2].

Table 1 presents an example of the kind of information we obtain with our method. The table shows the values of argument's co-occurrence with the verb for three Spanish verbs using the WordNet hierarchy. These numbers were obtained following the methodology that is described in detail in Section 3. Note that synsets that have greater chance of being an argument for a verb have a greater value, such as *drink liquid*. In contrast, lower values indicate that a synset is less likely to be an argument for the corresponding verb (v. gr. *drink reading, read food* or *drink surface*). These combinations were found due to mistakes in the training corpus or due to several unrelated senses of a word. For example, *gin* can be also a *trap* that in turn is a *device*. This may lead to **drink device*. When big corpora are used for training, this noise is substantially reduced in contrast with correct patterns, allowing for disambiguation of word senses based on the sentence's main verb.

Table 1 also shows that synsets located higher in WordNet hierarchy have higher values, as they accumulate the impact of the hyponym words that are below them (see for example *communication, liquid* or *action*). A simple ad-hoc strategy of weighting values in WordNet's hierarchy will be described also in Section 3.

In the following sections we will show how we obtain information like that shown in Table 1, and then we will illustrate the usefulness of our method applying this information to word sense disambiguation (WSD).

2 Related Work

One of the first works on selectional preference extraction linked to WordNet senses was Resnik's [3]. It is devoted mainly to word sense disambiguation in English. Resnik assumed that a text annotated with word senses was a resource difficult to obtain, so he based his work on text tagged only morphologically. Subsequently, Agirre and Martinez [4, 5] worked linking verb usage with their arguments. In contrast with Resnik, Agirre and Martínez assumed the existence of a text annotated with word senses: Sem-Cor, in English. Other supervised WSD systems include JHU [6], which won the Senseval-2 competition, and a maximum entropy WSD system by Suarez and Palomar [7]. The first system combined, by means of a voting-based classifier, several WSD subsystems based on different methods: decision lists [8], cosine-based vector models, and Bayesian classifiers. The second system selected a best-feature selection for classifying word senses and a voting system. These systems had a score around 0.70 on the Senseval-2 tests.

We take into account that a resource such as Sem-Cor is currently not available for many languages (in particular, Spanish), and the cost of building it is high. Accordingly, we follow Resnik's approach, in the way of assuming that there is not enough quantity of text annotated with word senses. Furthermore, we consider that the WSD process must be completely automatic, so that all the text we use is automatically tagged with morphological and part-of-speech (POS) tags. Accordingly, our system is fully unsupervised.

Table 2. Selected combinations extracted from VCC

	verb	relation	noun	English gloss
1	*contar*	*con*	*permiso*	'to have permission'
2	*pintar*	<	*pintor*	'painter paints'
3	*golpear*	>	*balón*	'kick ball'
4	*solucionar*	>	*problema*	'solve problem'
5	*dar*	>	*señal*	'give signal'
6	*haber*	>	*incógnita*	'there is unknown quantity'
7	*poner*	*en*	*cacerola*	'put in pan'
8	*beber*	*de*	*fuente*	'drink from source'
9	*beber*	>	*vodka*	'drink vodka'

Previous work on unsupervised systems has not achieved the same performance as with supervised systems: Carroll and McCarty [9] present a system that uses selectional preferences for WSD obtaining 69.1% precision and 20.5% recall; Agirre and Martinez [10] present another method, this time unsupervised. They use recall as the only performance measure, reporting 49.8%; Resnik [3] achieves 40% correct disambiguation.

In the next sections we describe our method and measure its performance.

3 Methodology

In order to obtain the selectional preferences linked to an ontology, we used the hypernym relations of Spanish EuroWordNet[1] 1.0.7 (S-EWN) as ontology, and the corpus described in [11] as a training corpus (VCC). This corpus of 38 million words is supposed to combine the benefits of a virtual corpus (e.g. the web as corpus), with those of a local corpus, see details in [11].

The text was morphologically tagged using the statistical tagger TnT by Thorsten Brants [12] trained with the corpus CLiC-TALP. This tagger has a performance of over 92%, as reported in [13].

After the text was tagged morphologically, several combinations were extracted for each sentence: (1) verb + noun to the left (subject), (2) verb + noun to the right (object), and (3) verb NEAR preposition + noun. Here, + denotes adjacency, while NEAR denotes co-occurrence within a sentence. Table 2 shows an example of the information obtained in this way. The symbol > means that the noun is to the right of the verb; the symbol < means that the noun appears to the left of the verb.

Once the combinations have been extracted, the noun for each combination was looked up in WordNet and an occurrence for the corresponding synset (with every sense) was recorded. Also the occurrence was recorded for each hyperonym of each its sense. A weighting factor was used so that words higher in the hierarchy (up to the root *entity*) have lower impact than the words in the lower part of the hierarchy. We used the weighting factor $\dfrac{1}{level}$. For example, for *drink vodka* found in the text, an occurrence of the combination *drink vodka* is recorded with the weight 1, also occurrences of *drink liquor* with the weight 0.5, *drink alcohol* with 0.33, etc. are recorded. For each combination, the weights of its occurrences are accumulated (summed up).

Currently we have acquired 1.5 million of selectional preferences patterns linked to the WordNet synsets. Each pattern consists on a verb, a preposition (in some cases), and a synset. An example of the information obtained can bee seen in Figure 1. *Channel* has 6 senses listed by WordNet: *way, conduit, clear, conduit* (anatomic), *transmission, depression*, and *water*. The sense marked with the highest number of occurrences is *conduit*, while the one with fewer occurrences is *transmission*, in the sense of *channel of transmission* or *TV channel*, for example; one cannot *cross* a TV channel. Now consider *libro* 'book'; this Spanish word has five senses: *stomach, product, section, publication* and *work / play*. The first sense refers to the name in Spanish for an internal part of body. We can see that this is the sense with fewer occurrences (one cannot *read* an *organ*). The sense with the greatest number of occurrences is that related to *written_language*. This information can be used to disambiguate the sense

---

[1] S-EWN was Developed jointly by the University of Barcelona (UB), the Nacional University of Open Education (UNED), and the Polytechnic University of Catalonia (UPC), Spain.

atravesar canal: 'cross channel'

02342911n → **way** 3.00 → trough 8.83 → artifact 20.12 → unanimated_obect 37.10 → entity 37.63

02233055n → **conduit** 6.00 → way 3.00 → trough 8.83 → artifact 20.12 → unanimated_object 37.10 → entity 37.63

03623897n → **conduit** 5.00 → anatomic_structure 5.00 → body_part 8.90 → part 7.22 → entity 37.63

04143847n → **transmission** 1.67 → communication 3.95 → action 6.29

05680706n → **depression** 2.33 → geological_formation 2.83 → natural_object 14.50 → unanimated_object 37.10 → entity 37.63

05729203n → **water** 4.17 → unanimated_object 37.10 → entity 37.63

leer libro: 'read book'

01712031n → **stomach** 3.50 → internal_organ 3.00 → organ 3.08 → body_part 3.75 → part 4.35 → entity 41.51

02174965n → **product** 14.90 → creation 13.46 → artifact 34.19 → unanimated_object 36.87 → entity 41.51

04214018n → **section** 23.33 → writing 33.78 → written_language 25.40 → communication 55.28 → social_relation 43.86 → relation 42.38 → abstraction 44.18

04222100n → **publication** 16.58 → work 7.95 → product 14.90 → creation 13.46 → artifact 34.19 →unanimated_object 36.87 → entity 41.51

04545280n → **play** 4.50 → writing 33.78 → written_language 25.40 → communication 55.28 →social_relation 43.86 → relation 42.38 → abstraction 44.18

Fig. 1. Ontology with usage values for the combinations in Spanish *atravesar canal* 'cross channel' and *leer libro* 'read book'. Synsets labels were translated here from Spanish to English for the reader's convenience

of the word, given the verb with which it is used. In the next section we describe an experiment we ran to measure the performance of this method in the task of WSD.

4   Application to WSD

Senseval is a series of competitions aimed to evaluation of word sense disambiguation programs, organized by the ACL-SIGLEX. The last competition took place in 2001 (the next one being scheduled for 2004). The data for this competition are available on-line. This competition included, among 10 languages, Spanish data, to which we applied our method. The evaluation set comprises slightly more than 1,000 sentences. Each sentence contains one word, for which the correct sense, among those listed for it in WordNet, is indicated.

Our evaluation showed that 577 of 931 cases were resolved (a recall of ~62%). Of those, 223 corresponded in a fine-grained way to the sense manually annotated (precision ca. 38.5%). These results are similar to those obtained by Resnik [3] for English, who obtained on average 42.55% for the relations verb – subject and verb – object only. Note that these results are much better than random selection of senses (around 28% as reported in [3]).

4.1 Discussion

Our results are lower than those of some other WSD systems. For example, Suarez and Palomar [7] report a score of 0.702 for noun disambiguation for the same evaluation set of Senseval-2. However, their system is supervised, whereas ours is unsupervised. In comparison with existing unsupervised WSD systems (i.e. [3, 9, 10]) our method has a better recall, though lower precision in some cases. The latter is due the strategy of our method that considers only verb – noun relations, when sometimes the word sense is strongly linked to the preceding noun. This is particularly true for pairs of nouns that form a single prepositional phrase. For example, in the training text the following sentence appears: *La prevalecía del principio de libertad frente al principio de autoridad es la clave de Belle Epoque* 'The prevalence of the liberty principle in contrast with the authority principle is the key of Belle Epoque'. In this case, the sense of *autoridad* 'authority' is restricted more strongly by the preceding noun, *principio* 'principle', in contrast with the main verb: *es* 'is'. To determine the sense of *autoridad* by means of the combinations *is < authority* and *is of authority* is not the best strategy to disambiguate the sense of this word.

In order to improve our method, it is necessary to include information on the usage of combinations of nouns. This is part of our future work.

5 Other Applications

Besides WSD, the information of selectional preferences obtained by this method can be used to solve important problems, such as syntactic disambiguation. For example, consider the phrase in Spanish *Pintó un pintor un cuadro*, lit. 'painted a painter a painting' meaning 'a painter painted a painting'. In Spanish it is possible to put the subject to the right of the verb. There is ambiguity, as it is not possible to decide which noun is the subject of the sentence. As Spanish is a language with rather free word order, even *Pintó un cuadro un pintor*, lit. 'painted a painting a painter' has the same meaning.

To decide which word is the subject (*painting* or *painter*) it is possible to consult the ontology linked with selectional preferences constructed with the method presented in this paper. First, we find statistically that the subject appears to the left of the verb in 72.6% of the times [14]. Then, searching for *un pintor pintó* 'a painter painted' returns the following chain of hypernyms with occurrence values: *painter* → *artist* 1.00 → *creator* 0.67 → *human_being* 2.48 → *cause* 1.98. Finally, the search of *un cuadro pintó* 'a painting painted' returns *scene* → *situation* 0.42 → *state* 0.34. That is, *painter* (1.00) is more probable as subject than *painting* (0.42) for this sentence. A large-scale implementation of this method is a topic of our future work.

6 Conclusions

We have presented a method to extract selectional preferences of verbs linked to an ontology. It is useful to solve natural language text processing problems that require information about the usage of words with a particular verb in a sentence. Specifically, we presented an experiment that applies this method to disambiguate word senses. The results of this experiment show that there is still a long way to improve unsupervised WSD methods using selectional preferences; however, he have identified specific points to improve our method under the same line of pattern-based statistical methods combined with knowledge.

References

1. P. Resnik. Selection and Information: A Class-Based Approach to Lexical Relationships. TesisDoctoral, University of Pennsylvania, December (1993)
2. P. Resnik. Selectional constraints: An information-theoretic model and its computational realization. Cognition, 61 (1996) 127–159
3. P. Resnik. Selectional preference and sense disambiguation, ACL SIGLEX Workshop on Tagging Text with Lexical Semantics: Why, What, and How?, Washington, D.C., USA, April 4-5 (1997)
4. E. Agirre, D. Martinez. Learning class-to-class selectional preferences. In: Proceedings of the Workshop Computational Natural Language Learning (CoNLL-2001), Toulousse, France, 6-7 july (2001)
5. E. Agirre, D. Martinez. Integrating selectional preferences in WordNet. In: Proceedings of the first International WordNet Conference, Mysore, India, 21-25 January (2002)
6. D. Yarowsky, S. Cucerzan, R. Florian, C. Schafer, R. Wicentowski. 2001. The Johns Hopkins SENSEVAL-2 System Description. In: Preiss and Yarowsky, eds.: The Proceedings of SENSEVAL-2: Second International Workshop on Evaluating Word Sense Disambiguation Systems, Toulouse, France, (2001) 163–166
7. A. Suárez, M. Palomar. A Maximum Entropy-based Word Sense Disambiguation System. In: Hsin-Hsi Chen and Chin-Yew Lin, eds.: Proceedings of the 19th International Conference on Computational Linguistics, COLING 2002, Taipei, Taiwan, vol. 2 (2002) 960–966
8. D. Yarowsky. Hierarchical decision lists for word sense disambiguation. In Computers and the Humanities, 34(2) (2000) 179–186
9. J. Carroll, D. McCarthy. Word sense disambiguation using automatically acquired verbal preferences. In Computers and the Humanities, 34(1-2), Netherlands, April (2000)
10. E. Agirre E, D. Martínez. Unsupervised WSD based on automatically retrieved examples: The importance of bias. In Proceedings of the Conference on Empirical Methods in Natural Language Processing, EMNLP, Barcelona, Spain (2004)
11. A. Gelbukh, G. Sidorov, L. Chanona. Corpus virtual, virtual: Un diccionario grande de contextos de palabras españolas compilado a través de Internet. In: Julio Gonzalo, Anselmo Peñas, Antonio Ferrández, eds.: Proc. Multilingual Information Access and Natural Language Processing, International Workshop, in IBERAMIA-2002, VII Iberoamerican Conference on Artificial Intelligence, Seville, Spain, November 12-15, (2002) 7–14
12. T. Brants. TnT: A Statistical Part-of-Speech Tagger. In Proceedings of the 6th Applied Natural Language Processing Conference, Seattle, Washington, USA (2000)
13. R. Morales-Carrasco, A. Gelbukh. Evaluation of TnT Tagger for Spanish. In Proc. Fourth Mexican International Conference on Computer Science, Tlaxcala, Mexico, September 08-12 (2003)
14. J. Monedero, J. González, J. Goñi, C. Iglesias, A. Nieto. Obtención automática de marcos de subcategorización verbal a partir de texto etiquetado: el sistema SOAMAS. In Actas del XI Congreso de la Sociedad Española para el Procesamiento del Lenguaje Natural SEPLN 95, Bilbao, Spain (1995) 241–254

Advanced Relevance Feedback Query Expansion Strategy for Information Retrieval in MEDLINE

Kwangcheol Shin[1], Sang-Yong Han[1,*], Alexander Gelbukh[1,2,**], and Jaehwa Park[1]

[1] School of Computer Science and Engineering,
Chung-Ang University, 156-756, Seoul, Korea
kcshin@archi.cse.cau.ac.kr, {hansy,jaehwa}@cau.ac.kr
[2] Center for Computing Research,
National Polytechnic Institute, Zacatenco 07738 DF, Mexico
www.Gelbukh.com

Abstract. MEDLINE is a very large database of abstracts of research papers in medical domain, maintained by the National Library of Medicine. Documents in MEDLINE are supplied with manually assigned keywords from a controlled vocabulary called MeSH terms, classified for each document into major MeSH terms describing the main topics of the document and minor MeSH terms giving more details on the document's topic. To search MEDLINE, we apply a query expansion strategy through automatic relevance feedback, with the following modification: we assign greater weights to the MeSH terms, with different modulation of the major and minor MeSH terms' weights. With this, we obtain 16% of improvement of the retrieval quality over the best known system.

1 Introduction

Relevance feedback is a classic information retrieval (IR) technique that reformulates a query based on documents selected by the user as relevant [10]. Relevance feedback techniques have been recently an active research area in IR.

We experimented with the MEDLINE database maintained by the National Library of Medicine, which is widely used in medical research. It contains ca. 12 million abstracts on biology and medicine collected from 4,600 international biomedical journals. To each document in this database, keywords called MeSH (Medical Subject Headings) are manually added to describe its content for indexing in a uniform manner. This is a specific features of MEDLINE that other databases do not have [5].

In this paper we suggest new a retrieval technique for MEDLINE based on relevance feedback using modulating MeSH terms in query expansion. We show that our technique gives 16% improvement in the quality of retrieval over the best currently known system.

The paper is organized as follows. Section 2 explains the MEDLINE database and MeSH indexing, as well as the vector space model and the relevance feedback technique. Section 3 discusses related work. Section 4 describes the proposed technique to modulate the MeSH terms' weights in relevance feedback-based query expansion. Section 5 presents our experimental results, and Section 6 draws conclusions.

---

* Corresponding author.
** The third author is currently on Sabbatical leave at Chung-Ang University.

A. Sanfeliu et al. (Eds.): CIARP 2004, LNCS 3287, pp. 425–431, 2004.
© Springer-Verlag Berlin Heidelberg 2004

2   Background

2.1   MEDLINE and MeSH

MEDLINE, a premier bibliography database of National Library of Medicine (NLM, www.nlm.gov), covers the fields of medicine, nursing, dentistry, veterinary medicine, the health care system, the preclinical sciences, and some other areas of the life sciences. It contains bibliographic citations and author abstracts from over 4,600 journals published in the United States and in 70 foreign countries. It has approximately 12 million records dating back to 1966 [5].

MeSH is the acronym for *Medical Subject Headings*. It is the authority list of the vocabulary terms used for subject analysis of biomedical literature at NLM [6]. The MeSH controlled vocabulary, a distinctive feature of MEDLINE, is used for indexing journal articles. It imposes uniformity and consistency to the indexing of biomedical literature. MeSH is an extensive list of medical terminology. It has a well-formed hierarchical structure. MeSH includes major categories such as anatomy/body systems, organisms, diseases, chemicals and drugs, and medical equipment. Expert annotators of the NLM databases, based on indexed content of documents, assign subject headings to each document for the users to be able to effectively retrieve the information that explains the same concept with different terminology [5].

MeSH terms are subdivided into MeSH Major headings and MeSH Minor headings. MeSH Major headings are used to describe the primary content of the document, while MeSH Minor headings are used to describe its secondary content. On average, 5 to 15 subject headings are assigned per document, 3 to 4 of them being major headings [6].

To use the current MEDLINE search engine, users give their keywords as a query to the system. The system automatically converts such a query to a Boolean query and retrieves data from the MeSH field of the documents. The current system does not use the full text of the documents.

2.2   Vector Space Model

The vector space model has the advantage over the Boolean model (used currently in the search engine provided with MEDLINE) in that it provides relevance ranking of the documents: unlike the Boolean model which can only distinguish relevant documents from irrelevant ones, the vector space model can indicate that some documents are very relevant, others less relevant, etc.

In the vector space model [8] the documents are represented as vectors with the coordinates usually proportional to the number of occurrences (*term frequency*) of individual content words in the text. Namely, the following procedure is used for converting documents into vectors:

The vector space model for the entire document collection is determined by the $d \times n$-dimensional matrix $\| w_{ij} \|$, where d is the number of significant words in all documents of the collection (stopwords, i.e.., the functional words and the words with too high and too low frequency, are excluded), n is the number of documents in the collection, and w_{ij} is the weight of the i-th term in j-th document. For these weights, usually the *tf-idf* (*term frequency–inverse document frequency*) value is used:

$$tf\text{-}idf = \frac{f_{ij}}{\max f_{ij}} \log \frac{n_i}{n} \tag{1}$$

where f_{ij} is the frequency of the term i for the document j and n_i is the number of the documents where the term i occurs.

Using such vectors to represent documents, we can measure the similarity between two documents (vectors) using the cosine measure (the cosine of the angle between the two vectors) widely used in information retrieval. This measure is easy to understand and its calculation for sparse vectors is very simple [8]. Specifically, the cosine measure between the user query and a document is used to quantitatively estimate the relevance of the given document for the given query.

The cosine similarity between two vectors x_i and x_j is calculated as their inner product:

$$s(x_i, x_j) = \frac{x_i^T x_j}{\| x_i \| \| x_j \|} = \cos \theta \tag{2}$$

where θ is the angle between the two vectors. To simplify calculations in practice, the vectors are usually normalized so that their norm $\| x \|$ be 1. The similarity is in the range between 0 and 1. If the two documents have no words in common, the similarity is 0; the similarity between two copies of same document is 1.

2.3 Query Expansion Using Relevance Feedback

To improve the quality of ranking, a number of strategies is used, among which is query expansion: the system automatically adds to the user query certain words (in some very broad sense synonymous to the original ones) that bring relevant documents not matching literally with the original user query.

In the relevance feedback technique, the query is modified using information in a previously retrieved ranked list of documents that have been judged for relevance by the user. A number of methods, such as those suggested by Rocchio and Ide, have been studied within this broad strategy. Using Rocchio's method [11], the new query is derived from old query according to the below formula:

$$\vec{q}_m = \alpha\vec{q} + \frac{\beta}{|D_r|} \sum_{\forall \vec{d}_j \in D_r} \vec{d}_j - \frac{\gamma}{|D_n|} \sum_{\forall \vec{d}_j \in D_n} \vec{d}_j \tag{3}$$

D_r : *Set of relevant documents, as identified by the user, among the retrieved documents*

D_n : *Set of irrelevant documents, as identified by the user, among the retrieved documents*

α, β, γ : *Tuning parameters*

The parameter α represents the relative importance of terms in the original query; β and γ are parameters regulating the relative importance of relevant irrelevant information for query expansion.

Ide [10] uses a slightly different formula:

$$\vec{q}_m = \alpha\vec{q} + \beta \sum_{\forall \vec{d}_j \in D_r} \vec{d}_j - \gamma \max_{irrelevant}(\vec{d}_j) \tag{4}$$

2.4   Related Work

The best known retrieval technique for MEDLINE is the one introduced by Srinivasan in a series of recent articles focusing on two areas of the retrieval process, indexing [1] and query expansion [2, 3]. Here we briefly introduce this method.

Srinivasan constructs two index vectors for each document: a vector of the (significant – not stopwords) words in the title and abstract (*ta*-vector) and a vector of the (significant) words of the MeSH terms (*m*-vector). With a title-abstract vocabulary of *p* words and a MeSH vocabulary of *q* words, a document is represented as:

$$\vec{d}_j = (w_{1j}, w_{1j}, ..., w_{pj}); (c_{1j}, c_{1j}, ..., c_{qj})$$

She generates a single *ta*-vector for each query, since she considers the user's initial free-text query more suitable for searching the title and abstract field.

$$q_{old} = (w_{1q}, w_{2q}, ..., w_{tq}).$$

Her query expansion strategy consists in adding an *m*-vector to each query representation. This expanded query is used to compute the ranking as a weighted sum of the vector inner products of the corresponding vectors in the documents and queries:

$$\text{Similarity}(d, q) = \sigma * \text{similarity}(\text{ta - vectors}) + \text{similarity}(\text{m - vectors}), \tag{5}$$

where σ is a parameter that allows one to change the relative emphases on the two types of vectors during retrieval.

Thus, her query expansion consists in adding the MeSH terms of the retrieved documents to the original query:

$$q_{new} = (w_{1q}, w_{2q}, ..., w_{tq}); (c_{1q}, c_{2q}, ..., c_{pq})$$

Note that the *ta*-vectors in q_{old} and q_{new} are always identical. The retrieval process considers both *ta*-vectors and *m*-vectors from the documents and queries as in (5).

3   Modulating MeSH Term Weights

As explained before, MEDLINE data contains MeSH keywords classified for each document into major (more important) and minor (less important) ones as shown in Table 1.

Table 1. A sample of MEDLINE data

MJ	BONE-DISEASES-DEVELOPMENTAL: co. CYSTIC-FIBROSIS: co. DWARFISM: co.
MN	CASE-REPORT. CHILD. FEMALE. HUMAN. SYNDROME.
AB	Taussig et al reported a case of a 6-year-old boy with the Russell variant of the Silver-Russell syndrome concomitant with cystic fibrosis. We would like to describe another patient who...

Our idea is to modulate the weight of MeSH terms in each document vector in query expansion, since these terms are more important than the ordinary words in the text of the document. Indeed, a keyword assigned by the reviewer "stands for" several words in the document body that "voted" for this generalized keyword. For example, for the text "... *the patient is* _allergic_ *to ... the patient shows* _reaction_ *to ... causes* _itch_ *in patients* ..." the annotator would add a MeSH term *allergy*. Though this term appears only once in the document description, it "stands for" three occurrences in the text, namely, *allergic*, *reaction*, and *itch*. Our hypothesis is that increasing its weigh would more accurately describe the real frequency of the corresponding concept in the document and thus lead to better retrieval accuracy.

It is well known that relevance feedback, which uses the terms contained in relevant documents to supplement and enrich the user's initial query, gives better results than first retrieval result [10]. In this paper, we use a modified relevance feedback model:

$$\vec{q}_m = \alpha \vec{q} + \sum_{\forall \vec{d}_j \in D_r} (\vec{\beta}_j + \vec{d}_j) \tag{6}$$

D_r : *Set of relevant documents, as identified by the user, among the retrieved documents*

Here by × we denote coordinate-wise multiplication of the two vectors. We give different weights to MeSH terms and to general terms:

$$\beta_{ij} \leftarrow \begin{cases} (\delta + \tau\delta) & : term\ i\ is\ MeSH\ Major\ term\ in\ \vec{d}_j \\ (\delta - \tau\delta) & : term\ i\ is\ MeSH\ Minor\ term\ in\ \vec{d}_j \\ 0 & : otherwise \end{cases} \tag{7}$$

δ, τ : *Tuning parameters*

4   Experimental Results

For the experiments we use the well-known Cystic Fibrosis (CF) dataset, which is a subset of MEDLINE. It has 1,239 medical data records and 100 queries with relevant documents provided for each query. A sample query is shown in Table 2, with relevant document numbers (e.g., 139) and the relevant scores ranging from 0 to 2 obtained from 4 specialists manually evaluating the query and the data (e.g., 1222 stands for the score 1 assigned by the first expert and 2 by all others).

Table 2. Part of CF queries

QU	What are the effects of calcium on the physical properties of mucus from CF patients?				
RD	139 1222	151 2211	166 0001		
	311 0001	370 1010	392 0001		
	439 0001	440 0011	441 2122		
	454 0100	461 1121	502 0002		
	503 1000	505 0001			

We used the MC program [8] to produces vectors from the documents. Stopwords and the terms with frequency lower than 0.2% and higher than 15% were excluded. With this, the CF collection had 3,925 terms remaining. Then the *tf-idf* value was calculated for each document and the vectors were normalized; this produced 1,239 document vectors.

For applying the user's initial query, we formed two datasets, one consisting of only abstracts and another one consisting of abstract and MeSH terms, to compare our technique with Srinivasan's one which searches only in the abstracts when performs retrieval according to the initial query.

Table 3. Test result by applying initial query

	Abstract	MeSH+Abstract
R = the number of relevant docs in collection	4819	4819
#R = number of relevant docs among best R	1343	1511
Sum of scores of #R	4819	6155
#R / R = R-precision	0.279	**0.314**

Table 3 shows the results on first iteration (the original, not expanded query). We show the average R-Precision on 100 queries and the total value of the relevant scores (taken from the CF collection) of the *R* highest-ranked documents, where *R* is the total number of the documents known to be relevant in the collection. We considered a document to be known to be relevant if it was assigned non-zero score by at least one of the four human experts, see Table 2. One can note 12.51% of improvement in R-precision on MeSH+Abstracts data.

Now, to verify our query expansion technique, we used the documents known to be relevant within the *R* highest-ranked ones (their number is denoted #R), thus simulating the user's relevance feedback. Table 4 shows the result using Srinivasan's technique, and Table 5 shows the result using our technique.

Table 4. Query expansion results with Srinivasan's technique

σ	0.0	0.4	0.6	**0.7**	0.8	1.0	1.2
R = number of correct in the collection	4819	4819	4819	**4819**	4819	4819	4819
#R = number of correct docs among best R	2094	2110	2115	**2117**	2115	2108	2100
sum of scores of #R	8424	8528	8559	**8571**	8568	8528	8481
#R / R = R-precision	0.435	0.438	0.439	**0.439**	0.439	0.437	0.436

Table 5. Query expansion results with our technique

δ (τ = δ / 20)	0.3	0.4	0.5	0.6	**0.7**	0.8	0.9	1.0
R = number of correct in collection	4819	4819	4819	4819	**4819**	4819	4819	4819
#R = number of correct among best R	2446	2452	2450	2455	**2456**	2448	2441	2440
sum of scores of #R	9445	9466	9411	9455	**9416**	9373	9321	9312
#R / R = R-precision	0.508	0.509	0.508	0.509	**0.510**	0.508	0.507	0.506

One can note a 16% improvement over Srinivasan's technique, which is the best currently known technique.

5   Conclusions

We have shown that assigning different weights to major and minor MeSH headings in relevance feedback technique on MEDLINE data gives the results superior to the best known technique, which ignores the difference between the major and minor MeSH heading, treating them in the same way. Our technique shows a 16% improvement in R-precision.

References

1. Srinivasan P. Optimal document-indexing vocabulary for MEDLINE. Information Processing and Management, 1996; 32(5):503-514.
2. Srinivasan P. Query expansion and MEDLINE. Information Processing and Management, 1996; 32(4): 431-443.
3. Srinivasan P. Retrieval feedback in MEDLINE. Journal of the American Medical Informatics Association, 1996; 3(2):157-167.
4. MEDLINE Fact Sheet. www.nlm.nih.gov/pubs/factsheets/medline.html.
5. Lowe H.J., Barnett O. Understanding and using the medical subject headings (MeSH) vocabulary to perform literature searches. J. American Medical Association, 1995; 273:184.
6. Dhillon I. S. and Modha, D. S. *"Concept Decomposition for Large Sparse Text Data using Clustering," Technical Report* RJ 10147(9502), IBM Almaden Research Center, 1999.
7. Dhillon I. S., Fan J., and Guan Y.,: Efficient Clustering of Very Large Document Collections. Data Mining for Scientific and Engineering Applications, Kluwer Academic Publishers, 2001.
8. Frakes W. B. and Baeza-Yates R., *Information Retrieval: Data Structures and Algorithms.* Prentice Hall, Englewood Cliffs, New Jersey, 1992.
9. Ide E., "New experiments in relevance feedback" In G. Salton, editor, The SMART Retrieval System, 337-354, Prentice Hall, 1971.
10. Salton G. and. McGill M. J., *Introduction to Modern Retrieval.* McGraw-Hill Book Company, 1983.
11. Rocchio, J. (1971). Relevance feedback in information retrieval, In G. Salton (Ed.), *The SMART Retrieval System-Experiments in Automatic Document Processing* (Chap 14). Englewood Cliffs, N J: Prentice Hall.

Detecting Inflection Patterns in Natural Language by Minimization of Morphological Model*

Alexander Gelbukh[1,2], Mikhail Alexandrov[1], and Sang-Yong Han[2,**]

[1] National Polytechnic Institute, Mexico
www.Gelbukh.com, dyner1950@mail.ru
[2] Chung-Ang University, Korea
hansy@cau.ac.kr

Abstract. One of the most important steps in text processing and information retrieval is stemming – reducing of words to stems expressing their base meaning, e.g., *bake, baked, bakes, baking* → *bak-*. We suggest an unsupervised method of recognition such inflection patterns automatically, with no a priori information on the given language, basing exclusively on a list of words extracted from a large text. For a given word list V we construct two sets of strings: stems S and endings E, such that each word from V is a concatenation of a stem from S and ending from E. To select an optimal model, we minimize the total number of elements in S and E. Though such a simplistic model does not reflect many phenomena of real natural language morphology, it shows surprisingly promising results on different European languages. In addition to practical value, we believe that this can also shed light on the nature of human language.

1 Introduction

Nowadays huge amounts of information are available in more and more languages. For example, in May 2004 the number of official languages of the European Union reached 20 and will grow soon. The need of processing multidisciplinary documents in so many languages results in growing interest to knowledge-poor methods of text processing.

One of the most important modules in a system dealing with natural language, such as information retrieval or document classification system, is stemming. The task of a stemmer algorithm is to map the words having the same base meaning but differing in grammatical forms, to the same letter string that can be used to identify the word independently of its morphological form. As the common identifier of a set of word-forms, their common initial substring is usually used, e.g., *bake, baked, bakes, baking* → *bak-*. Often morphological derivations of the word are included in the set: *bake, baked, bakes, baking, baker, bakery* → *bak-*.

Though the quite problem is important for English, it is much more important for processing texts in very many other languages, among which are almost all European languages. Indeed, while in English there are only four morphological variants of a

---

* Work done under partial support of the ITRI of Chung-Ang University, Korea, and for the first author, Korean Government (KIPA) and Mexican Government (SNI, CONACyT, CGPI-IPN). The first author is currently on Sabbatical leave at Chung-Ang University.
** Corresponding author.

A. Sanfeliu et al. (Eds.): CIARP 2004, LNCS 3287, pp. 432–438, 2004.

verb, in Spanish verbs have 65 forms, while in Russian 250 (mostly due to participles), which are to be mapped to a common stem by the stemmer.

Manual construction of the corresponding dictionaries or rules is a tedious and labor-consuming task, especially for languages for which little linguistic resources are available (there are ca. 5,000 languages in the world). An attractive alternative is automatic learning of the necessary models from the texts themselves.

The languages spoken in the world can be roughly classified as follows:

- Inflective languages. Words in such languages consist of a stem and a number of suffixes and/or prefixes. The number of suffixes (or prefixes) for words of a given part of speech is fixed (or several different variants may exist), thus the number of different combinations of suffixes (prefixes) is fixed, e.g.: Eng. *ask-ed*, Span. *pregunt-aba-s* 'you were asking', *pregunt-e-n-se* 'please you (many) ask yourself'. Most European languages, except for Finnish, Hungarian, and Basque, are of this type.
- Agglutinative languages. Words in such languages consist of a stem and a potentially infinite number of suffixes attached to it as needed, e.g. Turkish *Türk-yali-lastir-a-ma-di-k-lar-i-mi-z-dan* '*one of those that we could not have possibly turned into a Turkish*', with the stem *Türk-* and a set of suffixes. Examples of such languages are Hungarian, Turkish, Korean, Aztec, etc.
- Isolating languages. Words in such languages do not change, so that each word is its own stem. Examples of such languages are Chinese or Vietnamese.
- Intraflective languages. In such languages the root meaning of a word is expressed with consonants, while the grammatical variations with vowels intermixed with the consonants, e.g., Arabic *kitab* 'book' consists of a stem *k-t-b* 'book-' and a morpheme -i-a- expressing grammatical meaning. Examples of such languages are Arabic and Hebrew.
- Incorporating languages. In such languages words consist of many stems glued together by complicated rules. Such a word represents the meaning of a whole sentence. Examples of such languages are Sanskrit, Chukchee, and some North American native languages.

In this paper we only deal with inflective languages, though we believe that our methods can be adjusted to the languages of other classes. We present an unsupervised approach to automatic construction of a stemmer basing only on a list of words extracted from large enough text.

The paper is organized as follows. In Section 2 we discuss the previous work on the topic, in Section 3 we explain our algorithm, and in Section 4 present the experimental results. Section 5 draws conclusions and lists some future work directions.

2   Previous Work

There are three main approaches to stemming:
- Dictionary-based,
- Rule-based, and
- Statistical-based.

Dictionary-based approach. It provides the highest quality of results at the cost of the highest development expenses. This approach implies the development of a dictionary listing all known words of a given language along with their inflection classes and other necessary information for generation of all their morphological forms [2]. A theoretical advantage of a dictionary-based approach is that it deals correctly with the words that look like inflected forms but in fact are not. For example, *darling* looks like a form of a verb **to darl*, while in fact it is not.

However, the main advantage of the dictionary-based approach is its correct treatment of exceptions, which can be individual (*men* → *man*) or regular (*stopping* → *stop*, Span. *conozco* 'I know' → *conocer* 'to know', Rus. *molotka* 'of hammer' → *molotok* 'hammer').

A weakness of the dictionary-based approach is the treatment of words absent in the dictionary. In this case one usually has to resort to a supplementary rule-based algorithm. Obviously, the need to develop, maintain, and process in runtime a large dictionary and/or a complex analysis system is the main practical disadvantage of such approaches.

Rule-based approach. This approach can be well exemplified by the well-known Porter stemmer [4]. This stemmer uses a complex cascades system of manually tuned rules such as:

1. $(*v*)$ *ING* →
2. BL → *BLE*
3. $(*d$ and not $(*L$ or $*S$ or $*Z)) →$ single letter
4. $(m = 1$ and $*o) → E$

etc.

The left-hand side of these transformation rules is a condition that fires the rule. It is an expression, usually containing a pattern to be matched with the string at hand. If the condition is met, the corresponding part of the string is substituted with another substring. The first rule above describes deletion (empty right-hand part) of a suffix *-eng* given that the string contains a vowel (v) preceding this suffix, possibly separated from it by an arbitrary substring (*). The second rule prescribes addition of -e after *-bl*. The third rule deletes repetition of the consonant in the words like *stopped*; *d* stands for this double consonant. In the fourth rule, *m* stands, roughly speaking, for the number of non-ending vowels, and *o* for a special form of the last syllable of the string.

The rule-based approach is much less expensive in terms of necessary linguistic resources, and yet powerful enough to correctly process many of regular exceptions; other exceptions can be treated with a small dictionary. Still, rule-based approach requires detailed analysis of the linguistic properties of the language at hand and careful manual construction of the rules.

Statistical-based approach. This approach allows for fast and totally automatic development of a stemmer for a new language. Most approaches of this type use supervised learning techniques, which rely on a set of manually prepared training examples [1]. However, collecting and selection of such training examples can be problematic. In addition, the absence of examples of a specific type can lead to lacunas in the learned data resulting in massive errors.

In this paper we suggest an unsupervised approach to learning stemming rules from a list of words extracted from a corpus of the given language. Since the approach is unsupervised, it does not rely on subjective expert judgments. Just because of this, we believe that the possibility of learning morphological information from the texts without human intervention can shed some light on the nature of human languages.

As an example of a previous work on unsupervised learning of morphology [3] can be mentioned. However, unlike [3], we do not apply complex heuristics and do not use statistical considerations. Instead, we try to find the absolute minimum number of the elements (stems and endings, not letters) which describe the given language.

3   The Algorithm

Given a word list, we find the set of possible stems and endings of the language at hand. Then, we can decompose any word – either from the same list or an unseen one – into a stem and ending. In case of ambiguity we select a combination of the most frequent stem and ending (the global ambiguity can be solved by mutual reinforcement method). Below we concentrate on the problem of finding the sets of stems and endings of the given language.

Problem formulation. We rely on the following two hypotheses:
1. The words of the language are simple concatenations of one stem and one (possibly complex) suffix (or prefix). Thus, we currently ignore any sandhi phenomena (such as *lady* + *es* = *ladies*), suppletivism (*foot* / *feet*) and other complications of real language morphology.
2. Language is constructed in such a way that minimal learning effort is necessary for its acquisition; in particular, it has the minimal necessary amount of stems and endings. The stems and endings are "re-used" to form many combinations: *ask*, *ask-ed*, *ask-ing*, *bak-e*, *bak-ed*, *bak-ing*.

Mathematically, the task of finding the corresponding set of stems and endings can be formulated as follows: Given a set V of letter strings extracted from a text, find two sets of strings, S (standing for stems) and E (standing for endings), such that any word $w \in V$ is a concatenation of a suitable stem and ending: $w = s + e$, $s \in S$, $e \in E$, and $|S| + |E|$ has the minimum value over all sets with such properties, where $|X|$ is the number of elements in the set X. In other words, find minimum sets S and E generating V, i.e., such that $V \subseteq S + E$.

If we suppose in addition that the language is suffixal (and not prefixal), we can additionally require that of all possible pairs S and E with the same $|S| + |E|$ preferable are those with smaller $|E|$.

Genetic algorithm. Unfortunately, we are not aware of a less-than-exponential algorithm for finding the sets S and E. So we conducted experiments using a genetic algorithm to find an approximate solution; any other method of optimization could be used as well.

First, we experimented with chromosomes of the length $|V|$ whose genes are the points of division of the individual wordforms from V; for example, a gene 3 at the position corresponding to *darling* stands for the division hypothesis *dar-ling*. We used simple crossover and random mutation. For each such set of division hypotheses, we calculated the total number of stems $|S|$ and endings $|E|$. To reflect our preference for smaller E (versus smaller S), we considered as fitness function

$$|S| + 0.000001|E| \to \min,$$

the coefficient only affecting the choice between chromosomes with the same $|S| + |E|$.

However, such a search space proved to be too large. To reduce the search space for sake of performance, we considered chromosomes with binary values indicating the presence or absence of a certain stem or ending in S or E. For this, we construct the maximal sets S' and E' of all possible prefixes and all possible suffixes of all strings from V. From them, we remove all those elements that occur only once. Indeed, a decomposition of a $w \in V$ into $w = s + e$, where either s or e occurs only once, can be substituted by a decomposition $w = w + \lambda$, where λ is an empty ending, without changing $|S| + |E|$.

Note that when an element is excluded from S' or E', the frequency of another element – the second half of the decomposition of a word w – decreases and can become 1, so that this element will also be excluded. Such iterative exclusion of elements from S' and E' further reduces their size, finally producing the sets S'' or E'' with such a property that for any element $s \in S''$ there are at least two different $e \in E''$ such that $s + e \in V$, and similarly for E''.

With this, we form binary chromosomes of the length $|S''| + |E''|$ so that a value of 1 stands for the inclusion of the corresponding element in S or E, correspondingly. If for a given selection of S and E, some word $w \in V$ cannot be decomposed, we consider the whole word w a new element of S. This gives us the following fitness function:

$$|S| + 0.000001|E| + |V \setminus (S + E)| \to \min.$$

The last member of the expression stands for the non-decomposable (with the given random selection of S and E) words from V, which we add to S on the fly.

Since the search space with such a method is considerably reduced, we can find better approximate solutions. In addition, we observed significant gain in quality when we removed not only the endings occurring once but all too rare endings, e,g., all endings occurring less than $|V|/1000$ times. This is possible since we suppose that all endings used in the language are rather productive (are used many times).

Note that due to eliminating the stem or ending candidates that occur only once, our algorithm will usually correctly deal with difficult words such as *darling*. Indeed, even if *-ing* is a likely ending, *darl-* is not a frequent stem. Thus, the algorithm will prefer decomposition of this word into the stem *darling-* and an empty ending.

4   Experimental Results

We applied our algorithm, as described at the end of the previous section, to the official list of words permitted in crossword games such as Srabble. The list has 113,809 wordforms; the found $|S| + |E| = 60917$. Here is an example of the divisions obtained:

abject-	abjur-ing	ablaze-	abluent-s	abnegat-ing
abject-ly	abla-te	ab-le	ablush-	abnegat-ion
abjectness-	abla-ted	ablegate-	ablut-ed	abnegat-ions
abjectness-es	abla-tes	ablegate-s	ablut-ion	abnormal-
abjurat-ion	abla-ting	able-r	ablut-ions	abnormalit-ies
abjurat-ions	abla-tion	able-s	ab-ly	abnormalit-y
abjur-e	ablation-s	able-st	abmho-	abnormal-ly
abjur-ed	ablativ-e	ablings-	abmho-s	abnormal-s
abjur-er	ablativ-es	ablins-	abnegat-e	
abjur-ers	ablau-t	abloom-	abnegat-ed	
abjur-es	ablaut-s	abluen-t	abnegat-es	

One can see that the results are not perfect but quite promising. Note that the examples shown here is not an optimal solution; if we run our genetic algorithm for a longer time, we will find a better solution. As compared with Porter stemmer [4] the result is not as good. However, unlike manually tuned Porter stemmer, our algorithm was presented with only 114 thousand of English wordforms and found the presented decomposition in a fully unsupervised manner.

We also apply the same algorithm to a small Spanish wordlist extracted from *Don Quijote*, of only 22,966 words; the found $|S| + |E| = 7959$. Here is an example of obtained decomposition:

ablándate-	abolla-do	aborrec-imiento	abrasa-n	abra-zada
abland-áis	abomin-ábamos	aborrezco-	abra-sar	abra-zado
abland-ó	abomin-able	abr-áis	abrasa-rla	abraza-miento
abland-aba	abomin-ado	abr-í	abrasa-rnos	abraza-ndo
abland-aban	abomin-o	ab-ría	abrasa-sen	abra-zar
abland-ado	abon-asen	ab-rían	abra-semos	abraza-rá
abland-an	abon-o	abrí-la	abrazándo-le	abraza-ra
abland-ar	aborrascadas-	abr-ís	abrazándo-nos	abraza-rle
abland-ara	aborrec-í	ab-ra	abrazándo-se	abraza-rme
abland-arme	aborrec-ía	abracé-	abrazáro-nle	abraza-ron
abland-aron	aborrec-e	ab-ran	abrazáro-nse	abraza-rse
abland-arte	aborrec-en	abra-só	abrazár-selos	abraza-se
abland-e	aborrec-ió	abra-sa	abra-zó	abr-azo
abobado-	aborrec-ible	abrasa-da	abrazól-a	abr-azos
abolengo-	aborrec-ida	abrasa-das	abrazól-e	
aboll-é	aborrec-ido	abrasa-dores	abrazól-os	
abolla-da	aborrec-idos	abra-sados	abraza-ba	

One can observe that accent alternations in Spanish verb stems present certain problems to our algorithm. However, given so small word list and the fact that the presented solution is not optimal (which can explain some random anomalies), the results seem promising.

We also apply our algorithm to some other inflective languages, such as Russian, with similar results.

5   Conclusions and Future Work

We have presented an unsupervised algorithm for recognizing the morphological structure of an inflective language, with application to stemming. Currently our algorithm ignores many phenomena of the real natural language morphology, such as sandhi (including Spanish accent alternations), suppletivism, or letter-phoneme correspondence; dealing with such phenomena will be a topic of our future work. We also believe that a similar approach can be applied to some other types of languages, such as agglutinative ones, with suitable modifications.

An interesting direction of future work is to detect, in an unsupervised manner, the syntactic classes of words, roughly corresponding to parts of speech. This can be done by clustering the contexts where the words with certain endings occur. With this, we expect to improve the behavior of our model on difficult words such as *darling*.

We will also try different algorithms for finding better approximate solutions problem formulated in Section 3, for example, simulated annealing.

References

1. M. Alexandrov, X. Blanco, A. Gelbukh, P. Makagonov. Knowledge-poor Approach to Constructing Word Frequency Lists, with Examples from Romance Languages. *Procesamiento de Lenguaje Natural* **33**, 2004.
2. A. Gelbukh, G. Sidorov. Approach to construction of automatic morphological analysis systems for inflective languages with little effort. In: Computational Linguistics and Intelligent Text Processing (CICLing-2003). *Lecture Notes in Computer Science* **2588**, Springer-Verlag, pp. 215–220.
3. J. Goldsmith. Unsupervised Learning of the Morphology of a Natural Language. *Computational Linguistics*, **27** (2), 2001.
4. M.F. Porter. An algorithm for suffix stripping. *Program*, **14** (3): 130–137, 1980.

Study of Knowledge Evolution in Parallel Computing by Short Texts Analysis

Pavel Makagonov[1] and Alejandro Ruiz Figueroa[2]

[1] Postgraduate Division of Mixteca University of Technology, Huajuapan de León, Oaxaca, 69000, México
mpp@mixteco.utm.mx
[2] Institute of Electronic and Computation of Mixteca University of Technology Huajuapan de León, Oaxaca, 69000, México
figueroa@nuyoo.utm.mx

Abstract. The problem of measuring and predicting the future of various branches of science is discussed. We propose an economical approach that is useful for the estimation of the stage of development for any branch of "normal" science with the help of abstract flow analysis. For this goal it is necessary to collect large amounts of abstracts uniformly distributed in years. As abstracts are poor knowledge objects, we use the procedure of aggregation in its annual sum of texts as an elemental unit for cluster analysis. For cluster analysis we use the tool kit «Visual Heuristic Cluster Analysis for Texts» developed earlier by one of the co-authors, with K. Sboychakov. To determine the topic of the cluster, we propose to use chapters of manuals and articles principal in the procedure of pattern recognition.

1 Introduction. Problems of Scientometric and Practical Demands

The problem of resource distribution between different branches of investigation call for evaluation and quantification of the scientific activity, its productivity and results. Public institutes involved in the process of sharing of restricted economical resources for investigation need tool kits for the analysis of effectiveness of their policy of investment and to help to improve it according to a plan.

In fact it is not possible to predict the time and the place of the appearance of new inventions, but it is possible to predict the development of "normal" science [1] that is gradually improving results and that these results warrant capital investment in investigation.

"Normal" science is less uncertain than the forefront of science. "Normal" science bases on antecedent results (the primaries of which as a rule are unexpected, unforeseen) and a study of predecessors gives us the possibility to predict the tendency of development of different (distinguishable) branches of science and gives a reason to correct financial planning.

Quantitative parameters of the system life cycle can be described as an S-curve [2]. When the system reaches the limits of its possible development it changes qualitatively or is substituted by another system. "Normal" science is growing in the stage of system development and declining about the moment of obsolescence.

A. Sanfeliu et al. (Eds.): CIARP 2004, LNCS 3287, pp. 439–445, 2004.

We propose a method that does not have the ability to predict a character of qualitative changes but can be used for fixing a time when interest in the subject of investigation falls precipitously or begins to grow up. To implement this approach it is necessary to have the criteria of the prospects for the branch of science or for the subject of investigation.

For problems of this type different methods of Scientometric and Bibliometric Mapping [3, 4, 5, and 6] are used. These methods are laborious, and demand a great quantity of articles that must be paid for in advance. Large scientific bodies, Government organizations and big companies can use these articles because of their financial ability. Our idea is to develop a simple tool kit that can be used by public institutes that are responsible for the financial support of scientific investigation and by investigators who are in the initial part of their activity, and who only have access to free abstracts of articles on the Internet, and need to investigate different branches of their science.

2   Preparing Samples for Revealing Models of Scientific Nowledge Flows

Our approach is based on an analysis of a corpus of articles' texts or at least abstracts' texts for a sufficient period of years in a special circle of problems or in a partial branch of science.

Every topic has a typical time period of substantial development. We chose a topic that has a rather short history of development (about 30 years) and has developed in the last 10 years very intensively. This topic is Parallel, Simultaneous, Concurrent, and Distributed Computing.

The characteristics almost coincide with the title of the book "Foundations of Multithreaded, Parallel, and Distributed Programming" [7]. The author of this book earlier, in 1991, issued another book with the title «Concurrent Programming Principles and Practices». So, even the names of these two books show us changes in the point of view of the same subject.

Information on this topic is accessible on the Internet for free. With the availability of this information we collected 710 abstracts on the mentioned topic for the years from 1990 until 2004 (about 50 per year) in the Digital library of IEEE [8].

The criteria for selection of abstracts into the corpus of texts was the presence of one of the key words of the topic (Parallel, Simultaneous, Concurrent, and Distributed) or those equivalents (multithreads, supercomputer, hypercube, cluster of computers etc.) of the same level of abstraction of the "ontology" of this topic.

Our task was to reveal clusters of words that give us a lower level of abstraction (ontology) for our topic.

3   Method of Analysis of Poor Knowledge Data

We used the toolkit Visual Heuristic Cluster Analysis for texts (VHCA for texts) [9] as an elemental step of methodology (algorithm).

We used this tool kit to obtain a Domain oriented dictionary (DOD) for the texts corpus and an image of every text as a vector of quantities of words from the DOD presented in the text [9].

These images were used to form three matrices:

1. matrix "text/word" with quantity of words of the DOD (column) in every text (row) as elements of it;
2. matrix "word/word" with quantity of texts which contain the pairs of words from column and row as elements of it;
3. matrix "text/text" with quantity of the same words of the DOD in every pair of texts as elements of it.

For construction of the DOD with VHCA for texts we select the words which satisfy the following criteria:

1. The relative frequency of a word in the corpus of texts must be K0 times greater than the relative frequency of the same word in the frequency list of common used lexis (in our case K0=400%).
2. Criterion K1 defines the upper boundary for the minimum of texts' quantity that contains a given word at least once.
3. Criterion K2 defines the lower boundary for the maximum of texts' quantity that contains a given word. (The goal is to exclude common scientific words for all subtopics.)

It is known that abstracts contain about 150-250 words and in very poor condition when K0 = 100% only about 2 - 8 words per one text (abstract) are new candidates to DOD. Real options of K0, K1, and K2 reduce this number 2- 5 times.

That is why abstracts are considered as poor knowledge objects (texts).

To obtain objects with enriched knowledge we join all abstracts of every year to one annual text and obtain about   100 words as new candidates to the DOD.

In figure 1 we present the matrix "text/word" where every text is the sum of abstracts of the same year. Every non-zero element of the matrix is substituted by a rectangle with corresponding darkness of grey color in according to scale located in the left part of the figure.

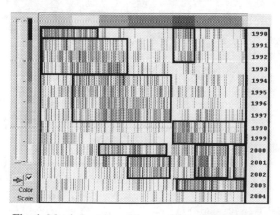

Fig. 1. Matrix text /word for annual sums of abstracts

This matrix is obtained in condition for DOD forming: K1 = 14%; K2= 86% of abstracts. The matrix is presented after clustering with the above mentioned tool kit VHCA. It is then possible to see the tight groups (clusters) of words for some groups of annual texts. If we construct the matrix of the "text/word" type directly for abstracts, we obtain a very rarefied matrix or a poor knowledge object.

The matrix of figure 1 was used for the calculation of the matrix "text/text" presented in figure 2 with outlined clusters of annual texts.

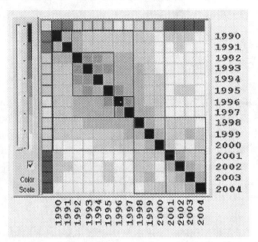

Fig. 2. Matrix "text/text" for annual sums of abstracts

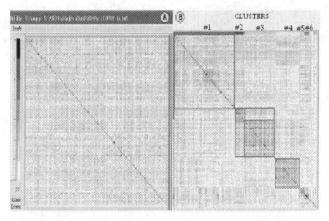

Fig. 3. Matrix "text/text" for 710 abstracts of different years (A) before and (B) after clustering

For a uniform aggregate of texts we can consider this part of our investigation almost complete, but our annual texts are a mixture of different topics (according to the method of preparation) and we can assume a greater diversity of topics for the same years.

For a more detailed investigation of an inhomogeneous aggregate of texts it is possible to obtain greater detail. For this goal we prepare the matrix "text/text" for every

710 abstracts. In figure 3a and 3b this matrix is presented before and after clustering. In figure 3b one can distinctly see 4 large clusters of abstracts that are evidently connected with more partial topics.

The quantity of abstracts in large clusters is represented in figure 4.

The deviation of the number of abstracts in clusters gives us information about the change of interest over time (during years) for topics that are connected with every cluster. The only problem is to get to know the contents of these topics.

For this goal we prepared the set of annual texts for every rich cluster. Every annual text contains a sum of abstracts from the same cluster for the same year. We can do it only for the clusters that contain a large amount of abstracts. Otherwise we would obtain poor knowledge texts. This new set of annual texts can be analyzed by the same method that we use for the initial corpus of texts.

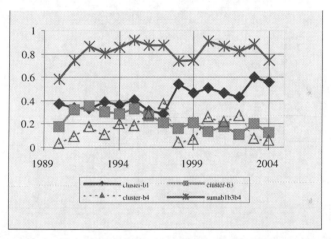

Fig. 4. The quantity of abstracts in large clusters

The difference is that new annual texts are more uniform (homogeneous) themselves. For this reason it is possible to reveal more definitively the topic of every new cluster of annual investigations. Indeed, with help of VHCA we can now obtain partial DODs of new clusters. And these DODs are dictionaries of subtopics that the experienced investigator can reveal by analyzing their contents.

Now the problem is what to do if we do not have an "experienced investigator" at our disposal? In the case of the absence of this specialist it is possible to use the same (or another) tool kit for pattern recognition. For this goal one can combine a new corpus of texts that contain:

1. a set of chapters of manuals or articles with different partial topics (and different sets of special words);
2. a set of annual sums of abstracts for different clusters, which are obtained in previous steps.

The results of this step for patterns and annual texts of two large clusters are presented in figure 5. The visible links (a) between annual texts of different clusters can be explained by using scientific words that are more common in articles than in textbooks. Texts of cluster #3 have fewer links with manuals than cluster #1.

The possible reason is that we do not have correspondent patterns in our aggregate or, alternatively, the topic corresponding to this cluster is a new one or is a discussion of very general problems without special words of partial subjects.

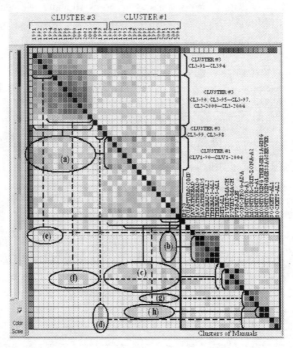

Fig. 5. Matrix "text/text" for patterns and annual texts of two large clusters

Cluster #1 has rather strong links (b) with topic Threads in a later years; with topics MPI (Message Passing Interface) and PVM (Parallel Virtual Machine) in almost all years (c) with the exception of 1998 and 1999, and with topic Monitor and Monitoring (g) and (h).

Cluster #3 has only poor links (e) with Java Threads, with the topic "Sockets" in 1999 (d), and with PVM (f).

Part of the words in manuals can be distributed between different clusters of annual texts. In this case it is possible to count the percentage of representation of every manual topic in every cluster of annual texts.

4   Conclusion

This article exposes only a short description of the proposed method of revealing prospective topics of "normal" science. We have postponed the problem of pattern quality. Those patterns could be selected by experts or with the tool kit used here (or with some other "standard instrument"). In any case, it is necessary to select texts enriched with words in a very narrow subject with minimal intersection of vocabulary with other patterns. This is the subject of future research.

The other problem is common scientific terminology. It can be an obstacle for more refined clustering in the case of poor knowledge texts, but there are some approaches for the solution of this problem.

The third problem is an eagerness of authors to synthesize new complex words that are ignored by our method. It is possible to include in the DOD such words as hypercube, multithreads, supercomputer, etc. in the same row with "cube, thread, computer". There are texts with exotic words that which could be dropped as nonexistent or as errors in writing, if the operator could not add those worlds to the DOD without confidence.

To obtain certain results with our method for poor knowledge data it is necessary to use only clusters with numerous abstracts (not articles). For small but important clusters it is still necessary to buy full texts of articles corresponding to abstracts.

This research is being partially supported by National Council for Science and Technology – CONACYT, México under project N-39011-A. We greatly appreciate the help given to us by Ms. Lorraine Parkin for reviewing the text.

References

1. La Estructura de las revoluciones científicas. Thomas S. Kuhn. Editorial Fondo de Cultura Económica de España. 2000(1962). Traducción: A. Contín. ISBN:84-375-0046-X, pp 320.
2. The Geography of Economic Development: Regional Changes, Global Challenges. Timothy J. Fik. A Division of the McGraw-Hill Companies, pp 260-265.
3. Bibliometric Mapping as a Science Policy and Research Management Tool. Ed C. M. Noyons. DSWO PRESS. Science Studies. 1999 Leiden University , The Netherlands, pp 225.
4. http://148.216.10.83/VIGILANCIA/capitulo_4.htm.
5. http://bvs.sld.cu/revistas/aci/vol10_4_02/aci040402.htm.
6. http://www.campus-oei.org/salactsi/elsa6.htm
7. Foundations of Multithreaded, Parallel, and Distributed Programming. Gregory R. Andrews, University of Arizona. Addison-Wesley 2000.
8. http://search2.computer.org/advanced/simplesearch.jsp
9. Makagonov P., Alexandrov, M., Sboychakov, K. A toolkit for development of the domain-oriented dictionaries for structuring document flows. In: H.A. Kiers et al (Eds.), "Data Analysis, Classification, and Related Methods", Springer, 2000 (Studies in classification, data analysis, and knowledge organization), pp. 83-88.

JERARTOP: A New Topic Detection System[*]

Aurora Pons-Porrata[1], Rafael Berlanga-Llavori[2],
José Ruiz-Shulcloper[3], and Juan Manuel Pérez-Martínez[2]

[1] Universidad de Oriente, Santiago de Cuba, Cuba
aurora@app.uo.edu.cu
[2] Universitat Jaume I, Castellón, Spain
{berlanga,martinej}@lsi.uji.es
[3] Advanced Technologies Application Center, MINBAS, Cuba
jshulcloper@cenatav.co.cu

Abstract. In this paper we present an on-line detection system, named *JERARTOP*, which goes beyond traditional detection systems, because it generates the implicit knowledge of a stream of documents. This knowledge is expressed as a taxonomy of topics/events, which is automatically built by the system in an incremental way. Moreover, the proposed detection system also annotates each detected topic using a set of predefined subjects, as well as it provides a summary for the topic. The experimental results demonstrate its usefulness and its effectiveness as a detection system.

1 Introduction

Topic Detection and Tracking (TDT) is a new line of research that comprises three major sub-problems: segmenting speech-recognized TV/radio broadcasts into news stories, detecting novel events, and tracking the development of an event according to a given set of sample stories of that event [1]. Starting from a continuous stream of newspaper articles, the *Event Detection* problem consists in determining for each incoming document, whether it reports on a new event, or it belongs to some previously detected event.

One of the most important issues in this problem is to define what an *event* is. Initially, an event can be defined as something that happens at a particular place and time. However, many events occur along several places and several time periods (e.g. the whole event related to a complex trial). For this reason, researchers in this field prefer the broader term of *Topic*, which is defined as an important event or activity along with all its directly related events [2]. In this context, a *Topic Detection System* aims at discovering the topics reported in a stream of newspaper articles. For this purpose, incremental unsupervised clustering algorithms have been widely applied, such as the *K-Means*, *Single-Pass*, *1-NN* and others [3, 4, 5, 6].

In this paper we address three main problems that currently event detection systems present, namely: 1) they make irrevocable clustering assignments and therefore the set of detected topics can depend on the arrival order of the documents, 2) they do not take into account the different abstraction levels at which events and topics can be represented, and 3) they do not provide any summary of the detected topics, so that users can know quickly the cluster's contents.

---

[*] This work has been partially funded by the research project CICYT (TIC 2002-04586-C04-03).

A. Sanfeliu et al. (Eds.): CIARP 2004, LNCS 3287, pp. 446–453, 2004.

The proposed solution consists of a new on-line detection system named *JERARTOP*. It generates incrementally the implicit knowledge of the incoming documents. This knowledge is expressed as a hierarchy of topics, that is, our system identifies not only the topics but also the structure of events they comprise. Moreover, the proposed system also categorizes each hierarchy topic with respect to a set of predefined subjects, and it provides a summary for it.

The remainder of the paper is organized as follows: Section 2 presents the global architecture of our system. Section 3 describes the representation of documents taking into account their temporal and place components, a similarity measure for these documents and the clustering algorithms. The description methods are presented in Section 4 and our experiments are showed in Section 5. Finally, conclusions are presented in Section 6.

2 Global Architecture

The global architecture of our detection system is presented in Figure 1. Starting from a continuous stream of newspaper articles, the system first processes them to get a proper representation to cluster them according to their semantics. The steps included in this pre-processing are the following ones: document texts are tokenised, abbreviations, proper names and some simple phrases are recognised, stop-words are removed, part-of-speech tags are added and common words are replaced by their lemmas. All these elements are called terms and they will form a vector with their text frequency. Additionally, the system also extracts some useful metadata such as the publication dates and the places mentioned in the texts. Thus, the document representation can take into account the time and place properties.

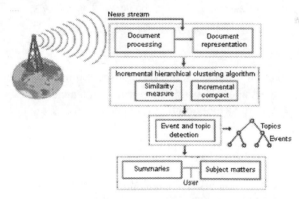

Fig. 1. Global architecture of the detection system *JERARTOP*.

3 Document Clustering Algorithm

Each incoming document d^i is represented in our system with three components:

- *A vector of weighted terms* $T^i = (TF_1^i, ..., TF_n^i)$, where the terms represent the lemmas of the words appearing in the content of the document, and TF_k^i is the relative frequency of the term t_k in d^i.

- A *vector of publication dates*. This vector is only formed by one publication date when comparing documents instead of cluster representatives.
- A *vector of weighted places* $(TF_{p_1^i},...,TF_{p_{l_i}^i})$, where $TF_{p_k^i}$ is the absolute fre-

quency of the place p_k in d^i and $k=1,...,l_i$. Place names are automatically extracted from the content of the documents by using a thesaurus. They are represented by their paths within the thesaurus, where each level indicates a geographic region.

Automatic document clustering, as in event detection, is based on a similarity measure and a clustering criterion. The cosine measure mostly uses to compare two documents. In our case, we consider that two documents refer to the same event if their contents, places and time references approximately coincide.

To compare the term vectors of two documents d^i and d^j we use the cosine measure: $S_T(d^i,d^j) = \cos(T^i,T^j)$.

To compare the time vectors of two documents we propose the following function:

$$D(d^i,d^j) = \min_{f^i \in FR^i, f^j \in FR^j} \left\{ d(f^i,f^j) \right\},$$ where $d(f^i,f^j)$ is the number of days be-

tween both and FR^i is the set of all publication dates f^i of the document d^i.

To compare the place vectors of two documents we propose the following Boolean function:

$$S_P(d^i,d^j) = \begin{cases} 1 & \text{if } \exists\, p_q^i, p_t^j \text{ such that they have a common prefix} \\ 0 & \text{otherwise} \end{cases}$$

Finally, the global similarity measure can be defined as follows:

$$S(d^i,d^j) = \begin{cases} S_T(d^i,d^j) & \text{if } S_P(d^i,d^j)=1 \wedge D(d^i,d^j) \le \beta_{time} \\ 0 & \text{otherwise} \end{cases}$$

where β_{time} is the maximum number of days that are required to determine whether two articles refer to the same or to different events. This measure tries to capture the idea that two documents reporting a same event should have a high semantic similarity, time proximity and place coincidence.

Hierarchical Document Clustering

One of the main novelties of *JERARTOP* is that it applies an incremental hierarchical clustering algorithm to the detection problem. This algorithm attempts to build a hierarchy of topics by clustering successively the representatives of the clusters obtained in the previous hierarchy level. In this way, the higher is the hierarchy level we have less details in the detected topics. The lowest level of the hierarchy is intended to allocate the smallest detectable events, which are groups of tightly related documents. The rest of the levels contain cluster representatives. The representative of a cluster c, denoted as $\bar{c}$, is also a document, represented as $(T^{\bar{c}}, F^{\bar{c}}, P^{\bar{c}})$, which is calculated as the union of the documents in c.

JERARTOP uses as the basic clustering routine the compact clustering algorithm presented in [7], which is based on the incremental construction of β_0-compact sets. In this way the system ensures that the detected sets are independent of the document arrival order.

In order to ensure this property in the hierarchy, the system must revise all the detected topics in the hierarchy every time a new document arrives. For this purpose, the system first applies the clustering routine in the lowest level of the hierarchy. New clusters could appear and other existing could disappear. When clusters are removed from any level of the hierarchy, their representatives must be removed from the clusters in which they were located in the next level. Similarly, when new clusters are created, their representatives must be calculated. The members of the clusters where changes took place (that is, some cluster representatives were eliminated) as well as all new representatives, must be queued in order to incorporate them to the set of existing clusters in this level of the hierarchy. For that purpose, we apply the clustering routine again. This process is repeated until the top level on the hierarchy is reached [8].

4 Cluster Description Methods

In order to determine at a glance whether the content of an event are of user interest, we propose a new summarization method based on Testor Theory [9]. Starting from a set of document clusters, each one representing a different event or topic, our method selects the frequent terms of each cluster that are not included in the other clusters. Once these terms have been selected, the system extracts all the sentences that contain the selected terms. Finally, in order to improve the coherence and organization of the summaries, we sort the extracted sentences according to the publication date of the news and their position in the text.

For each cluster c, we construct a matrix $MR(c)$, whose columns are the most frequent terms in the representative $\bar{c}$ and its rows are the representatives of all clusters, described in terms of these columns. In order to calculate the typical testors, we considered two classes in the matrix $MR(c)$. The first class is only formed by $\bar{c}$ and the second one is formed by all remaining cluster representatives. The comparison criterion applied to all the features is:

$$d(v_{i_k}, v_{j_k}) = \begin{cases} 1 & if \ v_{i_k} - v_{j_k} \geq \delta \\ 0 & otherwise \end{cases},$$

where v_{i_k}, v_{j_k} are the frequencies in the cluster representative i and j in the column corresponding to the term t_k respectively, and δ is an user-defined parameter.

Then, a summary of an event c consists of a set of sentences extracted from the documents in c, in which the highest quantity of terms that belong to the maximum length typical testors of the matrix $MR(c)$ occurs. Moreover, the sentences that cover the calculated typical testor set are also added to the summary.

In addition to this, *JERARTOP* also assigns subject matters to each detected topic of the hierarchy. For this purpose, we have adopted the subjects proposed by the International Press Telecommunications Council (IPTC)[1]. The IPTC Subject Reference System provides a list of internationally acceptable subject names, subject matter names and some subject detail names for categorizing the content of news.

---

[1] http://www.iptc.org/

To assign IPTC subjects to detected topics, we make use of the synsets of the lexical database *WordNet²*. We have used the different relationships between synsets in order to annotate each synset of *WordNet* with an IPTC code. More specifically, we first manually associate to each IPTC subject a proper synset. Then the system automatically propagates this IPTC code to all the directly related synsets and its hyponyms. Notice that not all the synsets will have associate an IPTC code.

Finally, in order to assign an IPTC subject to each detected topic, the system applies the following method. Given the cluster representative of the topic, the system first obtains a tuple with the synsets associated to the term vector. Notice that these terms can have several senses, and therefore some disambiguation method must be applied to reduce the number of ambiguous synsets. In this work we have used the method presented in [10]. Afterwards, the system determines the 10 IPTC subjects that annotate more synsets in the disambiguated representative. As the IPTC subjects are organized into taxonomy, each selected IPTC subject votes for its ancestors in this taxonomy. The vote is the number of the synsets annotated with this subject in the representative. Finally, the IPTC subject that has the maximum number of votes is selected. The final subject of the cluster will be the IPTC that satisfies the following conditions:

- It is one of the 10 IPTC subjects initially selected.
- It is a descendent of the IPTC subject that received the maximum number of votes.
- It annotates the greater number of the synsets in the cluster representative among all descendents of the IPTC subject that received the maximum number of votes.

The intuitive idea of this method is to select firstly, the more general IPTC subject that annotates the greater number of terms in the document cluster and then, inside this subject matter, to select the most particular subject.

5   Experiments and Results

The effectiveness of our detection system has been evaluated using two collections. The first one contains 554 articles published in the Spanish newspaper "El País" during June 1999. We have manually constructed a hierarchy of topics. In this work we only deal with the two first levels of this hierarchy, called the *Event Level* and *Topic Level* respectively. In the first level we have identified 85 non-unitary events. From these events we have identified 58 topics. The collection covers 21 events associated to the end of the "Kosovo War" along with their immediate consequences, the visit of the Pope to Poland, the elections in several countries, among others.

To evaluate the results we use two measures of the literature that compare the system-generated clusters with the manually labeled topics, namely: the F1-measure and the Detection Cost [2]. Table 1 shows the minimum topic-weighted cost and the maximum F1-Measure obtained by our system on the "El País" dataset in both levels of the hierarchy. The first line shows results for the base system using the cosine metric. Line 2 shows results when using our similarity measure instead of cosine distance. Our similarity measure performs much better with respect the F1-Measure, improving the results by 0.06 in both levels. As a consequence, we can conclude that the time and spatial components improves notably the quality of the system-generated topics. These components do not affect to the Detection Cost.

---

² http://www.cogsci.princeton.edu/~wn/

Table 1. The obtained results in "El País" collection.

System	Event Level		Topic Level	
	Detection Cost	**F1-Measure**	**Detection Cost**	**F1-Measure**
Base cosine	0.0027	0.7237	0.0039	0.7572
JERARTOP	0.0026	0.7848	0.0039	0.8114

Figure 2 shows a snippet of the created hierarchy by *JERARTOP*. This hierarchy is represented as a XML file containing for each topic the events that it comprises and its subject matter. Each event contains also the titles of the news, its subject matter and its summary. The carried out experiments demonstrate the usefulness of the description methods. The summaries capture the main ideas about each topic and an appreciable reduction of words is also achieved (superior to 85% in most of the topics). In case of the subject matters, we evaluate the results obtained in each topic in good (G), bad (B) and not too bad (R). Table 2 shows for some topics of this collection, the obtained subject and its evaluation. Considering alone the good answers, the method obtains a precision of 71%, whereas if we also consider as good those classified as not too bad, we obtain a precision of 88%.

```
- <Topic Id= "Cluster_134" Level= "1">
    <Subject IPTC= "Politic & Treaty and International Organisations & alliances" />
  - <Event Id= "Cluster_166" Level= "1">
      <Description Summary= "Ni siquiera una conversación telefónica celebrada la semana pasada entre
      Chirac, Aznar y el presidente argentino, Carlos Menem, ha modificado la decisión francesa de retrasar la
      apertura de negociaciones con Chile y con el Mercosur. El viceministro de Exteriores alemán, Günther
      Verheugen, expresó el deseo de la presidencia alemana de aprobar los mandatos de negociación antes de
      esa cita que reunirá a los jefes de Estado o de Gobierno de todos los países de América Latina y del
      Caribe y de la UE. Los países de Mercosur y Chile advirtieron a la UE el pasado fin de semana en México
      que quieren un acuerdo de libre comercio y que esperan que la cumbre de Río adopte compromisos claros
      en ese sentido. Fue él quien lanzó en 1997 la idea de reunir en una cumbre a los líderes de América Latina
      y Europa. La diplomacia española ha mantenido un breve y discreto silencio sobre el enfrentamiento que
      se registró el pasado viernes en Colonia, Alemania, entre el presidente del Gobierno español, José María
      Aznar, y el presidente francés, Jacques Chirac, sobre el mandato de negociación con Mercosur. Aunque la
      cumbre es mucho más que Mercosur -asistirán 17 Jefes de Estado y de Gobierno de Latinoamérica, 16 del
      Caribe y 15 de la UE-, las negociaciones con el bloque en el que están Brasil y Argentina son el
      escaparate de las relaciones de Europa con el resto del continente." />
      <Subject IPTC= " Politic & Treaty and International Organisations & alliances" />
      <Document>Francia trata de retrasar la negociación de un pacto comercial de la UE con América Latina.
      </Document>
      <Document>El portazo de la UE a Mercosur amenaza el futuro de las relaciones con América
      Latina.</Document>
      <Document>América Latina busca en la UE la salida a las crisis financieras cíclicas.</Document>
    </Event>
  - <Event Id= "Cluster_343" Level= "1">
      <Subject IPTC= "Politic & Treaty and International Organisations & alliances" />
      <Document>Francia culpa a España del bloqueo de la negociación entre la UE y Mercosur.</Document>
    </Event>
  </Topic>
```

Fig. 2. A snippet of the created hierarchy.

Moreover, our system has been evaluated using the TDT2 dataset, version 4.0. This corpus consists of 6 months of news stories from the period January to June

Table 2. Evaluation of the obtained subjects.

Topic	Subject	Eval.	Topic	Subject	Eval.
Elections in South Africa	Government /President	R	The murder of the bishop Gerardi	Crime/Homicide	G
Ocalan's trial	Justice/Trials	G	Electric belt in USA	Economy & Finance /Clothing	B
Cachemira's conflict	Conflicts and war	G	Earthquake in Mexico	Disaster/ Earthquake	G

1998. The news stories were collected from six different sources. Human annotators identified a total of 193 topics in the TDT2 dataset. 9824 English stories belong to one of these topics, the rest are unlabeled. The collection TDT2 is not annotated in different abstraction levels. Therefore we only have the manual classification at Topic Level. Again, we build a hierarchy of two levels.

Table 3 shows the minimum topic-weighted and normalized costs and the maximum F1-Measure for our system on the TDT2 dataset. Again, the better results are obtained when we use our similarity measure. We consider that the results obtained by *JERARTOP* are very good if we compare them with those obtained by the existent detection systems (see evaluation results in [11]).

Table 3. The obtained results in TDT2 collection.

System	Cost	Norm Cost	F1-Measure
Base cosine	0.0047	0.235	0.730
JERARTOP	0.0054	0.2688	0.779

6 Conclusions

In this paper we presented a new detection system. The most important novelty is the construction of a hierarchy of topics and events with different abstraction levels. This hierarchy allows users to discover the temporal structure of topics and events, that is, to identify not only the topics but also the possible smaller events they comprise. Unlike the detection systems proposed in the literature, this approach avoids the definition of what a topic is, since is the user who navigating by the created hierarchy decides in what level he explores the knowledge of interest.

A new similarity measure between documents considering the places, the temporality and contents of the news is also introduced.

Additionally, we propose two description methods of the obtained clusters at any level of the hierarchy. Thus, *JERARTOP* categorizes each node of the created hierarchy on the pre-specified subject matters and it provides a summary of the associated contents in each one of them. These methods are helpful to a user in order to determine at a glance whether the content of an event is of interest.

The obtained results for the F1-measure and the detection cost also demonstrate the validity of our algorithms for topic detection tasks. *JERARTOP* not only obtains similar results to the best systems in TDT2 evaluation but rather it also offers additional information: the hierarchy of topics and events along its description.

References

1. Allan, J.; Carbonell, J.; Doddington, G.; Yamron, J. and Yang, Y.: Topic Detection and Tracking Pilot Study: Final Report. In *Proceedings of DARPA Broadcast News Transcription and Understanding Workshop*, pp. 194-218, 1998.
2. National Institute of Standards and Technology. The Topic Detection and Tracking Phase 2 (TDT2) evaluation plan. version 3.7, 1998.
3. Carbonell, J.; Yang, Y.; Lafferty, J.; Brown, R.D.; Pierce, T. and Liu, X.: CMU Report on TDT-2: Segmentation, detection and tracking. In *Proceedings of DARPA Broadcast News Workshop*, pp.117-120, 1999.
4. Yamron, J.: Dragon´s Tracking and Detection Systems for TDT2000 Evaluation. In *Proceedings of Topic Detection & Tracking Workshop*, pp.75-80, 2000.
5. Allan, J.; Lavrenko, V.; Frey, D. and Khandelwal, V.: UMASS at TDT 2000. In *Proceedings TDT 2000 Workshop*, 2000.
6. Brants, T.; Chen, F. and Farahat, A.: A System for New Event Detection. Annual ACM Conference on Research and Development in Information Retrieval. In *Proceedings of the 26th annual international ACM SIGIR conference on Research and Development in Information Retrieval*, SIGIR'03, Toronto, Canada, 2003.
7. Pons-Porrata, A.; Berlanga-Llavori, R. and Ruiz-Shulcloper, J.: On-line event and topic detection by using the compact sets clustering. *Journal of Intelligent and Fuzzy Systems, Number* 3-4, pp.185-194, 2002.
8. Pons-Porrata, A.; Berlanga-Llavori, R. and Ruiz-Shulcloper, J.: Building a hierarchy of events and topics for newspaper digital libraries. *LNCS 2633*, Springer-Verlag, 2003.
9. Pons-Porrata, A.; Ruiz-Shulcloper, J. and Berlanga-Llavori, R.: A method for the automatic summarization of topic-based clusters of documents. *LNCS 2905*, Springer Verlag, pp. 596-603, 2003.
10. Pons-Porrata, A.; Berlanga-Llavori, R. and Ruiz-Shulcloper, J.: A new word sense disambiguation method using WordNet. *Proceedings of X Conference of the Spanish Association for the Artificial Intelligence*, Volumen II (In Spanish), pp. 63-66, 2003.
11. Fiscus, J.G.; Doddington, G.; Garofolo, J.S. and Martin, A.: Nist's 1998 topic detection and tracking evaluation (tdt2). In *Proc. of the DARPA Broadcast News Workshop*, 1998.

Fractal-Based Approach for Segmentation of Address Block in Postal Envelopes

Luiz Felipe Eiterer[1], Jacques Facon[1], and David Menoti[1,2]

[1] PUCPR-Pontifícia Universidade Católica do Paraná
Rua Imaculada Conceição 1155, Prado Velho
80215-901 Curitiba-PR, Brazil
{eiterer,facon,menoti}@ppgia.pucpr.br
[2] UFMG Universidade Federal de Minas Gerais
DCC Departamento de Ciência da Computação
Av. Antônio Carlos, 6627 31.270-010, Belo Horizonte-MG, Brazil
menoti@dcc.ufmg.br

Abstract. In this paper, an address block segmentation approach based on fractal dimension FD is proposed. After computing the fractal dimension of each image pixel by the 2D variation procedure, a clustering technique based on K-means is used to label pixels into semantic objects. The evaluation of the efficiency is carried out from a total of 200 postal envelope images with no fixed position for the address block, postmark and stamp. A ground-truth strategy is used to achieve an objective comparison. Experiments showed significant and promising results. By using the 2D variation procedure for three ranges of neighbor window sizes ($r = \{3, 5\}$, $r = \{3, 5, 7\}$, and $r = \{3, 5, 7, 9\}$), the proposed approach reached a success rate over than 90% on average.

1 Introduction

It is well known that the proper addressing allows mail pieces to be processed quickly and more efficiently. We also know that this task is not a mystery. When the mail piece meets size requirements, address block and zip code are filled in correctly and the proper amount of postage is obeyed, it moves easily through the mechanized sorting process saving labor and time. Therefore, despite of all rules mentioned above, why is so difficult to increase mail sorting automation? Some reasons like wide variety of postal envelope attributes (layouts, colors and texture), the handwritten address block which appears mixed up with postmarks or stamps are factors that increase the complexity of an efficient mail sorting system.

Several authors have dealt with the problem of locating address blocks in envelope images. For instance, Yu et al in [1] present a method for locating address blocks from magazine envelopes based on the following assumptions: The address is written on a light-colored label, generally skewed. Moreover, the label may be stuck on the magazine, under the plastic envelope or displayed in a plastic window provided in the envelope. The address block follows the left alignment rule. The contrast between the ink and the spaces between characters varies according to the equipment used (laser or matrix printer, or even a typewriter). And the magazine and envelope ensemble contains other text messages in addition to the address block. The authors segment magazine envelopes using an Otsu's modified method which reduces the influence of the grayscale

A. Sanfeliu et al. (Eds.): CIARP 2004, LNCS 3287, pp. 454–461, 2004.
© Springer-Verlag Berlin Heidelberg 2004

distributions. Then a connected component analysis based on BAG strategy is used to identify individual blocks of text. Some heuristics are used to eliminate false address block candidates. Finally, a recognizer is used to locate the address block. Experiments on 53 IBM magazine envelopes and 52 other ones showed that the method was successful in locating the correct address block in 71.70% and 92.86%, respectively.

Recently, Yonekura et al [2] present a method for postal envelope segmentation combining the 2-D histogram and morphological clustering. A new filter based on the morphological grayscale dual reconstruction is proposed to the 2-D histogram calculation and the proposed clustering is based on the watershed transform criterion. Experiments on a database composed of 300 complex postal envelope images, with creased background and no fixed position for the handwritten address blocks, postmarks and stamps showed that the method was successful in locating the correct address block in 75%.

The goal of this paper is to propose and to evaluate a new postal envelope segmentation method based on Fractal Dimension FD clustering. The aim is to locate and segment handwritten address blocks, postmarks and stamps with no *a priori* knowledge of the envelope images (Figure 1). The Fractal Dimension clustering is carried out by means of the K-means. A ground-truth segmentation is employed to evaluate the accuracy of this approach.

This paper is organized as follows: Section 2 shortly reviews fractal-based techniques to solve the segmentation challenge. Section 3 describes the grayscale image fractal dimension method used in our approach. The proposed method based on the K-means is detailed in Section 4. Section 5 presents some experimental results and discussions. In addition, the proposed segmentation method is evaluated by means of ground-truth images in Sections 5.1 and 5.2. Finally, some conclusions are drawn in Section 6.

2   Fractal-Based Techniques for Segmentation Challenge

Fractals are very useful in modeling roughness and self-similarity properties of surfaces in Image Processing. The fractal dimension gives a measure of the roughness of

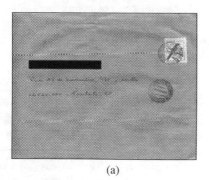
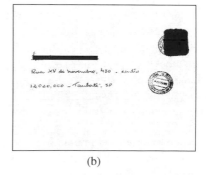

| (a) | (b) |

Fig. 1. Example of envelope image segmentation: (a) Envelope image, (b) Ground-truth handwritten address block, postmark and stamps

a surface. Intuitively, the larger the fractal dimension, the rougher the texture is. Some authors have developed recent practical applications in segmentation challenges. For instance, Diayana et al [3] have compared three microcalcification detection methods in digital mammogram. They showed that the fractal analysis based on morphological dilation and erosion in 8×8 image blocks is a promising approach.

Andrew Ringler [4] has used a local fractal dimension FD approach to segment oceanic images into *water* and *no-water* classes. By using the 2D variation procedure for each image pixel, the author has successfully segmented ocean waves to detect dolphin and swimmers and to perform human search and rescue.

Samarbandu et al [5] have proposed an initial study of bone X-Rays images through a morphological fractal analysis. This FD approach, where only the dilation is used, has demonstrated the feasibility of detecting bone structures independent of scale.

3   Fractal Dimension for Grayscale Images

Since the nature of textured surfaces is not deterministic, the computation of grayscale image fractal dimension FD is not an easy task. Some methods were proposed for estimating the FD for grayscale images. To better understand how the fractal dimension FD can be computationally estimated, let first explain the most popular method, the DBC differential box-counting method [6]. Consider an $M \times M$ pixel image as a surface in (x, y, z) space where $P(x, y)$ represents the pixel position and z is the pixel intensity. One can partition the (x, y) space into a grid of $s \times s$ size pixels. An estimate of the relative scale is $r = s/M$. At each grid position, one stacks cubes of size s, numbering each box sequentially from 1 up to the box containing the highest intensity in the image over the $s \times s$ area. Denoting the minimum and maximum gray levels for the image at position (i, j) by k and l respectively, one can define $n_r(i, j) = l - k + 1$. A parameter $N(r)$ is then estimated by summing over the entire grid as $N(r) = \sum_{(i,j)} n_r(i, j)$. The above procedure is repeated for a number of values of $r(s)$. The slope estimation of the graph $log(N(r))$ versus $log(1/r)$ by the least-squares method provides the fractal dimension FD.

Among the Fractal-based approaches available in literature, one could observe that the 2D variation procedure is not very complex and has shown to be promising in complex images (see [4]). It is the reason why it has been chosen. The 2D variation procedure, proposed by [7], similar to the differential box-counting method, analyses the pixel environment at different distances r. The squares with different sizes r are running pixel by pixel across the image from left to right and from top to bottom. The algorithm determines the minimum min and maximum max gray values within the square of size r. Since the intensity value v of a pixel p is related to the height of the objects in the image, one can meaningfully define at p a volume $r \times r \times v$. By defining the difference volume of p as $r \times r \times (max - min)$, one can denote $V(r)$ as the sum of differences between the maximum and minimum for scale r for the entire image, resulting in a power law: $V(r) = const \ r^s$. In the Richardson-Mandelbrot plot ($log(V(r))$ versus $log(r)$), the dependence of this volume $V(r)$ should be linear with the square size r. By using the least-squares method to this linear regression, one can compute the slope s of this line and then deduce FD:

$$FD = 3 - s/2 \qquad (1)$$

We applied the 2D variation procedure onto postal envelope images for three ranges of neighbor window sizes ($r = \{3, 5\}$, $r = \{3, 5, 7, \}$, and $r = \{3, 5, 7, 9\}$). It results in an image I_{FD} where the FD of each pixel stays in the range $[2.0, 3.0]$ (see Equation 1).

4   Clustering

We are aiming at automatic clustering, where the handwritten address block, postmark and stamp classes should be extracted from the image through their fractal dimension. For this purpose, we use the K-means clustering which is a robust unsupervised algorithm often applied to the problem of image texture segmentation. The K-means clustering is an algorithm for partitioning N data points into k disjoint clusters C_j containing N_j data points so as to minimize the sum-of-squares error. Each cluster in the partition is defined by its member data points and by its centroid. The centroid for each cluster is the point to which the sum of distances from all data points in that cluster is minimized. The K-means clustering uses an iterative algorithm that minimizes the sum of distances $S_d = \sum [C_j(P) - P]^2$ from each data point P to its cluster centroid C_j, over all clusters. This algorithm moves data points between clusters until the sum cannot be decreased further. The result is a set of clusters that are as compact and well-separated as possible. It is comprised of a simple re-estimation procedure as follows [8] [9]:

1. First, the data points are assigned at random to the k sets;
2. Second, the centroid is computed for each set.

These two steps are alternated until a stopping criterion is reached (i.e. when there is no further change in the assignment of the data points). Details of the minimization can be controled using several optional input parameters to K-means, including those for the initial values of the cluster centroids, and for the maximum number of iterations.

The input parameters used in our K-means clustering approach are:

- Number of features: only one, the FD itself;
- Number of clusters : 3 clusters which are the handwritten address block, postmark and stamp one, the background one and the noise one;
- Number of iterations: 10;
- Convergence criterion: 0.0001.

It is well-known that the K-means algorithm suffers from initial starting conditions effects (initial clustering effects). One can find in literature some researches about the initialization optimisation of iterative partitional clustering [10]. In our approach, min, $(max + min)/2$ and max are used to initialize the values of cluster centroids, where max and min are the FD buffer maximum and minimum values, respectively. The convergence of the K-means algorithm onto the image I_{FD} results in the labeled image I_{Kmeans} where each pixel is labeled into the 3 clusters.

5   Experiments

A database composed of 200 complex postal envelope images, with no fixed position for the handwritten address blocks, postmarks and stamps was used to evaluate the efficiency of the proposed approach. Each image has about 1500×2200 pixels and was digitized at 300 dpi. We could verify that the address blocks, stamps and postmarks represent only 1.5%, 4.0% and 1.0% of the envelope area, respectively and that the great majority of pixels of these images belong to the envelope background (approximatively 93.5%).

5.1   Evaluation Strategy of the Proposed Method

A ground-truth strategy was employed to evaluate the accuracy of the proposed approach. The ideal result (ground-truth segmentation) regarding the handwritten address block, postmark and stamp class has been generated for each envelope image (Figure 1-(b)). The comparison between the ground-truth segmentation and the results obtained by the proposed approach was carried out pixel by pixel. We have computed each obtained result with the ideal segmentation in terms of identical pixels at the same location. We have also computed the average of all obtained results for each class.

5.2   Numerical Results and Discussion

Figures 2 and 3 show interesting address block, stamp, postmark segmentations in case of envelope images with creased background and wrong layout (Figure 2-(a)), with many stamps and postmarks (Figure 2-(b)), and without stamp (Figure 3). In spite of the background complexity, and independently of the semantic classes, the address blocks, stamps and postmarks are very well segmented. As explained before, the evaluation of the approach was carried out by comparing pixel by pixel the ground-truth segmentation and the results obtained.

The average segmentation rates for each class are showed in Table 1. This table shows how the accuracy of the algorithm changes if the box size range r is changed. Best values are obtained for range $r = \{3, 5, 7, 9\}$, where the segmentation successfully recovered address blocks ($97.24\% \pm 13.64\%$) postmarks ($91.89\% \pm 17.22\%$). The most important figures are the ones related to the address block, since for practical purposes the classes of stamp, and postmark would be discarded in the end and it would not harm the result. It is possible to conclude that, independently of the layout and background in the input images, the segmentation recovered the address blocks and postmarks with great success. It can be seen that the segmentation did not recovered the stamps as expected. It is caused by the fact that the stamps contain some complex drawings, gray level differences (dark objects and bright background).

6   Conclusions

The use of fractal dimension in postal envelope segmentation was proposed. After computing the fractal dimension for each image pixel, the resulting fractal image is then

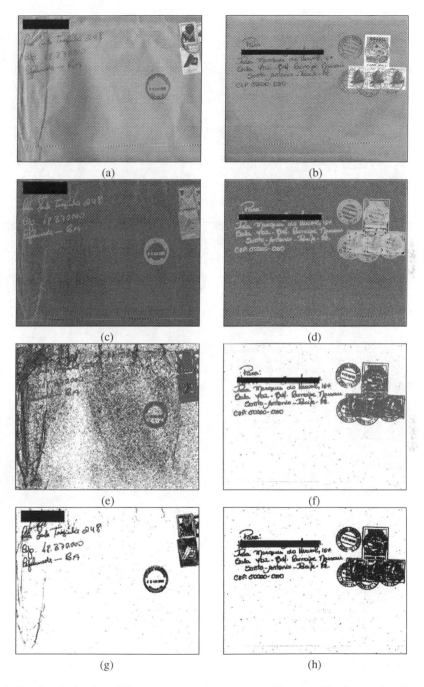

Fig. 2. Results obtained to different envelope images: (a) with creased background and wrong layout, (b) with many stamps and postmarks: (c)-(d) Fractal Images, (e)-(f) K-means clustering, (g)-(h) Handwritten address blocks, postmarks and stamps

Table 1. Average results with identification of regions (pixel by pixel accuracy)

Box sizes	Accuracy pixel by pixel ($\mu \pm \sigma$)		
	$r = \{3,5\}$	$r = \{3,5,7\}$	$r = \{3,5,7,9\}$
Address Block	92.61% $\pm$ 13.61%	96.05% $\pm$ 10.89%	97.24% $\pm$ 13.64%
Stamp	48.86% $\pm$ 13.84%	59.76% $\pm$ 15.68%	66.34% $\pm$ 16.90%
Postmark	82.02% $\pm$ 19.66%	88.97% $\pm$ 17.58%	91.89% $\pm$ 17.22%

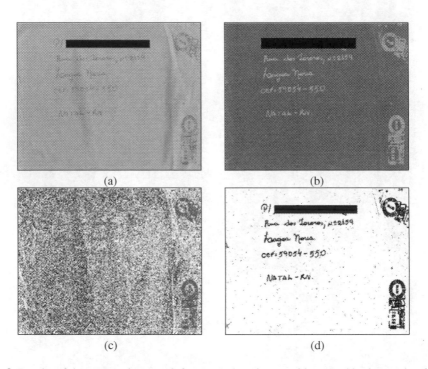

(a)   (b)

(c)   (d)

Fig. 3. Results of the proposed approach for an envelope image with creased background and no stamp: (a) Envelope image, (b) Fractal Image, (c) K-means clustering, (d) Handwritten address block and postmarks

clustered by K-means procedure. By comparing the obtained results with the ideal ones (ground-truth segmentation), it is possible to conclude that the proposed approach is robust if we consider the *handwritten address block* and *postmark* classes without *a priori* knowledge about the position of each semantic class. The 2D variation procedure was shown to be appropriate in our purpose. In spite of its simplicity, the centroid initialization in K-means was shown to be efficient in the segmentation challenge. In addition, since this method does not use a priori knowledge, it can be employed to segment other types of document images. Future works will focus segmentation of magazine envelopes with plastic covers.

Acknowledgments

We would like to acknowledge support for this research from PUCPR, CNPq/MCT and the Brazilian Post Office Agency (Correios Brasileiros).

References

1. Yu, B., Jain, A., Mohiuddin, M.: Address block location on complex mail pieces. Technical Report MSUCPS:TR97-12, Dept. of Computer Science, Michigan State University (1997)
2. Yonekura, E., Facon, J.: Postal envelope segmentation by 2-d histogram clustering through watershed transform. ICDAR 2003, 7th International Conference on Document Analysis and Recognition 1 (2003) 338–342
3. Diayana, W.M., Larcher, J., Besar, R.: A comparison of clustered microcalcifications automated detection methods in digital mammogram. ICASSP (2003) 385–388
4. Ringler, A.: Texture segmentation by local fractal dimension as applied to oceanic search and rescue. IEEE ICICS, International Conference on Information Communications Signal Processing 2 (2003) 975–979
5. Samarbandu, J., Acharya, R., Hausmann, E., Allen, K.: Analysis of bone x-rays using morphological fractals. IEEE Transactions on Medical Imaging 12 (1993) 466–474
6. Chaudhuri, B., Sarkar, N., Kundu, P.: Improved fractal geometry based texture segmentation technique. IEE Proceedings 140 (1993) 233–241
7. Dubuc, B., Quiniuo, J., Roques-Carmes, C., Tricot, C., Zucker, S.: Evaluating the fractal dimensions of profile. Phys. Rev. 39 (1989) 1500–1512
8. Bishop, C.: Neural Networks for Pattern Recognition. Oxford University Press (1995)
9. Jain, A., Dubes, R.: Algorithms for Clustering Data. Prentice Hall: New Jersey (1988)
10. Fayad, U., Reina, C., Bradley, P.: Initialization of iterative refinement clustering algorithms. 4th KDD98- International Conference on Knowledge Discovery and Data Mining (1998)

A Proposal for the Automatic Generation of Instances from Unstructured Text

Roxana Danger[1], I. Sanz[2], Rafael Berlanga-Llavori[2], and José Ruiz-Shulcloper[3]

[1] University of Oriente, Santiago de Cuba, Cuba
roxana@csd.uo.edu.cu
[2] Universitat Jaume I, Castellón, Spain
berlanga@uji.es
[3]Institute of Cybernetics, Mathematics and Physics, La Habana, Cuba
recpat@icmf.inf.cu

Abstract. An ontology is a conceptual representation of a domain resulted from a consensus within a community. One of its main applications is the integration of heterogeneous information sources available in the Web, by means of the semantic annotation of web documents. This is the cornerstone of the emerging *Semantic Web*. However, nowadays most of the information in the Web consists of text documents with little or no structure at all, which makes impracticable their manual annotation. This paper addresses the problem of mapping text fragments into a given ontology in order to generate ontology instances that semantically describe this kind of resources. As a result, applying this mapping we can automatically populate a Semantic Web consisting of text documents that concern with a specific ontology. We have evaluated our approach over a real-application ontology and a text collection both in the Archeology domain. Results show the effectiveness of the method as well as its usefulness.

1 Introduction

The Semantic Web (SW) project is intended to enrich the current Web by creating knowledge objects that allow both users and programs to better exploit the Web resources [1]. The cornerstone of the Semantic Web is the definition of an ontology that conceptualizes the knowledge within the resources of a domain [2]. Thus, the contents of the Web will be described in the future by means of a large collection of semantically tagged resources that must be reliable and meaningful.

Nowadays most of the information in the Web consists of text documents with little or no structure at all, which makes impracticable their manual annotation [3]. As a consequence, automatic or even semi-automatic resource tagging will become a necessary and urgent task to populate the contents of the SW.

For this purpose, we can benefit from the research works done in both the automatic document classification and the Information Extraction areas. In the former area, several methods have been proposed to automatically classify documents according to a given taxonomy of concepts (e.g. [4]). However, these methods require a big amount of training data, and they do not generate *instances* of the ontology. In the latter area, much work has been focused on recognizing predefined entities (e.g. dates, locations, names, etc.), as well as on extracting relevant relations between them by using natural language processing. However, current Information Extraction (IE) systems are restricted to extract flat and very simple relations, mainly to feed a rela-

A. Sanfeliu et al. (Eds.): CIARP 2004, LNCS 3287, pp. 462–469, 2004.
© Springer-Verlag Berlin Heidelberg 2004

tional database. In an ontology, relationships are more complex as they can involve nested concepts and they can have associated inference rules.

This paper addresses the problem of mapping text fragments into a given ontology in order to generate the ontology instances that semantically describe them. Our proposal is based on generating a specific mapping between text fragments and the subgraphs of the ontology that better fit them. As in current IE systems, we also recognize predefined entities that can be directly associated to ontology concepts. These entities are extracted by applying a set of pre-defined regular expressions. However, in contrast to these systems, our approach does not use any syntactic nor semantic analysis to extract the relations appearing in the text. As a consequence, the proposed method performs very efficiently, and as the results show, it achieves a good effectiveness.

2   Generation of Ontology Instances

In this work we have adopted the formal definition of ontology from [6]. This definition distinguishes between the conceptual schema of the ontology, which consists of a set of concepts and their relationships, and its associated resource descriptions, which are called *instances*. In our approach, we represent both parts as oriented graphs, over which the ontology inference rules are applied to extract and validate complex instances.

2.1   Preliminary Concepts

The next paragraphs present the definitions of the concepts used when generating partial and complete instances from the words and entities appearing within a text fragment.

Definition 1. An *ontology* is a labeled oriented graph $G = (N, A)$ where the set of nodes N contains both the concept names and the instance identifiers, and A is a set of labeled arcs between them representing their relationships. Specifically, the labels *is_a* and *instance_of* account for the taxonomy and classification relationships respectively. Additionally, over this graph we introduce the following restrictions according to [6]:

- The set of the ontology concepts C is the subset of nodes in N that are not pointed by any arc labeled as "*instance_of*".
- The taxonomy of concepts C consists of the subgraph that only contains the *is_a* arcs. It defines a partial order over the elements of C, denoted with $\leq_C$.
- The relation signature is a function $\sigma: R \rightarrow C \times C$, which contains the subsets of arc labels that involve only concepts.
- The function *dom*: $R \rightarrow C$ with $dom(r) = \Pi_1(\sigma(r))$ gives the domain of a relation $r \in R$, whereas *range*: $R \rightarrow C$ with $range(r) = \Pi_2(\sigma(r))$ gives its range.
- The function dom_C: $C \rightarrow 2^{|\gamma|}$ gives the domain of definition of a concept.

As an example, Figure 1 shows an ontology to describe artifacts made by artists and where they are exhibited. Double line arrows represent the taxonomy relation $\leq_C$, single line arrows denote the different relationships between concepts, dotted line arrows represent the partial order $\leq_R$, and finally shaded nodes represent instances.

In order to express the proximity of two concepts c and c' we define the following relevance function:

$$Rel(c,c') = 1 - \log_{|C|} \min \{d_T(c,c'),\ d_R(c,c')\}$$

where $d_T(c,\ c')$ and $d_R(c,\ c')$ are the distances between the two concepts c and c' through paths across the taxonomy and the relations in R, respectively.

For the sake of simplicity, we will represent these graphs only with the set of arcs, which are triples of the form $(n_1, label, n_2)$, omitting the set of nodes.

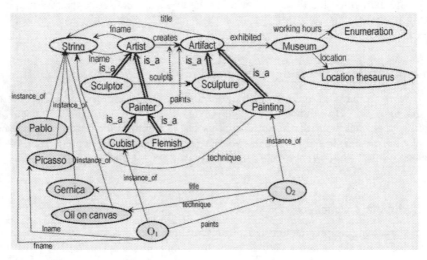

Fig. 1. Example of an ontology graph.

Definition 2. We denote with $I|_o^c$ an *instance related to the object o of the class c or simply an instance*, as the subgraph of the ontology that relates the node o with any other, and there exists an arc $(o, instance\_of, c) \in A$.

$$I|_o^c = \{ (o,r,o')/(o,\ instance\_of,\ c) \in A, \exists r \in R, \sigma(r) = (c^*,c'),$$

$$o \in dom_c(c^*), o' \in dom_c(c'), c^* \leq_C c, \neg\exists r', c^* \leq_C dom(r') \leq_C c\}$$

Notice that the arc $(o, instance\_of, c)$ is not included in the instance subgraph.

An instance is empty if the object o only participates in the arc $(o, instance\_of, c)$, which is represented as the set $\{(o, *, *)\}$

According to the ontology of Figure 1, the following sets are examples of instances:

$$I|_{o_1}^{cubist} = \{(o_1, fname, "Pablo"),(o_1, lname, "Picasso"),(o_1, paints, o_2),(o_1, paints, o_3)\}$$

$$I|_{o_2}^{painting} = \{(o_2, techniques, "Oil\ on\ canvas")\}$$

$$I|_{o_3}^{painting} = \{(o_3, techniques, "Oil\ on\ canvas"),(o_3, exibited, o_4)\}$$

In the next paragraphs we introduce several definitions to operate over instance subgraphs by applying the ontology inference rules over the taxonomy and the concept relations. These operations are intended to merge the partial information extracted from the text (concepts and relationships) in order to form maximal and coherent graphs covering as much as possible the text terms.

Definition 3. We call a *specialization of the instance* $I\big|_o^c$ to the class c', $c \leq_c c'$, denoted with $I\big|_{o \to o'}^{c \to c'}$, the following instance:

$$I\big|_{o'}^{c'} = \{\, (o', r, x) / (o, r, x) \in I\big|_o^c, \neg\exists r' \in R, r \leq_R r', dom(r) \leq_C c', range(r) = c_x,$$
$$x \in dom_C(c_x), o' \in dom_C(c')\}$$

Basically, this definition says that an instance can be specialized by simply renaming the object with a name from the target class in all the instance triples that do not represent an overridden property.

For example, the specialization of the instance

$$I\big|_o^{artist} = \{\, (o, fname, "Pablo"), (o, lname, "Picasso"), (o, creates, o_2), (o, creates, o_3)\}$$

to the class *painter* is:

$$I\big|_{o'}^{painter} = I\big|_{o \to o'}^{artist \to painter} = \{(o', fname, "Pablo"), (o', lname, "Picasso")\}$$

Definition 4. We call an *abstraction of the instance* $I\big|_o^c$ to the class c', $c' \leq_c c$, denoted with $I\big|_{o \uparrow o'}^{c \uparrow c'}$, the instance

$$I\big|_{o'}^{c'} = \{(o', r, x) / (o, r, x) \in I\big|_o^c, \exists r, c_x, dom(r) \leq_C c', range(r) = c_x, x \in dom(c_x)\}\,.$$

Similarly to the previous definition, we can obtain an abstract instance by selecting all the triples whose relation name can be abstracted to a relation of the target class c' and renaming accordingly the instance object.

For example, the abstraction of the instance $I\big|_{o_1}^{cubist}$ to the class painter is the following subgraph:

$$I\big|_{o'}^{painter} = I\big|_{o_1 \uparrow o'}^{cubist \uparrow painter} = \{(o', fname, "Pablo"), (o', lname, "Picasso"), (o', paints, o_2),$$
$$(o', paints, o_3)\}$$

Definition 5. We call *union of the instances* $I_1\big|_o^c$ and $I_2\big|_{o'}^{c'}$, and denote it by $I_1\big|_o^c \cup I_2\big|_{o'}^{c'}$ the set:

$$I_1\big|_o^c \cup I_2\big|_{o'}^{c'} = \begin{cases} I_1\big|_o^c \cup I_2\big|_{o'}^{c'} & \text{if } I_1\big|_o^c \neq \{(o,*,*)\} \wedge I_2\big|_{o'}^{c'} \neq (o',*,*) \vee (\neg c \leq_c c' \wedge \neg c' \leq c) \\ I_1\big|_{o \to o'}^{c \to c'} & \text{if } I_2\big|_{o'}^{c'} = \{(o',*,*)\} \wedge c \leq_c c' \\ I_1\big|_o^c & \text{if } I_2\big|_{o'}^{c'} = \{(o',*,*)\} \wedge c' \leq_c c \\ I_2\big|_{o'}^{c'} & \text{if } I_1\big|_o^c = \{(o,*,*)\} \wedge c \leq_c c' \\ I_2\big|_{o' \to o}^{c' \to c} & \text{if } I_1\big|_o^c = \{(o',*,*)\} \wedge c' \leq_c c \end{cases}$$

Definition 6. We call *difference of the instances* $I_1|_o^c$ and $I_2|_{o'}^{c'}$, denoted with

$I_1|_o^c \stackrel{-}{\div} I_2|_{o'}^{c'}$, the following set: $I_1|_o^c \stackrel{-}{\div} I_2|_{o'}^{c'} = \begin{cases} I_1|_o^c - I_2|_{o\uparrow o}^{c\uparrow c} & \text{if} & c \leq_c c' \\ I_1|_o^c - I_2|_{o'\to o}^{c'\to c} & \text{if} & c' \leq_c c \end{cases}$

Definition 7. We call *symmetric difference of the instances* $I_1|_o^c$ and $I_2|_{o'}^{c'}$, denoted with $I_1|_o^c \stackrel{-}{\div} I_2|_{o'}^{c'}$, the result of $I_1|_o^c \stackrel{-}{\div} I_2|_{o'}^{c'} \, \hat{\cup} \, I_2|_{o'}^{c'} \stackrel{-}{\div} I_1|_o^c$.

Definition 8. We say that two instances $I_1|_o^c$ and $I_2|_{o'}^{c'}$, related to the objects o and o' of classes c and c', respectively, $c \leq_C c'$, are *complementary* if they satisfy at least one of the following two conditions:

1. $(\neg \exists (o', \ r, \ x), \ (o', \ r, \ x') \ \in \ I_1|_{o\to o'}^{c\to c'} \div I_2|_{o'}^{c'}, \ x \neq x', \ r \text{ is biyective})$ and $(\neg \exists (o, r, x), (o', r', x') \in I_1|_o^c \, \hat{\cup} \, I_2|_{o'}^{c'}, r \leq_R r', r \neq r', x \neq x')$ or

2. at least one of the instances $I_1|_o^c$ or $I_2|_{o'}^{c'}$ is empty.

Two instances are complementary if there not exist contradictions between the values of their similar relations.

For example, the following instances are complementary:

$I|_o^{artist} = \{(o, fname, "Pablo"), (o, lname, "Picasso")\}$

$I|_{o'}^{painter} = \{(o', paints, o_2), (o', paints, o_3)\}$

Definition 9. We say that two complementary instances $I_1|_o^c$ and $I_2|_{o'}^{c'}$ are *unifiable* in

$I|_{o_u}^{c'} = I_1|_{o\to o_u}^{c\to c'} \, \hat{\cup} \, I_2|_{o'\to o_u}^{c'\to c'}, \ c \leq_C c'$.

For example, $I|_o^{artist}$ and $I|_{o'}^{painter}$ are unifiable, producing the following instance:

$I|_{o_u}^{painter} = I|_{o\to o_u}^{artist\to painter} \, \hat{\cup} \, I_2|_{o'\to o_u}^{painter\to painter} = \{ (o_u, fname, "Pablo"),$

$(o_u, lname, "Picasso"), (o_u, paints, o_2), (o_u, paints, o_3)\}$

Definition 10. We say that two instances, $I_1|_o^c$ and $I_2|_{o'}^{c'}$ are *aggregable* in

$I|_o^c = I_1|_{o\to o}^{c\to c^*} \cup \{(o, r, o'')\}$, if $\exists r \in R, \ \sigma(r) = (c^*, c''), \ c \leq_C c^*, \ c'' \leq_C c'$, and o'' is the name of the instance $I|_{o''}^{c''} = I_2|_{o'\to o''}^{c'\to c''}$.

For example, $I|_o^{artist}$ and $I|_{o_2}^{painting}$ are aggregable in

$I|_o^{painter} = I|_{o\to o}^{artist\to painter} \cup \{(o, paints, o'')\} = \{(o, fname, "Pablo"),$

$(o, lname, "Picasso"), (o, paints, o'')\}$

where $I|_{o''}^{painting} = \{(o'', techniques, "Oil on canvas")\}$

2.2 Extracting Instances from Texts

Let T be a text fragment formed by the sequence of terms $(w_1,...,w_n)$, which can be either words or extracted entities. It is worth mentioning that stop-words are removed from this sequence, and the different word forms are reduced to their lemmas. We will denote with $I\big|_{o,[i,j]}^c$ the instance described by the subsequence of terms between w_i and w_j $(j \geq i)$.

In this context, two instances of the text T, $I_1\big|_{o,[i_1,j_1]}^c$ and $I_2\big|_{o',[i_2,j_2]}^{c'}$, with $c \leq_C c'$, are unifiable if they are complementary according to Definition 8, and there not exists any instance related to them. In this case, the unification of both instances is the following instance:

$$I\big|_{o_u,[\min\{i_1,i_2\},\max\{j_1,j_2\}]}^{c'}, \text{ where } I\big|_{o_u}^{c'} = I\big|_{o}^c \uplus I\big|_{o'}^{c'}.$$

For example, let us consider the following text, where the extracted entities have been denoted with pairs *entity-type:entity*,

```
fname:Pablo lname:Picasso was a very famous painter, specifically
he was an eminent cubist. In his paintings title:Woman and
title:Guernica he used oil on canvas.
```

From this text, we can identify the following partial instances:

$$I\big|_{o_1,[1,7]}^{painter} = \{(o_1, fname,"Pablo"),(o_1, lname,"Picasso")\}$$

$$I\big|_{o_2,[13,13]}^{cubist} = \{(o_2,*,*)\} \qquad I\big|_{o_3,[16,17]}^{painting} = \{(o_3, title,"Woman")\}$$

$$I\big|_{o_4,[18,18]}^{atifact} = \{(o_4, title,"Guernica")\} \qquad I\big|_{o_5,[21,23]}^{painting} = \{(o_5, techniques,"Oil on canvas")\}$$

According to the previous definitions, the instances $I\big|_{o_1,[1,7]}^{painter}$ and $I\big|_{o_2,[13,13]}^{cubist}$ are complementary and they are unifiable in

$$I\big|_{o_2,[1,7]}^{cubist} = \{(o_2, fname,"Pablo"),(o_2, lname,"Picasso")\}$$

Moreover, the instance $I\big|_{o_2,[1,13]}^{cubist}$ can aggregate $I\big|_{o_3,[16,17]}^{painting}$ and $I\big|_{o_4,[18,18]}^{atifact}$, being the result the following one

$$I\big|_{o_2,[1,23]}^{cubist} = \{(o_2, fname,"Pablo"),(o_2, lname,"Picasso"),$$

$$(o_2, paints, o_3),(o_2, paints, o_4)\}$$

Taking into account the definitions above, the system generates the set of instances associated to each text fragment as follows. Firstly, it constructs all the possible partial instances with the concept, entity and relation names that appear in the text fragment. Then it tries to unify partial instances, substituting them by the unified ones. Finally, instances are aggregated to form complex instances. The following algorithm resumes all the process.

1. For each concept c in the ontology appearing in the text
   a. Create an empty instance of c
   b. Let $R_{concepts} = \{c' \mid Rel\,(c', c) \geq 3\}$ be the relevant concepts related to c
   c. For each value/entity, v, appearing in the text so that it participates in a relation r of a concept c', in $R_{concepts}$, create an instance $I\big|_{o'}^{c'} = \{(o', r, v)\}$
2. Apply Definitions 9, 10 and the considerations remarked in Section 2.2, to merge complementary instances and to group aggregable instances.

Alg. 1. Algorithm for generating ontology instances.

3   Experiments

In order to validate the proposed approach, we have tested it over an ontology for the Archeological Research[1]. This ontology contains 164 concepts, 92 relations, and 390 predefined literal values. The number of entity types that can be recognized is around 20 (e.g. dates, locations, numbers, measures, etc.). We have selected 16 excavation reports from [8] as the test document collection.

In this work we evaluate the quality of the extracted instances by computing the percentage of the correct ones and the percentage of missing ones. For this purpose, we have manually annotated 15 complete instances from these text collection. Table 1 shows the global results[1] obtained by applying different ways of fragmenting the document contents, namely: sentences, paragraphs and sections.

Table 1. Precision and missing percentages for different levels of fragmentation.

	Number	Number of generated instances	Precision (%)	Missing (%)
Sentences	7262	5841	96.1	15.3
Paragraph	4441	3923	94.6	16.8
Section	254	4157	84.2	15.6

From these results, we can conclude that when we use sentences and paragraph to fragment documents, the proposed method performs very effectively, extracting a good number of instances. When we use the logical sections of documents, the precision notably decreases, as the ambiguity of relations increases. The obtained missing percentages can be attributed to the linguistic references to objects that currently are no detected by our method.

4   Conclusions

This work presents a new approach to the automatic generation of ontology instances from a collection of unstructured documents. This approach does not use any grammar nor extraction rules to obtain the ontology instances. Instead, our system tries to form correct partial instances by taking words and entities appearing in texts and automatically relating them. This makes our approach very efficient. Our experiments on a real-application show that we can obtain a good extraction precision, but it de-

---

[1] http://tempus.dlsi.uji.es/TKBG/Arqueologia.rdfs, http://tempus.dlsi.uji.es/TKBG/Instancias.rdf

pends on the fragmentation level used to find the mapping between fragments and the ontology. As future work, we plan to include further techniques of current IE systems for detecting concept references, which can help us to combine partial instances even if they stem from different documents.

Acknowledgements

This work has been partially funded by the research project of the Spanish Program of Research CICYT TIC2002-04586-C03.

References

1. Berners-Lee, T., Hendler, J., Lassila, O. "The Semantic Web". Scientific American, 2001.
2. Gruber, T.R. "Towards Principles for the Design of Ontologies used for Knowledge Sharing", International Journal of Human-Computer Studies Vol. 43, pp. 907-928, 1995.
3. Forno, F., Farinetti, L., Mehan, S. "Can Data Mining Techniques Ease The Semantic Tagging Burden?", SWDB 2003, pp. 277-292, 2003.
4. Doan, A. et al. "Learning to match ontologies on the Semantic Web". VLDB Journal 12(4), pp. 303-319, 2003.
5. Appelt, D. "Introduction to Information Extraction", AI Communications 12, 1999.
6. Maedche, A., Neumann, G. and Staab, S. "Bootstrapping an Ontology based Information Extraction System". Studies in Fuzziness and Soft Computing, Springer, 2001.
7. Danger, R., Ruíz-Shulcloper, J., Berlanga, R. "Text Mining using the Hierarchical Structure of Documents" Current Topics in Artificial Intelligence (CAEPIA 2003), Lecture Notes in Computer Science (In Press), 2004.
8. Dirección General del Patrimonio Artístico. http://www.cult.gva.es/dgpa/

An Electronic Secure Voting System Based on Automatic Paper Ballot Reading

Iñaki Goirizelaia, Koldo Espinosa, Jose Luis Martin,
Jesus Lázaro, Jagoba Arias, and Juan J. Igarza

University of the Basque Country
School of Engineering, Bilbao
Alda. Urquijo s/n 48013 Bilbao, Spain
jtpgoori@bi.ehu.es

Abstract. A secret and secure ballot is the core of every democracy. We all feel proud of being able to decide the future of our countries by making appropriate use of our right to vote in an election. However, how can we improve the efficiency of the voting process? Democratic governments should have mechanisms which ensure the integrity, security and privacy of its citizens at the polls during an election process. This paper describes a new electronic secure voting system, based on automatic paper ballot reading, which can be utilized to offer efficient help to officials and party representatives during elections. It presents how the system is organized, it also describes our OCR system and how it is implemented to read paper ballots, and it ends showing some experimental results.

1 Introduction

Due to the rapid growth of computer networks and advances in cryptographic techniques, electronic polling over the Internet is now becoming a real option for voters who have access to the Net. However, electronic democracy must be based on electronic voting systems that have the following properties as described by Cranor et al [1]: *Accuracy, Invulnerability, Privacy, Verifiability and Convenience.* Internet voting systems are still under development and we think that it will take time before they can become widely available to all citizens [2], [4]. This paper describes a new electronic voting system that is accurate, invulnerable, private, verifiable, convenient and compatible with electoral tradition in our country. It uses OCR techniques to automatically read paper ballots and GSM techniques to transmit electoral results to the central electoral office where results coming from all voting boxes will be counted.

2 A Proposal for an Electronic Voting System Architecture

Any new proposal for a new Voting Systems should take into account all of the characteristics defined in [1] and it should pay special attention to two key points, "No Digital Division" and compatibility with electoral tradition in each country.

The electronic voting system that we present allows to make compatible traditional voting methods with automatic reading of paper ballots, automatic vote counting

A. Sanfeliu et al. (Eds.): CIARP 2004, LNCS 3287, pp. 470–477, 2004.

system and a way of transmitting election results by using GSM network to the Data Center where final count of all the data coming from all the Electronic Ballot Boxes takes place.

Figure 1 shows the proposed architecture. On the left, Electronic Ballot Boxes (EBB) are shown, i.e. computer systems based on OCR techniques that automatically read the paper ballots, fully compatible with traditional paper ballots, and voters use them to cast their ballots. Once the election is over, each EBB will transmit its results through the GSM network by using Short Message Service (SMS) that allows short messages to be sent in a secure way from the ballot box to the Short Message Service Center (SMS-C). These messages are stored in memory until they are read by the API specific functions of the SMS-C server that are executed under control of the application being executed in the Vote Server.

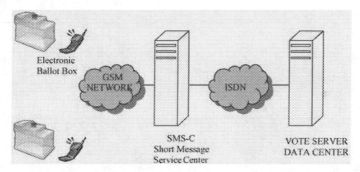

Fig. 1. Architecture for electronic voting system

3   Automatic Paper Ballot Reading

The ballot box is identical to a traditional one in our country, the only exception being that an electronic lid has been added. This lid has two input slots for ballots; one for validation and one for counting. The ballot adheres to traditional ballot papers with one electoral possibility printed on it and a special strip where a non-visible text is written (Fig. 2). This text is visible using ultraviolet light. After checking the correspondence between the visible and non-visible text, the ballot is folded, occulting only the visible text (Fig. 2). Therefore the proposed system absolutely fulfills the privacy requirement. This ballot is introduced to the first slot and once it has been recognized and validated by the electronic lid, it is introduced to the second slot. The vote is then counted.

3.1   Image Acquisition and Preprocessing System

The main function of the circuit is accomplished when a digital image of what a camera is seeing is saved in a memory. Due to the critical application of the system, the image has to be processed to obtain the required quality so that the optical recognition of characters is fast and accurate.

In order to achieve the objectives stated above the image is treated on two different planes. The first involves the optical part of the image capture. The system uses an

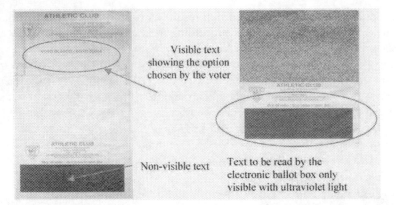

Visible text showing the option chosen by the voter

Non-visible text   Text to be read by the electronic ballot box only visible with ultraviolet light

Fig. 2. An example of ballot for the electronic voting system and ballot after being folded ready to be introduced into the ballot box

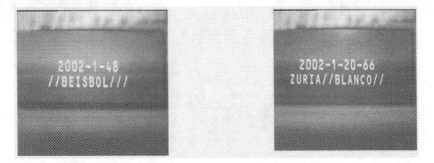

Fig. 3. Images of the paper ballot grabbed using ultraviolet light

adequate illumination and optical filter to obtain the best possible image. Once the image has been digitalized, it enters the second plane where it is treated to obtain a good monochrome picture which will later be read by OCR software. In this application, the characters are black over white background but the procedure would be similar if the characters were white over black background . Figure 3 shows images of paper ballots grabbed by our system using ultraviolet light and ready to be read by the OCR.

The digital processing of the image is done in four different stages: *Correction of non-uniform illumination, Adaptive image enhancement, Adaptive binarization, and Median filtering.*

3.2 Optical Character Recognition Algorithm

The ballot is automatically read by means of an OCR software specifically designed to accomplish this task. There are several research works that were taken into account to design and implement our OCR system. Some works offer solutions based on the smallest distance [5], other works are related to the use of Bayes statistic classifier or correlation techniques [6]. There has been a great deal of effort in the field of neuronal nets like it is shown for instance in [7]. Structural methods have been also proposed like in [8] [9]. Finally, several authors proposed methods that combine different techniques [10].

The reading process is based on the fact that each character can be uniquely identified by several features which need to be obtained from the digital image of the ballot. The image of the text to be read is taken by use of ultraviolet light. Aforesaid text is invisible with ordinary light.

The first step of the recognition process consists of extracting from each character the following features: number of groups, number of regions in each group, and position of corners for each region.

A group is composed of a set of horizontal consecutive lines of pixels where all the lines belonging to the same group have the same number of transitions from white to black. The number of regions in a group is equal to the number of transitions from black to white that the group has. Coordinates of corners for all the regions are defined by the position of the first and last pixel of the first line and first and last pixel of the last line. For example, figure 4 shows the character 2 where we have three different groups.

During the following step we try to classify the character by using two kinds of features: simple features and complex features. Using simple features we reduce the number of possible candidates and complex features permitting us to undoubtedly classify the character.

Simple features are extracted processing the character line by line: the number of enclosures and its position in the character; number of concavities, its shape and position in the character; number of groups; number of regions per group. These simple features are used to define a key that allows us to search for the character through the decision tree. If this key only matches one character the identification process finishes indicating that it was possible to identity the character. Should this not be the case, more complex features need to be obtained from the character.

Fig. 4. Groups, regions and floating mask

The process of finding complex features for a character is based on the use of floating masks [3] which are specific for each feature. Therefore, the number of floating masks depends on the number of Complex features to be found, and this depends on the number of characters to be recognised. Depending on the Simple features, the system has to be able to decide which floating masks have to be applied to the character in order to identify it among all the candidates that share the same Simple features. One mask is a group of pixels strategically distributed, in such a way that allows, comparing with other pixels of the image, an extraction of information about a certain feature of the image.

The mask is a floating mask because it moves over the image. It slides over the character, testing, in adequate points, the presence or not of the feature. There is a movement direction and a floating one. The movement direction is fixed and it is one of the four main directions on the plane. The floating direction will be one of the two perpendicular directions to the movement one, depending on the concrete position of the mask inside the image.

Masks are formed by grid elements, which together define matrixes. Each grid element is equivalent to a pixel and has an associated value: 0 or 1. Testing the feature consists of comparing the value of each grid element with the value of the pixel that is under it at any given time. If values equate then the test is positive, otherwise it will be negative.

Grid elements belong to any of the following three different matrixes:

1. Control matrix: By testing this matrix the floating direction is decided and also, the decision to carry out additional tests by using other matrixes of the mask is taken.
2. Full Coincidence matrix: It searches for a full coincidence of the matrix and image.
3. Partial Coincidence matrix: It searches for a partial coincidence of the matrix and image.

Figure 4 shows an example of a floating mask formed by a Control matrix, and a Full Coincidence matrix, the latter consisting of just one element. This basic mask may be used to detect a horizontal line located at the bottom of the character (for instance in characters 2 or L).

The Mask starts its movement from an initial position inside the image, which is defined during the design process (this will be determined by the desired features that we are looking for). First of all, a control test is performed. If the Control Matrix and the image are coincident the control test is positive. In this case, the Full Coincidence matrix test is carried out. A negative result in this test means that the feature has not been found and the mask should then move one position in the movement direction. If in the new position the control test is negative, the mask advances one position in the floating direction.

These steps are constantly repeated until, either the Full Coincidence matrix test is positive, the mask reaches a final position fixed in the design process, or the Control matrix leaves the character window. This last possibility always happens when the feature cannot be found in the image.

There are several characters where the use of floating masks is absolutely necessary to solve ambiguities among them. Let's consider the following example where we show how to distinguish between the number 8 and the character B (see figure 5). First step consists of designing the appropriate mask to use in this case. It is clear that the main difference between the number 8 and the letter B is the discontinuity that we find in the left side of the number 8 that cannot be found in the letter. This means that the floating masks should be designed to find that characteristic that uniquely identifies number 8. Figure 5 shows one mask that can be used in this case.

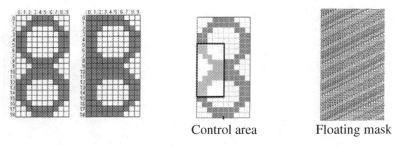

Control area   Floating mask

Fig. 5. Characters to be identified by using floating mask

The characteristic that we are looking for is located in a well known position of the segmented character. Therefore, we define a control area where the mask is going to be used (see figure 5). The mask starts its movement in this control area from the left bottom corner.

4 Paper Ballot Automatic Reading Experimental Results

Our system has been tested mainly using OCR-B characters font size 18 because paper ballots are written using that font. Floating masks were designed for this font type and size but, as we can see, our system is very robust to variable font sizes. Table 1 shows testing results of our system applied to automatic paper ballot reading. It is important to notice that there are only 8 characters that generate wrong readings, / ,\ 0, 2, (,), S and O. If we analyze the path followed by the floating mask during its movement, right reading ratios are dramatically increased (see table 2).

Table 1. Reading results using floating masks designed for OCR-B 18

Character Font size 18	Number of readings	Correct reading rate	Wrong reading rate
0	5000	96,16%	3,84% (identified as O)
2	5000	98,44%	1,56% (identified as Z)
O	5000	97,66%	2,34% (identified as 0)
S	5000	99,42%	0,58% (identified as 5)
(	5000	99,34%	0,66% (identified as I)
)	5000	99,26%	0,74% (identified as I)
/	5000	99,24%	0,76% (identified as I)
\	5000	99,3%	0,7% (identified as I)
All other characters	5000	100%	

Paper ballots are written using OCR-B font size 18 and, as it is shown in table, reading results are very good. Our electronic vote system based on automatic paper ballot reading has been checked in several election processes and results were excellent. Wrong reading ratio is almost zero, because our system is prepared to correct one character bad reading. Don't forget that in several countries electoral options are well known before the electoral day (closed lists), and it is possible to create a Data Base with all these options.

Table 2. Reading results using floating masks designed for OCR-B 18 and analyzing paths followed by floating masks

Character Font size 18	Number of readings	Correct reading rate	Wrong reading rate
0	5000	99,9%	3,84% (identified as O)
2	5000	100%	
O	5000	99,94%	2,34% (identified as 0)
S	5000	100%	
(	5000	100%	
)	5000	100%	
/	5000	100%	
\	5000	100%	
All other characters	5000	100%	

5 Conclusions

Today many researchers are working to develop new voting systems. It is clear that there is a risk. Internet voting systems could be attacked, electronic voting machines could go wrong and the election process could become a total disaster. While it is true that this may happen, it is also true that we need to continue working in this field and should not be deterred by these risks.

The new voting system that we present here has already been checked in limited election processes. It represents a step forward in the development of new electronic voting systems. So far the results have proved to be very good. We have developed a new framework for voting based on an electronic voting system that is able to automatically read ballots. This electronic voting system can be described as an evolution of traditional voting systems where no human is needed to count votes.

Our proposal is based on a new implementation of an OCR system that uses the floating mask concept to read paper ballots. Our experimental tests prove that our system reads with 100 % of good readings.

We believe that this new framework fulfills all of the properties required by electronic voting systems that have been stated in this paper. Research in the field should continue because digitally literate people should use digital equipment to cast their votes.

Acknowledgment

Authors would like to thank the Basque Government for their support and funding of this project.

References

1. Cranor, L.F., Cytron, R.K., Sensus: A security-Conscious Electronic Polling System for the Internet. Proceedings of the Hawaii International Conference on Systems Sciences, Wailea Hawaii USA, January 7-10, 1997.

2. California Internet Voting Task Force. "A report on the feasibility of Internet voting". California Secretary of State Bill Jones.
http://www.ss.ca.gov/executive/ivote/final_report.htm, January 2000.

3. Bao-Chang P., Si-Chang W., Guang-Yi Y. "A Method of Recognising Handprinted Characters". Computer Recognition and Human Production of Handwriting, *World Scientific Publ. Co.*, 37-60. 1989.

4. Voting. "What is What could be". Calthech MIT Voting Technology Project.
http://web.mit.edu/voting/, July 2001.

5. Lee, E.W.; Chae, S.I.; "Fast design of reduced-complexity nearest neighbor classifiers using triangular inequality. IEEE, Transactions on Pattern Analysis and Machine Intelligence, pp. 562-566. Mayo, 1998.

6. González, R.C., Woods, R.E. "Digital Image processing". Addison-Wesley / Ediciones Díaz de Santos. 1996.

7. Oh, I.S., Lee, J.S., Suen, C.Y. "Analysis of Class Separation and Combination of Class-Dependent Features for Handwriting Recognition". IEEE, Transactions on Pattern Analysis and Machine Intelligence, pp. 1089-1094. October, 1999.

8. Gdalyahu, Y., Weinshall, D. "Flexible Syntactic Matching of Curves and Its Application to Automatic Hierarchical Classification of Silhouettes". IEEE, Transactions on Pattern Analysis and Machine Intelligence, pp. 1312-1327. December, 1999.

9. Phillips, I.T., Chhabra, A.K. "Empirical Performance Evaluation of Graphics Recognition Systems". IEEE, Transactions on Pattern Analysis and Machine Intelligence, pp. 849-870. September, 1999

10. Kittler, J., Hatef, M., Duin, R.P.W., Matas, J. "On Combining Classifiers". IEEE, Transactions on Pattern Analysis and Machine Intelligence, pp. 226-239. March, 1998.

A Fast Algorithm
to Find All the Maximal Frequent Sequences in a Text

René A. García-Hernández, José Fco. Martínez-Trinidad,
and Jesús Ariel Carrasco-Ochoa

National Institute of Astrophysics, Optics and Electronics (INAOE)
Puebla, México
{renearnulfo,fmartine,ariel}@inaoep.mx

Abstract. One of the sequential pattern mining problems is to find the maximal frequent sequences in a database with a β support. In this paper, we propose a new algorithm to find all the maximal frequent sequences in a text instead of a database. Our algorithm in comparison with the typical sequential pattern mining algorithms avoids the joining, pruning and text scanning steps. Some experiments have shown that it is possible to get all the maximal frequent sequences in a few seconds for medium texts.

1 Introduction

The *Knowledge Discovery in Databases* (KDD) is defined by Fayyad [1] as "the non-trivial process of identifying valid, novel, potentially useful and ultimately understandable patterns in data". The key step in the knowledge discovery process is the data mining step, which following Fayyad: "consisting on applying data analysis and discovery algorithms that, under acceptable computational efficiency limitations, produce a particular enumeration of patterns over the data". This definition has been extended to *Text Mining* (TM) like: "consisting on applying text analysis and discovery algorithms that, under acceptable computational efficiency limitations, produce a particular enumeration of patterns over the text". So TM is the process that deals with the extraction of patterns from textual data. This definition is used by Feldman [2] to define *Knowledge Discovery in Texts* (KDT). In both KDD and KDT tasks, especial attention is required in the performance of the algorithms because they are applied on a large amount of information. In especial the KDT process needs to define simple structures that can be extracted from texts automatically and in a reasonable time. These structures must be rich enough to allow interesting KD operations [2].

The frequent sequences are of interest in some areas, such as data compression, human genome analysis and in the KDD process. But some of these areas are more interested in the maximal frequent sequences (MFS) because these areas search the longest pattern that could match or that could be extracted from the database. The *sequential pattern mining problem* is defined by Agrawal [3] as the problem of finding MFS in a database; this is a data mining problem. Therefore, we are interested in finding all the MFS in a text, in order to do text mining for the KDT process.

MFS have received special attention in TM because this kind of patterns can be extracted from text independently of the language. Also they are human readable patterns or descriptors of the text. MFS can be used to predict or to determine the causality of an event. For information retrieval systems, MFS can be used to find keywords; in this case, the MFS are key phrases. MFS allow constructing links between docu-

A. Sanfeliu et al. (Eds.): CIARP 2004, LNCS 3287, pp. 478–486, 2004.

ments in an automatic way. MFS could help in the definition of stop-phrases instead of stop-words. Also, they can be used for text summarization.

In this paper, we propose a fast algorithm which gets all the MFS from a simple structure. This structure is relatively easy to extract from the text.

The paper organization is as follows: In section 2, the problem definition is given. In section 3 the related works are presented. Section 4 describes our algorithm and in section 5 a complexity analysis of it is presented. Section 6 presents some experiments. Section 7 gives a discussion about our algorithm. Finally, in section 8 the conclusions and future work are given.

2 Problem Definition

A *sequence S* is an ordered list of at least two elements called *items*. The ith element or item in the sequence is represented as s_i. A sequence is *frequent* if it appears in the text twice or more. And S is *maximal* if S is not a subsequence of any other frequent sequence. The number of elements in a sequence S is called the *length* of the sequence and is denoted by $|S|$. A sequence with length k is denoted as *k-sequence*.

Let $P=p_1p_2...p_n$ and $S=s_1s_2...s_m$ be sequences, P is contained or is a subsequence of S, denoted $P \subseteq S$, if there exists an integer $1 \leq i$ such that $p_1=s_i$, $p_2=s_{i+1}$, $p_3=s_{i+2},...,p_n=s_{i+(n-1)}$. P is a *proper subsequence* of S, $P \subset S$, if P is a subsequence of S, but $P \neq S$.

Let $X \subseteq S$ and $Y \subseteq S$ then X and Y are *mutually excluded* if X and Y do not share items i.e., if $(x_n=s_i$ and $y_1=s_j)$ or $(y_n=s_i$ and $x_1=s_j)$ then $i<j$.

Given a text T expressed as a sequence and a user-specified threshold β. A sequence S is *β-frequent* in T, if it is contained at least β times in T in a mutually excluded way.

In this paper, we are interested in the problem of finding all the maximal *β-frequent* sequences in a text.

3 Related Work

Most of the algorithms that get all MFS [3,4,5,6] have been developed to work in a database of sequences. In [7], an algorithm was developed for a text collection, which is different from finding all the MFS into a single text. The algorithms for getting all MFS can be classified as Apriori-based (typical) and Pattern-growth methods [8].

Into the typical methods the first approach was the AprioriAll algorithm [3] and some approaches, like GSP [9], were after developed. These typical algorithms operate in a bottom-up breadth-first way. These methods use the joining, pruning and text scanning steps, for the candidate generation phase. In the fig.1a the general algorithm for the Apriori methods is shown. The fig. 1b shows an example of the different *k-sequences* that are generated for this kind of algorithms. The subindex in the sequences of fig. 1b indicates the frequency of each sequence.

Unlike the typical methods, the pattern-growth methods avoid the joining, pruning and scanning steps. These pattern-growth methods try to find the MFS more directly, expanding the growth of the *k-sequences*, beginning with *2-sequences*. For this reason, these methods are faster than the typical methods, when there are long sequences. Examples of this category are the PrefixSpan [5] and SPADE [6] algorithms

Input: DB and β support; **Output:** MFS list
1-sequences={set of frequent 1-sequences}
   While *k-sequences* is not empty **do**
      k-sequences = **Joining** ((*k-1*)*-sequences*)
      k-sequences = **Pruning**(*k-sequences*)
      k := *k* + 1
   End-while
Return *Maximal sequences*

(a)

TEXT: " esadeladesad" β=2	
2-Sequence	es$_2$, sa$_2$, ad$_3$, de$_2$, el$_1$, la$_1$,
Pruning	es$_2$, sa$_2$, ad$_3$, de$_2$,
Joining	esa$_2$, sad$_2$, ade$_2$, des$_1$
Pruning	esa$_2$, sad$_2$, **ade$_{2,}$**
Joining	esad$_2$,sade$_1$,
Pruning	**esad$_2$**

(b)

Fig. 1. a) General algorithm for the typical methods; b) Example of how to get the MFS with the joining and pruning steps for the text "esadeladesad"

4   Proposed Algorithm

Our algorithm belongs to pattern-growth methods class; because it uses a bottom-up strategy without candidate generation. The main idea consists in to generate only all the distinct pairs of items from the text, i.e. the *2-sequences*, and do not lose the relation between them, in order to allow the growth of the sequences. The input data of the algorithm are a text (T) and a β threshold. The proposed algorithm has three phases. These phases are as follows:
Phase 1. - Get the alphabet from the text. The algorithm gets an *id* for each different item (chars or words) from the text.

Phase 2: Algorithm to construct the array structure
Input: A text T **Output:** The *array* structure
For *all the pairs [t$_i$,t$_{i+1}$]* ∈ T **do**
     PositionNode.Pos ←*index* ← *array [t$_i$,t$_{i+1}$]*;   *// if [t$_i$,t$_{i+1}$] it is not in array, add it*
     array[index].Positions ←**New** *PositionNode*   // new node
     array[index].Freq ← *array[index].Freq*+ 1   // increase the frequency
     array[LastIndex].Positions.NextIndex←*index*; // keep the index of the pair
     array[LastIndex].Positions.NextPos←*PositionNode*;//link the new node
     LastIndex ← *index*;   //keep the last index
End-for

Fig. 2. Algorithm to construct the *array* structure (phase 2)

Phase 2. - Construct an array structure for text representation (fig. 2). The algorithm constructs an *array* structure from the text T. Each element of the *array* contains two *id*'s corresponding to a distinct pair (t_i,t_{i+1}), the *frequency* of this pair and a list of the *positions* where this pair appears in the text (see fig. 3a). Each *position* node of the *positions* list contains the position where the pair appears, together with the *next-index* of the following pair in each position (see fig. 3b). The phase 2 works as follows: for each item t_i get the *index* of the pair (t_i,t_{i+1}) in the *array* and in this position add a *Position* node at the end of the list of *positions*. Increase the frequency (*Freq*) of this pair and link this *position* node with the previously added *position* node in order to build the *NextPos* list, which stores the text representation. In fig. 3a an example of this array is shown.

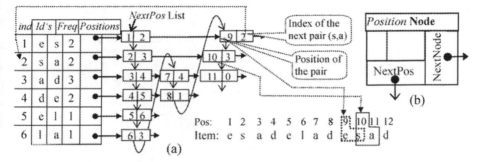

Fig. 3. a) *Array* for the text: "esadeladesad". b) Node for *Positions* list

Phase 3: Algorithm to find all MFS

Input: *Array* from phase 2, β support   **Output:** MFS list

Actual←1 //index of the array where it is the first element of NextPos List

  while Actual ≠ 0 **do**

    if Array[Actual].Frequency ≥ β, **then**   //if the pair has frequency ≥ β

      temporal ← Copy_list (array[Actual].Positions) //create a similar list

      PMS ← Array[Actual].Id₁ + Array [Actual].Id₂   //initial elements of the PMS

      Pos ← Array [Actual].NextIndex   //The first time Pos←1

      while Pos ≠ 0 **do**   //expand the pair

        temporal ← **Get common nodes**((temporal.Pos+1) , (Array[Pos].Positions.Pos))

        if | temporal | ≥ β, **then**   //if temporal has a number of nodes ≥ than β

          if Pos = Array, **then** there is a cycle,

            PMS ← **Cycle**(β, temporal, array, Actual, Pos) //call to Cycle function

            if the PMS cannot grow **then** exit from the while

          else PMS ← PMS + Array[Pos].Id₂ // expand the PMS

        Pos ← Array[Actual].NextIndex

      end-while

      delete all the MFS ⊆ PMS

      if (PMS ⊄ MFS) **then** MFS←Add(PMS)

      Actual ← Array[Actual].NextIndex

  End-while

Fig. 4. Algorithm to find all MFS (phase 3)

Phase 3. – Find all MFS (fig. 4). For each element *i* of the *NextPos list,* check if it has a frequency ≥ β, in order to determine if this pair can become a possible maximal sequence PMS. If frequency ≥ β then grow forward all the elements in the *NextPos* list w.r.t *i*. If after this growth there is (in the *NextPost* list) a number of elements ≥ β, then the PMS can grow. When the PMS cannot grow it is added to the MFS list if only if the PMS is not a subsequence of any previously stored MFS, and all the MFS that are subsequence of the PMS are deleted from the MFS list. The table 1 shows how the algorithm finds the first four MFS for the example of the fig. 3a.

In the example of figure 3a, the generated PMS does not contain cycles since all its pairs are different. For our algorithm each PMS can be classified as a PMS with and without cycles. A *cycle* is detected when the first pair is repeated if it happens, the *cycle* function is used to get the PMS. The cycle function guarantees the *mutually excluded* property. If the PMS obtained from *cycle* function can grow, then it is treated as a PMS without cycles, because it could grow.

Table 1. Example of how to get a PMS for the text "esadeladesad" with the structure presented in figure 2.a, using the algorithm of figure 4 with β=2. Since the first pair "es" has two ocurrences in the text (frequency ≥ β) in the positions 1 and 9 (*temporal* list), this pair becomes the new PMS. Then, the next item is "a" for both ocurrences. Therefore, the PMS can grow in one (PMS="esa"), it is, the positions are increased in one (*temporal={2,10}*). The same happends w.r.t. the "d" item and the PMS="esad". Since the next item has frequency < β the PMS cannot grow and it is store. Then, this process is repeated to get more PMS

Actual	Pos	temporal	PMS_Freq	Action	PMS
1	**1**	1,9	2	PMS_Freq ≥ β, PMS=Pair=T_{pos} + T_{pos+1}	es
2	2	2,10	2	PMS_Freq ≥ β, Grow PMS= PMS + T_{pos+1}	esa
3	3	3,11	2	PMS_Freq ≥ β, Grow PMS= PMS + T_{pos+1}	**esad**
4	4	4	1	PMS_Freq is not ≥ β, Store the PMS	
2	**2**	2,10	2	PMS_Freq ≥ β, PMS=Pair=T_{pos} + T_{pos+1}	sa
3	3	3,11	2	PMS_Freq ≥ β, Grow PMS= PMS + T_{pos+1}	**sad**
4	4	4	1	PMS_Freq ≥ β, Store the PMS	

Cycle function: Algorithm to find the PMS with cycles
Input: β support, *temporal, array, Actual, aux;*   **Output:** A PMS
CycleSize ← *Array[aux].Pos-Array[Actual].Pos;* //size of the cycle
Intervals ← From *temporal* find the intervals of groups of cycles
ActualGrpSize ← Size of the interval where [*Array[actual].Pos-Array[aux].Pos*] ∈ *Intervals*
While *ActualGrpSize* ≥ 2 **do**
    For each *Interval* get the *frequency* w.r.t. *ActualGrpSize*
        if Σ *frequencies* ≥ β **then** PMS←T[*Array[actual].Pos*] +...+T[*Array[actual].Pos÷ActualGrpSize*]
            if *ActualGrpSize* was not decremented **then** the PMS can grow
                temporal ← Rebuild *temporal* with (*end of Intervals* -1) in which the frequency = 1
            return (PMS, *temporal*);
    end-for
end-while
The *frequency* is calculated as follows:
        Used-Periods ← Ceiling (*ActualGrpSize* / *CycleSize*);
        Period ← *GrpSize* analyzed / *CycleSize*
    if *Used-Periods.remainder* = *Period.remainder* and *Period.remainder* >0 **then**
        Period←*Period* +1
Frequency = *Period* / *Used-Periods*

Fig. 5. Algorithm for finding a PMS with cycles

Cycle function (fig. 5). Using the *size of the cycle* (number of elements between the first and the repeated pair) find all the groups of occurrences of the cycle in order to build a list of *intervals* with the beginning and end of such positions. Using this list of intervals it is possible to find the longest PMS. Given the *size of the interval*, this function tests in decreasing way (because we search the longest PMS) how many PMS are contained in each interval, therefore the sum of this local frequency becomes the total frequency that must be ≥ β. In such case, the PMS has as size the *size of the interval* that can appear β times into the text. If the *size of the interval* was not decremented then it is a PMS that can grow. The table 2 shows an example of how to find a PMS with cycles.

Table 2. Example of the PMS obtained from the *cycle* function for the text "abcabcabMabc GabcabcabMabc" with β =2. When the algorithm of phase 3 detects that the initial pair "ab" is repeated in the PMS="abcab", then the *cycle* function is activated. In step 1, all the groups of occurrences of cycles are found. In the Step 2, the *CycleSize* and *ActualGrpSize* are caculated. In the Step 3, the frequency of apparition is computing for each group using *CycleSize* and *ActualGrpSize*. In the Step 4, if the total frequency ≥ β, then the length of the PMS is *ActualGrpSize* and the PMS starts in the originial inital position, but if total frecuency < β, then decrement *ActualGrpSize* and return to step 3. In this example, the PMS obtained from *Cycle function* is "abcabcab". But, if *ActualGrpSize* is not decremented, then the PMS obtained is treated as a PMS without clycles and the phase 3 gets the PMS="abcabcabMabc"

Text:	a	b	c	a	b	c	a	b	M	a	b	c	G	a	b	c	a	b	c	a	b	M	a	b	c
Position	1	2	3	4	5	6	7	8	9	10	11	12	13	14	15	16	17	18	19	20	21	22	23	24	25

Given the above text, the following steps are generated (similar process of the Table 1)

Actual	Pos	Temporal	PMS-Freq	Action	PMS
1	1	1,4,7,10,14,17,20,23	8	PMS-Freq ≥ β, PMS=Pair=T_{pos} + T_{pos+1}	ab
2	2	2,5,11,15,18,24	6	PMS-Freq ≥ β, Grow PMS= PMS + T_{pos+1}	abc
3	3	3,6,16,19	4	PMS-Freq ≥ β, Grow PMS= PMS + T_{pos+1}	abca
1	4	4,7,17,20	4	PMS-Freq ≥ β, Grow PMS= PMS + T_{pos+1}	**abcab**

Step 1: The *cycle* function is activated since the first value of *Actual* is repeated:

From *temporal* list it is possible to get the *intervals* of positions of the groups of occurrences of the cycle:{4 ,   7,   17,   20 } =*temporal*

1	2	3	4	5	6	7	8	9	10	11	12	13	14	15	16	17	18	19	20	21	22	23	24	25
a	b	c	a	b	c	a	b	M	a	b	c	G	a	b	c	a	b	c	a	b	M	a	b	c

[1 , 8] ◄——— Groups ———► [14 , 21]

Step 2: The *CycleSize* and *ActualGrpSize* values are needed to calculate the frequency of each interval:

The *CycleSize*=3;(size of the repeated string)

1	2	3	4	5	6	7	...
a	b	c	a	b	c	a	...

ActualGrpSize=8 (size of the interval in which is contained the actual positions that are analized, that is [1,4] ∈ [1,8], therefore *ActualGrpSize*=(8-1)+1=8)

Step 3: Using the algorithm of fig. 5 the frequency for each interval is calculated:
For [1-8] the frequency = 1; and for [14-21] the frequency = 1

Step 4: Since (∑ frequencies) ≥ β , then the |PMS|= *ActualGrpSize* and the PMS=$T_{(m-1)+i}$ where 1≤ i≤ *ActualGrpSize* and m is the first value of *Pos*, in this case the PMS="abcabcab". Since *ActualGrpSize* was not decremented, the PMS can growth and must be treated as a PMS without cycles. The process continue so on, finally the PMS obtained is "abcabcabMabc"

5   Complexity Analysis for the Proposed Algorithm

Let T a Text and $n=|T|$, then the required space in the worst case is $O(n)$ because no additional space is needed, Only the space for the array structure is used. As example, if n =100,000 chars (approx. 50 pages), the required space is approx. 3 MB. The time complexity to get the MFS is $O(kn)$ where k is the length of longest the PMS, in the worst case $k=n/2$ in such case the complexity is $O(n^2)$, but in the practice the PMS's are not very long, for example in [7] the longest PMS has a length of 22.

6 Experiments

From the collection given in [10] we chose the text "Autobiography" by Thomas Jefferson corresponding to: 243,115 chars, 31,517 words (approx. 100 pages), 5,499 different words and 18,739 different pairs. Also, we chose the text "LETTERS" by Thomas Jefferson with around 1,812,428 chars and 241,735 words (approx. 800 pages). In both texts the stop words were not removed and only the numbers and punctuation symbols were omitted. In order to show the behavior of the processing time against the number of words in the text, we compute the MFS using our algorithm for the minimum threshold value, $\beta =2$. Each chart in fig. 6 corresponds to one text, processing different quantities of words. The figure 6a starts with 5,000 words and uses an increment of 5,000, in order to see how the processing time grows when the number of processed words is augmented in the same text. In the fig. 6b, an increment of 40,000 words was used in order to see how the processing time grows for a big text. Also, in both charts the time for phases (1 and 2) is shown.

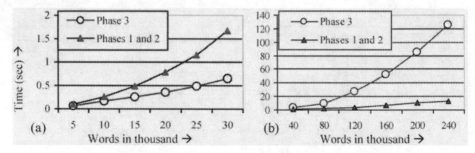

Fig. 6. Processing time for: a) "Autobiography" and, b) "LETTERS"

For the same documents the whole text was processed to find all the MFS, in order to appreciate (fig. 7) how the performance of our algorithm is affected for different values of the β threshold. Fig. 7a shows the time in seconds for "Autobiography" and fig. 7b for "LETTERS".

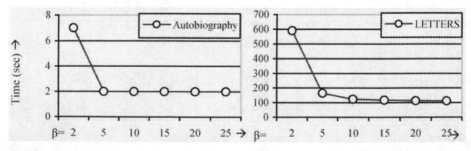

Fig. 7. Time performance for different values of β for: a) "Autobiography" and b) "LETTERS"

Furthermore, we have included in fig. 8 an analysis of the growth of the amount of MFS obtained from the same texts for different values for β.

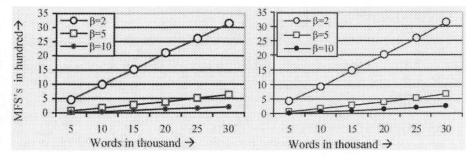

Fig. 8. Amount of MFS generated for different values of β for: a) "Autobiography" and, b) "LETTERS"

Additionally to these experiments, we processed the biggest text from the collection [10] "An Inquiry into the nature ..." by Adam Smith with 2,266,784 chars corresponding to 306,156 words (approx. 1000 pages) with β=2, all MFS were obtained in 353 sec. approx. 5.88 min.

7 Discussion

The sequential pattern mining algorithms have been designed for working on a database. The comparison of our algorithm against this kind of algorithm is difficult since they have different assumptions and they were not designed to work on one text. First, with respect to the space the typical methods have a reasonably performance for 2-sequences, but the performance drastically decrease when any of the MFS becomes longer because if a l-sequence is a MFS, it implies the presence of 2^l-2 candidates (as example if $l=100$ then $2^{100}-1{\approx}10^{30}$), and each candidate must be explicitly examined [4,5]. The pattern-growth methods, for example PrefixSpan [5], need to get the frequent prefixes in order to keep all the projected databases, but it is very expensive. In contrast, our algorithm does not need to generate any extra auxiliary set of sequences or projected databases. Consequently, the required space for our algorithm is much smaller than pattern-growth methods. Moreover, our algorithm avoids the text scan to see if a sequence is frequent or it exists in the source. Our algorithm goes directly to find the PMS. Finally in comparison with others algorithms, our algorithm can run different values for β using the same structure; getting better times.

8 Conclusions

This paper proposes a fast algorithm to find all the MFS in one text, requiring only the β parameter. The algorithm uses a simple structure and does not need to use hash tables or any other auxiliary structure. In texts with cycles the algorithm uses the *cycle* function to become faster. As future work we are going to adapt this algorithm to work over a text collection, in order to allow a fair comparison against the other methods. Since our algorithm constructs an alphabet at phase 1, and the following phases work over this alphabet, it can be applied on any data represented as a sequence, for example DNA sequences in human genome analysis.

Acknowledgement

This work was financially supported by CONACyT (Mexico) through project J38707-A.

References

1. Fayyad, U., Piatetsky-Shapiro G. "Advances in Knowledge Discovery and Data mining". AAAI Press, 1996.
2. Feldman, R and Dagan, I. "Knowledge Discovery in Textual Databases (KDT)", *In Proceedings of the 1st International Conference on Knowledge Discovery (KDD-95)* 1995.
3. Agrawal, R and Srikant, R. "Mining Sequential Patterns" in *Proceedings of the International Conference on Data Engineering*, 1995.
4. Lin, Dao-I. Fast Algorithms for Discovering the Maximum Frequent Set, Ph. Thesis, New York University, 1998.
5. Pei, J, Han, et all: "PrefixSpan: Mining Sequential Patterns Efficiently by Prefix-Projected Pattern Growth" in *Proc International Conference on Data Engineering* (ICDE 01), 2001.
6. Mohammend j. Zaki, SPADE: An Efficient Algorithm for Mining Frequent Sequences, Machine Learning, Kluwer Academic Publishers, 2000.
7. Ahonen, H. "Finding All Maximal Frequent Sequences in Text". *ICML-99 Workshop: Machine Learning in Text Data*, 1999.
8. Antunes, C., Oliveira A. Generalization of Pattern-growth Methods for Sequential Pattern Mining with Gap Constraints. *Third IAPR Workshop on Machine Learning and Data Mining MLDM´2003*, 2003.
9. Srikant, R., and Agrawal, R. Mining sequential patterns: Generalizations and performance improvements. *In 5th Intl. Conf. Extending Database Discovery and Data Mining*, 1996.
10. Public domain documents from American and English literature as well as Western philosophy. http://www.infomotions.com/alex/

Refined Method for the Fast and Exact Computation of Moment Invariants

Humberto Sossa[1] and Jan Flusser[2]

[1] Centro de Investigación en Computación - IPN
Av. Juan de Dios Bátiz s/n, Esquina con Miguel Othón de Mendizábal
Colonia Nueva Industrial Vallejo, C. P. 07700, México, D. F. Mexico
[2] Institute of Information Theory and Automation
Academy of Sciencies of the Czech Republic
Pod vodárenkou vezi 4. 182 08 Prage 8, Czech Republic

Abstract. Geometric moments have been proven to be a very efficient tool for description and recognition of binary shapes. Numerous methods for effective calculation of image moments have been presented up to now. Recently, Sossa, Yañez and Díaz [Pattern Recognition, 34(2):271-276, 2001] proposed a new algorithm based on a morphologic decomposition of the image into a set of closed disks. Their algorithm yields approximative results. In this paper we propose a refinement of their method that performs as fast as the original one but gives exact results.

1 Introduction

Image moments and various types of moment-based invariants play a very important role in object recognition and shape analysis [3], [1]. The $(p+q)$th order Cartesian geometric moment M_{pq} of a two-dimensional grey-level image $f(x,y)$ (for short 2-D moment) is defined as

$$M_{pq} = \int_{-\infty}^{\infty} \int_{-\infty}^{\infty} x^p y^q f(x,y) dx dy \qquad p,q = 0,1,2,\cdots \qquad (1)$$

In a binary image the characteristic function takes only the values 1 or 0, supposing that for the interest region R holds $f(x,y)=1$. Thus, the definition simplifies to the form

$$M_{pq} = \iint_R x^p y^q dx dy, \qquad (2)$$

In the discrete case, the double integral must be replaced by a summation. The most common way how to do that is to employ the rectangular (i.e. zero-order) method of numeric integration. Then (1) turns to the well-known form

$$m_{pq} = \sum_{x=1}^{N} \sum_{y=1}^{N} x^p y^q f_{ij}, \qquad (3)$$

where N is the size of the image and f_{ij} are the grey levels of individual pixels $(x,y) \in Z^2$. Finally, for binary region R we get

A. Sanfeliu et al. (Eds.): CIARP 2004, LNCS 3287, pp. 487–494, 2004.

$$m_{pq} = \sum_{(x,y)\in R}\sum x^p y^q. \tag{4}$$

Fast and exact computation of 2-D geometric moments of binary objects has been considered as an important problem for its importance in numerous image-processing applications.

Since direct calculation of discrete moments from eq. (4) is time-consuming (it requires $O(pqN^2)$ operations), a large amount of effort has been spent in the last decade to develop more effective algorithms.

Recently, Flusser [2] pointed out that the formula (4), commonly used in the literature for the calculation of the discrete moments of a rectangular block yields inaccurate results. In the same paper, Flusser presented a correction of the method originally proposed by Spiliotis and Mertzios [6].

In this paper we show that the recent method by Sossa et al. [5] also suffers by this inaccuracy and we propose how to correct it. We use the same block-wise image representation as Sossa et al. proposed in [5] but we present a different scheme to calculate the block moments. We show that the new method yields more accurate results than the original one.

2   Original Method by Sossa et al.

In [5], a novel approach to the calculation of geometric moments of binary image was introduced. This method was based on morphologic erosion of the original shape.

The method performs in three basic steps:

1. Decompose the given image into a union of disjoint disks;
2. Compute the geometric moments for each of these disks;
3. Obtain the final moments as a sum of the moments computed for each disk.

Various metrics defined on a discrete plane can be employed in Step 1. The use of different metrics leads to different image decompositions. Sossa et al. used d_8 "maximum" metric defined as

$$d_8(P_1,P_2) = \max\{|x_1 - x_2|, |y_1 - y_2|\} \tag{5}$$

where P_i is a point whose coordinates are (x_i, y_i). It should be noted that a circular disk in d_8 metric is a square in Euclidean metric. The basic algorithm used by Sossa et al. to obtain the desired decomposition of a binary region $R \subset Z^2$ iteratively erodes R until the maximal disk completely contained in the original region R is obtained. Then this disk is eliminated from the region R and the remaining shape is assigned to R. The algorithm repeats this procedure until R becomes empty.

To calculate the moments of a disk D_p^r of radius r with center (X_c, Y_c) in $p \in Z^2$, Sossa et al. used eq. (4). The explicit formulae for the first ten geometric moments of this disk in d_8 metric are:

$$m_{00} = (2r+1)^2 \qquad m_{10} = m_{00}X_c \qquad m_{01} = m_{00}Y_c \qquad m_{11} = m_{10}Y$$

$$m_{20} = \frac{m_{00}}{3}\left(3X_c^2 + r(r+1)\right) \qquad\qquad m_{02} = \frac{m_{00}}{3}\left(3Y_c^2 + r(r+1)\right)$$

$$m_{21} = m_{20}Y_c \qquad\qquad m_{12} = m_{02}X_c \qquad\qquad (6)$$

$$m_{30} = m_{10}\left(X_c^2 + r(r+1)\right) \qquad m_{03} = m_{01}\left(Y_c^2 + r(r+1)\right)$$

To obtain these expressions, Sossa et al. used the well-known formulae for sums of integer powers:

$$\sum_{k=1}^{n} k = \frac{n}{2}(n+1), \ \sum_{k=1}^{n} k^2 = \frac{n}{6}(n+1)(2n+1), \ \sum_{k=1}^{n} k^3 = \left[\frac{n}{2}(n+1)\right]^2.$$

For details on the Sossa et al. method we refer to [5].

3 Refined Method

In this Section, we present a refinement of Sossa et al. method, which uses different formulae for calculation of disk moments. To explain the idea, we recall the original definition of moments in the continuous domain:

$$M_{pq} = \int_{-\infty}^{\infty}\int_{-\infty}^{\infty} x^p y^q f(x,y)\,dxdy \qquad\qquad (7)$$

where $f(x,y)$ is, in this case, the characteristic function of a disk. Clearly, eq. (4) is only an approximation of eq. (7). An error $\left|M_{pq} - m_{pq}\right|$ is introduced due to the zero-order approximation and numeric integration of $x^p y^q$ over each pixel of the disk. Below we show how to calculate the geometric moments of a disk exactly without any approximation.

Given a closed disk D_p^r of radius r with center (X_c, Y_c) in $p \in Z^2$ with corner pixels centered in $(X_c - r, Y_c - r)$, $(X_c + r, Y_c - r)$, $(X_c - r, Y_c + r)$ and $(X_c + r, Y_c + r)$. The characteristic function of this disk is

$$f(x,y) = \begin{cases} 1 & \text{if } (x,y) \in (X_c - r - 0.5, X_c + r + 0.5)\times(Y_c - r - 0.5, Y_c + r + 0.5) \\ 0 & \text{otherwise.} \end{cases}$$

According to eq. (7), the exact moments of the disk D_p^r are given as

$$\begin{aligned} M_{pq} &= \int_{-\infty}^{\infty}\int_{-\infty}^{\infty} x^p y^q f(x,y)\,dxdy \\ &= \frac{1}{(p+1)(q+1)}\left[(X_c + r + 0.5)^{p+1} - (X_c - r - 0.5)^{p+1}\right]\cdot \qquad (8) \\ &\quad \left[(Y_c + r + 0.5)^{q+1} - (Y_c - r - 0.5)^{q+1}\right] \end{aligned}$$

The reader can easily see that the corrected set of expressions for the first ten moments of the closed disk D_p^r becomes:

$$M_{00} = (2r+1)^2 \qquad M_{10} = M_{00}X_c \qquad M_{01} = M_{00}Y_c \qquad M_{11} = M_{10}Y$$

$$M_{20} = \frac{M_{00}}{3}\left(3X_c^2 + r(r+1) + 0.25\right) \qquad M_{02} = \frac{M_{00}}{3}\left(3Y_c^2 + r(r+1) + 0.25\right)$$

$$M_{21} = M_{20}Y_c \qquad\qquad\qquad M_{12} = M_{02}X_c$$

$$M_{30} = M_{10}\left(X_c^2 + r(r+1) + 0.25\right) \qquad M_{03} = M_{01}\left(Y_c^2 + r(r+1) + 0.25\right)$$

$$(9)$$

4 Comparison of the Two Methods

While eq. (8) provides exact results, eq. (4) calculates some moments with errors due to the approximation. It can be shown that there is always $M_{pq} \geq m_{pq}$; the error $M_{pq} - m_{pq}$ depends on the values of p and q. Comparing eqs. (9) and (6), we can evaluate this errors easily, for instance

$$
\begin{aligned}
M_{20} - m_{20} &= \frac{1}{3}\left(6X_c^2 r + 3X_c^2 + 2r^3 + 3r^2 + 1.5r + 0.25\right)(2r+1) - \\
&\quad \frac{1}{3}\left(6X_c^2 r + 3X_c^2 + 2r^3 + 3r^2 + r\right)(2r+1) \\
&= \frac{1}{3}(2r+1)(0.5r + 0.25) \\
&= \frac{1}{12}m_{00}.
\end{aligned}
$$

Similarly,

$$M_{02} - m_{02} = \frac{m_{00}}{12}, \ M_{30} - m_{30} = \frac{m_{10}}{4}, \ M_{21} - m_{21} = \frac{m_{01}}{12},$$

$$M_{12} - m_{12} = \frac{m_{10}}{12}, \ M_{03} - m_{03} = \frac{m_{01}}{4}. \qquad (10)$$

On the other hand, for some moments both methods produce exact results:

$$M_{00} - m_{00} = 0, \ M_{01} - m_{01} = 0, \ M_{10} - m_{10} = 0, \ M_{11} - m_{11} = 0. \qquad (11)$$

5 Impact on the Values of the Invariants

In object recognition we rarely use directly the geometric moments as the features because they are sensitive to particular position of the object in the image plane. Instead, we employ certain functions of moments, called moment invariants, that are invariant to expected intraclass variations of the objects. Typically, shift and rotation invariance is required in many practical tasks. In this Section, we analyze how the values of various moment invariants differ depending on if m_{pq} or M_{pq} are used.

Probably the most popular set of moment invariants was derived by Hu [3]. These features are invariant to translation and rotation of the object. In continuous domain the first two are defined as

$$\phi_1 = \mu_{20} + \mu_{02}, \; \phi_2 = (\mu_{20} - \mu_{02})^2 - 4\mu_{11} \qquad (12)$$

where

$$\mu_{pq} = \int_{-\infty}^{\infty} \int_{-\infty}^{\infty} (x - x_t)^p (y - y_t)^q f(x,y)dxdy \qquad (13)$$

is the central moment of the object $f(x,y)$ and (x_t, y_t) are the coordinates of the object centroid. Hu also showed that scaling invariance can be achieved via normalization of each central moment by $\mu_{00}^{(p+q+2)/2}$.

It can be easily observed that both algorithms give the same position of object centroid:

$$x_t \equiv \frac{m_{10}}{m_{00}} \equiv \frac{M_{10}}{M_{00}} \; \text{and} \; y_t \equiv \frac{m_{01}}{m_{00}} \equiv \frac{M_{01}}{M_{00}},$$

Thus, central moments are affected exactly in the same way as geometric moments. However, since μ_{10} and μ_{01} equal zero by definition, the relations (10) simplify to the form

$$M_{20} - \mu_{20} = \frac{m_{00}}{12}, \; M_{02} - \mu_{02} = \frac{m_{00}}{12},$$

$$M_{30} - \mu_{30} = 0, \; M_{21} - \mu_{21} = 0, \; M_{12} - \mu_{12} = 0, \; M_{03} - \mu_{03} = 0$$

where μ_{pq} denotes the central moments calculated by traditional method while M_{pq} stands for the central moments calculated by the refined method.

Now we can observe an interesting fact: The only Hu's invariant whose values depend on the method of calculation is the first one. Clearly,

$$\phi_1(M_{pq}) - \phi_1(\mu_{pq}) = \frac{\mu_{00}}{6}.$$

ϕ_3, ϕ_4, ϕ_5 and ϕ_7 contains only 3rd-order moments, so they cannot be affected. ϕ_2 and ϕ_6 stay also constant due to the error cancellation effect. The same observation can be found in [4].

Another set of invariants called affine moment invariants (AMI's) was proposed by Flusser and Suk [1]. They are more general than Hu's invariants because they are invariant not only to rotation and scaling but to general affne transformation. Thanks to this, they can be successfully used in object recognition on images deformed by slant or anisotropic scaling. The first six AMI's are shown below.

$$I_1 = (\mu_{20}\mu_{02} - \mu_{11}^2)/\mu_{00}^4$$

$$I_2 = (\mu_{30}^2\mu_{03}^2 - 6\mu_{30}\mu_{21}\mu_{12}\mu_{03} + 4\mu_{30}\mu_{12}^3 + 4\mu_{21}^3\mu_{03} - 3\mu_{21}^2\mu_{12}^2)/\mu_{00}^{10}$$

$$I_3 = (\mu_{20}(\mu_{21}\mu_{03} - \mu_{12}^2) - \mu_{11}(\mu_{30}\mu_{03} - \mu_{21}\mu_{12}) + \mu_{02}(\mu_{30}\mu_{12} - \mu_{21}^2))/\mu_{00}^7$$

$$
\begin{aligned}
I_4 = {}& (\mu_{20}^3\mu_{03}^2 - 6\mu_{30}\mu_{11}\mu_{12}\mu_{03} - 6\mu_{20}^2\mu_{02}\mu_{21}\mu_{03} + 9\mu_{20}^2\mu_{02}\mu_{12}^2 \\
& + 12\mu_{20}\mu_{11}^2\mu_{21}\mu_{03} + 6\mu_{20}\mu_{11}\mu_{02}\mu_{30}\mu_{03} - 18\mu_{20}\mu_{11}\mu_{02}\mu_{21}\mu_{12} \\
& - 8\mu_{11}^3\mu_{30}\mu_{03} - 6\mu_{20}\mu_{02}^2\mu_{30}\mu_{12} + 9\mu_{20}\mu_{02}^2\mu_{21}^2 + 12\mu_{11}^2\mu_{02}\mu_{30}\mu_{12} \\
& - 6\mu_{11}\mu_{02}^2\mu_{30}\mu_{21} + \mu_{02}^3\mu_{30}^2)/\mu_{00}^{11}
\end{aligned}
$$

$$I_5 = (\mu_{40}\mu_{04} - 4\mu_{31}\mu_{13} + 3\mu_{22}^2)/\mu_{00}^6$$

$$I_6 = (\mu_{40}\mu_{04}\mu_{22} + 2\mu_{31}\mu_{22}\mu_{13} - \mu_{40}\mu_{13}^2 - \mu_{04}\mu_{31}^2 - 3\mu_{22}^3)/\mu_{00}^9$$

We can easily prove that, for the same reason as in the previous case, I_2 stays the same irrespective of the calculation algorithm. However, other AMI's change if M_{pq} are used instead of μ_{pq}. We can observe that, for instance,

$$I_1(M_{pq}) - I_1(\mu_{pq}) = \frac{\mu_{00}}{12}(\mu_{20} - \mu_{02}) + \frac{\mu_{00}^2}{144}.$$

Similar (but more complicated) relations can be derived for other AMI's too.

Summarizing the above analysis, we can conclude that when using Hu's invariants, one does not need to use the refined algorithm for moment calculation (with exception of ϕ_1). On the other hand, the AMI's should be computed using the refined method if accurate values are required.

6 Numerical Experiments

In this Section, we experimentally demonstrate the difference between classical and new formula for moment calculation. From the theoretical analysis given above implies that some moments and moment invariants are identical regardless of the fact whether eq. (4) or eq. (8) is used. In this experiment we show the differences between second-order central moments, first Hu's invariant ϕ_1 and six affne moment invariants $I_1,\ldots,I_6$ for three binary images.

In Fig. 1, one can see our test objects called "Plane", "Duck", and "Snake", respectively. In Table 1, the relative errors of the moments and of the invariants are shown. The errors we have investigated are defined as follows:

$$e_1 = \frac{M_{20} - \mu_{20}}{M_{20}}, \quad e_2 = \frac{M_{02} - \mu_{02}}{M_{02}}, \quad e_3 = \frac{\phi_1(M_{02}) - \phi_1(\mu_{02})}{\phi_1(M_{02})},$$

$$e_{j+3} = \frac{I_j(M_{02}) - I_j(\mu_{02})}{I_j(M_{02})}, \quad j = 1,\ldots,6.$$

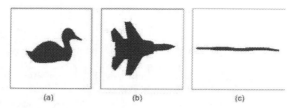

Fig. 1. Test objects used in the experiment: Plane(left), Duck(middle), and Snake(right).

Table 1. Relative differences between traditional and new formulae for moment calculation. For simplicity, all values were multiplied by 10^4.

	e_1	e_2	e_3	e_4	e_5	e_6	e_7	e_8	e_9
Plane	0.16	0.23	0.19	0.40	0	0.21	0.63	0.91	1.63
Duck	0.19	0.41	0.26	0.81	0	0.41	1.24	2.08	3.27
Snake	0.18	54.89	0.37	56.73	0	-6.52	2.02	2.21	145.07

The most important observation that is based on this experiment can be summarized in the following way. For elongated objects (where elongation is parallel to one of the axes) the relative errors can be high and might, in some cases, cause misclassification. An extreme case is a one-pixel thick horizontal line, for which $\mu_{02} = 0$ but M_{02} is proportional to its length. Relative errors of other objects are much smaller, as can be seen in Table 1 when comparing Plane or Duck to Snake. Thus, when dealing with elongated objects, it is recommended to use the refined formula (8) for moment calculation. On the other hand, for objects having "regular" shapes traditional computation according to eq. (4) can be used without significant loss of accuracy.

7 Conclusion

In this paper, we presented a new method for calculating geometric moments and, consequently, of moment invariants of binary objects. This method is a refinement of Sossa et al. algorithm that was based on a decomposition of the object into disjoint disks. In the original paper by Sossa et al., zero-order approximation was used for numerical integration when calculating moments of the disks. In this paper we proposed an exact formula with no approximation. We analyzed (both theoretically and experimentally) the differences between these two formulae and the influence of the refined method on the values of moment invariants. We demonstrated that for some shapes the new method yields a significant increase in accuracy.

Acknowledgment

Financial support of this research was provided by the National Council of Science and Technology of Mexico (CONACYT) under projects No. 41529 and 40114Y, by the National Polytechnic Institute of Mexico (IPN) under project No. 20030658 and by the Grant Agency of the Czech Republic under the project No. 102/00/1711.

References

1. J. Flusser and T. Suk, Pattern recognition by affne moment invariants, Pattern Recognition, 26(1):167-174, 1993.
2. J. Flusser, Refined moment calculation using image block representation, IEEE Transactions on Image Processing, 9(11):1977-1978, 2000.
3. M. K. Hu, Visual pattern recognition by moment invariants, IRE Transactions on Information Theory, 8:179-187, 1962.
4. W. G. Lin and S. S. Wang, A note on the calculation of moments, Pattern Recognition Letters, 15(11):1065-1070, 1994.
5. H. Sossa, C. Yañez and J. L. Díaz, Computing geometric moments using morphological erosions, Pattern Recognition, 34(2):271-276, 2001.
6. I. M. Spiliotis and B. G. Mertzios, Real-time computation of 2-D moments on binary images using image block representation, IEEE Transactions of Image Processing, 7(11):1609-1615, 1998.

Skeletonization of Gray-Tone Images
Based on Region Analysis

Luca Serino

Istituto di Cibernetica "E. Caianiello", CNR, 80078 Pozzuoli (Napoli), Italy
ls@imagm.cib.na.cnr.it

Abstract. A problem often present in skeletonization of gray-tone digital images is that the obtained skeleton includes an excessive number of branches. In this respect, a regularization process should be performed in order to partially, or totally, remove branches which are not meaningful in the problem domain. In this paper, we propose a skeletonization algorithm which is active only on a suitable subset of the image, mainly constituted by regions understood as relevant from a perceptual point of view. The notion of dominance of a region, which is defined in terms of geometrical features, gray-value and adjacency relations, plays a central role in the selection of the regions of the subset. The obtained skeleton turns out to be more representative and its simpler structure will allow one to perform the regularization phase with a reduced computational effort.

1 Introduction

Generally, the skeleton of a gray-tone digital image could be defined as a set having a "graph-like" structure which, ideally, should represent a sketch of the subset of the image which is understood as the foreground in a specific problem domain. However, since it is often difficult to distinguish clearly which regions belong to the foreground, the obtained skeleton may include branches found in correspondence with non significant regions, and its structure may result too busy for representation purposes. In this respect, the representation power of the skeleton can be improved noticeably by taking into account a regularization process, which modifies the skeleton structure by using context information and domain knowledge [1], [2], [3].

In this paper, we propose a skeletonization algorithm which is active only on a suitable subset of the image, mainly constituted by regions understood as relevant from a perceptual point of view. Purpose of this selection of the image subset is to highlight the regions which are more likely to belong to the foreground. The advantages inherent in this approach with respect to previous work, e.g., [4], are: i) a reduced computational effort during skeletonization, since the skeleton is searched only in a subset of the image. ii) a skeleton having a simpler structure and therefore more representative. iii) a reduced computational effort during the regularization phase, since the skeleton is likely to be constituted by a smaller number of branches.

To find the regions belonging to the image subset of interest, we introduce the notion of dominant region. This notion involves geometrical features, gray-value and adjacency relations of a region, and turns out to be useful in classifying a region as perceptually more relevant than (some of) its adjacent regions. The image subset will consist of the dominant regions and of a number of other regions, called induced regions. The induced regions, although not perceptually meaningful, are important because are placed along an ideal path connecting a dominant region with another

A. Sanfeliu et al. (Eds.): CIARP 2004, LNCS 3287, pp. 495–502, 2004.

dominant region with higher gray-value, and their presence allow connectedness preservation during the pixel removal phase.

The proposed skeletonization algorithm follows the scheme described in a previous paper [4], which allows a computationally convenient analysis of the regions to be processed. Besides the region selection phase, it includes a labeling phase guided by distance transformation [5], [6], [7], and a pixel removal phase accomplished by topology preserving reduction operations [8], [9].

2   Preliminaries

Let G be a gray-tone digital image. Pixels in G are assigned one out of a finite number of increasing integer values g_k k=0,1,...,N, which indicates for any pixel p the gray-value or status $g(p)$ of the pixel itself. We assume that G is bordered by a frame of pixels with gray-value higher than g_N. In the following, pixels will be described as darker as their gray-value is higher.

The neighbors of p are its 8-adjacent pixels. They constitute the neighborhood $N(p)$ of p and are denoted by $n_1, n_2, ..., n_8$, where the sub indexes increase clockwise from the pixel n_1 placed to the left of p.

A gray-tone digital image is a mosaic constituted by regions, which we regard as maximal 4-connected sets of pixels with the same gray-value.

Two regions in the mosaic are adjacent if they are 4-adjacent.

The area of a region is the number of its pixels.

The perimeter of a region is the number of its pixels 4-adjacent to the adjacent regions.

The length of the common border between a region and an adjacent one is the number of its pixels 4-adjacent to that region.

A "higher neighboring component" (shortly, HNC) of a region R is a maximal connected set of adjacent regions, each having gray-value higher than the one of R.

A "lower neighboring component" (shortly, LNC) of a region R is a maximal connected set of adjacent regions, each having gray-value lower than the one of R.

3   Regions

In a gray-tone image where there is no *a priori* knowledge of its contents, we consider the darker areas as foreground and those clearer as background. To regard a region as darker does not depend on its real gray-value, but only on the existence of neighboring regions with lower gray-value. In a broad sense, darker regions are perceptually more relevant and, under certain conditions, we say that they dominate the neighboring regions.

In order to detect the dominant regions, it is preliminarily convenient to distinguish four types of regions: top, bottom, saddle and slope.

- A top is a region with gray-value higher than the gray-value of all its adjacent regions.
- A bottom is a region with gray-value lower than the gray-value of all its adjacent regions.
- A saddle is a region for which there exist at least either two HNCs or two LNCs.
- A slope is a region for which there exists exactly one HNC and one LNC.

Since the perceptual relevance of a region depends on the local context in which it is placed, the tops assume a determinant role since they are characterized by a locally maximum gray-value. Thus, all tops should be represented by branches of the skeleton. On the contrary, the bottoms have a locally minimum gray-value and are very likely to be part of the background. Such regions should not be represented by branches of the skeleton.

More questionable is the decision regarding saddles and slopes.

A saddle is a region that separates two HNCs (or two LNCs) and may correspond either to an abrupt change of gray-value with respect to the gray-values of these components or to a smooth transition between those gray-values. Whichever the case, we regard a saddle as part of the background if its gray-value is closer to the gray-values of the LNCs than to the ones of the HNCs, and as part of the foreground if this is not true, i.e., the saddle appears sharply defined. Thus, a saddle cannot be considered automatically as a dominant region, and certain measurements have to be performed to this purpose. See Fig. 1 (a,b).

Slopes correspond to perceptually relevant regions if they are elongated and mostly surrounded by regions with a suitably lower gray-value, i.e., are sharply defined. In this case, they are dominant regions and skeleton branches should be found in correspondence with them. In other cases, they could be understood as belonging either to the foreground or to the background, depending on the context. Particularly, we regard them as part of the foreground if they are useful (to contribute) to establish a connection between dominant regions with different gray-values.

To define the set of the dominant regions, we propose the four criteria below, which take into account gray-value, elongation, and local context.

c1: the region is not a bottom;
c2: the region is a top;
c3: the region is a sharp saddle;
c4: the region is an elongated and sharp slope;

Then, we say that a region is dominant if the following condition is verified:

$$c1 \text{ AND } (c2 \text{ OR } c3 \text{ OR } c4)$$

Once the dominant regions have been found, it is important to establish which other regions can be understood as belonging to the foreground, and whose detection can be induced by the presence of the dominant regions. For instance, if we identify an elongated slope as a dominant region, then it is important that it be connected to the part of the foreground (i.e., already detected dominant regions) of which it is perceived as a protrusion. To this purpose, it is necessary to consider as belonging to the foreground also the slopes placed between the protrusion and the foreground. Once detected, an induced region will induce in turn other regions with higher and higher gray-values until a dominant region is found. See Fig. 1c.

4 Skeletonization

The skeletonization process can schematically be divided in 5 phases. The first phase regards the preprocessing. The aim is to simplify the input image by using an iterative merging process, which creates macro regions including input regions whose gray-values can vary only within a given range [10]. We don't discuss this phase since it is described in detail in a previous paper [4]. The second phase regards the extraction of

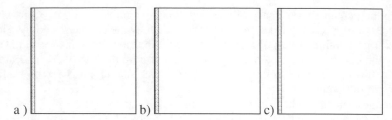

Fig. 1. a-b) Region A is a saddle. Depending on the context, A can be dominant (a) or not (b). c) Region A is a bottom. Region H is a top. Regions B-G are slopes. Slopes D, E, F, and G are induced from the elongated and sharp slope C.

data characterizing the regions. The third phase regards the detection of both the dominant regions and the regions induced by these ones. The fourth phase regards the extraction of the skeleton from the regions previously selected. We will only briefly outline this phase, since it is not significantly different from a similar one described in detail in [4]. The last phase regards the post processing, tailored to originate a one-pixel-thick skeleton.

4.1   Data Characterizing Regions

During this phase we collect useful data regarding the regions. In order to keep these data, we use a list R of records; every record of R has 10 fields and contains the data concerning a region. The first field is a natural number that is ascribed to the region and has the role of ID of the region; the fields from 2 to 5 contain respectively the gray-value, the area, the length of the common border with the regions having lower gray-value, the length of the common border with the regions having higher gray-value; the fields 6 and 7 contain numbers 0, 1 or 2 depending on whether the number of HNCs (LNCs) is $= 0$ or $= 1$ or > 1; the fields 8 and 9 points to two other lists of records: the first one points to a list containing the ID of the adjacent regions of the examined region; the second points to a list C of records keeping the coordinates of the pixels of the region. Finally the last field is a Boolean field that will assume true or false value depending on whether the region will be considered as foreground or background.

Since it is important to access the data regarding a region also by starting from the ID value, we have chosen as ID the progressive numbers starting from 1. In this way, we can use an array of pointers in which the generic element "i" points to the record containing the data of the i-th region.

The extraction from the image G of the data of interest regarding every region is carried out in two steps, and in different ways.

The first step is concerned with a raster scan of the image G during which, every time that a new region is detected, the progressive number is ascribed as ID to the region, and a new record is created where the ID and the gray-value of the region are inserted. All the pixels of the region are then detected and labeled with their ID in a new array F. While the pixels of a region are detected, the border pixels regarding the region itself are inserted into the list C and the value of the area is also computed. Once the entire region has been examined, also this value will be inserted in the relative field of the record.

The second step is concerned with the analysis of the list R, in order to assign to every region the ID of the adjacent regions and the lengths of the common border with its adjacent regions. To this purpose, we consider, for every region, the list C of the border pixels. Every member of C is a pair of coordinates characterizing a pixel in F. The set of the regions 4-adjacent to the border pixels identifies the regions adjacent to the examined region. Every time that a new adjacent region is found, its ID is inserted in the list of the region under examination. By analyzing the 4-neighbors of the pixel in F it is also possible to know the gray-value of the adjacent regions. Therefore, after analyzing the list C, the length of the common border with the regions with higher and lower gray-values will be known and these lengths can be inserted in the relative fields of the record.

The R list is analyzed again in order to detect, for every region, the HNCs and the LNCs; in particular, it is necessary to know the number (0, 1, >1) of HNCs and LNCs. First, we consider the case of the HNCs. The description is referred to a generic region found when scanning the list R, since the procedure is the same for all the regions. We consider the list of the adjacent regions and construct a new list L of regions including only the regions with gray-value higher than the one of the examined region. If L is empty, the number of HNCs is equal to zero, else we analyze L in order to check, by considering the adjacency of the regions stored in L, whether all these regions constitute only one connected set in the image F. To this purpose, we consider a new list L', initially empty. We remove the first element from L and place it in L'. For every region E of L, we consider its list of adjacent regions in order to detect whether an element of L' is in it. If this happens, we remove the region E from L and insert it in L'. When the analysis of all the elements of L terminates, one of the following three cases can occur. i) The list L is empty; in this case the procedure terminates and the number of components found is equal to 1. ii) The list L is not empty, but at least one removal has been done; in this case L must be scanned again. iii) The list L is not empty and no removal has been done; in this case the procedure terminates and the number of components found is greater of 1.

The procedure to detect the LNCs is analogous; the only difference occurs in the construction of L, where the elements with lower gray-value will be inserted.

4.2   Selection of Dominant and Induced Regions

The conditions c1, c2, c3, c4 mentioned above (see section 3) are taken into account to decide whether a region is dominant.

The first condition says that the region should not be a bottom. This information is available since if a region is a bottom, the number of its LNCs is equal to 0.

The second condition says that the region should be a top. Also this information is available since a top has the number of HNCs equal to 0.

The third condition says that the region should be a sharp saddle. If the region is a saddle the number of HNCs (LNCs) is equal at least to 2. If this is the case, it is necessary to check whether this region is sharp. To this purpose, it is necessary to have a measure for the "nearness" of the saddle with respect to the HNCs and with respect to the LNCs. In our opinion, a crucial role in defining the quality of the context for the HNCs (LNCs) is played both by the gray-value of the regions that constitute the HNCs (LNCs) and by their spatial extensions. Thus, we ascribe to the HNCs (LNCs) a weight equal to the sum of the products between the gray-value and the area of every region of the HNCs (LNCs), divided by the area of the HNCs (LNCs). We indicate such values with d_hnc and d_lnc respectively. If there results that $d\_hnc<d\_lnc$, that is if the gray-value of the region is nearer to d_hnc than to d_lnc, we take the region as a dominant region. In order to evaluate d_hnc and d_lnc, only the data regarding the gray-values and the areas of the adjacent regions are necessary; thus one scan of the list of the adjacencies of the considered region is sufficient.

The fourth condition says that the region should be a sharp and elongated slope, understood as a protrusion. We note that, if the region is a slope, the number of HNCs and of LNCs must be equal to 1, therefore this information is available. With regard to the sharpness, we follow the procedure used for the saddles. What remains to evaluate, is whether the slope is a protrusion. Our criterion is to estimate the ratio between the respective lengths of the common border with LNC and with HNC. If this ratio is greater than a threshold, the slope is a protrusion. In this paper, we have chosen a threshold value equal to 3. This ratio is readily available since the data regarding the lengths of the common borders are already known.

To select the dominant regions is therefore sufficient one scan of the list R, then a true or false value will be inserted depending on whether the region is dominant or not.

Once the dominant regions have been detected, the induced regions should be found. In fact, every dominant region induces the adjacent regions with higher gray-value to become themselves dominant regions.

In order to find the induced regions, it is necessary to consider a process starting from the detected dominant regions. Thus, we perform one more scan of the list R during which, every time that we detect a dominant region, we begin an iterative process. This process starts from the dominant region and analyzes step by step the regions with higher gray-values adjacent to the created induced regions, and proceeds until an already detected dominant region (possibly, a top) is found. In Fig. 2, a pre-processed input image is shown (a), together with the extracted dominant and induced regions (b).

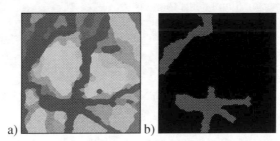

Fig. 2. a) Preprocessed input image. b) Dominant and induced regions.

4.3 Skeleton Extraction and Post Processing

The dominant regions and the induced regions are the only regions involved in the skeletonization process. The skeletonization procedure that we use was introduced in [4]. There, the skeleton was computed by applying topology preserving reduction operations to the pixels of the image, which is analyzed region by region. We outline below the modifications to bring to that algorithm in order to allow its use in the framework of this paper. The algorithm described in [4] is performed in three phases: region labeling, end point detection and pixel removal. Regarding the region labeling phase, this is replaced by the phases described in subsections 4.1 and 4.2 to which one has to add, with the same modalities described in [4], the computation of the distance transform for every region. Regarding the end point detection phase, no change is needed. As for the pixel removal phase, the only modification consists in estimating, every time that a new region is considered, if the region is of interest; if this is not the case, its analysis is skipped and the process continues on the remaining regions. The set obtained at the end of this phase is not ensured to be one-pixel-thick, so that a post processing phase is required. The image is considered as a binary image where the skeleton constitutes the foreground and its complement the background, so it is suffi-cient to apply well-known topology preserving reduction operations designed for binary images [8] to the set obtained above, during one raster scan of the image.

5 Conclusions

In this paper we have proposed a skeletonization algorithm for gray-tone images, based on region analysis. The aim of this analysis has been to try to foresee which regions could reasonably be understood as belonging to the foreground, so as to ex-clude the remaining ones from the skeletonization process. We have characterized four types of regions, by taking into account the gray-values of the regions and their spatial relations with the adjacent regions. We have also proposed some criteria to highlight a number of regions, called dominant regions, that are perceptually relevant and should be part of the foreground. The process of region selection foresees the detection of further regions, called induced regions, which allow one to link to each other the dominant regions. The dominant regions and the induced regions constitute the image subset on which the skeletonization algorithm is applied. The resulting skeleton (see Fig.3) is more representative than a skeleton obtained by considering all the regions of the image. Moreover, its simpler structure allows one to implement with a reduced computational effort the regularization phase, which should necessar-ily be considered to obtain a skeleton meaningful in the problem domain.

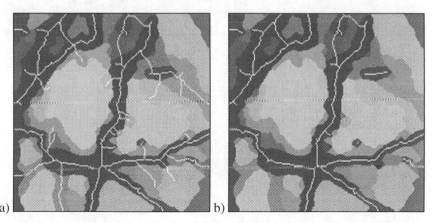

Fig. 3. Skeleton, superimposed on the preprocessed input, computed by considering all the regions (a) and by considering only the dominant and induced regions (b).

References

1. G. Bertrand, J.-Ch. Everat, M Couprie, Image segmentation through operators based on topology, J. Electronic Imaging **6** (1997) 395-405.
2. C. Arcelli, L. Serino, Regularization of graphlike sets in gray-tone digital images, Int. J. Pattern Recognition and Artificial Intelligence **15** (2001) 643-657.
3. L. Najman, M. Schmitt, Geodesic saliency of watershed contours and hierarchical segmentation, IEEE Trans. on PAMI **18** (1996) 1163-1173.
4. C. Arcelli, L. Serino, Topology preservation and tricky patterns in gray-tone images, in: I. Nyström, G. Sanniti di Baja, S. Svensson (Eds.), Discrete Geometry for Computer Imagery, LNCS 2886, Springer, Berlin, 2003, pp. 298-307.
5. A. Rosenfeld, On connectivity properties of greyscale pictures, Pattern Recognition **16** (1983) 47-50.
6. J. Piper, E. Granum, Computing distance transformations in convex and non-convex domains, Pattern Recognition **20** (1987) 599-615.
7. G. Borgefors, Distance transformations in digital images, Computer Vision, Graphics and Image Processing **34** (1986) 344-371.
8. C. Arcelli, G. Sanniti di Baja, Skeletons of planar patterns, in: T.Y. Kong, A. Rosenfeld, (Eds), Topological Algorithms for Digital Image Processing. North Holland, Amsterdam, 1996, pp. 99-143.
9. V. Ranwez, P. Soille, Order independent homotopic thinning for binary and grey tone anchored skeletons, Pattern Recognition Letters **23** (2002) 687-702.
10. Y. Wang, P. Bhattacharya, On parameter-dependent connected components of gray images, Pattern Recognition **29** (1996) 1359-1368.

JSEG Based Color Separation of Tongue Image in Traditional Chinese Medicine

Yonggang Wang[1], Yue Zhou[1], Jie Yang[1], and Yiqin Wang[2]

[1] Institute of Image Processing & Pattern Recognition,
Shanghai Jiaotong University, Shanghai, China, 200030
{yonggangwang,zhouyue,jieyang}@sjtu.edu.cn
[2] School of Basic Medicine, Shanghai University of TCM, Shanghai, China, 200032
wangyq@stcm.edu.cn

Abstract. The process of color separation of tongue image in traditional Chinese medicine (TCM) is decomposed into two steps: region partition and color classification. In the first step, a partition method based on JSEG is proposed to obtain homogenous regions in the tongue. In the second step, a priori template and some standard color patches are designed to assist the classification according to a priori knowledge from the TCM experts, where the nearest neighbour classifier is applied for color classification. The experimental results show that the proposed approach is greatly promising to computerized tongue diagnosis.

1 Introduction

Traditional Chinese medicine (TCM) consists of a systematized methodology of medical treatment, where much special physiological information could be obtained through analyzing the patient's tongue. The experienced TCM doctors usually incline to use the information of the patient's tongue to determine his disease and health conditions. Unfortunately, the traditional tongue diagnosis has been impeded because this diagnostic process involves a great deal of subjective information and experiential knowledge. Recently, more and more attention has been focused on building objective standards for tongue diagnosis and as a result, several tongue diagnosis systems based on image analysis theory [1–4] have been developed for the purpose of the diagnosis and treatment of patients. These systems include a series of algorithms for tongue image processing, e.g. color calibration, tongue extraction, color separation of tongue image, etc. The purpose of color calibration is to keep the consistency and repeatability of colors transmitted from image acquiring device (e.g. digital camera) to monitor so as to facilitate doctor's diagnosis and further image processing. Some standard color patches are usually used to build the calibration model. Before analyzing the tongue features, tongue extraction process is needed to cut out the tongue body from its surroundings. Here we mainly discuss the color separation algorithm of substance and coat which cover on the surface of tongue. It is very important to carry out the quantitative analysis of the tongue image.

A. Sanfeliu et al. (Eds.): CIARP 2004, LNCS 3287, pp. 503–508, 2004.

However, some drawbacks exist in these algorithms as follows. First, these algorithms carry out pixel-wise color recognition in the tongue image, which abandons the spatial correlations between pixels and neglects the local properties in the tongue image. Second, they are not fully associated with a priori knowledge of TCM. Third, such supervised classifiers as SVM and supervised FCM [3, 4] are adopted to classify the colors of substance and coat, and thereby much tedious work like sample collecting and learning need be implemented.

The impetus of this research is to suggest a new algorithm to overcome the problems mentioned above. We decompose the process of color separation of the tongue image into two steps, i.e. region partition and color classification. In the first step, JSEG, a newly proposed method for unsupervised segmentation, is used to partition the tongue into several homogenous regions. Next in the second step, a priori template induced by the TCM experts' experience, is designed and applied to detect tongue substance and coat. A nearest neighbour classifier is used to color classification. Note that the color patches which have been used in color calibration and designed according to a priori knowledge, are used as the reference samples in the nearest neighbour classifier. Fig. 1 show a part of these color patches.

Fig. 1. Some color patches

This paper is organized as follows. Section 2 depicts the JSEG based region partition method. Section 3 discusses the color classification using a priori template and much expert's knowledge. Section 4 tests the proposed algorithm and section 5 concludes the paper.

2   JSEG Based Region Partition

2.1   Local Properties of Tongue Image

In the tongue image, the colors of the tongue substance are classified as light pink, rose pink, red and purple. And the coat colors are classified as white, yellow, brown and black. In general, the light pink substance and flimsily white coat are considered to be healthy. It can be observed that the tongue image is a typical kind of color-texture image and has locally different color distribution. Moreover, according to TCM principles, the conclusions drawn by doctors are a kind of region-based description of color distribution of tongue substance and coat. Following this logic, we firstly divide the tongue image into various homogenous regions with similar colors and textures. On the basis of this partition, we represent the colors in every region quantitatively so that some important features, e.g. substance colors, coat colors as well as their distribution, could be obtained.

2.2   JSEG Algorithm

JSEG is a new method for unsupervised segmentation of color-texture regions in images which is presented in [5]. The basic idea of the JSEG method is to separate the segmentation process into two stages: color quantization and spatial segmentation. In the first stage, colors in the image are quantized to several representative classes that can be used to differentiate regions in the image. This quantization is performed in the color space without considering the spatial distributions of the colors. Then, the image pixel values are replaced by their corresponding color class labels, thus forming as a special kind of texture composition. In the second stage, a criterion for "good" segmentation is applied to local windows in the class-map. This results in the "J-image", in which high and low values correspond to possible boundaries and interiors of color-texture regions. A region growing method is then used to segment the image based on the multiscale J-images. The decoupling of color similarity from spatial distribution in the JSEG allows for the development of more tractable algorithms for each of the two processing stages. In fact, one of the good color quantization algorithms, called PGF [6], has been used in the original JSEG method. The JSEG algorithm is tested to show very robust to a variety of images.

In our research, the JSEG algorithm is used to partition different regions on the surface of the tongue image. Fig. 2 shows a partition example. Obviously in the result image, the tongue body is segmented into four regions, where region C corresponds to its substance while regions A, B and D correspond to its coat.

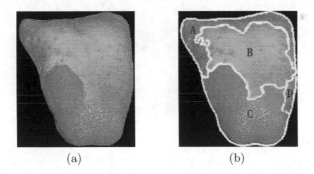

(a)   (b)

Fig. 2. An example of JSEG based region partition: (a) a tongue image and (b) its partition result

3   Color Classification

The distribution of substance and coat on the surface of tongue has properties of complexness and diversity, although, some principles could be derived. Most of the previous work didn't consider these principles. Hence, their classification accuracy was not too high. In our research, we have applied a priori knowledge as much as possible to improve the accuracy.

3.1   Priori Template

Under the guide of the TCM experts, together with a great deal of observation, we summarize several principles about the distribution of substance and coat in tongue as follows. i) There usually exists much coat at the root of tongue. ii) There usually exists much substance at the tip of tongue. iii) As regard to the two sides of tongue, the probability of substance is larger than that of coat. iv) There is a transition of dark to light, i.e. thick to thin coat from the root to the tip of tongue. v) In a tongue body, generally, the amount of coat is more than substance.

According to these principles, we design a template to assist the following color separation. This template, shown in Fig. 3, divides a tongue into six parts whose sizes are labeled in detail. Part I is tongue root region, part II is middle-

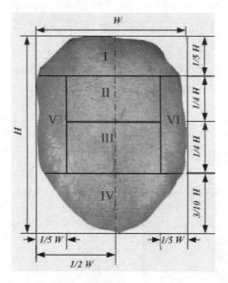

Fig. 3. Priori template

root region, part III is middle-tip region, part IV is tip region and parts V and VI are tongue side regions respectively. Besides, we plan out the following priority strategies for each sub-region R_i obtained from the JSEG based partition.

– If R_i falls into part I, it will be classified into the coat class as long as 10% of its pixels have coat colors.
– If R_i falls into part II, it will be classified into the coat class as long as 40% of its pixels have coat colors.
– If R_i falls into part III, it will be classified into the substance class as long as 40% of its pixels have substance colors.
– If R_i falls into part IV, it will be classified into the substance class as long as 20% of its pixels have substance colors.
– If R_i falls into part V or VI, it will be classified into the substance class as long as 30% of its pixels have substance colors.

Note that R_i will be considered to fall into a certain part only if more than 75% of its pixels fall into this part.

3.2 Substance and Coat Color Classification

To determine the color label of a pixel in the tongue image, a nearest neighbour classifier is used. The classifier is widely used in pattern recognition tasks (see Chapter 4 in [7]). As mentioned in the beginning, we use the color patches in Fig. 1 as the reference samples. These color patches are designed in the color calibration stage by the experienced TCM experts and contain the usual colors of substance and coat in TCM tongue diagnosis. Since in the JSEG method the CIE LUV color space is adopted, here we evaluate the distances of pixels' features in this space. The color space has a perceptually uniform property where the image components are reasonably uncorrelated with each other. Euclidean distance in this space is used to classify any pixel in each homogeneous sub-region into its nearest neighbour color class corresponding to the least distance. Then the priority strategies above are applied and the class of the sub-region belonging to substance or coat is determined.

4 Experimental Results

The proposed algorithm is tested in our computerized tongue diagnosis system. This system provides a stable and consistent sampling environment which includes several main components as follows: standard light source with 5000K color temperature, Canon-G5 CCD digital camera with a resolution of 1024×768 pixels, Dell Dimension8200 workstation, dark chest with face supporting structure as well as tongue image analysis software. Using this system, we have collected thousands of tongue images from clinical patients. The colors occurring in different zones of each tongue image are judged simultaneity by more than three experienced TCM doctors. To avoid a large variation among different doctors for the same tongue image, we pick out over 600 samples with consistent evaluation on colors by those doctors and test the proposed algorithm on them. Over 90% of the color separation results are coincident with the doctors' conclusions.

Fig. 4 gives two examples by our method. We adopt pseudocolors to represent the different color classes of substance and coat after color separation, e.g. light pink corresponding to light pink substance, grey corresponding to white coat, yellow corresponding to yellow coat and black corresponding to black coat.

5 Conclusions

Tongue color separation is an important stage in tongue diagnosis systems based on image analysis. In this paper, a new method is proposed, which fully considers the local property of the tongue image as well as a priori knowledge. The basic idea of this method is to decompose the color separation problem into two steps,

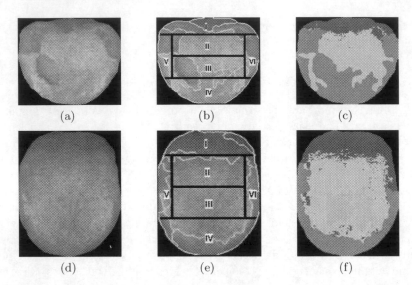

Fig. 4. Examples of color separation. (a) and (d) are the original tongue images; (b) and (e) are JSEG based partition results superimposed with the priori template; (c) and (f) are color separation results in a pseudocolors representation

region partition and color classification. In the first step, the tongue image is divided into various homogenous sub-regions by the aid of the JSEG algorithm. In the second step, a nearest neighbour classifier is used to further determine these sub-regions to belong to the substance or coat class. Finally, the approach proposed here is tested to show much potential to computerized tongue diagnosis.

References

1. Jang, J.H., Kim, J.E., Park, K.M., et al: Development of the digital tongue inspection system with image analysis. In: IEEE Proc. of the 2nd Joint EMBS/BMES Conf. Volume I., Houston, TX, USA (2002) 1033–1034
2. Chiu, C.C.: A novel approach based on computerized image analysis for traditional chinese medical diagnosis of the tongue. Computer Methods and Programs in Biomedicine **61** (2000) 77–89
3. Zhao, Z.X., Wang, A.M., Shen, L.S.: An automatic tongue analyzer of chinese medicine based on color image processing. In: The 4th Int. Conf. on Electronic Measurement and Instruments Conf. Proc., Harbin, China (1999) 830–834
4. Wang, Y.G.: Research on pragmatizing the tongue image analysis instrument of traditional chinese medicine. Master's thesis, Beijing Polytechnic University (2001)
5. Deng, Y.N., Manjunath, B.S.: Unsupervised segmentation of color-texture regions in images and video. IEEE Trans. on PAMI **23** (2001) 800–810
6. Deng, Y.N., Kenney, C., Moore, M.S., et al: Peer group filtering and perceptral color image quantization. In: Proc. IEEE Int. Symp. Circuits and Systems. Volume 4., Orlando, FL (1999) 21–24
7. Duda, R.O., Hart, P.E., Stork, D.G.: Pattern classification. Second edn. John Wiley & Sons, New York (2001)

Estimation of High Resolution Images
and Registration Parameters
from Low Resolution Observations*

Salvador Villena[1], Javier Abad[2], Rafael Molina[2], and Aggelos K. Katsaggelos[3]

[1] Dpto. de Lenguajes y Sistemas Informáticos, Universidad de Granada,
18071 Granada, Spain
svillena@ugr.es
[2] Dpto. de Ciencias de la Computación e I.A., Universidad de Granada,
18071 Granada, Spain
{abad,rms}@decsai.ugr.es
[3] Dept. of Electrical and Computer Engineering, Northwestern University,
Evanston, IL 60208-3118
aggk@ece.nwu.edu

Abstract. In this paper we consider the problem of reconstructing a high resolution image from a set of undersampled and degraded frames, all of them obtained from high resolution images with *unknown* shifting displacements between them. We derive an iterative method to estimate the unknown shifts and the high resolution image given the low resolution observations. Finally, the proposed method is tested on real images.

1 Introduction

High resolution images can, in some cases, be obtained directly from high precision optics and charge coupled devices (CCDs). However, due to hardware and cost limitations, imaging systems often provide us with only multiple low resolution images. In addition, there is a lower limit as to how small each CCD can be, due to the presence of shot noise [1] and the fact that the associated signal to noise ratio (SNR) is proportional to the size of the detector [8].

Over the last two decades research has been devoted to the problem of reconstructing a high resolution image from multiple shifted undersampled, and degraded frames (see [4] for a recent review). A key part of the high resolution reconstruction problem is the estimation of the shifts between the images.

Most of the reported approaches on shift estimation for super-resolution, first estimate the displacement vectors either by interpolating the low resolution observations and then finding the registration parameters or by finding the low resolution registration parameters in the low resolution domain and then interpolating them (consider [4] again), where the high resolution image and the registration parameters are estimated simultaneously, can be found in [10, 9, 12, 2].

---

* This work has been partially supported by the "Comisión Nacional de Ciencia y Tecnología" under contract TIC2003-00880.

A. Sanfeliu et al. (Eds.): CIARP 2004, LNCS 3287, pp. 509–516, 2004.

In this paper, starting from the low to high resolution method described in [6, 11], we propose a new iterative method to alternatively estimate the registration parameters and to obtain a high resolution image from a set of low resolution observations.

The paper is organized as follows. The problem formulation is described in section 2. The process to estimate the displacements between the images is described in section 3. Once the registration parameters have been obtained the application of the Bayesian paradigm to calculate the MAP high resolution image and estimate the regularization hyperparameters is described in section 4. The iterative estimation of the registration parameters and the high resolution image is discussed in section 5. Experimental results are described in section 6. Finally, section 7 concludes the paper.

2   Problem Formulation

Consider a set $\mathbf{g} = \{\mathbf{g}_1, \ldots, \mathbf{g}_Q\}$ of $Q \geq 1$ low resolution images with $N_1 \times N_2$ pixels. The low resolution sensors obtaining the low resolution images are shifted with *unknown* horizontal and vertical displacements with respect to each other by values proportional to $(T_1/L) \times (T_2/L)$, where $T_1 \times T_2$ is the size of each low resolution sensing element and L denotes the high resolution magnification factor. Our aim is to reconstruct an $M_1 \times M_2$ high resolution image, $\mathbf{f}$, with $M_1 = L \times N_1$ and $M_2 = L \times N_2$, from the set of low resolution observations.

We now relate the low resolution observed images in $\mathbf{g}$ to the unknown high resolution image $\mathbf{f}$ we want to estimate. Since the low resolution sensors obtaining the low resolution images are shifted with *unknown* horizontal and vertical displacements with respect to each other by values proportional to $T_1/L \times T_2/L$ we have that each $\mathbf{g}_i$, $i = 1, \ldots, Q$ results from $\mathbf{f}$ through motion compensation, filtering, and subsampling:

$$\mathbf{g_q} = \mathbf{AHC}(\mathbf{d_q})\mathbf{f} + \epsilon_\mathbf{q} \qquad q = 1, \ldots, Q, \tag{1}$$

where $\mathbf{C}(\mathbf{d_q})$ is the $(M_1 \times M_2) \times (M_1 \times M_2)$ matrix defined by $\mathbf{C}(\mathbf{d_q})\mathbf{f}(a, b) = \mathbf{f}(a + \mathbf{d}_\mathbf{q}^x, b + \mathbf{d}_\mathbf{q}^y))$, where $\mathbf{d_q} = (\mathbf{d}_\mathbf{q}^x, \mathbf{d}_\mathbf{q}^y)$ denotes horizontal and vertical displacements, matrix $\mathbf{H}$ of size $(N_1 \times N_2) \times (LN_1 \times LN_2)$ describes a high resolution filtering operation, $\mathbf{A}$ is the downsampling matrix with size $N_1 N_2 \times (M_1 M_2)$ and $\epsilon_\mathbf{q}$ a random independent noise with variance $\beta_\mathbf{q}^{-1}$.

Matrices $\mathbf{A}$ and $\mathbf{H}$ are assumed to be known. $\mathbf{AH}$ models optical distortion together with CCD pixel resolution [11]. The matrix $\mathbf{H}$ is assumed to be block-circulant and $\mathbf{C}(\mathbf{d_q})$ will be approximated by a block-circulant matrix as well.

Our problem can now be formulated as the estimation of the set of displacements, $\mathbf{d} = \{\mathbf{d}_1, \ldots, \mathbf{d_q}\}$, and the high resolution image $\mathbf{f}$. In order to perform this task we will proceed in two steps; first we will estimate the displacements $\mathbf{d}$ and then the high resolution image $\mathbf{f}$.

3   Estimation of the Displacement Vectors

To obtain the high resolution image $\mathbf{f}$, we need to accurate estimate the pixel displacement $\mathbf{d_q}$ in (1). In this paper we estimate the registration parameters as follows. From (1), we first consider for each $\mathbf{q} \in \{1, \ldots, Q\}$, the following low to high resolution observation model with just one observation,

$$\mathbf{g_q} = \mathbf{AHu_q} + \psi_\mathbf{q} \qquad q = 1, \ldots, Q \,, \tag{2}$$

where $\mathbf{u_q}$ is an $M_1 \times M_2$ high resolution image, $\mathbf{H}$ and $\mathbf{A}$ have been defined in (1) and $\psi_\mathbf{q}$ is random independent noise with variance $\mu_\mathbf{q}^{-1}$.

We then use as prior model for $\mathbf{u_q}$ a simultaneous autoregression (SAR) [7], that is,

$$p(\mathbf{u_q}|\alpha_\mathbf{q}) = \frac{1}{Z_{prior}(\alpha_\mathbf{q})} \exp\left\{ -\frac{1}{2}\alpha_\mathbf{q} \parallel \mathbf{C\,u_q} \parallel^2 \right\}, \tag{3}$$

where the parameter $\alpha_\mathbf{q}$ measures the smoothness of the 'true' image, $Z_{prior}(\alpha_\mathbf{q})$ $= (\prod_{i,j} \lambda_{ij}^2)^{-1/2}(2\pi/\alpha_\mathbf{q})^{(M_1 \times M_2)/2}$ and $\lambda_{ij} = 1 - 2\phi(\cos(2\pi i/M_1) + \cos(2\pi j/M_2))$, $i = 1, 2, \ldots, M_1$, $j = 1, 2, \ldots, M_2$ and $\mathbf{C}$ is the Laplacian.

Then we select as estimate of $\mathbf{u_q}$,

$$\hat{\mathbf{u}}_\mathbf{q} = \arg\min_{\mathbf{u_q}} \left\{ \alpha_\mathbf{q} \parallel \mathbf{C\,u_q} \parallel^2 + \mu_\mathbf{q} \parallel \mathbf{g_q} - \mathbf{AHu_q} \parallel^2 \right\} \tag{4}$$

The high resolution estimate $\hat{\mathbf{u}}_\mathbf{q}$ is found together with estimates of $\alpha_\mathbf{q}$ and $\mu_\mathbf{q}$ using the method described in [6, 11, 5].

One of the $\hat{\mathbf{u}}_\mathbf{q}$'s (call it $\hat{\mathbf{u}}$) is an initial estimate of $\mathbf{f}$, and we proceed with the estimation of the registration parameters $\mathbf{d} = \{\mathbf{d_1}, \ldots, \mathbf{d_q}\}$. In this paper we have used the following two approaches.

3.1   Method I: Global Correlation

Given $\hat{\mathbf{u}}_\mathbf{q}$ and the initial estimate, $\hat{\mathbf{u}}$, of the high resolution image $\mathbf{f}$ we calculate the registration parameters between $\hat{\mathbf{u}}_\mathbf{q}$ and $\hat{\mathbf{u}}$ by finding

$$(\hat{\mathbf{d}}_\mathbf{q}^x, \hat{\mathbf{d}}_\mathbf{q}^y) = \arg\max_{\mathbf{d}_\mathbf{q}^x, \mathbf{d}_\mathbf{q}^y} C_{\hat{\mathbf{u}}_\mathbf{q}, \hat{\mathbf{u}}}(\mathbf{d}_\mathbf{q}^x, \mathbf{d}_\mathbf{q}^y), \tag{5}$$

where

$$C_{\hat{\mathbf{u}}_\mathbf{q}, \hat{\mathbf{u}}}(\mathbf{d}_\mathbf{q}^x, \mathbf{d}_\mathbf{q}^y) = \sum_{n_1} \sum_{n_2} \hat{\mathbf{u}}_\mathbf{q}(n_1, n_2)\hat{\mathbf{u}}(n_1 + \mathbf{d}_\mathbf{q}^x, n_2 + \mathbf{d}_\mathbf{q}^y) \tag{6}$$

3.2   Method II: Local Correlation

Given $\hat{\mathbf{u}}_\mathbf{q}$ and $\hat{\mathbf{u}}$ we compute a set of points of interest in image $\hat{\mathbf{u}}_\mathbf{q}$ (see for instance [3]). Then, for each pixel location (n_x, n_y), corresponding to a point of interest, consider a block of small size centered around it and search for the location of the best-matching block of the same size in a limited area around pixel (n_x, n_y) in image $\hat{\mathbf{u}}$.

Let $\mathbf{d_q}(i)$ for $i = 1, \ldots,$ points of interest be the set of obtained registration parameters; we then create the list $L = \{\mathbf{d_q^n}, n = 1, \ldots, N\}$, of the N most frequently appearing values of the registration parameters (N should cover a high percentage of the points of interest). For each $\mathbf{d_q^n}$ find the correlation between the central part of $\hat{\mathbf{u}}_{\mathbf{q}}$ of size $M_1/2 \times M_2/2$ and the same area in image $\hat{\mathbf{u}}$ displaced by $\mathbf{d_q^n}$. Select the registration parameter maximizing this correlation.

4   Bayesian Analysis

Once we know the registration vector $\mathbf{d}$, from (1), the probability density function of $\mathbf{g_q}$, with $\mathbf{f}$ the 'true' high resolution image, is given by

$$p(\mathbf{g_q}|\mathbf{f}, \beta_{\mathbf{q}}) = \frac{1}{Z(\beta_{\mathbf{q}})} \exp\left[-\frac{\beta_{\mathbf{q}}}{2} \parallel \mathbf{g_q} - \mathbf{W_q}\mathbf{f} \parallel^2\right], \tag{7}$$

where $Z(\beta_{\mathbf{q}}) = (2\pi/\beta_{\mathbf{q}})^{(N_1 \times N_2)/2}$, $\beta_{\mathbf{q}}$ is the inverse of the noise variance and $\mathbf{W_q} = \mathbf{AHC}(\mathbf{d_q})$.

Since we have multiple low resolution images, the probability density function of $\mathbf{g}$ given $\mathbf{f}$ is

$$p(\mathbf{g}|\mathbf{f}, \underline{\beta}) = \prod_{\mathbf{q}} p(\mathbf{g_q}|\mathbf{f}, \beta_{\mathbf{q}})$$

$$= \frac{1}{Z_{noise}(\underline{\beta})} \exp\left[-\frac{1}{2} \sum_{\mathbf{q}} \beta_{\mathbf{q}} \parallel \mathbf{g_q} - \mathbf{W_q}\mathbf{f} \parallel^2\right] \tag{8}$$

where $\underline{\beta} = (\beta_1, \ldots, \beta_Q)$ and $Z_{noise}(\underline{\beta}) = \prod_{\mathbf{q}} Z(\beta_{\mathbf{q}})$.

As prior model for $\mathbf{f}$ we use the simultaneous autoregression (SAR) defined in (3), that is

$$p(\mathbf{f}|\alpha) = \frac{1}{Z_{prior}(\alpha)} \exp\left\{-\frac{1}{2}\alpha \parallel \mathbf{C}\mathbf{f} \parallel^2\right\}, \tag{9}$$

Note that this SAR model is equivalent to the use of the Laplacian operator to regularize the high resolution image estimate.

The Bayesian analysis is performed to estimate the hyperparameters, α and $\underline{\beta}$, and the high resolution image. In this paper we use the following two steps:

Step I: Estimation of the Hyperparameters

$\hat{\alpha}$ and $\hat{\underline{\beta}}$ are first selected as

$$\hat{\alpha}, \hat{\underline{\beta}} = \arg\max_{\alpha, \underline{\beta}} \mathcal{L}_{\mathbf{g}}(\alpha, \underline{\beta}) = \arg\max_{\alpha, \underline{\beta}} \log p(\mathbf{g}|\alpha, \underline{\beta}), \tag{10}$$

where $p(\mathbf{g}|\alpha, \underline{\beta}) = \int_{\mathbf{f}} p(\mathbf{f}|\alpha)p(\mathbf{g}|\mathbf{f}, \underline{\beta})d\mathbf{f}$.

The solution to this equation is obtained with the EM-algorithm with $\mathcal{X}^t = (\mathbf{f}^t, \mathbf{g}^t)$ and $\mathcal{Y} = \mathbf{g} = [\mathbf{0} \ \mathbf{I}]^t \mathcal{X}$.

Step II: Estimation of the High Resolution Image

Once the hyperparameters have been estimated, the estimation of the high resolution image, $\mathbf{f}_{(\hat{\alpha},\hat{\beta})}$, is selected to minimize

$$\hat{\alpha} \parallel \mathbf{Cf} \parallel^2 + \sum_{\mathbf{q}} \hat{\beta}_{\mathbf{q}} \parallel \mathbf{g}_{\mathbf{q}} - \mathbf{W}_{\mathbf{q}}\mathbf{f} \parallel^2, \tag{11}$$

which results in

$$\mathbf{f}_{(\hat{\alpha},\hat{\beta})} = \mathbf{Q}\left(\hat{\alpha},\hat{\beta}\right)^{-1} \sum_{\mathbf{q}} \hat{\beta}_{\mathbf{q}} \mathbf{W}_{\mathbf{q}}^{t} \mathbf{g}_{\mathbf{q}}, \tag{12}$$

where $\mathbf{Q}(\hat{\alpha},\hat{\beta}) = \hat{\alpha}\mathbf{C}^t\mathbf{C} + \sum_{\mathbf{q}} \hat{\beta}_{\mathbf{q}}\mathbf{W}_{\mathbf{q}}^{t}\mathbf{W}_{\mathbf{q}}$.

The estimation process we are using could be performed within the so called hierarchical Bayesian approach (see [6]) by including priors on the unknown parameters α and β. Note that the prior model in (9) plays an important role in the estimation of the high resolution image and the hyperparameters when an incomplete set ($\sum_{\mathbf{q}} \beta_{\mathbf{q}}\mathbf{W}_{\mathbf{q}}^{t}\mathbf{W}_{\mathbf{q}}$ singular) of low resolution images is used [5]. Note also that equation (12) can be solved using the method proposed in [6].

5   Iterative Registration and Image Estimation

Combining the methods proposed in section 3 to estimate the registration parameters, $\mathbf{d}$, and the algorithm to estimate the high resolution image, $\mathbf{f}$, described in section 4, we can obtain an iterative procedure to estimate both of them.

Let $\mathbf{d}^0$ be the displacement vector obtained by applying the methods described in section 3 and $\mathbf{f}^0$ the image estimate obtained by the method described in section 4 when $\mathbf{d} = \mathbf{d}^0$. Then re-estimate the displacement vector $\mathbf{d}^k$ by using $\hat{\mathbf{u}}_{\mathbf{q}}$ obtained in section 3 and replacing $\hat{\mathbf{u}}$ (the initial estimate of the high resolution image obtained in section 3), by $\mathbf{f}^{k-1}$. Recalculate $\mathbf{f}^k$ for this new displacement vector $\mathbf{d}^k$ using the method described in section 4. The iterative procedure ends when $\parallel \mathbf{f}^k - \mathbf{f}^{k-1} \parallel^2 / \parallel \mathbf{f}^{k-1} \parallel^2$ is less than a prescribed bound.

6   Experimental Results

A number of experiments were performed with the proposed algorithms over a set of images to evaluate their performance to estimate the high resolution image and registration parameters.

According to (1) the high resolution image in Fig. 1a, $\mathbf{f}$, was first shifted to obtain a set of 16 high resolution images, $\mathbf{f}_{l1,l2}(x,y) = \mathbf{f}(x + l1, y + l2)$, $(x,y) \in \{0,\ldots,M_1\} \times \{0,\ldots,M_2\}$, $l1, l2 = 0,\ldots,3$. Then each $\mathbf{f}_{l1,l2}$ was blurred using a motion blur of length 10 and downsampled by a factor of four. Gaussian noise was added to each low resolution image to obtain three sets of sixteen low resolution images, $\mathbf{g}_{l1,l2}$, with signal to noise ratio (SNR) equal to 20, 30 and 40dB.

Table 1. Estimated registration parameters for the low resolution image set with SNR of 20dB, by global correlation (first table) and local correlation (second table)

Table 2. Estimated registration parameters for the low resolution image set with SNR of 30dB, by global correlation (first table) and local correlation (second table)

GLOBAL CORRELATION. ESTIMATED SHIFTS IN TABLE			
Real shifts	0	1	2	3
0	(0,0)	(0,0)	(0,0)	(0,0)
1	(0,0)	(0,0)	(0,0)	(0,0)
2	(0,0)	(0,0)	(0,0)	(0,0)
3	(2,0)	(1,0)	(1,0)	(1,0)

GLOBAL CORRELATION. ESTIMATED SHIFTS IN TABLE			
Real shifts	0	1	2	3
0	(0,0)	(0,0)	(0,0)	(0,0)
1	(0,0)	(0,0)	(0,0)	(0,0)
2	(0,0)	(0,0)	(0,0)	(0,0)
3	(1,0)	(1,0)	(1,0)	(1,0)

LOCAL CORRELATION. ESTIMATED SHIFTS IN TABLE			
Real shifts	0	1	2	3
0	(0,0)	(0,1)	(0,2)	(0,3)
1	(1,0)	(1,1)	(1,2)	(1,3)
2	(2,0)	(2,1)	(2,2)	(2,3)
3	(3,0)	(3,1)	(3,2)	(3,3)

LOCAL CORRELATION. ESTIMATED SHIFTS IN TABLE			
Real shifts	0	1	2	3
0	(0,0)	(0,1)	(0,2)	(0,3)
1	(1,0)	(1,1)	(1,2)	(1,3)
2	(2,0)	(2,1)	(2,2)	(2,3)
3	(3,0)	(3,1)	(3,2)	(3,3)

In order to test the performance of the proposed algorithms we ran the registration algorithms in section 3 and the reconstruction method described in section 4 on different sets of q randomly chosen low resolution images with $1 \leq q \leq 16$. For comparison purposes, Fig. 1b depicts the zero-order hold upsampled image of $g_{0,0}$ for 30dB SNR (PSNR=13.68dB) while the bilinear interpolation of $g_{0,0}$ is shown Fig. 1c (PSNR=14.22dB).

Tables 1 and 2 show, at convergence of the method described in section 5, the estimated displacement vectors obtained using the methods described in sections 3.1 and 3.2 for the 20dB and 30dB cases, respectively. The estimated registration parameters did not change between the first and second iteration of the method.

The estimated high resolution image for the 30dB case using local correlation and 6 low resolution images is depicted in Fig. 1d (PSNR = 21.03dB).

7   Conclusions

In this paper we have presented an iterative method to estimate the registration parameters and reconstruct a high resolution image from a set of shifted low resolution observation. The method has been tested on synthetic images and has provided good estimates of both the high resolution image and displacement vectors.

The proposed method works for the case of shift displacements between the high resolution images. Extension to homographies, of particular interest for plane surfaces like registration plates or text, is under study.

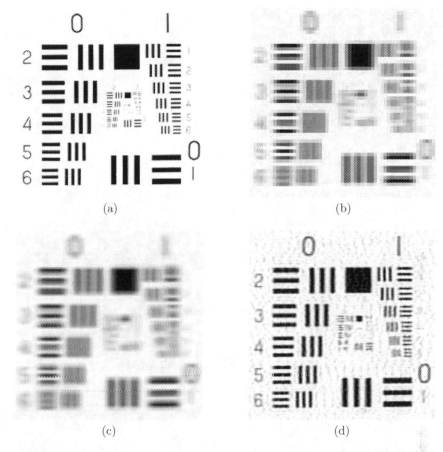

Fig. 1. (a) original image (b) zero order hold, (c) bilinear interpolation, (d) image obtained with the proposed method using 6 low resolution images

References

1. K. Aizawa, T. Komatsu, and T. Saito. A scheme for acquiring very high resolution images using multiple cameras. In *IEEE Conference on Audio, Speech and Signal Processing*, volume 3, pages 289–292, 1992.
2. C. M. Bishop, A. Blake, and B. Marthi. Super-resolution enhancement of video. In *C. M. Bishop and B. Frey (Eds.), Proceedings Artificial Intelligence and Statistics*, 2003.
3. C.J. Harris and M. Stephens. A combined corner and edge detector. In *Proceedings 4th Alvey Vision Conference*, pages 147–151, 1988.
4. M. G. Kang and S. Chaudhuri, editors. *Super-resolution image reconstruction*. IEEE Signal Processing Magazine, vol. 20, no. 3, 2003.
5. J. Mateos, M. Vega, R. Molina, and A.K. Katsaggelos. Bayesian image estimation from an incomplete set of blurred, undersampled low resolution images. In *1st Iberian Conference on Pattern Recognition and Image Analysis (IbPRIA2003), LNCS 2652*, pages 445–452, 2003.

6. R. Molina, M. Vega, J. Abad, and A.K. Katsaggelos. Parameter estimation in bayesian high-resolution image reconstruction with multisensors. *IEEE Trans. on Image Processing*, 12:1655–1667, 2003.

7. B.D. Ripley. *Spatial Statistics*. John Wiley, New York, 1981.

8. H. Stark and P. Oskoui. High-resolution image recovery from image-plane arrays, using convex projections. *Journal of the Optical Society A*, 6(11):1715–1726, 1989.

9. B. C. Tom, N. P. Galatsanos, and A. K. Katsaggelos. Reconstruction of a high resolution image from multiple low resolution images. In S. Chaudhuri, editor, *Super-Resolution Imaging*, chapter 4, pages 73–105. Kluwer Academic Publishers, 2001.

10. B. C. Tom and A. K. Katsaggelos. Reconstruction of a high-resolution image by simultaneous registration, restoration, and interpolation of low-resolution images". In *Proceedings of the IEEE International Conference on Image Processing*, volume 2, pages 539–542, 1995.

11. M. Vega, J. Mateos, R. Molina, and A.K. Katsaggelos. Bayesian parameter estimation in image reconstruction from subsampled blurred observations. In *IEEE International Conference on Image Processing (ICIP-2003)*, volume II, pages 969–973, 2003.

12. N.A. Woods, N.P. Galatsanos, and A.K. Katsaggelos. Em-based simultaneous registration, restoration, and interpolation of super resolved images. In *Proceedings of the IEEE International Conference on Image Processing*, volume II, pages 303–306, 2003.

Automatic Lung Surface Registration
Using Selective Distance Measure in Temporal CT Scans

Helen Hong[1], Jeongjin Lee[2], Kyung Won Lee[3], and Yeong Gil Shin[2]

[1] School of Electrical Engineering and Computer Science BK21: Information Technology,
Seoul National University, San 56-1 Shinlim 9-dong Kwanak-gu, Seoul 151-742, Korea
hlhong@cse.snu.ac.kr
[2] School of Electrical Engineering and Computer Science, Seoul National University
{jjlee,yshin}@cglab.snu.ac.kr
[3] Dept. of Radiology, Seoul National University Bundang Hospital, 300, Gumi-dong,
Sungnam-si, Kyunggi-do, Korea
lkwrad@radiol.snu.ac.kr

Abstract. In this paper, we propose a novel technique of lung surface registration for investigating temporal changes such as growth rates of pulmonary nodules. For the registration of a pair of CT scans, a proper geometrical transformation is found through the following steps: First, optimal cube registration is performed for the initial gross registration. Second, for allowing fast and robust convergence on the optimal value, a 3D distance map is generated by the local distance propagation. Third, the distance measure between surface boundary points is repeatedly evaluated by the selective distance measure. Experimental results show that the performance of our registration method is very promising compared with conventional methods in the aspects of its computation time and robustness.

1 Introduction

Chest computed tomography (CT) is a sensitive method for detecting pulmonary nodules [1]. In clinical practice, radiologists often compare current chest CT with previous one of the same patient to investigate temporal changes such as growth rates of pulmonary nodules. However, it is often very difficult even for radiologists to identify subtle changes, particularly in lesions that involve overlap with anatomic structures such as ribs, vessels, heart, and diaphragm. The automatic detection of corresponding regions in temporal CT scans would be very useful for detecting and tracing pulmonary nodules

Several methods have been suggested for the automated matching of temporal lung CT images. In Betke et al. [2-4], anatomical landmarks such as the sternum, vertebrae, and tracheal centroids are used for initial global registration. Then the initial surface alignment is refined step by step by an iterative closest point (ICP) process. However most part of the computation time for the ICP process is to find the point correspondences of lung surfaces obtained from two time interval CT scans. Hong et al. [5] proposed an efficient multilevel method for surface registration to cope with the problem of Betke [2]. The multilevel method first reduces the original number of points and aligned them using an ICP algorithm. In addition, they proposed a midpoint approach to define point correspondences instead of using the point with the smallest Euclidean distance as in the original ICP algorithm. However the midpoint

A. Sanfeliu et al. (Eds.): CIARP 2004, LNCS 3287, pp. 517–524, 2004.

approach has a tradeoff between accuracy and efficiency, because additional processing time is needed to find the second closest point and compute the midpoint. Mullaly et al. [6] developed a multi-criterion nodule segmentation and registration methods that facilitate the identification of corresponding nodules in temporal chest CT scans. The method requires additional nodule segmentation and measures for multi-criterion. Gurcan et al. [7] developed an automated global matching of temporal thoracic helical CT scans. The method uses three-dimensional anatomical information such as the ribs but did not require anatomical landmark identification or organ segmentation. However it is difficult to align correctly since the method uses only the reduced information obtained by Maximum Intensity Projection (MIP) images of two time-interval CT scans.

Current approach still needs some progress in computational efficiency and accuracy for investigating changes of lung nodules in temporal chest CT scans. In this paper, we propose a novel technique of lung surface registration to speed-up the computation time and increase robustness. Our proposed registration method for aligning a pair of CT images is composed of three procedures. First, optimal cube registration is performed to correct gross translational mismatch. This initial registration does not require any anatomical landmarks. Second, a 3D distance map is generated by local distance propagation, which derives fast and robust convergence on the optimum value. Third, the distance measure between surface boundary points is evaluated repeatedly by the selective distance measure. Then the final geometrical transformations are applied to align lung surfaces in the current CT scans with lung surfaces in the previous CT scans. Experimental results show that our method is dramatically faster than the chamfer matching-based registration and more robust in the sense that the algorithm always converges to an optimum value.

The organization of the paper is as follows. In Section 2, we discuss how to correct gross translational mismatch. Then we propose a local distance propagation and selective distance measure to find exact geometrical relationship in the two time interval images. In Section 3, experimental results show how the method rapidly and robustly aligns lung surfaces of current and previous CT scans. This paper is concluded with a brief discussion of the results in Section 4.

2   Lung Surface Registration

For the registration of the current CT study, called target volume, with the previous study, called template volume, we apply the pipeline shown in Fig. 1 to the temporal CT scans. At first, lung surfaces are automatically segmented from each volume and saved as binary volumes. In the second step, initial alignment is performed using the optimal cube registration for correcting the gross translational mismatch. In the third step, initial alignment is repeatedly refined by the selective distance measure and optimization. In order to find exact geometrical relationship between two time interval volumes, the target volume is moved during the iterative alignment procedure. Interpolating the target volume at grid positions of the template volume is required for the each iteration depending on the transformation. After registration, lung surfaces of template and target volume are displayed by data mixing and volume rendering.

In our method, we have two assumptions as follows: 1) Each CT scan is acquired at the maximal respiration. 2) The entire lung regions are included in each CT scan. Based on this assumption, in general, rigid transformation is sufficient for the registration of temporal chest CT scans. We use rigid transformation – three translations and three rotations about the x-, y-, z-axis.

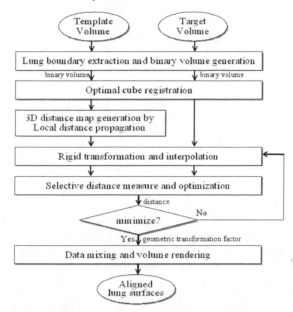

Fig. 1. The pipeline of automatic lung surface registration

2.1 Optimal Cube Registration

According to the imaging protocol and the patient's respiration and posture, the position of lung surfaces between template and target volume can be quite different. For the efficient registration of such volumes, an initial gross correction method is usually applied. Several landmark-based registrations have been used for the initial gross correction. To achieve the initial alignment of the lung surfaces, these landmark-based registrations require landmark detection and point-to-point registration of corresponding landmarks. These additional processes much degrade the performance of the whole system.

To minimize the time and maximize the effectiveness for initial registration, we propose a simple method of global alignment using the circumscribed boundary of lung surfaces. An optimal cube of bounding volume which includes left and right lung surfaces is generated as shown in Fig. 2. For initial registration of two volumes, we align centers of optimal cubes.

Our optimal cube registration dramatically reduces the processing time since initial alignment is performed without any anatomical landmark detection. In addition, our method leads to robust convergence to the optimal value since the search space is limited near optimal value.

2.2 Local Distance Propagation

In a surface registration algorithm, the calculation of distance from a surface boundary to a certain point can be done using a preprocessed distance map based on the

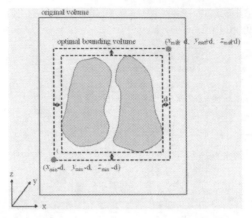

Fig. 2. The generation of an optimal cube

chamfer matching. The method reduces the generation time of a distance map by an approximate distance transformation instead of a Euclidean distance transformation. However the computation time of distance is still expensive by two-step distance transformation using forward and backward mask. In particular, the generation of a 3D distance map of whole volume dataset is unnecessary when the initial alignment almost corrects the gross translational mismatch. From this observation, we propose a local distance propagation for the efficient generation of a distance map.

For generating a 3D distance map, we approximate the global distance computation with repeated propagation of local distances within a small neighborhood. To approximate Euclidean distances, we consider 26-neighbor relations for a 1-distance propagation as seen in Eq.(1). The positive distance value of the 3D distance map tells how far it is apart from the surface boundary points. The local distance propagation shown in Fig. 3 is applied to the surface boundary points only in the template volume.

$$DP(i) = \min\{DP(i-1)+1, DP(i-1)\} \tag{1}$$

Fig. 4 shows the result of a 3D distance map using local distance propagation. The generation time is considerably reduced since pixels only need to be propagated in the direction of increasing distances to the maximum neighborhood. In addition, we do not need the backward propagation which reduces the size of neighborhoods used.

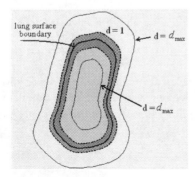

Fig. 3. Local distance propagation

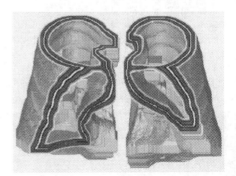

Fig. 4. The result of 3D distance map

2.3 Selective Distance Measure and Optimization

The distance measure is used to determine the degree of resemblance of surface boundaries of template and target volume. To get the distance measure, the current approach needs to calculate the root mean square of distance differences of whole values in a distance map. Whereas, our selective distance measure(SDM) only uses distance values near to the surface boundary that can be found in the already generated a 3D distance map. Since distance values in the selected regions are used, we can reduce the computation time for the distance measure and optimization.

As can be seen in Eq. (2), the distance value $D_{target}(i)$ of target volume is subtracted from the distance value $D_{template}(i)$ of the 3D distance map of template volume. We assume that $D_{target}(i)$ are all set to 0. N_C is the total number of surface boundary points in target volume. Then SDM reaches minimum when surface boundary points of template and target volume are aligned correctly.

$$SDM = \frac{1}{N_C} \sum_{i=0}^{N_C-1} \left| D_{template}(i) - D_{target}(i) \right| \qquad (2)$$

We use the Powell's method for evaluating SDM. Since the search space of our distance measure is limited to the surrounding lung surface boundaries, we do not need to use a more powerful optimization algorithm such as simulated annealing.

3 Experimental Results

All our implementation and test were performed on an Intel Pentium IV PC containing 2.4 GHz CPU and 1.0 GBytes of main memory. Our registration method has been applied to three pairs of successive CT scans whose properties are described in Table 1. The performance of our method is evaluated with the aspects of visual inspection, accuracy and robustness.

Table 1. Experimental datasets

Patient		Image size	Slice number	Pixel size (mm)	Slice thickness
Patient 1	Previous chest CT	512 x 512	358	0.64 x 0.64	2.0
	Current chest CT	512 x 512	316	0.66 x 0.66	2.0
Patient 2	Previous chest CT	512 x 512	300	0.57 x 0.57	2.0
	Current chest CT	512 x 512	330	0.55 x 0.55	2.0
Patient 3	Previous chest CT	512 x 512	101	0.62 x 0.62	2.0
	Current chest CT	512 x 512	113	0.64 x 0.64	2.0

Fig. 5 shows the effectiveness of the optimal cube for initial registration. The positional difference between lung surfaces of template and target volume shown in Fig. 5 (a) are much reduced as shown in Fig. 5 (b) by the optimal cube registration. This initial registration is further refined until lung surfaces of template and target volume are aligned exactly like a Fig. 6 (c) and (d).

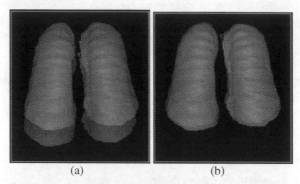

(a)   (b)

Fig. 5. The results of optimal cube registration (a) initial position (b) after initial registration

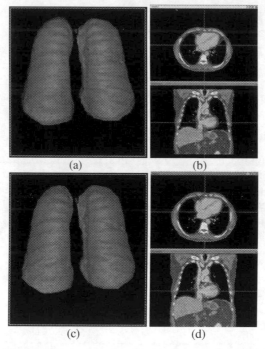

(a)   (b)

(c)   (d)

Fig. 6. The results of lung surface registration (a) after initial registration in 3D view (b) after initial registration in axial and coronal view (c) after surface registration in 3D view (d) after surface registration in axial and coronal view

Fig. 7 shows how we can reduce the registration time and the error measure, the sum of squared distance difference (SSD), using the optimal cube registration. After the first iteration, the SSD of our method is significantly reduced by optimal cube registration compared to chamfer matching-based surface registration. Moreover in the early iterations the SSD of our method (Method 2) is much smaller than that of chamfer matching-based surface registration (Method 1), as shown in Fig. 8.

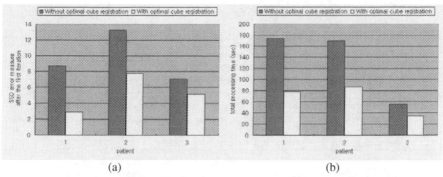

(a)   (b)

Fig. 7. The effectiveness of the optimal cube registration (a) SSD error measure (b) total processing time

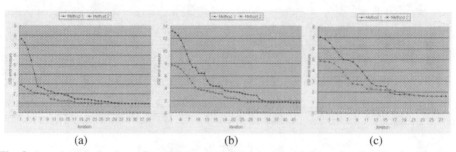

(a)   (b)   (c)

Fig. 8. Accuracy evaluation using SSD per iteration (a) patient 1 (b) patient 2 (c) patient 3

The total processing time is summarized in Table 2 where execution time is measured for the generation of a distance map, the distance measure and optimization.

The robustness of the selective distance measure (SDM) criterion has been evaluated by comparing SDM measure traces (represented by square dot line) with chamfer distance measure (CDM) traces (represented by diamond dot line). As shown in Fig. 9, the changes of SDM measure are smooth near to the minimal position, but CDM measure is changed rapidly. This means that SDM measure is more likely to converge to an optimum value.

4 Conclusion

We presented a novel technique of lung surface registration of a pair of chest CT scans. Using the optimal cube registration, the initial gross registration can be done much fast and effectively without any detection of anatomical landmarks. Selective distance measure using a 3D distance map generated by the local distance propagation allows rapid and robust convergence on the optimal value. Three pairs of temporal chest CT scans have been used for the performance evaluation with the aspects of visual inspection, accuracy and robustness. In the early iterations, the SSD of our method is much smaller than that of chamfer matching-based registration by using optimal cube registration and selective distance measure. Experimental results also show that SDM measure has more chance of converging to an optimum value than CDM measure. Our method can be successfully used for investigating temporal changes such as growth rates of pulmonary nodules.

Table 2. Total processing time

Patient		3D distance map generation	Distance measure and optimization	Total processing time
Patient 1	Method 1	46	120	166
	Method 2	5	72	77
Patient 2	Method 1	41	122	163
	Method 2	7	78	85
Patient 3	Method 1	11	43	54
	Method 2	4	34	38

(sec)

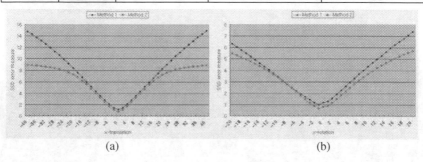

(a)   (b)

Fig. 9. Comparison of our proposed method and chamfer distance-based surface registration (a) the error in x-translation (b) the error in x-rotation

Acknowledgements

This work was supported in part by the Korea Research Foundation under the Brain Korea 21 Project. The ICT at Seoul National University provides research facilities for this study.

References

1. Yankelevitz, D.F., Reeves, A.P., Kostis, W.J., Binsheng, Z., henschke, C.I., Small Pulmonary Nodules: Volumetrically Determined Growth Rates Based on CT Evaluation, Radiology, Vol. 217 (2000) 251-256.
2. Betke, M., Hong, H., Ko, J.P., Automatic 3D Registration of Lung Surfaces in Computed Tomography Scans, Proc. Of Medical Image Computing and Computer-Assisted Intervention (MICCAI) (2001) 725-733.
3. Betke, M., Hong, H., Ko, J.P., Automatic 3D Registration of Lung Surfaces in Computed Tomography Scans, CS Technical Report 2001-004, Boston University.
4. Betke, M., Hong, H., Thomas, D., Prince, C., Ko, J.P., Landmark Detection in the Chest and Registration of Lung Surfaces with an Application to Nodule Registration, Medical Image Analysis, Vol. 7 (2004) 265-281.
5. Hong, H., Betke, M., Teng, S., Multilevel 3D Registration of Lung Surfaces in Computed Tomography Scans – Preliminary Experience, Proc. Of International Conference on Diagnostic Imaging and Analysis (ICDIA) (2002) 90-95.
6. Mullaly, W., Betke, M., Hong, H., Wang, J., Mann, K., Ko, J.P., Multi-criterion 3D Segmentation and Registration of Pulmonary Nodules on CT: a Preliminary Investigation.
7. Gurcan, M.N., Hardie, R.C., Rogers, S.K., Dozer, D.E., Allen, B.H., Hoffmeister, J.W., Automated Global Matching of Temporal Thoracic Helical CT Studies: Feasibility Study, Proc. of International Congress Series, Vol. 1256 (2003) 1031-1036.

An Enhancement to the Constant Range Method for Nonuniformity Correction of Infrared Image Sequences*

Jorge E. Pezoa, Sergio N. Torres, Juan P. Córdova, and Rodrigo A. Reeves

Department of Electrical Engineering, University of Concepción
Casilla 160-C, Concepción, Chile
{jpezoa,storres}@die.udec.cl
jcordova@udec.cl
rreeves@die.udec.cl
http://nuc.die.udec.cl/

Abstract. A statistical technique for adaptive nonuniformity correction of infrared image sequences has been developed. The method, which relies on our previously developed constant range nonuniformity correction method, estimates the nonuniformity parameters using two recursive estimation techniques. The method selects an estimation algorithm using a decision rule based on a threshold value computed from the collected infrared images. The strength of the method lies in its simplicity, low computational complexity, and its good trade-off between nonuniformity correction and ghosting artifacts reduction. The ability of the enhanced constant range technique to compensate for nonuniformity noise is demonstrated by using video sequences of infrared imagery with both real and synthetic nonuniformity.

1 Introduction

Since the 1970's, infrared (IR) imaging technology has proven to be an invaluable tool in a wide range of industry, medical, and military applications. IR cameras have been used for temperature measurements, IR signature analysis, tracking applications, medical and military usage, stress measurements, detection and prediction of failures modes within machinery, etc. For several technical and economical reasons, the focal plane array (FPA), an integrated circuit containing an array of IR photodetectors, is the most commonly used sensor technology employed in IR cameras [1].

However, the performance of the whole imaging system is strongly affected by the main disadvantage of the FPA: the random spatial response of each

* This work was partially supported by the 'Fondo Nacional de Ciencia y Tecnología' FONDECYT of the Chilean government, project number 1020433 and by Grant Milenio ICM P02-049. The authors wish to thank Ernest E. Armstrong (OptiMetrics Inc., USA) for collecting the data, and the United States Air Force Research Laboratory, Ohio, USA.

A. Sanfeliu et al. (Eds.): CIARP 2004, LNCS 3287, pp. 525–532, 2004.

individual photodetector in the array under the same uniform input [1, 2]. This nonuniformity (NU), produced by mismatches during the fabrication process of the IR sensor, can considerably degrade the quality of IR images, since it results in a fixed-pattern-noise (FPN) that is superimposed on the true image. Furthermore, the problem is made worse because the NU is not totally stationary, but instead it drifts slowly and randomly over time. This temporal drift can take, from minutes to hours, depending on the technology used.

It is well known that the NU correction (NUC) of IR images is a great advantage for any kind of post processing analysis such as pattern recognition, image restoration, image registration, etc. [3]. To compensate for the NU, two categories of NUC methods have been developed: calibration-based and scene-based NUC methods. Calibration-based methods need to steer the FPA away from the target to an uniform black-body radiation source used as a reference. This is very unlikely in real time applications; it forces the interruption of the normal imaging operation. On the other hand, scene-based techniques require image sequences with motion or changes in the actual scene to be able to perform the NUC. If the motion requirement is not fully satisfied, these approaches produce a lower quality NUC than calibration-based techniques. In addition, when an object does not move enough, a ghost image of itself, also called a ghosting artifact, can be observed over the corrected IR images even when the object has left the field of view [1, 2].

In this paper, an extension of our previously developed constant range (CR) scene-based NUC method is presented [4]. The enhanced CR (ECR) improves the CR method by adding two extra features: an exponential windowing (EW) estimation algorithm, and a decision criteria to adaptively change the estimation algorithm. Read-out mean and variance are recursively estimated with an EW algorithm, which converges faster than the one used in the CR method. The EW algorithm produces a faster update for the estimation because it weights the recent data most heavily; however, it also produces an oscillating effect over the estimation. Changing between the traditional CR's estimation method and the EW algorithm is decided by thresholding the incoming read-out frames. Thus, the ECR NUC method obtains a good trade-off between the speed and the quality of the estimation. As a result, these features naturally can help reduce the ghosting artifacts produced by the scene-based NUC. To test the scheme, the ECR technique is applied to sequences of IR images with both simulated and real NU and the performance of the scheme is tested using the root mean square error (RMSE) between the corrected and the uncorrected frames and the image quality parameter Q-factor [5].

This paper is organized as follows. Section 2 presents the linear model for an FPA and the CR NUC method. Also, the ECR NUC method is introduced. In Section 3 the ECR algorithm is tested with sequences of IR data with both, simulated and real NU, and the performance parameters are computed. The conclusions of the paper are summarized in Section 4.

2   The Enhanced Constant Range Nonuniformity Correction Method

In this section the mathematical models of an IR-FPA and the CR NUC method are presented. Using this background, the ECR algorithm is developed and theoretical calculations about its performance are derived.

2.1   The Mathematical Model of an Infrared Focal Plane Array

Most NUC methods consider, for a single operating point, the linear model given in [1]. In this model, the mathematical relationship between the read-out IR data Y_k^{ij} in the $ij - th$ detector of the FPA, and at time k, with the input irradiance T_k^{ij} can be written as:

$$Y_k^{ij} = A^{ij} T_k^{ij} + B^{ij} \tag{1}$$

where A^{ij} and B^{ij} are the gain and bias for ij-th detector in the array, respectively. A^{ij} and B^{ij} can be modelled as constants when no significant drift on the NU is considered and this condition is satisfied capturing a couple of minutes of data. Finally, the input T_k^{ij} represents the irradiance collected at the k-th frame time by the ij-th IR detector of the FPA. For simplicity of notation, the pixel superscripts ij will be omitted with the understanding that all operations are performed on a pixel-by-pixel basis.

2.2   The Constant Range Algorithm

The task of any NUC method is to estimate A and B using the information obtained from Y_k. To achieve this estimation, additional information is required, therefore, assumptions about T are necessary. The key assumption in the CR method is that the input irradiance is an uniformly distributed random variable within each sequence of frames and all detectors are exposed to, approximately, the same range of input irradiance. Assuming a common range $[T_{min}, T_{max}]$, it allows us to estimate the gain and the bias for each pixel to within unknown but global scale and offset factors. So, T_{min} and T_{max} can be considered known parameters, and they depend only on the camera used to collect the IR information [4]. Finally, this condition can be easily met, for example, in the presence of motion.

Using the CR assumption, the method estimates the gain and the bias based on the following equations [4]:

$$\hat{A} = \frac{\hat{\sigma}_Y}{\hat{\sigma}_T} \tag{2}$$

$$\hat{B} = \hat{m}_Y - \frac{\hat{\sigma}_Y}{\hat{\sigma}_T} \hat{m}_T \tag{3}$$

where $\hat{m}_T$ ($\hat{\sigma}_T$) and $\hat{m}_Y$ ($\hat{\sigma}_Y$) are the estimated expected values (the standard deviation) of T and Y, respectively. In [4], $\hat{m}_T$ and $\hat{\sigma}_T$ are estimated a priori with the CR assumption, and $\hat{m}_Y$ and $\hat{\sigma}_Y$ are recursively estimated using:

$$\hat{m}_{Y,k} = \frac{Y_k + (k-1)\ \hat{m}_{Y,k-1}}{k} \tag{4}$$

$$\hat{\sigma}_{Y,k} = \frac{|Y_k - \hat{m}_{Y,k}| + (k-1)\ \hat{\sigma}_{Y,k-1}}{k} \tag{5}$$

2.3   The Proposed Enhancement on the Constant Range Method

The system model (1) considers the gain and the bias as stationary-unknown parameters. But, it was stated that the NU changes slowly and randomly over time. Therefore, the estimation provided by any NUC method must follow this drift. In [2], the following EW recursive estimation algorithm for $\hat{m}_Y$ and $\hat{\sigma}_Y$ is presented:

$$\hat{m}_{Y,k} = (1-\alpha)\ Y_k + \alpha\ \hat{m}_{Y,k-1} \tag{6}$$

$$\hat{\sigma}_{Y,k} = (1-\alpha)\ |Y_k - \hat{m}_{Y,k}| + \alpha\ \hat{\sigma}_{Y,k-1} \tag{7}$$

where α, $0 < \alpha < 1$, is the time constant of the filter that controls the exponential window of the read-out data. Because an EW algorithm emphasizes recent data, it provides the NUC method with the ability to follow changes in the operating point and, besides, it helps the algorithm to reduce ghosting artifacts [2]. However, a faster convergence of the estimator may reduce the quality of the NUC.

The ECR NUC method computes $\hat{m}_Y$ and $\hat{\sigma}_Y$ using either (4,5) or (6,7) equations. It selects which estimation algorithm to use based on a threshold value. The algorithm detects the changes, per pixel, between the current and the previous read-out data, and it compares the difference with the threshold. If the change is greater than the threshold, then the ECR employs the EW estimation algorithm to accelerate the convergence of the estimation. On the other hand, if no significative change in Y_k is observed, the algorithm (4,5) has been shown to yield a good estimation [4]. Furthermore, in real situations, the difference between consecutive frames is very low due to the sample rate of the camera; then, the threshold comparison is performed between the k-th and the $k + \Delta k$-th frames. It can be seen from the foregoing analysis that only two parameters of the algorithm need to be tuned: the threshold value and the stride value Δk.

Finally, the ECR algorithm does not require a great computing time effort; it only needs fourteen additions, fourteen multiplications and five logical instructions, for each pixel at each frame.

3   Performance Analysis

In this section the ECR NUC method is tested using sequences of IR images corrupted with simulated and real NU. The NUC performance is evaluated using the performance indexes RMSE and Q-factor [5] computed between the reference (an IR sequence calibrated with black bodies) and the corrected IR video sequence. For the Q-factor, the dynamical range is $[-1, 1]$, where $+1$ represents the best performance [5]. The sequence used during the tests is a video of terrestrial mid-wave IR imagery ($3 \sim 5 \ \mu$m) collected with a 128×128 InSb FPA cooled camera (Amber Model AE-4128). The video contains 4000 frames captured at a rate of 30 fps, and each pixel is quantized in 16-bit integers: $[Y_{min}, Y_{max}] = [0, 65535]$. In addition, the sequence was corrected using calibration-based techniques and will be used as reference when needed.

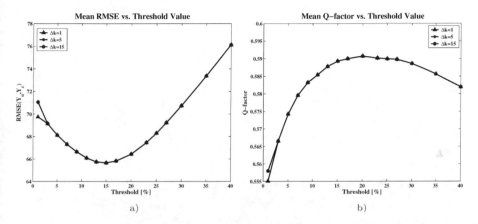

Fig. 1. Performance of the NUC methods under simulations. a) The mean RMSE for the sequence of IR data vs. the threshold value. b) The mean Q-factor for the sequence of IR data vs. the threshold value. (The $\triangle$ sign means a stride value $\Delta k = 1$. The $\bullet$ sign means a stride value $\Delta k = 5$. The $\circ$ sign means a stride value $\Delta k = 15$.)

In all simulations, the gain and the bias are considered as spatially and mutually uncorrelated Gaussian random variables with mean values of one and zero, respectively. Different levels of nonuniformity are introduced by varying the standard deviation of the gain and the bias. Finally, all our simulations were made following the standard procedures given in [2, 4].

The ECR algorithm depends on the following quantities: the threshold value and the stride parameter Δk. To tune these values, the ECR method was applied to a video of frames with simulated NU. Threshold values between 1 and 40% of Y_{max} were tested for the following strides: $\Delta k = \{1, 2, 3, 4, 5, 8, 10, 12, 15\}$. For the EW estimation algorithm used in the ECR method, the α time constant of the filter was established to be 0.99, in accord to the results obtained in [2]. Figs. 1a) and b) plot the results for the mean RMSE and the mean Q-factor of the video of frames vs. the threshold values considered, for the stride values of 1, 5, and 15 frames. The results show that a good choice for the threshold is between 15 and 20% of the maximum quantization value used by the IR camera. Further, our computations demonstrate that no significant enhancement in the RMSE and the Q-factor is obtained for the stride values evaluated.

Using the previous results, the ECR NUC method was tested with a new sequence of IR data also corrupted with synthetic NU. The threshold value and the stride value of the ECR were chosen as 15% of Y_{max} and 1 frame, respectively. In Figs. 2b), c), d) and e) an example of the real, the corrupted and the corrected IR images obtained with simulations can be observed. It can be noted that, to the naked eye, the ECR produces a better NUC than the CR method. Again, a visual inspection shows that the image corrected with the ECR algorithm is less affected by the ghosting than the one corrected with the CR method. A subjective evaluation, computed with the performance parameters RMSE and Q-factor, agrees also with the objective evaluation. Fig. 3a) and b) illustrate the time evolution of these parameters. The ECR method produces a lower RMSE than the CR method. Furthermore, the ECR's RMSE is lower than the one obtained with a CR method that utilizes an EW estimation algorithm instead of the traditional algorithm (4,5). The same behavior is seen when the Q-factor is computed: the ECR NUC method achieves the best values. In addition, a closer look at Figs. 2d) and e) shows a ghost image of the Fig. 2a) imposed over the corrected images. However, it can also be noted that the proposed algorithm produces less ghosting artifacts than the CR method.

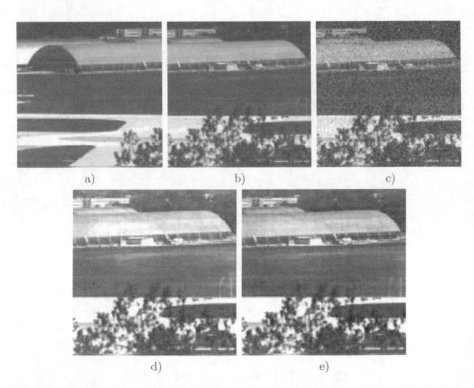

Fig. 2. Performance of the ECR NUC method under simulations. a) The 1560-th frame of the reference IR image sequence b) The 1680-th frame of the reference c) The 1680-th frame corrupted with synthetic NU d) The 1680-th frame corrected using the CR method e) The 1680-th frame corrected using the ECR method. Note in images d) and e) the effect of the ghosting artifact introduced by the 1560-th frame.

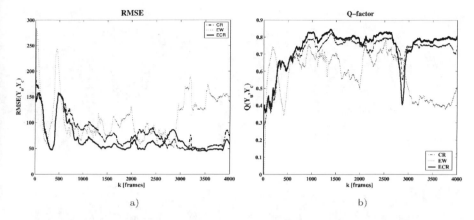

Fig. 3. Performance of the NUC methods under simulations. a) The evolution of the RMSE between the reference and the corrected frames of IR data. b) The evolution of the Q-factor between the reference and the corrected frames of IR data (CR means constant range NUC method. EW means CR with exponential windowing. ECR means enhanced constant range).

A block of frames with real NU was also used to test the performance of the ECR NUC method. According to the previous simulations and after several tests, we obtain the best results for the following parameters: $\alpha = 0.99$, a threshold value of 17% of Y_{max}, and $\Delta k = 3$. Figs. 4a) and d) show examples of the raw frame captured by the camera. Figs. 4b) and e) are their corresponding frames corrected using the CR method, and Figs. 4c) and f) are corrections made with the ECR algorithm. The results show that the ECR method effectively compensates the NU and produces, to the naked eye, a better NUC than the CR algorithm. Similar results are obtained for the performance parameters. As an example, the computed RMSE of the 2280-th frame for the CR method is 0.123% of Y_{max}, whereas the ECR algorithm obtains a 0.064%. The computed Q-factor for this frame are 0.607 and 0.668 for the CR and the ECR method, respectively. Besides, the images in Fig. 4b) and c) show that the ECR method produces less ghosting artifacts than the CR method. Finally, it can be seen from Fig. 4 that the proposed method inherits the valuable CR ability of compensating for malfunctioning pixels.

4   Conclusions

In this paper an enhanced version of our previously developed constant range nonuniformity correction method is proposed. The algorithm estimates the gain and the bias of the infrared sensors with two estimation techniques and, using the read-out data, adaptively selects which one to employ. The method is quite simple, utilizes low computational resources and needs to tune only two parameters. Our evaluations, using infrared video sequences corrupted with both real

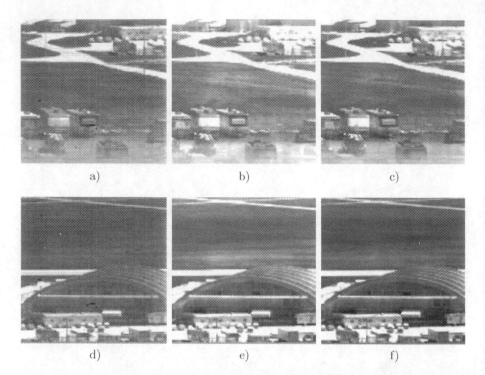

Fig. 4. Performance of the ECR NUC method under real NU. a) The 2280-th frame with real NU b) The 2280-th frame corrected with the CR method c) The 2280-th frame corrected with the ECR method d) The 2680-th real frame e) The 2680-th frame corrected using the CR method f) The 2680-th frame corrected using the ECR method.

and simulated nonuniformity, have shown that the approach not only performs an efficient nonuniformity correction of the sequences, but also it produces compensated images with better quality than the original constant range method.

References

1. Holst, G.: CCD arrays, cameras and displays. SPIE Optical Engineering Press. Bellingham. (1996).
2. Harris, J., Chiang, Y-M.: Nonuniformity Correction of Infrared Image Sequences Using the Constant-Statistics Constraint. IEEE Transactions on Image Processing. **8**. (1999) 1148–1151.
3. Armstrong, E., Hayat, M., Hardie, R., Torres, S., Yasuda, B.: The Advantage of Non-Uniformity Correction Pre-Processing on Infrared Image Registration. Application of Digital Image Processing. **XXII**. (1999).
4. Torres, S., Reeves, R.: Scene-Based Nonuniformity Correction Method Using Constant-Range. Performance and Analysis. Proc. SCI 2002/ISAS 2002. **IX**. (2002).
5. Wang, Z., Bovik, A.: A Universal Image Quality Index. IEEE Signal Processing Letters. **20**. (2002) 1–4.

Color Cartographic Pattern Recognition Using the Coarse to Fine Scale Method

Efrén González-Gómez and Serguei Levachkine

Centre for Computing Research (CIC) - National Polytechnic Institute (IPN)
UPALMZ, CIC Building, 07738, Mexico City, Mexico
efren@esfm.ipn.mx, sergei@cic.ipn.mx

Abstract. Hard problem of cartographic pattern recognition in fine scale[1] maps, using information that comes from coarse scale[2] maps, is considered. The maps are raster-scanned color maps of different thematic, representing the same territory in coarse and fine scale respectively. A solution called *Coarse-to-Fine Scale Method* is proposed. This method is defined in terms of *means*: coarse scale maps and their *information*; *concepts*: image associated function, cartographic knowledge domain and cartographic pattern; and *tools*: a set of clustering criteria of the *Logical Combinatorial Pattern Recognition*.

1 Introduction. Formal Statement of the Problem

In this paper we present the main ideas of the C2FS (*Coarse-to-Fine Scale*) method of color cartographic pattern recognition. This method has been originated from unsolved problem of the vector description of raster objects. To date, it is hard to see the ways to obtain even a partial, but general, i.e. applied to any type of raster objects, solution of the problem; see survey papers [2][4][7] for detail discussion. In certain sense, the C2FS method represents a promising alternative.

Let us suppose that we have a vector image I_1 (or already recognized raster image) in scale $1:s_1$ of a given territory $\mathbf{T}$ and a raster image I_2 of $\mathbf{T}$ to be vectored (recognized) in scale $1:s_2$, and $s_1 > s_2$ (e.g. $s_1 = 100,000$ and $s_2 = 50,000$). Our goal is to use the information from I_1 in vectorization of I_2. Note that I_1 can be considered as a "generalization"[3] of I_2: $I_1 = G(I_2)$, i.e. if an object $O_2 \in I_2$, then there can exist $O_1 \in I_1$, such that $O_1 = G(O_2)$. We denote Ω - the set of all such objects O_2 from I_2 and Θ - the compliment of Ω in I_2: $I_2 = \Omega \cup \Theta$. We also put $\omega = G(\Omega)$ and note that $\omega \subseteq I_1$. Obviously, to vector objects from Ω and Θ we need two different strategies. The objects from Ω can be vectored, using the features (position, color or colors, shape, etc.) of the vector objects from ω. After, the objects of Ω have being vectored we can vector the objects from Θ by one of the recognition modules [2][7] as a "new" cartographic material.

---

[1] Inferior to 1:200,000.

[2] Superior to 1:200,000.

[3] We do not discuss here what this generalization is.

A. Sanfeliu et al. (Eds.): CIARP 2004, LNCS 3287, pp. 533–540, 2004.
© Springer-Verlag Berlin Heidelberg 2004

2 Theoretical Background

The theoretical background of the C2FS method is based on the following definitions:

Definition 1. A digital image is a matrix $\|M(i,j)\|_{n \times m}$ such that $0 \le i \le n$, $0 \le j \le m$; and $M(i,j) = (r, g, b)$, where r, g, b are elements of the set $\{0,1,..., 255\}$.

Definition 2. Let **I** be a digital image according to the definition 1, then *Image Associated Function* (IAF) f_1: $Z \times Z' \to M$ to **I** is defined as follows:

a) IAF domain is $Z \times Z'$ where $Z=\{0,1,..., n\}$ and $Z'=\{0,1,..., m\}$.
b) IAF co-domain is a set M *without repeated elements*, which is composed of the elements of $M(i,j) \in$ **I**.
c) IAF is assigned to each pair (i, j) in $Z \times Z'$ the corresponding value given by the matrix $\|M(i,j)\|$. In other words, $f_I(i,j) = M(i,j)$, $\forall (i,j) \in Z \times Z'$.

Definition 3. *Cartographic Knowledge Domain* (CKD) is a finite space of attributive, topologic, logical and spatial data, which are associated with raster cartographic objects presented in maps [9][4].

Definition 4. Let **I** be a digital image according to definition 1 and let f_1: $Z \times Z' \to M$ be IAF. *Cartographic Pattern* (CP) **P** in **I** is a function such that

1) $\mathbf{P} = f_1|_{Z_p}$: $Z_p \to M_p$, where $Z_p \subseteq Z \times Z'$ and $M_p \subseteq M$. In other words, **P** is the restriction of IAF f_I to some set Z_p.
2) A concept from CKD can be assigned to the set Z_p or M_p.

Whereas **P** only fulfills condition 1, it is a candidate to be a CP.

These definitions are served as a compliment to clustering criteria coming from *Logical Combinatorial Pattern Recognition*: β_0**-Connected**, β_0**-Compacted**, β_0**-Complete Maximal [1][3]** to segment and recognize the image. We apply the clustering criteria only to IAF *co-domain* because this contains much less elements than the total number of pixels presented in the digital image (raster map).

Clustering criteria. Next, we analyze mentioned above clustering criteria and the similarity measures in application to color cartographic image processing. To our knowledge, this is one of the first works in this direction; see **[2][3][8]** for belief.

We use the following notations. Let **I** be a digital cartographic image; f_I be an Image Associated Function, f_i: $Z \times Z' \to M$; Γ: $U \times U \to [0,1]$ be a *Similarity Function*, where U is a finite space of objects to classify; β_0 be nonnegative real number.

A subset G_i in U is called β_0**-Connected**, if $\forall O_r$, $O_s \in G_i$, then there exist $O_{i_1},..., O_{i_q} \in G_i$ such that $O_r = O_{i_1}$, $O_s = O_{i_q}$ and $\forall p \in \{1,..., q-1\}$ $\Gamma(O_{i_p}, O_{i_{p+1}}) \ge \beta_0$. Moreover, if $O_k \in U$ and $\exists O_j \in G_i$ such that $\Gamma(O_k, O_j) \ge \beta_0$ then $O_k \in G_i$.

In cartographic digital images, this criterion can be used to find groups in co-domain M, defined by the elements that allow a gradual transition in terms of the

---

[4] For example, attributive data like type of border, name of state, surface, population, administrative unit, among others; geometric data like contours, coordinates, etc. [2].

similarity function. While for cartographic patterns, this can be used when the patterns are defined by colors that go from "clear" blue to "dark" blue, for instance. A problem comes when there are gradual transitions between colors in the image and each color of that transition is used to represent a different cartographic pattern. Notice that this problem depends on the image context and can be solved by using other two criteria that are defined in the following.

A subset G_i in U is called β_0-**Compacted**, if $\forall\ O_j \in G_i\ \exists\ O_i \in G_i$ such that $O_i \neq O_j$ and $\Gamma(O_i, O_j)$ takes the maximum value.

In other words, the objects in a β_0-Compacted set are most similar objects with respect to the similarity function. As we have already mentioned, the applications of β_0-Connected criterion depend on the image context. To make it context–independent, we can successively apply the β_0-Compacted criterion and/or the following criterion.

A subset G_i in U is called β_0-**Complete Maximal** iff $\forall O_i$, $O_j \in G_i$, the similarity function Γ computed for both elements is greater or equal than β_0, and if $\Gamma(O_k, O_p) \geq \beta_0$, where $O_k \in G_i$, then $O_p \in G_i$.

According to our experiments, this criterion has a disadvantage that if it is applied to the digital image before other two criteria it can generate more than necessary groups in the co-domain. On the other hand, it can be applied to β_0-Connected groups iteratively extracting more precisely the groups of interest (finer clustering); that is its advantage. Once again, the use of each single criterion depends on the image context, while their combination may not.

Summing-up the clustering criteria analysis, we note the following:

- Elements of the IAF co-domain can be grouped/structured in different groups depending on the clustering criteria.
- Groups/structures obtained by the application of a criterion Π[5] can result in the union of groups/structures formed by another criterion Π'. In other words, successive application of clustering criteria leads to gradually finer structuring of the IAF co-domain. Thus, a hierarchy under *inclusion* relation between the groups is settled down, in which "general" ("coarse") groups are at superior level (β_0-Connected criterion) and "specific" ("fine") groups are at inferior level (β_0- Compacted and/or β_0- Complete Maximal criteria) [1].

On the other hand, these criteria are general and abstract. To apply them in image processing, we should make them specific and concrete for the pixel clustering. Thus, we use a criterion of similarity and *modified* HSI color space. Indeed, in normal HSI space, if the intensity is equal to zero then the saturation is indeterminate, and if the saturation is zero then hue is indeterminate. In the modified HSI space, we remove the singularities, i.e. intervals where the saturation and hue are indeterminate[6].

---

[5] Π, Π' is one of the three criteria: β_0-Connected, β_0-Compacted or β_0-Complete Maximal.
[6] More general approach to modified non-linear color spaces see in [6].

Similarity criterion and similarity function. Let I be a cartographic digital image. Let $f_I \colon Z{\times}Z' {\to} M$ be IAF. The *Similarity Criterion* C: $M{\times}M{\to}[0,1]$ is defined as follows: let p, q $\in$ M; we denote by I(k), S(k) and H(k) the intensity, saturation and hue respectively of some point k $\in$ M, then C(p, q):

$$C(p,q) = \begin{cases} C_1(p,q) = \begin{cases} C_3(q)\, if\ I(p) \le N \\ C_4(p,q)\, otherwise \end{cases} & if\ \ |I(p)-I(q)| \le C \\ \qquad 0 & otherwise \end{cases}$$

where :

$$C_3(q) = \begin{cases} 1\ if\ I(q) \le N \\ 0\ otherwise \end{cases}$$

$$C_4(p,q) = \begin{cases} C_5(q)\ if\ I(p) \ge B \\ C_6(p,q)\ otherwise \end{cases}$$

$$C_5(q) = \begin{cases} 1\ if\ I(q) \ge B \\ 0\ otherwise \end{cases}$$

$$C_6(p,q) = \begin{cases} C_7(q)\, if\ S(p) \le R\ y\ I(q) \ne 0 \\ 1 - |I(p)-I(q)|\ \ If\ S(p) \le 0.03\ and\ I(q) = 0\ \ \ or\ \ \ S(q) \le 0.03 \\ 1 - \sqrt{(S(p)\cos(H(p)) - S(q)\cos(H(q)))^2 + (S(p)\sin(H(p)) - S(q)\sin(H(q)))^2}\ \ otherwise \end{cases}$$

$$C_7(q) = \begin{cases} 1\ if\ S(q) \le R \\ 0\ otherwise \end{cases}$$

Using this similarity criterion, it is possible to define the *Similarity Function* only in terms of this criterion. Unique feature used in definition of *C* is color. However, we can define another criterion C_a and consider other features besides of color, constructing C_a and corresponding similarity function.

According to the similarity criterion above, the similarity function coincides with the criterion C(p, q). C(p, q) for elements p, q from the IAF co-domain are computed as follows; refer formulas above.

a) If the absolute value of difference between their intensities is more than some threshold C the value of similarity function is equal to zero.
b) Otherwise, if this value is less than C, then if both intensities are less or equal than some another threshold N (average of all colors close to "black") or the difference is more or equal than yet another threshold B (average of all colors close to "white"), then the value of similarity function is equal to one[7].
c) If ¬a ∧¬b, then the saturation of p and q are considered as follows.

---

[7] This can be interpreted as averaging of clear and dark tonalities.

c1) If both saturation are less or equal than some threshold R, then the value of similarity function is equal to one.

c2) If one of saturation is less or equal than R, then the value of similarity function is equal to one minus the absolute value of the difference of intensities.

c3) If $\neg c1 \wedge \neg c2$, then the saturation as well as hue are determinate, forming two vectors for p and q in polar coordinates (saturation (radii), hue (angle)). In this case, the value of similarity function is equal to one minus the Euclidean distance between these two vectors; see also formula above.

Figure 1 shows the results obtained with the application of the clustering criteria (first β_0-Connected and then β_0-Complete Maximal), which use just defined the similarity function, to segment a complex color image.

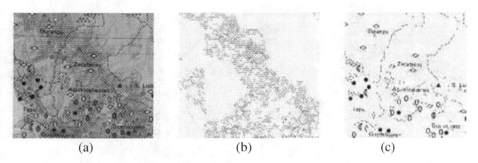

(a)   (b)   (c)

Fig. 1. (a) Source Image. (b) and (c) Segmentation of the objects of interest.

3 Application of the C2FS Method to Cartographic Pattern Recognition

Let **I** be a digital cartographic image $\|M(i, j)\|_{nxm}$. First we should compute the Image Associated Function as follows. Let $Z = \{0,..., n\}$, $Z' = \{0,..., m\}$, consider the Cartesian product $Z \times Z'$ and the difference of the sets A and B: A-B = $\{x \in A \mid x \notin B\}$. Next the following steps are employed:

1. Let $p_0 = 0$, $q_0 = 0$, then the sets are defined:

$G_0 = \{ M(x, y) \mid M(x, y) = M(p_0, q_0)\}$ and

$G'_0 = \{(x, y) \mid M(x, y) \in G_0\}$.

2. Let $(p_1, q_1) \in Z \times Z' - G'_0$, then the sets are defined:

$G_1 = \{ M(x, y) \mid M(x, y) = M(p_1, q_1)\}$ and

$G'_1 = \{(x, y) \mid M(x, y) \in G_1\}$.

3. Let $(p_2, q_2) \in Z \times Z' - G'_0 \cup G'_1$, then the sets are defined:

$G_2 = \{ M(x, y) \mid M(x, y) = M(p_2, q_2)\}$ and

$G'_2 = \{(x, y) \mid M(x, y) \in G_2\}$.

4. The process continues until the first natural number k such that $Z \times Z' - G'_0 \cup$
   $G'_1 \cup G'_2 \cup ... \cup G'_{k+1} = \emptyset$ is found. It can be demonstrated that sets G'_i, $i \in$
   $\{0,...,k\}$ generate a partition of set $Z \times Z'$. We call the union $\cup_i G'_i$ a *primitive partition*.

To relax the equality condition that is requested in the definition of sets G_i, $i \in$ $\{1,..., k\}$, we set up the generalized sets G_i^ε as follows: $G_i^\varepsilon = \{ M(x, y) \mid \|M(x, y) - M(p_i,q_i)\| \leq \varepsilon\}^8$, where $\|\bullet\|$ could be any metric. In this work we use the "Manhattan" metric, i.e. $\|(x, y, z,) - (p, q, r) \| = |x - p| + |y - q| + |z - r|$; $|\bullet|$ denotes the absolute value.

It is more convenient to work with the co-domain of the Image Associated Function because it does not contain repeated elements thus allowing avoid excessive computing. For example, consider figure 2.

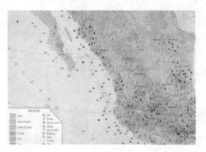

Fig. 2. Cartographic map: size $914 \times 539 = 492646$ pixels.

The number of elements in the co-domain of the Image Associated Function, considering the sets G_i^ε, with $\varepsilon=20$, is 120. In other words, we only use 0.02% of the total number of the image pixels to build primitive partition. To this partition, we apply the clustering criteria to extract and recognize the objects of interest in maps[9].

Cartographic Pattern Recognition. Suppose that a cartographic pattern P_{TE} already recognized by a computer system in a cartographic map in a coarse scale exists. The recognition of P_{TE} implies that corresponding attributive, geometric, topologic data are known and, therefore, form the Cartographic Knowledge Domain (CKD). Information of special interest is its location with respect to some coordinate system, color or colors, shape, etc. We use this information to recognize or assign a concept from CKD, e.g. "Lerma River" to P_{FE} presented in the fine scale map. Note that the characteristics of P_{TE} and P_{FE} are conceptually similar, e.g. they have the same name, although they can be distinct as functions according to definition 4.

---

[8] Notice that when $\varepsilon = 0$, the sets G_i^ε are converted in the sets G_i; that is why we call them "generalized".

[9] Note that primitive partition in vector image of region maps, for example, is immediate and provides the region recognition as well, i.e. this is simultaneous segmentation-recognition [5]

Information about the location of $\mathbf{P}_{TE}$ is used to find a candidate to be "fine" carto-graphic pattern $\mathbf{P}_{FE}$. Notice that $\mathbf{P}_{FE}$ is generated by the application of the clustering criteria. This way, once $\mathbf{P}_{FE}$ has been located the system is assigned to it the concept defined by "coarse" cartographic pattern $\mathbf{P}_{TE}$, finally reaching $\mathbf{P}_{FE}$ recognition under that concept. For example, suppose that a cartographic map in coarse scale provides information with which the following CKD is build: {name: "Palm"; location: (84,101)}. CKD affirms that it is possible to find in the image coordinates (84,101) a cartographic pattern denominated "Palm". Notice that the location, extraction and recognition are immediate because the classification has been employed over all im-age pixels by means of the Image Associated Function co-domain; see figure 3.

(84,101)

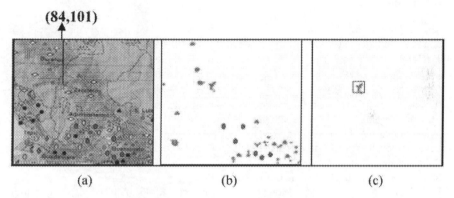

(a)   (b)   (c)

Fig. 3. Recognition of a cartographic pattern visually classified as punctual. (a) Original image. (b) Image obtained after applying the criterion β_0-Connected, $\beta_0=0.9$. (c) Recognition of the pattern (function) "Palm".

4 Conclusion

Color cartographic pattern recognition by a computer system remains a hard task [4]. This is closely related to the spatial data vectorization for GIS-ready information [2]. In this context, the coarse-to-fine scale method represents a promising alternative to carry it out. Indeed, a typical situation in GIS development is that spatial data in a coarse scale are available, and GIS-developer needs to transform (recognize) them into finer scale. For example, Mexico has full-territory coverage by recognized to-pographic maps in scale 1:50,000, but not in 1:25,000; this is a commonality for many countries [4]. Moreover, the C2FS method is in essence a simultaneous seg-mentation-recognition system [5][7].

The method attempts to incorporate the external (interpretative) knowledge to the segmentation-recognition process; an early approach with the same core was [10].

We believe that this work is not a yet another paper about (YAPA) cartographic pattern recognition. This assertion is also based on "universality" of our method: this was initially designed to recognize cartographic patterns into fine scale maps, however, further development shown that it is possible to recognize patterns independently of the map scale by modifying the cartographic knowledge domain.

Of course, the method has certain limitations. One of them is that it is required a lazy user's intervention to establish the clustering criteria parameters. This common problem in image processing and pattern recognition, however, is not a great obstacle for further method's development by adding more pattern features to the criteria. Although, the method has actually been designed at basic level (considers unique color feature), requiring further development (consider other features such as shape), it is technically sound, according to the obtained results.

References

1. Martínez-Trinidad, J.F., Guzmán-Arenas, A.: The Logical Combinatorial Approach to Pattern Recognition, an Overview through Selected Works. *Pattern Recognition*, Vol. 34, No. 1. (2001) 741-751
2. Levachkine, S.: Raster to Vector Conversion of Color Cartographic Maps for Analytical GIS. In: Llados, J. (ed.): Proc. 5th IAPR International Workshop on Graphics Recognition (GREC 2003) July 30-31, 2003, Barcelona, Catalonia, Spain (2003) 77-91
3. Martínez-Trinidad, J.F., Ruiz-Shulcloper, J.: Fuzzy Clustering of Semantic Spaces. *Pattern Recognition*, Vol. 34, No. 4. (2001) 783-793
4. Levachkine, S. P., Polchkov, E.A.: Integrated Technique for Automated Digitization of Raster Maps, *Revista Digital Universitaria*, Vol. 1, No. 1. (2000). Available on-line at http://www.revista.unam.mx/vol.1/art4/index.html
5. Levachkine, S., Torres, M., Moreno, M., Quintero, R.: Simultaneous Segmentation-Recognition-Vectorization of Meaningful Geographical Objects in Geo-Images. Lecture Notes in Computer Science. Vol. 2905, Springer-Verlag (2003) 635-642
6. Angulo, J., Serra, J.: Mathematical Morphology in Color Spaces Applied to the Analysis of Cartographic Images. In: Levachkine, S., Serra, J., Egenhofer, M. (eds.), Semantic Processing of Spatial Data, Research on Computing Science, Vol.4. (2003) 59-66
7. Levachkine, S., Velázquez, A., Alexandrov, V., Kharinov, M.: Semantic Analysis and Recognition of Raster-scanned Color Cartographic Images. Lecture Notes in Computer Science, Vol. 2390. Springer-Verlag (2002) 178-189
8. Lazo-Cortés, M., Ruiz-Shulcloper, J., Alba-Cabrera, E.: An Overview of the Evolution of the Concept of Testor. *Pattern Recognition*, Vol. 34, No. 4. (2001) 753-762
9. Torres-Ruiz, M., Levachkine, S.: Semantics Definition to Represent Spatial Data. In: Levachkine, S. *et al.* (eds.), *Proc. International Workshop on Semantic Processing of Spatial Data* (GEOPRO 2002), 3-4 December 2002, Mexico City, Mexico (2002)
10. Meyers G.K., Chen, C.-H.: Verification–based Approach for Automated Text and Feature Extraction from Raster-scanned Maps. Lecture Notes in Computer Science, Vol. 1072. Springer-Verlag (1996) 190-203

Cerebral Vessel Enhancement Using Rigid Registration in Three-Dimensional CT Angiography

Helen Hong[1], Ho Lee[2], Sung Hyun Kim[3], and Yeong Gil Shin[2,4]

[1] School of Electrical Engineering and Computer Science BK21: Information Technology,
Seoul National University, San 56-1 Shinlim 9-dong Kwanak-gu, Seoul 151-742, Korea
hlhong@cse.snu.ac.kr
[2] School of Electrical Engineering and Computer Science, Seoul National University
{holee,yshin}@cglab.snu.ac.kr
[3] Dept. of Radiology, Seoul National University Bundang Hospital, 300, Gumi-dong,
Sungnam-si, Kyunggi-do, Korea
kimsungh@radiol.snu.ac.kr
[4] INFINITT Co., Ltd., Taesuk Bld., 275-5 Yangjae-dong Seocho-gu, Seoul 137-934, Korea

Abstract. In this paper, we propose a robust 3D rigid registration technique for detecting cerebral aneurysms, arterial stenosis, and other vascular anomalies in a brain CT angiography. Our method is composed of the following four steps. First, a set of feature points are selected using a 3D edge detection technique within skull base. Second, a locally weighted 3D distance map is constructed for leading our similarity measure to robust convergence on the maximum value. Third, the similarity measure between feature points is evaluated repeatedly by selective cross-correlation. Fourth, bone masking is performed for effectively removing bones. Experimental results show that the performance of our method is very promising compared to conventional methods in the aspects of its visual inspection and robustness. In particular, our method is well applied to vasculature anatomy of patients with an aneurysm in the region of the skull base.

1 Introduction

Computed tomography (CT) angiography [1-3] is a useful and noninvasive imaging technique for the evaluation of both the intra- and extracranial vasculature. If the injection of a bolus of intravenous contrast material is timely controlled, CT scans can capture the arterial phase in a large volume of patient anatomy. This makes it possible to detect cerebral aneurysms, arterial stenosis, and other vascular anomalies in the intra- and extracranial arteries.

To get an arterial anatomy in three-dimensional views, source images from CT angiography are often displayed using volume rendering techniques [4-5]. A drawback of the volume rendering techniques is that extensive preprocessing is needed for bone removal. Although some software tools are available, the bone removal process is still time-consuming and often incomplete. In addition, separating arteries from bone or perivascular calcification are difficult particularly in the areas where arteries are contiguous with the bone. As a consequence, aneurysms in the region of the skull base are obscured by bone. These difficulties of bone removal limit the clinical application of volume rendering techniques.

A conventional approach of delineating vessels from bone is to subtract enhanced images which taken after injecting a contrast material from nonenhanced images. This

A. Sanfeliu et al. (Eds.): CIARP 2004, LNCS 3287, pp. 541–549, 2004.

subtraction technique assumes that tissues surrounding vessels do not change in position or density during exposure. However, even minor patient movement results in severe distortion or artifacts since the contrast between vessels and surrounding tissues is significantly smaller than that between bone and surrounding tissues. Without the proper handling of patient motion artifacts, the clinical application of a subtraction method is very limited. Even though the motion of a patient can be minimized by taking special precautions of either patient, acquisition system, or both [6], artifacts can not be entirely avoided. To reduce patient motion artifacts, we have to use a retrospective image processing techniques.

Several registration techniques have been proposed to reduce patient motion artifacts in brain CT angiography. A common registration method used in radiology is a manual method which translates and rotates images by interactive but tedious and time-consuming user interactions. In addition, this requires the clinical knowledge and experience. Pixel shifting [7] provides a solution in the situation where artifacts have been caused by gross two-dimensional translational motion. In most cases, patient motion is more spatial and complex and cannot be modeled by such a simple transformation. Yeung et al. [8] proposed a 3D feature detector and a 3D image flow computation algorithm for matching feature points between enhanced and nonenhanced images of brain CT angiography. The processing time for finding 3D feature points takes too much time since the interest index of each voxel position is found by comparing variance values in all 13 directions. Venema et al. [9] developed a global matching method using gray value correlation of skull bases in two time interval brain CT angiography. The alignment by minimizing the difference of intensity values of the both skull bases may not be accurate because the same pixel of individual CT scans may have different density. For the same purpose, Kwon et al. [10] proposed a mutual information-based registration. However, the limited information only using the area of skull base for similarity measure does not guarantee the exact alignment.

These registration methods can minimize patient motion artifacts, however, they still need some progress in computational efficiency and robustness for the clear visualization of cerebral vessels in CT angiography. In this paper, we propose a robust 3D rigid registration technique for the detection of cerebral aneurysms, arterial stenosis, and any other anomalies in brain CT angiography. Our method consists of the following four steps. First, a set of feature points is selected using a 3D edge detection technique within the skull base. Second, a locally weighted 3D distance map is constructed for leading our similarity measure to robust convergence on the maximum value. Third, the similarity measure between feature points is evaluated repeatedly by selective cross-correlation. Fourth, the bone masking process is performed for removing bones. Experimental results show that our method is more robust than the conventional methods.

The organization of the paper is as follows. In Section 2, we discuss how to extract and select feature points in an angiographic image. Then we propose a similarity measure and the optimization process to find exact geometrical relationship between feature points in the enhanced and nonenhanced images. In Section 3, experimental results show how the method accurately and robustly extracts the extra- and intracranial vessels from the brain CT angiography. This paper is concluded with a brief discussion of the results in Section 4.

2   3D Rigid Registration

Fig. 1 shows the pipeline of our method for the registration of enhanced and nonenhanced images. To find exact geometrical relationship between two volumes, one dataset is fixed as mask volume whereas other dataset is defined as contrast volume which taken after injecting a contrast material to mask volume. The contrast volume is moved during the iterative alignment procedure. Interpolating the contrast volume at grid positions of the mask volume is required for each iteration depending on the transformation. Since rigid transformation is enough to align the skull base, we use three translations and three rotations about the x-, y-, z-axis. After transformation, the mask is slightly widened by means of dilation with 1-pixel to allow partial-volume effects and acceptable small mismatch. Finally, extracted vessels are displayed by a conventional volume rendering technique.

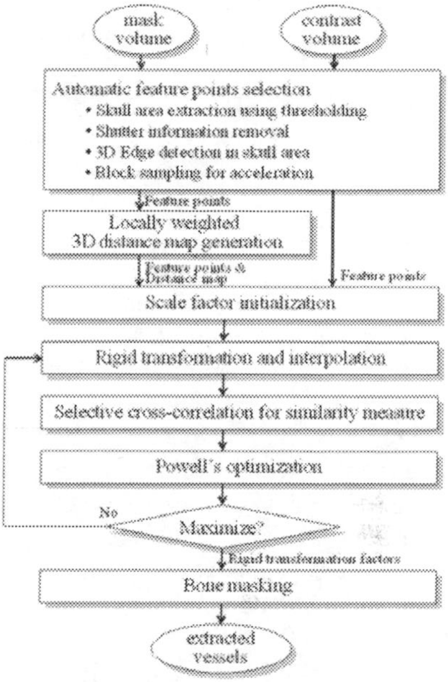

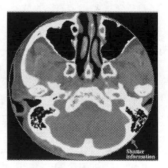

Fig. 1. The pipeline of 3D rigid registration

2.1   Feature Points Selection

A traditional approach of finding the correspondence between mask and contrast volume of brain CT angiography requires voxel by voxel correspondence test for entire volume. This is computationally expensive and cannot lead to a clinically accepted technique. Since artifacts almost appear in the region where strong edges are present in the subtracted image, we can accelerate the registration procedure by processing voxels belonging to image edge area only instead of all voxels in the volume.

Fig. 2. Shutter information in brain CT angiography image

Our feature identification uses a 3D operator for utilizing spatial relations in volume data. At first, in order to align skull base which represents rigid object boundaries in brain CT angiography, we only use pixels with a CT number above a chosen threshold. Shutter information of CT angiography shown in Fig. 2 is removed since it leads to misalignment by detecting the boundary of the shutter as a feature. Then 3D edge detection technique is applied to the skull base in mask and contrast volume, respectively. Just like their two-dimensional counterparts, 3D edges are usually defined as discontinuities of image intensity caused by the transition from one homogeneous 3D region to another 3D region of different mean intensity. The location of rigid object boundaries can be computed by detecting local maxima of the gray-level gradient magnitude. Since rigid object boundaries are scale-dependent image features, they can only be detected by using derivatives which allows finer tuning for detecting the required edge scale. Among detected features, algorithm selects a predefined number feature points enough to ensure even distribution of feature points in the skull base.

2.2 Locally Weighted 3D Distance Map Generation

Registration between selected feature points is likely to converge to local optimum near to global maximum depending on the initial position. To prevent this occurrence we need to find the optimum value of the similarity measure within the global search space. However, this approach increases the computation time by the proportion to the size of the search space. To minimize the search space and guarantee the convergence to the optimum value, we generate a locally weighted 3D distance map per each feature point. This map is generated only for the mask volume.

For generating 3D distance map, we approximate the global distance computation with repeated propagation of local distances within a small neighborhood mask. To approximate Euclidean distances, we consider 26-neighbor relations for a chessboard distance to be the same distance as 1-distance value. The chessboard distance is applied to each feature point in the mask volume. Then the weighting factor W_{xyz} is multiplied to the chessboard distance as like Eq. (1). The mask size N of locally weighted 3D distance map is fixed as $9\times9\times9$. Largest weighting factor is assigned to the center of mask while the smallest weighting factor to boundary of mask.

$$D_x =| M_x - C_x |, \quad D_y =| M_y - C_y |, \quad D_z =| M_z - C_z |$$

$$W_{xyz} = \frac{(N+1)}{2} - Max(D_x, D_y, D_z) \tag{1}$$

where M and C be the current and the center position of locally weighted-3D distance mask. D_x, D_y, D_z is the difference of x-, y-, and z-axis between the current and the center position in locally weighted 3D distance mask.

Fig. 3(a) shows the locally weighted 3D distance map when N is fixed as $5\times5\times5$. Fig. 3(c) shows the cut plane of the volume of a locally weighted 3D distance map when the distance map of Fig. 3(a) is applied to feature points as shown in Fig. 3(b). Each color shown in Fig. 3(c) represents the distance value of the locally weighted distance map.

2.3 Similarity Measure and Optimization

The similarity measure is used to determine the degree of resemblance of windows in successive frames. Several similarity measures have been devised and applied to angiographic images – the sum of squared intensity differences, cross-correlation, and the entropy of the difference image. However, most of these similarity measures are sensitive to mean gray-level offset and local dissimilarities caused by contrasted vessels. We propose the selective cross-correlation as a similarity measure which only

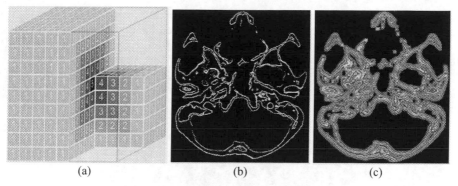

(a)   (b)   (c)

Fig. 3. A locally weighted 3D distance map

uses feature points near to skull base. Our approach reduces sensitivity to mean gray-level offset or local dissimilarities by incorporating distance information of a locally weighted distance map into the similarity measure.

As can be seen in Eq. (2), the local weighting factor of a 3D distance map in mask volume is multiplied to the distance in contrast volume. We assume that the distances of feature points in contrast volume, $D_C(i)$, are all set to 1. Then the selective cross-correlation SCC reaches maximum when feature points of mask and contrast volume are aligned correctly.

$$SCC = \frac{1}{N_C} \sum_{i=0}^{N_C-1} D_C(P_C(i)) W_M(T(P_C(i))) \qquad (2)$$

where N_C is total number of feature points in contrast volume, $P_C(i)$ is the position of i-th feature point in contrast volume. The weighting factor of the current feature point of contrast volume, $W_M(i)$, is obtained from the corresponding locally weighted 3D distance map in mask volume.

To evaluate the selective cross-correlation of large samples from volume dataset, we use the Powell's method. Since the search space of our similarity measure is limited to the surrounding skull base, we do not need a more powerful optimization algorithm such as simulated annealing. For example, Fig. 4 shows the process of optimizing the selective cross-correlation. Fig. 4(a) and (b) are feature points selected from mask and contrast volume, respectively. In the initial position in Fig. 4(c), the number of matching feature points is 6 pixels. Finally, the number of matching feature points becomes 12 pixels when the selective cross-correlation reaches the maximum value.

2.4 Bone Masking

A traditional approach for enhancing vessels after alignment is to subtract transformed contrast volume to mask volume. However it is very difficult to remove bone completely using a traditional subtraction technique since densities between mask and transformed contrast volume can be different even in the same pixel position. In addition, partial-volume effects near to bone area and slight amounts of mismatch make it possible to generate artifacts in subtraction images. For the more complete removal of bones, we propose a bone masking instead of a traditional subtraction technique.

Our bone masking process first identifies bone pixels in the mask volume by applying the threshold value of 1500HU. The identified bone pixels as mask is then slightly widened by means of dilation with 1-pixel to allow for partial-volume effects and slight amount of mismatch. Finally, pixels in contrast volume which are corresponding to pixels in mask volume are set to an arbitrarily low value. This results in the removal of bones in the volume rendering image of contrast volume.

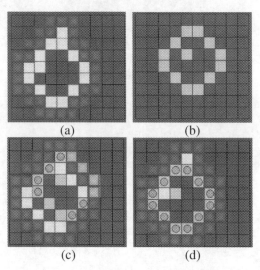

Fig. 4. The process of optimizing the selective cross-correlation (a) feature points in mask volume (b) feature points in contrast volume (c) initial position (d) final position

3   Experimental Results

All our implementation and test were performed on an Intel Pentimum IV PC containing 3.0 GHz CPU and 1.0 GBytes of main memory. Our method has been applied to nine sets of enhanced and nonenhanced images of brain CT angiography, as described in Table 1, obtained from MDCT (Multi-Detector Computed Tomography). We assume that image and pixel sizes are the same in enhanced and nonenhanced images.

Table 1. Experimental datasets

Patient #	Image size	Slice number	Pixel size	Slice spacing
1	512 x 512	185	0.30x 0.30	0.3
2	512 x 512	220	0.32 x 0.32	0.3
3	512 x 512	98	0.33 x 0.33	0.7
4	512 x 512	220	0.31 x 0.31	0.3
5	512 x 512	205	0.31 x 0.31	0.3
6	512 x 512	37	0.28 x 0.28	1.0
7	512 x 512	200	0.25 x 0.25	0.3
8	512 x 512	220	0.34 x 0.34	0.3
9	512 x 512	201	0.29 x 0.29	0.3

The performance of our method is evaluated with the aspects of visual inspection and robustness. The average processing time including volume rendering of nine sets is less than 60 seconds. Fig. 5 shows the two-dimensional comparison of a regular subtraction method and the proposed method. We can see many misalignments in Fig. 5 (c), whereas brain vessels are clearly depicted in Fig. 5 (d). Note that intracranial vessels mingling with bone in the middle part of brain are also well separated from skull base. The intracranial vessels in Fig 5 (c) were shrunk by the lack of alignment process of enhanced and nonenhanced images.

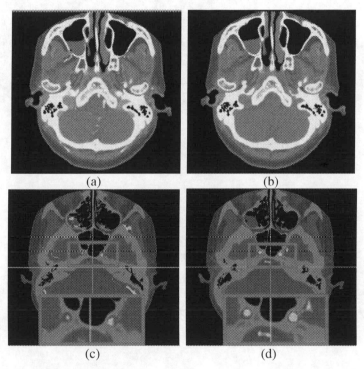

(a)   (b)

(c)   (d)

Fig. 5. Comparison of regular subtraction and the proposed method (a) enhanced image (b) nonenhanced image (c) regular subtraction (d) proposed method

Volumetric images resulted from regular subtraction and the proposed method are illustrated in Fig. 6. Both regular subtraction and the proposed method can reveal the vasculature in the skull base, which are obscured by bone. While the quality of regular subtraction image was substantially reduced by patient motion artifacts, our method can keep the quality of the original image. Our method would be useful for the visualization of the vasculature of the patients with an aneurysm in the region of the skull base.

The robustness of the selective cross-correlation (SCC) criterion has been evaluated by comparing SCC measure traces (represented by circle dot line) with cross-correlation (CC) measure traces (represented by square dot line). As shown in Fig. 7, the changes of SCC measure are smooth near to the maximal position, but CC measure is changed rapidly. This means that the CC measure for similarity evaluation is more likely to converge to the local maximum, whereas the SCC measure is more robust in converging to the global maximum.

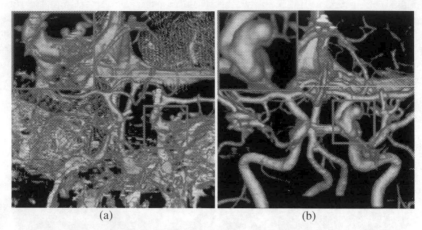

Fig. 6. Volume rendering images with an ROI of aneurysm in brain CT angiography (a) regular subtraction (b) proposed method

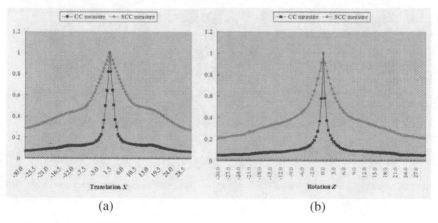

Fig. 7. Comparison of SCC and CC traces (a) for translation in the x-direction (b) for rotation in the z-direction.

4   Conclusion

To clearly visualize cerebral vessels, we have developed a system for aligning enhanced and nonenhanced images of brain CT angiography. Our methods include 3D feature point selection within the skull base, the generation of a locally weighted 3D distance map of each feature point, iterative 3D rigid registration to maximize the similarity measure, the SCC, between feature points, and bone masking. Our method has been successfully applied to the enhanced and nonenhanced brain images of nine different patients. Experimental results show that our registration is clinically useful by the fact that the method is very little influenced by image degradation occurred in bone-vessel interface. For all experimental patients, good visualization of cerebral vessels on the volume rendering image can be obtained. In particular, our method has been well applied to vasculature anatomy of patients with an aneurysm in the region of a skull base.

Acknowledgements

This work was supported in part by the Korea Research Foundation under the Brain Korea 21 Project and INFINITT Co., Ltd. The ICT at Seoul National University provides research facilities for this study.

References

1. Philip, M.W., Wardlaw, J.M., Easton, V., Can Noninvasive Imaging Accurately Depict Intracranial Aneurysms? A Systematic Review, Radiology, Vol. 217 (2000) 361-370.
2. Kato, Y., Katada, K., Hayakawa, M., Nakane, M., Ogura, Y., Sano, K., Kanno, T., Can 3D-CTA Surpass DSA in Diagnosis of Cerebral Aneurysm?, Acta Neurochir (Wien), Vol. 143 (2001) 245-250.
3. Jayaraman, M.V., Mayo-Smith, W.W., Doberstein, C.E., Intracanalicular Aneurysm of the Anterior Inferior Cerebellar Artery Revealed by Multi-Detector CT Angiography, AJNR Am J Neuroradiol, Vol. 24 (2003) 1338-1340.
4. Napel, S., Marks, M.P., Rubin, G.D., Dake, M.D., McDonnell, C.H., Song, S.M., Enzmann, D.R., Jeffrey, R.B., CT Angiography with Spiral CT and Maximum Intensity Projection, Radiology, Vol. 185 (1992) 607-610.
5. Philipp, M.O., Kubin, K., Mang, T., Hormann, M., Metz, V.M., Three-Dimensional Volume Rendering of Multidetector-Row CT Data: Applicable for Emergency Radiology, European Journal of Radiology (2003) 1-6.
6. Jayakrishnan, V.K., White, P.M., Aitken, D., Crane, P., McMahon, A.D., Teasdale, E.M., Subtraction Helical CT Angiography of Intra- and Extracranial Vessels: Technical Considerations and Preliminary Experience, AJNR Am J Neuroradiol, Vol. 24 (2003) 451-455.
7. Wu, Q.X., Bones, P.J., Bates, R.H.T., Translational Motion Compensation for Coronary Angiogram Sequences, IEEE Trans. on Medical Imaging, Vol. 8, No. 3 (1989) 276-282.
8. Yeung, M.M., Yeo, B.L., Liou, S.P., Banihashemi, A., Three-Dimensional Image Registration for Spiral CT Angiography, Proc. of Computer Vision and Pattern Recognition (1994) 423-429.
9. Venema, H.W., Hulsmans, F.J.H., den Heeten, G.J., CT Angiography of the Circle of Willis and Intracranial Internal Carotid Arteries: Maximum Intensity Projection with Matched Mask Bone Elimination – Feasibility Study, Radiology, Vol. 218 (2001) 893-898.
10. Kwon, S.M., Kim, Y.S., Kim, T., Ra, J.B., Novel Digital Subtraction CT Angiography based on 3D Registration and Refinement, Proc. of SPIE Medical Image: Image Processing (2004).

Skeleton-Based Algorithm for Increasing Spectral Resolution in Digital Elevation Model

Rolando Quintero, Serguei Levachkine, Miguel Torres, and Marco Moreno

Centre for Computer Research, National Polytechnical Institute, Mexico City, Mexico
{quintero,sergei,mtorres,mmoreno}@cic.ipn.mx
http://geo.cic.ipn.mx, http://geopro.cic.ipn.mx

Abstract. In this work, we present an algorithm for increasing spectral resolution in DEM. The algorithm is based on the 8-connected skeleton of polygons formed by the contour lines and to prune this skeleton by translating it into a graph. This is an alternative to the processes of vector interpolation. With this approach, it is possible to find new elevation data from the information contained in DEM and generate new data with the same spatial resolution.

1 Introduction

Nowadays, Digital Elevation Models (DEM) have gained popularity in applications for simulating natural disasters. Nevertheless, these applications require a huge amount of data. In many cases, the available data do not present enough quality for simulation processes. The Statistics, Geography and Informatics National Institute of Mexico (INEGI) produces DEM with 50 meters of resolution [1][2], but some simulation processes require a better level of detail (1 meter is the standard). In all cases, DEM are generated by means of contours. These have different representations and thresholds of separation. For instance, in the topological maps of INEGI, the contours are separated by 10 meters and 5 meters near the coast. In Simulation processes like flooding simulations we need more detailed information (less than 1m. of resolution).

In this work, we propose an algorithm to increase spectral resolution of DEM for simulation processes; the algorithm is based on a skeletonization. In [3], we present an application to handle the huge quantity of data contained in DEM for real-time rendering by discriminating the less significant elevation data, without changing the *semantics* of the raster data. However, we cannot improve the quality of the more relevant data to obtain additional information. In [4], we extended the algorithm to increase the spatial resolution of DEM. In this paper, we introduce a method for increasing spectral resolution of DEM. It is important to lineout that the algorithms mentioned above were developed to be used with raster data sets, although similar considerations can be taken for vector data sets.

By using the algorithm presented in this work and the previous jointly, we can solve the problem of 3D data representation and generate virtual scenes, which are ready to navigate, either by simulations or by defined trajectories [5].

In the next section, we present some frameworks of the underlying theory of the skeletonization making different approaches. In Section 3, we give the pertinent considerations for the application of skeletonization in DEM and outline the proposed

A. Sanfeliu et al. (Eds.): CIARP 2004, LNCS 3287, pp. 550–557, 2004.

approach. In Section 4, some results and tests are presented and analyzed. Finally, Section 5 describes our conclusions.

2 Skeletonization

The skeleton of a region is defined by means of the Medial Axes Transform (MAT) proposed by Blum [6]. The MAT of a region R with edge B is defined as follows: Find the *nearest* neighbor for each point p of R, if p has more than one neighbor then p belongs to the medial axis (skeleton) of R. The concept *"nearest"* depends on a distance, while the results of MAT depend on the selection of a distance measure. Fig. 1 shows some examples that use Euclidean distance as measure [7].

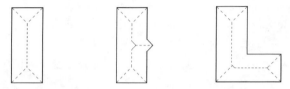

Fig. 1. Medial Axis of some simple geometrical shapes

Strictly speaking, the skeleton of a region should fulfill the following conditions:
- Be a connected subset of points from the original region.
- Represent the geometric characteristics of the original region.
- Preserve some topological characteristics of the original region, such as connectivity and holes.

In general, all skeletonization methods of binary images can be classified in two groups: *pixel-based* methods and *non-pixel-based* ones. In the first case, every pixel belonging to an object in the image is used for computation of the skeleton (thinning and distance transformations).

On the other hand, non-pixel-based methods attempt to determine analytically the symmetric points of a shape from opposite points in the shape edge. The thinning techniques provide different types of skeletons, depending on the connectivity desired for the skeleton. In general, there are four types of skeleton connectivity (Eqn. 1) They are: 8-connected, 4-connected, 6-right-connected and 6-left-connected.

$$d_8(p,q) = \max(|x-u|,|y-v|),$$
$$d_4(p,q) = |x-u|+|y-v|,$$
$$d_{6R}(p,q) = \max(|x-u|,|y-v|,|x-u+y-v|),$$
$$d_{6L}(p,q) = \max(|x-u|,|y-v|,|x-u-y+v|),$$

(1)

For a pixel p, from an image I, exists four types of neighborhoods, depending on the type of connectivity, they are denoted by v_8, v_4, v_{6R} y v_{6L}. In Fig. 2 the neighborhoods mentioned are depicted.

Thinning is the process that consists of deleting all pixels of a set of objects with region R and edge B, which fulfill the following conditions:
- Pixel p is not an extreme, i.e. it has just one neighbor belonging to the object.
- If p is deleted, the connectivity must not be affected.

（a）   （b）   （c）   （d）

Fig. 2. Set of neighbors for a pixel p using different connectivity criteria. (a) 8-connected. (b) 4-connected. (c) 6R-connected. (d) 6L-connected

A classic thinning algorithm consists of the following stages: First, determining the edge pixels. To determine these pixels, it is necessary to use a dual connectivity criteria (if we want a 8-connected skeleton, then we must use 4-connected criteria). Once determined the edge pixels, we must delete the pixels that are not necessary. The conditions for determining if a pixel p can be deleted are defined in Eqn. 2 (the rotated versions of masks are conditions too).

$$\sum p_i = 0 \wedge \sum p_j = 1 \wedge \sum p_k = 1, i \in \{3,7\}, j \in \{8,1,2\}, k \in \{6,5,4\},$$
$$\sum p_i = 0 \wedge \sum p_j = 1 \wedge \sum p_k = 1, i \in \{1,3\}, j \in \{2\}, k \in \{4,5,6,7,8\},$$

(2)

Eqn. 2 can be explained by the masks that result from all possible combinations of the equations (see Fig. 3). If an edge pixel gives a true result by applying any of the masks of Fig. 3, then this pixel cannot be deleted. Additionally, it is necessary to test if the pixel is an extreme one (Eqn. 3). If it is true, then the pixel cannot be deleted.

$$\sum p_i = 1, i \in \{1,3,5,7\},$$

(3)

This process is iteratively repeated, while we can delete pixels. The result of the process is the 8-connected skeleton of the original object.

a_1	a_2	a_3
0	p	0
b_1	b_2	b_3

b_1	0	a_1
b_2	p	a_2
b_3	0	a_3

a_1	0	1
a_2	p	0
a_3	a_4	a_5

a_3	a_2	a_1
a_4	p	0
a_5	0	1

a_5	a_4	a_3
0	p	a_2
1	0	a_1

a_5	a_4	a_3
0	p	a_2
1	0	a_1

Where:
$$\sum a_i = 1$$
$$\sum b_i = 1$$

Fig. 3. Masks used to obtain the 8-connected skeleton

3   Applying Skeletonization for Increasing DEM Spectral Resolution

In this paper, we propose the use of a skeletonization to obtain a new contour between two known ones. In previous section, we present the process to compute the skeleton of a binary image. In this section we define how to generate the new contour from the skeleton of the region between the two known contours. We will call this region *Equi-Heigth* region or EH regions.

Generally, we do not have the DEM of a whole world, i.e. we should work with DEM that describe a region. Due to this, many times the contours are interrupted in the edges of the image. Hence, the EH regions can be incomplete; in this case we have identified three cases (See Fig. 4):

- *Case A.* The contours that define EH region are completely inside of the image, forming a blob with at least one hole.
- *Case B.* The contours begin and end outside of the image, forming a strip across the image.
- *Case C.* The same as case B, but there are holes in the strip.

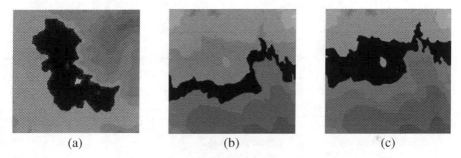

(a)   (b)   (c)

Fig. 4. Cases considered in the raster analysis

In Fig. 5 we present the skeletons obtained for EH regions of Fig. 4. As we can see, each skeleton has a lot of branches that are not suitable for being part of the contour. We can discriminate the noise branches (prune the skeleton). In same Fig. 5 the noise lines are in light gray, while the contour is in black.

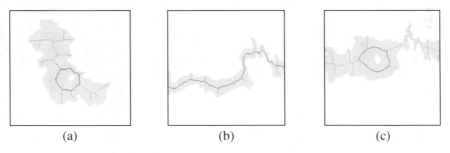

(a)   (b)   (c)

Fig. 5. The skeletons for the examples depicted in Fig. 4

Once having the skeleton, it is necessary to obtain the contour from it by pruning the skeleton. To perform this, we propose to generate a graph that describes the morphology of the skeleton. Thus, it is possible to find the contour of EH region by using a graph that describes the skeleton (see Fig. 6). In other words; it is possible to prune the skeleton using its graph; see in the following.

To generate the graph from the skeleton, we use on the fact that the skeleton is 8-connected. Let I be a binary image containing a skeleton and p_{ij} the value of the image matrix $I(i,j)$. The first element of the image f is defined by Eqn. 4.

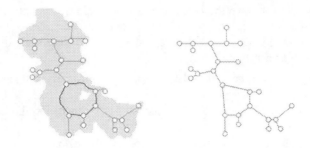

Fig. 6. Transformation of skeleton into graph

$$f = p_{ij} \ni p_{ij} \neq 0, p_{kl} = 0, k < i, l < j, \tag{4}$$

Let p be a pixel of the image and $n(p)$ the number of 8-connected neighbors. Then we define T as the set of terminal pixels (Eqn. 5). Similarly, we define A as the set of edge pixels (Eqn. 5) and R as the set of triad pixels (Eqn. 5). While, the set of vertices V is given by Eqn. 6.

$$T = \{p : n(p) = 1\},$$
$$A = \{p : n(p) = 2\}, \tag{5}$$
$$R = \{p : n(p) \geq 3\},$$
$$V = \{f\} \cup T \cup R. \tag{6}$$

Let p be an image pixel and $N(p)$ the set of the 8-connected neighbors of p, then we define a branch s by Eqn. 7. Also, $l(s)$ denotes the length of a branch s, and $first(s)$ and $last(s)$ defines the extreme elements of a branch s.

$$s = \{p_1, p_2, ..., p_n\} \ni p_i \in N(p_{i+1}), p_1 \in V, p_n \in V,$$
$$l(s) = card(s) = n,$$
$$first(s) = p_1, \tag{7}$$
$$last(s) = p_n.$$

We now define the graph representing the skeleton of the image as $G(V, E)$ where $E = \{s : s \text{ is a branch}\}$. Also, we define a path w on the graph G by Eqn. 8. Moreover, we define the length of a path $\lambda(w)$, the set of all paths in G as $W(G)$, and $\omega(G)$ is the longest path in G.

$$w = \{s_1, s_2, ..., s_n\} \ni s_i \in E, last(s_i) = first(s_{i+1}), i = 1, ..., n-1,$$
$$\lambda(w) = \sum_i l(s_i) \ni s_i \in w \tag{8}$$
$$\omega(G) = w_i \ni \lambda(w_i) \geq \lambda(w_j), w_i \in W(G), w_j \in W(G)$$

Once we have obtained the graph from skeleton, we simply take the following criteria for discriminating noise branches:

- If there are loops in graph, then all branches that are not in one loop are eliminated.

- If a branch is in more than one loop, then that branch is eliminated.
- If there are not loops in graph, then all branches outside of the longest path in graph are eliminated.

The next definitions are used to discriminate branches. A path b is a loop if $last(s_n)=first(s_1)$. So, let $B(G)$ be the set of all loops in graph G and $S_R(G)$ the set of redundant branches in G (Eqn. 9). Then we define the candidate contour C as is denoted in Eqn. 9.

$$
\begin{aligned}
S_R(G) &= \{s : s \in b_i, s \in b_j, i \neq j, b_i \in B(G), b_j \in B(G)\}, \\
C(G) &= \{s : s \in b, b \in B(G), s \notin S_R(G)\},
\end{aligned}
\tag{9}
$$

Finally, let C_N be the resulting contour within the skeleton, defined by Eqn. 10.

$$
C_N = \begin{cases} C(G) \Leftrightarrow C \neq \phi \\ w(G) \Leftrightarrow C = \phi \end{cases}.
\tag{10}
$$

4 Tests and Results

We have developed an application implementing the described process. The contours that have been obtained compose DEM. Nevertheless, we have found some pathological cases in the skeletonization as in well as the pruning process. Fig. 7 is depicted a pathological case in the skeletonization process: parasite branches (circled in Fig. 7.a). This case has been solved by applying some morphological operations (erosion, dilatation and aperture) to the image before obtaining the skeleton. The result is shown in Fig. 7.b.

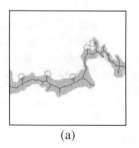 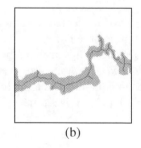

(a)   (b)

Fig. 7. Pathological case in the skeletonization

A pathological case of the pruning is illustrated in Fig. 8: there are no loops in the graph and there is a triad pixel near the edge of the image, Also the larger branch does not accomplish the edge of the image. Hence, the larger branch becomes parasite, so it does not belong to the contour. The problem can be easily solved by defining the set of edge pixels and requested the larger path in the graph begins and ends at edge pixel.

Fig. 9 shows the final step of processing of our algorithm. Moreover, Fig. 9.a depicts the found contour in the context of the DEM. This contour is integrated into DEM (Fig. 9.b).

Fig. 8. Pathological case in the pruning

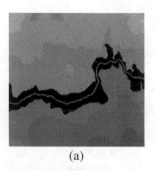

(a)   (b)

Fig. 9. Final result. (a) Contour discovered into original DEM. (b) Modified DEM according to the source

5   Conclusions

In this work, we have presented an algorithm for increasing spectral resolution in DEM. The algorithm is based on the 8-connected skeleton of polygons formed by the contour lines; and to prune this skeleton by transforming it into a graph.

The skeletonization algorithm provides 8-connected skeleton. We identify some pathological cases in which the skeleton has parasite branches. These branches do not affect the pruning algorithm. Nevertheless we reduce the number of parasites by applying morphological operations (erosion, dilatation and aperture) on the EH regions.

For the definition of the pruning algorithm, we describe the cases that can be DEM. This algorithm consists of the transformation of the skeleton into a graph. In the graph, the singular pixels (extreme, terminal and triad pixels) are the vertices and all other pixels form the edges of the graph. Once obtained the graph, criteria for deleting edges and vertices are defined. This conversion of the skeleton into graph can be used in other pruning algorithms, by changing the deletion criteria.

The algorithm is an alternative to the processes of vector interpolation. With this approach, it is possible to find new elevation data from the information contained in DEM, and generate new data with the same spatial resolution. The use of this approach jointly with the previous works [3][4] allow processing huge quantity of data contained in DEM for in simulation and visualization processes, optimizing its performance.

Acknowledgments

The authors of this paper wish to thank the Centre for Computing Research (CIC), General Coordination of Postgraduate Study and Research (CGEPI), National Polytechnic Institute (IPN) for their support. Additionally the authors wish to thank the reviewers for their pertinent comments.

References

1. Modelos Digitales de Elevación, Generalidades y Especificaciones, Instituto Nacional de Estadística, Geografía e Informática de México, Aguascalientes, México, 1999 (ISBN: 970-13-2511-7).
2. Normas Técnicas para la Elaboración de Ortofotos Digitales, Instituto Nacional de Estadística, Geografía e Informática de México, Aguascalientes, México, 1999 (ISBN: 970-13-2510-9).
3. Quintero, R., Guzman, G., Torres, M. and Moreno, M.: Spatial Analysis Based on 3D Rendering Techniques, *Proc. of 6th Association of Geographic Information Laboratories Europe conference on Geographic Information Science (AGILE 2003)*, Lyon, France, april 24 – 26, 2003.
4. Quintero, R., Moreno, M., Torres, M. and Levachkine, S.: Scale Changing of Digital Elevation Models using Bicubic Parametric Patches for Real-time Simulations, *Proc. of 8th Iberoamerican Congress on Pattern Recognition (CIARP 2003)*, La Habana, Cuba, 2003.
5. Reddy, M. and Leclerc, Y.: Enabling Geographic Support in Virtual Reality Modeling with Geo-VRML, Journal of Cartography and Geographic Information Science, 26(3), 1999.
6. Blum, H.: A transformation for extraction new descriptors of shape. *Proc. of symp. models for the perception of speech and visual form*, W. W. Dunn (Ed), MIT Press: Cambridge MA, 1967, pp. 362-380.
7. González, R. and Woods, R.: Digital image processing, Second Edition, Ed. Prentice Hall, 2002.

Landform Classification in Raster Geo-images

Marco Moreno, Serguei Levachkine, Miguel Torres, and Rolando Quintero

Geoprocessing Laboratory-Centre for Computing Research-National Polytechnic Institute,
Mexico City, Mexico
{marcomoreno,palych,mtorres,quintero}@cic.ipn.mx
http://geo.cic.ipn.mx, http://geopro.cic.ipn.mx

Abstract. We present an approach to perform a landform classification of raster geo-images to obtain the *semantics* of DEMs. We consider the following raster layers: slope, profile curvature and plan curvature, which have been built to identify the intrinsic properties of the landscape. We use a *multi-valued raster* to integrate these layers. The attributes of the multi-valued raster are classified to identify the landform elements. The classification approach is used to find the terrain characteristics of the water movement. Moreover, we describe the mechanisms to compute the primary attributes of digital terrain model. The method has been implemented into Geographical Information System–ArcInfo, and applied for Tamaulipas State, Mexico.

1 Introduction

Nowadays, Geographical Information Systems (GIS) are powerful and useful tools as means of information, visualization and research or as decision making applications [1]. Since the mid-1980s, with increasing popularity of GIS technology and availability of Digital Elevation Models (DEM), the potential of using DEM in studies of surface processes has been widely recognized [2]. DEM is playing an important role in many technical fields of GIS development, including earth and environmental sciences, hazard reduction, civil engineering, forestry, landscape planning, and commercial display. DEM has been used to delineate drainage networks and watershed boundaries to compute slope characteristics and to produce flow paths [3].

Contrasting with the traditional topographic map methods, the GIS approaches are relatively easy to apply in a consistent way on large landscape areas, because they allow summation of terrain characteristics for any region. To automate the procedure of terrain analysis, new methods and algorithms have been developed. The advantage of DEM analysis is that only one static parameter has to be captured to describe landscape processes. DEM are used in the measurement of geometry and landform. DEM has traditionally been applied to identify watersheds, drainages, hillslopes and other terrain object groups. The characteristics of terrain are distinguished by spatial relationships among and can be characterized by both its composition and configuration. We usually note that DEM are directly computed from the elevation model and *secondary compound attributes* which involve combination of primary attributes and constitute physically the spatial variability of specific processes that are presented in the landscape. While, *primary attributes* include slope, aspect, plan and profile curvature, flow-path length, and upslope contributing area. Most of these topographic attributes are computed from directional derivatives of a topographic surface.

A. Sanfeliu et al. (Eds.): CIARP 2004, LNCS 3287, pp. 558–565, 2004.

DEM are treated as field functions that consider a value at any position in a two dimensional space [4]. DEM is a particular type of raster geo-images. This raster describes thematic aspects of the terrain, which are represented by attributes (see Fig. 1). The geometric characteristics of DEM are the following: resolution, origin of coordinates, number of rows and columns, and lowest and highest coordinates.

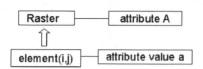

Fig. 1. Raster Data Model

In this paper, we propose an approach to make *landform[1]* classification based on geo-image processing by means of Spatial Analyzer Module (SAM). In Section 2 we describe SAM and its functionality. Section 3 describes how landform classification has been obtained. Some results are shown in Section 5. Our conclusions are outlined in Section 6.

2   Spatial Analyzer Module (SAM)

SAM is a special module, which has been designed to perform the spatial analysis procedures. SAM uses vector and raster data to make the spatial analysis. This module has been implemented using Arc Macro Language (AML) to ensure portability between computer platforms executing ArcInfo 7.0 or later. Initially, SAM was designed to compute Terrain Ruggedness and Drainage Density [3]. The present analysis consists of using different spatial data related to the case of study. SAM contains two components: *Analysis Block* is composed of a set of processes to make data analysis, *List of Procedures* stores the sequence of steps to execute the processes [5].

2.1   Analysis Block

It contains the functions to perform the spatial analysis. The functions are the following:

Grid Functions. They contain the set of functions for cell analysis, which include operations of the map algebra and functions to compute primary topographic attributes such as slope, aspect, plan and profile curvature and upslope contributing area.

- *Slope Function (CALCULATE_SLOPE)*: Slope identifies the maximum rate of change in value from each cell to its neighbors. An output slope grid can be computed as percent slope or degree of slope. Conceptually, the slope function fits a plane to the z-values (altitudes) of a 3 x 3 cell neighborhood around the processing or center cell. The direction of the plane (x,y-values) faces is the aspect for the

---

[1]   Landform is the result of various processes acting on the surface has also the function of a static boundary condition for processes in geomorphology, hydrology, meteorology, and others. Landform units can be extracted by delimiting homogeneous areas.

processing cell. The slope for the cell is computed from the 3 x 3 cell neighborhood using the average maximum technique [6]. If there is a cell location in the neighborhood with a *nodata* z value, the z value of the center cell will be assigned to the location. At the edge of the grid, at least three cells (outside of the grid's extent) will contain *nodata* as their z values. These cells will be assigned to the center cell's z value. The result is a flattening of the 3 x 3 plane that is fitted to these edge cells, which usually leads to a reduction in the slope. The formulas to compute the slope are:

$$Rise\_Run = \sqrt{\sqrt{\frac{dz}{dx}} + \sqrt{\frac{dz}{dy}}} ,$$ (1)

$$Slope = A\tan(Rise\_Run) * 57.29578 ,$$ (2)

where dz/dx and dz/dy are calculated using a 3 x 3 window (see Fig. 2) as described in equation 3 and 4:

$$\frac{dz}{dx} = ((a+2d+g)-(c+2f+i))/(8*X\_mesh\_spacing) ,$$ (3)

$$\frac{dz}{dy} = ((a+2b+c)-(g+2h+i))/(8*Y\_mesh\_spacing) ,$$ (4)

a	b	c
d	e	f
g	h	i

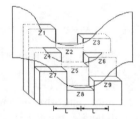

Fig. 2. 3 x 3 window to compute slope   **Fig. 3.** Description of elements to compute the curvature

◆ *Curvature Functions*: This functions compute the curvature in a DEM. The curvature functions can be used to describe the physical characteristics of a drainage basin to understand erosion and runoff processes. Two types of curvatures can be obtained by using SAM.

1) *Profile curvature (CALCULATE_PROFILE_CURVATURE)* is the curvature of topography from a cross-section view (perpendicular to contour lines). 2) *Plan curvature (CALCULATE_PLAN_CURVATURE)* is the curvature of topography from a map view (following contour lines). The curvature of a surface is computed on a cell-by-cell. For each cell, we use a fourth-order polynomial of the form [7]:

$$Z = Ax^2y^2 + Bx^2y + Cxy^2 + Dx^2 + Ey^2 + Fxy + Gx + Hy + I ,$$ (5)

Equation 5, it is used to fit a surface composed of a 3 x 3 window. The coefficients from *A* to *I* are calculated from this surface. The relationships between the coefficients and the nine values of elevation for every cell numbered are shown in Fig. 3, and they are defined by equations 6 to 14.

$$A = \frac{\left[\frac{(z1+z3+z7+z9)}{4} - \frac{(z2+z4+z6+z8)}{2} + z5\right]}{L4} ,$$ (6)

$$B = \frac{\left[\dfrac{(z1+z3-z7-z9)}{4} - \dfrac{(z2-z8)}{2}\right]}{L3}, \tag{7}$$

$$C = \frac{\left[\dfrac{(-z1+z3-z7+z9)}{4} + \dfrac{(z4-z6)}{2}\right]}{L3}, \tag{8}$$

$$D = \frac{\left[\dfrac{(z4+z6)}{2} + z5\right]}{L2}, \tag{9}$$

$$E = \frac{\left[\dfrac{(z2+z8)}{2} - z5\right]}{L2}, \tag{10}$$

$$F = \frac{(-z1+z3+z7-z9)}{4L2}, \tag{11}$$

$$G = \frac{(-z4+z6)}{2L}, \tag{12}$$

$$H = \frac{(z2-z8)}{L2}, \tag{13}$$

$$I = z5, \tag{14}$$

The output of the *CURVATURE* function is the second derivative of the surface (i.e., the slope of the slope), which is defined in equation 15.

$$Curvature = -2(D+E)*100, \tag{15}$$

The slope affects the overall rate of movement downslope. The *Profile curvature* impacts the acceleration and deceleration of the water flow. Therefore, it influences in the erosion and the deposition processes. The *Plan curvature* affects convergence and divergence of the water flow [8].

♦ *Overlay Function (OVERLAY)*. This operation has been designed to generate *multi-valued raster*, which can be used to combine different geo-images. It is to count rasters with more than one attribute and assign values to these attributes for each raster elements [4]. The representation schema of the data structure is shown in Fig. 4. It is important to note that two rasters can only be overlaid if they have the same geometry.

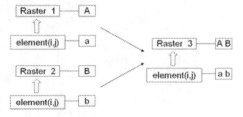

Fig. 4. Construction of multi-valued rasters

2.2 List of Procedures

It stores the set of procedures for each one of the analysis processes, describes the required data type and the constraints. SAM has a wide range of applications, not only to make *Landform classification* but also to perform the detection of *landslide* and *flooding* areas [3].

3 Landform Classification

Primary and *secondary attributes* have been used to classify DEM into different landforms. A method by Pennock described in [9] was implemented to automatic classification. The distribution of the landform elements is depicted in Fig. 5.

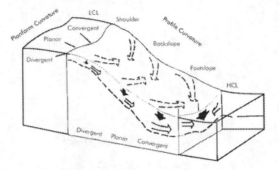

Fig. 5. Landform elements distribution

The slope, profile curvature and plan curvature have used to classify eleven different landforms (see Table 1). The landform classification is considered to evaluate the probable water movement and concentrations. Watershed is an area that drains water and other substances to common outlet as concentrated drainage. This area is normally defined as the total area flowing to a given outlet or pour point [8]. These areas are defined by *WATERSHED* function (Arc/Info).

Table 1. Classification of landform elements for a DEM with resolution of 10 m

Landform Elements	Acronym	Slope	Profile Curvature	Plan Curvature	Watershead
Divergent Shoulder	DHS	>0	>0.1	>0.1	NA
Planar Shoulder	PSH	>0	>0.1	>0.1 >-0.1	NA
Convergent Shoulder	CSH	>0	>0.1	>0.1	NA
Divergent BlackSlope	DBS	> 3.0	>-0.1 <0.1	>0.1	NA
Planar BackSlope	PBS	> 3.0	>-0.1 <0.1	>0.1 >0.1	NA
Convergent BackSlope	CBS	> 3.0	>-0.1 <0.1	>0.1	NA
Divergent FootSlope	DFS	>0	>-0.1	>0.1	NA
Planar FootSlope	PFS	>0	>-0.1	>0.1 >0.1	NA
Convergent FootSlope	CFS	>0	>-0.1	>0.1	NA
Low Catchment Level*	LCL	< 3.0	>-0.1	NA	< 500
High Catchment Level*	HCL	< 3.0	>-0.1	NA	> 500

The following pseudo-code has been designed to generate the *landform classification*:

```
program LFC{
  /* input layers
     dem        - Input Grid
     slope      - Grid to store the slope
     profcurv - Grid to store profile curvature
     plancurv - Grid to store plan curvature
     watershed -  Grid to store watershed area
     outgrid0  - Auxiliary grid
     outgrid1  - Auxiliary grid
     landformgrid - Grid to store Landform classification
  /* Landform classification process
     slope := CALCULATE_PLAN_CURVATURE(dem)
     profcurv := CALCULATE_PROFILE_CURVATURE(dem)
     plancurv:= CALCULATE_PLAN_CURVATURE(dem)
     outgrid0 := OVERLAY(profcurv, plancurv)
     outgrid1 := OVERLAY(slope, watershed)
     landformgrid := OVERLAY(outgrid0, outgrid1)
     classify (landform,landformgrid)
     visualize(landformgrid)
}
```

4 Results

By using SAM, we classify DEM. The algorithm has been applied to Tamaulipas State, Mexico. Some results are presented in this section. Tamaulipas State area is covered by DEM at two resolutions, 10 x 10 m and 100 x 100 m, generated in GEOLAB, interpolating line contours. The spatial data reference is UTM projection. In this case, we use two DEM of the same zone in two resolutions: 1) 1925 rows and 2410 columns (10 meter resolution), 2) 190 rows and 239 columns (100 meter resolution); see Fig 6. Fig. 6c and 6d show the landform classification of the DEM. The differences between these figures are due to the resolutions. Fig 6c has more level of detail than Fig 6d. The favorite value in both classifications is Planar Back Slope, meaning that the terrain is mainly planar (this is its semantics).

5 Conclusion

In this work, we propose the Spatial Analyzer Module integrated into GIS-application to analyze *landform characteristics* of geo-images. SAM generates primary attributes of DEM to detect landform elements in raster image data. In this approach, spatial and attributive data are used to generate raster. Using SAM, it is possible to define the essential characteristics of the raster spatial data.

This raster analysis is traditionally performed by using the methods based on topographic map-processing in manual way. Our approach significantly decreases the amount of time and effort required to quantify selected *terrain characteristics*. Other methods are designed to evaluate additional characteristics, which are different to the properties proposed in our approach. However, these methods can be integrated into SAM.

564   Marco Moreno et al.

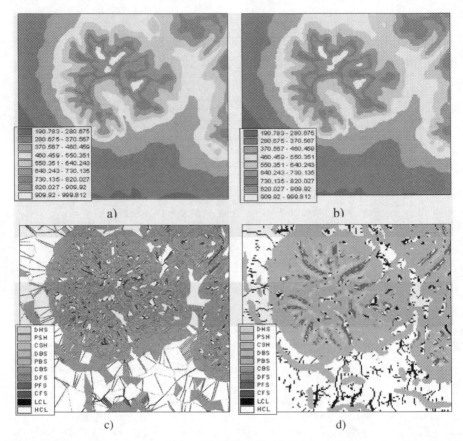

Fig. 6. a) DEM with resolution of 10 m, b) DEM with resolution of 100m, c) Landform classification of DEM with resolution of 10 m, d) Landform classification of DEM with resolution of 100 m

The generation of the *landform* layer facilitates the extraction-information of the spatial properties that can be used in other cartographic processes such as hydrological balance, automatic map description, identification of risk areas, map generalization, etc. Moreover, the *landform classification* approach is used to identify flooding areas and the path of the hydrological flows. Also, we can catch the *semantics* of DEM.

Acknowledgments. The authors of this paper wish to thank the CIC, CGPI, IPN and CONACYT for their support.

References

1. Goodchild, M.: Perspective: Browsing metadata, where do we go from here?, Vol. 10, Geo Info Systems, (2000), 30–31.
2. Wharton, G.: Progress in the use of drainage network indices for rainfall-runoff modelling and runoff prediction. Progress in Physical Geography, Vol. 18, (1994), 539-557.

3. Moreno, M., Levachkine, S, Torres, M. Quintero, R.: Geomorphometric Analysis of Raster Image Data to detect Terrain Ruggedness and Drainage Density. Speech and Image Analysis in A. Sanfeliu and J. Ruiz-Shulcloper (Eds), LNCS 2905, Springer-Verlag, Berlin Heidelberg, 2003, 643-650.
4. Molenaar, M.: An Introduction to the theory of spatial object modelling for GIS. Taylor & Francis, U.K., (1998).
5. Torres, M., Moreno, M., Menchaca, R. and Levachkine, S.: Making Spatial Analysis with a Distributed Geographical Information System, Series on APPLIED INFORMATICS - AI 2003, International Conference on Databases and Applications (DBA'2003), International Association of Science and Technology for Development (2003), 1245-12506.
6. Burrough, P.A.. Principles of Geographical Information Systems for Land Resources Assessment. Oxford University Press, New York, (1986).
7. Moore, I. D., Grayson, R. B., and Landson, A.: Digital Terrain Modelling: a Review of Hydrological, Geomorphological, and Biological Applications, Hydrological Processes. Vol. 5.3-30, (1999).
8. Zeverbergen, L. W., and C. R. Thorne: Quantitative Analysis of Land Surface Topography, Earth Surface Processes and Landforms, Vol. 12, (1987), 47-56.
9. Pennock, D.J., Zebarth, B.J. and de Jong, ELandform classification and soil distribution in hummocky terrain, Sasketchewan, Canada, Geoderma. 40, (1997), 297-315.

Homotopic Labeling of Elements
in a Tetrahedral Mesh for the Head Modeling

Jasmine Burguet and Isabelle Bloch

École Nationale Supérieure des Télécommunications
Département TSI – CNRS UMR 5141 LTCI
46 rue Barrault
75634 Paris Cedex 13, France
{jasmine.burguet,isabelle.bloch}@enst.fr

Abstract. In this paper we propose a method to obtain a tetrahedral model of the human head by labeling elements of a tetrahedral mesh. To work with meshes as regular as possible, we use the notion of Almost Regular Tesselation (ART) providing tetrahedral meshes with good quality elements. The proposed labeling method uses segmented M.R.I. containing main tissues of the head as input. The labeling is done under topological constraints in order to preserve topological arrangement of the head tissues. This process uses a notion of simple tetrahedra.

1 Introduction

In applications based on Electroencephalography (E.E.G.) and Magnetoencephalography (M.E.G.) data, electromagnetic field propagation is numerically calculated, for example using finite element methods. This computation is based on a meshed model of the head tissues generally obtained thanks to Magnetic Resonance Imaging (M.R.I.), in order to get realistic models. The purpose of this paper is to propose a method allowing us to build such head models, we focus particularly on the mesh generation description and the labeling of the tetrahedra according to the anatomical tissues. One main constraint of our method is the preservation of the topological arrangement of the head structures. Indeed, the literature mainly concerns the mesh construction, refinement or adaptation, but very few references deal with topological aspects, which is however an important criterion. The input image is a segmented M.R.I. containing the repartition of the main tissues of the head (for instance the brain, skull or scalp). Then we can assign the corresponding property (for example electrical conductivity) to each segmented tissue. The segmentation step is outside the scope of this paper but more details can be found in [1, 2]. Next we build the tetrahedral mesh. The quality of the tetrahedra influences the accuracy of the numerical computations. So bad shaped tetrahedra (sliver, cap or needle for instance) must be avoided. Ideally a Finite Element (F.E.) mesh should be entirely composed of regular tetrahedra, but unfortunately we cannot tessellate $\mathbb{R}^3$ only with equilateral tetrahedra. The common approaches to construct the meshes use a polyhedral representation of the boundary of the object to tessellate. The principle is the

A. Sanfeliu et al. (Eds.): CIARP 2004, LNCS 3287, pp. 566–573, 2004.

introduction of points in the interior of the object, and then a Delaunay tesselation is applied to generate the finite elements [3–6]. One drawback of these methods is the necessity of post-treatment to remove bad quality tetrahedra. The complexity of the head structures (see the brain for instance) and the use of M.R.I. (and so discrete surfaces instead of polyhedral ones) as input make the application of these methods very difficult. These are the reasons why we use for our purpose the Almost Regular Tesselation (ART) introduced by J. Pescatore which produces a tesselation made of good quality tetrahedra [2, 7]. Finally, after the tetrahedral mesh generation, we must label the tetrahedra according to their membership to the different segmented head tissues. It is a well known fact that a topology of interwoven spheres [8, 9] is a good approximation of the topology of head tissues. Therefore it is important to use a *homotopic* labeling method, i.e. a method under topological constraints, in order to prevent a bad configuration like a contact between the scalp and the brain. J. Pescatore proposed one based on the use of *simple* tetrahedra [2]. Using his algorithm, the topology of full sphere was guaranteed for the brain and the whole head. However a topology of empty sphere was not guaranteed for the skull or the scalp for instance. Up to now, no other methods takes care about the tetrahedral meshes topology. However, even if the segmented image satisfies the wanted topology, there is absolutely no guarantee that it is the case for the labeled mesh if we directly label the tetrahedra according to the segmentation, in particular if some segmented structures are very thin. Moreover, the numerical methods used to compute the electromagnetic field propagation are very sensitive to these bad configurations. So we propose a new labeling procedure that respects a spherical topology for all structures, that is the main contribution of our work.

The paper is organized as follows: Section 2 introduces the ART, presents the images we use as input and presents some initializations. Then Section 3 exposes the different topological tools we need for our method, like the tetrahedra simplicity or the notions of thinning/thickening. The labeling process is described in Section 4 and some results are proposed. Finally we discuss the obtained results and propose some perspectives to this work in Section 5.

2   Tetrahedral Mesh and Initializations from Segmented M.R.I.

Here we present the construction of a tetrahedral mesh called Almost Regular Tesselation (ART) (see [2, 7] for more details). A tetrahedral tesselation of $\mathbb{R}^3$ is *Almost Regular* if it is possible to tessellate $\mathbb{R}^3$ with tetrahedra such that each tetrahedron has a fixed connectivity. The principle of the ART construction is based on the following notion: a tetrahedron T is said to be *subdivision invariant* (SI) if we can divide T into 8 tetrahedra which are congruent to T (scaled by a factor $1/2$) by halving the edges of T. Note that the regular tetrahedron is not subdivision invariant. Figure 1 shows an example of SI tetrahedron. Using such a tetrahedron we can generate an ART having the following properties:

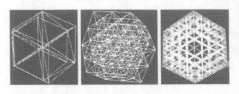

Fig. 1. Example of SI tetrahedron and its subdivision into 8 tetrahedra.

Fig. 2. ART construction with from left to right: $n = 0$, $n = 1$ and $n = 2$.

- it is structured: a tetrahedron has 4 neighbors per face, 18 neighbors per edge, 70 neighbors per vertex; a vertex is shared by 24 tetrahedra;
- it is conform: the intersection of two tetrahedra is either $\emptyset$, a face, an edge or a vertex.

To obtain a tesselation as regular as possible, we must use a SI tetrahedron having a good quality. There are several ways to evaluate this quality [10, 11], such as: $Q_{T_\alpha} = \alpha \frac{h_{max}}{\rho_T}$ where h_{max} is the largest edge of T, ρ_T the in-radius of T and α a regulation coefficient ($\alpha = \sqrt{6}/12$ for $Q_{T_\alpha} = 1$ if T is the regular tetrahedron). Since Q_{T_α} varies from 1 to ∞, we consider $Q_{T_\alpha}^{-1}$ that varies from 0 to 1. As shown in [7], we choose the following SI tetrahedron since it has an optimal quality (i.e. the closest to 1):

$$T^* = \left\{ \begin{pmatrix} 0 \\ 0 \\ 0 \end{pmatrix}, \begin{pmatrix} 1 \\ 0 \\ 0 \end{pmatrix}, \begin{pmatrix} \frac{1}{3} \\ \frac{2\sqrt{2}}{3} \\ 0 \end{pmatrix}, \begin{pmatrix} \frac{2}{3} \\ \frac{\sqrt{2}}{3} \\ \frac{2}{3} \end{pmatrix} \right\}, \quad Q_{T_\alpha^*}^{-1} = 0.866.$$

For our purpose, we build the ART initialization as the polyhedron P composed of 24 tetrahedra T^* sharing a common vertex. This vertex is chosen as the center of the segmented head $S(I)$, and we use a scale factor S to enlarge P until it contains entirely $S(I)$. Next, each tetrahedron is recursively subdivided n times until the desired precision is reached (see Figure 2). The final number of tetrahedra of the ART is $N_n = 24 * 8^n$ ($N_4 = 98304$ and $N_5 = 786432$). Moreover each tetrahedron of the ART has the same quality as T^*.

Our input images are segmented from M.R.I of human heads. Let I be a M.R.I. We suppose that the segmentation $S(I)$ of I contains n_t tissues of interest. In this paper we use a segmentation program developed in [1] producing segmented images under constraints to preserve the topology (see Figure 3). We associate an index j to each tissue, $1 \leq j \leq n_t$, such that the tissue j is bounded by the tissue $j + 1$, and $j = 1$ corresponds to the brain. The index $j = 0$ corresponds to the background of the image. Figure 4 presents the general scheme of the head and an example for $n_t = 3$.

Before the labeling, we associate to each tetrahedron t a vector $Tab(t)$ of size $n_t + 1$ containing the percentages of each component j (background or tissue) in t. The vectors are computed thanks to $S(I)$. The value $Tab(t)[0]$ corresponds to the percentage of background in t, $Tab(t)[1]$ to the percentage of brain and so on. For instance, if $n_t = 3$ and $Tab(t) = [0.11, 0.62, 0.27, 0.0]$, then t contains

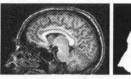 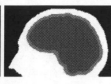 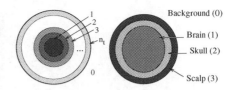

Fig. 3. M.R.I I (left) and segmentation $S(I)$ of I into Brain, Skull and Scalp.

Fig. 4. General scheme of the head for n_t tissues (left) and for $n_t = 3$ (right).

11% of background, 62% of brain, 27% of skull and 0% of Scalp. We define $P_{Head}(t) = \sum_{i=1}^{n_t} Tab(t)[i] = 1 - Tab(t)[0]$.

3 Topological Tools

3.1 Definitions

Our labeling method uses topological tools defined in [2,7]. First let us introduce some basic concepts. We suppose that vertices, edges, faces and tetrahedra contain their boundaries and they are also called $0-$, $1-$, $2-$ and $3-simplexes$, respectively. Let O be a set of tetrahedra and k an integer such that $k < 3$.

A k-simplex s is said to be *shared* if there exist two tetrahedra $t_1, t_2 \in O$ such that $s \in t_1 \cap t_2$. Otherwise, s is called *bare*. Let t be a tetrahedron. The *neighborhood* $V(t)$ of t is the union of all tetrahedra t_i such that $t_i \cap t \neq \emptyset$. We denote by $Bd(t)$ the *boundary* of t defined as the union of the whole faces of t. The *attachment set* of t $Bd_s(t)$ is the union of all the shared k-simplexes of t, and the *bare set* of t is $Bd_b(t) = Bd(t) \backslash Bd_s(t)$. Two simplexes s_1 and s_2 are said to be *adjacent* if and only if $s_1 \cap s_2 \neq \emptyset$. A set of simplexes $s_1, s_2, \ldots, s_k$ in which each s_i is adjacent to s_{i+1}, $1 \leq i < k$, is called a *path of simplexes* from s_1 to s_k. Then the set of tetrahedra O is said to be *connected* if for any pair of tetrahedra $t, t' \in O$, there exists a path of simplexes $s_1, s_2, \ldots, s_k$ such that $s_1 = t$, $s_k = t'$ and, for $i = 1, \ldots, k$, $s_i \in O$. A maximal connected subset of O is called *connected component* of O.

We suppose that O is connected. Following Kong [12] we define the *simplicity* of a tetrahedron as follows:

Definition 1. *Let t be a tetrahedron and O a connected set of tetrahedra. Then t is said to be* simple *if there exits a homotopy equivalence from O to $O \cup t$ or from O to $O \backslash \{t\}$.*

There exists a *local characterization* of the simplicity of a tetrahedron:

Theorem 1 (from [2]). *The tetrahedron t is simple in O if and only if $Bd_s(t)$ and $Bd_b(t)$ are not empty and are connected.*

In Figure 5, let us consider the tetrahedra t_1 and t_2 and their attachment sets. In (a), the tetrahedron t_1 is simple in O_1 since $Bd_s(t_1)$ and $Bd_b(t_1)$ are not empty and are connected. In (b), t_2 is not simple in O_2 because $Bd_s(t_2)$ is not connected.

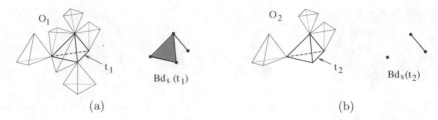

Fig. 5. Two tetrahedra t_1 and t_2 (left) and their attachment sets (right).

Fig. 6. Result of the head construction for $n = 4$ (middle) and $n = 5$ (right).

3.2   Homotopic Thinning / Thickening

Based on the use of simple tetrahedra, we define the following notions:

Definition 2. *We call* homotopic thinning *(resp.* homotopic thickening*) of a connected set of tetrahedra O the sequential deletion (resp. addition) of simple tetrahedra in O. A set of tetrahedra S' obtained by a homotopic thinning or homotopic thickening of a set S is said to be* homotopic *to S.*

One first application of these notions is the constitution of the set containing the tetrahedra of the head among all the tetrahedra of the ART. First we choose a tetrahedron t which belongs to the head. For example, if $n_t=3$, we choose a t such that $Tab(t) = [0.0, 1.0, 0.0, 0.0]$. Then we perform a homotopic thickening of the set $H = \{t\}$: we add to H simple tetrahedra x such that $P_{Head}(x) > \mu_{Head}$ where $\mu_{Head} \geq 0$ is a parameter of the method. For instance, if $Tab(x) = [0.71, 0.18, 0.11, 0.00]$ and $\mu_{Head} = 0.10$, then $P_{Head}(x) = 0.29 \geq \mu_{Head}$, so x can be added to H during the thickening if x is also simple. The resulting set corresponds to the head and is homotopic to a single tetrahedron, i.e. to a full sphere. We can see in Figure 6 the result of this labeling for $n = 4$ and $n = 5$, with $S = 160$ and $\mu_{Head} = 0$.

One new tool we propose to label the different tissues of the head is the original notion of *interior thinning*. First, a tetrahedron t is said to be *interior* to a set of tetrahedra O if $t \in O$ and if $V(t) \subset O$. Then we say that a tetrahedron is *removable* if it is simple and if it also satisfies another condition (for instance $\{Tab(t)[2](x) < 0.5\}$). An interior thinning of a set H begins with the choice of an interior tetrahedron t in H. Then, we apply a homotopic thinning to the set $H\backslash t$ (which is homotopic to an empty sphere) starting from t and deleting *removable* tetrahedra until stability. The corresponding pseudocode is:

- **list_of_tetrahedra** l_1 ← neighbors by face of t; //border of the thinning
- **list_of_tetrahedra** l_2 ← NULL;   //next border of the thinning
- **tetrahedron** t ← interior_tetrahedron;

   Iterate until stability
      for each tetrahedron x in l_1
         if x is removable **then** delete x from H and update l_2;
         else put x into l_2;
    l_1 ← l_2;
    l_2 ← NULL;

Since we delete only simple tetrahedra during this thinning, the set of deleted tetrahedra is homotopic to a full sphere whereas the set of remaining tetrahedra R is homotopic to an empty sphere. An example of the result of an interior thinning applied to the head H is shown in Figure 7 (a tetrahedron was removable if it was only simple, without additional condition).

Fig. 7. Result of an interior thinning of the head by deleting simple tetrahedra (light gray set).

4   Homotopic Tissues Labeling

We now propose a new complete labeling scheme. We label the tissues from the most exterior to the most interior one, thus from $j = n_t$ to $j = 1$. Let $O \subset H$ be the set of tetrahedra which are not yet labeled (initially $O = H$ and $j = n_t$).

First we choose a tetrahedron t interior to O such that $\text{Tab}(t)[1]=1$ (t contains only brain). Then we iterate the following process while $j > 1$:

1. We apply an interior thinning to the set O, a tetrahedron x being removable if it satisfies the two following properties:
   - x is simple,
   - there exists a tissue i such that $0 < i \leq n_t$, $i \neq j$, $Tab(t)[i] > Tab(t)[j]$.
   The tetrahedra of the remaining set R are labeled as j.
2. The set O becomes $O \backslash R$, j becomes $j - 1$, and we eventually update t.

Let us consider Figure 8. In (a) the set O and the interior tetrahedron t are shown. We see in (b) the result of the labeling for the tissue j. Next, in Figure 8 (c) and (d) we can see the labeling of tissue $j - 1$ obtained with the updated set O. After the labeling for all $j > 1$, we label the final set $O \backslash R$ (i.e. the removed tetrahedra during the labeling of tissue 2) with $j = 1$ (i.e. the brain).

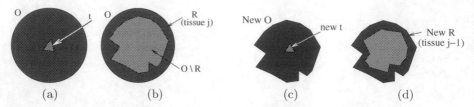

Fig. 8. Labeling of tissues such that $j > 2$.

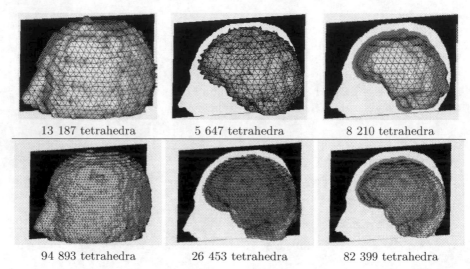

| 13 187 tetrahedra | 5 647 tetrahedra | 8 210 tetrahedra |
| 94 893 tetrahedra | 26 453 tetrahedra | 82 399 tetrahedra |

Fig. 9. Result of the head labeling for the scalp, skull and brain (from left to right), for $n = 4$ (top) and $n = 5$ (bottom), with $S = 160$.

After the labeling for all $j > 1$, we label the final set $O \backslash R$ (i.e. the removed tetrahedra during the labeling of tissue 2) with $j = 1$ (i.e. the brain).

In Figure 9, the results (exterior surfaces) of the topological labeling are shown for the scalp, skull and brain respectively (the number of tetrahedra for each tissue is also given).

5   Conclusion and Perspectives

We proposed in this paper a way to build a tetrahedral model of the head. First we constructed an ART mesh to tessellate a volume containing the head. Then, using a segmented M.R.I. of the head, we defined a homotopic process to label tetrahedra of the ART in order to get a tetrahedral head. Our method guarantees that the resulting head has a topology of interwoven spheres. Examples shown in the paper are obtained for $n_t=3$ tissues, but our method is adapted to any value of n_t, as soon as these tissues have a spherical topology (we can moreover consider the Cerebro-Spinal Fluid for example). But the use of a segmentation having a non-adequate topology (for example segmentation with isolated components or including the jaw in the skull) can produce results with bad a geometrical quality. One perspective of this work is to increase the robustness of our method for any type of segmented head, by releasing topological constraints during the labeling.

In several applications like the study of the impact of the exposure to electromagnetic waves from mobile phones on human health, we may want to focus our attention on precise places, like the ear. A multi-scale approach could be of high interest to model important localizations with a higher degree of accuracy.

References

1. Dokladal, P., Bloch, I., Couprie, M., Ruijters, D., Urtasun, R., Garnero, L.: Topologically Controlled Segmentation of 3D Magnetic Resonance Images of the Head by using Morphological Operators. Pattern Recognition **36** (2003) 2463–2478
2. Pescatore, J.: Maillages Homotopiques Tétraédriques des Tissus de la Tête pour le Calcul du Problème Direct en Électro/Magneto-Encéphalographie. PhD thesis, École Nationale Supérieure des Télécommunications (2001)
3. George, J.: Computer Implementation of the Finite Element Method. PhD thesis, Dept. of Computer Science Stanford University (1971)
4. George, P., Séveno, E.: The Advancing Front Mesh Method Revisited. Internation Journal in Numerical Methods in Engineering **37** (1994) 3605–3619
5. Peraire, J., Morgan, K.: Unstructured Mesh Generation Including Directional Refinement for Aerodynamics Flow Simulation. Finite Elements in Analysis and Design **25** (1997) 343–355
6. Bowyer, A.: Computing Dirichlet Tesselations. The Computer Journal **24** (1981) 162–167
7. Pescatore, J., Bloch, I., Baillet, S., Garnero, L.: FEM Tetrahedral Mesh of Head Tissues from MRI under Geometric and Topological Constraints for Applications in EEG and MEG. In: Human Brain Mapping HBM 2001, Brighton, UK (2001) 218
8. Munck, J.: The Potential Distribution in a Layered Anisotropic Spheroidal Volume Conductor. Journal of applied Physics **64** (1988) 464–470
9. Sarvas, J.: Basic Mathematical and Electromagnetic Concepts of the Biomagnetics Inverse Problem. Physics in Medical Biology **32** (1987) 11–22
10. Parthasarathy, V., Graichen, C., Hathaway, A.: A Comparison of tetrahedron Quality Measures. Finite Elements in Analysis and Design **15** (1993) 255–261
11. Martinez, E., Garnero, L., Bloch, I.: Refined Adaptive Meshes for the Localization of Cortical Activity. Technical Report 2003D001, Ecole Nationale Supérieure des Télécommunications (2003)
12. Kong, T.Y.: On Topology Preservation in 2D and 3d Thinning. Internation Journal of Patterne Recognition and Artificial Intelligence **9** (1995) 813–844

Grey Level Image Components
for Multi-scale Representation

Giuliana Ramella and Gabriella Sanniti di Baja

Istituto di Cibernetica E. Caianiello, CNR, Via Campi Flegrei 34,
80078, Pozzuoli (Naples), Italy
(g.ramella,g.sannitidibaja)@cib.na.cnr.it

Abstract. A method to identify grey level image components, suitable for multi-scale analysis, is presented. Generally, a single threshold is not sufficient to separate components, perceived as individual entities. Our process is based on iterated identification and removal of pixels, with different grey level values, causing merging of grey level components at the highest resolution level. A growing process is also performed to restore pixels far from the fusion area, so as to preserve as much as possible shape and size of the components. In this way, grey level components can be kept as separated also when lower resolution representations are built, by means of a decimation process. Moreover, the information contents of the image, in terms of shape and relative size of the components, is preserved through lower resolution representations, compatibly with the resolution.

1 Introduction

Grey level images are of large use in image analysis tasks. One of the main problems that have to be faced is image segmentation, necessary to distinguish foreground components from the background. The method to be used depends on problem domain. The easiest way, unfortunately seldom effective, is to fix a threshold and to assign to the foreground all pixels with grey level larger than the threshold, and to the background all remaining pixels, e.g., [1]. The result of this process is, generally, an image with a number of components different from the expected one. Actually, the threshold should assume different values in different parts of the image, to allow correct identification of foreground components. These methods are generally referred to as multi-threshold methods, e.g., [2,3]. An unwanted side effect of thresholding is that the size of foreground components is likely to be significantly reduced with respect to the perceived size. In fact, the same grey level distribution can characterise both the fusion area among foreground components perceived as individual entities, and (peripheral) parts of foreground components, located far from the fusion area. More sophisticated techniques, especially based on watershed transformation, generally produce better result [4-6]. These techniques, however, need a complex preliminary phase to identify the sources for watershed segmentation, as well as an equally complex post-processing phase necessary to reduce the unavoidable over-segmentation.

The method that we propose in this paper is a small addition to the literature on image segmentation. It is based on non-topological erosion and topological expansion, is computationally non expensive and in the experiments we have done performed quite well. Our method can be classified as a multi-threshold method. In fact, once the minimum and the maximum possible values of the threshold have been

A. Sanfeliu et al. (Eds.): CIARP 2004, LNCS 3287, pp. 574–581, 2004.
© Springer-Verlag Berlin Heidelberg 2004

fixed, depending on problem domain, the threshold is automatically increased and the thresholding process is repeated. An advantage with respect to other multi-threshold methods is that we avoid an excessive reduction of the size of foreground components. In fact, after each thresholding that actually produces a separation of foreground components, a growing process is accomplished, to restore pixels of the foreground components far from the fusion area. Our method has proved to be useful especially when a multi-scale approach to image analysis is followed. If a lower resolution image is obtained, by applying a decimation process to the non-segmented initial image, perceived individual grey level components tend to merge, producing one agglomerate where individual components are no longer distinguishable, especially at low resolution. In turn, if a decimation process is applied to a segmented image and care is taken to avoid merging of individual components, shape information is better preserved also at low resolution. We will show the performance of our segmentation method in the framework of multi-scale image analysis. To this purpose, we will illustrate a decimation process able to prevent merging among individual components, within the limits of decreasing resolution. To preserve topology through lower resolutions, we first identify and single out in the input image all significant foreground components. Then, after each decimation process, we use the segmented high resolution initial image as a reference set and open *canals* so as to separate foreground parts that constituted individual entities at the highest resolution.

2   Detecting Grey Level Components

Let G be the input grey level image, and let g denote any pixel of G as well as its grey level value. A starting value for the threshold, θ_i, needs to be fixed, depending on grey level distribution in the image. The value of θ_i should be such that all pixels with grey level $g \leq \theta_i$ can, without any doubt, be interpreted correctly as background pixels. A final value for the threshold, θ_f, needs also to be fixed. This value should be such that all pixels with grey level $g > \theta_f$ certainly belong to some component, perceived as a foreground component. In the most general case, the initial value θ_i can be set to the minimal grey level found in the image and the final value θ_f can be set to the maximal grey level, decreased by 1. Of course, the initial and final values of the threshold should be more carefully set, depending on user's needs. In particular, a very small initial value could cause the detection of a number of noisy components, erroneously interpreted as belonging to the foreground. In turn, the final value should be set in such a way to prevent excessive foreground fragmentation, which would split foreground components perceived as individual entities into a number of meaningless components. All pixels with grey level value g, such that $\theta_i < g \leq \theta_f$, can, in principle, be either foreground or background pixels. In particular, pixels having the same grey level in different parts of the image can be differently classified. The decision on whether they belong to foreground or background is taken during segmentation.

We iterate a process, based on non-topological erosion and topological expansion, which uses different threshold values, automatically obtained increasing the initial value by an increment δ. The increment δ can be set to any value greater than or equal to one, depending on problem domain. In particular, a small increment is preferable for images where grey level distribution of the foreground is in a large range and also small variations of grey level are significant.

Let $\theta_i=\theta_1$, θ_2, ..., $\theta_n=\theta_f$, be the n values of the threshold, where the threshold at the k-th iteration is $\theta_k = \theta_{k-1} + \delta$. In the following, we will describe the process done at the k-th iteration, which consists of two steps, namely i) non-topological erosion and ii) topological expansion. To separate foreground components that result to be merged in a fusion area characterised by a grey value corresponding to the current threshold value, pixels placed in the fusion area among components have to be identified and assigned to the background (i.e., their grey levels have to be lowered to the background value θ_1). To this purpose, non-topological erosion is accomplished. This is a process that assigns pixels belonging to the border of foreground components to the background, regardless of the topology changes possibly caused by this operation. Border pixels are identified as pixels having at least an edge-neighbour in the background, i.e., pixels with at least one edge-neighbour with grey level equal to θ_1. Non-topological erosion is iterated until border pixels are found. In particular, at the k-th iteration, pixels that are possibly placed in a fusion area are those with grey level g such that $\theta_1<g\leq\theta_k$. Among pixels with grey level in the current range of values, only those that, when inspected, result to be border pixels are assigned to the background.

Border pixels are examined in increasing grey level order and have their grey levels lowered to the background value θ_1, regardless on whether connectedness is preserved in their neighbourhood. However, the number of connected components of foreground pixels, i.e., with grey level greater than θ_1, in the neighbourhood of any removed pixel is counted. In fact, if more than one component is found, this indicates that the removed pixel was actually a fusion point among foreground components. If this is the case, a fragmentation counter f_c, initially set to zero, is increased by one. Each removed pixel is orderly stored in a suitable list L, to keep track of its coordinates and grey level. Removal is repeated on the image as far as border pixels with grey level in the current range of values are found. At the end of this process, the counter f_c is examined. If $f_c=0$, no fusion occurred for the current threshold, and all removed pixels should be recovered to preserve the information contents of the image. In turn, if $f_c\neq0$, some fusion actually occurred. Of course, not all pixels removed at the k-th iteration were actually responsible of fusion among components. Those far from the fusion area should be recovered. Thus, in any case, before proceeding to the successive iteration with a new threshold, topological expansion is performed, to restore size and shape of foreground components, which have been modified by non-topological erosion. Of course, recovery of foreground pixels is done in such a way to still maintain as separated the components that have been singled out. The process is straightforward if no fusion occurred at θ_k. All pixels previously stored in L are newly assigned their initial grey level in the image G.

In turn, if some fusion occurred, care should be taken when setting on G the pixels from L. To this purpose, pixels of L are examined in the opposite order with respect to their insertion order in L. For the current pixel p, the number of components of foreground pixels (i.e., pixels with grey level greater than θ_1) is counted after p is restored in G. If only one component is found, p is just assigned on G its initial grey level, as no fusion occurred in p. Otherwise, p is also suitably marked in G to point out that it was actually a fusion point.

Once all pixels of the list L have been processed and restored in G, the fusion marker is iteratively propagated onto successive neighbours of the marked pixels, provided that these neighbours are pixels that have been recovered from L. Marker propagation is performed to identify all pixels in the fusion area. Unfortunately, marker propagation may include in the fusion area more pixels than those whose removal is strictly necessary to separate foreground components. Since we aim at changing the status of the lowest possible number of pixels, a suitable process is performed to reduce the thickness of the set of marked pixels, so as to better preserve the original contents of G. Finally, all pixels still marked as fusion points are set to θ_1, which results in the separation of foreground components at θ_k.

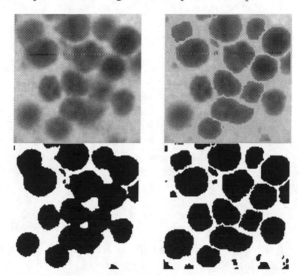

Fig. 1. Top: the input grey level image G, left, and the resulting image G_1, right. Bottom: binary images obtained from G, left, and G_1, right.

The threshold θ_k is incremented by δ and the (k+1)-th iteration of non-topological erosion and topological expansion are performed, to separate foreground parts at the successive threshold value. The process is iterated until all threshold values are used.

The effect of our segmentation process can be seen in Fig. 1. The two images in Fig.1 top, respectively show the input grey level image G (left) and the image G_1 (right), resulting after non-topological erosion and topological expansion. The two images in Fig. 1 bottom, show the binarizations of G and G_1. In the image to the right pixels with grey level equal to or smaller than θ_1 are set to 0 and the remaining pixels are set to 1, to point out which are the foreground components singled out by our process; in the image to the left a threshold value greater than θ_1 has been used for the binarization so as to favour segmentation, which however is not satisfactory. The values for θ_1, θ_n and δ have been heuristically selected, based on the image domain. In particular, $\theta_1=70$, $\theta_n=170$ and $\delta=5$.

3   A Topology Preserving Multi-scale Representation

As pointed out in Introduction, our segmentation method can find a useful application in multi-scale image analysis. Having a multi-scale image representation is of interest in a number of tasks, e.g., [7-11], since successively condensed representations of the information in the input image are available and the user can often work with a reduced data set, at low resolution, which still provides a reasonable representation of the most relevant regions.

Image pyramids are among the most common multi-scale representation systems [12]. Both continuous and discrete methods to build pyramids can be found in the literature. We here describe a discrete method to build a topology preserving pyramid.

Two important features to use pyramids in the framework of image analysis are shift invariance and topology preservation [13]. Representations at low resolution can differ significantly from the input image, when this is shifted or, better, when the partition grid used to performed decimation, is shifted along the image. It is, in fact, quite obvious that a different position of the partition grid generally leads to a significantly different image pyramid. Moreover, the mechanism used to build the pyramid can significantly alter, besides geometry and shape, also the topology of the input image, so that the representative power of lower resolution images would become questionable. Topology preservation is not considered in methods based on filters, [14,15], while is taken into account in generation methods of irregular pyramids. In this latter case, however, the father-child relation is lost or altered, [16, 17]. Our aim is to obtain an almost shift invariant and topology preserving grey level pyramid, without altering or destroying the father-child relation, and based on a regular tessellation. We introduced in [18] a method to generate a pyramid, starting from a binary image, which is shift invariant and topology preserving, within the limits of decreasing resolution. The method here illustrated is an extension of the one in [18] to the case of grey level images.

To build the pyramid, a recursive subdivision into quadrants of the $2^n \times 2^n$ grey level image, G_1, is performed. At each recursion step, resolution decreases by four and the process terminates when the image including one single pixel is built. This is the general scheme, but is obvious that resolution levels with less than 16 pixels in each dimension can be disregarded, as they would not be useful in shape analysis tasks. Thus, the pyramid construction will actually end as soon as the $2^4 \times 2^4$ image is built. The base of the pyramid is the input image G_1 at full resolution (128×128, for the example shown in this paper), the next level of the pyramid represents the image G_2 at a uniformly lower resolution (64×64) and so on. The apex of the pyramid is the 16×16 image G_4.

Pyramid construction is accomplished by using the image G_1 segmented by the process described in Section 2. Foreground components are assigned an identity label by means of connected component labelling. To build G_2, a partition grid is superimposed onto G_1. The grid consists of non-overlapping blocks of 2×2 pixels. Each block originates one pixel in G_2. The four pixels in a block are the *children*, and the pixel corresponding to the whole block in G_2 is the *parent*. The grey level value of a parent pixel is computed by taking into account number, positions and grey levels of its four children. The label identifying the foreground component to which children belong is also transferred to the parent pixel. When children belong to different components, a majority rule is used to decide the label for the parent pixel.

Depending on the position of the partition grid over G_1, a pixel p in the image G_1 belongs to one out of four possible blocks, including three out of the eight neighbours of p. In turn, each neighbour of p belongs to a different number of blocks, depending on its position with respect to p. Each edge-neighbour of p belongs to two different 2×2 blocks including p, while each vertex-neighbour belongs to exactly one such 2×2 block. See Fig. 2.

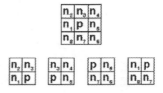

Fig. 2. The eight neighbours of p, top, and the four 2×2 blocks that can be obtained by shifting the partition grid.

The decimation filter is a 3×3 mask of weights, with central value 4, edge-neighbours valued 2 and vertex-neighbours valued 1. This multiplicative mask is centred on each pixel p of G_1 with even coordinates (2j, 2k), and the value of the corresponding parent pixel p' with coordinates (j, k) in G_2, is computed. The image G_2 is then re-scaled by linearly re-scaling its pixels to the range {0, 255} and the mask is applied to build G_3, and so on.

Since the multiplicative mask takes into account all possible 2×2 non-overlapping blocks, the resulting pyramid will be almost shift invariant. As concerns topology preservation, a decision is necessary on whether foreground or background components have to be favoured, since when resolution decreases it can be impossible to preserve both. We favour foreground components.

We use a landscape representation of the grey level image, where the grey level of a pixel is interpreted as the height in a topographic map. In this way, the image G_1 can be interpreted as consisting of a number of *islands*, some of which may include *lakes* and *craters*. Islands of G_1 close to each other can merge into a unique component in G_2, lakes and craters can be transformed into less deep craters, and new lakes can appear, due to deformation of *bays*. To preserve topology in the limits of reduced resolution, we use G_1 as a reference image and open suitable canals at lower resolutions to separate islands erroneously merged into a unique component. We also open spurious craters rather than filling them. In this way, the effect produced by the modified value distribution better resembles that of the original image. This opening is done at each resolution level before computing the next pyramid level, so as to avoid chain reaction effects.

To open canals in G_2, we check for each foreground pixel if a neighbour exists, having different identity label. In the affirmative, the pixel with the lowest grey level (and, hence, the lowest relevance) in the adjoining pair is assigned to the background.

A crater is a set of pixels with value strictly smaller than all values of the pixels on the 8-connected rim of the crater. Craters and lakes which do not correspond to craters and lakes in the full resolution image are interpreted as spurious entities, and are transformed into bays by iteratively identifying their bottom and by assigning to the rim of the bottom the grey level of the bottom.

The pyramid built for the grey level image shown in Fig.1, is illustrated in Fig. 3. Only levels 64×64, 32×32, and 16×16 are

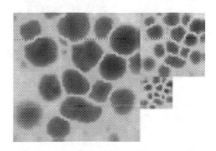

Fig. 3. The pyramid built for the grey level image shown in Fig.1. A zoom factor 2 is used.

shown, since level 128×128 is the image in Fig. 1 top right. A zoom factor 2 has been used to make visible these resolution levels. We note that foreground components are preserved also at low resolution.

4 Conclusion

We have introduced a method to single out foreground components, which is suitable in the framework of multi-scale grey level image analysis.

Foreground components detection is done by using an iterated process, based on non-topological erosion followed by topological expansion. A multi-scale representation is then built starting from this image. To limit translation dependency, the four different images that would be generated by shifting, in the four possible positions, the partition grid used to build lower resolutions are combined. Topology preservation is favoured by identifying on the highest resolution image all foreground components. This allows us to open canals to separate, at lower resolution, foreground parts that constituted individual entities at the highest resolution level. Naturally, topology is preserved compatibly with the resolution, through lower resolution pyramid levels.

The method we have developed was mainly intended to treat biological specimens, as the one shown in Fig.1. However, we think that our method could also be used in other fields, e.g., for document analysis. More in general, the method is adequate for application areas dealing with grey level images in which foreground components can be distinguished from the background.

References

1. Brink A.D., Thresholding of digital images using two-dimensional entropies, Pattern Recognition 25-8 (1992) 803-808.
2. O'Gorman L., Binarization and multithresholding of document images using connectivity, Graphical Models and Image Processing (1994) 56-6.
3. Papamarkos N., Strouthopoulos C., Andreadis I., Multithresholding of color and gray-level images through a neural network technique, Image and Vision Computing 18-3 (2000) 213-222.
4. Vincent L., Soille P., Watersheds in digital space: an efficient algorithm based on immersion simulations. IEEE Trans. PAMI 13- 6 (1991) 583-598.
5. Beucher S., Meyer F., The morphological approach to segmentation: the watershed transformation, in Mathematical Morphology in Image Processing, E. Dougherty ed., Marcel Dekker, Chap. 12 433-481 (1993).
6. Bleau A., Leon L.J., Watershed-based Segmentation and Region Merging, Computer Vision and Image Understanding 77 (2000) 317-370.
7. Yacoub S.B., Jolion J.M:, "Hierarchical line extraction", Proceedings of IEEE Conf. on Vision, Image and Signal Processing 142 (1995) 7-14.
8. Tan C.L., Loh S.K.K., "Efficient edge detection using hierarchical structures", Pattern Recognition, 26-1 (1993) 127-135.
9. Brzakovic D., Luo X.M., Brzakovic P., An approach to automated detection of tumors in mammograms. IEEE Transactions on Medical Imaging 9-3 (1990) 233-241.
10. Tan C.L., Ng P.O., Text extraction using pyramid. Pattern Recognition 31-1 (1998) 63-72.
11. Bosworth J., Koshimizu T., Acton S.T., Automated segmentation of surface soil moisture from landsat TM data, Proceedings of IEEE Southwest Symposium on Image Analysis and Interpretation (1998) 70-74.
12. Rosenfeld, A. (Ed.), Multiresolution Image Processing and Analysis. Springer-Verlag, Berlin (1984).

13. Bister M., Cornelis J., Rosenfeld A., A critical view of pyramid segmentation algorithms, Pattern Recognition Letters 11- 9 (1990) 605-617.
14. Burt P.J., The Pyramid as a Structure for Efficient Computation, in A. Rosenfeld, (ed.) Multiresolution Image Processing and Analysis, Springer-Verlag, Berlin (1984).
15. Greenspan H., Belongie S., Goodman R., Perona P., Rakshit S., Anderson C.H., Overcomplete steerable pyramid filters and rotation invariance, Proceeding IEEE Computer Vision and Pattern Recognition, Seattle, Washington (1994) 222-228.
16. Arman F., Pearce J.A., Unsupervised classification of cell images using pyramid node linking, IEEE Trans Biomedical Engineering 37- 6 (1990) 647-50.
17. Montanvert A., Meer P., Rosenfeld A., Hierarchical Image Analysis Using Irregular Tessellations, IEEE Trans. PAMI 13 – 4 (1991) 307-316.
18. Borgefors G., Ramella G., Sanniti di Baja G., Shape and topology preserving multi-valued image pyramids for multi-resolution skeletonization, Pattern Recognition Letters 22 (2001) 741-751.

Performance Improvement
in a Fingerprint Classification System
Using Anisotropic Diffusion

Gonzalo Vallarino, Gustavo Gianarelli, Jose Barattini, Alvaro Gómez,
Alicia Fernández, and Alvaro Pardo

Institute of Electrical Engineering
Faculty of Engineering
Universidad de la República
Montevideo, Uruguay

Abstract. In a previous work, [1], we evaluated a classification algorithm based on the Karu-Jain method [2] and compared the performance with a fully manual method used at the Dirección Nacional de Identificación Civil (DNIC). In this paper, we analyze the high performance improvement achieved using anisotropic diffusion instead of pure averaging for the directions smoothing. We also define a quality measure that shows high correlation with the experts' criteria. The results are evaluated over 2800 images extracted from a 4 million fingerprint card archive maintained by DNIC.

1 Introduction

This work is part of an ongoing collaboration between the Universidad de la República and the Dirección Nacional de Identificación Civil (DNIC) concerned with civil identification affairs in Uruguay. The goal of this joint project is to evaluate an automatic fingerprint classification system compatible with the manual method that has been used by DNIC for several years. DNIC's classification scheme is based on the Vucetich system that has four fundamental classes: Arch, Right and Left Loop, and Whorl. In [1] we presented the results obtained in a first stage of the project. In this work we analyze the improvements achieved using anisotropic diffusion for direction smoothing instead of mean filters. For classification we propose some modifications to the algorithm proposed by Karu and Jain [2]. This algorithm is based on a singularities approach. The classification uses some heuristic criteria applied on the number and position of singularities.

To evaluate the algorithm we use the database described in [1], which is a representative sample of more than 4 hundred individual fingerprint cards from the national archive held by DNIC. Each card has a ten-print image and the corresponding manual classification formula provided by human experts. Given the heterogeneity of fingerprints obtained from the database, it becomes mandatory to have a quality measure in order to reject bad impressions.

A. Sanfeliu et al. (Eds.): CIARP 2004, LNCS 3287, pp. 582–588, 2004.

We define a global quality measure that takes into account the whole fingerprint and a local quality measure that only uses the regions surrounding the singularities. To compute these measures we use Gabor Filters as described in [3]

The quality of a fingerprint image is estimated using global and local features and also the number of steps in the iterative smoothing process. Based on this quality measure the fingerprints are divided into three categories: good, poor and bad. We learn the decision thresholds using a training set categorized by the DNIC experts.

The paper is organized as follows: In section 2 we describe the fingerprint database. In section 3 we describe the anisotropic diffusion algorithm. In section 4 the classification algorithm. In section 5 we present the results and the performance of the algorithm tested on our database. In section 6 we present the quality measure. Finally, in section 7 we outline the conclusions of this work.

2   Fingerprint Database

DNIC holds the fingerprints of more than four million people. The fingerprints of each individual are stored in a paper card as shown in [1]. The card archive is indexed and physically ordered by the ten-fingerprint classification formula of each individual. In order to test the classification algorithm, the whole paper card archive was sampled and more than four hundred cards were digitized to obtain over 4000 fingerprint digital images. The cards were digitized at a resolution of 500 dpi and the fingerprints extracted to become 512×480 pixels images. In [1] we showed some statistics on the sample fingerprint database.

3   The Anisotropic Diffusion Algorithm

The direction vector field of the fingerprint is one of the most important features used in classification algorithms. Following [2] we perform a smoothing of the directions before classification. Instead of using a simple mean filter, we propose to use anisotropic diffusion. One of the main drawbacks with the mean filter is that it rapidly destroys singularities, especially deltas. Furthermore, the number of mean filtering iterations needed to obtain a reasonable direction field depends on each fingerprint.

On the other hand, anisotropic diffusion, is well known to respect singularities better than mean filtering. Also, it is known that during the evolution of the anisotropic diffusion singularities can disappear but never be created [5].

Although we obtained good results with the anisotropic diffusion filter, we are aware that there exist other diffusion algorithms that deal directly with directions and avoid artificial normalization steps. For example, this approach of direction diffusion was introduced in [6], and a complete framework for direction diffusion was introduced in [8]. In [8] Tang, Sapiro and Caselles introduce the algorithms for orientation diffusion based on the harmonic maps theory. In this way, they guarantee that during the continuous evolution, the diffused orientation remain living on the unit circle. Although, the same is not valid for the corresponding numerical implementations, some numerical advances have been recently made. We leave the study of this for future research.

For a continuous image $p : \Omega (\subset R^2) \to R$ the anisotropic diffusion evolution is given by the following PDE:

$$\frac{\partial p}{\partial t} = \nabla \left(\frac{\nabla p}{\sqrt{\beta^2 + ||\nabla p||^2}} \right) \tag{1}$$

For discrete images, we use the following numerical implementation (see [4] for details on this point):

$$\frac{p_{j,k}^{t+\Delta t} - p_{j,k}^{t}}{\Delta t} = D_j^- \left\{ \frac{D_j^+ p_{j,k}^t}{\sqrt{\beta^2 + \| D_k^+ p_{j,k}^t \|^2 + \| m(D_j^+ p_{j,k}^t, D_j^- p_{j,k}^t) \|^2}} \right\} + \ldots$$

$$\ldots + D_k^- \left\{ \frac{D_j^+ p_{j,k}^t}{\sqrt{\beta^2 + \| D_k^+ p_{j,k}^t \|^2 + \| m(D_j^+ p_{j,k}^t, D_j^- p_{j,k}^t) \|^2}} \right\} \tag{2}$$

where $D_j^\pm$ y $D_k^\pm$ are the forward and backward differences j and k, and the operator $m(.)$ is $m(x,y) = minmod(x,y) = min(x,y) [sign(|x|) + sign(|y|)]/2$. The numerical stability condition is easily computed to be:

$$\Delta t \leq \beta/4 \tag{3}$$

3.1   Implementation

In the numerical implementation we use the following parameters: $\beta = 0.01$ and $\Delta t = \beta/4.5$.

The anisotropic diffusion filter is applied to the matrices $R_{cos} = \cos(2\Theta)$ and $R_{sin} = \sin(2\Theta)$, where Θ is the direction angle. Since we are dealing with a direction that lives in the unit circle, after each iteration of the anisotropic diffusion filter we apply a normalization step. Finally the direction angle $\Theta(i,j)$ is obtained with: $\Theta(i,j) = 0.5 * atan(R_{sin}(i,j)/R_{cos}(i,j))$.

For the parameters mentioned above we empirically found that 200 iterations are enough to correctly classify poor fingerprints which are the majority in our database. This may not be an ideal stopping criteria for good fingerprints, and bad fingerprints. In the case of bad fingerprints, we usually need more iterations.

4   Classification Algorithm

In this section we describe the classification algorithm used. We modified the algorithm proposed by Karu and Jain [2] for a four-class problem.

We now describe its main steps and the modifications we have introduced. The first step is the computation of a directional image, corresponding to ridge directions at each pixel in the input image. All possible directions are quantized to eight discrete values equally spaced around the unit circle. Directions are then converted to vector form (i.e. (x,y) coordinate pairs), giving an appropriate representation to perform the smoothing operations described in Section 3. The original image is averaged in 8×8 windows giving a reduced directional image of size 64×60. Singularities are located computing the Poincaré index at every pixel (in the reduced image) in a 2×2 neighbourhood. Doing this we label each pixel as either: Ordinary, Delta, or Core point.

Based on the number and location of Delta and Core points, the fingerprint is adequately classified. As unwanted spurious singularities may appear in the first step we use an iterative approach where the directional image is successively smoothed, until we can classify it. The main drawback of the algorithm was the influence of spurious singularities that cause classification errors. Unwanted singular points come from many sources: low quality image within the fingerprint area, spurious artifacts outside the fingerprint area: typed words, lines, etc.

As a first pre-processing step, we normalize the image and make a segmentation to remove spurious elements. In a second step, we make some checking procedures to eliminate false singularities. This classification into the four classes (Arch, Left and Right Loop and Whorl) is done based on the number and position of the detected Deltas and Cores.

5   Results and Evaluation

In tables 1 to 4 we show the results of the classification algorithm over 2800 fingerprints which includes good, poor and bad ones. As we can see, the anisotropic diffusion algorithm performs better than the mean filter smoothing.

5.1   Test Platform

The algorithms were coded in C++ using the image processing library VIL which is part of VXL. The tests were conducted on an AMD Athlon 1300 MHz with

Table 1. Mean filter performance for singularities classification

	Arch	Left loop	Right loop	Whorl
		Mean filter performance		
Arch	73 (71.57%)	21 (2.41%)	12 (1.57%)	10 (0.99%)
Left loop	7 (6.86%)	816 (93.69%)	20 (2.62%)	69 (6.83%)
Right loop	21 (20.59%)	21 (2.41%)	706 (92.41%)	90 (8.91%)
Whorl	1 (0.98%)	13 (1.49%)	26 (3.40%)	841 (83.27%)
Total	102 (100%)	871 (100%)	764 (100%)	1010 (100%)

Table 2. Mean filter classification performance

Mean filter performance	
Correct classification	2436 (87.00%)
Wrong classification	311 (11.11%)
Not classified	53 (1.89%)
Total	2800 (100%)

Table 3. Anisotropic diffusion filter performance for singularities classification

	Anisotropic diffusion performance			
	Arch	Left loop	Right loop	Whorl
Arch	108 (84.38%)	39 (4.16%)	8 (0.94%)	3 (0.34%)
Left loop	9 (7.03%)	865 (92.32%)	15 (1.75%)	20 (2.28%)
Right loop	11 (8.59%)	16 (1.71%)	811 (94.85%)	22 (2.51%)
Whorl	0 (0%)	17 (1.81%)	21 (2.46%)	831 (94.86%)
Total	128 (100%)	937 (100%)	855 (100%)	876 (100%)

Table 4. Anisotropic diffusion filter classification performance

Anisotropic diffusion performance	
Correct classification	2615 (93.39%)
Wrong classification	181 (6.46%)
Not classified	4 (0.14%)
Total	2800 (100%)

Table 5. Mean filtering timing

Mean filter timing	
Number of images	2800
Total processing time	8503.42 sec.
Mean time per image	3.034 sec.

Table 6. Anisotropic diffusion filtering timing

Anisotropic diffusion timing	
Number of images	2800
Total processing time	17664.5 sec.
Mean time per image	6.306 sec.

256 MB of RAM running Red Hat 9.0 (kernel 2.4.20-8). In tables 5 and 6 we show the running times for both filtering approaches.

6   The Quality Measure

The DNIC database quality is very heterogeneous, as no objective quality requirement was imposed on the acquisition process. One of the goals of this project is to define a quality measure (QI) that enables to reject bad impressions in the digitalization steps and improve the average database quality by the substitution of bad cards.

For that aim, fingerprint images are divided in blocks of 16×16 pixels. A block class is defined using Gabor filters as in [3]. We obtain eight Gabor features for each block. A block is considered to have a good quality if the standard deviation of the eight features is lower than a given threshold (420) and otherwise it is considered bad.

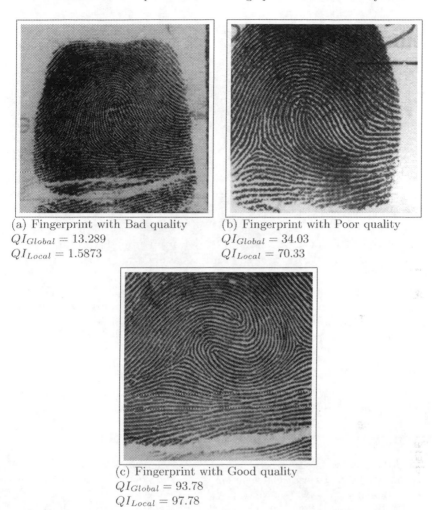

(a) Fingerprint with Bad quality
$QI_{Global} = 13.289$
$QI_{Local} = 1.5873$

(b) Fingerprint with Poor quality
$QI_{Global} = 34.03$
$QI_{Local} = 70.33$

(c) Fingerprint with Good quality
$QI_{Global} = 93.78$
$QI_{Local} = 97.78$

Fig. 1. Example of fingerprints discriminated by their quality index

The fingerprint is accepted or rejected taking into account the global and local measures and also the number of iterations during the smoothing process.

We define a global QI (QIglobal) taken into account the whole fingerprint quality and a local QI (QIlocal) estimated over the singularities areas. Each iteration penalizes the measures in ten percent. A fingerprint is considered good if both QI are over their respective threshold. The QI definitions:

$$QI_{global} = 1 - \frac{\text{number of bad quality front blocks}}{\text{number of front blocks}} \qquad (4)$$

$$QI_{local} = 1 - \frac{\text{number of bad quality front blocks in the mask}}{\text{number of front blocks in the mask}} \qquad (5)$$

The QI thresholds were learned from a training set done by the DNIC experts. A subset of fingerprints was drawn from the database. These fingerprints were analysed and categorized as good, poor or bad by the experts. This training set was used to learn the quality thresholds ($QI_{goodth}=50$ $QI_{regularth}=35$)

Perceptually the quality measure has shown to be consistent with the technicians criteria when we analyse the results over the database. We continue working looking forward this measure will work as a confidence index of the classification algorithm.

7   Concluding Remarks

In this work we studied and evaluated the performance improvement achieved after the modifications introduce in an automatic fingerprint classification algorithm. We defined a quality measure that has shown consistency with the technician's criteria. The modifications to the original algorithm are proposed and evaluated over images extracted from a 4 million fingerprint card archive held by DNIC.

Our future work will include improvements on the algorithm and further testing. For the anisotropic diffusion we will try working with vectors in S^2 to avoid the normalization in each step and we will also look for an automatic stopping criteria.

Acknowledgments

We want to acknowledge the DNIC staff, specially: Raúl Marcora , Jorge Millot, Graciela Nogueira and Raquel Abal.

References

1. Alberto Bartesaghi, Alicia Fernandez, and Alvaro Gomez. Performance evaluation of an automatic fingerprint classification algorithm adapted to a vucetich based classification system. In *LNCS 2091*, pages 259–265, 2001.
2. K. Karu and A. Jain. Fingerprint classification. *Pattern Recognition*, 29(3):389–404, 1996.
3. Lin Lin Shen, Alex Kot, and WaiMun Koo. *Quality Measures of Fingerprint Images*. School of Electrical and Electronic Engineering, Nanyang Technological University, Singapore, 2000.
4. A. Pardo and G. Sapiro. Vector Probability Diffusion. *IEEE Signal Processing Letters*, 8(4):106–109, April 2001.
5. P. Perona. Orientation Diffusion. *IEEE Transactions on Image Processing*, 7(3):457–467, March 1998.
6. P. Perona and J. Malik. Scale-space and Edge Detection Using Anisotropic Diffusion. *IEEE Transactions on Pattern Analysis and Machine Intelligence*,12(7):629–639, July 1990.
7. N. Ratha, K. Karu, S. Chen, and A. Jain. A real-time matching system for large fingerprint databases. *IEEE Pattern Analysis and Machine Intelligence*, 18(8), 1996.
8. B. Tang, G. Sapiro, and V. Caselles. Diffusion of general data on non-flat manifolds via harmonic maps theory: The direction diffusion case. *International Journal Computer Vision*, 36(2):149–161, February 2000.

Image Thresholding
via a Modified Fuzzy C-Means Algorithm

Yong Yang, Chongxun Zheng, and Pan Lin

Key Laboratory of Biomedical Information Engineering of Education Ministry,
Institute of Biomedical Engineering, Xi'an Jiaotong University, Xi'an 710049, P. R. China
greatyyy765@sohu.com

Abstract. In this paper, a modified fuzzy c-means (FCM) algorithm named weighted fuzzy c-means (WFCM) algorithm for image thresholding is presented. The algorithm is developed by incorporating the spatial neighborhood information into the standard FCM clustering algorithm. The weight indicates the spatial influence of the neighboring pixels on the centre pixel, which is derived from the k-nearest neighbor (k-NN) algorithm and is modified in two aspects so as to improve its property in the WFCM algorithm. To speed up the algorithm, the iteration in FCM algorithm is carried out with the statistical gray level histogram of image instead of the conventional whole data of image. The performance of the algorithm is compared with those of an existing fuzzy thresholding algorithm and widely applied between variance and entropy methods. Experimental results on both synthetic and real images are given to demonstrate the proposed algorithm is effective and efficient. In addition, due to the neighborhood model, our method is more tolerant to noise.

1   Introduction

Thresholding is an important technique for image segmentation based on the assumption that the objects can be distinguished and extracted from the background by their gray levels. The output of the thresholding operation is a binary image whose gray level 0 (black) will indicate the foreground and gray level 255 (white) will indicate the background, and vice versa. Many thresholding methods have been developed. A detailed survey can be found in references [1] and [2]. In general, threshold selection can be categorized into two classes, local methods and global methods. The global thresholding methods segment an entire image with a single threshold using the gray level histogram of image, while the local methods partition the given image into a number of sub-images and select a threshold for each of sub-images. The global thresholding techniques are easy to implement and computationally less involved, therefore they are superior to local methods in terms of many real image processing applications. The global thresholding methods select the threshold based on different criterions, such as Otsu's method [3], minimum error thresholding [4], and entropic method which was first proposed by Pun [5] and then modified and extended by Kapur et al. [6], etc.

Generally, all the above conventional one-dimensional (1D) histogram thresholding techniques work well when the two consecutive gray levels of the image are dis-

A. Sanfeliu et al. (Eds.): CIARP 2004, LNCS 3287, pp. 589–596, 2004.

tinct. However, all these 1D thresholding techniques did not combine the spatial information and the gray-level information of the pixels into the process for image segmentation. This drawback will lead to serious misclassification in the case of image thresholding, for the data in the image are inherently correlated. In addition, when the image is interrupted by noise and other artifacts the performance of these thresholding techniques will be poor or even fail.

Another important issue for image thresholding is that in real life situations great deals of images are ambiguous and usually have indistinguishable histogram. In these cases, the above classical thresholding techniques can not easy to find a criterion of similarity or closeness for thresholding. Since the fuzzy set theory was introduced, it has become a powerful tool to tackle this difficulty in image thresholding. Fuzzy set theory has been successfully applied to image thresholding to partition the image space into meaningful regions [7], [8], [9]. However, all the mentioned algorithms still do not include the contextual information in image thresholding.

In this paper, we proposed a new global image thresholding technique named weighted fuzzy c-means (WFCM) algorithm. It is formulated by incorporating the spatial neighboring information into the FCM algorithm. Experimental results support its effectiveness and efficiency.

2   Fast Fuzzy C-Means Algorithm

The Fuzzy C-means (FCM) algorithm is an iterative clustering method that produces an optimal c partition, which minimizes the weighted within group sum of squared error objective function $J_m(U,V)$ [10]:

$$J_m(U,V) = \sum_{k=1}^{n}\sum_{i=1}^{c}(u_{ik})^m d^2(x_k,v_i) \tag{1}$$

where $X = \{x_1,x_2,\cdots,x_n\} \subseteq R^p$, n is the number of data items, c is the number of clusters with $2 \le c < n$, u_{ik} is the degree of membership of x_k in the ith cluster, m is a weighting exponent on each fuzzy membership, v_i is the prototype of the centre of cluster i , $d^2(x_k,v_i)$ is a distance measure between object x_k and cluster centre v_i . A solution of the object function J_m can be obtained via an iterative process, which is carried as follows:

$$v_i^{(b)} = \frac{\sum_{k=1}^{n}\left(u_{ik}^{(b)}\right)^m x_k}{\sum_{k=1}^{n}\left(u_{ik}^{(b)}\right)^m} \tag{2}$$

$$u_{ik}^{(b+1)} = \frac{1}{\sum_{j=1}^{c}\left(\dfrac{d_{ik}}{d_{jk}}\right)^{2/(m-1)}} \tag{3}$$

where b is the loop counter. Since FCM algorithm is an iterative operation, it is very time consuming which makes the algorithm impractical used in image segmentation. To cope with this problem, the statistical gray level histogram of image is applied to the algorithm. Define the non-negative integrate set $G = \{L\min, L\min + 1, \cdots, L\max\}$ as gray level, where $L\min$ is the minimum gray level, $L\max$ is the maximum gray level, so the grayscale is $L\max - L\min$. For image size $S \times T$, at point (s, t), $f(s, t)$ is the gray value with $0 \le s \le S - 1$, $0 \le t \le T - 1$. Let $His(g)$ denote the number of pixels having gray level g, $g \in G$. The statistical histogram function is as follows:

$$His(g) = \sum_{s=0}^{S-1}\sum_{t=0}^{T-1} \delta(f(s,t) - g) \tag{4}$$

where $g = \{L\min, L\min + 1, \cdots, L\max\}$, $\delta(0) = 1$ and $\delta(g \ne 0) = 0$. With the statistical gray level histogram the membership function is still by (3), while the cluster centers are updated by:

$$v_i^{(b)} = \frac{\sum\limits_{g=L_{\min}}^{L_{\max}} \left(u_{ig}^{(b)}\right)^m His(g)g}{\sum\limits_{g=L_{\min}}^{L_{\max}} \left(u_{ig}^{(b)}\right)^m His(g)} \tag{5}$$

It is important to note that k in (3) now denotes the gray level as g. Since the FCM algorithm now only operates on the histogram of the image, it is faster than the conventional version which processes the whole data.

3   Weighted Fuzzy C-Means Algorithm

The general principle of the techniques presented in this paper is to incorporate the neighborhood information into the FCM algorithm. Since in the standard FCM algorithm for a pixel $x_k \in I$ where I is the image, the clustering of x_k with class i only depends on the membership value u_{ik}, if we consider a noisy image, the FCM does not have a method to overcome this problem. Considering the influence of the neighboring pixels on the central pixel, the fuzzy membership function given in (3) can be extended to

$$u_{ik}^* - u_{ik} p_{ik} \tag{6}$$

where $k = 1, 2, \cdots, n$, n is the number of image data, and p_{ik} is the probability of data point k belonging to cluster i, further referred to as weight in this paper which can be determined by the following neighborhood model. Therefore the degrees of membership u_{ik}^* and the cluster centers v_i are now updated via:

$$u_{ik}^* = \frac{p_{ik}}{\sum\limits_{j=1}^{c} \left(\dfrac{d_{ik}}{d_{jk}}\right)^{2/(m-1)}} \qquad (7)$$

$$v_i = \frac{\sum\limits_{k=1}^{n} \left(u_{ik}^*\right)^m x_k}{\sum\limits_{k=1}^{n} \left(u_{ik}^*\right)^m} \qquad (8)$$

The core idea now is to define the auxiliary weight variable p_{ik}, which is a priori information to guide the outcome of the clustering process. This paper proposes a method for determining the weight based on the neighborhood information inspired from k-nearest neighbor (k-NN) algorithm [11].

$$p_{ik} = \frac{\sum\limits_{x_n \in N_k^i} 1\Big/ d^2(x_n - k)}{\sum\limits_{x_n \in N_k} 1\Big/ d^2(x_n - k)} \qquad (9)$$

where N_k is the dada set of the nearest neighbors of central pixel k, and N_k^i is the subset of N_k composed of the data belonging to class i. In order to give an appropriate method to describe the probability of a data point belonging to any cluster, two improved implementations of the k-NN algorithm are introduced. First, the equation (9) is extended by considering the potential function of each feature vector [12].

$$K(x, x_k) = \frac{1}{1 + \alpha \|x - x_k\|^2} \qquad (10)$$

where α is a positive constant, and $\|x - x_k\|^2$ is the norm of the vector $(x - x_k)$. Then the potential is modified by assigning the proximity of feature vector to each prototype instead of the potential for feature vector to feature vector. Hence the new equation for the weight value is defined as:

$$p_{ik} = \frac{\sum\limits_{x_n \in N_k^i} 1\Big/ 1 + \alpha \cdot d^2(x_n - v_i)}{\sum\limits_{x_n \in N_k} 1\Big/ 1 + \alpha \cdot d^2(x_n - v_i)} \qquad (11)$$

where v_i is the prototype of cluster i. After the a-priori weight is determined, a new iteration step starts with this auxiliary variable p_{ik}. To prevent that the WFCM gets trapped in a local minima, the WFCM algorithm is initialized with the above fast FCM algorithm. Once the FCM is stopped, the WFCM algorithm continues with the values for the prototypes and membership values obtained from the fast FCM algorithm. When the algorithm has converged, a defuzzification process then takes place in order to convert the fuzzy partition matrix U to a crisp partition. A number of methods have been developed to defuzzify the partition matrix U, in which the maximum membership procedure is the most important. The procedure assigns object k to the class C with the highest membership:

$$C_k = \arg_i \{\max(u_{ik})\}, \ i = 1, 2, \cdots, c. \tag{12}$$

With this procedure, the fuzzy images are then converted to crisp image. For image thresholding, $c = 2$ in equation (12). We call this method is a soft threshoding scheme contrary to conventional hard threshold scheme which has been proven to be associated with loss of structure details on thresholding [7]. Although Jawahar et al. [7] has proposed a fuzzy thresholding method with FCM algorithm by finding the hard threshold in the intersection of both membership distributions (see equation (10) in [7]), it is easily verified that this technique is almost equivalent to thresholding the image using the maximum membership procedure.

4 Experimental Results

In this section, the results of the application of the WFCM algorithm are presented. The performance of the proposed method is compared with fuzzy thresholding method introduced by Jawahar et al. (see Section 3) and two well-known thresholding methods, including Otsu and Kapur et al. algorithms. For all cases, unless otherwise stated, the weighting exponent $m = 2.0$ and $\varepsilon = 0.0001$ in the FCM algorithm. We tried several values for α and found that a value of $\alpha = 1$ gives a convenient result. A 3×3 window of image pixels is considered in this paper, thus the spatial influence on the centre pixel is through its 8-neighborhood pixels. All the algorithms are coded in Microsoft Visual C++ Version 6.0 and are run on a 1.7GH$_z$ Pentium IV personal computer with a memory of 256 MB. Since we use the fast FCM algorithm, all the algorithms are implemented within 1 seconds.

In the first example, we generate a synthetic image with gray levels 0 and 255 for background and foreground respectively. The image was then corrupted by additive Gaussian noise such that the $SNR = 5$. Fig. 1 (a) is the original image and Fig. 1(b) is the degraded noisy images. Fig.1 (f) shows the result of proposed method. The results of Jawahar's method, Otsu's method and Kapur's method are displayed in Fig. 1 (c), (d) and (e), respectively. The results show the proposed method is an effective method and outperforms the other methods in the noisy situation. The number of misclassified pixels for different thresholding methods is counted during the experiments and is listed in Table 1. It can be seen from Table 1. that the total number of misclassification pixels for the proposed method is the least in the four different methods, and the total misclassification number for Jawahar's method, Otsu's method and Kapur's method is nearly the same which is about 18 times than that of the proposed method.

The second example is a T1-weighted magnetic resonance (MR) image as shown in Fig2 (a). Since the MR scanners usually produces normally distributed white noise [13], in order to extract the head from the background, the noise should be removed firstly that is often the first stage for segmentation of MR images. The results of

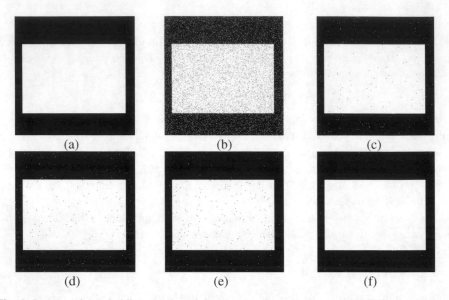

Fig. 1. Results of thresholding: (a) the original image; (b) noisy image with SNR=5; (c) by the Jawahar's method; (d) by the Otsu's method; (e) by the Kapur's method; (f) by the proposed method

Table 1. Number of misclassified pixels

Methods	Jawahar	Otsu	Kapur	Our mehtod
Foreground	61	83	141	0
Background	118	96	39	10
Total	179	179	180	10

thresholding by applying the different algorithms to the image appear in Fig. 2 (b)-(e). From these images, we can see that the Kapur's method was unable to correctly threshold the image. The Jawahar's method, Otsu's method and our method can extract the head from background, however with the first two methods some noise still exists especially in the cerebrospinal fluid (CSF) of the image.

In the last example, there is a standard test image named *camerman*, which is illustrated in Fig.3 (a). The result of the proposed method is presented in Fig.3 (e). The results for comparison are given in Fig.3 (b)-(d). As can be seen, the Jawahar's method and Otsu's method give almost the same result, while the Kapur's method can not accurately extract the object from the background as in the second example. However, it can be seen the proposed method performs best for segmenting the object from background with least spurious components and noise.

5   Conclusions

In this paper, we present a novel approach for image thresholding based on a modified FCM algorithm, i.e., WFCM algorithm. The method not only takes into account of the advantage of the fuzzy framework, but also considers the spatial relation

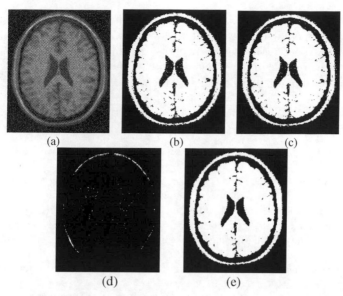

Fig. 2. Results of thresholding: (a) the original image; (b) by the Jawahar's method; (c) by the Otsu's method; (d) by the Kapur's method; (e) by the proposed method

Fig. 3. Results of thresholding: (a) the original image; (b) by the Jawahar's method; (c) by the Otsu's method; (d) by the Kapur's method; (e) by the proposed method

among pixels. The weight plays a key role in this algorithm, which is derived from k-NN algorithm and is modified to improve its property in the WFCM algorithm. The performance of the proposed method is compared with those of the Otsu's method, Kapur's method, and a fuzzy thresholding method proposed by Jawahar et al. Experiments with synthetic and real image show that WFCM algorithm can effectively extract object from background. Since the algorithm is initialized with fast FCM algorithm, the presented approach is as fast as the conventional 1D techniques. Also, owing to the incorporation of spatial information, the WFCM algorithm is less prone to noise. In fact, if the result of thresholding is an image with two gray values, the process can also be called bilevel segmentation. Future work will extend the algorithm to multi-level thresholding or segmentation.

References

1. S. K. Fu and J. K. Mu: A survey on image segmentation. Pattern Recognit., Vol. 13, (1981) 3–16.
2. P. K. Sahoo, S. Soltani, and A. K. C. Wong: A survey of thresholding techniques. Comput. Vis. Graph. Image Process., Vol. 41, (1988) 233–260.
3. N. Otsu: A threshold selection method from gray level histogram. IEEE Trans. Syst., Man, Cybern., Vol. SMC-9, (1979) 62–66.
4. J. Kittle and J. Illingworth: Minimum error thresholding. Pattern Recognit., Vol.19, (1986) 41–47.
5. T. Pun: A new method for gray level picture thresholding using the entropy of the histogram. Signal Process., Vol. 2, (1980) 223–237.
6. J. N. Kapur, P. K. Sahoo, and A. K. C. Wong: A new method for gray level picture thresholding using the entropy of the histogram. Comput. Vis. Graph. Image Process., Vol. 29, (1985) 273–285.
7. C. V. Jawahar, P. K. Biswas, and A. K. Ray: Investigations on fuzzy thresholding based on fuzzy clustering. Pattern Recognit., Vol. 30, (1997)1605–1613.
8. H. D. Cheng, J. Chen, and J. Li: Thresholding selection based on fuzzy c-partition entropy approach. Pattern Recognit., Vol. 31, (1998) 857–870.
9. M. S. Zhao, A. M. N. Fu, and H. Yan: A technique of three level thresholding based on probability partition and fuzzy 3-partition. IEEE Trans. Fuzzy Systems, Vol. 9, (2001) 469–479.
10. J. C. Bezdek: Pattern Recognition with Fuzzy Objective Function Algorithms. Plenum Press, New York, 1981.
11. T. M. Cover and P. E. Hart: Nearest neighbor pattern classification. IEEE Trans. Inform. Theory, Vol. IT-13, (1967) 21–27.
12. T. Tou Julius: Pattern Recognition Principles. Addison–Wesley Company, 1974.
13. W. A. Edelstein, P. A. Bottomley, and L. M. Pfeifer: A signal-to-noise calibration procedure for NMR imaging systems. Med. Phys., Vol.11, (1984) 180–185.

Video Object Segmentation Using Multiple Features

Alvaro Pardo

IIE & IMERL – Faculty of Engineering
Universidad de la República
CC 30, Montevideo, Uruguay
and Faculty of Engineering and Technologies
Universidad Católica del Uruguay

Abstract. In this paper we present an algorithm for semi-automatic object extraction from video sequences using multiple features. This work is part of an ongoing effort to study video segmentation using multiple features, and the relative contribution of each one of them. For this reason, the algorithm here presented will be very simple and made up from of the shelf algorithms. We will show that even with a simple algorithm, with the right steps, we can successfully segment video objects in moderate complex sequences.

1 Introduction

Video object segmentation is one of the most important and challenging problems in video analysis. Applications range from video surveillance and tracking, to video object-based coding and video databases.

Since the amount of literature about this subject is relatively vast, we will content ourselves with a review of the more relevant references, and the ones that are closely connected with our approach.

We can distinguish two main groups of algorithms: completely automatic algorithms, and the ones that require some interaction with the user. Among the later ones, we have all methods where the user must select the video object to be segmented along the sequence. Although these methods need the interaction with the user to select the object to be segmented, this interaction is indeed minimal. Is important to note that in this step the user introduces semantic information, or high level knowledge of the object. This is one of the reasons why these methods usually perform better than fully automatic ones. Usually, the system can aid the user with an initial coarse segmentation of the first frame. In addition, we can distinguish between region and boundary-based methods.

In existing approaches features may include only chromatic information, for example [1], or a combination of colour, spatial and motion information [2–6]. Usually these methods rely on statistical descriptions of the features. For example, Gaussian Mixture Models (GMM) are used in combination with maximum a posterior (MAP) to classify different regions in the sequence. This approach is simple and efficient when dealing only with colour information, however, when including spatial and motion information, the results tend to deteriorate at the

A. Sanfeliu et al. (Eds.): CIARP 2004, LNCS 3287, pp. 597–604, 2004.

object boundaries. The reasons for this problem are, on one hand the fact that GMM usually produce small errors that then are propagated to future frames. On the other hand, the difficulty to reliably update the spatial information [7]. To overcome these problems we propose: first to regularize the posterior probabilities of object and background using an isotropic probability diffusion algorithm [8]. Second, to decouple spatial information from motion estimation steps for the update of spatial information. That is, we will estimate the new object shape to feed an Expectation-Maximization step (EM) in order to learn the new GMM parameters.

This work is part of an ongoing project to study video segmentation using multiple features. One of the main goals is to investigate a common framework for all the features used. Although recently several authors presented novel and successful algorithms, we believe that there is still a lack of information in order to judge all the different existing approaches. Specially, usually is difficult to tell which part of the algorithm is responsible of the overall success or failure. For this reason we decided to investigate a simply structured algorithm, made up from of the shelf algorithms without using any fancy and/or complicated methods. In this way, we will be able to evaluate the individual contribution of each feature and each step of the whole process. As we will see in section 2 all the building blocks of our algorithm can be replaced with others.

The structure of the paper is as follows. In Section 2 we present the proposed approach. In Section 3 we summarize some practical issues. In Section 4 we present some examples, and finally in Section 5 we discuss some future work and conclusions.

2   Proposed Approach

Our work falls into the category of semi-automatic and region-based object segmentation based on GMM. At the beginning, the user must select the object of interest to be segmented along the sequence. We assume that whenever the object disappears from the scene or is completely occluded, the process must be re-initialised.

With the initial object and background classification, we learn the object and background GMM. This is similar in spirit to [4, 7, 6]. We describe object and background as a set of regions each one modelled with a Gaussian distribution. To learn the optimum parameters of the GMM we apply the well known EM algorithm [9]. The initial mean, and covariance matrices are estimated using the Kmeans algorithm [9]. Before describing the structure of our algorithm, we first describe the features used.

2.1   Features

The whole process relies on three different features: colour, position and motion. Each feature is different in nature and plays a different role in our method. This contrast with some existing approaches where the full set of features is combined into an unique feature vector [5, 4]. In our case we append into the same feature vector, colour and spatial information, while we leave motion information for the update of object shape.

Colour. Colour information is represented using the Lab space that is known to be perceptually meaningful. That means that distances in the Lab space correlate with perceived colour distances.

Position. The spatial information is given by the (x, y) object and background pixels coordinates. In our method position plays two roles. Firstly, it is included in a feature vector together with colour information. Second, position constitutes the shape information that will be used to estimate the motion of the object.

The feature vector of colour and position is normalized to $[0, 1]$ before applying Kmeans and EM. The number of components in each mixture is fixed along the whole process. As in [6] the Minimum Description Length can be sued to estimate the optimal number of Gaussians. We will come back to this point in Section 5.

Given a new frame we can update the object and background GMM with the EM algorithm using as initial values the ones of the previous frame. In this way we can cope with variations in object and background along the sequence. This is especially useful in cases where the object or the background changes its model. For example, when the object deforms or moves. If the object moves or zooms, its spatial distribution also moves. Therefore, this step is crucial in order to track the position of each Gaussian in the mixture.

Finally, the posterior probabilities of object and background are regularized with an isotropic vector probability algorithm [8]. This is also very important to avoid problems due to small errors during MAP classification.

Motion. Motion information is taken into account to estimate the objects shape. To track the object shape deformation we apply a simple block-matching algorithm between the previous and current frame. We use 3×3 blocks and a search area of ± 5 pixels. With the translation vectors obtained after the block-matching we estimate the objects shape that will be used to update the object and background GMM. Although simple, we observed that this process is quite robust and efficient. We also experimented with optical flow but it turned to be too unstable in complex and noisy scenes. In Section 5 we will come back to this point.

2.2   Algorithm Outline

1. Given the initial video object marked by the user, learn the models of object and background.
2. For all frames in the sequence:
   (a) Apply the block-matching motion estimation between frames $t - 1$ and t to obtain an estimation of the shape, $\hat{S}(t)$, at current frame t. After block-matching the estimated shape is regularized via mathematical morphology, its holes are filled, and the biggest connected component that matches the video object is selected.
   (b) Using the points in $\hat{S}(t)$ the GMM for object and background are updated with EM.

(c) Before applying the MAP step, we regularize the posterior probabilities using the isotropic vector probability algorithm [8]. Given the posterior probabilities $p(o|(x,y))$ and $p(b|(x,y))$ of the pixel (x,y) to be object and background, we define the probability vector:

$$\mathbf{p}(x,y) = (p(o|(x,y)), p(b|(x,y))).$$

The iterative regularization procedure is then:

$$\mathbf{p}^{k+1}(x,y) = \mathbf{p}^k(x,y) + 0.25 * \Delta\mathbf{p}^k(x,y)$$

where $\Delta\mathbf{p}$ is the Laplacian of $\mathbf{p}$ at (x,y).

(d) Apply a MAP step to obtain the shape of the object at frame t, $S(t)$
(e) Regularize the obtained shape as in step 2a.
(f) Continue to next frame.

3   Practical Issues

In this section we describe several practical issues that we encountered to be crucial for the algorithm presented, and some implementation details.

Initialization. Is very important to start the process with a good representation of the object and the background. We found out that if the initial models of the object and background do not correctly represent their content, the segmentation tends to deteriorate along frames. Hence, it is very important to start with good initial guesses for the Kmeans and therefore for EM.

Posterior probabilities regularization. We used the isotropic version of the algorithm presented in [8] with four iterations. Although we could use the anisotropic version of the same algorithm that respects borders in a better way, we decided to use this simple one to understand the importance of this step. In fact, this step turned out to be very important to obtain a clear segmentation close to the object border.

Motion. We also tested Horn-Schunck, and Lucas-Kanade [10] optical flow methods. However, it turned out that due to the amount of regularization imposed, these methods do not provide a good estimation of the shape. We are aware that there exist methods that allow the extraction of discontinuous optical flows. Nevertheless, since we wanted to use only standard algorithms we did not include them here.

4   Results

We now present some examples to show the performance of our algorithm. We selected two different sequences with different complexity. First, we have Claire sequence. In this case, the background is static and the object moves slowly from

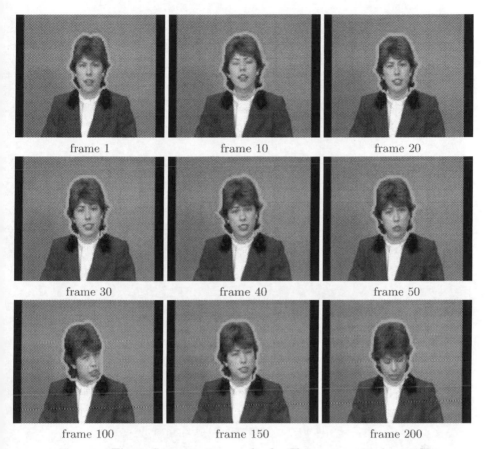

frame 1   frame 10   frame 20

frame 30   frame 40   frame 50

frame 100   frame 150   frame 200

Fig. 1. Segmentation results for Claire sequence.

frame to frame. As we can see in Figure 1 the algorithm successfully extracts the object along the sequence. Although these results may not be very impressing since this sequence is relatively simple to segment, it is important to note that we are not segmenting the whole body of Claire but her head. This is indeed a harder problem since we need to clearly separate the head and body's features. As already discussed in Section 2 a bad description of object and background leads to misleading results. In this case, the head object tends to include the rest of the body as we increase the number of frames. As we can see in Figure 1, the algorithm proposed successfully segment the head object along the sequence without expanding it to include parts of the image originally marked as background.

The second example is the Foreman sequence (Figure 2). In this case, both, the object and the background move and slowly change. Once again, the results are very stable during the whole sequence. We also show in Figure 3 that the proposed algorithm can cope with occlusions. When the hand occludes the face it is included in the object. Then when it moves away the algorithm success-

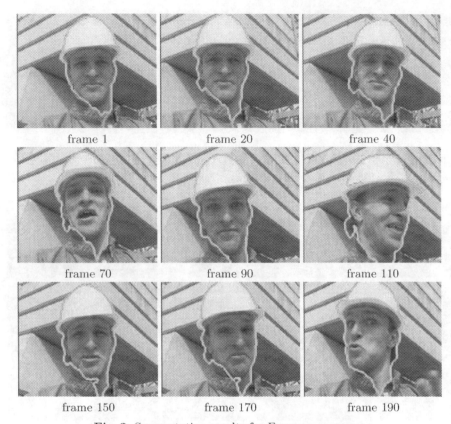

Fig. 2. Segmentation results for Foreman sequence.

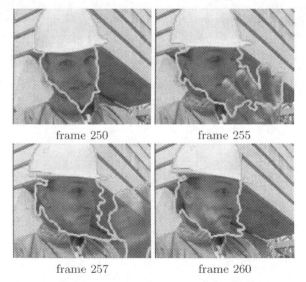

Fig. 3. Segmentation results for Foreman sequence in presence of occlusion.

fully selects the head as the main object. This is done mainly using the motion estimation and the position feature in the Gaussian mixture model.

5   Conclusions and Future Work

We showed how using a simple algorithm based on of the shelf algorithms; we can obtain good results in video object segmentation. In addition, we showed how to overcome some problems of GMM via using posterior probability regularization, and decoupled shape and model updating.

Regarding the relative contribution of each feature to the overall performance, we found out, as note in [7], that colour information alone is not very reliable. For this reason colour and spatial information must be appended into the same feature vector. Furthermore, to obtain a good classification a posterior probability regularization is essential.

On the other hand, shape updating must be very accurate in order to be used in the MAP classification step. Otherwise, the results close to object borders tend to deteriorate. Due to this observation, we did not include a shape probability in the MAP classification. In future work we will study other methods for shape motion estimation, for example affine versions of the Lucas-Kanade algorithm [11].

Finally, another important thing is the initialisation of the whole process and the possible change in the number of Gaussians. The initial condition of the EM determines the quality of the results. Therefore, for the future we leave the inclusion of method such as the ones presented in [12]. With respect with a varying number of Gaussians, we will explore the use of MDL. Although, feasible, this solution seems to be computationally demanding.

References

1. Marlow, S., Oconnor, N.:   Supervised Object Segmentation and Tracking for MPEG4 VOP Generation.   In: ICPR00 - International Conference on Pattern Recognition. Volume 1. (2000) 1125–1128
2. Castagno, R., Ebrahimi, T., Kunt, M.: Video Segmentation Based on Multiple Features for Interactive Multimedia Applications. IEEE Transactions on Circuits and Systems for Video Technology **8** (1998) 562–571
3. Gu, C., Lee, M.C.: Semiautomatic Segmentation and TRacking of Semantic Video Objects. IEEE Transactions on Image Processing **8** (1998) 572–584
4. Everingham, M., Thomas, B.: Supervised Segmentation adn Tracking of Nonrigid Objects using a Mixture of Histograms Model. In: ICIP01 - International Conference on Image Processing. (2001) 62–65
5. Khan, S., Shah, M.: Object Based Segmentation of Video using Color, Motion and Saptial Information. In: CVPR2001 - Int. Conf. Computer Vision and Pattern Recogbition. Volume 2. (2001) 746–751
6. Greenspan, H., Goldberger, J., Meyer, A.: Probabilistic Space-Time Video Modeling via Piecewise GMM. IEEE Transactions on Pattern Analysis and Machine Intelligence **26** (2004) 384–396

7. Thirde, D., Jones, G., Flack, J.: Spatio-Temporal Semantic Object Segmentation using Probabilistic Sub-Object Regions. In: BMVC2003 - British Machine Vision Conf. (2003)

8. Pardo, A., Sapiro, G.: Vector Probability Diffusion. IEEE Signal Processing Letters **8** (2001) 106–109

9. Duda, R., Hart, P., Stork, D.: Pattern Classification. Second edn. John Wiley and Sons (2000)

10. Barron, J., Fleet, D., Beauchemin, S.: Performance of Optical Flow Techniques. International Journal of Computer Vision **12** (1994) 43–77

11. Baker, S., Matthews, I.: Lucas-Kanade 20 Years on: A Unifying Approach. International Journal of Computer Vision **56** (2004) 221–255

12. Figueiredo, M., Jain, A.: Unsupervised Learning of Finite Mixture Models. IEEE Transaction on Pattern and Machine Intelligence **24** (2002) 381–396

Thinning Algorithm to Generate k-Connected Skeletons

Juan Luis Díaz de León, C. Yánez, and Giovanni Guzmán

Digital Image Processing Laboratory
Centre for Computing Research (CIC)
Mexico City, Mexico
{jdiaz,cyanez,jguzman1}@cic.ipn.mx

Abstract. This paper presents a novel algorithm intended to generate k-connected skeletons of a digital binary image using a new mask set. These skeletons may be 4 or 8 connected. The new algorithm performs a thinning process that finish when it is not possible to eliminate additional pixels without breaking the connectivity. The end-point criterion and a 3x3 masks set are used to decide if a pixel is eliminated. The proposed masks set for each kind of connectivity covers all the necessary cases, and guarantee to obtain a one pixel wide and k-connected skeleton without parasitic branches. The new algorithm yields some advantages to developers. It is not just oriented to written characters or some kind of object in particular; this means that the algorithm can be adapted easily to any application generating good results. Besides, the user can work with different classes of connectivity; note that several recent algorithms use 4-connectivity while 8-connectivity is used for others. Additionally, the skeletons produced by the new algorithm are immune to structured noise around the processed objects.

1 Introduction

Skeletonization is an important technique used in many areas in digital image processing. Its goal is to reduce an object R within an image in order to generate an object S (commonly called skeleton) whose thickness is just 1 pixel and it is generally connected, preferable on a specific metric. It is well known that the general topologic characteristics based on connectivity are not sufficient to describe a given object, because the skeleton of a simple connected object can be just a point, like was raised by Rosenfeld [1], and the representation yielded it is useless in many applications. For this reason, it is recommendable to take into account the objects geometric properties as Pavlidis's end-point condition [2]. This condition helps to preserve the "geometric form" of the object in the final skeleton.

Actually, there exist two types of algorithms to obtain the skeleton from a given image: the pixel based algorithms, and the not pixel based ones [3]. In the former manner, each background pixel takes part on the compute of the skeleton. Thinning algorithms [4, 5] and the distance transforms [4, 6] belong to this kind of techniques. Most of the more efficient methods are based on thinning techniques.

The basic principle of the thinning methods is to eliminate repeatedly those points from the contour of an object of such a way that the elimination of such points don't alter the object connectivity, and respect the local end-point condition, just as is done in the classic Pavlidis algorithm [2]. In order to decide if the elimination of a pixel alters or not, the connectivity of the object, it is useful to use local connectivity criterions, considering a neighborhood centered at the pixel to be analyzed. These criterions are usually formulated in terms of digital geometry [7], or by means of masks [8].

A. Sanfeliu et al. (Eds.): CIARP 2004, LNCS 3287, pp. 605–612, 2004.

In general, after thinning it is no possible to perform the original object reconstruction and, despite this technique preserves connectivity, there exist two problems where the actual study focuses, namely: the algorithms execution time, and the resulting object shape. The former point it is no critic, because the well-known advances in the speed of the devices used on the computers, and the possibility of use parallel algorithms as the one developed by Zhang and Suen [9]. With respect to the second point, a potential problem is the appearance of parasitic branches, which were not in the original object. On this topic focused the work of Díaz de León [10], Lü and Wang [11], Abdulla, Saleh and Morad [12] among others.

The goal of this work is to present a new sequential thinning algorithm for skeletonizing binary images. The approach is based on the use of masks that allow to determine if a pixel could be or could not be eliminated, taking into account a connectivity criterion and avoiding the elimination of end points. This algorithm is efficient with respect to processing time; that is made possible thanks to the use of only logical binary operations instead of arithmetic operations.

The remainder of the document is organized as follows: in section 2 some important concepts are cited, and the general strategy of the proposed thinning algorithm is formulated. In section 3 the masks used in connectivity of type 4 and 8, are deduced. In section 4 the system proofs are presented, and finally, in section 5 the conclusions on the present paper are given.

2 Preliminaries and General Strategy

Next we will introduce some important concepts about digital geometry. Let $p = (x, y)$, $q = (u, v)$ be points in Z^2. The following metrics in Z^2 are widely used:

$$
\begin{aligned}
d_4 &= |x - u| + |y - v|, \\
d_8 &= máx(|x - u|, |y - v|), \\
d_{6R} &= máx(|x - u|, |y - v|, |x - u + y - v|), \\
d_{6L} &= máx(|x - u|, |y - v|, |x - u - y + v|).
\end{aligned}
\tag{1}
$$

Each one of these metrics $d_k, k \in \{4, 6L, 6R, 8\}$, induce a symmetric and not reflexive relation N_k in Z^2, which is defined by $(p, q) \in N_k \Leftrightarrow d_k(p, q) = 1$. The structure (Z^2, N_k) is usually called the k-neighborhood graph, and the points p, q are k-neighbors if $(p, q) \in N_k$; additionally, $N_k(p)$ denotes the set of all k-neighbors of p. In the graph (Z^2, N_k) the connectivity concept from the indirect graphs theory is applied. Then, a subset $R \subseteq Z^2$ is k-connected if for each arbitrary $p, q \in R$, exists a sequence of points in $R, p = a_1, a_2, ..., a_n = q$, where a_i y a_{i+1} are k-neighbors for $i = 1, ..., n-1$.

Now, let R be a k-connected subset in Z^2. A point p in R is called end point in R if it has just one k-neighbor in R. Note that the only element in a set containing just one point in Z^2, is an end point. Besides, if R has at least two points, then $p \in R$ is an end point in R if p has exactly one k-neighbor in R. The idea behind the thinning is to remove iteratively points in R preserving not only the connectivity, but also preserving the end point condition into the actual points set through each iteration. It is clear that the contour in R are candidates to be eliminated without altering the connectivity. Recalling, p is a contour point in R if p has a k'-neighbor q fulfilling $q \notin R$, where

$k'= 8$ if $k = 4$, $k'= 4$ if $k = 8$, and $k'= k$ if $k \in \{6L,6R\}$. Thanks to the way the contour is defined, it is possible to warranty that the contour is k-connected.

The general strategy of the algorithm is as follows:

1. $R_0 = R; i = 1; R_i := R$.

2. Determine the contour C from R_i.

3. For $p \in C$: If p fulfills the k-condition:

4. "p is not an end point in R_i, and $R_i \setminus \{p\}$ is k-connected", then $R_i = R_i \setminus \{p\}$.
   Repeat step 3 with the remain points in the contour.

5. If $R_i = R_{i-1}$, then stop; R_{i-1} is the k-skeleton of R. Else, increase i in 1, do
   $R_i = R_{i-1}$, and go to step 2.

3 Thinning Masks

Next, for a 4-connected skeleton the T_4 masks set will be deduced. Let suppose that R is a 4-connected subset in (Z^2, N_4). The needed masks must cover all possible local configurations, where 4-connectivity and end points shall be preserved. As a starting point, at least 6 masks are required, which are shown in the Figure 1.

$$P_1 = \begin{bmatrix} X & 0 & X \\ 1 & p & 1 \\ X & 0 & X \end{bmatrix}, \ P_2 = \begin{bmatrix} X & 1 & X \\ 0 & p & 0 \\ X & 1 & X \end{bmatrix}, \ P_3 = \begin{bmatrix} X & X & X \\ X & p & X \\ 0 & 1 & 0 \end{bmatrix}, P_4 = \begin{bmatrix} X & X & 0 \\ X & p & 1 \\ X & X & 0 \end{bmatrix}, \ P_5 = \begin{bmatrix} 0 & 1 & 0 \\ X & p & X \\ X & X & X \end{bmatrix}, P_6 = \begin{bmatrix} 0 & X & X \\ 1 & p & X \\ 0 & X & X \end{bmatrix}$$

Fig. 1. Cases where p is needed to preserve 4-connectivity or as an end-point

The X symbol used along the entire document, denotes don't care condition. Note that the masks P_1 and P_2 are useful to cover local situations as the shown in the Figure 2.

$$\begin{bmatrix} 0 & 0 & 1 \\ 1 & p & 1 \\ 1 & 0 & 0 \end{bmatrix}, \begin{bmatrix} 1 & 0 & 0 \\ 1 & p & 1 \\ 0 & 0 & 1 \end{bmatrix}, \begin{bmatrix} 1 & 0 & 1 \\ 1 & p & 1 \\ 1 & 0 & 1 \end{bmatrix}, \begin{bmatrix} 0 & 0 & 0 \\ 1 & p & 1 \\ 1 & 0 & 1 \end{bmatrix}, \begin{bmatrix} 1 & 0 & 1 \\ 1 & p & 1 \\ 0 & 0 & 0 \end{bmatrix}, \begin{bmatrix} 1 & 1 & 0 \\ 0 & p & 0 \\ 0 & 1 & 1 \end{bmatrix}, \begin{bmatrix} 0 & 1 & 1 \\ 0 & p & 1 \\ 1 & 1 & 0 \end{bmatrix}, \begin{bmatrix} 1 & 1 & 1 \\ 0 & p & 0 \\ 1 & 1 & 1 \end{bmatrix}, \begin{bmatrix} 1 & 1 & 0 \\ 0 & p & 0 \\ 1 & 1 & 0 \end{bmatrix}, \begin{bmatrix} 0 & 1 & 1 \\ 0 & p & 0 \\ 0 & 1 & 1 \end{bmatrix}$$

Fig. 2. Some specific patterns covered by the masks P_1 and P_2

In all these patterns, the point p is needed to preserve 4-connectivity. In order to justify why the masks P_3, P_4, P_5, P_6 are needed, the patterns shown in the Figure 3 can be considered.

$$\begin{bmatrix} X & y & X \\ y & p & y \\ 0 & 1 & 0 \end{bmatrix}, \begin{bmatrix} X & y & 0 \\ y & p & 1 \\ X & y & 0 \end{bmatrix}, \begin{bmatrix} 0 & 1 & 0 \\ y & p & y \\ X & y & X \end{bmatrix}, \begin{bmatrix} 0 & y & X \\ 1 & p & y \\ 0 & y & X \end{bmatrix}$$

Fig. 3. Cases where the masks P_3, P_4, P_5, P_6 are used

In these cases, point p is necessary to connect any point labeled y with the pixel having intensity 1. If the all y labeled points are 0, then p is an end point, thus p won't be eliminated. The points labeled as X are not relevant in 4-connectivity. Additionally, it is a must to be sure that the skeleton doesn't have parasitic branches, as some of the configurations shown in the Figure 4.

$$\begin{bmatrix} X & 1 & 1 \\ 0 & p & 0 \\ 0 & 0 & 0 \end{bmatrix}, \begin{bmatrix} 0 & 0 & X \\ 0 & p & 1 \\ 0 & 0 & 1 \end{bmatrix}, \begin{bmatrix} 0 & 0 & 0 \\ 0 & p & 0 \\ 1 & 1 & X \end{bmatrix}, \begin{bmatrix} 1 & 0 & 0 \\ 1 & p & 0 \\ X & 0 & 0 \end{bmatrix}$$

Fig. 4. Possible cases of parasitic branches

Independently of the value in X, the pixel p must be eliminated, because the branches having length 1 are prone to cause structural noise on the generated skeleton. The pixel p can be deleted due to any configuration in the Figure 4 does not fulfill any of the patterns covered by the masks from the Figure 1.

By analyzing the Figure 5 (pixels labeled 3 belonging to the contour), it is clear that only one of the two points labeled as r is necessary within the skeleton being thus redundant the other r labeled point; however, if the all points are analyzed in parallel with the six masks in the Figure 1 both points will be eliminated, resulting in a non-connected skeleton.

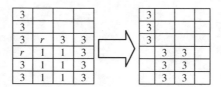

Fig. 5. Redundant connectivity case

Fortunately the previous problem is solved due to the asynchronous execution of the algorithm. This is, one of the r labeled points is analyzed first and then considered redundant being thus eliminated; after that, when the other r labeled point is analyzed, this is not redundant anymore and thus preserved. The remainder cases not covered by the masks in the Figure 1, are covered with the masks in the Figure 6.

$$A_1 = \begin{bmatrix} X & 0 & X \\ 1 & p & x \\ 0 & y & X \end{bmatrix}, \quad A_2 = \begin{bmatrix} 0 & x & X \\ 1 & p & y \\ X & 0 & X \end{bmatrix}, \quad A_3 = \begin{bmatrix} 0 & 1 & X \\ y & p & 0 \\ X & x & X \end{bmatrix}$$

$$A_4 = \begin{bmatrix} X & 1 & 0 \\ 0 & p & x \\ X & y & X \end{bmatrix}, \quad A_5 = \begin{bmatrix} X & y & 0 \\ x & p & 1 \\ X & 0 & X \end{bmatrix}, \quad A_6 = \begin{bmatrix} X & 0 & X \\ y & p & 1 \\ X & x & 0 \end{bmatrix}$$

$$A_7 = \begin{bmatrix} X & x & X \\ 0 & p & y \\ X & 1 & 0 \end{bmatrix}, \quad A_8 = \begin{bmatrix} X & 0 & X \\ y & p & 1 \\ X & x & 0 \end{bmatrix}, \quad \text{with } x \wedge y = 0$$

Fig. 6. Masks that cover the remainder cases for 4-connectivity

For these new masks, x or y must have a zero value in order to avoid single pixel length branches. These new masks eliminate all possible redundancy in the skeleton, and the 4-connectivity is preserved, since the algorithm is sequential. By adding the masks in the Figures 1 and 6, results 14 masks in total, but the last ones can be combined with P_1, P_2 by means of Boolean operations in order to obtain the masks shown in the Figure 7.

$$B_1 = \begin{bmatrix} a & b & X \\ 1 & p & e \\ c & d & X \end{bmatrix}, B_2 = \begin{bmatrix} c & 1 & a \\ d & p & b \\ X & e & X \end{bmatrix}, B_3 = \begin{bmatrix} X & d & c \\ e & p & 1 \\ X & b & a \end{bmatrix}, B_4 = \begin{bmatrix} X & e & X \\ b & p & d \\ a & 1 & c \end{bmatrix}$$

where $c \wedge d = 0, a \wedge b = 0, b + d + e = 1$

Fig. 7. Simplified masks

Notice that the masks P_1 and P_2 are particular cases of B_1, B_3 and B_2 , B_4 respectively, given $c = a = 0$ y $e = 1$. Also, A_1, A_2, A_3, A_4, A_5, A_6, A_7 and A_8 are particular cases of B_1, B_2, B_3 y B_4; furthermore, if the pixel opposed to the one labeled 1 has value 1 in the masks P_3, P_4, P_5 and P_6, the results are also particular cases of B_1, B_2, B_3, B_4.

These masks include all the possible configurations of end points. This means that P_3, P_4, P_5 and P_6 can be replaced by a unique mask, which is shown in the Figure 8. As a consequence, the masks set: $T_4 = \{B_1, B_2, B_3, B_4, B_5\}$ is the final masks set for the 4-connected thinning algorithm.

$$B_5 = \begin{bmatrix} 0 & h & 0 \\ e & p & g \\ 0 & f & 0 \end{bmatrix}, \text{with } e + f + g + h = 1$$

Fig. 8. Mask grouping the cases of P_3, P_4, P_5, P_6

To cover all the cases for the type 8 connectivity, at least the cases shown in the Figure 9 are required.

$$P_1 = \begin{bmatrix} 1 & 0 & X \\ 0 & p & X \\ X & X & X \end{bmatrix}, P_2 = \begin{bmatrix} X & 0 & 1 \\ X & p & 0 \\ X & X & X \end{bmatrix} P_5 = \begin{bmatrix} 0 & 0 & X \\ 1 & p & X \\ 0 & 0 & X \end{bmatrix}, P_6 = \begin{bmatrix} X & X & X \\ 0 & p & 0 \\ 0 & 1 & 0 \end{bmatrix}$$

$$P_3 = \begin{bmatrix} X & X & X \\ X & p & 0 \\ X & 0 & 1 \end{bmatrix}, P_4 = \begin{bmatrix} X & X & X \\ 0 & p & X \\ 1 & 0 & X \end{bmatrix} P_7 = \begin{bmatrix} X & 0 & 0 \\ X & p & 1 \\ X & 0 & 0 \end{bmatrix}, P_8 = \begin{bmatrix} 0 & 1 & 0 \\ 0 & p & 0 \\ X & X & X \end{bmatrix}$$

Fig. 9. Former masks for the type 8 connectivity

If at least one of the pixels marked with the don't care value (X) has an intensity of 1, the p pixel must remain in order to keep connectivity. If none of these pixels is one, p is an end point, and it must not be eliminated. Additionally, the two masks shown in the Figure 10 are needed, since they are cases where the connectivity must be preserved, and they aren't covered by the masks in the Figure 9.

$$P_9 = \begin{bmatrix} X & 0 & X \\ 1 & p & 1 \\ X & 0 & X \end{bmatrix}, P_{10} = \begin{bmatrix} X & 1 & X \\ 0 & p & 0 \\ X & 1 & X \end{bmatrix}$$

Fig. 10. Additional masks

The order in which the algorithm scans the image affects to some of the former 4 masks from the mentioned above. For example, if the scanning is done *top–down* (left to right, and upper to bottom), the P_1 must be changed by the mask shown in the Figure 11.

$$P_1 = \begin{bmatrix} 1 & 0 & d \\ 0 & p & e \\ h & g & f \end{bmatrix} \text{, with } d+e+f+g+h>0$$

Fig. 11. Mask changed due to the order of the image scan

With respect to masks P_5, P_6, P_7 and P_8, when the pixel located in opposition to the pixel marked with 1 has value 1, particular cases of the masks P_9 and P_{10} arises as is shown in the Figure 12a. If on the contrary, this opposite pixel has a zero value but some of their lateral pixels are 1-valued, then a special case of the former 4 masks (P_1, P_2, P_3 and P_4) arise. This situation is shown in the Figure 12b.

$$\begin{bmatrix} 0 & 0 & X \\ 1 & p & 1 \\ 0 & 0 & X \end{bmatrix}, \begin{bmatrix} X & 1 & X \\ 0 & p & 0 \\ 0 & 1 & 0 \end{bmatrix}, \begin{bmatrix} X & 0 & 0 \\ 1 & p & 1 \\ X & 0 & 0 \end{bmatrix}, \begin{bmatrix} 0 & 1 & 0 \\ 0 & p & 0 \\ X & 1 & X \end{bmatrix}$$
(a)

$$\begin{bmatrix} 0 & 0 & X \\ 1 & p & 0 \\ 0 & 0 & X \end{bmatrix}, \begin{bmatrix} X & 0 & X \\ 0 & p & 0 \\ 0 & 1 & 0 \end{bmatrix}, \begin{bmatrix} X & 0 & 0 \\ 0 & p & 1 \\ X & 0 & 0 \end{bmatrix}, \begin{bmatrix} 0 & 1 & 0 \\ 0 & p & 0 \\ X & 0 & X \end{bmatrix}$$
(b)

Fig. 12. (a) Particular cases of P_9 y $P_{10.}$ (b) Particular cases of the former four masks

Because of this, the masks P_5, P_6, P_7 and P_8 are only necessary for configurations as the ones shown in the Figure 13a. The masks P_5, P_6, P_7 and P_8 can be eliminated and replaced by a unique one. This new mask is shown in the Figure 13b.
Finally, the masks set for 8-connectivity is $T_8 = \{P_1, P_2, P_3, P_4, P_9, P_{10}, P_{11}\}$.

$$\begin{bmatrix} 0 & 0 & 0 \\ 1 & p & 0 \\ 0 & 0 & 0 \end{bmatrix}, \begin{bmatrix} 0 & 1 & 0 \\ 0 & p & 0 \\ 0 & 0 & 0 \end{bmatrix}, \begin{bmatrix} 0 & 0 & 0 \\ 0 & p & 1 \\ 0 & 0 & 0 \end{bmatrix}, \begin{bmatrix} 0 & 0 & 0 \\ 0 & p & 0 \\ 0 & 1 & 0 \end{bmatrix}$$
(a)

$$P_{11} = \begin{bmatrix} 0 & a & 0 \\ d & p & b \\ 0 & c & 0 \end{bmatrix} \text{, with } a+b+c+d=1$$
(b)

Fig. 13. (a) Cases where the masks P_5, P_6, P_7 and P_8 are used. (b) Mask that replace them

4   Final Tests and Results

The proposed algorithm was implemented in the Integrated Development Environment (IDE) C++ Builder release 5.0. We probe the technique using two types of images: synthetics and real. In both cases, we obtained good results. In Figure 14, we shown the result using a synthetic image, generated with a commercial drawing tool.

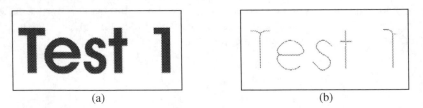
(a)   (b)

Fig. 14. Algorithm test. (a) Image to process. (b) 8-connected algorithm

In some practical cases, like the one shown in Figure 15, it is convenient to apply the opening morphological operator, using a structured element of size 3 x 3, to remove parasitic pixels which can generate not desired branches in the final skeleton.

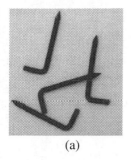
(a)

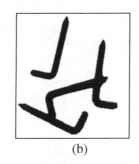
(b)

(c)

Fig. 15. (a) Source image. (b) Thresholding and opened image (c) 8-connected skeleton

5 Conclusions

In this paper an efficient thinning algorithm is presented, using a small set of templates that allow us to decide when a contour pixel can be removed without losing connectivity. One advantage of our proposal is that due to the low time obtained, the algorithm can be applied in systems with strong time constrains such as real time applications. A very important fact is that the templates are not affected by the presence of structured noise and the final skeleton preserves a topological structure based on a single metric space.

Acknowledgments

The authors of this paper wish to thank to the Centre for Computing Research (CIC), the General Coordination of Postgraduate Study and Research (CGEPI) and to the National Polytechnic Institute (IPN) for their support. Additionally, the authors wish to thank the reviewers of this work for their pertinent comments.

References

1. Rosenfeld, "Characterization of parallel thinning algorithms", Information and Control, 29, pp. 286 – 291, 1975.
2. T. Pavlidis, "Algorithms for Graphics and Image Processing", Ed. Computer Science Press, 1982.
3. J. J. Zou, H.-H. Chang, H. Yan, "Shape skeletonization by identifying discrete local symmetries", Pattern Recognition, vol. 34 pp. 185 – 1905, 2001.
4. R. W. Smith, "Computer processing of line images: a survey", Pattern Recognition, vol. 20, pp. 7 – 15, 1987.
5. L. Lam, S.-W. Lee, C. Y. Suen, "Thinning methodologies – a compressive survey", IEEE Tran. Pattern A., vol. 14, pp. 869 – 885, 1992.
6. F. Leymarie, M. D. Levine, "Simulating the grassfire transform using an active contour model", IEEE Trans. Pattern A., vol. 14, pp. 56 – 75, 1992.
7. H. Tamura, "A comparison of line thinning algorithms from the digital viewpoint", Proc. of 4th ICPR, pp. 715 – 719, 1987.

8. E. S. Deutsch, "Thinning algorithms on rectangular, hexagonal, and triangular arrays", Communications of the ACM, vol. 15, pp. 827 – 837, 1972.
9. T. Y. Zhang, C.Y. Suen, "A fast parallel algorithm for thinning digital patterns", Image Processing and Computer Vision, vol. 27, pp. 236 – 239, 1984.
10. J. L. Díaz de León S, "Algoritmos de esqueletización de imágenes digitales binarias", Master thesis, Mexico, 1993.
11. H. E. Lü, S. P. Wang, "A comment on a fast parallel algorithm for thinning digital patterns", Image Processing and Computer Vision, vol. 29, pp. 239 – 242, 1986.
12. W.H. Abdulla, A. O. Saleh, A. H. Morad, "A preprocessing algorithm for hand written character recognition", Pattern Recognition Letters, vol. 7, pp. 13 – 18, 1988.
13. R. González, E. Woods, "Digital Image Processing", Second Edition, Prentice Hall.

Image Processing
Using the Quaternion Wavelet Transform

Eduardo Bayro-Corrochano and Miguel Angel de La Torre Gomora

Computer Science Department, GEOVIS Laboratory
Centro de Investigación y de Estudios Avanzados
CINVESTAV, Guadalajara, Jalisco 44550, Mexico
edb@gdl.cinvestav.mx

Abstract. The contribution of this work is to generalize the real and complex wavelet transforms and to derive for the first time a quaternionic wavelet pyramid for multi-resolution analysis using three phases. The paper can be very useful for researchers and practitioners interested in understanding and applications of the quaternion wavelet transform.

1 Introduction

This work presents the basics and the practicalities of the Quaternion Wavelet Transform (QWT). Along the lines of Mallat [7, 6], we developed a pyramidal model to disentangle symmetries of 2D signals (images) in the quaternion algebra, getting for each level one approximation and three decompositions (horizontal, vertical and diagonal). Different to the complex wavelet transform, the quaternionic wavelet transform provides three phases for a powerful image analysis while using the phase concept.

In the literature [8, 10] the QWT belongs to the theoretical arena where the quaternion mother wavelet is the Haar function, a very inefficient kernel. In our approach we use the more efficient quaternion Gabor kernel and we introduce the multiresolution analysis using the quaternion phase concept. In this regard modulated quaternion Gabor filters are used for computing a pyramid of phases with different resolutions. In the experimental part we show a hierarchical region-based matching algorithm using discrete QWT to estimate optical flow.

2 Quaternions

The quaternion algebra $I\!H$ was invented by W. R. Hamilton in 1843 [4, 1]. It is an associative non-commutative four-dimensional algebra

$$I\!H = \{ q = s + x i + y j + z k \mid s, x, y, z \in \mathbb{R} \}, \tag{1}$$

where the orthogonal imaginary numbers i, j and k obey the following multiplicative rules

$$i^2 = j^2 = -1, \; k = ij = -ji \; \rightarrow \; k^2 = -1. \tag{2}$$

A. Sanfeliu et al. (Eds.): CIARP 2004, LNCS 3287, pp. 613–620, 2004.

The conjugated of a quaternion is given by

$$\bar{q} = s - xi - yj - zk \tag{3}$$

For the quaternion q we can compute its partial angles as $\arg_i(q) = s\tan 2(x, s)$, $\arg_j(q) = s\tan 2(y, s)$, $\arg_k(q) = s\tan 2(z, s)$, and its partial modules and its projections on its imaginary axes as $mod_i(q) = \sqrt{s^2 + x^2}$, $mod_j(s) = \sqrt{s^2 + y^2}$, $mod_k(q) = \sqrt{s^2 + z^2}$, $mod_i(q)\exp(i\arg_i(q)) = s + xi$, $mod_i(q)\exp(j\arg_j(q)) = s + yj$ and $mod_k(q)\exp(k\arg_k(q)) = s + zk$.

In a similar way as the complex numbers which can be expressed in a polar representation, we can also represent a quaternion $q = r + xi + yj + zk$ in a polar form

$$q = |q|e^{i\phi}e^{k\psi}e^{j\theta}, \tag{4}$$

where the phases ranges are delimited as follows $(\phi, \theta, \psi) \in [-\pi, \pi[\times[-\frac{\pi}{2}, \frac{\pi}{2}[\times, \pi[-\times[-\frac{\pi}{4}, \frac{\pi}{4}]$.

For a unit quaternion $q = q_0 + q_x i + q_y j + q_z k$, $|q| = q\bar{q} = 1$, its phase can be evaluated first by computing

$$\psi = -\frac{arcsin(2(q_x q_y - q_0 q_z))}{2} \tag{5}$$

and then by checking that it adheres to the following rules:

- If $\psi \in]-\frac{\pi}{4}, \frac{\pi}{4}[$, then $\phi = \frac{arg(q\mathcal{T}_j(\bar{q}))}{2}$ and $\theta = \frac{arg(\mathcal{T}_i(\bar{q})q)}{2}$.
- If $\psi = \pm\frac{\pi}{4}$, then select either $\phi{=}0$ and $\theta = \frac{arg(\mathcal{T}_k(\bar{q})q)}{2}$ or $\theta{=}0$ and $\phi = \frac{arg(q\mathcal{T}_k(\bar{q}))}{2}$.
- If $e^{i\phi}e^{k\psi}e^{j\theta} = -q$ and $\phi \geq 0$, then $\phi \to \phi - \pi$.
- If $e^{i\phi}e^{k\psi}e^{j\theta} = -q$ and $\phi < 0$, then $\phi \to \phi + \pi$,

where we use the three nontrivial involutions [3] $\mathcal{T}_i(q) = -iqi = q_0 + q_x i - q_y j - q_z k$, $\mathcal{T}_j(q) = -jqj = q_0 - q_x i + q_y j - q_z k$, and $\mathcal{T}_k(q) = -kqk = q_0 - q_x i - q_y j + q_z k$.

3   Quaternion Wavelet Transform

The quaternion wavelet transform is a natural extension of the real and complex wavelet transform taking into account the axioms of the quaternion algebra, the quaternionic analytic signal [2] and the separability propriety. The QWT is applied for signals of 2-D or bigger dimensions.

The multi-resolution analysis can be also straightforwardly extended to the quaternionic case; we can improve therefore the power of the phase concept which in the real wavelets is not possible and in the case of the complex is limited to only one phase. Thus, in contrast to the similarity distance used in the complex wavelet pyramid [9], we favor the quaternionic phase concept for top-down parameter estimation.

For the quaternionic versions of the wavelet scale function h and the wavelet function g we choose two quaternionic modulated Gabor filters in quadrature as follows

$$h^q = g(x, y, \sigma_1, \varepsilon) \exp(\mathbf{i} \frac{c_1 \omega_1 x}{\sigma_1}) \exp(\mathbf{j} \frac{c_2 \varepsilon \omega_2 y}{\sigma_1}) = h^q_{ee} + h^q_{oe} \mathbf{i} + h^q_{eo} \mathbf{j} + h^q_{oo} \mathbf{k}, \quad (6)$$

$$g^q = g(x, y, \sigma_2, \varepsilon) \exp(\mathbf{i} \frac{\tilde{c}_1 \tilde{\omega}_1 x}{\sigma_2}) \exp(\mathbf{j} \frac{\tilde{c}_2 \varepsilon \tilde{\omega}_2 y}{\sigma_2}) = g^q_{ee} + g^q_{oe} \mathbf{i} + g^q_{eo} \mathbf{j} + g^q_{oo} \mathbf{k}. \quad (7)$$

Note that the horizontal axis x is related with $\mathbf{i}$ and the vertical axis y is related with $\mathbf{j}$, both imaginary numbers of the quaternion algebra fulfill the equation $\mathbf{k} = \mathbf{ji}$.

The right parts of the equations (6) and (7) obey a natural decomposition of a quaternionic analytic function: the subindex oo stands for even-even a symmetric filter, eo even-odd or oe odd-even both stand for unsymmetrical filters and oo odd-odd stand for a unsymmetrical filter as well. Thus we can see clearly that h^q and g^q of equations (6) and (7) are powerful filters for disentanglement of the symmetries of the 2-D signals. It is clear that for exploting the phase concept, complex wavelets can use only one phase, where as the quaternionic wavelets offer three phases.

3.1 Quaternionic Wavelet Pyramid

For the 2-D image function $f(x, y)$, a quaternionic wavelet multi-resolution will be written as

$$f(x, y) = A^q_n f + \sum_{j=1}^{n} [D^q_{j,1} f + D^q_{j,2} f + D^q_{j,3} f]. \quad (8)$$

The upper index q stands for indicating quaternion 2-D signal. We can characterize each approximation function $A^q_j f(x, y)$ and the difference components $D^q_{j,p} f(x, y)$ for $p = 1, 2, 3$ by means of a 2D scaling function $\mathbf{\Phi}^q(x, y)$ and its associate wavelet functions $\mathbf{\Psi}^q_p(x, y)$ as follows

$$A^q_j f(x, y) = \sum_{k=-\infty}^{+\infty} \sum_{l=-\infty}^{+\infty} a_{j,k,l} \mathbf{\Phi}^q_{j,k,l}(x, y), \quad (9)$$

$$D^q_{j,p} f(x, y) = \sum_{k=-\infty}^{+\infty} \sum_{l=-\infty}^{+\infty} d_{j,p,k,l} \mathbf{\Psi}^q_{j,p,k,l}(x, y) \quad (10)$$

where

$$\mathbf{\Phi}^q_{j,k,l}(x, y) = \frac{1}{2^j} \mathbf{\Phi}^q(\frac{x-k}{2^j}, \frac{y-l}{2^j}), \quad (j, k, l) \in \mathbb{Z}^3, \quad (11)$$

$$\mathbf{\Psi}^q_{j,p,k,l}(x, y) = \frac{1}{2^j} \mathbf{\Psi}^q_p(\frac{x-k}{2^j}, \frac{y-l}{2^j}) \quad (12)$$

and

$$a_{j,k,l}(x,y) = < f(x,y), \mathbf{\Phi}^q_{j,k,l}(x,y) >, \quad d_{j,p,k,l} = < f(x,y), \mathbf{\Psi}^q_{j,p,k,l}(x,y) > . \quad (13)$$

In order to carry out a separable quaternionic multi-resolution analysis, we decompose the scaling function $\mathbf{\Phi}^q(x,y)_j$ and the wavelet functions $\mathbf{\Psi}^q_p(x,y)_j$ for each level j as follows

$$\mathbf{\Phi}^q(x,y)_j = \phi^{\boldsymbol{i}}(x)_j \phi^{\boldsymbol{j}}(y)_j, \qquad (14)$$

$$\mathbf{\Psi}^q_1(x,y)_j = \phi^{\boldsymbol{i}}(x)_j \psi^{\boldsymbol{j}}(y)_j, \quad \mathbf{\Psi}^q_2(x,y)_j = \psi^{\boldsymbol{i}}(x)_j \phi^{\boldsymbol{j}}(y)_j, \qquad (15)$$

$$\mathbf{\Psi}^q_3(x,y)_j = \psi^{\boldsymbol{i}}(x)_j \psi^{\boldsymbol{j}}(y)_j, \qquad (16)$$

where $\phi^{\boldsymbol{i}}(x)_j$, $\psi(x)^{\boldsymbol{i}}_j$ are 1-D complex filters applied along the rows and columns respectively. Note that in the ϕ and ψ we use the imaginary number $\boldsymbol{i}, \boldsymbol{j}$ of quaternions that fulfill $\boldsymbol{ji} = \boldsymbol{k}$. By using these formulas we can build quaternionic wavelet pyramid. Figure 1 shows the two primary levels of the pyramid (fine to coarse). According the equation (16) the approximation after the first level $A^q_1 f(x,y)$ is the output of $\mathbf{\Phi}^q(x,y)_1$, the differences $D^q_{1,1}f, D^q_{1,2}f, D^q_{1,3}f$ are the outputs of $\mathbf{\Psi}^q_{1,1}(x,y), \mathbf{\Psi}^q_{1,2}(x,y)$ and $\mathbf{\Psi}^q_{1,3}(x,y)$. The procedure continues through the j levels decimating the image at the outputs of the levels (indicated in the Figure 1 within a circle).

The quaternionic wavelet analysis from level $j-1$ to level j corresponds to the transforming of one quaternionic approximation to a new quaternionic approximation and three quaternionic differences, i.e.

$$\{A^q_{j-1}\} \to \{A^q_j, D^q_{j,p}, p = 1, 2, 3\}, \qquad (17)$$

compare that we do not use the idea of mirror tree [5]. As a result, the quaternionic wavelet tree is the compact and economic processing structure to be used for the case of n-D multi-resolution analysis.

The procedure of quaternionic wavelet multi-resolution analysis depicted partially in Figure 1 is as follows

- convolve the 2-D real signal at level j and convolve it with the scale and wavelet filters H^q_j and G^q_j along the rows of the the 2-D signal.
- H^q_j and G^q_j are convolved with the columns of the previous responses of the filters H^q_j and G^q_j.
- Subsample the responses of these filters by a factor of two ($\downarrow 2$).
- The real part of the approximation at level j is taken as input at the next level j, this process continues through the all levels $j = 1, ..., n$ repeating the steps 1→4.

4   Applications

The estimation of the disparity using the concept of local phase begins with the assumption that a couple of successive images are related as follows

$$f_1(x) = f_2(x + \mathbf{d}(x)), \qquad (18)$$

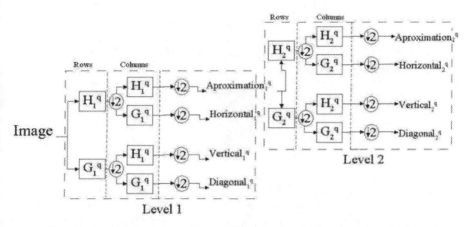

Fig. 1. Abstraction of two levels of the quaternionic wavelet pyramid

where $\mathbf{d}(x)$ is the unknown vector. Assuming that the phase varies linearly (here we see the importance of shifting invariant filters), the displacement $\mathbf{d}(x)$ can be computed as

$$d_x(x) = \frac{\phi_2(x) - \phi_1(x) + n(2\pi + k)}{2\pi u_{ref}}, \qquad d_y(x) = \frac{\theta_2(x) - \theta_1(x) + m\pi}{2\pi v_{ref}}, \qquad (19)$$

with reference frequencies (u_{ref}, v_{ref}) that are not known a priori. Here $\phi(x)$ and $\theta(x)$ are the first two components of the quaternionic local phase of the quaternionic filter. We choose $n, m \in \mathbb{Z}$, so that d_x and d_y are within a valid range. Depending on m, k is defined as

$$k = \begin{cases} 0, \text{ if } m \text{ is even} \\ 1, \text{ if } m \text{ is odd} \end{cases} \qquad (20)$$

A good disparity estimation is achieved if (u_{ref}, v_{ref}) are well chosen. There are two methods of dealing with the problem: i) the constant model where u_{ref} and v_{ref} are chosen as the central frequencies of the filters; ii) the model for the complex case called the local model, it supposes that the phase takes the same value $\Phi_1(x) = \Phi_2(x+d)$ in two correspondent points in both images, thus one estimates d by approximating Φ_2 via a first order Taylor's series expansion about $\mathbf{x}$:

$$\Phi_2(\mathbf{x} + \mathbf{d}) \approx \phi_2(\mathbf{x}) + (\mathbf{d} \cdot \nabla)\phi_2(\mathbf{x}), \qquad (21)$$

where we call $\Phi - (\phi, \theta)$. Solving equation (21) for $\mathbf{d}$ we obtain the estimated disparity of the local model. In our experiments we assume that ϕ varies along the $\mathbf{x}$ direction and θ along y. Using this assumption the disparity (equation (19)) can be estimated using the following reference frequencies

$$u_{ref} = \frac{1}{2\pi}\frac{\partial \phi_1}{\partial x}(x), \qquad v_{ref} = \frac{1}{2\pi}\frac{\partial \theta_1}{\partial y}(x). \qquad (22)$$

If locations where u_{ref} and v_{ref} are equal to zero, the equations (22) are undefined. One can neglect these localities using a sort of confidence mask.

As an application we will show the estimation of the optical flow of the Rubik cube image sequences. We used the following scaling and wavelet quaternionic filters

$$h^q = g(x, \sigma_1, \varepsilon) \exp(i\frac{c_1\omega_1 x}{\sigma_1}) \exp(j\frac{c_2\varepsilon\omega_2 y}{\sigma_1}) \qquad (23)$$

$$g^q = g(x, \sigma_2, \varepsilon) \exp(i\frac{\tilde{c}_1\tilde{\omega}_1 x}{\sigma_2}) \exp(j\frac{\tilde{c}_2\varepsilon\tilde{\omega}_2 y}{\sigma_2}) \qquad (24)$$

with $\sigma_1 = \frac{\pi}{6}$ y $\sigma_2 = \frac{5\pi}{6}$ so that the filters are in quadrature and $c_1 = \tilde{c}_1 = 3$, $\omega_1 = 1$ y $\omega_2 = 1, \varepsilon = 1$. The resulting quaternionic mask will also be sub-sampled through the levels of the pyramid. For the estimation of the the optical flow we use two successive images of the image sequence, thus two quaternionic wavelet pyramids are generated. For our examples we computed 4 levels. According to equation (17) at each level of each pyramid we obtain 16 images accounting for the four quaternionic outputs (approximation Φ and the details Ψ_1 (horizontal), Ψ_2 (vertical),Ψ_3 (diagonal)). The phases are evaluated according to the equations (2). Figure 2 shows the magnitudes and phases obtained at a level j using two successive Rubik's images.

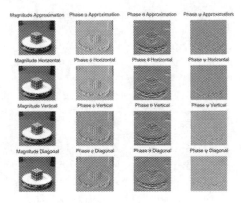

Fig. 2. The magnitudes and phase images for the Rubik's sequence at certain level j: (upper row) the approximation Φ and (next rows) the details Ψ_1 (horizontal), Ψ_2 (vertical),Ψ_3 (diagonal)

After we have computed the phases, we proceed to estimate the disparity images using the equations (19), where the reference frequencies u and v are calculated according to equation (22). We apply the confidence mask as shown in Figure 3.a.

After the estimation of the disparity has been filtered by the confidence mask, we proceed to estimate the optical flow at each point computing a velocity vector in terms of the horizontal and vertical details. Now, using the information of the diagonal detail, we adjust the final orientation of the velocity vector. Since the

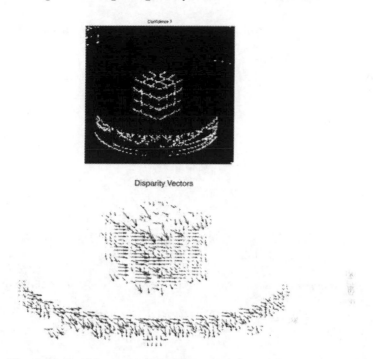

Fig. 3. a) Confidence mask. b) Estimated optical flow

procedure starts from the higher level (top-down) the resulting matrix of the optical flow vectors is expanded in size equal to the next level. The algorithm estimates the optical flow at the new level, the result is compared with the one of the expanded previous level. The velocity vectors of the previous level fill gaps in the new level.

This procedure is continued until the bottom level. In this way the estimation is refined smoothly, the well defined optical flow vectors are passing from level to level increasing the confidence of the vectors at the finest level. It is unavoidable that some artifacts survive at the final stage. A final refinement can be applied imposing a magnitude thresholding and certainly deleting isolated small vectors.

Figure 3 presents the optical flow for an image couple of the Rubik's image sequence. Note that we present all the optical flow vectors that we get with our procedure. We have checked results of some other authors using their own Mat-Lab routines of complex wavelets, and we have detected that their results were presented after deleting many small vectors or the ones in conflicting locations like in the corners of the Rubik's cube.

Our experiment shows that the procedure using quaternionic wavelet pyramid and the phase concept for the parameter estimation work very well.

5   Conclusion

This paper presents the theory and practicalities of the quaternion wavelet transform. The Mallat's multi-resolution analysis has been extended using the quaternion wavelets. A big advantage of the approach is that it offers three phases at each level of the pyramid, which can be used for a powerful top-down parameter estimation. The authors believe that the paper can help to push forward the research and applications of hyper-complex wavelet transforms.

Acknowledgments

The authors were supported by the project 49 of CONACYT-Fondo Sectorial de Investigación en Salud y Seguridad Social.

References

1. Bayro-Corrochano E., 2001. *Geometric Computing for Perception Action Systems*, Springer Verlag, Boston.
2. Bülow T., 1999. *Hypercomplex Spectral Signal Representations for the Processing and Analysis of Images.* PhD. thesis, University Christian Albrechts university of Kiel.
3. Chernov V. M., 1995. *Discrete orthogonal transforms with the data representation in composition algebras.* In Scandinavian Conference on Image Analysis, Uppsala, Sweden, pp. 357-364.
4. Hamilton W.R., 1969. *Elements of Quaternions.* Longmans Green, London 1866. Chelsea, New York.
5. Magarey, J.F.A. and Kingsbury, N.G. 1998. *Motion estimation using a complex-valued wavelet transform.* IEEE Trans. Image Proc. **6**, 549-565.
6. S. Mallat *A Wavelet Tour of Signal Processing.* Academic Press, San Diego, CA, Second Edition, 1998.
7. Mallat S.,1989. *A Teory for multiresolution signal decomposition: the wavelet representation.* IEEE Trans. Patt. Anal. and Mach. Intell., 11(7):674-693, July.
8. Mitrea M., 1994. *Clifford Waveletes, singular Integrals and Hardy spaces.* Lecture notes in mathematics 1575, Spinger Verlag.
9. Pan H.-P., 1996. *Uniform full information image matching complex conjugate wavelet pyramids.* XVIII ISPRS Congress, Viena, July 1996, vol. XXXI.
10. Traversoni L., 2001. *Image Analysis using Quaternion Wavelet,* in Geometric Algebra in Science and Engineering Book, E. Bayro Corrochano and G. Sobczyk, Springer Velag, Chap. 16.

Improving Pattern Recognition Based Pharmacological Drug Selection Through ROC Analysis*

W. Díaz[1], María José Castro[2], F.J. Ferri[1,**], F. Pérez[3], and M. Murcia[3]

[1] Dept. Informàtica, Universitat de València, 46100 Burjassot, Spain
ferri@uv.es
[2] Dept. Sistemes Informàtics i Computació, Universitat Politècnica de València 46071 València, Spain
[3] Dept. Química Física, F. Farmàcia, Universitat de València, 46100 Burjassot, Spain

Abstract. The design of new medical drugs is a very complex process in which combinatorial chemistry techniques are used. The goal consists of discriminating between molecular compounds exhibiting or not certain pharmacological activities. Different machine learning approaches have been recently applied to different drug design problems leading to competitive results in pointing at particular compounds with high probability of exhibiting activity. The present work first deeps into the natural trade-off between accuracy in the much less populated active group and false alarm rate which could lead to too many expensive laboratory tests. Preliminary results show how different classification techniques are suited for this particular problem and throw light to keep improving the results by considering also the acceptance/rejection trade-off.

1 Introduction

The design of new medical drugs with desired chemical properties is a challenging and very important problem in the pharmaceutical industry. The traditional approach for formulating new compounds requires the designer to test a very large number of molecular compounds, to select them in a blind way, and to look for the desired pharmacological property. Therefore, it is very useful to have tools to discriminate the pharmacological activity of a given molecular compound so that the laboratory experiments can be directed to those molecular groups in which there is a high probability of finding new compounds with the desired properties.

All methods developed for this purpose are based on the fact that the activity of a molecule derives from its structure and therefore it is possible to find a relationship between this structure and the properties that the molecule exhibits [9]. Thus, the way the molecular structure is represented has special relevance.

---

* This work has been partially funded by spanish project TIC2003-08496.
** Contacting author

A. Sanfeliu et al. (Eds.): CIARP 2004, LNCS 3287, pp. 621–628, 2004.

In Chemical Graph Theory, molecular structures are represented as doubly labelled graphs which can be conveniently characterized by a number of specific topological indices [6]. In this work, a reduced set of 62 topological indices [7] are considered.

These or similar representations have already been applied to different discrimination problems in drug design (analgesic, antidiabetic, antibacterial, etc.) but the cost/benefit problem and the corresponding discrimination thresholds have always been selected at hand based on previous a priori knowledge on the particular problem.

This paper describes several Machine Learning approaches (LDA analysis, naive Bayes classifier and neural networks) to solve a particular problem of property discrimination (antibacterial activity) based on the structural representation of the molecule. A detailed analysis is then performed in order to determine the suitability and adaptability of these methods for the particular task from the point of view of the cost/benefit trade-off.

2   The Molecular Representation Space

As an alternative to the methods based on the "exact" description of the electronic properties of a molecule calculated by mechanical-quantum methods, the molecular topology describes the molecule as a set of indices. These topological indices are numerical descriptors that encode information about the number of atoms and their structural environment. This representation is derived from the hydrogen-suppressed molecular formula seen as a graph and it requires a relatively low calculation effort [1, 2, 6].

The molecular topology considers a molecule as a planar graph where atoms are represented by vertices and chemical bonds are represented by edges. The chosen set of molecular descriptors should adequately capture the phenomena underlying the properties of the compound. In this and other related works, a set of 62 indices has been selected [7, 8, 10]. Fourteen of these indices are related to the molecular attributes of the compound; for example, the total number of atoms of a certain element (carbon, nitrogen, oxygen, sulphur, fluorine, chlorine, . . .), the total number of bonds of a certain type (simple, double or triple), the number of atoms with a specific vertex degree, distance between the bonds, etc. . .

The remaining forty-eight indices include different topological information, such as the number of double bonds at distance 1 or 2, and the minimum distance between pairs of atoms, which are counted as the number of bonds between atoms. These indices are classified into six groups which are associated to the most frequent elements that constitute the molecules with pharmacological activity: nitrogen, oxygen, sulphur, fluorine, chlorine, bromine, and a general group in which the distances between pairs of atoms are considered without identifying the type of atom.

This molecular representation has shown its ability for discriminating and predicting different kinds of pharmacological properties. Nevertheless, it is known that certain indices are more important that others for detecting particular cases. For example, it has been shown that only eight out of the above topological indices are enough to predict antibacterial activity with about 80% accuracy (and about 90% inactivity accuracy or 10% false alarm rate) [8].

As we are trying to extract conclusions as general as possible from the empirical evaluation carried out, we will not use this kind of information in the experiments and the whole set of topological descriptors will be considered. This means that the methods with a natural tendency to extract a few good features (as multilayer neural networks) will have more chances to obtain better results.

3   The Antibacterial Activity Discrimination Problem

The particular discrimination problem was to determine whether a molecule has antibacterial activity or not. To this end, three different classification thechniques have been considered: LDA analysis [8], Multilayer Perceptrons [3] and Gaussian Naive Bayes [4] as a reference.

A dataset of 434 samples with potential pharmacological activity has been used in this work. This particular dataset is basically balanced which is not representative of the a priori probability of antibacterial activity in real pharmacological design trials.

In order to obtain results as significant as possible, repeated cross-validation has been used to compute all accuracies. In particular, the dataset was split five times into training and test set in a 70%-30% proportion and the corresponding results averaged. Every partition has been performed randomly, taking into account that the percentages of active and inactive samples were the same as in the original sample.

Instead of performing new experiments, the results with LDA analysis have been directly taken from a previous work [8] which used a different (and slightly more representative) dataset and can be considered as the best results to date for this particular problem.

New experiments have been performed with a naive Bayes classifier [4] to use them as a reference. Finally, multilayer perceptrons (MLPs) were used to discriminate antibacterial properties of the molecules.

The 62 topological indices were used to obtain feature vectors in which values were linearly normalized to the interval $[0, 1]$ in an independent way. As in previous works [8], each feature vector was labeled with 1 (indicating that the molecule has antibacterial properties) and -1 (the molecule is inactive).

The training of the MLPs were carried out using the neural software package "SNNS: Stuttgart Neural Network Simulator" [12]. The network topology, training algorithm and parameter settings were chosen from a previous work [3] which was not particularly aimed at looking for antibacterial activity.

More specifically, the results presented have been obtained by using the standard Backpropagation algorithm with a learning rate equal to 0.05 and a topology of 62 input units, 2 hidden units and one output unit. The hyperbolic tangent function was used in order to keep outputs in the interval $[-1, 1]$ as in the LDA analysis [8].

The Naive Bayes implementation used was taken from the data mining and machine learning package Weka [11]. The outputs were normalized also to the $[-1, 1]$ interval to keep all results and discrimination thresholds comparable.

4   The Cost Benefit Trade-Off

It is important to note that we are interested not only in achieving a high accuracy in classification but also a convenient compromise between true positive and false alarm rates. The high economical costs due to the pharmacological tests on each candidate molecule in drugs research makes an important issue to keep the number of false positives as low as possible, even if this implies to reject some true positives.

Table 1. Confusion matrix corresponding to LDA [8]. All undetermineds are taken from molecules predicted as active. Consequently, accuracies for both active and inactive groups without a reject option are 81.95% and 92.58%, respectively.

	predicted		
	active	undetermined	inactive
active	70.83%	11.12%	18.05%
inactive	5.94%	1.48%	92.58%

As already mentioned, orientative figures for previous results on this problem are about 80% of true positives and 10% of false positives. The whole confusion matrix obtained for antibacterial prediction using LDA in [8] is shown in Table 1. Nevertheless, the emphasis of the experimentation in this work is on studying how the classifiers behave as we constrain one of the two above figures. In other words, we are interested in obtaining a Receiver Operating Characteristic (ROC) curve and looking for the best parameter settings of each classification scheme.

Given a particular classifier whose output consists of a continuous value in a specified interval (as in the cases considered in this work), the ROC curve is defined as the plot of the true positive rate (TP) against false positive rate (FP) considering the threshold used in the classifier as a parameter. The so-called ROC space is given by all possible results of such a classifier in the form (FP,TP). The performance of any classifier (with the corresponding threshold included) can be represented by a point in the ROC space. ROC curves move from the "all-inactive" point (0,0) which corresponds to the highest value of the threshold to the "all-active" point (1,1) given by the lowest value for the threshold. The straight line between these two trivial points in the ROC space corresponds to the family of random classifiers with different a priori probabilities for each class. The more a ROC curve separates from this line, the better the corresponding classification scheme is. As ROC curves move away from this line, they approach the best possible particular result that corresponds to the point (0,1) in the ROC space which means no false alarms and highest possible accuracy in the active class.

The ROC curve is a perfect tool to find the best trade-off between true positives and false positives and to compare classifiers in a range of different situations. A number techniques to obtain different measures from ROC curves have been also developed.

5   Experiments, Results and Discussion

The above mentioned classification methods have been applied to the training sets taken from the available data set and the corresponding (continuous) outputs have been obtained for the test data. For each partition into train and test, a ROC curve is obtained. Figure 1 shows the corresponding averaged ROC curves for the three classification schemes considered. In the particular case of LDA, the curve corresponds to a unique partition in train and test data as explained in [8].

The ROC curve corresponding to LDA shows that, apart from the already mentioned $(0.08, 0.82)$ classifier with discrimination threshold set to zero, there are other possible convenient classifiers as the one with point $(0.005, 0.72)$ in ROC space which uses a higher discrimination threshold, namely 0.61.

More importantly, the (particularly simple) Multilayer Perceptron considered, significantly outperforms the LDA results along the whole range of the curve. Particular (averaged) results that can be mentioned are $(0.05, 0.95)$ and $(0.10, 0.82)$ that involve discrimination thresholds very close to 1.

Finally, results obtained with the Gaussian Naive Bayes are clearly and significantly worse than the others and have been included as a reference only.

The threshold averaged ROC curves have been computed as explained in [5]. The corresponding intervals for a 95% confidence level have also been computed and are shown in Figure 2 for the case of Multilayer Perceptron.

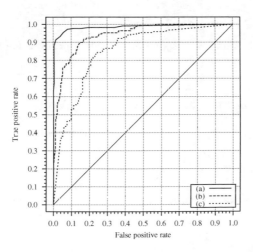

Fig. 1. Averaged ROC curves for a) Multilayer Perceptron, b) LDA, and c) Gaussian Naive Bayes.

Further experimentation including a reject option as in [8] shows that there is still room for improving these results. In particular, the results in Table 1 are obtained by rejecting outputs in the interval $[-0.5, 0.5]$ which means rejecting about 7% of the cases if the data set was balanced. We have carried out an exhaustive computation of ROC curves for all possible percentages of rejection for a particular dataset partition in the case of Multilayer Perceptron. From all curves (in fact, classifiers) obtained, we have selected those with 0% (the original ROC curve), 15% and 20% rejection rate. Results for two particular partitions of the data are shown in Figure 3. As can be seen, the curves are getting better as rejection rate increases. Although these results are still preliminary and valid only for a specific partition of the (by the way quite reduced) data set, this family of curves could eventually be used to look for more convenient classifiers for the problem at hand.

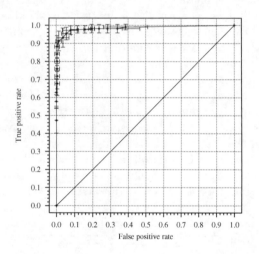

Fig. 2. Averaged ROC curve corresponding to the multilayer perceptron approach along with 95% confidence intervals.

6   Concluding Remarks and Further Work

In this work a classical ROC analysis has been performed on a particular drug activity discrimination problem. Preliminary results show that this kind of analysis is very interesting and can significantly improve the overall costs in the whole drug design methodology. In particular, very simple Multilayer Perceptron is shown to significantly improve previously used approaches in a wide range of situations.

In order to obtain more confident results significant also from a pharmacological point of view, the whole experimentation in this work needs to be repeated with a larger and more representative data set. Also, ROC analysis including the whole range of possible rejects is under consideration. This will lead to a

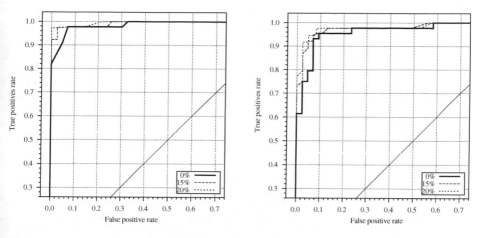

Fig. 3. ROC curves obtained at 0%, 15% and 20% rejection rates for two particular partitions of the available data set using Multilayer Perceptron.

ROC surface into a three dimensional ROC space given by true positive rate, false alarm rate and reject rate and would lead to a full characterization of the discrimination problem in drug design applications.

References

1. A.T. Balaban, I. Motoc, D. Bonchev, and O. Makenyan. Topological indices for structure-activity correlations. *Top. Curr. Chem.*, 114:21–55, 1983.
2. S.C. Basak, S. Bertelsen, and G. Grunwald. Application of graph theoretical parameters in quantifying molecular similarity and structure-activty studies. *J. Chem. Inf. Comput. Sci.*, 34:270–276, 1994.
3. M. J. Castro, W. Díaz, P. Aibar, and J. L. Domínguez. Prediction and Discrimination of Pharmacological Activity by Using Artificial Neural Networks. In F. J. Perales, A. J. C. Campilho, N. Pérez de-la Blanca, and A. Sanfeliu, editors, *Pattern Recognition and Image Analysis*, volume 2652 of *LNCS*, pages 184–192. Springer-Verlag, 2003. ISSN 0302-9743.
4. R. O. Duda, P. E. Hart, and D. G. Stork. *Pattern Classification.* John Wiley and Sons, second edition, 2001.
5. Tom Fawcett. Roc graphs: Notes and practical considerations for researchers. *Machine Learning*, submitted(http://www.hpl.hp.com/personal/Tom_Fawcett/papers/ROC101.pdf), 2004.
6. J. Gálvez, R. García-Domenech, J.V. de Julián-Ortiz, and R. Soler. Topological approach to drug design. *J. Chem. Inf. Comput. Sci.*, 35:272–284, 1995.
7. J. Jaén-Oltra, M.T. Salabert-Salvador, F.J. García-March, F. Péz-Giménez, and F. Tomás-Vert. Artificial neural network applied to prediction of fluorquinolone antibacterial activity by topological methods. *J. Med. Chem.*, 43:1143–1148, 2000.

8. M. Murcia-Soler, F. Pérez-Giménez, F.J. García-March, M.T. Salabert-Salvador, W. Díaz-Villanueva, and P. Medina-Casamayor. Discrimination and selection of new potential antibacterial compounds using simple topological descriptors. *J. Mol. Graph. Model.*, 21:375–390, 2003.

9. P.G. Seybold, M. May, and U.A. Bagal. Molecular structure-propertiy relationships. *J. Chem. Educ.*, 64:575–581, 1987.

10. F. Tomás-Vert, F. Pérez-Giménez, M.T. Salabert-Salvador, F.J. García-March, and J. Jaén-Oltra. Artificial neural network applied to the discrimination of antibacterial activity by topological methods. *J. Mol. Struct. (THEOCHEM)*, 504:272–276, 2000.

11. Ian H. Witten and Eibe Frank. *Data Mining: Practical machine learning tools with Java implementations.* Morgan Kaufmann, San Francisco, 2000.

12. A. Zell et al. *SNNS: Stuttgart Neural Network Simulator. User Manual, Version 4.2.* Institute for Parallel and Distributed High Performance Systems, University of Stuttgart, Germany, 1998.

Adaboost to Classify Plaque Appearance in IVUS Images

Oriol Pujol, Petia Radeva, Jordi Vitrià, and Josepa Mauri

Computer Vision Centre and Dept. Informàtica
Universitat Autònoma de Barcelona
08193 Bellaterra (Barcelona), Spain
petia@cvc.uab.es, jordi@cvc.uab.es

Abstract. Intravascular Ultrasound images represent a unique tool to analyze the morphological vessel structures and make decisions about plaque presence. Texture analysis is a robust way to detect and characterize different kind of vessel plaques. In this article, we make exhaustive comparison between different feature spaces to optimally describe plaque appearance and show that applying advanced classification techniques based on multiple classifiers (adaboost) significantly improves the final results. The validation tests on different kind of plaques are very encouraging.

1 Introduction

The composition and structure of the vessel change with age, hypertension, diabetes mellitus and many other factors. Until this moment, it is feasible to discriminate different morphological structures of the vessel as calcium deposits, fatty, fatty fibrous and fibrous materials. Today, it is not completely clear what the vulnerable plaque is. The common researcher opinion is that a vulnerable plaque consists of: lipid core, fibrous cap, presence of inflammatory cells and is affected by the vessel remodelling and its 3D morphology. Still a complete morphological, mechanical and chemical information is necessary in order to characterize the vulnerable plaque in a robust way.

IVUS displays the morphology and histological properties of a cross-section of a vessel. Figure 1 shows a good example of IVUS images. It is generally accepted that the different kind of plaque tissues distinguishable in IVUS images is threefold: *Calcium formation* is characterized by a very high echoreflectivity and absorbtion of the emitted pulse from the transducer. This behavior produces a deep shadowing effect behind calcium plaques. In the figure, calcium formation can be seen at three o'clock and from five to seven o'clock. *Fibrous plaque* has medium echoreflectivity resembling that of the adventitia. This tissue has a good transmission coefficient allowing the pulse to travel through the tissue, and therefore, providing a wider range of visualization. This kind of tissue can be observed from three o'clock to five o'clock. *Soft plaque* or *Fibro-Fatty plaque* is the less echoreflective of the three kind of tissues. It also has good transmission

A. Sanfeliu et al. (Eds.): CIARP 2004, LNCS 3287, pp. 629–636, 2004.

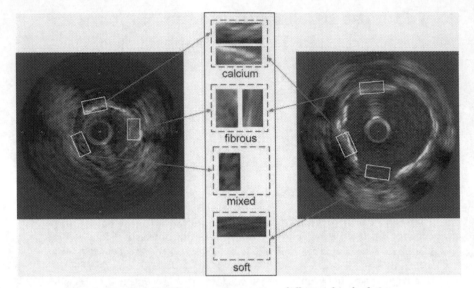

Fig. 1. Typical IVUS images presenting different kind of tissues

coefficient allowing to see what is behind this kind of plaque. Observing the figure, a soft plaque configuration is displayed from seven o'clock to three o'clock.

Textural analysis is one of the closest related processes in computer vision to the physicians expertise when dealing with IVUS images; due to the fact that plaque discrimination is performed using, mostly, morphological issues. Visual textural analysis is a difficult, subjective and time-consuming process highly depending on the specialist. Therefore, there is an increasing interest of the medical community in developing automatic tissue characterization procedures of IVUS images. The problem of automatic tissue characterization has been widely studied in different medical fields. The unreliability of gray level only methods to achieve good discrimination among the different kind of tissues forced us to use more complex measures, usually based on texture analysis.

Several researching groups have reported different approximations to characterize the tissue of intravascular ultrasound images [1] [2] [3]. Most of the literature found in the tissue characterization matters use texture features, being co-occurrence matrices the most popular of all feature extractors. Further work has been done trying to use other kind of texture feature extractors and IVUS images. And, although not specifically centered on tissue characterization, the usage of different texture features in plaque border assessment is reported. This work can be easily extrapolated to tissue characterization. In [6], derivative of gaussian, wavelets, co-occurrence matrices, Gabor filters and cumulative moments are evaluated and used to classify blood from plaque. The work highlights the discriminative power of co-occurrence matrices, derivatives of gaussian and cumulative moments. Other works such as [7] provide some hints on how to achieve a fast framework based on local binary patterns and fast high-performance classifiers. This last line of investigation overcomes one of the most significant drawbacks of the texture based tissue characterization systems, the speed, as texture descriptors are inherently slow to be computed.

In this paper we make an exhaustive comparison study of different feature spaces: *co-occurrence matrix measures, statistical descriptors, local binary patterns*, etc. The originality of the paper consists in applying a novel classification method to analyze the optimal feature space. Applying adaptive boosting techniques allow us to deal with high dimensional spaces by using an intelligent feature selection process while training the classifier. This technique is proven to optimize the final classification results when compared to standard supervised pattern recognition techniques.

2   Feature Spaces

Plaque recognition is usually approached as a texture discrimination problem. We focus our study on two different kind of texture descriptors. The first class of texture descriptors is formally acknowledged to be fully representative and highly discriminant. In this class we place co-occurrence matrices descriptors [9] and a bank of filters approach, based on derivatives of gaussian [11]. The second class is less recognized since the techniques involved are relatively new. This class comprehends descriptors characterized by its low complexity and, therefore, fast to be computed. This gain in speed, however has a cost, the lost in accuracy of the description. In this category we are placing, cumulative moments [10] and local binary patterns [12].

These sets of techniques include examples of the two most important lines of work when dealing with texture, the statistical approach (co-occurrence matrices measures and cumulative moments) and the kernel-based approach (bank of filters and local binary patterns). The first line of work are concerned with density estimation techniques or parameters. The second line of work is centered on sampled forms of analytic functions. In this sense, the local binary patterns approach is the less conventional of the methods, but we have chosen to include it in the kernel-based approach for sake of simplicity.

3   Adaboost Classification Process

Adaptative Boosting (AdaBoost) is an iterative arcing method that allows the designer to keep adding "weak" classifiers until some desired low training error has been achieved [13] [14] [8]. At each step of the process, a weight is assigned to each of the feature points. These weights measure how accurate the feature point is being classified at that stage. If it is accurately classified, then its probability of being used in subsequent learners is reduced, or emphasized otherwise. This way, AdaBoost focuses on difficult training points at each stage. The classification result is a linear combination of the "weak" classifiers. The weight of each classifier is proportional to the amount of data that classifies in a correct way. As an additional feature, AdaBoost is capable of selecting the features with best performance.

The general algorithm is described as follows:

- Determine a supervised set of feature points $\{x_i, c_i\}$ where $c_i = \{-1, 1\}$ is the class associated to each of the features classes.
- Initialize weights $w_{1,i} = \frac{1}{2m}, \frac{1}{2l}$ for $c_i = \{-1, 1\}$ respectively, where m and l are the number of feature points for each class.
- For $t = 1..T$:
  - Normalize weights

  $$w_{t,i} \leftarrow \frac{w_{t,i}}{\sum_{j=1}^{n} w_{t,i}}$$

  so that w_t is a probability distribution.
  - For each feature, j train a classifier, h_j which is restricted to using a single feature. The error is evaluated with respect to w_t, $\epsilon_j = \sum_i w_i |h_j(x_i) - c_i|$.
  - Choose the classifier, h_t with the lowest error ϵ_t.
  - Update the weights:

  $$w_{t+1,i} = w_{t,i} \beta_t^{e_i}$$

  where $e_i = 1$ for each well-classified feature and $e_i = 0$ otherwise. $\beta_t = \frac{\epsilon_t}{1-\epsilon_t}$. Calculate parameter $\alpha_t = -log(\beta_t)$.
- The final "strong" classifier is:

$$h(x) = \begin{cases} 1 & \sum_{t=1}^{T} \alpha_t h_t(x) \geq 0 \\ 0 & \text{otherwise} \end{cases}$$

Therefore, the strong classifier is the ensemble of a series of simple classifiers ("weak"). Parameter α_t is the weighting factor of each of the classifiers. The loop ends when the classification error of a "weak" classifier is over 0.5, the estimated error for the whole "strong" classifier is lower than a given error rate or if we achieve the desired number of "weaks". The final classification is the result of the weighted classifications of the "weaks". The process is designed so that if $h(x) > 0$, then pixel x belongs to one of the classes.

Figure 2 shows the evolution of the error rates for the training and the test feature points. Figure 2(a) shows the test error rate. One can observe, that the overall error has a decreasing tendency as more "weak" classifiers are added to the process. Figure 2(b) shows the error evolution of each of the "weak" classifiers. The figure illustrates how the error increases as more "weak" classifiers are added. Figure 2(c) shows the error rate of the system response on the training data. As it is expected, the error rate decreases to very low values. This, however does not ensure a test classification error of such accuracy.

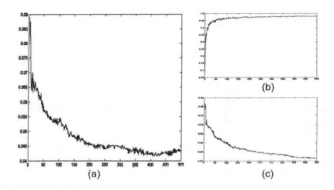

Fig. 2. Error rates associated to the AdaBoost process. (a) Test error rate. (b) "Weak" single classification error (c) Strong classification error on the training data

4   Experimental Results and Conclusions

One of the main problems in the IVUS scientific community is the lack of a standard reference set for validation of the IVUS tissue classification. Regarding this matter, we have devoted a great amount of time in collaboration with expert physicians to create a database with ten thousand samples of each of the four tissues acknowledged by experts, soft tissue, fibrous tissue, mixed tissue and calcium. Those samples have been extracted from 20 different patients, using a *Clearview* device from Boston Scientifics Corp. and a 40 MHz *Atlantis* catheter. Using this database, several texture descriptors have been selected.

Particularly, we have chosen: First, derivatives of gaussian filter bank, up to the third derivative. A five level multi-resolution framework is used, with scales $\{0.2, 0.5, 1, 2, 4\}$. For each scale, a set of directional derivatives is extracted. Second, a set of descriptors of the co-occurrence matrices at angles $\{0, 45, 90, 135\}$ with neighborhoods of 11×11 pixels and distance for the co-occurrence pair of $D = 2$ and a 17×17 pixels neighborhood with a distance of $D = 3$. In third place, a tissue description set based on local binary patterns and local variance, using radius 1 with 8 samples, radius 2 with 16 samples and radius 3 with 24 samples. And finally, a feature space based on cumulative moments, with moments up to $(9, 9)$.

Regarding the Adaboost procedure, we use a composition of 500 classifiers in the original feature space for each description set. The classification process is performed in the following way: Given the data samples in the desired feature space, a training subset is selected (images of the 40% of the total patient cases). This subsets are used to feed the Adaboost training step. As a result, a set of parameterized classifiers is obtained. The linear combination of those classifiers describes the "strong" decision rule. Each sub-classifier, "weak", is combined with a mixing value proportional to the classification error measured at the stage of its incorporation to the ensemble. The "weak" classifier used for our study is a ROC based classification process.

To compare the performance of the boosting method we have selected a well-known classifier, Fisher Linear Discriminant Analysis. The results of this classifier are our ground-truth, to which we refer in order to compare the results of the Adaboost technique.

Plaque discrimination	Feature Set	Initial Error	Final Error
fibrous vs. calcium	BOF	33.13%	13.09%
fibrous vs. calcium	COOC25	20.90%	13.74%
fibrous vs. calcium	COOC38	20.67%	11.04%
fibrous vs. calcium	LBP	24.76%	21.81%
fibrous vs. calcium	MOM	43.62%	38.04%
soft vs.calcium	BOF	17.75%	5.80%
soft vs.calcium	COOC25	9.81%	7.27%
soft vs.calcium	COOC38	8.88%	4.29%
soft vs.calcium	LBP	15.31%	14.68%
soft vs.calcium	MOM	45.49%	33.00%
mixed vs. calcium	BOF	26.29%	9.79%
mixed vs. calcium	COOC25	16.36%	12.44%
mixed vs. calcium	COOC38	15.91%	7.46%
mixed vs. calcium	LBP	20.54%	19.15%
mixed vs. calcium	MOM	44.16%	35.75%
soft vs. fibrous	BOF	28.63%	26.41%
soft vs. fibrous	COOC25	27.58%	27.53%
soft vs. fibrous	COOC38	26.57%	25.98%
soft vs. fibrous	LBP	31.62%	30.93%
soft vs. fibrous	MOM	44.41%	38.43%
fibrous vs. mixed	BOF	37.74%	36.28%
fibrous vs. mixed	COOC25	39.99%	37.33%
fibrous vs. mixed	COOC38	39.40%	35.65%
fibrous vs. mixed	LBP	41.31%	40.90%
fibrous vs. mixed	MOM	43.42%	40.92%
soft vs. mixed	BOF	40.44%	37.36%
soft vs. mixed	COOC25	37.72%	33.09%
soft vs. mixed	COOC38	35.42%	29.29%
soft vs. mixed	LBP	39.35%	39.01%
soft vs. mixed	MOM	46.45%	41.26%

Fig. 3. Classification of plaques

The table in figure 3 shows the figures for the error rate in our problem. The characterization of the calcium tissue seems to be the less difficult one since the calcium tissue has a very high echo-reflectivity and homogeneity (see 3). When compared with the fibrous plaque, the Adaboost procedure refines the classification increasing the recognition rates to an average of 88%. On the other hand, it is surprising that LBP has a relative good performance, close to 80%, making it an ideal candidate if we aim for fast processing. The recognition rate of the high complexity spaces in the soft versus calcium problem is pretty high,

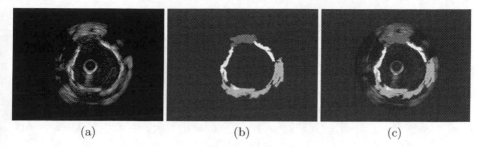

(a)   (b)   (c)

Fig. 4. Example of classification in a real image. (a) Original image. (b) Classification result masks. (c) Classification masks over the original image

and it is further increased by the AdaBoost process, up to an average over 95%. Three important remarks can be made looking at the figures. First, there is a huge improvement in performance using derivatives of gaussian, of about 12%. Second, LBP still has pretty good results: over 85%. Third, MOM still performs bad in this stage. LBP lowers its error rate by 30% and BOF lowers its error rate by 20%. The discrimination between calcium and mixed plaque are not as good as the soft versus calcium problem, but are better than the fibrous versus calcium one. This is logical if we recall that the mixed tissue is a combination of both fibrous tissue and lipid tissue in an interleaved way. COOC25 seems to perform the worst of the trio formed by the high complexity classifiers. If we compare this results to the ones obtained using FLD, BOF lowers its error rate by 20%, and COOC38 by 10%. Discriminating soft vs. fibrous plaque, the AdaBoost process does not help very much. This fact, seems to show that the way data is distributed in the feature spaces is clearly entwined. This fact hinders the process of the combination of classifiers. In this case, the comparison of the results with the reference of Fisher, improves the recognition rate by 10%. Discriminating fibrous vs. mixed plaque as well as the soft vs mixed plaques are by far the most complex ones. The difference between mixed and pure plaque is simply the spatial overall distribution of the tissues. Most of the methods we have tried are purely local, and therefore are destined to fail in this problem. In fact, we have seen that the mixed label is also the most disagreed of the plaques among the experts labelling. It is remarkable the fact that COOC38 is able to distinguish both plaques with an average recognition rate of over 70%. This is due to the fact that COOC38 use a 17×17 neighborhood and therefore is susceptible to pick up the spatial distribution of the entwined fibrous and soft plaques. The fibrous vs. mixed and soft vs. mixed using linear discriminant analysis can not be made, since the results show that the decision is nearly random (recognition rates of about 55%). However, using AdaBoost the problem seems to have a weak solution, that is, a solution of nearly 70% of recognition. Figure 4 shows an example of the classification result using the fibrous (light gray), calcium (white) and soft tissue (dark gray) classifiers.

636   Oriol Pujol et al.

5   Discussion and Conclusions

In summary, AdaBoost is a very high performance classifier, the results show that plaque characterization based only on texture can not be made accurately if we want recognition rates over 85%. Furthermore, the most different kind of tissue, calcium is easily identified even without context information, with an overall accuracy of over 95%. However, mixed plaques are really difficult to distinguish. This points out that if we want to classify mixed plaques, texture descriptors alone are not suitable for the task. The "fake-plaque" effect (plaque resembling other tissues) opens the possibility to create a new kind of classification process that takes into account the particular test set to infer context information and therefore adapt the classification process to the particularities of the test set.

References

1. Arul, P. and Amin, V., Characterization of beef muscle tissue using texture analysis of ultrasonic images, Proc. XIIth Southern Biomed. Eng. Conf., pp. 141-143, 1993.
2. Mavromatis, S., Mammographic mass classification using textural features and descriptive diagnostic data, Digital Signal Processing, 2002. DSP 2002. 2002 14th Int. Conf. on, Vol. 1, pp. 461-464, 2002.
3. Donohue, K. and Forsberg, F., Analysis and classification of tissue with scatterer structure templates, Ultrasonics, Ferroelectrics and Frequency Control, IEEE Trans., Vol. 46, No. 2, pp. 300-310, 1999.
4. de Korte, C. L. and van der Steen, A. F. W., Identification of atherosclerotic plaque components with intravascular ultrasound elastography in vivo: a yucatan pig study, Circulation, Vol. 105, No. 14, pp. 1627-1630, 2002.
5. Zhang, X. and Sonka, M., Tissue characterization in intravascular ultrasound images, IEEE Transactions on Medical Imaging, Vol. 17, No. 6, pp. 889-899, 1998.
6. Pujol, O. and Radeva, P., Automatic segmentation of lumen in IVUS images: An evaluation of texture feat. extrac., Proc. for IBERAMIA 2002, pp. 159-168, 2002.
7. Pujol, O. and Radeva, P., Near real time plaque segmentation of ivus, Proceedings of Computers in Cardiology, pp. 159-168, 2003.
8. Pujol, O. and Rosales, M. and Radeva, P., Intravascular Ultrasound Images Vessel Characterization using AdaBoost, Functional Imaging and Modelling of the Heart. Lecture Notes on Computer Science 2674, pp. 242-251, 2003.
9. Haralick, R., Shanmugam, K. and Dinstein, I., Textural features for image classification, IEEE Trans. System, Man, Cybernetics, Vol. 3, pp. 610-621, 1973.
10. Tuceryan, M., Moment based texture segmentation, PRL, V. 15, pp. 659-668, 1994.
11. Lindeberg, T., Scale-Space Theory in Computer Vision, Kluwer Academic P., 1994.
12. Ojala, T., Pietikainen, M. and Maenpaa, T., Multiresolution gray-scale and rotation invariant texture classification with local binary patterns, IEEE Transactions on Pattern Analysis and Machine Intelligence, Vol. 24, No. 7, pp. 971-987, 2002.
13. Schapire, R. E., The boosting approach to machine learning. an overview, MSRI Workshop on Nonlinear Estimation and Classification, 2002.
14. Viola, P. and Jones, M., Rapid object detection using a boosted cascade of simple features, Conf. on Computer Vision and Pat. Recog., p. 511-518, 2001.
15. Sonka, M. and Zhang, X., Segmentation of intravascular ultrasound images: A knowledge-based approach, IEEE T. Med. Im., Vol. 17, No. 6, pp. 889-899, 1998.

SVM Applied to the Generation
of Biometric Speech Key

L. Paola García-Perera, Carlos Mex-Perera, and Juan A. Nolazco-Flores

Computer Science Department, ITESM, Campus Monterrey
Av. Eugenio Garza Sada 2501 Sur, Col. Tecnológico
Monterrey, N.L., México, C.P. 64849
{paola.garcia,carlosmex,jnolazco}@itesm.mx

Abstract. In this research we present a new scheme for the generation
of a biometric key based on Automatic Speech Technology and Support
Vector Machines. Keys are produced by making a distinction among the
voice attributes of the users employing hyperplanes. It is described how
the key is conformed and the reliability of the method. We depict an
experimental evaluation for different values of the parameters. Among
the different kernels for the Support Vector Machine, the RBF obtained
the best results.

1   Introduction

Human body characteristics such as fingerprints, retinas and irises, facial structure, and voice recognition are just some of the many biometric fields being
researched today. These characteristics are unique to each individual, then they
are a good choice for developing biometric keys. The goal of the biometric key is
to produce a password using the intrinsic attributes of some specific user characteristic with the consequence that remembering a complex password would
not be necessary. Since voice is a natural process and it can produce different
utterances in short time, it gives advantages among other biometrics. For instance, to assure user's identity the system can always request to him a random
passphrase, avoiding the use of recorded voice by an unauthorised person. In this
research we focus on voice and its characteristics to properly develop a reliable
biometric key. This type of key generation has several applications in security
purposes; for instance, biometric authentication and access to networks.

Through the years an extensive research has been done in the voice field. One
of the branches is focused on the Automatic Speech Recognition (ASR), which
deals with the computerised modelling of the human voice to obtain a transcript
of what it is said. The previous research and advances done in the field together
with the SVM techniques act as a basis for this investigation.

The main challenge of this research is to produce a biometric key that should
repeatedly be equal for the same user utterance under certain conditions. Monrose *et. al* [6] showed a method to produce this key. The main point of their
research was to map the voice features and providing a binary-classifying plane

A. Sanfeliu et al. (Eds.): CIARP 2004, LNCS 3287, pp. 637–644, 2004.

generate a descriptor from them. However, it had a serious drawback, the search of the partition plane was difficult due to the fact that infinite planes were possible. The key depended strictly on the plane chosen, this means that the key of the user was unknown until the plane was set. The number of trials to produce a suitable plane might be too large before obtaining the desired result. A more flexible way to produce a key is always attractive. Control of the assignation of the key values can enhance the cryptographic performance. It is also interesting to explore the possibility to produce a key by the use of an algorithm that can handle all the voice important attributes without discarding any of them.

In the next section we present our proposal. Section 3 through 5 describe the fundamental elements of the feature generation and SVM techniques. Section 6 examines the experimental methodology and the final section presents the results and discusses future research problems.

2   Proposal

The purpose of this proposal is to produce a biometric key from the attributes of the voice signal and the spoken user passphrase. The imperative challenge lies in the search of suitable set of planes that can significantly partition the handled data and give a key as a result.

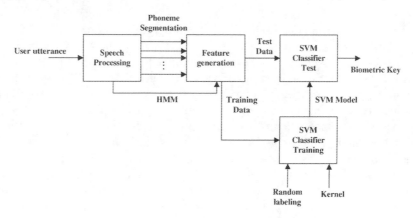

Fig. 1. System Architecure

A general view of the mechanism is shown in Figure 1. In the first stage, *speech processing* employing Automatic Speech Recognition techniques is used to extract the model parameters and the sets of phoneme frames of each user utterance. Manipulating both new sets of data the features are conformed. The *Support Vector Machine* classifier (SVM) will produce a new model according to the kernel and bit specifications. Finally, using the SVM model the key is generated. Each part will be discussed in the following sections.

3   Speech Processing

The speech data is processed using Automatic Speech Recognition [11]. ASR provides two important results for the purpose of this research: an acoustic model named Hidden Markov Model (HMM) that has the inherent characteristics of real speech, and a set of phoneme-based segmented data. The HMM can be seen as a finite state machine, where output distributions are commonly represented by Gaussian Mixture Densities with means and covariances as important parameters.

Let P be the set of phonemes, the states and the gaussians will make reference to this set. The phonemes were chosen as the sound units to be modelled since its possible to generate larger keys than working with the complete word. C_P will denote the set of the central gaussian of the middle state vectors given by the HMM. This vector was chosen because the middle state is the most stable part of the phoneme representation.

4   Feature Generation

After obtaining the phoneme-based segmented data, the segment sets $\{R_{i,j}\}$ where i is the index associated to each phoneme and j is the j-th user, are conformed. Then, the feature vector is defined as $\psi_{i,j} = \mu(R_{i,j}) - C_i$, where $\mu(R_{i,j})$ is the mean vector of the data in the $R_{i,j}$ segment, and C_i is the matching phoneme mean vector of the model. Let us denote the universe set as $\Psi = \{\psi_{i,j} \mid 1 \leq i \leq \ell, 1 \leq j \leq n\}$, where ℓ refers to the number of all the possible phonemes and n is the number of all users.

Let D_p be a subset of Ψ containing all features related to a certain phoneme p. Thus, $D_p = \{\psi_{i,j} \mid i = p, 1 \leq j \leq n\}$. The final subsets D_p are the input to the following step.

5   Support Vector Machine

This part of our research refers to the Support Vector Machine (SVM) technique used to produce a key. The SVM was chosen among others because a classifier that can separate sparse data and tolerate missclassification was needed.

The SVM is a method widely used for classification derived by Vapnik and Chervonenkis [1, 3]. The goal of basic SVM is to obtain a model of vector classification in one of two classes. Two stages conform the SVM process: training and testing. Before the training process, the data should be formatted in vectors, and each vector is labelled according to its class. The following set of pairs are defined $\{x_i, y_i\}$; where $x_i \in R^n$ are the training vectors and $y_i = \{-1, 1\}$ are the labels, see Figure 2.

For the data depicted in Figure 2 one can obtain a canonical form for (w, b) of the unique separating hyperplane satisfying $y_i(w^T x_i + b) \geq 1$. The extension to the nonlinear technique consists on the nonlinear mapping of the input data into a high dimensional space. This transformation is denoted as function $\phi(x)$ and

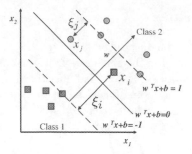

Fig. 2. Support Vector Machine

allows us to work in a huge dimensional space without doing explicit computation in this space. Then, the construction of the linear hyperplane is done. For the nonlinear case, $y_i[w^T\phi(x_i) + b] \geq 1$, and the optimisation problem is as follows,

$$\min_{x_i,b,\xi} \frac{1}{2}w^T w + C \sum_{i=1}^{l} \xi_i \tag{1}$$

$$\text{subject to } y_i(w^T\phi(x_i) + b) \geq 1 - \xi_i \tag{2}$$

$$\xi_i \geq 0$$

where ξ_i is a slack variable and C is a positive real constant known as a tradeoff parameter between error and margin.

It is possible to transform Equations 1 and 2 into a dual problem in the Lagrange multipliers α_i. Thus,

$$\sum_{i=1}^{l} \alpha_i - \frac{1}{2} \sum_{i=1,j=1}^{l} \alpha_i \alpha_j y_i y_j \langle \phi(x_i), \phi(x_j) \rangle \tag{3}$$

$$\sum_{i=1}^{l} \alpha_i y_i = 0, C \geq \alpha_i \geq 0. \tag{4}$$

The value of $\alpha_i \in R$ is close related to the training point x_i and it represents the strength with which that point is associated in the final decision function, α_i can be solved as a quadratic programming (QP) problem. Only a subset of the points will be associated with a non-zero α_i. These points are called *support vectors* and are the points that lie closest to the separating hyperplane.

The vectors are mapped into a higher dimensional space by function ϕ. However exact specification of ϕ is not needed: instead, the expression known as kernel $K(x_i, x_j) \equiv \phi(x_i)^T \phi(x_j)$ is defined. There are different types of kernels, but the most common are

- linear $K(x_i, x_j) = x_i^T x_j$
- polynomial $K(x_i, x_j) = (\gamma x_i^T x_j + r)^d, \gamma > 0$

- Radial Basis Function (RBF) $K(x_i, x_j) = e^{(-\gamma||x_i - x_j||^2)}, \gamma > 0$
- Sigmoid function $K(x_i, x_j) = tanh(\gamma x^T x_j + r)$

where γ, r and d are parameters.

The decision function is expressed as

$$y(x) = sign[\sum_{k=1}^{\#SV} \alpha_k y_k K(x_i, x) + b]. \tag{5}$$

The parameters of the kernels should be tunned to find the best classification of the training data. When convergence is reached, the kernel and its final parameters are evaluated using Equation 5 and the test data. The statistics can give a guide on the performance of the classifier and decide to tune or stop.

The Support Vector Machine has been used for several applications, including biometrics [10, 9]. In this research we employ it for searching a function that can be able to transform a vector produced by one phoneme to a binary number (key bit) assigned randomly.

The methodology used to implement the SVM training is as follows. Suppose that $/AH/$ is the unique phoneme that can be uttered from all users. The one bit label $\{-1, 1\}$ is assigned to each $D_{/AH/}$. However, if one user utters the phoneme $/AH/$ several times, the value of the bit will remain the same. For instance, $f(D_{/AH/}) = 1$ will be 1 for the utterances of the same user. The process is similar for the rest of the users, but the value of the bit $f(D_{/AH/})$ can change from user to user. The procedure is generalised for all the phonemes. Afterwards, the kernel parameters are tunned. In the test stage we evaluate the model produced by the SVM using unknown data. The statistics are made in terms of errors per phoneme according to different quantity of users.

As shown, the key is constructed using the phonemes of each word, and a random bit labeling. If the key has freedom of assignation the entropy grows significantly. This research considers just binary classes, however, an M-ary bit labeling per phoneme might be possible for future research. The final key could be obtained by concatenating the bits produced by each phoneme. For instance, if a user utters two phonemes: $/F/$ and $/AH/$, the final key is $K = \{f(D_{/F/}), f(D_{/AH/})\}$, thus, the output is formed by two bits.

6   Experimental Methodology

The experiments were performed using the YOHO database [2, 4]. YOHO contains the voice utterances of 138 speakers of different nationalities speaking three pairs of numbers in each utterance. For instance, "Thirty-Two, Fourty-One, Twenty-Five".

The utterances are processed using the Hidden Markov Models Toolkit (HTK) by Cambridge University Engineering Department [5]. We employ HTK as an automatic speech recogniser. The important results of the speech processing stage are the twenty means of the phonemes given by the HMM and the phoneme-based segmentation of the utterances. The phonemes used are: $/AH/$,

/AX/, /AY/, /EH/, /ER/, /EY/, /F/, /IH/, /IY/,/K/, /N/, /R/, /S/, /T/, /TH/, /UW/, /V/, /W/. The model of each phoneme is composed by three states, and three gaussians per state. The mean of the central gaussian of the middle state of each phoneme and the phone-based segments of the utterances are the input for the feature generator. Following the method already described, the subsets D_p are formed. It is important to note that the cardinality of each set D_p can be different since the number of the same phoneme utterances can vary from user to user. Subsets from each D_p were formed for training and test SVM phases. For training, the number of vectors picked for generating the model is the same. Each user has the same probability to produce the correct bit per phoneme. The number of test vectors that each user provided can be different.

Then, the assignation of $\{1, -1\}$ is performed. For simulation purposes, a distribution of equal number of 1's and -1's is given among the users. Then, the data is ready to be classified. SVMLight by Thorsten Joachims was used to implement the classifier [12]. We explored the performance of the linear, polynomial and RBF kernels. Suitable values of the parameters are choosen to produce the minimum amount of errors.

7   Experimental Results

One of the first stages in the experimental part was the selection of the parameters for the SVM. The behaviour of the SVM is given in terms of the average classification accuracy on test data for a given number of users. The average classification accuracy is computed by the ratio

$$\eta = \frac{\text{matches on test data for all phonemes and users}}{\text{number of trials}}. \tag{6}$$

In Figure 3 values for η using the linear ($d = 1$), polynomial ($d > 1$), and RBF ($\gamma = 0.007$) kernels are shown. It can be observed that the best results for the polynomial and linear case are obtained if the value of d is equal to 2 or 3. As long as d increases, i.e. 5, the accuracy of the SVM is reduced, classification is not performed for $d = 7$. Moreover, analysing the RBF kernel, it can easily concluded that its behaviour is better than the linear or polynomial kernels although the increment of the number of users reduces the value of η.

The RBF kernel can model closed decision surfaces [8], which may occur in the speech case in view of the nature of the data. However a deeper research is suggested. Parameters γ and C must be adjusted in order to maximise η. From several experiments was concluded that a suitable value of C is 6. To see the behaviour of the SVM for different values of γ, some experiments were done. Figure 4 displays such results using $C = 6$ for 10 users. If γ decreases, it leads to a smoother decision surface; as γ increases, the variance of the RBF decreases and produces a narrow support region (increment of the support vectors). The accuracy has its maximum values when $\gamma = 0.007$ and $\gamma = 0.009$.

As exposed the RBF kernel is a good solution in the generation of the key since it can give the maximum values for η, however an extra study should be done to produce the same effect when incrementing the users.

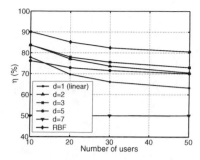

Fig. 3. η for different number of users and several types of kernels

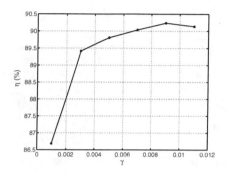

Fig. 4. η for different values of γ, $C = 6$, and 10 users

8   Conclusion

We have presented a method to produce a biometric key from voice based on a
phoneme segmentation, where one key bit was assigned to each user phoneme.
Combined techniques of ASR and Support Vector Machines have been used
in this work. To our knowledge, Monrose *et. al* [6] has shown a first method to
produce this key. The main advantage of our approach over Monrose work is that
key bits can be selected and assigned for each user before the partition plane is
computed. Thus, key bits are freely assigned regardless of the parameters value
for the algorithms used in our method.

From the experiments conducted on several groups of users, it is concluded
the feasibility of the use of the SVM to classify data vectors derived from users
voice where the classes are labeled arbitrarily.

Among all the kernels used in the tests, RBF had the best performance, as
discussed. The method to distinguish phonemes of specific users is quite good.
However error correction mechanisms has to be considered in future research
since the bits of the key must not present any error, although the number of
users increment. Adding extra bits for error correction demands more phonemes
in the passphrase but it might reduce the possibility of wrong key production.

Besides, future studies on a M-ary key can be useful to increase the number
of different keys available for each user given a fixed number of phonemes in the
passphrase.

Acknowledgments

The authors would like to acknowledge the Cátedra de Seguridad, ITESM, Campus Monterrey and the CONACyT project CONACyT-2002-C01-41372 who partially supported this work.

References

1. Boser, B., I. Guyon, and V. Vapnik. A training algorithm for optimal margin classifiers. In Proceedings of the Fifth Annual Workshop on Computational Learning Theory, 1992.
2. Campbell, J. P., Jr. Features and Measures for Speaker Recognition. Ph.D. Dissertation, Oklahoma State University, 1992.
3. Cortes, C. and V. Vapnik. Support-vector network. Machine Learning 20, 273–297, 1995.
4. Higgins, A., J. Porter and L. Bahler. YOHO Speaker Authentication Final Report. ITT Defense Communications Division, 1989.
5. HTK Hidden Markov Model Toolkit home page. http://htk.eng.cam.ac.uk/
6. F. Monrose, M. K. Reiter, Q. Li , S. Wetzel. Cryptographic Key Generation From Voice. Proceedings of the IEEE Conference on Security and Privacy, Oakland, CA. May, 2001.
7. R. Morris and K. Thompson. Password security: A case history. Communications of the ACM, 22(11):594–597, 1979.
8. K.-R. Müller, S. Mika, G. Rätsch, K. Tsuda, and B. Schölkopf. An introduction to kernel-based learning algorithms. IEEE Neural Networks, 12(2):181-201, May 2001.
9. E. Osuna, R. Freund, and F. Girosi. Support vector machines: Training and applications. Technical Report AIM-1602, MIT A.I. Lab., 1996.
10. E. Osuna, R. Freund, and F. Girosi, Training Support Vector Machines: An Application to Face Recognition, in IEEE Conference on Computer Vision and Pattern Recognition, pp. 130-136, 1997.
11. L.R. Rabiner and B.-H. Juang. Fundamentals of speech recognition. Prentice-Hall, New-Jersey, 1993.
12. T. Joachims, SVMLight: Support Vector Machine, SVM-Light Support Vector Machine http://svmlight.joachims.org/, University of Dortmund, November 1999.

Causal Networks for Modeling Health Technology Utilization in Intensive Care Units*

Max Chacón and Brenda Maureira

Informatic Engineering Department, University of Santiago de Chile,
Av. Ecuador 3659, PO Box 10233, Santiago, Chile
{mchacon,bmaureira}@diinf.usach.cl

Abstract. This study presents the application of Bayesian networks (Bn) to explain Neonatal Intensive Care Unit relationships. Information was compiled retrospectively from the medical records at two neonatal intensive care units of 523 neonates (63 deaths). A total of 31 variables were used for the model, eleven to characterize admission conditions and severity of illness as well as the 20 technologies. With mortality as the output variable, the K2 search algorithm and Geiger-Heckerman quality measures were used in the training that generated the Bn. Evidence propagation was used to assess the training, which yielded a sensitivity of 77.78% and a specificity of 91.30%, in the classification of mortality. Clinical criteria, correlations and logistical regression were used to analyse the relationships the model provided. The Bn found clinically coherent relationships as recognizable conditions that directly affect mortality such as congenital malformations are seen and it exposes the least effective technologies among those studied, bicarbonate treatment.

1 Introduction

Effectiveness in medical technology is essential for improving the quality of health-care [1]. When multiple medical technologies are used together, such as in premature births, Intensive Care Units (ICU), Acute Immune Deficiency Syndrome (AIDS) or multiple failure [2], it is necessary to establish the sequence (or causal order) in which the technologies are applied, to evaluate an individual technology's impact on the outcome. The limitations of using non-causal models in this area have become apparent [3-4].

Having a model that represents the causal way in which medical technologies are applied, delivers valuable clinical evidence concerning medical practices. In addition it offers the possibility of determining how changes to the order in which technologies are employed, impact the outcome, through the use of simulations.

Techniques such as decision analysis, Markov chains and path analysis have been used to describe the interaction of multiple technologies when few technologies are under scrutiny [4-5]. Such methods cannot cope with the surge in combinations when using more than five technologies, and do not have sufficiently efficient pruning mechanisms to be able to derive an easily interpretable model.

The current work explores the use of Bayesian networks (Bn) as an alternative to modelling the causal relationships in the utilization of multiple technologies. We have chosen a typical problem that requires the use of multiple technologies; Neonatal

---

* This study has been supported by FONDECYT (Chile) project N° 1990920 and DICYT - USACH.

Intensive Care Units (NICU). These units have proven their effectiveness at reducing neonatal mortality. Yet the continual rise in the introduction of new technologies in such units has not been adequately addressed. Little is known about how these technologies are used in daily medical practices, particularly in developing countries.

In medicine most Bayesian network applications centre on automatic diagnosis and in aiding treatment [6-7]. However, no Bayesian network applications are known of that assess health technologies. The closest study to the current work is that of Sierra et al [8], in which Bayesian networks are applied to intensive care units (ICU) aiming to improve the classification of patients within a unit, but the work does examine the use of ICU medical technologies.

In ICU there is no clear indication of the causal order in which the technologies are applied within the ICU; currently it is only possible to recognize the initial variables (admission conditions and the severity of the ailment) and the network's output variables (such as morbidity or mortality). Our proposal is to use structural learning for the Bn to determine just how medical technologies are used in the unit and how these relate to mortality.

2   Methods

2.1   Data Collection and Pre-processing

Data was collected retrospectively, from the medical records of the Fernandes Figueira Institute and the Pediatric Center of Lagoa, two neonatal intensive care units (NICU) in Rio de Janeiro, Brazil. A complete list of the variables collected is given in Table 1, which corresponds to health conditions at birth or admission, diagnostic hypotheses, and technology utilization. While the list is not exhaustive, the technologies selected, including both diagnostic and therapeutic means, were representative of the NICU armamentarium of the early 90s. Technologies used in nearly 100 % of the neonates, such as incubators and sedation, were not analysed. Cases involving internment over 45 days were also not included.

Initially, 78 different diagnostic hypotheses were found and these were grouped into the eight main diagnostic categories listed in Table 1. A consultant neonatologist who classified the neonate's condition as not affected, mild or severe for each diagnostic category reviewed each medical record. For the category congenital malformations, the number of different malformations was added up, assuming mild = 1 and severe = 2. These eight diagnostic variables, along with birth weight, gestational age, and the Apgar score (5th min), were used as a proxy for severity of illness.

Diagnostic methods and clinical procedures such as blood transfusions are examples of discrete technologies. The measure of the intensity of usage of these technologies was taken as the number of applications of the specific technology to each neonate. On the other hand, technologies that tend to be used on a continuous basis, such as drugs or mechanical ventilation, had their "dosage" measured by the total length of their application in days (Table 1). The day each treatment began was also recorded.

The Bayesian network adopted in this study requires the variables the model comprises to be represented by discrete values, which would later be transformed into binary values. For *birth weight* three ranges are used: low, normal and overweight; four states are defined for *gestational age* considering morphological criteria and foetal maturity. The 10 values for the *Apgar score* are grouped into four states. Diagnostic hypotheses are coded directly in three states; absent = 0, medium = 1 and severe = 2, apart from congenital malformations for which six values are used, and correspond to the maximum value of the sum of the ailments found in the database. Medical technology usage (diagnostic and therapeutic) can be represented directly with binary values, taking 0 as not having used the technology and 1 as having used the technology, irrespective of how extensively it is employed. Finally, the output variable, mortality, considers 0 as surviving and 1 as dead.

Table 1. List of input variables and regression coefficients whit mortality.

Variable	Mean ± SD	Regress. Coeffi.	Variable	Mean ± SD	Regress. Coeffi.
Birth/admission weight (Weight)	2321 ± 865 [grams]	-11,81 *	Electrolytes (Elect)	2.20 ± 2.77 [events]†	15,76 *
Gestational age (GAge)	36 ± 3 [weeks]	-4,45	White blood cell count (WBCC)	2.42 ± 1.98 events†	-0,15
Apgar 5th min. (Apgar)	7.2 ± 2.2	-6,68 *	Antibiotics (Antib)	13.5 ± 13.4 [days]*	-6,70
Congenital malformations (ConMa)	0.19 ± 0.72 [sum]	17,27 *	Inotropic agents (InoAg)	0.97 ± 4.22 [days]*	10,54 *
Obstetrical conditions (ObsCo)	0.02 ± 0.17 [class]#	-2,44	Diuretics (Diure)	1.89 ± 7.54 days*	-2,03
Respiratory conditions (ResCo)	0.82 ± 0.68 [class]#	-0,29	Anticonvulsive therapy (Antic)	1.63 ± 6.95 [days]*	7,89
Asphyxia (Asphy)	0.36 ± 0.64 [class]#	1,22	Sodium bicarbonate (SodBi)	0.29 ± 1.12 [days]*	26,16 *
Cardiovascular conditions (CarCo)	0.03 ± 0.23 [class]#	-5,66 *	CPAP (CPAP)	0.71 ± 1.81 [days]*	-1,64
Haematologic conditions (HaeCo)	0.16 ± 0.46 [class]#	0,91	Oxygen therapy (oxihood) (Oxiho)	0.79 ± 1.61 [days]*	-24,58 *
Infections (Infec)	0.19 ± 0.59 [class]#	-4,82 *	Mechanical ventilation (MecVe)	0.91 ± 3.10 [days]*	-3,80
Metabolic conditions (MetCo)	0.07 ± 0.28 [class]#	-3,11	Phototherapy (Photo)	2.18 ± 2.94 [days]*	-3,38
Blood gases (BloGa)	4.49 ± 3.30 [events]†	4,44	Intravenous solutions (InSol)	4.85 ± 5.30 [days]*	4,55
X rays (XRays)	2.76 ± 8.40 [events]†	6,92	Parenteral nutrition (PaNut)	1.75 ± 4.54 [days]*	0,28
Ultrasound (UlSou)	0.79 ± 1.09 [events]†	-6,59	Packed red cells transfusion (PRCT)	0.52 ± 1.69 [events]†	14,39 *
Microhaematocrit (MiHem)	8.55 ± 8.72 [events]†	-18,77 *	Exchange transfusion (ExTra)	0.08 ± 0.38 [events]†	6,98
Blood culture (BloCu)	2.05 ± 1.71 [events]†	0,26			

Note: 7 diagnostic categories have been coded as 14 binary variables thus increasing the total number of input variables to 31.

classified as absent = 0, mild = 1, or severe = 2.
† *number of applications of technology to each neonate.*
* *total number of days of use in each neonate. *Significant coefficients at 5%.*

2.2   Bayesian Network Analysis

A Bayesian network is a directed acyclical graph whose nodes represent stochastic variables and the arc the conditioned dependencies between two related variables. The procedure for modelling a problem using Bn can be divided into two steps, learning and the propagation of evidence.

The learning process on which this work focuses involves two principal tasks: induction of a graphical model that best represents the problem at hand (structural learning), and the extraction of conditional probabilities that define a graphical model's dependencies (parametrical learning).

Learning, based on a database, is two-part process. First, a search algorithm tries to determine the possible parents of each node (conditional dependence of a precedent variable) and, second, a measure (or metric) of quality. The measure of quality calculates how successful the network is from the data. For its part, the search algorithm attempts to identify the structure offering the best measure of quality. As a rule, this is an NP-Complete problem and certain heuristic approximations are used to restrict the search space and so avoid the combinatorial explosion.

Structural learning is needed to find the order of technology application. We employed the most commonly used search algorithm at present for discrete variables, called K2 [8-10]. This algorithm searches for a network structure on the basis of discrete data, considering that the input variables are independent and that these are initially ordered. Wit this restriction there are $2^{n(n-1)/2}$ possible structures for representing a problem with n variables. The basic idea is to use a measure of quality to evaluate the quality of the network formed. In initial stages all the nodes lack parents, but in later stages those nodes that maximize the value of the measure of quality are added to the parental set. The process stops when addition of new nodes results in no improvement of quality or when the maximum number of parents u has been reached, this number being fixed for a particular problem. The complexity of the worst case for this algorithm is O(n4), when the maximum number of parents u is equal to the number of variables n.

Two different measures of quality were tried, the first was obtained from the Geiger-Heckerman measure (G-H) while the second is known as the Cooper-Herskovits measure (C-H) [11-12].

All of the algorithms used in this work were executed in release 12.1 of MATLAB software version 6.0 for the PC.

2.3   Initial Order and Evaluation

One of the K2 algorithm's requirements is that the variables that will comprise the Bayesian network are ordered first. Normally, expert opinion is sought when undertaking this initial ordering. For our purposes though, it was possible to employ the distribution of the first application of technologies during a patient's internment in the NICU as our criteria. To quantify these values we considered the first day of application of each technology, as the point when the technology had been applied in at least 80% of cases.

The dependability of network learning has to be determined when choosing the best network and to compare the measures of quality used. Thus, it was necessary to run a group of cases independently of the training group and to assess the results. Evidence propagation was performed using an exact method of general propagation, known as "clustering" [10]. Training was carried out using 85% of the cases in the training set (445 cases) and 15%, selected at random, for the test set (78, 69 survivors and 9 deaths).

The general lack of work presenting the relationships of how neonatal intensive care units are used and the clinical knowledge required of such units makes quantitative means of comparison necessary. For such purposes, first the correlations of 23 real variables from the model are calculated (Admission weight, Gestational age, Apgar and the 20 technologies) followed by a logistical regression of the 31 variables shown in Table 1, using mortality as the output variable.

3   Results

Data were collected on 523 cases corresponding to 268 cases (48 deaths) from the Fernandes Figueira Institute and 255 (15 deaths) from the Paediatric Centre of Lagoa. The mean ± SD of the admission weight was 2320 ± 865 g (range 670-5680 g) and the gestational age was 36 ± 3 weeks (range 24-43 weeks). Table 1 gives the distribution of the other variables.

Training began with an initial ordering of the variables. The first 11 (admission conditions), used to approximate the severity of illness, are the primary candidates, as they are obtained at the point of admission to the unit. The technologies were then ordered, as described, by date of application. Table 2 shows the initial ordering, considering the day most of the technologies had been applied.

The process of generating the Bayesian network took a maximum of u=10 parents for each node as the training parameter. Two networks were then obtained, one for each measure of quality with the training group (445 cases). Evidence propagation was then applied to the remaining 15% of cases (78 cases) to the two models. The results of the classification for the test group, expressed by sensitivity and specificity are presented in Table 3 for both measures of quality used.

While the two network structures are very similar, sensitivity and specificity analysis shown in Table 3 differ in that the G-H measure is more sensitive to the detection of deaths, and provides us the best tool for classifying the survival of a patient.

Table 2. Initial order of application of the technologies.

Technology	0Day	Technology	1Day
Intravenous solutions	2	Mechanical ventilation	4
Blood culture	2	Exchange transfusion	5
Blood gases	2	Diuretics	6
Microhaematocrit	2	CPAP	6
X rays	2	Parenteral nutrition	7
White blood cell count	2	Anticonvulsive therapy	7
Antibiotics	2	Inotropic agents	7
Electrolytes	3	Sodium bicarbonate	7
Phototherapy	4	Ultrasound	8
Oxygen therapy	4	Packed red cells transfusion	8

Table 3. Results of the classification when applying propagation of the evidence with 15% of the test group cases, for the two quality measures.

Measure	Sensitibity	Specifity
Cooper-Herskovits	55.56%	92.75%
Geiger-Heckerman	77.78%	91.30%

For the comparative analysis the correlations are doing for the 12-variable subgroup (from a total of 23 real variables). Results of the logistical regression on mortality are presented in Table 1.

Structural learning algorithms provided results ordering the parent nodes for each variable, using the probability of adding a new parent node and the probability once the node is added. For easier graphical interpretation we preferred to show a graph, simply showing the order in which each parent of the variable was chosen in the arc (between the parent and child). The graph for the network obtained from the G-H measures is shown as Figure 1.

4 Discussion

We will centre analysis of the results on comparison with basic existing neonatological relationships, correlations between the real variables of the studied data set, and the logistical regression of mortality (Table 1).

The first significant relationship provided by the chosen network (Figure 1) is that between *birth weight* and *gestational age*. This is well known in neonatology, since both variables are representative of immaturity and a high correlation exists between the two (r=0.75).

Asphyxia dependency on the *Apgar score* is accounted for, as the states of *asphyxia* are required as a component in calculating the *Apgar* points. The path that flows from *asphyxia* up to *anticonvulsive therapy* is also clearly explainable, as severe *asphyxia* induces convulsions.

The exchange transfusion dependence on haematologic conditions and birth weight is explained in the knowledge that this therapeutic technology is used in situations of incompatible blood with the mother, low birth weight and in cases of underdeveloped digestive systems that cause jaundice, which then requires a full blood transfusion.

One group of relationships that stand out include variables belonging to respiratory disorders.

Respiratory conditions as the parent of blood gases and x rays, which are the parents of mechanical ventilators and oxygen therapy, complete a classical cycle in medicine: problem (respiratory disorders), diagnosis (blood gases and x rays) and therapy (mechanical ventilators and oxygen therapy). All dependencies are confirmed by the correlations up 0.63. It is also possible to follow a route for cases in which respiratory infection is suspected that would require diagnosis using x rays, a dearer technology than blood gases, followed by a course of antibiotics to treat the infection. It is also worth noting that while CPAP ventilation therapy is applied after oxygen therapy, the former presents no relationship with mechanical ventilation.

The relationship between microhematocrit and antibiotics (r=0.97), and between antibiotics and electrolytes (r = 0.88) present the highest correlations. It is possible to

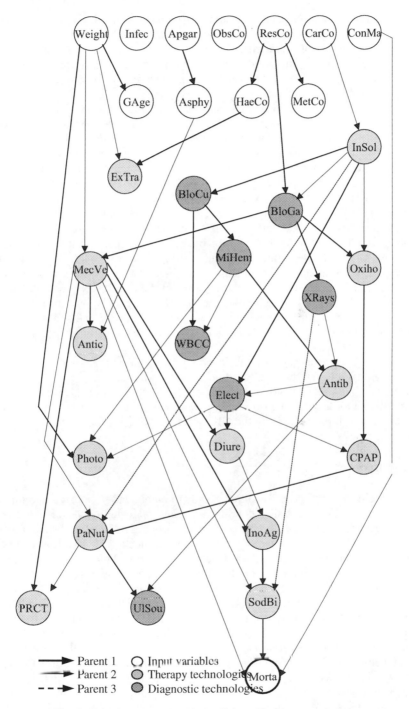

Fig. 1. Bayesian network with the Geiger-Heckerman measure.

explain this as both microhematocrits and electrolytes (r=0.8) are employed as antibiotic control technologies. Yet the Bayesian network affords further information on indicating that the microhematocrit is conducted before the use of antibiotics, while the electrolytes is applied afterwards. On examining the network however, it is possible to conclude that this relationship is, in reality, indirect, as it arises from the relationship caused by using antibiotics.

The only admission condition variables that are directly linked to mortality are congenital malformations, which is confirmed by high regression coefficient values (Table 1). The lack of technology intervention in this relationship indicates the effectiveness of technologies used in such disorders. In a significant number of cases of congenital malformations, and especially in more severe cases, medical intervention contributes little to patient recovery.

Various admission conditions, such as low birth weight, respiratory or cardiovascular conditions lead to the use of bicarbonate following the application of several diagnostic and therapeutic technologies. The relationship here with mortality is unequivocal and direct. Logistical regression sets bicarbonate as the variable most closely related with mortality. The clinical explanation for this is that this treatment technology is applied to compensate for acidosis of the blood arising from respiratory insufficiency. Use of bicarbonate treats the symptoms of the respiratory problem, but does not manage to revert the demise of the patient. The lower relationship between mechanical ventilators and mortality and the existence of multiple paths in the Bayesian network, reveal that this technology is more effective than bicarbonate at altering the initial morbid outlook.

A general comparison between the logistical regression model and Bayesian network of Figure 1, clearly shows a regression model's limitations at representing such problems, since the regressions solely manage to identify variables that are directly and only linked to the outcome (mortality), but do not manage to represent the series of causal relationships that exist in the NICU before the results are known.

5   Conclusions

The network shown in Figure 1 enables people to obtain and to interpret the relationships clearly between admission conditions, usage of technology and outcome, in forming a better idea than is possible with conventional statistical methods of a complex usage of technologies in medical establishments such as in ICUs. It is also possible to trace out an idea of the effectiveness of certain technologies with regard to others, on comparing their direct or indirect association with the results.

A method is surely needed though to quantify the impact of the technologies upon results; a direct measure of effectiveness. This would require designing a method that enables the simulation of amendments to the application of a technology in the Bayesian network, and to establish the impact of such modifications on the results. A simple way of generating such a method would be to eliminate arcs or nodes in the trained Bayesian network and then use a propagation of evidence that would allow the propagation of cases in networks with different structures to those for which they were trained. This would make it possible to quantify the simulation of changes representing the non-deployment or different ways of employing a particular technology to a group of patients.

References

1. Evans, RW Health care technology and the inevitability of resource allocation and rationing decisions, JAMA. 249 (1983) 2047-2053.
2. Slonim, AD; Patel, KM; Ruttimann, UE & Pollack, MM The impact of prematurity: A perspective of pediatric intensive care units, Crit. Care Med. 28 (2000) 848-853.
3. Almeida, RT; Panerai, RB; Carvalho, M & Lopes, JMA. Analysis of multiple technologies in neonatal care, Int. J. Techol. Assess. Health Care. 7 (1991) 22-29.
4. Panerai, RB; Chacón-Pacheco, ML & Almeida, RT Path Analysis in Health Technology Assessment, International Society of Technology Assessment in Health Care, Seventh Ann. Meet., Helsinki, Finland, (1991).
5. Panerai, RB; Almeida, RT; Portela, MC; Carvalho, M; Coura-Filho, M & Costa,TP Estimating the effectiveness of perinatal care technologies by expert opinion, Int. J. Techol. Assess. Health Care. 7 (1991) 367-378.
6. Kahn, CE Jr; Roberts, LM; Shaffer, KA & Haddawy, P. Construction of Bayesian Network for mammographic diagnosis of breast cancer. Comput. Biol. Med. 27(1) (1997) 19-29.
7. Sierra, B & Larranaga, P. Predicting survival in malignant skin melanoma using Bayesian networks automatically induced by genetic algorithms. An empirical comparison between different approaches. Artif. Intell. Med. 14(1-2) (1998) 215-230.
8. Sierra. B; Serrano, N; Larranaga. P; Plasencia, EJ; Inza, I; Jimenez, JJ; Revuelta, P & Mora, ML. Using Bayesian networks in the construction of a bi-level multi-classifier. A case study using intensive care unit patients data. Artif. Intell. Med. 22(3) (2001) 233-248.
9. Heckerman, D Bayesian networks for knowledge discovery, In: *Advances in Knowledge Discovery and Data Mining*, Fayyad, UM.; Piatesky-Shapiro, G; Padhraic, S. and Uthurusamy, R. (Eds.), Mit Press, Melo Park, CA. 273-305, (1996).
10. Castillo E; Gutiérrez, JM & Hadi, AS. Expert systems and probabilistic network models. Springer-Verlag, New York, (1997).
11. Gaiger, D & Heckerman, D. A characterization of the Dirichlet distribution with application to learning Bayesian networks. *In: proceedings of the Eleventh Conference on Uncertainty in Artificial Intelligence*. Morgan Kaufmann Pub., San Francisco, CA, (1995) 196-207.
12. Cooper GF & y E. Herskovits E A Bayesian Method for the induction of probabilistic networks from data. Machine Learning. 9 (1992) 309-347.

Medical Image Segmentation
by Level Set Method Incorporating Region
and Boundary Statistical Information

Pan Lin, Chongxun Zheng, Yong Yang, and Jianwen Gu

Institute of Biomedical Engineering, Key Laboratory of Biomedical Information Engineering
of Education Ministry, Xi'an Jiaotong University, xi'an 710049, China
Linpan99@sohu.com

Abstract. Level set methods are powerful numerical techniques for image segmentation and analysis. This method requires the definition of a speed function that governs curve evolution. However, the classical method only used image gradient, edge strength, and region intensity to define the speed function. In this paper, we present a new speed function for level set framework. The new method integrates the image region statistical information and image boundary statistical information instead of the conventional method that uses spatial image gradient information. The new speed function gives the level set method a global view of the boundary information within the image. The method here proposed is particularly well adapted to situations where edges are weak and overlap, and images are noisy. A number of experiments on ultrasound, CT, and X-ray modalities medical images were performed to evaluate the new method. The experimental results demonstrate the reliability and efficiency of this new scheme.

1 Introduction

The level set approach were introduced by S. Osher and J. A. Sethian[1] in 1988. These methods have recently become one of the most studied techniques for medical image segmentation. Level sets are designed to handle problems in which the evolving interfaces can develop sharp corners and cusps, change topology and become very complex. In the level set approach, the convergence to the final result may be relatively independent of the initial shape, and branches, splits and merges can develop without problems as the front moves. Generally, the method may be applied even where no a priori assumptions about the object's topology are made. Most of the challenges in level set approach result from the need to construct an adequate model for the speed function.

But the classical level set speed function models rely on the edge gradient information to stop the curve evolution; these models can detect only objects with edges defined by gradient. Also, in practice, the discrete gradients are bounded and then the stopping function is never zero on the edges, and the curve may pass through the boundary. On the other hand, if the image is very noisy, then the isotropic smooth the edges too.

A. Sanfeliu et al. (Eds.): CIARP 2004, LNCS 3287, pp. 654–660, 2004.

To address this problem speed functions that take into account probability density functions of regions inside and outside the structures of interest have been proposed [3,4,5,6,7]. This class of solution is well adapted to situations where adjacent structures have different intensity distributions but are challenged by applications that require the segmentation of structures surrounded by other structures with similar intensity values and separated by weak edges.

In this paper, a new speed function model is proposed, which based on the image region and boundary gradient information. The region information is achieved at a global level by a statistical characterization. The boundary finding part is handled by the gradient information. Since the gradient defines a measure of no-homogeneity in the pixel neighborhood, it is modeled as a potential function that generates a Gibbs distribution of a Markov random field [9]. The experimental results show that incorporating region intensity information and gradient information into the level set framework, an accurate and robust segmentation can be achieved.

2 Level Set Method

The level set method was proposed by Osher and Sethian[1], The main idea in the level set method is to describe a closed curve Γ in the image plane as the zero level set of a higher dimensional function $\phi(x,t)$ in $\Re^3$, The value of ϕ at some point x is defined by

$$\phi(x,t=0) = \pm d \tag{1}$$

where d is the distance from x to $\Gamma(t=0)$, and the sign in (1) is chosen whether the point x lies outside or inside the initial hypersurface. $\Gamma(t=0)$. In this manner, Γ is represented by the zero level set $\Gamma(t) = \{x \in R^2 \mid \phi(x,t) = 0\}$ of the level set function, and the initial function $\phi(x,t=0)$ with the property that $\Gamma(0) = \{x \in R^2 \mid \phi(x,t=0) = 0\}$. The evolution of $\phi(x,t)$ can be modeled as

$$\frac{\partial \phi}{\partial t} + F\|\nabla \phi\| = 0 \text{ With } \phi(x,t=0) \tag{2}$$

The speed function F plays the major role in the evolution process. The speed function F depends on factors like the image gradient. A common choice for F is:

$$F = P(I)(1 - \varepsilon k) \tag{3}$$

where, $0 < \varepsilon < 1$ is a constant, I is the image intensity and k is the curvature obtained from divergence of the gradient of the normal vector to the front. The term $P(I)$ is an image-dependent halting criteria calculated as:

$$P(I) = e^{-|\nabla G_\sigma * I|} \tag{4}$$

where $\nabla G * I$ denotes the image convolved with a Gaussian smoothing filter whose characteristic width is σ. This halting criterion allows model to stop on high image gradient by reducing speed function to zero, thus aligning it to the object boundary.

Given the initial value, it can be solved by means of difference operators in a fixed grid via

$$\phi_{ij}^{n+1} = \phi_{ij}^{n} - \Delta t \cdot h \cdot \left(\max\left(F_{ij}, 0\right)\nabla^{+} + \min\left(F_{ij}, 0\right)\nabla^{-}\right) \tag{5}$$

where n is the iterative time, h is the grid step, Δt is the time step, F_{ij} is the speed value of pixel (i, j), ϕ_{ij}^{n} is the level value of pixel (i, j) at time n and where

$$\nabla^{+} = [\max(D_{ij}^{-x}\phi, 0)^2 + \min(D_{ij}^{+x}\phi, 0)^2 + \max(D_{ij}^{-y}\phi, 0)^2 + \min(D_{ij}^{+y}\phi, 0)^2]^{\frac{1}{2}} \tag{6}$$

$$\nabla^{-} = [\max(D_{ij}^{+x}\phi, 0)^2 + \min(D_{ij}^{-x}\phi, 0)^2 + \max(D_{ij}^{+y}\phi, 0)^2 + \min(D_{ij}^{-y}\phi, 0)^2]^{\frac{1}{2}} \tag{7}$$

$$D_{ij}^{-x}\phi = \frac{\phi_{ij}^{n} - \phi_{i-1j}^{n}}{\Delta x} \quad D_{ij}^{+x}\phi = \frac{\phi_{i+1j}^{n} - \phi_{ij}^{n}}{\Delta x} \tag{8}$$

$$D_{ij}^{-y}\phi = \frac{\phi_{ij}^{n} - \phi_{ij-1}^{n}}{\Delta y} \quad D_{ij}^{+y}\phi = \frac{\phi_{ij+1}^{n} - \phi_{ij}^{n}}{\Delta y} \tag{9}$$

This implementation allows the function ϕ to automatically follow topological changes and corners during evolution.

3   The Proposed Level Set Speed Function

The key idea was to utilize the probability density function inside and outside the structure to be segmented. The pixel in the neighborhood of the segmenting structure was responsible for creating a pull/push force on the propagating front. The boundary finding part is handled by the gradient information. Since the gradient defines a measure of no-homogeneity in the pixel neighborhood, it is modeled as a potential function that generates a Gibbs distribution of a Markov random field. We chosen the original speed given by Malladi[2] for its simplicity as :

$$F = h_I(v - \rho k) \tag{10}$$

where v represents an external propagation force, k is the local curvature of the front and acts as a regularization term. The weighting ρ expresses the importance given to regularization. The term h_I is the data consistency and act as a stopping criterion at the location of the desired boundaries; which is defined according to the intensity of the image data.

3.1   Image Region Statistical Characterization

Suppose that a image is partitioned into N pixel, labeled by the integers $1, 2, \cdots, N$. In most application, the pixel locations or sites will form a regular square lattice. Further suppose that each pixel variable, $x_i, 1 \le i \le N$ can take any real value, $x_i \in R$. The values of the pixel variables are called intensities and arbitrary shading will be denoted $x = \{x_1, x_2, \cdots, x_N\}$, hence $x \in R^N$. In general it is not possible to observe x directly, instead the observed image y is a degraded copy of x.

$$y_i = x_i + \varepsilon_i \quad , \quad 1 \le i \le N \tag{11}$$

where $\varepsilon_i \sim N(0, \sigma^2)$, and ε_i and ε_j are independent when $i \ne j$. Hence the conditional distribution of Y given X and σ with density function:

$$P(Y \mid X) = \frac{1}{\sqrt{2\pi}\sigma} \exp\{-\frac{1}{2\sigma^2} \sum_{i=1}^{N} (y_i - x_i)^2\} \tag{12}$$

The sign of v determines the direction of the external propagation force.

$$v = Sign\{a_i p_i(I) - (1 - a_i) p_e(I)\} \tag{13}$$

$$p(y_s \mid x_s) \propto \begin{cases} \dfrac{1}{\sqrt{2\pi}\sigma_{in}} \exp(-\dfrac{(I(x) - \mu_{in})^2}{2\sigma^2_{in}}) & inside\,object \\[3mm] \dfrac{1}{\sqrt{2\pi}\sigma_{out}} \exp(-\dfrac{(I(x) - \mu_{out})^2}{2\sigma^2_{out}}) & outside\,object \end{cases} \tag{14}$$

where $p_i(I)$ and $p_e(I)$ denote the likehood of intensity inside and outside the object, and a_i is the prior of a image to be inside the object. Where $\mu_{in}, \mu_{out}, \sigma^2_{in}$ and σ^2_{out} are respectively the mean and the variance of the image intensity.

3.2 Image Boundary Statistical Characterization

Let Y be the observed image, X the ideal image, and N is an additive Gaussian noise present in the image. That can be described as:

$$Y = X + N \tag{15}$$

The gradient image is corrupted by false-edges due to noise. The plausibility of false edges follows a Rayleigh distribution. In order to distinguish real edges from false ones, Voorhees [8] proposed to statistically estimate a threshold that separates these two populations.

We assume the plausibility of the true edges being described by a single distribution. One must normalize the gradient values in order to keep both gradient and statistics measures in the same numerical range. Therefore, we define the normalized gradient at a given position y_s as follows

$$\tilde{g}(y_s) = \frac{g(y_s)}{\mu} \tag{16}$$

where μ is the mean of the Rayleigh distribution.

The segmentation field, x, has an isotropic nature and its distribution is strictly defined in a local neighborhood. Thereafter, we can use MRF model. Based on the Hammersley-Clifford theorem, the density of x is given by a Gibbs density using the form:

$$p(x) = \frac{1}{Z} e^{-(\sum_c V_c(X))} \tag{17}$$

where Z is a normalization factor, or partitioning function. $V_c(x)$ is a sum of functions, one of each pixel in x, which describes the interaction of each pixel with its neighbors. The clique potentials V_c depend only on the pixels that belong to clique C. Since the gradient defines a measure of non-homogeneity and is evaluated in the immediate neighborhood of y_s, its response could be handled as being a transformation that maps the gray-level of y_s to the potential function $V_c(x_s)$. This relation is carried out in a proportional formulation as follows:

$$V_c(x_s) \propto \tilde{g}(y_s) \tag{18}$$

So, the MRF field henceforth be written in the following as:

$$p(x_s) = \frac{1}{Z} e^{-\tilde{g}(y_s)} \tag{19}$$

3.3 Level Set Speed Function of the Proposed Model

We can integrate the boundary probability and region homogeneity information to define new speed function. The estimation of these parameters to find the boundary is posed as an optimization process, By applying the Bayesian formulation the objective function measures the strength of the data consistency term h_I at a point s is defined as decreasing function as following:

$$p(x_s \mid y_s) \propto p(x_s) p(y_s \mid x_s) \tag{20}$$

where $p(x_s)$ is the boundary probability term in (19), $p(y_s \mid x_s)$ is the object region probability term in (14). It is clear that (20) combines the statistical and the gradient-based measure in order to find the optimal segmentation. The new consistency term h_I at point s proportion to the combined probability $p(x_s \mid y_s)$ of the closest point on the current interface. The final expression of the new term h_I will be:

$$h_I(s) = \exp\{-k \cdot p(x_s \mid y_s)\} \tag{21}$$

So the new speed function can be defined as:

$$F = h_I(v - \rho k) = (v - \rho k) \cdot \exp\{-k \cdot p(x_s \mid y_s)\} \tag{22}$$

4 Experimental Results

To demonstrate the performance of our new speed function for the level set framework, we carried out a series of experiments on medical images.

We describe a number of 2D images from which we extract the contours using the proposed method, which we have previously described. We have chosen images from some kinds of modalities medical images, US, CT, and X-ray images to demonstrate our methods.

As we can see, the US image quality is very poor and the region boundaries seem to be very fuzzy. Fig.1 shows the results on a US image with both strong and fuzzy region boundaries. Fig.1 (a) shows the original image, Fig.1 (b) shows the initial curve, Fig.1(c) shows the Intermediate iterations process, Fig.1 (d) shows the result of the proposed method. The examples presented show that the algorithm we propose is able to cope with ultrasound images that are notoriously difficult to segment because of speckle noise as well as with images with low signal-to-noise ratio and poorly defined edges.

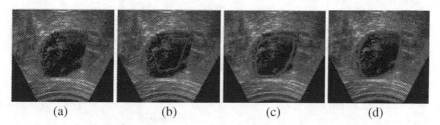

(a)   (b)   (c)   (d)

Fig. 1. US image segmentation results; (a)original image; (b) initial curve; (c) intermediate iterations; (d) our proposed method result.

We also applied our method on CT image of the liver as shown in Fig.2 and Fig.3. In every instance, a pair of image is presented. The human liver and brain images illustrate the performance of our methods for the segmentation of structures with similar intensity values that are separated by weak edges.

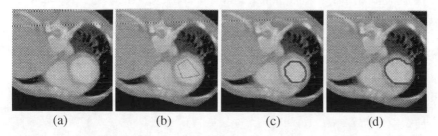

(a)   (b)   (c)   (d)

Fig. 2. CT liver image segmentation results; (a)original image; (b) initial curve; (c) intermediate iterations; (d) our proposed method results.

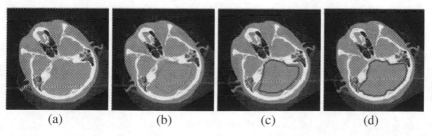

(a)   (b)   (c)   (d)

Fig. 3. CT brain image segmentation results; (a)original image; (b) initial curve; (c) intermediate iterations; (d) our proposed method results.

Fig.4 shows the results of applying our methods for finding boundary of the X-ray carpal bone image with object overlap. This segmentation is a critical operation in the automatic skeletal age assessment system. The results clearly demonstrate the superior segmentation quality of our approach.

As mentioned above, the proposed method seems ideal for use on a wide variety of medical imagery. The power of this method in extracting feature from even fuzzy boundary and overlap boundary medical images has been demonstrated.

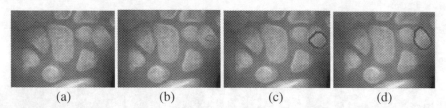

(a)   (b)   (c)   (d)

Fig. 4. Results of contour extracting from X-ray carpal bone image; (a)carpal bone; (b) initial curve; (c) intermediate iterations; (d) our proposed method result.

5   Conclusions

In this paper, we have proposed a new speed function for level set framework. The new models modify the level set speed function utilizing region intensity information and gradient information. The scheme here proposed is particularly well adapted to situations where edges are weak and overlap, and images are noisy. The method has been tested with numerical real modalities medical images, such as US, CT and X-ray images. The experimental results show the reliability of the approach.

References

1. S. J. Osher and J. A. Sethian. Fronts propagating with curvature dependent speed: Algorithms based on Hamilton-Jacobi formulations. *J. Comput. Phys*, vol. 79, pp. 12–49, 1988.
2. R. Malladi, J. Sethian, and B. Vemuri. Shape modeling with front propagation: A level set approach. *IEEE T-PAMI*, vol. 17, no. 2, pp. 158-175, 1995.
3. A. Chakraborty, L. Staib, and J. Duncan. Deformable boundary finding in medical image by integrating gradient and region information. *IEEE T-MI*, vol. 15, no. 6, pp. 859-870, 1996.
4. R. Ronfard. Region-based strategies for active contour models. *International Journal of Computer Vision*, vol. 13, no. 2, pp. 229-251, 1994.
5. C.S .Poon and M. Braun. Image segmentation by a deformable contour model incorporating region analysis. *Phys. Med. Biol*, vol. 42, no. 9, pp. 1833-1841, 1997.
6. C. Xu, A. Yezzi. Jr, and J. Prince. On the relationship between parametric and geometric active contours. *Technical Report JHU/ECE* 99-14, Dec. 1999.
7. C. Baillard and C. Barillot. Robust 3D segmentation of anatomical structures with level sets. *Proceedings of MICCAI 2000*, pp. 237-245, 2000.
8. H.Voorhees and T.Poggio. Detecting textons and texture boundaries in natural images. *Proc.of the International Conference on Computer Vision*, pp.250-258, 1987.
9. S. Geman and D. Geman. Stochastic relaxation, Gibbs distributions and the Bayesian restoration of images. *IEEE Trans. on Pattern Analysis and Machine Intelligence*, Vol.6, pp.721-741, 1984.

Measurement of Parameters of the Optic Disk in Ophthalmoscopic Color Images of Human Retina

Edgardo M. Felipe Riverón[1] and Mijail del Toro Céspedes[2]

[1] Center for Computing Research, National Polytechnic Institute,
Juan de Dios Batiz s/n, P.O. 07738, Mexico
edgardo@cic.ipn.mx
[2] Havana University, Havana, Cuba
mijail_dt@yahoo.es, mijail@ausa.gae.com.cu

Abstract. The objective of this paper is to measure some important parameters of the optic disk (or optic papilla) in ophthalmoscopic color images of human retinas. The approach consists of locating the optic disk automatically, segmenting its contour and the contour of the depression-like feature caused by glaucoma, called an excavation or cup. Then the corresponding areas are measured to calculate the ratio Cup/Disc and the relative displacement of the centroids of both regions. To achieve these objectives, noise is filtered, luminance is normalized, and a thresholding technique is used. The results obtained will aid the work of ophthalmologists by increasing the quality of automatic diagnosis of glaucoma, one of the main causes of blindness worldwide.

1 Introduction

There are three visible structural anatomical elements present in the rear pole of the retina: the macula, the optic disk (or optic papilla), and the vascular network, composed of the thicker and darker red vein network, and the thinner arterial network of clearer reddish tone (Fig. 1).

The optic disk or papilla is the clearest area in images of the rear pole of the retina. In a normal papilla, the vascular network coming out from the choroids travels through the center of the nervous fibers that constitute the optic nerve, which travels through a tube-like structure toward the brain. Due to glaucoma, caused frequently by an abnormal increase of the intraocular pressure, an *excavation* (or *cup*) is created in the papilla. This excavation produces a thickening of the wall of the papilla, which moves the cluster of veins and arteries toward the nasal side of the affected eye (Fig. 2). In time, the optic nerve is damaged, causing first loss of peripheral vision and later complete loss of vision in those patients suffering from this disease.

The papilla and the excavation areas in the rear pole constitute the objects and areas of interest (AOI) in this work. Figure 2 shows how the thickening of the wall of the papilla assumes a yellowish coloration, while the excavation stands out even more. The thick area of orange coloration is called the *neural ring*.

Glaucoma is one of the most prevalent illnesses of the retina in the world and one that, if not diagnosed on time, often leads to total blindness [1]. More than 66 million people in the world are affected by glaucoma [2]. The search for computerized image processing techniques to help diagnose this illness is an area of considerable interest. The work reported in this paper is a step in that direction.

A. Sanfeliu et al. (Eds.): CIARP 2004, LNCS 3287, pp. 661–668, 2004.

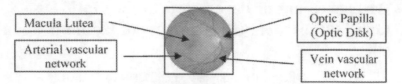

Fig. 1. Anatomic structural elements of the retina

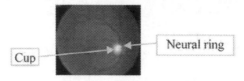

Fig. 2. Image of the optic disk or papilla in a human retina with glaucoma

2   The Problem

Our task deals with the localization and isolation of the optic disk in images of the retina. Any strategy applied to achieve this purpose should be independent of lack of uniformity in illumination, and be invariant to translation, rotation and scale in the images being analyzed. In the method described in the following sections, the border of the optic disk and that of the excavation mentioned earlier are segmented, and the position of their centroids is calculated. Finally, a relative shift between centroids and the ratio Cup/Disk of corresponding areas are computed, from which ophthalmologists are given an objective index of the presence or absence of glaucoma.

3   Previous Works

The successful localization and segmentation of the optic disk in images of the rear pole of human retina has been treated previously in the literature. Different methods like tracking of the optic disk have been described through a pyramidal decomposition and search of the contour based on the Hausendorff distance, where the region of the optic disk is found by means of multiscale analysis or of a pyramidal approach using a simple wavelet transformation [3]. The automatic localization of the papilla has also been achieved by means of the analysis of principal components. This technique is based on groupings by regions the brightest of pixels in the image [4].

Because the papilla is nearly elliptical, the Hough Transform has been applied also to the detection of this type of shape [5].

The border of the optic disk has also been detected by means of active contours (snakes), which simulate the adjustment from an elastic curve to the borders of the objects of interest in an image [7]. This has been applied in the detection of the optic disk in retina images, where they combine a priori knowledge about the papilla and its approximate size, keeping in mind the individual characteristics of the image.

4   Sequence of Operations

All color images used in this work and reported here were obtained from the same source and have 300 dpi of spatial resolution, 24 bits/pixel and were normalized to a size of 720 x 576 pixels. In total there were 107 images from 34 cases.

The operations carried out during the complete process were:

- Automatic localization of the papilla.
- Determination of centroids and reduction in size the image.
- Preprocessing (homogenizing gray levels of the background and noise cleaning).
- Measurements.

4.1 Automatic Localization of the Papilla

Because the color images used in this work are represented in the RGB color model, the papilla is located automatically by means of the thresholding method of Otsu [8] [9] from the green plane of the image. With a binary opening using a flat disk structure element (SE) of 5 pixels of diameter, the isolated components were cleaned and the small basins inside the AOI were filled using a binary closing operation.

4.2 Determination of the Centroids and Reduction of the Image

All images in this work are considered isotropic, that is, with objects having uniform characteristics in all dimensions. This allows us to compute easily the position of centroids. To obtain the coordinates of a centroid, we applied an *external border* morphological operation with a flat cross shape SE of 3 x 3 pixels. We then computed the centroid of the resulting convex polygon using the following general expressions for the area (Eq. 1) and for the coordinates X and Y (Eqs. 2 and 3) shown in Table 1 [10].

X_i and Y_i are the components x and y of pixel i in the polygon of N pixels. The only restriction to using the formula for computing the area in the case of several polygons is that there can be no overlap among them, a condition that is generally satisfied in practice.

Table 1. Expressions for calculating the position of the centroid

$$A = \frac{1}{2} \sum_{i=0}^{N-1} (X_i Y_{i+1} - X_{i+i} Y_i) . \text{ Polygon area.} \tag{1}$$

$$C_x = \frac{1}{6A} \sum_{i=0}^{N-1} (X_i + X_{i+1})(X_i Y_{i+1} - X_{i+1} Y_i) . \text{ X Component.} \tag{2}$$

$$C_y = \frac{1}{6A} \sum_{i=0}^{N-1} (Y_i + Y_{i+1})(X_i Y_{i+1} - X_{i+1} Y_i) . \text{ Y Component.} \tag{3}$$

Fig. 3. Automatic localization of the papilla

After the position of the centroid is calculated, we proceed to crop the original color image from the original 720 x 576 pixels to 200 x 200 pixels around the centroid, which guarantees that the optic disk is contained completely in the subimage. This subimage is our AOI (Fig. 3).

4.3 Homogenizing Gray Levels of the Background

In general, the capture of images was not focused directly toward the papilla. For that reason the area where it is located in an image is not of uniform illumination. To compensate for this, an algorithm to homogenize the background was applied to facilitate the subsequent segmentation by thresholding (Fig. 4).

The located subimage was subdivided into k x k cells, and on the basis of the average of gray levels of the corresponding pixels (Eqs. 4a-4d), it was determined which of them was the darkest (Eq. 5). After this, a calculation is performed (Eq. 6) to determine how many levels missed each pixel of remaining grids to be equally dark than the average of the darkest. Equation 7 shows the expression used to calculate the magnitude to be added to each pixel of each grid to achieve the homogenizing (See Table 2).

Fig. 4. Darker and lighter zones around the optic papilla

Table 2. Expressions for homogenizing the uneven background

$$S_{(0,0)} = \sum_{i=0}^{wc} \sum_{j=0}^{hc} g_{ij} \tag{4a}$$

$$S_{(0,k-1)} = \sum_{i=0}^{wc} \sum_{j=h-hc}^{h} g_{ij} \tag{4b}$$

$$S_{(k-1,0)} = \sum_{i=w-wc}^{w} \sum_{j=0}^{hc} g_{ij} \tag{4c}$$

$$S_{(k-1,k-1)} = \sum_{i=w-wc}^{w} \sum_{j=h-hc}^{h} g_{ij} \tag{4d}$$

$$S = \min(S_{(0,0)}, S_{(0,k-1)}, S_{(k-1,0)}, S_{(k-1,k-1)}) \tag{5}$$

$$V_{m,n} = \frac{S - S_{(i,j)}}{wc \cdot hc} \qquad i,j = \{0,k-1\} \tag{6}$$

$$V_{(m,n)} = \frac{(V_{(m,k-1)} - V_{(m,0)})n}{k-1} + V_{(m,0)} : 0 < n < k-1, 0 \le m \le k-1 \tag{7}$$

In our case the size of the subdivision selected was 20 x 20 cells (Fig. 5). To eliminate the noise in images, a Gaussian filter was applied with a flat square window of 5 x 5 pixels and standard deviation $\sigma = 0.8$ pixels, followed by an averaging filter with a flat square window of the same size [5] [12].

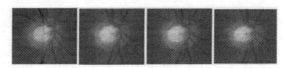

Fig. 5. Results of the homogenizing for 2 x 2, 4 x 4, 10 x 10, and 20 x 20 cells

4.4 Segmentation of Contours of the Papilla and the Excavation

Finally, the best results to segment the papilla and the excavation were achieved by a strategy that combines segmentation by thresholding according to Otsu [8], and the sequential application of binary opening, closing and external border. This procedure we called OACE, formed by the Spanish initials of Otsu, Opening, Closing and External border (Fig. 6). When using Otsu's method to threshold an image, a value ε taken from the histogram is needed to regulate the level of the total variation of the sample. In this study the value ε oscillated in the range [0.1-0.2] with a mean value of 0.15 for the papilla, and between [0.03-0.06] with a mean value 0.045 for the segmentation of the excavation area. They proved to be adequate in most of cases.

Fig. 6. Thresholding by Otsu with $\varepsilon = 0.15$ for the papilla and $\varepsilon = 0.05$ for the excavation

When detecting the contour of the papilla in binary images, it was observed that in some cases there were present isolated small spurious components (shown by arrows in Fig. 7a). To eliminate these components an opening was applied with a flat disk of 5 pixels in diameter. To restore the original image (now without the artifacts) a reconstruction operation by binary dilation with a similar SE was used.

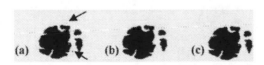

Fig. 7. (a) Thresholded image. (b) Binary opening. (c) Reconstruction by binary dilation

The vascular cluster present inside the papilla causes in the binary images after segmentation the separation among the components of the papilla and the small gulfs in the excavation. To enhance the shape of these components a closing was applied with flat disks SE of different sizes: 13 pixels for the papilla and 43 pixels for the excavation (Figs. 8c and 8f).

Fig. 8. (a) and (d) Papilla and excavation after Otsu. (b) and (e) After closing with a flat disk of 13 pixels of diameter. (c) and (f) Idem with a flat disk of 43 pixels of diameter

Subsequently, to extract the external borders of the papilla and the excavation, the morphological operation External Border was applied with a flat cross SE of 3x3 pixels, as shown in Fig. 9. Figure 10 shows both contours overlapping separately the original image.

Fig. 9. (a) External border of the papilla. (b) Idem of the excavation

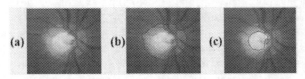

Fig. 10. Contours after applying OACE. (a) Original image. (b) $\varepsilon = 0.17$. (c) $\varepsilon = 0.052$

4.5 Measurements

By means of the Equation 1, the area occupied by the papilla and excavation was calculated in pixels. To determine the coordinates of the centroids, Equations 2 and 3 were used, starting from the corresponding contours. Because of the papilla has a nearly elliptic shape, the contour was approximated by an ellipse (Fig. 11).

One form to detect the presence of the glaucoma is through the so called Cup / Disk ratio, where the excavation is not more than the sinking that takes place in the papilla with respect to the normal level of the retina. The relationship Cup / Disk offers us a normal / abnormal index, based on the division of the optic disk in 10 sections, starting from the geometric center of the ellipse that bounds the optic disk.

Fig. 11. Ellipse that is better adjusted to the papilla

From the ellipses that better adjust the papilla (EExt) they were calculated (Fig. 12a):

- The Euclidean distances in pixels from the border of the excavation (blue), until the border of the ellipse EExt (red), in N, S, E and W directions [13].
- The Cup /Disk ratio.
- The distances between centroids of the two areas occupied by the papilla and the excavation, to obtain the displacement that takes place among them.

Global results are shown in Table 3 for 107 glaucomatous images analyzed. The percentage of effectiveness was of 94 %.

Table 3. Results obtained when OACE method was applied to 107 glaucomatous images

Task	Images
Optic disk detection	101
Excavation detection	105
Both contours	97

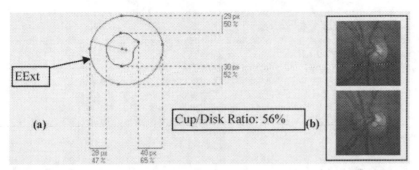

Fig. 12. (a) Indication and results of the measurements. (b) Two cases where OACE failed

5   Conclusions

This work has been oriented toward the measurements of parameters of the optic disk in real images of human retinas. The optic disk was located automatically, and its contour and the contour of any excavations present were segmented in order to measure the areas and relative displacements between correspondent centroids, as the main parameters indicative of the presence of glaucoma. A homogenizing algorithm was applied to equalize the illumination of the areas surrounding the papilla. Gaussian and averaging filters were used to reduce the random noise present in the original images. For the detection of contours of the papilla and the excavation, we used a strategy that combines segmentation using the thresholding method of Otsu, together with the binary operators of opening, closing and external border. The areas of the papilla and the excavation were measured, as were the relative displacement of correspondent centroid. Finally, the contour of the papilla was approximated by an ellipse to calculate the desired relationship Cup / Disk.

References

1. Alemañy Martorell, J., Marrero Faz, E., Villar Valdés, R., Oftalmología. Capítulo 14 (1980).
2. Lubinus Badillo, F. G., Mantilla Suárez, J. C., Valencia, A., Rueda, J. C., Estudio de la circulación retrobulbar con imagen doppler a color en pacientes con glaucoma asimétrico (2002).
3. Gagnon, L., Lalonde, M., Beaulieu, M., Boucher, M.-C. Procedure to detect anatomical structures in optic fundus images, Computer Research Institute of Montreal; Dept. of Ophthalmology, Maisonneuve-Rosemont Hospital (2001).
4. Li H. Chutatape O., Automatic Location of Optic Disk in Retinal Image. School of Electrical and Electronic Engineering (1999).

5. Molina, R., Introducción al Procesamiento y Análisis de Imágenes Digitales, en http://www-etsi2.ugr.es/depar/ccia/mia/complementario/Procesamiento_Imagenes/node14.html
6. McLaughlin, R. A., Technical Report – Randomized Hough Transform: Improved Ellipse Detection with Comparison (1995).
7. Mendels, F., Heneghan, C., and Thiran, J. P., Identification of the Optic disk boundary in retinal images using active contours (2000).
8. Otsu, N., A threshold Selection Method from Gray-Level Histogram. IEEE Trans Systems, Man and Cybernetics SMC-9:62-66 (1976).
9. Rodriguez, R. and Alarcon, T. E, Color Segmentation Applied to the Study of the Angio-genesis (2002).
10. Vincent, L., Componentes de SIGAU, Capítulo 5 (1999).
11. Vincent, L., Morphological grayscale Reconstruction in Images Analysis: Applications and Efficient Algorithms, IEEE Transactions on Images Processing, Vol 2, pp. 176-201 (1993).
12. Image Processing Learning Resources: www.dai.ed.ac.uk\HIPR2\mean.htm
13. Felipe-Riverón, E. M., Medidas de distancias, curso sobre Conceptos básicos sobre procesamiento de imágenes, CIC-IPN (2002).

Global Interpretation and Local Analysis to Measure Gears Eccentricity

Joaquín Salas

CICATA-IPN
salas@ieee.org

Abstract. This paper presents a data-driven approach to profile fitting where global constraints are imposed to local measurements. The local measurements are obtained from partial analysis of the objects under consideration. Prior knowledge of the object under analysis provides global constraints. To illustrate these concepts, it is developed the exercise of measuring a gear's boundary from its teeth profile. A framework is developed to extract local parameters from frame to frame and to enforce morphologic constraints over the whole sequence. It is shown how a combination of accurate local processing techniques and global knowledge can solve the tradeoff between what can be perceived locally and interpreted globally.

1 Introduction

Suppose that one is given the task to obtain the geometric properties of a circular object, *i.e.*, compute a circle's center and radius. A possible approach may be to grab an image, detect its contour and from it approximate both its center and its radius. But say, that now one is willing to challenge the hypothesis about the circularity of the boundary. A possible approach may be to zoom in the object's boundary, to reveal more detail, and grab a sequence of images while the object rotates. Then, the problem becomes to find the set rotations and translations that relate features found among the images. Indeed, as the detail level is increased more frames are needed to represent the periphery. If one proceeds from frame to frame the overall error will increase because each transformation adds up some estimation error that accumulates through the sequence. This paper presents a data-driven approach to profile fitting where global constraints are imposed to local measurements. The local measurements are obtained from partial analysis of the objects under consideration. The global constraints are obtained from knowledge about the objects that we are dealing with. In our case, internal spur gears, *i.e.*, they have teeth that are straight and parallel to the axis of rotation and on the inside of a hollow cylindrical shape.

In a seminal work, David Marr[1] introduced the concept of top-down and bottom-up approaches to computer vision systems. Since then, there has been a considerable interest on the integration of global constraints (see Ullman[2] for a description of high-level vision problems), which are usually associated with shape and spatial relations, and local properties, such as the extraction of certain

A. Sanfeliu et al. (Eds.): CIARP 2004, LNCS 3287, pp. 669–676, 2004.

Fig. 1. Experimental Setup. A gear is placed in front of a camera. Then, the gear is rotated manually very slowly while grabbing snapshots. The gear is standing on a metallic base. This causes considerable friction. Before being used the images are corrected using Zhang[5] camera calibration procedure.

physical properties. In this study, global constraints about a gear's circularity are applied to local measurements about the transformation from frame to frame. First, snapshots are acquired while the gear rotates. Each image has information about a few teeth (see Figs. 1 and 2). The translation from frame to frame is computed by applying an iterative registration procedure to the points in the gear's border. The rotation is computed with a closed form equation. Once, the local measurements are acquired, global coherence is enforced. The periodicity of the gear's teeth is used to correct the error accumulation carried out from frame to frame. Methods to measure a gear's profile may be classified as intrusive or non-intrusive. For instance, intrusive methods include a gauge pin that physically touch the gear's surface and translate the relative displacement into depth measurements[3]. Non-intrusive methods include optical comparators that magnify the object by projecting the shadow on a flat screen [4]. Our approach takes the best of both methods, leading to a non-invasive, high-accuracy system to measure an object's profile.

A central problem that we deal with is registration. Registration is the problem of finding the transformation that leads a data set into another. Because its pervasiveness in domains such as Computer Vision, Pattern Recognition, Medical Image Analysis and Remotely Sensed Data Processing, much effort has been devoted to solve it[6]. Significant progress has been made and nowadays registration is used for images that come from different sensors, viewpoints, times and patterns. Despite the variety of applications and categories, registration usually involves finding the transformation of a two-dimensional image patch. This transformation may be affine, perspective, projective or polynomial. In [7], Maintz and Viegever present an extensive overview of registration methods. In most cases, the registration transformation is usually found by establishing an optimization criterion. Although it has been observed that high dimensional

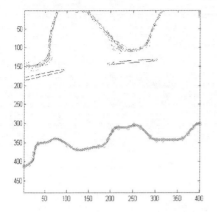

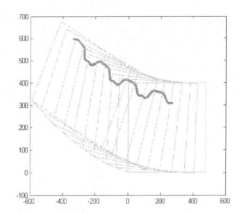

(a) Typical contour image used in the experimentation. It includes the set of profile points and the piecewise approximation with line segments.

(b) Locally, the approach is to find the geometric transformation from frame to frame. Globally, *a priori* knowledge about the object geometry is incorporated into the interpretation.

Fig. 2. Local measurements (a) are integrated by a set of constraints which leads to a global interpretation(b).

transformations involved in deformable registration generally make the problem ill-conditioned [8]. Shi and Tomasi[9] noted that even including the rotation transformation in the optimization criterion can lead to numerical instability. Following these observations, in this study translation and rotation are computed one after the other in an iterative loop. One of the most popular optimization criteria, and the one used in this paper, is the sum of the squared differences. Nevertheless, other optimization criteria are possible. For instance, Haker *et al*[10] use a Monge-Kantorovich distance that leads to a parameter free formulation. Another property of their formulation is that the optimal mapping equals the inverse mapping. This property is also found in other methods, for instance in[11]. In this study, a registration procedures derived from optimizing the sum of the squared differences is presented. The method is used to register two point sets from vector-valued functions. One-dimensional registration has been preluded in the context of projection based methods. Alliney and Morandi[12] presented a method that uses only the row and column projections of an image. They proposed to calculate the Fourier transform to compute phase correlation.

The rest of this document is organized as follows. In §2, it is described a registration procedure to compute the local properties of rotation and translation. Then, in §3, the global constraint about circularity is enforced. Next, in §4, the experimental results are shown. Finally, the document concludes.

2   Local Processing

In this section, a framework to compute the border transformation from frame to frame is introduced. First a vector-valued procedure for point set registration to

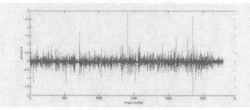 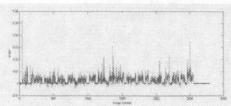

(a) Radio displacements. It is possible to appreciate abrupt changes about every 50 frames or so. This motion is due because we manually executed the gear's rotation.

(b) Angle displacements. Note the quasi-periodic bursts about every 100 frames or so.

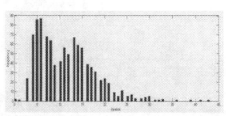

(c) Frequency of the number of iterations. In the average, the number of iterations was 11.49 with an standard deviation of 6.2548.

Fig. 3. Registration of vector-valued curve segments.

compute the translation is developed. Then a closed form equation to estimate the rotation is presented.

2.1   Translation

In [9], Shi and Tomasi introduced a procedure for region based feature tracking. In a similar way, here it is introduced a method for vector-valued point set registration. Let $\mathbf{f}(s) = [x_f(s), y_f(s)]^T$ and $\mathbf{g}(s) = [x_g(s), y_g(s)]^T$ be two vector-valued functions, the problem is to compute their best match in a short portion C of the curve S. The following similarity function is used

$$e(\delta) = \int_C \| \mathbf{f}(s) - \mathbf{g}(s + \delta) \|^2 \, ds \tag{1}$$

The term $e(\delta)$ is minimum when $\partial e(\delta)/\partial \delta = 0$, thus

$$\frac{\partial e(\delta)}{\partial \delta} = 2 \int_C \frac{\partial \mathbf{g}^T(s + \delta)}{\partial \delta} [\mathbf{g}(s + \delta) - \mathbf{f}(s)] \, ds \tag{2}$$

A possible way to express $\mathbf{g}(s + \delta)$ is by expanding it in terms of its Taylor's series and taking its linear order terms while neglecting higher order ones. Thus $\partial e(\delta)/\partial \delta$ can be approximated as

$$\frac{\partial e(\delta)}{\partial \delta} \approx 2 \int_C \mathbf{h}(s)^T (\mathbf{g}(s) + \delta \mathbf{h}(s) - \mathbf{f}(s)) ds \tag{3}$$

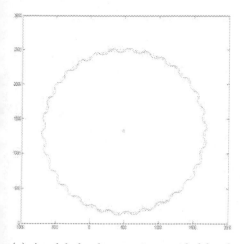

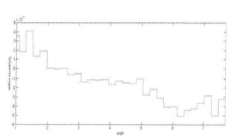

(a) As global coherence is provided local transformations are corrected. The dotted line signals the computed pitch circle. The center is in (483.2, 1324.6) and the radius is 1,177.6 pixels.

(b)Gear's eccentricity measured as the distance from the centroid to the boundary points relative to the computed radius. The values are between -5.9870×10^{-3} and 4.8334×10^{-3} relative to the radius distance.

Fig. 4. Iterative boundary measurements. In (a) the coherence constraint lead to a better fit in a global scale. In (b) this particular gear's eccentricity is presented.

where $\mathbf{h}(s) = \partial \mathbf{g}(s)/\partial s$. In the previous equation, the term δ represents the solution given the linear behavior assumption. Nonetheless, for real data, it is required to iterate until convergence is achieved. Thus δ, the relative displacement along the curve, is given by

$$\delta_{k+1} = \delta_k + \frac{\int_C [\mathbf{f}(s) - \mathbf{g}(s)]^T \mathbf{h}(s)ds}{\int_C \mathbf{h}(s)^T \mathbf{h}(s)ds} \tag{4}$$

2.2   Rotation

Here, a closed form equation to compute de angle between curve segments is derived. The transformation between a point $\mathbf{x} \in \mathbf{f}(s)$ and another point $\mathbf{y} \in \mathbf{g}(s)$ is given by

$$\mathbf{y} = R(\alpha)(\mathbf{x} - \mathbf{t}) \tag{5}$$

where $\mathbf{t}$ is the vector that makes coincide the center of rotation for both curves and $R(\alpha)$ is a 2×2 rotation matrix that depends on the angle α. A dissimilarity function relative to the different angle may be

$$\xi(\alpha) = \int_C \| \mathbf{y} - R(\alpha)(\mathbf{x} - \mathbf{t}) \|^2 \, ds \tag{6}$$

In order to find the minimum, $\xi(\alpha)$ is derived with respect to α. Expanding this result gives

$$\frac{\partial \xi(\alpha)}{\partial \alpha} = 2 \int_C [y_1, y_2] \begin{pmatrix} \sin \alpha \cos \alpha \\ -\cos \alpha \sin \alpha \end{pmatrix} \begin{pmatrix} x_1 - t_1 \\ x_2 - t_2 \end{pmatrix} ds \tag{7}$$

where $\mathbf{y}(s) = [y_1, y_2]^T$, $\mathbf{x}(s) = [x_1, x_2]^T$ and $\mathbf{t} = [t_1, t_2]^T$ respectively. Solving for α gives the following equation

$$\tan \alpha = -\frac{\int_C [y_1(x_2 - t_2) - y_2(x_1 - t_1)] \, ds}{\int_C [y_1(x_1 - t_1) - y_2(x_2 - t_2)] \, ds} \tag{8}$$

3   Global Correspondence

The scheme developed in the previous section is numerically error prone because the computations carry imprecisions from frame to frame. In this section, a framework for global coherence is developed. It is possible to observe that once defined a centroid and a radius, profile segments must couple smoothly as the border is processed. So we use the periodicity present in the border polar representation. Let $d(\theta)$ the function describing the objects border in polar coordinates. Then, its Fourier transform can be expressed as

$$D(f) = \sum_{k=0}^{N} d(\theta_k) e^{-2j\pi f \theta_k} \tag{9}$$

where N is the number of points in the border. Then

$$f_0 = \max_f \| D(f) \|^2 \tag{10}$$

is the frequency that describes the teeth periodicity. The number of teeth M observed is

$$M = N f_0 \tag{11}$$

Due to error propagation, the angle may have been overshot or undershot. To normalize it, the angle is multiplied by the factor

$$c = \frac{2\pi M}{T \theta_{\max}} \tag{12}$$

where T is the number of teeth in the gear and $\theta_{\max}$ is the maximum angle in the border sequence.

4   Experimental Results

A gear is placed in front of a camera (see Fig. 1). Then, the gear is rotated, manually, very slowly while grabbing 2,801 snapshots. The gear is standing on a metallic base. This causes considerable friction. Before being used the images are corrected using Zhang[5] camera calibration procedure. The center of rotation is expected to move from frame to frame. The gear used for experimenting is spur and internal.

The border is detected using Canny's edge detector. To avoid interrupted curves the edge image is dilated using a kernel $s = \begin{pmatrix} 1 & 1 \\ 1 & 1 \end{pmatrix}$. The resulting set of points is represented by a set of line segments using a divide and conquer strategy. The line segments are in turn used to represent the vector-valued functions. In Fig. 2, it is show a typical contour image. It includes the set of profile points and the piecewise approximation with line segments. For this particular image there are 401 border points that are reduced to 48 lineal segments. In the whole sequence 1,680,600 boundary points are collected.

The initial estimation of the centroid $(\overline{x}, \overline{y})$ and radius r is computed using Nelder's simplex[13]. The translation and rotation of the vector-valued curves is computed from frame to frame. In Fig. 3, these results are presented. As it was expected, it is possible to appreciate abrupt changes about every 75 frames or so. The angular coordinates vary between about cero and 0.01 degrees. The radius changes between -0.5 and 0.5 pixels from frame to frame. In the average, the number of iterations is 11.49 with an standard deviation of 6.2548. The frame to frame registration provided a good base to compute correspondence over larger steps. The angle computation is rather good because at the end the angle missed by an offset of 4.5%. In Fig. 4(a) the reconstructed image of the gear's boundary is presented. Then, in Fig. 4(b) the estimated gear's eccentricity is presented. The eccentricity is defined as the relative variation in radial distance from the centroid. The values are between -5.9870×10^{-3} and 4.8334×10^{-3} relative to the radius distance (1,177.6 pixels). Since the model of the circle is computed over all the collected points, the circle tends to pass through the gear's pitch.

5   Conclusion

This paper presents a data-driven approach to profile fitting where global constraints are imposed to the local measurements. As the level of detail in the image increases, less reliable for tracking is the information at a particular window resolution. It is demonstrated how a combination of accurate local processing techniques with clear global constraints can negotiate with this trade-off.

As an example, an application to measure the eccentricity in internal spur gears is presented. Gears are fundamental in a myriad of mechanical devices. In the context of this study, the gears are an excellent example because they have to be measured with high precision. Thus on the one hand, they demand high resolution. On the other hand, they exhibit information useful for tracking. The proposed approach iteratively finds the geometric transformation between frames allowing, later on, to enforce global coherence.

It has been shown that the method measures the eccentricity in the border's profile. Also, the method has been shown robust against change in rotation speed, and small variations between the gear's and the camera's reference systems.

References

1. David Marr. *Vision.* W. H. Freeman, 1982.
2. Shimon Ullman. *High-Level Vision.* MIT Press, 1995.
3. Bruce A. Wilson. *Dimensioning and Tolerancing Handbook.* Genium Publishing, 1995.
4. S. J. Martin, M. A. Butler, and C. E. Land. Ferroelectric Optical Image Comparator using PLZT Thin Films. *Electronics Letters,* 24(24):1486–1487, 1988.
5. Zhengyou Zhang. A Flexible New Technique for Camera Calibration. *IEEE Transactions on Pattern Analysis and Machine Intelligence,* 22(11):1330–1334, 2000.
6. Lisa Gottesfeld Brown. A Survey of Image Registration Techniques. *ACM Computing Surveys,* 24(4):325–376, 1992.
7. Maintz and Viergever. A Survey of Medical Image Registration. *Medical Image Analysis,* 2(1), 1998.
8. F. Kruggel M. Tittgemeyer, G. Wollny. Visualising Deformation Fields Computed by Non-Linear Image Registration. *Computing and Visualization in Science,* 5(1):45–51, 2002.
9. Jianbo Shi and Carlo Tomasi. Good Features to Track. In *IEEE Conference on Computer Vision and Pattern Recognition,* pages 593–600, 1994.
10. Steve Haker, Allen Tannenbaum, and Ron Kikinis. Mass Preserving Mappings and Image Registration. *Lecture Notes in Computer Science,* 2208:120, 2001.
11. G.E. Chirstensen and H.J. Johnson. Consistent Image Registration. *IEEE Transactions on Medical Imaging,* 20(7):568 –582, July 2001.
12. S. Alliney and C. Morandi. Digital Image Registration using Projections. *IEEE Transactions on Pattern Analysis and Machine Intelligence,* 8(2):222–233, 1986.
13. William H. Press, William T. Vetterling, Saul A. Teukolsky, and Brian P. Flannery. *Numerical Recipes in C++: the Art of Scientific Computing.* Cambridge University Press, 2002.

Two Floating Search Strategies to Compute the Support Sets System for ALVOT

Erika López-Espinoza, Jesús Ariel Carrasco-Ochoa, and José Fco. Martínez-Trinidad

Computer Science Department
National Institute of Astrophysics, Optics and Electronics
Luis Enrique Erro No. 1 Sta. María Tonantzintla, Puebla, CP 72840, México
{danae,ariel,fmartine}@inaoep.mx

Abstract. In this paper, two strategies to compute the support sets system for the supervised classifier ALVOT (voting algorithms) using sequential floating selection are presented. ALVOT is a supervised classification model based on the partial precedence principle, therefore, it needs, as feature selection, a set of features subsets, this set is called support sets system. The sequential floating selection methods for feature selection find only one relevant features subset. The introduced strategies search for a set of features subsets to generate a support sets system. Both strategies are compared between them and against the feature selection method based on testor theory, which is commonly used to compute this system. Results obtained with both strategies on different databases from UCI and on the faces database from Olivetti Research Laboratory (ORL) in Cambridge are presented.

1 Introduction

The feature selection problem traditionally consists in searching for one subset of features which improves or maintains the efficiency of the classifier. In the case of classification methods based on partial precedence, comparisons among the objects are made through subdescriptions previously specified. These methods do not take account whole comparisons between object descriptions. Partial conclusions about the similarity among the objects are considered to reach a final conclusion. Therefore a Support Sets System (SSS) is required.

ALVOT [1] is a supervised classification model developed in the framework of the Logical Combinatorial Pattern Recognition (LCPR) [1]. This classifier is based on the partial precedence principle, therefore it requires a SSS that indicates the subdescriptions that will be considered to make partial comparisons. An important characteristic of this classifier is that it can work with descriptions in terms of quantitative and/or qualitative variables, admitting incomplete descriptions [1]. The feature selection into the LCPR is commonly carried out by mean of the testor theory [1, 3]. A subset of typical testors can be used to form the SSS, nevertheless, the algorithms to compute the set of all typical testors are of exponential complexity with regard to the number of features, thus the computation of all typical testors, in problems where the objects are described in terms of high dimensionality n-uples, becomes computationally expensive or unfeasible.

In this work, two strategies to select the SSS for ALVOT using Sequential Floating Selection (SFS) [2] are proposed. In order to evaluate the performance of the subsets of selected features, the ALVOT classification rate is used, in addition it allows us to work with mixed and incomplete data. Experiments with different databases using the proposed strategies will be shown.

A. Sanfeliu et al. (Eds.): CIARP 2004, LNCS 3287, pp. 677–684, 2004.
© Springer-Verlag Berlin Heidelberg 2004

2 Foundations

2.1 Sequential Floating Selection

The SFS algorithms are part of the feature selection methods that use the Wrapper strategy. In this strategy the selection is made using a classifier to evaluate the efficiency of the subsets of selected features (J).

There are two ways to do a floating search, the Sequential Floating Forward Selection (SFFS) and the Sequential Floating Backward Selection (SBFS) [2].

The idea behind of SFFS consists in to initiate with an empty set of features, and to make the best inclusion of the feature that maximizes the classifier's efficiency, and after to make features exclusions as long as the resulting subset improves the classification efficiency compared to the subset obtained in the previous step. The algorithm finishes when it finds the subset with the desired cardinality.

In SBFS the idea is the same, but instead of initiating with an empty set of features it initiates with the whole set and exclusions followed by inclusions are done.

The algorithm of SFFS [2] is as follows.

1. *Initialization*: $Y = \phi, \; k = 0$

   Stop when k equals the number of required features.
   (in practice it is possible begin with $k=2$ applying two inclusions)

2. *Inclusion:* Select the most significant feature.

$$x^+ = \arg\max_{x \in X \setminus Y_k} [J(Y_k \cup \{x\})]$$

$$Y_{k+1} = Y_k \cup \{x^+\}; \; k = k+1$$

3. *Exclusion:* Select the least significant feature.

$$x^- = \arg\max_{x \in Y_k} [J(Y_k \setminus \{x\})]$$

If $J(Y_k \setminus \{x^-\}) > J(Y_k)$ then

$$Y_{k-1} = Y_k \setminus \{x^-\}; \; k = k-1$$

   go to step 3
   else
   go to step 2.

The SBFS algorithm can be obtained from SFFS by starting with the whole features set and substituting inclusion by exclusion and exclusion by inclusion.

2.2 ALVOT

ALVOT [1] is an algorithm developed into LCPR [1] to do supervised classification based on the *partial precedence principle*.

The classification is made through six stages:

1. Definition of support sets system.
2. Definition of similarity function.
3. Object evaluation function for a fix support set.
4. Class evaluation function for a fix support set.
5. Class evaluation function for the whole support sets system.
6. Solution rule.

In the first stage the SSS is defined. The SSS can be understood as any set of features subsets that indicates which parts of the objects will be compared in the classification stage. Each subset is a support set.

The similarity function is defined in the second stage. This function determines how subdescriptions will be compared and it should reflect how the comparisons among the objects are made in the real world.

Object evaluation function for a fix support set determines how much information is given by the similarity of a new object with each one of the sample objects, for a fix support set. The result of this function is called the vote given by each sample object to a new object with regard to a fix support set.

Class evaluation function for a fix support set summarizes all object evaluations for a new object within each class, for a fix support set. The result of this function is called the vote given by each class to a new object with regard to a fix support set.

Class evaluation function for the whole support sets system summarizes all class evaluations for a new object for whole the support sets system. The result of this function is called the vote given by each class to a new object with regard to the whole support sets system.

Finally the solution rule is applied, this function takes all votes for each class and decides which class or classes the new object belongs to.

2.3 Typical Testors

Into LCPR, feature selection is commonly carried out by mean of the testor theory [1, 3]. Typical testors or a subset of them can be used as SSS for the ALVOT classifier.

A features subset T is a testor if and only if considering the features from T there are no similar subdescriptions among objects from different classes, i.e., objects from class i are not similar to objects from class j, where $i \neq j$.

A testor T is a typical testor (irreducible) if and only if eliminating any feature from T the resultant set is not a testor. It means that there is not any other testor T' such that $T' \subset T$.

Typical testors are irreducible features combinations which allow distinguishing objects from different classes. We may think that if a feature appears in many irreducible combinations or typical testors, it will be more indispensable to distinguish classes. Based on this idea Zhuravlev formulated his feature's weight definition as the relative frequency of the occurrence of each feature in the set of all typical testors.

Let τ be the number of typical testors in a sample and let $\tau(i)$ be the number of typical testors where the feature x_i appears. Then the feature's weight (relevance) of x_i is as follows:

$$P(x_i) = \frac{\tau(i)}{\tau}, i = 1,...,n .$$ (1)

3 Proposed Strategies

As we have seen ALVOT requires a SSS to make the comparisons among the objects that will be classified.

Now we introduce two new strategies based on SFS to compute SSS for ALVOT. We only expose the algorithms for SFFS; the modifications apply also for SBFS.

3.1 Strategy 1

In the first strategy, the subset with the best classification efficiency for each cardinality i is searched (where $i=1,...,number\_features$), i.e., the subset of cardinality 1 with the best classification efficiency is searched, after the best subset of cardinality 2 is searched, this process continues until the best subset of cardinality equal to the total amount of features (N) is found, finally the best p subsets are selected as a SSS.

In this strategy the SSS may have at most one subset of cardinality i for each i.

The modified algorithm with the first strategy is as follows:

1. *Initialization* $Y = \phi$, $k = 0$, $S = \phi$, N;

   p = number of subsets to search
2. For $i = 1$ to N
   2.1. While Y don't have the cardinality i

   Inclusion: $x^+ = \arg\max_{x \in X \setminus Y_k}\left[J\left(Y_k \cup \{x\}\right)\right]$

   $Y_{k+1} = Y_k \cup \{x^+\}$; $k = k+1$

   Exclusion: $x^- = \arg\max_{x \in Y_k}\left[J\left(Y_k \setminus \{x\}\right)\right]$

   If $J(Y_k \setminus \{x^-\}) > J(Y_k)$ then

   $Y_{k-1} = Y_k \setminus \{x^-\}$; $k = k-1$

   go to step Exclusion
   else
   go to step Inclusion
   2.2. $S = Select\_the\_best\_p\text{-subsets } (S \cup Y_i)$

3.2 Strategy 2

The second strategy generates a SSS selecting the best p subsets from whole evaluated subsets during the entire floating search. This strategy admits a SSS with more than one subset with the same cardinality, while in the first strategy only one subset of cardinality i is permitted for each i. The maximum cardinality of SSS in the first strategy is limited to the number of features n, while in this strategy the SSS can be $\gg n$.

The modified algorithm with the second strategy is as follows:

1. Initialization, $Y=\phi$, $k=0$, $S = \phi$;

   Stop when k equals the number of required features.
   (in practice it is possible to begin with $k=2$ applying two inclusions)
   p = number of subsets to search
2. *Inclusion:* Select the most significant feature.

   $x^+ = \arg\max_{x \in X \setminus Y_k}\left[J\left(Y_k \cup \{x\}\right)\right]$

   $S = Select\_the\_best\_p\text{-subsets } (S \cup (Y_k + \{x\})\,)$ para $x \in X \setminus Y_i$

   $Y_{k+1} = Y_k \cup \{x^+\}$; $k = k+1$

3. *Exclusion:* Select the least significant feature.

   $x^- = \arg\max_{x \in Y_k}\left[J\left(Y_k \setminus \{x\}\right)\right]$

   $S = Select\_the\_best\_p\text{-subsets } (S \cup (Y_k \setminus \{x\})\,)$ where $x \in X \setminus Y_i$

   If $J(Y_k \setminus \{x^-\}) > J(Y_k)$ then

$$Y_{k-1} = Y_k \setminus \{x^-\}; \quad k = k - 1$$

go to step 3

else

go to step 2

4 Experimental Results

In this section, some experiments using both strategies are presented. The experiments were carried out on databases from [4] and on the faces database from [5].

ALVOT was used to measure the efficiency of selected subsets. In the experiments the test sample is equal to the training sample.

In the experiments the typical testors were selected based on their relevance using the equation (1). The relevance of typical testor is computed with equation (2):

$$R(\tau_j) = \frac{\sum\limits_{x_i \in \tau_j} P(x_i)}{|\tau_j|}. \tag{2}$$

where τ_j is a typical testor, $|\tau_j|$ is the cardinality of this testor and $P(x_i)$ is the feature's weight of x_i see (1).

The first experiment was carried out with the ZOO database. This database contains 101 animals grouped in 7 classes, each description is given in terms of 16 features, where 15 are Boolean and 1 is nominal. The best classification efficiency is reached using the strategy 2 with SBFS, obtaining a 100% recognition rate with SSS of 14 subsets. On the other hand, in this sample there are 32 typical testors, choosing support sets systems with 4 typical testors or more the classification efficiency is maintained. The results are shown in the figure 1.

The second experiment was carried out with the HEPATITIS database. This database has 155 objects in 2 classes described through 19 features, where 6 are numeric and 13 are Boolean. This database has incomplete descriptions (missing data). The best classification efficiency was obtained using the strategy 2 with SFFS with a SSS of 12 subsets. The number of computed typical testors was 35. The best classification efficiency was obtained using 10 testors as SSS (figure 2).

The third experiment was carried out with the FLAGS database. This database contains 193 objects in 8 classes and described with 28 features, 15 are nominal, 2 are numeric and 11 are Boolean. In this sample 1469 typical testors were found and the best classification efficiency was obtained with a SSS of 3 testors. The best classification efficiency was obtained using the strategy 2 with SFFS and a SSS of 12 subsets (figure 3).

The fourth experiment was carried out with the SPECTF Heart Data database. This database contains 80 objects grouped in 2 classes described with 22 Boolean features. 26 typical testors were found and the best classification efficiency was obtained with only one testor as SSS. The best classification efficiency is reached using the strategy 2 with SFFS and a SSS of 4 subsets (figure 4).

The last experiment was carried out with the faces database from Olivetti Research Laboratory (ORL) in Cambridge [5]. This database contains 10 different images of 40 subjects and the size of each image is 92x112. The figure 6 shows images of two subjects from ORL database.

An image may be considered as a vector of dimension N^2 (size of the image), in this case a vector of dimension 10304 is equivalent to a point in a 10304-dimensional space. To work with the set of vectors from all the images is unfeasible, due to this different methods are used to reduce the dimension of an image. In this work the Principal Component Analysis (PCA) method is used [6-8]. Once the principal components of the images set are obtained, the proposed strategies are applied to obtain the SSS for ALVOT.

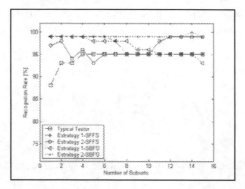

Fig. 1. Floating Methods and Typical Testors for ZOO.

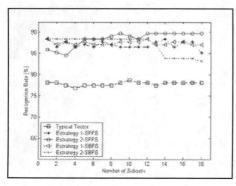 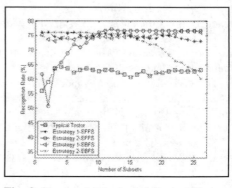

Fig. 2. Floating Methods and Typical Testors for HEPATITIS.

Fig. 3. Floating Methods and Typical Testors for FLAGS.

In this experimentation 150 images of 15 subjects were used from ORL database. Once the principal components were computed 26 eigenvectors which capture the 80.366% of the information were considered. In this case all features are numeric. Taking account the 26 eigenvectors 145951 typical testors were found and the best classification efficiency was obtained using a system with 21 typical testors. Both forward strategies obtained the best efficiency, nevertheless, with the second strategy this efficiency may be obtained using a SSS of cardinality smaller than the first. The classification efficiency is shown in the figure 5.

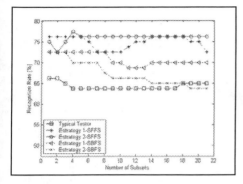
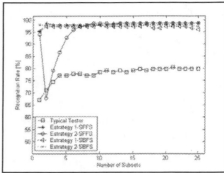

Fig. 4. Floating Methods and Typical Testors for SPECTF.

Fig. 5. Floating Methods and Typical Testors for ORL.

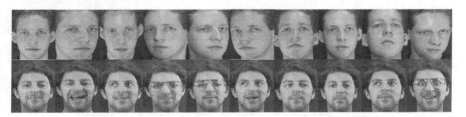

Fig. 6. Examples of subjects that exists in the ORL database.

5 Conclusions

In this paper, two strategies to compute the support sets system for the supervised classifier ALVOT using sequential floating selection were presented. In the experiments the two proposed strategies to compute the support sets system have better performance than using typical testors. The best classification efficiency for ALVOT may be obtained computing the SSS with the second strategy. Using our methods it is possible to find a SSS with lesser cardinality which increases the classification efficiency of ALVOT.

Another point to highlight is the fact that the number of typical testors is bounded exponentially, so that in some cases they can be too many to be useful in the classification stage. Contrarily, in the proposed method the size of the support sets system is one of the parameters, which allows fixing the size of the system according to the practical requirements.

Generally in the floating methods, the classifier used to evaluate the classification efficiency of selected subsets only works with numeric information. In this work, ALVOT is used to evaluate the classification efficiency of subsets, because ALVOT allowed us to carry out experiments with mixed and incomplete data.

Future work includes determining the optimum value of p (SSS's cardinality) to find the SSS that maximizes the classification efficiency of ALVOT.

Acknowledgement

This work was financially supported by CONACyT (México) through the project J38707-A.

References

1. J. Ruiz Shulcloper, Adolfo Guzmán Arenas y J. Fco. Martínez Trinidad, "Enfoque Lógico Combinatorio al Reconocimiento de Patrones", Editorial Politécnica, ISBN: 970-18-2384-1, 1999.
2. P.Pudil, F.J.Ferri, J.Novovièová, and J.Kittler. "Floating Search Methods for Feature Selection with Nonmonotonic Criterion Functions", In: Proceedings of the 12th International Conference on Pattern Recognition, Jerusalem, Israel, 1994. Los Alamitos, IEEE Computer Society Press, 279-283, 1994.
3. M. Lazo-Cortes, J. Ruiz-Shulcloper and E. Alba-Cabrera, "An overview of the evolution of the concept of testor", Pattern Recognition, 34(4), 2001, 753-762.
4. Machine Learning Databases, University of California, Irivne, Deparment of Information & Computation Science, http://ftp.ics.uci.edu/pub/machine-learning-databases/
5. A. L. Cambridge, Olivetti Research Laboratory face database http://www.uk.research.att.com/facedatabase.html
6. L. Sirovich and M. Kirby, "Low-Dimensional Procedure for the Characterization of Human Faces", Journal of the Optical Society of America A,, Vol. 4, pp 519, 1987.
7. M. Kirby and L. Sirovich, "Application of the Karhunen-Loève Procedure for the Characterization of Human Faces", IEEE Transactions on Pattern Analysis and Machine Intelligence, 12(1), 1990.
8. M. Turk and A. Pentland, "Eigenfaces for Recognition", Journal of Cognitive Neuroscience. V. 3, pp. 71-86, 1991.

Feature Selection Using Typical ε: Testors, Working on Dynamical Data

Jesús Ariel Carrasco-Ochoa[1], José Ruiz-Shulcloper[2],
and Lucía Angélica De-la-Vega-Doría[1]

[1] Computer Science Department
National Institute of Astrophysics, Optics and Electronics
Luis Enrique Erro No. 1 Sta María Tonanzintla, Puebla, CP: 72840, Mexico
{ariel,lucia}@inaoep.mx
[2] Advanced Technologies Application Center, MINBAS (Cuba)
jshulcloper@cenatav.co.cu

Abstract. Typical ε:testors are useful to do feature selection in supervised classification problems with mixed incomplete data, where similarity function is not the total coincidence, but it is a one threshold function. In this kind of problems, modifications on the training matrix can appear very frequently. Any modification of the training matrix can change the set of all typical ε:testors, so this set must be recomputed after each modification. But, complexity of algorithms for calculating all typical ε:testors of a training matrix is too high. In this paper we analyze how the set of all typical ε:testors changes after modifications. An alternative method to calculate all typical ε:testors of the modified training matrix is exposed. The new method's complexity is analyzed and some experimental results are shown.

1 Introduction

Yu. I. Zhuravlev introduced the testor concept to Pattern Recognition problems [4]. Upon which a new research line was opened [3]. Specially, there are many researches pointing to the development and application of algorithms for calculating all typical testors of a given matrix. Testors can be applied on the problem of feature selection for supervised classification; working in situations where there are qualitative and quantitative features and may be incomplete object descriptions. Zhuravlev's concept was defined for Boolean features. After, this concept was extended to any kind of features, but anyway all comparison criteria have to be Boolean. Another limitation of Zhuravlev´s testor concept is that the implicit similarity function is the total coincidence, but in some problems two objects could be similar even if they are different in some features, this type of similarity functions are called one threshold similarity functions. So a new testor concept was developed for one threshold similarity functions, the ε:testor concept [3].

Using typical ε:testors to solve the feature selection problem, has as inconvenient the high complexity of algorithms for computing all typical ε:testors, which makes impossible to use those in situations where the training matrix changes frequently. In this paper we analyze the behavior of the set of all typical ε:testors when the comparison matrix changes. Also we propose an alternative method for adjusting this set after modifications, and a new incremental algorithm for computing the set of all typical

A. Sanfeliu et al. (Eds.): CIARP 2004, LNCS 3287, pp. 685–692, 2004.

ε:testors. The new methods' performance is shown. Finally complexity analysis of the adjusting method is done.

2   Typical ε: Testors and Feature Selection

Into the framework of the Logical Combinatorial Pattern Recognition [1], feature selection is done using typical testors [1,2,3].

Let TM be a training matrix with **m** objects described using **n** features of any type $(x_1,...,x_n)$ and grouped in **r** classes. Let M be a dissimilarity Boolean matrix (0=similar,1=dissimilar), obtained from feature by feature comparisons of all the pairs of objects from TM belonging to different classes. M has **n** columns $(x_1,...,x_n)$ and **k** rows $(f_1,...,f_k)$.Testors and Typical Testors are defined as follows:

Definition 1. A subset of features T is a testor of M if and only if when all features are eliminated, except those from T, there is not any row of M with only 0´s.

Definition 2. A subset of features T is a typical testor of M if and only if T is a testor of M and there is not any other testor of M T' such that $T' \subset T$.

As it was mentioned, these definitions have as implicit similarity function the total coincidence, where two objects are similar if they are similar in all their features.

For a one threshold similarity function with threshold=ε, two objects are similar if they are different in less than ε features. For a one threshold similarity function with threshold=ε, ε:Testors and Typical ε:Testors are defined as:

Definition 3. A subset of features T is an ε:testor of M if and only if when all features are eliminated, except those from T, there is not any row with less than ε 1´s..

Definition 4. A subset of features T is a typical ε:testor of M if and only if T is a ε:testor of M and there is not any other ε:testor of M T' such that $T' \subset T$.

Each ε:testor is a set of features such that there is not a pair of objects from different classes which are similar for a one threshold similarity function with threshold=ε. Typical ε:testors are irreducible ε:testors, this is, all features are essential for class separation. Therefore, typical ε:testors can be used as feature selection.

3   Working on Dynamical Environments

The main problem of the ε:testor concept is that all algorithms for computing the set of all typical ε:testors are of exponential complexity with regards to the number of features. So, using them for feature selection on problems where data change frequently (Dynamical Data) is inadequate.

For this cause, it is necessary to find a new method for adjusting the set of all typical ε:testors when there are some changes on data. The search of this new method is called sensitivity analysis [5].

It is known [5] that all possible alterations to a training matrix TM can be summarized in 4 cases: delete a feature; add a feature; delete an object; add an object, or in successive compositions of them. All possible alterations on TM may have an effect on the comparison matrix M; it is shown in the table 1.

Table 1. Modifications on the training matrix TM and their effects on the comparison matrix M.

Alteration on TM	Effect on M
Delete a feature	The corresponding column is eliminated.
Add a feature	The corresponding column is added.
Delete an object	Rows that come from the comparisons with the deleted object are eliminated.
Add an object	Rows that come from the comparisons with the new object are added.

Clearly, possible modifications to the comparison M also can be reduced to the same 4 cases. For this reason, we only study how the set of all typical ε:testors changes because of each one of this 4 types of alterations.

A consequence of the typical ε:testor concept (definition 4) is the following:

Let $t=\{ x_{i_1} ,..., x_{i_s} \}$ be a typical ε:testor of M, then there are $r<s$ rows (associated to t) $F_t=\{ f_{i_1} ,..., f_{i_r} \}$ such that:

1. For each feature $x_{i_j} \in t$ there is a row $f_{i_k} \in F_t$ such that $|(t\backslash\{ x_{i_j} \})\cap f_{i_k} |<\varepsilon+1$

2. For each row $f_{i_k} \in F_t$ there is a feature $x_{i_j} \in t$ such that $|(t\backslash\{ x_{i_j} \})\cap f_{i_k} |<\varepsilon+1$

Also, for each row $f_{i_k} \in F_t$, $F_t\backslash\{ f_{i_k} \}$ does not fulfill these conditions. F_t can be not unique. We denote by F_t the set of all possible F_t.

In order to simplify the notation, we suppose that the comparison matrix is a set of rows, and each row is a set of those features which there is a 1 in the corresponding column. (for example if **n**=5 then (1 0 1 1 0) is the set $\{x_1,x_3,x_4\}$).

The behavior of the set of all typical ε:testors, when the comparison matrix M changes, is described in the following theorems (sensitivity theorems):

Let M be a dissimilarity comparison matrix whit values into {0,1}.

Theorem 1. Let M' the obtained matrix when the column x_i is eliminated from M, then $T'=T\backslash T_i$ where:

   T' is the set of all typical ε:testors of M'
   T is the set of all typical ε:testors of M
   T_i is the set of all typical ε:testors of M which contains the feature x_i.

Theorem 2. Let M' the obtained matrix when the column x_{n+1} is added to M, then $T'=T\cup T'_{n+1}$ where:

   T' is the set of all typical ε:testors of M'
   T is the set of all typical ε:testors of M
   T'_{n+1} is the set of all typical ε:testors of M' which contains the feature x_{n+1}.

Theorem 3. Let M' the obtained matrix when the row f_i is eliminated from M, then $T'=(T\backslash T_0)\cup T_1$ where:

   T' is the set of all typical ε:testors of M'
   T is the set of all typical ε:testors of M

$T_0 = \{t \in T \mid$ there is $F_t \in F_t$ with $f_i \in F_t$ and there is no a row set $\{f_{j1},...,f_{js}\} \subseteq M,$
$f_i \notin \{f_{j1},...,f_{js}\}$ such that $(F_t \setminus \{f_i\}) \cup \{f_{j1},...,f_{js}\} \in F_t \}$

$$T_1 = \bigcup_{M'' \in M^{(i)}} TT(M'')$$

where:

TT(M'') is the set of all typical ε:testors of M'',

$M^{(i)}$ is the set of all matrices that can be constructed with all rows of $M \setminus \{f_i\}$, all columns where f_i has 0, and ε columns where f_i has 1.

Theorem 4. Let M' the obtained matrix when the row f_{k+1} is added to M, then $T'=(T \setminus T_0) \cup T_1$ where:

T' is the set of all typical ε:testors of M'

T is the set of all typical ε:testors of M

$T_0 = \{t \in T \mid |t \cap f_{k+1}| \leq \varepsilon \}$

$T_1 = \{t' \mid t'=t \cup E,\ t \in T_0,\ t \cap E = \varnothing,\ E \subseteq f_{k+1},\ |E|=\varepsilon-|t \cap f_{k+1}|+1$ and there is not any t_0
      ε:testor of M' with $t_0 \subset t' \}$

Proofs for these 4 theorems can be found in [6].

4 Proposed Methods

Based on the sensitivity theorems it is possible to define a method for adjusting the set of all typical ε:testors when a modification on the comparison matrix M occurs. For each kind of modification the adjusting method works as follows:

- If a column is eliminated, the set of all typical ε:testors of the new matrix is obtained taking the set of all typical ε:testors of the original matrix and discarding such testors which contain the eliminated column.
- If a column is added, the set of all typical ε:testors of the new matrix is obtained taking the set of all typical ε:testors of the original matrix and adding all typical ε:testors that contain the added column. These new typical ε:testors must be calculated with an adapted traditional algorithm, by example ε:BT [3,6].
- If a row f_i is eliminated, the set of all typical ε:testors of the new matrix is obtained applying the following process:

   Verifying for each typical ε:testor t, of the original matrix, if $|t \cap f_i| \neq \varepsilon+1$ or $|t \cap f_i| = \varepsilon+1$ and $t \setminus \{x_k\}$ is not an ε:testor of the new matrix, for all $x_k \in (t \cap f_i)$, then t is a typical ε:testor of the new matrix, otherwise t is discarded. Additionally, building all different submatrices M'' of the new matrix, taking all columns where f_i has 0 and ε columns where f_i has 1. Calculate the set of all typical ε:testors of each M''. The set of all typical ε:testors of the new matrix is obtained from the union of the original set of the typical ε:testors, which are not discarded, with the sets of all typical ε:testors of all the matrices M''.

- If a row f_{k+1} is added, the set of all typical ε:testors of the new matrix is obtained applying the following process to each typical ε:testor of the original matrix.

    Let t be a typical ε:testor of the original matrix, if the added row f_{k+1} is such that $|t \cap f_{k+1}| \geq \varepsilon + 1$, then t is a typical ε:testor of the new matrix; if not, t must be substituted by the new typical ε:testors obtained from $t' = t \cup E$, where $E \subseteq f_{k+1}$, $|E| = \varepsilon - |t \cap f_{k+1}| + 1$, $t \cap E = \varnothing$, and t' is not a superset of any other ε:testor.

Additionally, based on the theorem 4, we define a new incremental algorithm for calculating all typical ε:testors as follows: Take the first row of the comparison matrix M, all subset of exactly ε features, taken from the columns where this row has 1, are the initial typical ε:testors, then add all other rows applying the adjusting method.

5 Experimental Tests

Performance of the adjusting method was proved. Runtimes of the adjusting method were compared against runtimes of ε:BT algorithm and the incremental algorithm based on theorem 4. First, some synthetic tests were done in order to show the new method performance, figures 1-4 show the results of these tests.

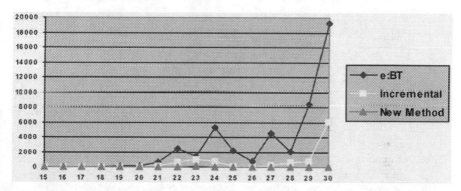

Fig. 1. Runtimes in hundredths of second for deleting a row with ε=1, for matrixes from 15 to 30 columns.

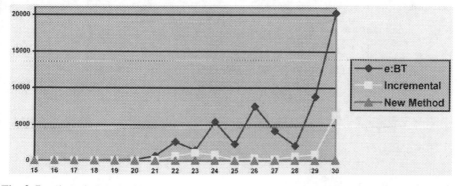

Fig. 2. Runtimes in hundredths of second for adding a row with ε=1, for matrixes from 15 to 30 columns.

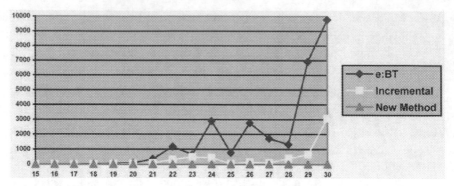

Fig. 3. Runtimes in hundredths of second for deleting a row with ε=1, for matrixes from 15 to 30 columns.

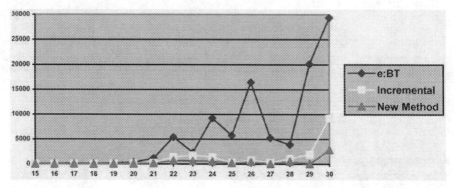

Fig. 4. Runtimes in hundredths of second for adding a column with ε=1, for matrixes from 15 to 30 columns.

These synthetic tests were done with a randomly generated matrix for each different number of columns.

Additional tests were done with the "annealing" problem [7]. This problem has 798 objects described through 38 features: 6 real-valued; 3 integer-valued; and 29 nominal-valued. There are several missing values. This problem has mixed incomplete data descriptions. Comparison criteria were:

For real-valued features:

$$C_i(v_1, v_2) = \begin{cases} 1 & \text{if } |v_1 - v_2| > \sigma_i \\ 0 & \text{otherwise} \end{cases}$$

where σ_i is the standard deviation of the sample data for the feature x_i.

For integer-valued and nominal-valued features:

$$C_i(v_1, v_2) = \begin{cases} 1 & \text{if } v_1 \neq v_2 \\ 0 & \text{otherwise} \end{cases}$$

Using these comparison criteria, we got a basic matrix [3], from the comparison matrix, with 38 columns and 45 rows. Some tests where done with this matrix applying the adjusting method, the new incremental algorithm, and ε:BT algorithm. Table 2 shows the results of these tests.

Table 2. Runtimes in hundredths of second for the "annealing" problem with ε=1,2,3. (# of T. ε:T means number of typical ε:testors).

Problem	Modification	Adjusting Method	Incremental	ε:BT	# of T. ε:T.
		ε=1			
"annealing" 38x45	Original	NA	294	13290	2968
	Adding column	759	323	14298	3120
	Deleting column	<1	247	11446	2529
	Adding row	1	296	13548	2968
	Deleting row	8	272	12472	2970
		ε=2			
"annealing" 38x45	Original	NA	16446	139532	29135
	Adding column	15956	18937	158125	32103
	Deleting column	3	13726	114613	23968
	Adding row	7	16520	142122	29135
	Deleting row	118	15927	136174	29176
		ε=3			
"annealing" 38x45	Original	NA	793903	939564	184772
	Adding column	165847	954793	1122892	213907
	Deleting column	17	681475	734084	145979
	Adding row	44	801726	956008	184772
	Deleting row	1175	788636	916909	185167

Finally, complexity analysis of the new methods was done. The table 3 shows the complexity of the new methods for each kind of modification and for the incremental algorithm.

Table 3. Complexity of the new methods.

Modification	New method´s complexity
Delete a column	W
Add a column	2^{n-1}
Delete a row	$kw + \binom{n-y}{\varepsilon} 2^{y+\varepsilon}$
Add a row	$\binom{n-y}{\varepsilon} w^2$
Incremental Algorithm	$M \binom{n-y}{\varepsilon} w^2$

where n is the number of columns of the new matrix,
     k is the number of rows of the new matrix,
     w is the number of typical ε:testors of the original matrix,
     y is the number of 0's in the row added or deleted,
     ε is the epsilon of the similarity function,
     m is the number of rows of the comparison matrix

6 Conclusions

As result of this work, it is possible to use typical ε:testors for feature selection in problems where modifications appear frequently. The new method allows adjusting the set of all typical ε:testors faster than applying any traditional algorithm, this can be appreciated from complexities, and it was corroborated with experimentation.

Also, a new incremental algorithm for calculating all typical ε:testors were proposed. In all experiments this new incremental algorithm had a better performance than ε:BT algorithm.

Acknowledgement

This work was financially supported by CONACyT (Mexico) through project I38436-A.

References

1. Martínez-Trinidad J. F. and Guzmán-Arenas A. "The logical combinatorial approach to pattern recognition an overview through selected works", Pattern Recognition, Vol 34, No. 4, pp. 741-751, 2001.
2. Ruiz-Shulcloper J. and Lazo-Cortés M. "Mathematical Algorithms for the Supervised Classification Based on Fuzzy Partial Precedence", Mathematical and Computer Modeling, Vol. 29, No. 4, pp. 111-119, 1999.
3. Lazo-Cortes M., Ruiz-Shulcloper J. and Alba-Cabrera E. "An overview of the evolution of the concept of testor", Pattern Recognition, Vol. 34, No. 4, pp. 753-762, 2001.
4. Dmitriev A.N., Zhuravlev Y.I., Krendeliev F.P. "About mathematical principles of objects and phenomena classification", Diskretni Analiz Vol 7, pp. 3-15, 1966. (In Russian).
5. Carrasco-Ochoa J. A. and Ruiz-Shulcloper J. "Sensitivity Problems of the Set of Typical Testors of a Boolean Matrix", Proceedings of the III Iberoamerican Symposium on Pattern Recognition", SIARP 98, pp. 257-266, Mexico, 1998 (in Spanish).
6. Carrasco-Ochoa J. A. "Sensitivity in Logical Combinatorial Pattern Recognition", PhD Thesis, CIC-IPN, Mexico, 2001
7. http://www-old.ics.uci.edu/pub/machine-learning-databases/

Supervised Pattern Recognition
with Heterogeneous Features

Ventzeslav Valev

Saint Louis University
College of Art and Sciences
Department of Mathematics and Computer Science
St. Louis, MO 63103, USA
valevv@slu.edu

Abstract. In this paper, we address the supervised pattern recognition problem with heterogeneous features, where the mathematical model is based on construction of thresholds. Non-Reducible Descriptors (NRDs) for fuzzy features are obtained through the use of a threshold value, which is calculated based on the distance between patterns. For solving the problem with real features the mathematical model for construction of thresholds is based on parallel feature partitioning. Boolean formulas are used to represent NRDs.

1 Introduction

We assume that a phenomenon to be studied using the available information is in the form of *patterns*. Let us denote by M, the set of all such patterns Q. M is viewed as a union of a finite number of subsets $K_1, K_2, \ldots, K_l$ which are called *classes*. We assume that classes do not intersect, but they can overlap. However, the information available pertains only to the partitioning of some subset $M' \subset M$, called the *training set*. We assume that there are m patterns in M', which are divided into l classes, and each pattern Q contains n features of the pattern described. This information is organized as a table which we call the *training table*, denoted by $T_{n,m,l}$, assuming that there are m_1 patterns in class K_1, m_2 patterns in class K_2, ..., m_l patterns in class K_l. The first m_1 rows of $T_{n,m,l}$ will correspond to patterns in K_1, the next m_2 rows will correspond to patterns in K_2, and so on.

The *supervised pattern recognition problem* is formulated as follows. Using the training set, the class membership of patterns in the training set, and the description Q, assign a pattern $Q \in M \backslash M'$ to one of the classes $K_1, \ldots, K_l$.

As a rule, all models for solving pattern recognition problem use the concepts of similarity or dissimilarity. These concepts are used in the mathematical models of learning procedures and in the decision rules. Usually, for measuring similarity or dissimilarity, a metric in the pattern space is introduced. When describing complex patterns, different types of features are used. Properties of different patterns are measured and these measurements are usually performed

A. Sanfeliu et al. (Eds.): CIARP 2004, LNCS 3287, pp. 693–700, 2004.

in different scales. Generally speaking, features can take values from the following sets: $\{0,1\}$; $\{0,1,\ldots,d-1\}$, d - integer, $d > 2$; R, where R is the set of all real numbers; fuzzy interval $[0,1]$.

As a rule, all models for solving pattern recognition problem are oriented towards one type of feature. Introducing a metric in a space with different types of features produces methodological difficulties. These difficulties are related to calculating the distance between two feature vectors, having components obtained as a result of the measurement of apparently incomparable quantities.

The methodological difficulties discussed above may be avoided in different ways. One possible methodological approach is to transform the feature space. Another approach is to transform some of the features from one type to another. The solution of the pattern recognition problem in both cases is constructed in the transformed space. Another group of methods are directed to search the solution of the supervised pattern recognition problem in the initial feature space. Some of them use a geometrical approach based on feature partitioning. Usually, each feature is considered separately and it is divided into segments [1]. Many models acquire decision rules, often expressed in logical form, but also in other forms like schemata. Other models use a set of representative instances [2], hyperrectangles (exemplars) [3], [4], or decision trees [5].

In the present paper binary description for fuzzy features are obtained through the use of a threshold value, which is calculated based on the distance between patterns defined in a manner similar to Hamming distance between binary features. For solving the problem with real features the mathematical model for construction of thresholds is based on feature partitioning. In contrast with the sequential methods, here all features are considered in parallel.

After transforming all the pattern descriptions into binary a mathematical model based on Non-Reducible Descriptors (NRDs) is applied. An NRD is a descriptor of minimal length. In other words, an NRD contains information on the smallest number of features that are necessary to describe a pattern uniquely.

The rest of the paper is organized as follows. In section 2, we present procedure for construction NRDs. In section 3, our model for construction NRD for fuzzy features is presented. Finally, in section 4, a method for transforming real features into binary or k-values based on parallel feature partitioning is proposed.

2   Non-reducible Descriptors

For ease of reference, we include here some definitions similar to the ones introduced in previous related work [6]. We will also describe briefly the computational procedure of [6] for the construction of all NRDs for pattern recognition problems with binary features. This will enable us to present the procedure for problems with fuzzy and real features in a simple and straightforward manner.

For pattern recognition problems with binary features, each pattern Q is represented in the training table by means of a sequence $t_1, t_2, \ldots, t_n$ with $t_i \in \{0,1\}$. Each member of this sequence corresponds to the presence or absence of the corresponding feature $x_1, x_2, \ldots, x_n$.

Definition 1. Let $Q_r = (t_{r,1}, t_{r,2}, \ldots, t_{r,n})$. The subsequence $(t_{r,j_1}, t_{r,j_2}, \ldots, t_{r,j_d})$, $j_d \leq n$ is called a *descriptor* for the pattern $Q_r \in K_i$ if there does not exist any other pattern $Q_s \in K_p$, $p = 1, 2, \ldots, i-1, i+1, \ldots, l$ in the training table with the same subsequence.

Definition 2. A given descriptor is called a *Non-Reducible Descriptor* (NRD) if none of its arbitrarily chosen proper subsequences is a descriptor.

Definition 2 means that if an arbitrarily chosen feature is removed, then this descriptor loses its property of being a descriptor. Therefore, an NRD is a descriptor of minimal length. Next, we assume that the NRD of pattern Q_r is given by $t_{j_1}, t_{j_2}, \ldots, t_{j_d}$.

Next, we need some more definitions for formulating the problem of constructing the NRDs for the patters $Q_r \in K_i$ for some i, $1 \leq i \leq l$. Let m' denote the number of patterns not belonging to K_i.

Definition 3. The *dissimilarity matrix* for a pattern $Q_r \in K_i$ is a binary matrix $L_r = [l_{v,j}]$; $v = 1, \ldots, m'$, $j = 1, \ldots, n$, with

$$l_{v,j} = \begin{cases} 1, \text{ if } t_{r,j} \neq t_{v,j}, \\ 0, \text{ otherwise,} \end{cases}$$

where $t_{r,j}$ and $t_{v,j}$ are the values of feature j of $Q_r \in K_i$ and $Q_v \notin K_i$, respectively.

Note that since the classes are pairwise disjoint, it follows that every row of the matrix L_r contains at least one unit.

Definition 4. The number of features d in an NRD is called its *rank* and is denoted by NRD^d.

Definition 5. Columns $j_1, j_2, \ldots, j_d$ of an arbitrary $\{0, 1\}$-matrix A of order $m \times n$ form a *covering* of M if there does not exist a row p, $p = 1, 2, \ldots, m$, such that $a_{p,j_q} = 0$ for $q = 1, 2, \ldots, d$.

The following procedure of [6], restated using the terminology presented above, is very useful in formulating the pattern recognition problem with binary features in terms of dissimilarity matrices.

The problem for constructing all NRDs for an arbitrary pattern Q_r is equivalent to permuting the rows and columns of the dissimilarity matrix L_r to obtain a matrix L'_r of order $m' \times n$ of the form

$$L'_r = \begin{bmatrix} E_d & P_1 \\ P_2 & P_3 \end{bmatrix},$$

satisfying the following properties:

a) Submatrix E_d is an identity submatrix of order d, and no further permutations of rows and columns of L_r will result in a larger identity submatrix comprising E_d;

b) The columns of the submatrix P_2 form a covering of P_2; in other words, each row of P_2 has at least one unit.

Therefore, E_d is the maximal identity submatrix, where d is the rank of the constructed NRD. Note that the above problem always has a solution because each row of the dissimilarity matrix L_r must contain at least one unit due to the pairwise disjointedness of the classes.

Example. Patients are characterized as suffering from strep-throat or flu depending on the presence or absence of a combination of the following symptoms: sore throat (feature x_1), cough (x_2), cold (x_3), and fever (x_4). Let K_1 denote the class of patients suffering from strep-throat, and K_2, the class of patients suffering from flu. The following training table consists of information pertaining to 7 patients, the first two in K_1, and the last five in K_2. The information pertaining to each patient is represented as a row in the following training table. A 1 in a particular column represents the presence of the corresponding symptom, and a 0 represents the absence of that symptom. Thus, in the notation of this paper, $Q_1, Q_2 \in K_1$, and $Q_3, \ldots, Q_7 \in K_2$.

$$T = \begin{array}{c} \begin{array}{cccc} x_1 & x_2 & x_3 & x_4 \end{array} \\ \left[\begin{array}{cccc} 1 & 1 & 0 & 0 \\ 1 & 0 & 1 & 0 \\ \hline 0 & 0 & 1 & 1 \\ 1 & 0 & 1 & 1 \\ 0 & 0 & 1 & 0 \\ 0 & 1 & 1 & 0 \\ 0 & 1 & 1 & 1 \end{array}\right] \end{array}.$$

For the object Q_1, the sequence $(t_{1,1}, t_{1,2}, t_{1,4}) = (1, 1, 0)$ is a descriptor. The sequence $(t_{1,1}, t_{1,2}) = (1, 1)$ is an NRD for the object Q_1, and it is expressed by the conjunction $x_1 x_2$. Also, the sequence $(t_3) = (0)$ is an NRD for the object Q_1, and it is expressed by the conjunction $\bar{x}_3$. Similarly, for the object Q_2, the sequence $(t_{2,1}, t_{2,3}, t_{2,4}) = (1, 1, 0)$ is descriptor. Also, the sequence $(t_{2,1}, t_{2,4}) = (1, 0)$ is an NRD for the object Q_2, and it is expressed by the conjunction $x_1 \bar{x}_4$.

This would mean that, based on the first patient's symptoms and diagnosis, the presence of sore throat and cough are sufficient to diagnose a patient with strep-throat. Similarly, based on the second patient's symptoms and diagnosis, the presence of sore throat and the absence of fever are sufficient to diagnose a patient with strep-throat as well.

In the next sections we will consider how to transform fuzzy features and real features into binary.

3   Fuzzy Features

Since the training table is not a $\{0, 1\}$-matrix for pattern recognition problems with fuzzy features, the previous definition of the dissimilarity matrix (for binary features) does not apply directly. Therefore, we need to extend this concept appropriately for the case of fuzzy features [7]. Once this is accomplished, the procedure for construction of NRDs may be applied as well. For this purpose, we make the following definition. For simplifying the notation we will assume that all features in the training table are fuzzy. Otherwise, we will apply the proposed model only to the fuzzy part of the descriptions.

Definition 6. The *distance matrix* for a pattern $Q_r \in K_i$ is the $m' \times n$ numerical matrix $D_r = [d_{v,j}]$ with $d_{v,j} = |t_{r,j} - t_{v,j}|$, where $t_{r,j}$ and $t_{v,j}$ are the values of feature j of $Q_r \in K_i$ and $Q_v \notin K_i$, respectively.

Note that since there are totally m patterns in the training table, m such distance matrices can be obtained, one for each pattern. In order to obtain binary dissimilarity matrices, we would like to determine a *threshold distance value* ε. We accomplish this as follows:

a) In each distance matrix, determine the maximal element for each row.
b) Define ε as the minimal element among all the maximal elements obtained from the distance matrices.

We have used this procedure for determining ε in order to ensure that the dissimilarity matrices will have at least one unit in each row. We are now ready to define dissimilarity matrices for fuzzy features.

Definition 7. The *dissimilarity matrix* for the pattern $Q_r \in K_i$ is the $m' \times n$ binary matrix $L_r = [l_{v,j}]$, with

$$l_{v,j} = \begin{cases} 1, & \text{if } d_{v,j} \geq \varepsilon, \\ 0, & \text{otherwise,} \end{cases}$$

where $d_{v,j}$ is the value in matrix D_r.

However, if the value corresponding to the feature x_j in a descriptor is at least ε it denotes the presence of the feature x_j, and therefore will be represented by the occurrence of x_j in the NRD. Similarly, if this value is smaller than ε, then it denotes the absence of x_j, and therefore will be represented by the occurrence of the feature $\bar{x}_j$ in the NRD.

4   Real Features

We will consider the case when all features take value from the set of real numbers R. Otherwise, we will apply the proposed model only to the real part of the descriptions. Without loss of generality, we will discuss the pattern recognition problem with two classes K_1 and K_2. Let the set M' be entirely contained in a restricted closed region D. Let $K_1 \cap K_2 = \emptyset$, $K_1 = \{Q_1, \ldots, Q_r\}$, $K_2 = \{Q_{r+1}, \ldots, Q_m\}$.

Let us assume that for each feature x_j, $j = 1, 2, \ldots, n$ the threshold set $E_j = \{\varepsilon_j^1, \ldots, \varepsilon_j^{v(j)}\}$ is given. The set element ε_j^s belongs to the region defined for the feature x_j and $\varepsilon_j^s \neq \varepsilon_j^t$ for $s \neq t$. Let $\varepsilon_j^1 < \ldots < \varepsilon_j^{v(j)}$.

Accordingly, the problem for transforming the feature space by feature partitioning is related to the construction of the sets $\tilde{E}_1, \ldots, \tilde{E}_n$ [8]. This solution means that for each coordinate axis x_j a subset $\tilde{E}_j \subseteq E_j$ is constructed, comprising of k_j elements $\{\varepsilon_j^{i_1}, \ldots, \varepsilon_j^{i_{k_j}}\}$, $\varepsilon_j^{i_1} < \ldots < \varepsilon_j^{i_{k_j}}$, $k_j \leq v(j)\}$ exists, so that the total number of thresholds is minimal. The sets $\tilde{E}_1, \ldots, \tilde{E}_n$ are called threshold sets and their members, thresholds. The problem for construction the threshold sets $\tilde{E}_1, \ldots, \tilde{E}_n$ is discussed next.

On each coordinate axis x_j, $j = 1, \ldots, n$ the values of the corresponding features from the descriptions of the training patterns $Q_1, \ldots, Q_m$ are plotted. Among all possible open intervals, restricted by two neighboring values, only those whose ends belong to the description of patterns from different classes are considered. Let the number of intervals for the jth coordinate axis be $v(j)$. Let

$$n_1 = \sum_{j=1}^{n} v(j),$$

From each open interval considered, one arbitrary threshold value, for example, the middle of the interval is chosen. In this way, for each coordinate axis j the sequence of threshold values $\varepsilon_j^1, \ldots, \varepsilon_j^{v(j)}$ is obtained. From this sequence the set $\tilde{E}_j$ has to be constructed. Let to each threshold component ε_j^t the binary variable x_j^t be assigned, according to the rule:

$$x_j^t = \begin{cases} 1, \text{ if } \varepsilon_j^t \text{ is chosen as a threshold,} \\ 0, \text{ otherwise,} \end{cases}$$

for $t = 1, 2, \ldots, v(j)$; $j = 1, 2, \ldots, n$.

Let us consider the ordered set of all possible pairs (Q_p, Q_q), where $Q_p \in K_1$, $p = 1, 2, \ldots, r$; $Q_q \in K_2$, $q = r + 1, r + 2, \ldots, m$. Obviously

$$|\{(Q_p, Q_q)\}| = r(m - r).$$

Let

$$m_1 = r(m - r).$$

The matrix $C = [c_{ij}^t]_{m_1 \times n_1}$ is constructed according to the rule:

$$c_{ij}^t = \begin{cases} 1, \text{ if } i\text{th pair of patterns differs in the } j\text{th} \\ \quad \text{coordinate axis by the threshold value} \\ \quad \varepsilon_j^t, \\ 0, \text{ otherwise.} \end{cases}$$

where $i = 1, 2, \ldots, m_1$; $j = 1, 2, \ldots, n_1$; $t = 1, 2, \ldots, v(j)$.

The matrix C is arranged in the following way. The first group of $v(1)$ columns contains information for the feature x_1, next group $v(2)$ - for the feature x_2 and so on, the last group $v(n)$ - for x_n. Each group of $v(j)$ columns, $j = 1, \ldots, n$, contains information for the thresholds $\varepsilon_j^1 < \ldots < \varepsilon_j^{v(j)}$ of the set E_j. Columns in each group are ordered sequentially in ascending order of thresholds. In the sequential rows of the matrix C, is written information for the pairs (Q_1, Q_{r+1}), (Q_1, Q_{r+2}), $\ldots$, (Q_1, Q_m), (Q_2, Q_{r+1}), $\ldots$, (Q_r, Q_m) according to the above rule.

The matrix C has the following properties by its construction: i) each row contains at least one unit, ii) each column contains at least one unit.

Let us suppose that for each feature x_j, $j = 1, 2, \ldots, n$, k_j thresholds, $1 \leq k_j \leq v(j)$ are chosen. This condition may be written as follows:

$$\sum_{t=1}^{v(j)} x_j^t = k_j; \; j = 1, 2, \ldots, n.$$

for $k_j = 1, 2, 3, \ldots, v(j)$.

From the condition $K_1 \cap K_2 = \emptyset$ it follows that each pair (Q_p, Q_q) differs at least by one coordinate. For ith pair this condition may be written as follows:

$$\sum_{j=1}^{n} \sum_{t=1}^{v(j)} c_{ij}^t \, x_j^t \geq 1; \; i = 1, 2, \ldots, m_1.$$

Now we can formulate the following problem. Find out the solution for the transformation of the feature space such that for each feature x_j no more than k_j, $k_j \leq v(j)$, thresholds, are constructed and

$$\sum_{j=1}^{n} k_j \; \rightarrow \; min.$$

It means that a binary vector $x^* = (x_1^1, \ldots, x_1^{v(1)}, \ldots, x_n^1, \ldots, x_n^{v(n)})$, with dimension n_1 is found, which minimizes:

$$\sum_{j=1}^{n} \sum_{t=1}^{v(j)} x_j^t \; \rightarrow \; min,$$

at the conditions:

$$1 \leq \sum_{t=1}^{v(j)} x_j^t \leq k_j, \; j = 1, 2, \ldots, n,$$

$$\sum_{j=1}^{n} \sum_{t=1}^{v(j)} c_{ij}^t \, x_j^t \geq 1, \; i = 1, 2, \ldots, m_1.$$

The formulated problem is an integer-valued optimization problem. Its geometrical interpretation is as follows. Let us construct the minimal n-dimensional parallelepiped, containing the region D in R^n. Let the threshold sets $\tilde{E}_1, \ldots, \tilde{E}_n$ be given. Let us construct for each threshold the $(n-1)$-dimensional plane, perpendiculiar to the corresponding coordinate axis. As a result of crossing the n-dimensional parallelepiped containing the region D is covered by the minimal number of hyperparallelepipeds. Their number is equal to $(k_1 + 1) \ldots (k_n + 1)$. Each parallelepiped either contains patterns belonging to only one of the classes or it is the empty one. From the condition $K_1 \cap K_2 = \emptyset$ it follows that the above feature partitioning problem always has a solution. If n thresholds are constructed as a result, then we can transform pattern descriptions into binary. If more than n thresholds are obtained as a result, then the NRD may be expressed using the tools of the k-valued logic.

5   Conclusions

In this paper, a mathematical models has been proposed in the case of heterogeneous features when it is difficult to introduce metric. We have shown how the dissimilarity matrix model for the pattern recognition problem with binary features may be used to construct the Non-Reducible Descriptors for patterns in a problem with fuzzy features. For real features a mathematical model based on parallel feature partitioning has been proposed. The model is based on partitioning the feature space using minimal number of nonintersecting regions. This is achieved by solving the integer-valued optimization problem, which leads to the construction of minimal covering. The proposed models may be used in a variety of fields, including medicine, molecular biology and social sciences.

References

1. H.A.Güvenir, I.Sirin, Classifiation by feature partitioning. Machine Learning **23** (1996)4767.
2. D.W.Aha, D.Kibler, M.K.Albert. Instance-based learning algorithms. Machine Learning **6** (1991)7766.
3. L.Rendell. A new basis for state-space learning systems and successful implementation. Artifiial Intelligence **20** (1983)369392.
4. S.Salzberg. A nearest hyperrectangle method. Machine Learning **6** (1991)251276.
5. J.R.Quinlan. Induction of decision trees. Machine Learning **1** (1986)81106.
6. V.Valev and P.Radeva. A Method of solving pattern or image recognition problem by learning Boolean formulas, Proceedings of 11th International Conference on Pattern Recognition, Hague, Netherlands, August 30 - September 3, 1992, IEEE Computer Society Press **II** (1992)359362.
7. V.Valev, A.Asaithambi. Fuzzy non-reducible descriptors, International Journal on Machine GRAPHICS &VISION **12** No. 3 (2003)353361.
8. V.Valev. Supervised pattern recognition by parallel feature partitioning. Pattern Recognition **37** No. 3 (2004)463467.

Author Index

Lecture Notes in Computer Science

For information about Vols. 1–3184

please contact your bookseller or Springer